Also by Dorothy Hart

THOU SWELL, THOU WITTY

Also by Robert Kimball

COLE (editor)
REMINISCING WITH SISSLE AND BLAKE (co-author)
THE GERSHWINS (co-author)
THE UNPUBLISHED COLE PORTER (editor)
THE COMPLETE LYRICS OF COLE PORTER (editor)

THE COMPLETE LYRICS OF LORENZ HART

THE
COMPLETE
LYRICS OF
LORENZ
HART

EDITED BY
DOROTHY HART AND
ROBERT KIMBALL

WITH AN APPRECIATION BY
ALAN JAY LERNER

ALFRED A. KNOPF

NEW YORK

1986

THIS IS A BORZOI BOOK
PUBLISHED BY ALFRED A. KNOPF, INC.

Copyright © 1986 by Dorothy Hart and
Robert Kimball
Introduction by Dorothy Hart copyright © 1986
by Dorothy Hart

All rights reserved under International and
Pan-American Copyright Conventions.
Published in the United States by Alfred A. Knopf,
Inc., New York, and simultaneously in Canada by
Random House of Canada Limited, Toronto.
Distributed by Random House, Inc., New York.

Copyright information on the lyrics of Lorenz Hart
appears in the Index, starting on page 299.

Library of Congress Cataloging-in-Publication Data
Hart, Lorenz, 1895–1943.
The complete lyrics of Lorenz Hart.
Includes index.
1. Music, Popular (Songs, etc.)—United States—Texts.
2. Musical revues, comedies, etc.—Librettos—Excerpts.
I. Kimball, Robert. II. Hart, Dorothy. III. Title.
ML49.H15K5 1986   782.81'2   86-45367
ISBN 0-394-54680-6

Manufactured in the United States of America
First Edition

For Teddy and our son,
Lorenz Hart II

Dorothy Hart

For my wife, Abigail,
and our children, Philip and Miranda,
and
In memory of Richard Rodgers
and Robert Luther Barlow

Robert Kimball

CONTENTS

CONTENTS

CONTENTS

ix

AN APPRECIATION

Contained within the pages of this book is the tragically abbreviated life of a diminutive giant.

I cannot say I knew him well, for that takes more than the four years between the day I met him, when he was preparing *Pal Joey* in 1939, and when he died, in 1943. But I came to know him well enough to love him, feel the pain of his loneliness, and silently weep for a man who seemed deprived of the happiness his lyrical gifts gave to others.

He was immensely kind to me during those four years. He read my lyrics, encouraged me, telephoned producers and told them about me, and, from time to time, would drop a bit of his long experience into a conversation which I tucked away and to this day, after all these years, I return to for guidance.

But the memories of one man are inconsequential compared to the living memory of his lyrics. Frequently, aficionados and practitioners of the musical theater play the pointless game of comparisons. Was Ira Gershwin "better" than Cole Porter? Was Hammerstein "superior" to Larry? As I say, it is pointless because they were all master craftsmen, each with an expression of his own. I am exhilarated by the gaiety, style, and surprising passion of Cole, overwhelmed by the wonderfully slangy sentimentality and ingenious versatility of Ira, touched by the disarming simplicity of Berlin, and forever impressed by Oscar Hammerstein's dramatic ability. Yet there is a tenderness in some of Larry's lyrics that always catches me off guard and brings a tear to my eye. His wit was delicious and pithy. When the subject was love—the love he never knew—well, there is that tear.

One very late night when he had been at the bar longer than he should have, and his eyes were shadowed by the black circles of depression, he turned to me and said, "I've got a lot of talent, kid. If I cared, I probably could have been a genius." Whether he cared or not, he was as close to being one as lyric writing has produced.

There are those who once met are never forgotten. I found that out from Larry.

ALAN JAY LERNER
London
June 11, 1985

INTRODUCTION

As someone once remarked, Richard Rodgers seemed more like a stockbroker than a composer. He also happened to be a musical genius. He went to the piano the way other men went to the office. Lorenz Hart went to work like a schoolboy who would rather be out in the street playing catch, always looking longingly out the window, but when he was young Larry was full of enthusiasm and dedication for the theater.

In school and at camp, he was involved in diverse activities. If he couldn't play baseball because he was five foot nothing, he became the business manager of the team. If he wasn't in a school play (though more often than not he saw to it that he was), he sold tickets. When he went off to summer camp he arrived with a suitcase containing the complete works of Shakespeare—not a pair of socks or a change of underwear. Larry was already stagestruck. Because of his height he felt more adequate creating laughter than playing tennis and competing with larger boys. When he became the dramatic counselor at camp, the kids called him, with obvious disgust, "the Rehearser." He never let up, though the camp boys grumbled about missing their swim in the lake. Only his brother Teddy (whom I later married) shared his enthusiasm and desire to go on with the show.

At Columbia University he directed, acted in, wrote, and produced many musicals. He eagerly worked on amateur shows for the Akron Club, an organization made up of young businessmen and businesswomen, very popular in the years before radio and television. He spent five years adapting and translating German and Viennese operettas for the Shuberts. (One of these shows was *Liliom,* produced with great success by the Theatre Guild, starring Joseph Schildkraut. Because Larry was on salary—fifty dollars a week—he received no credits. Later Rodgers and Hammerstein had an even greater success with their version, renamed *Carousel.*)

By 1926 Larry was collaborating with Richard Rodgers, and that year he wrote the lyrics (and some librettos) for six Broadway shows, and then two scores a season after that for the nearly twenty years he and Dick worked together.

Larry inherited his boundless energy from his father, Max Hart. As newly arrived immigrants from Hamburg, Max and Frieda married in their late teens. Max belonged to local political clubs, and with his expansive if somewhat vulgar personality, he found himself on the way to modest success. The family moved uptown to a brownstone on East 106th Street from a tenement on the Lower East Side. There Max became a close friend of Mayor Theodore Van Wyck (after whom Teddy was named), Lillian Russell and her husband, Alexander Moore (Ambassador to Spain), John Dos Passos (father of the author), and Willie Hammerstein (father of Oscar).

A final move to the more affluent neighborhood of West 119th Street fit Max's flamboyant tastes even better. Max loved to receive Larry's friends, and show business personalities found their way there at the end of an evening. Among the regulars were Gene Zukor, son of the producer Adolph Zukor, and Mel Shauer. The Hart home was bohemia uptown—lots of young people playing songs and reciting poetry. When his father suffered a heart attack, Larry moved the family to a modern apartment building—his success enabled him to care for his parents with great generosity.

Until Teddy and I married in 1938 the two brothers shared a bedroom; Larry was never reconciled to coming home to a darkened apartment, and Teddy was one of the few people who matched his late-night habits. In the world of the theater, early-morning hours were for the birds.

Richard Rodgers was different. In their later years together he would arrive at Larry's house at 10 a.m. and more often than not would have to roll Larry out of bed. Larry's drinking had increased and he usually had an obvious hangover. This was never Larry's finest hour. He continually grumbled to me about Dick's lack of understanding. But though it was often difficult to get Larry to begin work, once he started he was anything but lazy. Despite their differences of temperament and lifestyles, Dick and Larry's years of close, close contact—working together, living together, traveling around the world, prior to and after Dick's marriage—made for a very special relationship.

George Kaufman was quoted as saying that a professional collaboration was like a marriage without sex. Though Dick often treated Larry like a recalcitrant child, and Larry called Dick "the Teacher" who tried to make him behave, in the lightning-like rapidity of their writing and composing styles they were remarkably alike. When Florenz Ziegfeld, during a *Simple Simon* rehearsal, suggested that "the boys" write a song that wasn't too "highbrow," Larry and Dick repaired to the men's lounge—within the hour "Ten Cents a Dance" was turned in. When Jack Robbins asked Larry to write a commercial lyric for a song from the MGM movie *Manhattan Melodrama* after three sets of lyrics had already been turned in, Larry said, with obvious sarcasm, "You mean like 'Blue Moon'?"—very shortly thereafter, one of Rodgers and Hart's most enduring standards was delivered.

Only Dick could keep up with Larry's incredible creativity. Gene Kelly recalls in awe a *Pal Joey* rehearsal at which a song was discarded, as often happened. Another one was needed immediately. A disgruntled Dick looked around for Larry, who had just dashed in breathlessly, late as usual. Advised of the problem, Larry grabbed a piece of wrapping paper from a nearby chorus girl. "Zip" was written in a few minutes and went into rehearsal that day. George Balanchine felt it was unnecessary for Larry to "hang around" rehearsal halls because whatever had to be done, Larry did in minutes, whereas other writers might struggle and sweat for days.

Robert Russell Bennett, the great orchestrator, once asked Larry how he got his inspiration for those "lovely lyrics." Larry shrugged. "A stub of pencil and a sheet of paper."

Which came first, the music or the lyric? There was never any set rule. If a melody Dick was experimenting with at the piano caught Larry's ear, he grabbed a lead sheet and came up with a lyric. If Larry came up with an idea and Dick nodded, that was it. I never knew Larry to speak other than with great affection and reverence for Dick.

When Larry was a very young child, his father, Max Hart, had taken him to the old Hammerstein Theater, to Broadway shows, and to the German-speaking theater on Fourteenth Street. Dick told me on several occasions that Larry's instinct for the musical theater was incredibly true. He knew when to stop the story to bring in a song. He knew talent. At an audition for showgirls, when Vivienne Segal exclaimed over the beauty of the girls, Larry said, "Talent is beautiful."

He took the time and interest to nurture the early careers of Alan Jay Lerner and Arthur Schwartz.

But in the later years, as his drinking increased, he simply lost interest in his work. Finally, on a rainy and blustery November night in 1943, I went with Larry to the opening night of the revival of *A Connecticut Yankee*. During intermission Larry slipped into a neighborhood bar for a drink, eluding me. At the end of the show I caught up with him and took him to my apartment—Teddy, who was performing in *One Touch of Venus,* joined us a few minutes later. He put his brother to bed on the living-room sofa. Sometime during the night Larry slipped out and found his way back to his apartment at the Delmonico (at Fifty-ninth Street and Park Avenue), where he collapsed and was taken to the hospital. He died of pneumonia three days later on November 22.

I fell in love with Scott Fitzgerald and Lorenz Hart in my very early teens. Their gift for lyrical language appealed to the romantic in me. They made language live. It wasn't until many years later that I recognized a similarity in their temperaments. Fitzgerald, though a beautiful young man who had great success with the ladies, and Larry, a tiny, not too attractive romantic with no success at all with the female sex, approached their work with similar casualness. They both had a clinical tendency to melancholia, which was emphasized by their heavy drinking. Perhaps it was Richard Rodgers's workaholic methods, which Larry resented, that made their tremendous volume of work happen; Fitzgerald left only several novels of importance. Both their lives ended tragically at too early an age. Had Larry been the recipient of Fitzgerald's looks, his great zest for life, his realization of the happiness that eluded him, he might have had more self-control in his drinking. Josh Logan called him a "darling man," Dick Rodgers called him a "good man," George Balanchine called him the "Shelley of America." That I adored him is obvious.

Dorothy Hart

INTRODUCTION

When Richard Rodgers and Lorenz Hart burst upon the scene with their effervescent scores for *The Garrick Gaieties* and *Dearest Enemy* in 1925, Broadway was at the start of its most exciting and productive era.

It was an age of innocence and exuberance, variety and abundance. There were wonderful stars like Marilyn Miller, Bert Lahr, Will Rogers, and Florence Mills. It was the time of the lavish, tasteful, and elegant stage productions of Florenz Ziegfeld and George White and of the fabulous songs of Jerome Kern, Irving Berlin, Cole Porter, George and Ira Gershwin, Vincent Youmans, and, of course, Rodgers and Hart.

The explosive 1920s were the glory years of the American musical. Virtually every hotel had its own dance orchestra, and the Broadway stage was the vehicle for much of the best and most enduring American music of this century. For example, when Rodgers and Hart's *Dearest Enemy* bowed on September 18, 1925, it was only one of several notable mid-September openings. Vincent Youmans's *No, No, Nanette* (September 16), Rudolf Friml's *The Vagabond King* (September 21), and Jerome Kern and Oscar Hammerstein's *Sunny* (September 22) also premiered in that six-day period.

For Rodgers and Hart 1926 was even better. It was their *annus mirabilis.* Six shows. Three premieres in December alone, culminating with the consecutive-night, Christmas-week openings of *Peggy-Ann* and *Betsy.* Over 90 songs!

Rodgers and Hart had three Broadway openings in the astonishing 1927–28 season, the most extraordinary in Broadway history, when 264 shows (53 of them musicals) opened in 70 theaters and played before an estimated audience of 15 to 20 million people. (The 1985–86 season had 33 new shows and an attendance of 6.5 million.) During the spectacular Christmas week of December 1927 (a year in which seven new theaters—the Alvin, the Golden, the Majestic, the Royale, the St. James, the Hammerstein, and the Ziegfeld—opened their doors), 11 shows bowed on a single night, December 26.

If you were reasonably active, you could have seen all of the following, and many other equally illustrious performers, live on Broadway in 1927–28: Judith Anderson, Fred and Adele Astaire, Busby Berkeley, Humphrey Bogart, Mary Boland, Shirley Booth, James Cagney, Louis Calhern, Eddie Cantor, Ina Claire, George M. Cohan, Claudette Colbert, Katharine Cornell, Irene Dunne, Ruth Etting, Lynn Fontanne, John Gielgud, Ruth Gordon, Sidney Greenstreet, Texas Guinan, Adelaide Hall, Walter Hampden, Helen Hayes, William Holden, Lou Holtz, Miriam Hopkins, Ruby Keeler, Dennis King, Bert Lahr, Eva Le Gallienne, Archie Leach (Cary Grant), Beatrice Lillie, Alfred Lunt, Jeanette MacDonald, Marilyn Miller, Victor Moore, Helen Morgan, Eleanor Powell, George Raft, Edward G. Robinson, Bill "Bojangles" Robinson, Lillian Roth, Fritzi Scheff, Barbara Stanwyck, Franchot Tone, Spencer Tracy, Thomas "Fats" Waller, Clifton Webb, Mae West, Peggy Wood, and Ed Wynn.

If you were interested in attending a musical show in the late 1920s, there was a work for virtually every taste and much more abundance and variety than we have today. There were new European operettas, American operettas, English musicals, Victor Herbert and Gilbert and Sullivan revivals, old Viennese operettas, extravaganzas, big revues, intimate revues, Negro revues, and vastly different kinds of musical comedy, ranging from the sophisticated offerings of Cole Porter to the old-style farce comedies of George M. Cohan, from the "best things in life are free" frolics of De Sylva, Brown, and Henderson to the fantasy adventures of Rodgers and Hart.

In late 1918 or early 1919 twenty-three-year-old Lorenz Hart met sixteen-year-old composer Richard Rodgers. They were introduced by a mutual friend, Phillip B. Leavitt, a graduate of the Columbia College class of 1918, who was active in the Akron Club, for which Rodgers had written music. Soon thereafter Rodgers and Hart became collaborators.

Together they wrote amateur shows and even charity benefits and synagogue entertainments. And as they wrote—sometimes too much too quickly—they perfected their craft. Songs written in this period were shifted from show to show, appearing in as many as four different productions, and Hart often set several lyrics to a single Rodgers melody.

It was Phillip Leavitt again who introduced them to the producer Lew Fields of the great team of Weber and Fields. Fields took one of their first song collaborations, "Any Old Place with You," and interpolated it into the 1919 show *A Lonely Romeo.* It became the first published Rodgers and Hart song.

Some months later Fields entrusted them with the score for the 1920 musical *Poor Little Ritz Girl.* Yet soon after its Boston tryout most of Rodgers and Hart's songs were replaced by the work of lyricist Alex Gerber and composer Sigmund Romberg. Success on Broadway had to wait.

In 1922 Rodgers, Hart, and two other Columbia boys, Herbert Fields and Oscar Hammerstein II, wrote a musical called *Winkle Town.* The show was never produced, but the names of its creators are worth noting, and the Rodgers and Hart score is filled with numbers (the best known of which is "Manhattan") that later appeared in their Broadway shows.

The cycle of college and amateur shows ended in the spring of 1925 when Rodgers and Hart were asked to write the score for *The Garrick Gaieties,* a satirical revue to be put on by young artists of the Theatre Guild. Its success and the triumph of "Manhattan" were the making of Rodgers and Hart.

Teaming again with Herbert Fields, son of Lew Fields and brother of lyricist Dorothy Fields, Rodgers and Hart worked on a series of youthful, original musicals noted for the charm and fresh vitality of their music, the unprecedented brilliance of their lyrics, and the unusual variety of stories and situations. Perhaps more than any of their contemporaries, Rodgers, Hart, and Fields in their collaborations established fresh patterns for the American musical without radically altering its basic conventions.

If *The Garrick Gaieties* (1925) marked a transition between the first and second phases of their careers, the second, and most prolific, part of their partnership continued until the coming of the Depression and the team's departure for Hollywood in the spring of 1931.

The Hollywood years, 1931–35, which Rodgers especially loathed, saw them working for hire under the usual well-paid film industry conditions; they wrote what the studios asked them to write, frequently penning songs for several projects at the same time and having no close involvement with any film. Often enough during their unusually trying months at MGM their songs simply were not used. But they were able, in the enchanting *Love Me Tonight* (1932) with director Rouben Mamoulian and in *The Phantom President* (1932) and *Hallelujah,*

I'm a Bum (1933), to perfect what Hart called rhythmic dialogue, in which the songs flowed in and out of the stories in natural ways. Surely the success of these experiments paved the way for Rodgers's later work with Hammerstein.

The great years for Rodgers and Hart, the period in which they were the most successful songwriting team on Broadway, began with their return to New York to write *Jumbo* in 1935. *Jumbo* kicked off an almost uninterrupted series of hit shows—*On Your Toes* (1936); *Babes in Arms* and *I'd Rather Be Right* in 1937; *I Married an Angel* and *The Boys from Syracuse,* perhaps their greatest score, in 1938; *Too Many Girls* in 1939; the magnificent *Pal Joey* in 1940; and *By Jupiter* in 1942.

With *Pal Joey* and *By Jupiter* the glory years were over for Rodgers and Hart. Rodgers had thrived on the team's successes, but the lovable, childlike Hart, no longer eager to work, fearful of solitude, became increasingly immersed in drink and had proceeded far down a path to self-destruction. When he refused to work on the musical version of Lynn Riggs's play *Green Grow the Lilacs,* which became *Oklahoma!,* Rodgers found a new collaborator in the team's longtime mutual friend, Oscar Hammerstein II.

Many people believe that *Oklahoma!* opened after Hart died. Not so. He was present at the New York premiere on March 31, 1943, and in one of the most touching moments in Rodgers's autobiography, *Musical Stages,* the composer recounts: "After the final curtain we all went over to Sardi's to await the New York *Times* review. As we jostled our way into the restaurant, I saw a little man break through the crowd. It was Larry. Grinning from ear to ear, he threw his arms around me. 'Dick,' he said, 'I've never had a better evening in my life! This show will still be around twenty years from now!' And I knew he meant it."

The work of Larry Hart, said his friend and colleague Ira Gershwin, "sings for itself, and we listen to one of the most original lyricists of our time or any other." Hart was a master craftsman. His versification was immensely skillful. His use of exterior/interior, male and female rhymes and all the other techniques of light verse was carried off with breathtaking ease. His handling of foreign phrases, his irreverence, and his gentle mixture of sweet and pungent sentiments were fresh and wonderfully original treats to the audiences of his many shows.

But Lorenzo the magnificent, the little giant of Broadway lyricists, was also a "sentimental sap," in the words of one of his own lyrics, and in these tender moments he gave expression to the feelings of a sensitive artist. Beyond their fabled brilliance, many of his lyrics, most of his best, are love songs. Throughout his career love is his central theme. (Examine the treatment of love and death in his final lyric, "To Keep My Love Alive," and find it present, too, almost twenty-five years earlier in "Don't Love Me Like Othello.") No lyric writer was more romantic than Larry Hart. It is sad that a man who wrote such poignant and eloquent love songs could not find happiness in love for himself.

Among the most recognizable of Hart love songs are the "instantaneous love" lyrics in which love comes in a sudden, often dramatic rush: consider such gems as "My Heart Stood Still," "You Took Advantage of Me," "Did You Ever Get Stung?," "I Didn't Know What Time It Was," and, even, "Bewitched, Bothered and Bewildered."

One of the most quintessential Hart themes is the expression of a need to find love and happiness somewhere else, often away from the heart of the city. He sounded it repeatedly, from the early "Peek-in Pekin" and "Love's

Intense in Tents" to "The Blue Room," "Mountain Greenery," "A Tiny Flat Near Soho Square," "A Tree in the Park," "On a Desert Island with Thee," "There's a Small Hotel," and even "Den of Iniquity"—all these are among the most enchanting and timeless of the Rodgers and Hart creations.

There are also some exquisite songs in which pure elation is hauntingly expressed: "Wait Till You See Her," "The Most Beautiful Girl in the World," "My Funny Valentine," "My Romance," and "I'll Tell the Man in the Street." Note how far from conventional ideals most of these loved ones are.

As Hart grew older, he wrote more often about loneliness, loss, and rejection. These themes, expressed in "Atlantic Blues," "Where's That Rainbow?," "A Ship without a Sail," and "He Was Too Good to Me," occur frequently in the last years, which also saw the creation of "Glad to Be Unhappy," "Spring Is Here," "It Never Entered My Mind," and "Nobody's Heart." As the years passed, the zest was gone. With fame and wealth, Hart became more and more a lost boy, and as he got older, his height (under five feet) bothered him increasingly.

People around him got married and had families. He seemed alone. Six months after his mother died, he, too, was gone. In the end, the great tormented lyricist who brought such joy and consolation to others felt he was Nobody's Hart.

Hart left no manuscripts or notebooks and never dated the lyric sheets that survive alongside Rodgers's piano scores. He gave no thought to posterity. Rodgers, who lived until 1979, saved much more, but his lifelong creativity and his total concern with the work at hand gave him little time to worry about the past. In fact, when I first met Rodgers in 1959, he seemed disinclined to say much about his years with Hart. But as he grew older, he seemed to become more retrospective, more interested in his earlier output. On one of his last tryout forays to New Haven—for *Two by Two* in 1970—he agreed to speak to interested Yale students about the American musical theater. Near the appointed meeting place, a large poster, advertising a revue of "Songs by Rodgers and Hart," caught his eye. "I can't believe it," Rodgers said, looking at the poster. "Larry's been dead for twenty-seven years. Why are young people born after he died interested in those early songs?" Yet he seemed touched by their interest, and I know that as he reached back to gather recollections for his autobiography, he had more reason to understand the affection people have for the songs of Rodgers and Hart.

For many years, Dorothy Hart, Teddy's widow, has been tirelessly gathering her brother-in-law's work. Many collectors have aided her in her search. I know and share her frustration at finding that so much of Larry Hart's legacy has vanished. Part of the reason relates to the lack of importance Americans give their past and the lack of understanding at the time of how much of value was being created in the musical theater.

Nonetheless, we have done what we could, unearthing many previously unknown works, including more than one hundred titles not listed in the marvelously detailed and comprehensive *Richard Rodgers Fact Book.* Yet, at least one hundred songs, music as well as lyrics, are still missing.

The major sources for this volume have been the detective work of Dorothy Hart and the files of Richard Rodgers preserved by Dorothy Rodgers and the Rodgers and Hammerstein Office. These include many unpublished Hart lyrics.

Of central importance are the songs printed by Rodgers and Hart's music publishers (Chappell, Famous, T. B. Harms, Edward B. Marks, Robbins, and Warner Brothers), scripts, song manuscripts, film sound tracks, and radio air checks. Tams-Witmark, which licensed many of the early shows, has some important material.

A substantial body of unpublished work and some previously unknown Rodgers and Hart songs came to light in 1982 at the Warner Brothers Music warehouse in Secaucus, New Jersey. This rediscovery included more than thirty manuscripts in Rodgers's hand and some holograph lyrics by Hart.

Over the years Rodgers made a number of gifts to the Music Division of the Library of Congress in Washington, D.C. This collection also includes some copyright registration copies of songs which were deposited at the Library of Congress for Rodgers and Hart shows.

Music libraries at a number of film studios, notably MGM, Paramount, Warner Brothers, and RKO, have preserved scores that were used in their films.

Some of the missing Hart lyrics are likely to be ghosts and shadows, titles of works that were never written or lyrics that were the work of other early Rodgers collaborators, such as Frank Hunter, Milton Bender, Dorothy Crowthers, Herbert Fields, or even, in some instances, Rodgers himself.

Whenever possible, we have relied on written sources for the lyrics in this book. But, in a very few cases, where no manuscripts or scores have survived we have had to depend on sound-track recordings and radio air checks, which cannot always be clearly deciphered or understood and in some cases reflect a singer's conscious or unconscious changes in the lyric. The few examples of this process in the book are included because we felt an incomplete or slightly inaccurate version was better than none at all.

Most of the Rodgers and Hart songs were written for particular shows or films, and the lyrics appear here chronologically in the productions for which they were written. But many lyrics, particularly in the early years of their collaboration, were shifted from one show to another. Some were used in three or four productions. The rule we have followed is to place the lyric in this book within the production for which it was first intended. Therefore, "Manhattan" is part of *Winkle Town* (1922) instead of *The Garrick Gaieties* (1925) and "My Heart Stood Still" is printed here as part of *One Dam Thing After Another* (1927) rather than *A Connecticut Yankee* (1927).

Most relevant information is contained in the headnotes, such as who introduced a song, when it was published, its subsequent history and alternate titles.

ROBERT KIMBALL

CHRONOLOGY

1895

MAY 2   Lorenz Milton Hart born in New York City to Frieda Isenberg and Max Hart (married in November 1886). One child, Jimmy, born earlier, died in infancy.

1897

SEPTEMBER 25   Hart's younger brother, Theodore Van Wyck Hart, born.

1902

JUNE 28   Richard Rodgers born in New York City.

1908

SUMMER   The Hart brothers attend Weingart Institute, a summer-camp school in the Catskills. They return there for the summer of 1909.

1910

SUMMER   First summer for the Hart brothers at Camp Paradox in the Adirondack Mountains of New York. They return for the summers of 1911–1913.

1911

NOVEMBER   Earliest surviving verse, written for his parents' twenty-fifth wedding anniversary and for *The Columbia News*, the newspaper-literary magazine of the Columbia Grammar School in New York City, where he was a student.

1912

FALL   The Hart brothers tour Europe and spend three months in Germany.

1914

SPRING   Lorenz graduates from Columbia Grammar and begins studies at the Columbia School of Journalism in New York.

1916

Adapts and translates songs from operetta *Die Tolle Dolly*.

1917

APRIL 17   *Hello Central*, an operetta with lyrics and adaptation by Lorenz Hart, is registered for copyright.

1918

SUMMER   Dramatic counselor at Brant Lake Camp in the Adirondack Mountains, New York. Returns to Brant Lake for summers of 1919 and 1920.

FALL.   Phillip Leavitt introduces Richard Rodgers to Lorenz Hart. Exact date of first meeting of Rodgers and Hart is unknown but almost certainly took place not later than the winter of 1918–1919.

1919

MARCH 8   *Up Stage and Down*, an amateur show with music by Rodgers, is presented in the Grand Ballroom of the old Waldorf-Astoria Hotel at Thirty-fourth Street and Fifth Avenue in New York City.

MAY 18   *Up Stage and Down*, revised and retitled as *Twinkling Eyes*, is presented at the Forty-fourth Street Theatre, New York City. Show is directed by Lorenz M. Hart.

SPRING   Richard Rodgers and Lorenz Hart become songwriting team.

AUGUST 26   "Any Old Place with You," music and lyrics by Rodgers and Hart, is their first song to appear in a Broadway show (*A Lonely Romeo*).

DECEMBER 19   "Any Old Place with You" is registered for copyright and becomes the first published song by Rodgers and Hart.

1920

MARCH 6   *You'd Be Surprised*, Akron Club show with music by Rodgers and lyrics mostly by Hart, is presented at the Plaza Hotel, New York City. Second performance at Plaza Hotel, April 11, 1920.

MARCH 24–27   *Fly with Me* presented by the Players Club of Columbia University as the "Varsity Show of 1920" at the Grand Ballroom of the Hotel Astor, New York City.

MAY 29   First performance of *Poor Little Ritz Girl* (music and lyrics by Rodgers and Hart) at the Shubert-Wilbur Theatre, Boston.

JULY 28   Revised *Poor Little Ritz Girl* (music by Rodgers and Sigmund Romberg; lyrics by Hart and Alex Gerber) opens at the Central Theatre, New York City; 119 performances.

DECEMBER 8   *The Lady in Ermine*, operetta with adaptation and English lyrics by Hart, is registered for copyright by United Plays, Inc.

1921

FEBRUARY 10   *Say Mama*, Akron Club show, presented at the Brooklyn Academy of Music. Second performance February 12, 1921, at the Hotel Plaza, New York City.

APRIL 20–23   *You'll Never Know* is presented by the Players Club of Columbia University as the "Varsity Show

of 1921" at the Grand Ballroom of the Hotel Astor, New York City.

JUNE 1–2   *Say It with Jazz* (music by Rodgers; lyrics by Hart and Frank Hunter) presented by the Institute of Musical Art at the Institute, New York City.

1922

JUNE 2–3   *Jazz à la Carte*, music by Rodgers and Gerald Warburg, lyrics by Frank Hunter and Lorenz Hart, presented by the Institute of Musical Art at the Institute, New York City.

SUMMER   At work on *Winkle Town*, with music by Rodgers and book by Oscar Hammerstein II and Herbert Fields. Score includes "Manhattan." Show is unproduced, but many of its songs find life in later productions.

1923

MARCH 2   *The Blond Beast*, written by Henry Myers and staged by Lorenz Hart, opens at the Plymouth Theatre, New York City.

MARCH 19–24   *Half Moon Inn* is presented by the Players Club of Columbia University as the "Varsity Show of 1923" at the Grand Ballroom of the Hotel Astor, New York City. Hart contributed some lyrics to the production.

MARCH 25   *If I Were King*, with music by Rodgers and some lyrics by Hart, presented by the Dramatic Art Department of the Benjamin School for Girls at the Thirty-ninth Street Theatre, New York City.

MAY 31–JUNE 1   *A Danish Yankee in King Tut's Court*, with music by Rodgers and some lyrics by Hart, presented by the Institute of Musical Art at the Institute, New York City.

1924

MARCH 20   *Temple Belles*, with music by Rodgers and some lyrics by Hart, presented as the Purim entertainment at the Park Avenue Synagogue, New York City.

MARCH 24   First performance of *The Jazz King* (later retitled *Henky*, and finally known as *The Melody Man*) at the Kurtz Theatre, Bethlehem, Pennsylvania. Tryout also includes performances in Harrisburg, Pennsylvania; Johnstown, Pennsylvania; Wheeling, West Virginia; Toledo, Ohio; Detroit, Michigan; Cleveland, Ohio; Chicago; and Brooklyn.

MAY 13   *The Melody Man*, with two songs by Rodgers and Hart, opens at the Ritz Theatre, New York City (transfers to the Forty-ninth Street Theatre, in June); 56 performances.

1925

FEBRUARY 8   *Bad Habits of 1925* (amateur show) presented at the Heckscher Foundation, 104th Street and Fifth Avenue, New York City.

MAY 17   *The Garrick Gaieties* (1925) opens at the Garrick Theatre, New York City; 211 performances.

JULY 20   First performance of *Dear Enemy* (retitled *Dearest Enemy*) at the Colonial Theatre, Akron, Ohio.

AUGUST 6   "Anytime, Anywhere, Anyhow," a song by Rodgers and Hart, is interpolated in the Broadway show *June Days* (Astor Theatre, New York City).

SEPTEMBER 18   *Dearest Enemy* opens at the Knickerbocker Theatre, New York City; 286 performances.

1926

JANUARY   *The Fifth Avenue Follies* opens at the Fifth Avenue Club, New York City; number of performances unknown.

MARCH 8   First performance of *The Girl Friend* at the Apollo Theatre, Atlantic City, New Jersey.

MARCH 17   *The Girl Friend* opens at the Vanderbilt Theatre, New York City; 301 performances.

MAY 10   *The Garrick Gaieties* (1926) opens at the Garrick Theatre, New York City; 174 performances.

SUMMER   Rodgers and Hart travel to Europe for vacation (Italy, Switzerland, and France) and to England for work on *Lido Lady* for London.

OCTOBER 4   First performance of *Lido Lady* at the Alhambra Theatre, Bradford, England.

DECEMBER 1   *Lido Lady* opens at the Gaiety Theatre, London; 259 performances.

DECEMBER 13   First performance of *Peggy-Ann* at the Walnut Street Theatre, Philadelphia.

DECEMBER 20   First performance of *Betsy* at the National Theatre, Washington, D.C.

DECEMBER 27   *Peggy-Ann* opens at the Vanderbilt Theatre, New York City; 333 performances.

DECEMBER 28   *Betsy* opens at the New Amsterdam Theatre, New York City; 39 performances.

1927

MAY 19   *One Dam Thing After Another* opens at the London Pavilion; 237 performances.

JULY 27   *Peggy-Ann* opens at Daly's Theatre, London; 130 performances.

SEPTEMBER 30   First performance of *A Connecticut Yankee* at the Stamford Theatre, Stamford, Connecticut.

NOVEMBER 3   *A Connecticut Yankee* opens at the Vanderbilt Theatre, New York City; 418 performances.

DECEMBER 12   First performance of *She's My Baby* at the National Theatre, Washington, D.C.

1928

Lorenz Hart's father, Max, dies.

JANUARY 3   *She's My Baby* opens at the Globe Theatre, New York City; 71 performances.

APRIL 9   First performance of *Present Arms* at the Shubert Theatre, Wilmington, Delaware.

APRIL 26   *Present Arms* opens at Lew Fields' Mansfield Theatre, New York City; 155 performances.

AUGUST 27   First performance of *Chee-Chee* at the Forrest Theatre, Philadelphia.

SEPTEMBER 25   *Chee-Chee* opens at Lew Fields' Mansfield Theatre, New York; 31 performances.

1929

JANUARY 31   "I Love You More Than Yesterday" and "Sing" by Rodgers and Hart are interpolated in the New York run of *Lady Fingers*; 132 performances.

FEBRUARY 25   First performance of *Spring Is Here* at the Shubert Theatre, Philadelphia.

MARCH 11   *Spring Is Here* opens at the Alvin Theatre, New York City; 104 performances.

MAY   "Masters of Melody," a short film with songs and appearances by Rodgers and Hart, is released.

SEPTEMBER 15   First performance of *Me for You* at the Shubert Detroit Opera House, Detroit.

SEPTEMBER 28   *Me for You* closes in Detroit. With a new book, many new songs, and some new performers, *Me for You* is transformed into *Heads Up!*

OCTOBER 10   *A Yankee at the Court of King Arthur* (London production of *A Connecticut Yankee*) opens at Daly's Theatre, London; 43 performances.

OCTOBER 25   First performance of *Heads Up!* at the Shubert Theatre, Philadelphia.

NOVEMBER 11   *Heads Up!* opens at the Alvin Theatre, New York City; 144 performances.

1930

JANUARY 27   First performance of *Simple Simon* at the Colonial Theatre, Boston.

FEBRUARY 18   *Simple Simon* opens at the Ziegfeld Theatre, New York City; 135 performances.

FEBRUARY–MARCH   Rodgers and Hart write four numbers for the film version of *Follow Through*, their first motion picture assignment. Their songs are deleted before the film is released.

MARCH 5   Richard Rodgers and Dorothy Feiner marry in New York.

MAY 1   *Heads Up!* opens at the Palace Theatre, London; 19 performances.

JULY   Film version of *Spring Is Here* is released.

SEPTEMBER   Film version of *Follow Through* is released. *Leathernecking* (film version of *Present Arms*) is released.

OCTOBER   Film version of *Heads Up!* is released.

OCTOBER 13   First performance of *Ever Green* at the King's Theatre, Glasgow, Scotland.

DECEMBER 3   *Ever Green* opens at the Adelphi Theatre, London; 254 performances.

1931

JANUARY 19   First performance of *America's Sweetheart* at the Shubert Theatre, Pittsburgh.

FEBRUARY 10   *America's Sweetheart* opens at the Broadhurst Theatre, New York City; 135 performances.

MARCH   *The Hot Heiress* is released.

MAY 19   "Rest Room Rose," Rodgers and Hart song, is interpolated into Billy Rose's *Crazy Quilt* on Broadway, where it is sung by Fanny Brice.

NOVEMBER   Rodgers and Hart in Hollywood to begin work on *Love Me Tonight*.

1932

AUGUST   *Love Me Tonight* is released.

SEPTEMBER   *The Phantom President* is released.

1933

Rodgers and Hart in Hollywood.

JANUARY   *Hallelujah, I'm a Bum* is released.

FEBRUARY 21   "When You're Falling in Love with the Irish" written for *Peg O' My Heart*. Dropped from film.

FEBRUARY–APRIL   Rodgers and Hart at work with Moss Hart on MGM film *I Married an Angel*. Several songs are written, but the picture is abandoned.

MAY–NOVEMBER   Rodgers and Hart write songs for MGM films *Meet the Baron*, *Dancing Lady*, and *Hollywood Party*.

OCTOBER   *Meet the Baron* is released. Rodgers and Hart songs not used in film.

NOVEMBER   *Dancing Lady* with one Rodgers and Hart song is released.

1934

Rodgers and Hart in Hollywood.

FEBRUARY   *Nana*, with one Rodgers and Hart song, is released.

FEBRUARY–APRIL   Hart translates lyrics for film version of *The Merry Widow*. Rodgers and Hart contribute new (unused) songs for film.

MARCH   Rodgers and Hart write songs for film *Manhattan Melodrama*.

MAY   *Manhattan Melodrama*, with one Rodgers and Hart song, is released. *Hollywood Party* is released. Film includes only four of more than twenty songs that Rodgers and Hart wrote for the film.

JUNE   *Evergreen* (film version of *Ever Green*) is released.

JULY–AUGUST   Rodgers and Hart write most of score for *Mississippi*.

OCTOBER   *The Merry Widow*, with English lyrics by Hart, is released.

DECEMBER   "Blue Moon" is published.

1935

FEBRUARY 7   Hart returns to New York from Hollywood.

FEBRUARY 24   "What Are You Doing in Here?" sung as part of *The Post-Depression Gaieties* at New Amsterdam Theatre, New York City; 1 performance.

APRIL   *Mississippi* is released.

APRIL 29   "You Are So Lovely and I'm So Lonely" sung in non-musical *Something Gay*, at Morosco Theatre, New York City; 72 performances.

OCTOBER 22   Radio show *Let's Have Fun*, with two new songs by Rodgers and Hart, is broadcast.

NOVEMBER 16   First performance of *Jumbo* at the Hippodrome, New York City; 233 performances.

1936

MARCH 21   First performance of *On Your Toes* at the Shubert Theatre, Boston.

APRIL 11   *On Your Toes* opens at the Imperial Theatre, New York City (transfers to the Majestic Theatre, November); 315 performances.

JUNE   *Dancing Pirate* is released.

NOVEMBER 27   First performance of Rodgers and Hart's symphonic narrative *All Points West* performed by Paul Whiteman and the Philadelphia Orchestra with Ray Middleton as soloist at the Academy of Music, Philadelphia.

1937

MARCH 31   First performance of *Babes in Arms* at the Shubert Theatre, Boston.

APRIL 14   *Babes in Arms* opens at the Shubert Theatre, New York City (transfers to the Majestic Theatre, October); 289 performances.

APRIL 19   *On Your Toes* opens at the Coliseum, London; 123 performances.

SUMMER   Rodgers and Hart in Hollywood to write score for *Fools for Scandal*.

OCTOBER 11   First performance of *I'd Rather Be Right* at the Colonial Theatre, Boston.

NOVEMBER 2   *I'd Rather Be Right* opens at the Alvin Theatre, New York City (transfers to the Music Box Theatre, May 1938); 290 performances.

1938

JANUARY 10   Theodore (Teddy) Hart marries Dorothy Lubou.

MARCH   *Fools for Scandal* is released.

APRIL 14   First performance of *I Married an Angel* at the Shubert Theatre, New Haven.

MAY 11   *I Married an Angel* opens at the Shubert Theatre, New York City; 338 performances.

SEPTEMBER 26   Rodgers and Hart appear on the cover of *Time* magazine.

OCTOBER   Lorenz Hart stricken with pneumonia.

NOVEMBER 3   First performance of *The Boys from Syracuse* at the Shubert Theatre, New Haven.

NOVEMBER 23   *The Boys from Syracuse* opens at the Alvin Theatre, New York City; 235 performances.

1939

FEBRUARY   Rodgers and Hart and George Abbott in Florida to work on show ideas.

SEPTEMBER   Film version of *Babes in Arms* is released.

OCTOBER   Film version of *On Your Toes* is released. No Rodgers and Hart songs are retained.

OCTOBER 2   First performance of *Too Many Girls* at the Shubert Theatre, Boston.

OCTOBER 18   *Too Many Girls* opens at the Imperial Theatre, New York City; 249 performances.

1940

MARCH 7   First performance of *Higher and Higher* at the Shubert Theatre, New Haven.

APRIL 4   *Higher and Higher* opens at the Shubert Theatre, New York City; 108 performances.

AUGUST   Film version of *The Boys from Syracuse* is released.

NOVEMBER   Film version of *Too Many Girls* is released.

DECEMBER 16   First performance of *Pal Joey* at the Forrest Theatre, Philadelphia.

DECEMBER 25   *Pal Joey* opens at the Ethel Barrymore Theatre, New York City (transfers to the Shubert Theatre in September 1941 and to the St. James Theatre in October 1941); 374 performances.

1941

JANUARY 9   Lorenz Hart in Miami, Florida, with Dorothy Hart.

MAY   *They Met in Argentina* is released.
Hart at work on musical version of Richard Shattuck's comedy thriller *The Snark Was a Boojum*. Never completed.

1942

FEBRUARY 28   Lorenz Hart in Doctors Hospital, New York City.

MAY 11   First performance of *All's Fair* (retitled *By Jupiter*) at the Shubert Theatre, Boston.

JUNE 2   *By Jupiter* opens at the Shubert Theatre, New York City; 427 performances (longest running of all Rodgers and Hart shows).

JULY   Film version of *I Married an Angel* is released.

1943

MARCH 11   First performance of *Away We Go!* (retitled *Oklahoma!*) by Rodgers and Hammerstein at the Shubert Theatre, New Haven.

MARCH 31   *Oklahoma!* opens at the St. James Theatre, New York City; 2,212 performances.

APRIL   Frieda Hart dies.

OCTOBER 28   First performance of new version of *A Connecticut Yankee* at the Forrest Theatre, Philadelphia.

NOVEMBER 17   *A Connecticut Yankee* (revised) opens at the Martin Beck Theatre, New York City; 135 performances. Lorenz Hart's last score.

NOVEMBER 19   Hart, ill with pneumonia, is taken to Doctors Hospital, New York City.

NOVEMBER 22   Hart dies at the age of forty-eight in Doctors Hospital, New York City.

ACKNOWLEDGMENTS

Our deepest thanks to Theodore S. Chapin, Managing Director of the Rodgers and Hammerstein Office, for his unfailing encouragement and support; to Philip Zimet and Frederic Ingraham, on behalf of the Lorenz Hart Estate; to the late Alan Jay Lerner for his Appreciation of his friend Lorenz Hart; to Dorothy F. Rodgers; to Louis Landerson, Alvin Deutsch, Paul H. Epstein, and Jamie Glauber, for major assistance in researching the Rodgers and Hart song copyrights; to Rodgers and Hart's music publishers Warner Brothers, Inc., Chappell & Co., Inc., Famous Music Corporation, T. B. Harms Company, Robbins Music Corporation, Edward B. Marks Music Company, and Bourne Company, for their collaboration in this book; to the Rodgers and Hammerstein Office, The Music Division of the Library of Congress, The Lincoln Center Library of the Performing Arts, Yale University Library, The Columbiana Collection of the Columbia University Library, The Museum of the City of New York, ASCAP (the American Society of Composers, Authors and Publishers), The Columbia Grammar School, The Museum of Modern Art, Tams-Witmark Music Library, Metro-Goldwyn-Mayer, and Paramount Pictures; to early Rodgers and Hart collaborators Irving Caesar and the late Morrie Ryskind; to original cast members of Rodgers and Hart shows, Eleanor Shaler Dickson, Joy Hodges, John Hundley, Gene Kelly, Edith Meiser, Barbara Newberry, Vivienne Segal, and the late Tilde Getze; to Tommy Krasker, for invaluable help at all stages of this book; and to many, many more including: Louis Aborn, Lois Ahrens, William Appleton, Elizabeth Auman, Ben Bagley, Bob Baumgart, Roderick Bladel, Phyllis Blohm, William Bolcom, Lester Boles, Jeffrey J. Brabec, Richard Buck, Victoria Clark, Henry Cohen, Michael Colby, Mary Corliss, Carol Cuellar, Lee Davis, Amber Edwards, Roberta Elkins, Peter Felcher, Nicole Friedman, Vivien Friedman, Donald Fowle, James Fuld, Mary Anne Gaetti, Bob Gersten, Stanley Green, Sidney Herman, Jack Holmes, Richard Jackson, Michael Kerker, Al Kohn, Miles Kreuger, Dale Kugel, the late Donald Leavitt, Willie Lerner, Richard Lewine, Joe Lewis, Lisa Lippmann, Don Madison, Charles Mathes, John McGlinn, Frank Military, Larry Moore, Maxine Newman, Paul Palmer, Joseph Petticrew, William Reilly, Irwin Robinson, John Shepard, Wayne Shirley, Bobby Short, Maxwell Silverman, Alfred Simon, Sally Sommer, Steven Suskin, Dorothy Swerdlove, Kay Swift, Andrea Traubner, Richard Traubner, Bill Tynes, Eldridge Walker, Jr., and Richard Warren, Jr.

Special gratitude to the late George Balanchine, who loved Lorenz Hart and urged that his lyrics be published; to Carol Kohler, for helping to prepare and type this manuscript; to Philip Kimball, whose keen ears detected many obscure and inaudible words on old radio air checks and sound track recordings, and to Philip's mother, Abigail Kimball, for her patience and fortitude; and to the late Robert Luther Barlow, whose knowledge and love of Rodgers and Hart's imperishable legacy inspired Robert Kimball to become a musical theater historian; and to Martha Kaplan, Robert Gottlieb, Nancy Clements, Dorothy Schmiderer, Andy Hughes, Sharon Zimmerman, and Robert Cornfield, who guided our good intentions into this book.

THE COMPLETE LYRICS OF LORENZ HART

Lorenz Hart, 1918

EARLY WORK | 1911–1919

MAX AND FRIEDA— SILVER WEDDING ANNIVERSARY

From the age of six, Hart had written verse for every family occasion. The oldest surviving example dates from 1911. November 6 of that year was his parents' twenty-fifth wedding anniversary. The celebration was held at Harastad Hall in the Bronx, and the family and a hundred or so political cronies were present. For the occasion Hart wrote his own words to the music of Irving Berlin's big hit song "Alexander's Ragtime Band."

VERSE 1

Oh, my hubby, put your hat on.
Better hurry, the taxi's waiting.
We are going, surely going
To the big array—Silver Wedding Day.
Better hurry, better hurry—
Lord, we don't want to come too late, dear.
Come now, somehow, better hurry along.

REFRAIN 1

So clink your glass, each lad and lass,
For Max and Frieda's wedding day.
Put on a smile, make life worthwhile—
Let each wrinkle shout Hooray!
For life is much too short and time will always
    fly—
One, two, twenty-five, the years go rolling by.
This is the bestest night of all—let the laughter
    fall.
Years of joy, Max a boy, at full two score is well.
And Mrs. Hart still plays her part,
Though her age I dare not tell.
But if you want to make the evening seem like
    the dear old times,
Clink your glass, each lad and lass,
To Max and Frieda's wedding day.

VERSE 2

Way, way back, dear, '86, dear,
Things were not just like they are now, dear—
I was young, dear, you were young, dear,
And we didn't plan to help the census man.
Silver streaks, dear, in my hair, dear,
But our hearts, dear, are as young as ever.
Come now, somehow, jolly up and be young.

REFRAIN 2

In diesen Haus lass Saus und Braus
Könige von allem sein.
Drink a pile, it's worth your while,
Hab die Katz im Morgenschein.
For life is much too short and the years are
    rolling by—
Eins, zwei, fünf-und-zwanzig,
Let the old times fly.
This is the bestest night of all
Let the laughter fall.
Nur einmal ist es erlaubt,
Dass der Mensch gut leben kann.
Die Zeit fliegt ja und Sorg beraubt
Alle Jugend von dem Mann.
So if you want to make the evening seem like the
    dear old times,
Clink your glass, each lad and lass,
Zu der Silberfestigung.

SCHOOL VERSE

Hart attended the Columbia Grammar School on West 93rd Street in New York City, graduating from high school in 1914. He would have completed his studies in June 1913, but he and his brother Teddy traveled in Europe, mostly Germany, in the fall of 1912. As a result, he needed an extra semester at Columbia Grammar. The following selections were printed in *The Columbia News*, the school's monthly paper. Hart was an associate editor of the *News* in 1913.

THE GOOBERGOO AND THE KANTAN

An allegory published in *The Columbia News*, November 1911.

Long, long ago, in the land of the Golden Pools lived a magnificent green Goobergoo. He dwelt in a wood-pond, like all other Goobergoos, who are the frogs of Fairyland, and sang the most beautiful songs. His mellow voice was known, far and wide, for its charming melodies.

> "An emerald Goobergoo I,
>   In the land of the Golden Pools,
>   My note, 'neath amber sky,
>   The elfin kingdom rules."

Thus sang the beautiful green Goobergoo, on his pebble in the wood-pond, in the land of the Golden Pools.

The Kantan was jealous, furiously jealous, and trouble brews when the wrath of the Kantan is aroused.

"Who is this insignificant creature that dares to rival me; who dares to insult the Kantan?"

But the beautiful green Goobergoo did not care a bit. What if the Kantan were a large bird with a long beak? He, the beautiful green Goobergoo, excelled in song.

> "The Kantan is indeed,
>   A large and mawkish bird,
>   Whose voice is sore in need
>   Of never being heard."

At this the Kantan became doubly furious, for he hated the gentle ballads of the Goobergoo. His delight was ragtime.

> "Oh, ma babe, waltz with me, kid.
>   Gee, you've got me off ma lid.
>   Kiddo, dear, you're sure the candy,
>   Come and spiel wid your boy Sandy."

One bleak day, the Kantan gobbled up the Goobergoo, and, to this day, the sweet singer of ballads lies vanquished by the ungainly bird of ragtime.

The beautiful wood-pond has dried up, and in its place stands a vaudeville theater managed by George M. Cohan.

THE BIBLE

Published in *The Columbia News*, November 1911.

All glorious epitome of light,
Illuminator of dark hours,
E'er strengthening our poor weak sight,
In the realm of celestial bow'rs.

True, strong men need not thee,
But who on earth is strong?
To man thou e'er shalt be
True guide 'twixt right and wrong.

THE MODERN STUDENT

Published in *The Columbia News*, January 1912.

Will Shakespeare thought that fellows creep
"Unwillingly to school,"
And must to pore o'er knowledge deep
Be driven like a mule.
The classics were the goals pursued
By boys in Willie's day,
The English tongue was far too rude
Save for the common play.

New teachings have sprung up since then,
We've buried all that rot,
We will no longer wield the pen!
We have the Turkey Trot.

We care not what old Tullius raves,
And really must confess:
He should have sunk beneath the waves
Ere Catiline's address.
The greatest Julius when he stood
Most mighty o'er the mass,
With all his tact he never could
Have thrown a forward pass.

At Homer who told tales of Troy
We raise an awful din,
We'd rather hear Sir Eddie Foy
Sing "Ragtime Violin."
Salome too was not the whirl
The Semites used to think,
Why Miss Deslys could make that girl
Sit down and take a drink.

For modes and ways have changed a bit
Since Shakespeare was a boy,
The empty fads have made a hit
And ignorance is joy.

WASHINGTON

Published in *The Columbia News,* February 1912.

Chiseled in stone, your stately mien,
Haughty, predominates the scene;
Your lips are firm, your eyes serene,
Father of our Country!

LINCOLN

Published in *The Columbia News,* February 1912.

Gently you gaze with kindly eye,
Careworn for Peace, your forehead high;
Hero, your name shall never die,
Savior of our Country!

THE ROCK OF REFUGE

Published in *The Columbia News,* April 1912.

When you're tired, and languid,
And limped and slow
From the drudge of all study, from
School. "Hall of Woe."
When you feel life, a dead weight,
There's one place to go,
And drown all your sorrow, the
"Ten-twenty show."

Oh! "ten-twenty show!"
Oh! temple of Loew!
Where the brave cowboy shoots the wild buffalo,
Where Virtue e'er triumphs; brave
Dick kills his foe,
It's death to the villain, in
The "ten-twenty show."

Oh! dramas ecstatic
In pictures dramatic,
Appeal to the mass and the aristocratic,
Your pulse beats the faster at "thrillers"
    emphatic.
In no time you'll change to a "filmofanatic."

Your view is, in fact, not confined to a screen,
For vaudeville holds sway, that execrable queen,
Great "Sandow" and "Venus," "Terpsichore,"
    too
Appear between pictures, in gold review.
Then, horror of horrors, the clog dancers prance
And kick on the boards in true variance,
To all forms of beauty and sanity too,
But are met with applause, be their merits e'er
    few!

Oh! ten-twenty show!
Oh! temple of Loew!
There's a world of diversity
Where the lesser stars glow.
If you're troubled and bothered
With the discords of life,
Come to this Rock of Refuge
And forget all your strife.

BASEBALL AND THE EXAMS—A "MIX-UP"

Published in *The Columbia News,* January 1913.

I lay one night, a-dreaming,
My homework still undone;
This world was but a baseball field
And I, it's "Mathewson."
Yes, master of the "drop" was I,
And of the "fadeaway,"
And Greek and Trig,
Poor Greek and Trig,
Seemed very far away.

Then entered Jinx, wizard of woe,
And uttered: "Entrance Board!"
The concrete stand changed into desks,
The fans to pupils. Laud!
And Jinx, he grabbed me by the ears,
Believe me I was awed.

"Young man, you know the Roman Wars?
Speak up, or you will flunk."
"Yes, sir," said I, "I've got a list";
But then I lost all spunk.
"In literature, what have you read?
Will Shakespeare, Poe or Swift?"
"I've read McCormick's 'Ode to Sterne'
And Goldberg's 'Daily Drift.' "

"What about German?" "Sure," said I,
"I know Hans Wagner well."
"I think you'll flunk," said Jinx at last;
He pushed me, and I fell,
Down in a cubic cube I fell
And hit a tangent post.
Oh! Dante's Hell is surely sweet
Compared to Jinx's roast.

The devils fooled with big test tubes,
Made H-2 SO-4;
It was so hot my baseball spikes
Melted upon the floor.
"Give me a chance, dear Jinx, just one,"
Begged I, and he replied,
"Tell me the platform of your choice,
The hobby you bestride."

"I am a Socialist, sir," I said.
And Jinx cried out with joy,
"We Devils all support that Cause,
Our blessing on you, boy!"
And while he spoke, a test tube broke—
A boom! A crash!!! A roar!!!

And from sheer fright I pulled my sheets
And bedding to the floor.

"It's half past eight, get up right now,
Or you'll be late again!"
I rubbed my eyes and wondered how
My nightmare left me sane.
But I have written seven strains
Of awful doggerel,
About some things you don't believe,
And, as you're right, farewell!

COMUS AT C.G.S.

Published in *The Columbia News*, March 1913.

A FRIVOLOUS MASK
by Lorenz MILTON Hart

THE PERSONS:

The Attendant Spirit . . . . Mr. Cook
Comus . . . . Andrew Charles Simmons
His Crew . . . . . . McCormick and Fellow Demons
The Lady . . . . Miss Bertie Brummer

[*Scene: An alluring gymnasium. Comus is discovered imploring the Lady in the most dulcet tones and with graceful gestures*]

COMUS: Nay, Lady Bertie—if I but wave this
wand,
Your nerves are all chained up in
tutti-frutti,
And you a statue such as Venus was.
Come, now, cast up the basketball.
LADY: Fool, do not boast.
Thou canst not touch the freedom of my
mind.
I'll play no ball with thy thrice-wicked
crew—
For I would study as the Auerbachs do.
COMUS: Why are you vexed, Bertie?
From these gates
'Fessor calls merrily—look at all his
treasurers:
There's Martin Sheridan in halftone cut,
And here's his sweater blue, and his tape
measures.
Come, join my crew, and "forward" be.
Forget your studies—come, be free!

LADY: Never, base Andrew! I will study on
Till, languishing, I drop from sheer
exhaustion.
[*Enter the Attendant Spirit*]
A.S.: O Simmons! Thou art vile!
Go get thee hence
Unto the Office—tell there thy offense.
Thou canst not tempt this fair one:
She is pure, and purer than that word.
Go! and endure
The harshest Saturday thou e'er hast
spent.
Go, thou vile Comus, and relent, relent!
LADY: Good angel, how can I thank thee now?
A.S.: Study thine Algebra. I can allow
No basketball—I can—nohow.*

*Not like Milton, we admit—more like Frank
Tenney—but we must rhyme this thing in
some manner.

[*Exeunt in extreme ecstasy. The Spirit trips merrily off.
The Lady must be careful not to trip or dance, unless
the stage boards are very strong*]

[*Reenter Comus and Crew*]
COMUS: Most merry band of roughnecks bold,
Most gallant, gleeful laddies,
Ye fouled right well in every game,
Even as did your daddies.
But they were here in years gone by,
Forgotten is their fumbling.
No better played they, lads, than ye.
Yea, ye need do no grumbling.
And Mac's the seeliest rascal here,
Your forward and your thinker.
On many a man of Berkeley's team
He hath bestowed a blinker.
Come, let's carouse and gallivant—
We need not Venus Brummer.
We'll bacchanal around this Gym
Till June brings on the Summer.
Throw schoolbooks to the winds till then,
We do not care for study.
Till June arrive—then, rascals, then
We'll cram our brain cells muddy.

[*Ed. note: At this point the writer was slightly disabled
by furious editors. He may continue this poem next
month*]

THE CROAK OF THE EDITOR'S RAVEN

Published in *The Columbia News*, March 1913.

(With apologies to E. A. Poe)

Once upon a midnight dreary, while he pondered,
weak and weary,
Over many a quaint and curious column of
athletic lore,
While he nodded, nearly napping, suddenly there
came a tapping
As of someone gently rapping, rapping at the
office door.
"A contributor," he muttered, "tapping at my
office door—
Bertie, sleek, and nothing more."

"Here, O Harold, I have written verse of magic
piquancy;
Hear the meter, mark the jingle, it is music to
your ear."
When he took it, lo! he found it full of faults
both light and grave.
"Oh! this job is not so pleasant," echoed Harold
with a leer;
"Bertie, you are not a poet," Harold muttered
like a seer.
Exit Bertie by the rear.

Every faulty "form-note" changing, every article
arranging.
Doubting, swearing, blotting blots no blotter did
before—
But the silence was unbroken, and the stillness
gave no token,
And the only accent spoken was the whispered
words "That bore!"
This, he muttered, and the echo whispered back
those words "That bore!"
"Gee!" quoth Harold. "Nevermore!"

"Wretch," cried Harold, "thing of evil! wretched
paper of the devil!
By A. Simmons' lanky shadow, by our Bertie's
fattened pouch,
Ne'er again will I sit watching, ne'er again
correct this botching!
Curse the *News* and all this trouble! Would that
Izzy Moyse were here!"
And he nodded, almost sleeping, as you now are,
reader dear.
Gone and vanished was that leer.

6

In his dreams, his pale lips parted, and they
   formed the words "Oh! dear,
Nevermore—oh, never fear!"

L'ENVOI

Published in *The Columbia News*, May 1913.

Spring swiftly sweeps the sands of Time
And Summer days are nigh,
When Work is o'er and Play is king
And Jollity can have its fling,
Heigh-ho, for the bright, blue sky!

For ocean strands or mountain glades
We're bound; we're glad we're free!
We leave school with a merry will
But though we're gone, the school's there still,
Resting sleepily.

Shall we return?
Some of us will;
The rest will ride along
On rockets through the sphere of space.
Will they fall?
Are they weak, are they strong?
But the school's there still,

Each morning finds
Its lagging, lazy lads
"Creeping like snails, unwillingly"
Even as did their dads.

So, after all, leave we or stay,
The school's there still, we know.
The pranks we played are played again
By the very sons of the selfsame men,
Heigh-ho, we are free, let's go!

SPUGS

Published in *The Columbia News*, December 1913.

Oh! Santa Claus, you merry myth,
The kiddies' keenest joy,
You are securely, surely loved
By every girl and boy.

But Pa, 'tis said, is not so fond
Of your beloved name,

For what he said of you last night
Was certainly a shame.

Why is it, Santa Claus, when you
Bring all the kiddies joy,
That Pa and Ma and Brother Hugh
You every year annoy?

THE MODERN GRIND ON HIS WAY TO THE NEW DEGREE

Published in *The Columbia News*, January 1914.

Tom has lost his pitching arm,
Tom has lost his slide,
Tommy never runs a mile
O'er the countryside.

Thomas grinds the day away,
Burns the midnight oil—
Auburn curls are turning gray,
'Tis tremendous toil.

He don't peg on Algebra,
He don't dig on Trig,
For his English and his Math
Tom don't care a fig.

Twelve points on the College books
For the "Castle Walk,"
"Hesitation" brings three more,
So the records talk.

Tom will get the "One-Step" soon,
In a month or two,
When his net amount of points
Reaches thirty-two.

When he gets the "Walton Glide,"
"Tango del Maurice,"
Tommy's learned enough to try
The "Genee Caprice."

Then in six months and a year
If his legs will last,
If the poor old concave Tom's
Body's like a mast—

Thomas then gets his degree,
D.P.D.D.
Doctor of Palais de Danse,
"One-Stepology."

. . .

So he grinds the day away,
Burns the midnight oil,
But the D.P.D.D.'s
Well worth Tommy's toil.

WALL STREET

Although the editors believe "Wall Street" was intended for *The Columbia News*, they were unable to discover it in any of the old copies of the publication.

Between the dark defiles of stone,
Amidst a dreary din,
The surging souls crowd endlessly—
Each doomed to die or win.
Small atoms in this striving sea,
The fate of nations spin.

The dark defiles of stone will hear
Again that dreary din,
But other surging mobs will crowd
And others die or win.
And some will fall down by the way
Who caused the world to spin.

In race and creed they vary all,
In motive, all are kin!
But short the time is theirs to surge
And for the world to spin!
The dark defiles of stone will hear
Another dreary din.

CAMP SONGS

Lorenz Hart was an active camper. In the summers of 1908 and 1909 he and his brother Teddy attended the Weingart Institute, a summer camp-school in the Catskills. From 1910 through 1913 they were at Camp Paradox in the Adirondacks. In 1917 he went to Brant Lake Camp as a dramatic counselor. His oldest surviving song lyrics date from his Brant Lake summers.

THE TALE OF THE LONE(SOME) PINE

Verse. Probably written at Camp Paradox.

Dashed off in a wild moment by Lorry Hart

'Twas a balmy summer evening
On the hillside August eighth,
And we opened up our tent flies
While the big moon smiled us faith.
It's the moon we have to thank, it's
All his fault we used no blankets,
While the silhouette of Lone Pine
Seemed to warn us like a wraith.

'Twas a balmy summer evening
When King Sarnoff blew his Taps:
"LIGHTS OUT!" (Jablow eats salami
While the little Kinberg naps.)
Rusty Robbins in his snoozing
Tells you what he dreams in shmoozing,
While the hillside all is quiet,
Unsuspicious little chaps.

Then the north wind came a-roaring,
And I turned around in bed,
"BANG!" the tent pole snapped, and, zowie!
Right on Moldy Silver's head.
Mamma Lipps put his camp hat on,
And he kept his coat of fat on.
Artie Bernstein said so many things
Much better left unsaid.

'Twas a balmy summer evening
While the wind blew Harvey's nose,
And Valensi almost fainted
When he counted just nine toes.
Uncle Bob sat with a new hick
In his now so-famous Buick,
And the wind blew off his glasses
While his fond affection froze.

MORAL

When Lone Pine is grimly warning,
Cover up well till the morning,
For you cannot fool the horse fly.

DEAR OLD SCHOOL DAYS

Lorenz Hart wrote this for the camp paper, when he was drama counselor at Brant Lake.

When the sky-hooks are connected,
And the tent-keys lock the tents,
Leery lessons we've neglected
Are assigned by learned gents.

When we study hist'ry's pages,
We think Charlemagne a quince.
What are all these princely sages
When you've seen the Brent Lek prince?

As we pore o'er Fenny Cooper,
We think Fenimore was drunker
Than old Nero, when this trooper
Went and named his hero Unca.

And geography is rotten.
I suppose I'll can that book,
For its author has forgotten
Where's the Isle of Abel Crook.

Mathematics, too, is futile.
I'll throw it in the shade,
For what statistician brutal
Knows the runs that Leslie made?

After school has made us weary,
Though this camping season's done,
Next July, all bright and cheery,
Yea bo! comes another one.

B-R-A

In 1919 Lorenz Hart wrote the book and lyrics for *B-R-A*, a Brant Lake Camp show described as "The Crazy Musical Comedy." Milton Thomas (Mickie Thomashefsky) wrote the music. Their songs included were "B-R-A," "Green and Gray," "Old Brant Lake," "He Lights Another Mecca" and "Our Cheerleader." Also written for the show, but missing, are: "I Used to Love Them All," "Tee Ta Tee," and "Horicon Hop."

VERSE

Every time the boys of Brant Lake Camp
Eat or drink or go on a tramp,
Win a scrap or have short-story nights,
Take a nap and get mosquito bites
On sunny days or drear

They give this little cheer.
That tells the world the Brant Lake boys are
    here.

REFRAIN

B-R-A begins the brand, boys,
That will always win the day.
B-R-A for brawn will stand, boys,
You start brains with B-R-A,
Not the B-R-A in brass, boys,
Nor the B-R-A in brag,
But the B-R-A in Brant, boys,
Never strikes a snag.
Beat this B-R-A you can't, boys,
It's in our grand old flag!

GREEN AND GRAY

VERSE

We are the boys who always win
Any old fight that we begin;
That's why we're proud to say
We're from Brant Lake Camp today.

REFRAIN

We will fight today
For the Green and Gray,
And our hearts are loyal and true,
When we meet the foe
We will let them know
What old Brant Lake Camp can do.
YEA BO!
With a battle roar,
We will ask for more,
Ever hungry for the fight.
The good old Green and Gray will fix you,
And it always fixes right!

OLD BRANT LAKE

VERSE

Far from the hills that call me tonight,
Bound by the rills of moonbeams golden bright
In memories, fond memories,
Dreaming, I delight.

When the moon shines down on the lake
And the tents are still,
Only silver stars are awake
All quiet on the hill.
The green hills are calling
My senses enthralling,
Then I smile for memory's sake
And dream of old Brant Lake.

HE LIGHTS
ANOTHER MECCA

VERSE

Of course you know our Uncle Joe,
He of the bearded chin;
Who only wears a shirt because
It keeps his muscles in.
At morning, noon, or night,
On dry days or on wet,
He flurries thru all worries
With a Mecca cigarette!

REFRAIN

He lights another Mecca at inspection time,
He lights one when they're blowing taps.
He lights a Mecca underneath your nose,
When you're snoozin' a couple o' naps.
When he's up at bat,
When he gets a fly,
When he hits the ball right in the eye,
Do you think he runs like you and I?
He lights another Mecca, that's all!

OUR CHEERLEADER

He can twist and squirm
When a base we steal,
Like the lubricant worm
Or the gooiest eel.
A Hula dancer has nothing on Eddie
When the team's going smooth
And the pitcher is steady.
His frantic motions, guiding our cheering,
Make us sure that a victory we're nearing.
When contorting himself into a trance,
He goes through the motions of a shimmy dance.

So here's to our cheerleader, our cotton-top blond,
The best little leader this side of the pond.

SHE'S CAMPING AT
RED WING

Other songs written at Brant Lake Camp by Hart and
Thomas were: "She's Camping at Red Wing," "The Green
Song," "The Gray Song," and "The Brant Lake Blues."

Red Wing, she's camping at Red Wing.
I'm tramping to Red Wing very soon.
Beaming, in her fanciful dreaming,
There's a little of roguish scheming,
Not unseeming.
Oceans of fondest emotions
Are waiting to find my rendezvous.
Wait, dear. I'll not be too late, dear.
My princess of Red Wing, I love you.

THE GREEN SONG

The blue sea turns green
When you see it's not serene.
There's green all over Ireland,
The blood-and-fire land.
Its foes have seen
The green Brant Lake hills.
Our hearts with memory thrills
When our war cry we raise.
It's a gray day for grays,
For the greens have no green in their eyes.

THE GRAY SONG

When the ocean is angry, it's gray, boys.
And when the storm clouds appear, they're gray.
And we will let those green heads chatter,
They have no gray matter.
Let them come our way!
We'll make those greens green with envy today,
  boys.
They're in our power, in terror they crave.
And after years they'll all come back much wiser,
Gray heads at old Brant Lake.

THE BRANT LAKE BLUES

I chase the green line in the sub,
I swim the point in my bathtub;
In that position I lose ambition,
Bo!
The city hits you in the face.
It's hotter than the other place.
And I am yearning for my returning;
My heart is burning,
So!
I miss Uncle Joe,
The best old pal that I know,
And funny old Chris,
Another fellow I miss.
I miss your flabby nose, O,
Crazy Bozo.
And if I go back there perhaps,
I'll never talk again at Taps.
I never will lose
Those dear old Brant Lake Blues.

CHESTERTOWN

This and the following song also were written for Brant
Lake Camp.

VERSE

Goodbye, Broadway,
I'm now a rustic churl;
I dream today 'neath new-mown hay
Because I've found the girl.

REFRAIN

I've got a girl in Chestertown,
Sweet as the mountain dew.
Two lips that never, never frown.
Her eyes are laughing, too.
She'll never want a limousine,
She only wants a kiss.
With my arms around a gingham gown
I'll get chesty in old Chestertown.

IN MEMORIAM

When dark, relentless shadows on our way
Leave us bewildered if the way is right,
We must prepare for night with every day.
Light without shade is never, never light.

And like a wiser bard our wonder grows,
At life's unfeeling and unfailing tide,
When youth's sweet-scented manuscript must close,
While old and dusty books are open wide.

But then you never knew that spring was o'er,
And never did you feel life's winter chill,
Though brief your interlude, you loved it more.
Who knows the purpose of the Master's will?

I LOVE TO LIE
AWAKE IN BED

Camp song. Date unknown. Music by Arthur Schwartz,
who later used the same melody for "I Guess I'll Have to
Change My Plan," lyric by Howard Dietz.

I love to lie awake in bed
Right after taps I pull the flaps above my head.
I rest my head upon my pillow—
Oh, what a light the moonbeams shed.
I feel so happy I could cry,
And tears are born within the corner of my eye.
To be at home with Ma was never like this.
I could go on forever like this.

I like to lie awake a while
And go to sleep with a smile.

CAMP WIGWAM
HIKING SONG

Music by Robert K. Lippmann. Date unknown. Privately
printed in the Camp Wigwam Song Book. Called to the
editors' attention by musical theatre historian Alfred
Simon. Lippmann was a counselor at Camp Wigwam, a
friend of Richard Rodgers, and an early collaborator with
Oscar Hammerstein II. Lippmann and Hammerstein had
songs in the 1917 Columbia Varsity Show *Home, James.*

Swing along, boys of Wigwam,
All together in step.
Tho' the sun is hot and dusty miles grow longer,
Will your will, boys, and your will will grow
    much stronger.
All good fellows are marching
As we sing the same old song.
For the doggone Wigwam kind
Never lag behind
As we swing along.

THE SANDMAN

In 1914 Hart began studies at the Columbia University
School of Journalism. He was active in university dramatics and wrote criticism for the Columbia *Spectator.* In the
1916 Columbia Varsity Show (*The Peace Pirates,* April
12–15, 1916, Hotel Astor Grand Ballroom, New York
City) he played the role of Mrs. Rockyford, wife of a
"jitney pacifist." Three years later he contributed a lyric
for "The Sandman" to the 1919 Varsity Show (*Take a
Chance,* April 28–30, May 1 and 3, 1919, Grand Ballroom, Hotel Plaza, New York City). The music is credited
to Roy Webb, Columbia 1910, in the show program and
libretto. Introduced by Leonard F. Manheim and ensemble.

VERSE

On twilight's wings
The cricket sings—
The Sandman's coming
With shades of night.
Each sleepy head
Goes off to bed
And quite a number
Dream in their slumber.
The Sandman brings
The joy of kings
To every sweetheart who's true.
And little deary,
If you are weary,
Then he will come to you.

REFRAIN

Sweetheart, sleep with sand in your eyes,
Dreaming of love's paradise,
And know the dreamy delight
Of some Arabian Night.
You dream you'll never, never, never arise
From the land where happiness lies.
And when your heart is weary,
I'll call the Sandman,
I'll call the Sandman,
And he will close your eyes.

Lorenz Hart and Richard Rodgers

RODGERS AND HART | 1919–1921

ANY OLD PLACE WITH YOU

Published December 1919. Rodgers and Hart's first published song and their first song in a Broadway show. Introduced by Alan Hale and Eve Lynn in *A Lonely Romeo* after being added to the show on August 26, 1919. At one time it was called "The Geography Song" and was printed with the third refrain in Camp Paradox's literary magazine *The Paradoxion*, November 1920.

VERSE 1

There is a railroad around Lovers' Lane
And the conductor is you.
My heart goes faster than any old train,
Right on schedule, too.
All is ready for our honeymoon.
I've a route in view.
Our express leaves morning, night and noon.
Travel with me, please do.

REFRAIN 1

We'll melt in Syria,
Freeze in Siberia,
Negligee in Timbuktu.
In dreamy Portugal
I'm goin' to court you, gal.
Ancient Rome we'll paint anew.
Life would be cheerier,
On Lake Superior.
How would Pekin do?
I'm goin' to corner ya
In California.
Any old place with you.

VERSE 2

We'll madly fly over hill and down dale
In little Cupid's express.
I'm at the throttle and I'll never fail
If you whisper "Yes."
Come with me and let me be your guide.
One plus one is one.
Then our headlights never can collide,
Till life's long road is done.

REFRAIN 2

From old Virginia,
Or Abyssinia,
We'll go straight to Halifax.
I've got a mania
For Pennsylvania,
Even ride in London hacks.

I'll call each dude a pest
You like in Budapest.
Oh, for far Peru!
I'll go to hell for ya,
Or Philadelphia,
Any old place with you.

REFRAIN 3

We'll board a special train
Right for the coast of Maine.
Thousand Islands we'll explore;
Our honeymoon I've planned
Touring the Rio Grande,
Then right off to Labrador;
Clothes won't encumber ya
Down in Colombia;
Chile's saucy too,
In Macedonia
Let's get pneumonia,
Any old place with you.

YOU'D BE SURPRISED, 1920

Presented by the Akron Club at the Plaza Hotel, New York, March 6, 1920, and April 11, 1920. Music by Richard C. Rodgers. Lyrics by Lorenz M. Hart and Milton G. Bender. Book by Milton G. Bender. Directed by Milton G. Bender. Orchestra conducted by Richard C. Rodgers. Cast headed by Carol King, Ralph G. Engelsman, Phillip B. Leavitt, Dorothy Fields, Etta Leblang, and Elise Bonwit.

The lyrics to "Princess of the Willow Tree" and "When We Are Married" were written by Milton G. Bender.

The following lyrics, some of which could have been written alone by, or in collaboration with, Milton G. Bender, are missing: "Spain" (introduced by the entire company), "You Don't Have To Be a Toreador" (Dorothy Fields, Phillip B. Leavitt, and Ralph G. Engelsman), "Poor Fish" (Etta Leblang), "My World of Romance" (Ira R. Schattman), "China" (the Sing Song Girls: Kathryn Mayer, Dorith Bamberger, Edna Brandt, Emily Guggenheim, Viola Mayer, Elise Bonwit, Carol King, Dorothy Fields, Ruth Glaser, Ethel Rogers, and Etta Leblang), "Aphrodite" (Julian Jacobs, Robert Cassell, and Abraham Rosenstein), "I Hate to Talk About Myself," "Little Girl, Little Boy," and "Flying the Blimp."

DON'T LOVE ME LIKE OTHELLO

Introduced by Carol King and Ralph G. Engelsman. Also introduced by Leonard Falk Manheim and F. Fraser Bond in *Fly with Me* (1920), and by Margaret Hamilton and Bernard Ocko in *Say It with Jazz* (1921). Same music but different lyric used for the refrain of "You Can't Fool Your Dreams" in *Poor Little Ritz Girl* (1920).

VERSE 1

SHE: My romantic fancy isn't hard to please,
That is why my heart belongs to you.
You may not be handsome, like a Grecian frieze,
If you're but affectionate, you'll do.
I don't want a Don Juan with kiss-and-kill-'em eyes;
History is warning me where the danger lies.

REFRAIN 1

Don't love me like Othello,
I'm much too young to die.
An Arrow collar fellow
Can never make me sigh.
Don't love me like King Bluebeard,
His technique was risqué.
And never try to be a caveman—
Don't rave, man,
Behave, man.
But you can treat me like a slave, man,
If you will love and obey.

VERSE 2

HE: Girlies never clamor to make love to me,
That is why you wear my little ring.
You may not emerge like Venus from the sea,
All you have to know is how to cling.
I don't want a Trilby with a larynx in her eyes;
History is warning me where the danger lies.

REFRAIN 2

Don't love me like Salome,
I'd hate to lose my head.
A Lorelei to comb me
On seaweed must be fed.
Don't love me like Lucretia,
She mixed her drinks, they say.

And never be a bob-haired new girl—
A true girl
Will do, girl.
If I'm to give my name to you, girl,
You'll have to love and obey.

KID, I LOVE YOU

Probably introduced by Etta Leblang. Also introduced by James Tedford and Robert N. West in *Fly with Me* (1920).

VERSE

What's the use of dreaming true,
I don't want the moon and you
As a music cue.
I've a song that means much more,
It will make you call encore,
Make you love it too,
It isn't hard to do,
When you've heard the words, I'll bet,
You'll admit you can't forget—

REFRAIN

Da da da da da da da da,
Da da da da,
Da da da da da da da da,
Da da da da,
Da da da da da da da,
Da da da da da da da,
Da da da da,
Kid, I love you.

VERSE 2

Never try to waste your time
Looking for a triple rhyme;
Jazz will drown that too.
Shake a wicked shoulder blade,
And your little song is made.
And the lyric's thru;
It isn't hard to do;
Sing, "Tee-oodle-um-bum-bo,"
That is all they want to know.

REPEAT REFRAIN

THE BOOMERANG

Introduced by Phillip B. Leavitt and Elise Bonwit. Also introduced by Rebekah Cauble and Marie Elise in the Boston tryout of *Poor Little Ritz Girl* (1920). Dropped before the New York opening.

VERSE

Once a dusky beauty
Thought her love untrue,
Found the painful duty
To remove him from view;
Poor dusky wife
Let fly a knife;
As she stood on the strand,
It came back to her hand;
When her cute little blackie
Started "Ballin' the Jackie,"
'Twas the old boomerang!

REFRAIN

With a bang
They discovered the boomerang!
Steps were taken by husband and wife
Like the returning knife
(Their toes began to tickle),
Whirl away!
Then the boy threw the girl away!
(Didn't say Good day)
He'd never yearn
For boomerang's return
And with a clash! crash!!
Cymbals clang
The boomerang!!!

BREATH OF SPRING

Introduced by Etta Leblang. Under the title "Breath of Springtime" it was also introduced in *Jazz à la Carte* (1922) by Helen Kuck and ensemble.

VERSE

Don't you know my love's a-glowing just for you
And I feel my heart's a-going buzz for you.
Skies are smiling and all our love beguiling.
Like a worm, a young maid's fancy turns in
    Spring.

REFRAIN

When you feel a breath of Springtime
All the sunbeams dance in glee
And the robin goes a throbbin'
With a happy melody
And the bobolink in admiration sends a [*whistle.*]
When the whole world's on vacation,
What can a girlie do
When you feel the breath of Springtime
And the breath of Spring is you.

FLY WITH ME, 1920

Produced by the Players Club of Columbia University as the "Varsity Show of 1920" at the Grand Ballroom of the Hotel Astor, New York, March 24–27, 1920. Music by Richard C. Rodgers. Lyrics and adaptation by Lorenz M. Hart. Book by Milton R. Kroopf and Phillip B. Leavitt. Directed by Ralph Bunker. Dances and musical numbers staged by Herbert L. Fields. Settings and costumes by William M. Weaver. Orchestra conducted by Richard C. Rodgers. Cast included Clarence D. O'Connor (Class of 1921), William T. Taylor (1921), Thomas J. Farrell, Jr. (1920), Leonard F. Manheim (1922), Percival E. Cowan (1922, Law), Carlos Contreras (1921, Arch.), James Tedford (1922), Robert N. West (1920), F. Fraser Bond (1921), and D. E. McFarlane (1922). For the lyric to "Don't Love Me Like Othello," see *You'd Be Surprised* (1920), page 12. For "Kid, I Love You," see *You'd Be Surprised* (1920), page 13. The lyric to "If I Only Were a Boy" is missing. Vocal score printed 1920.

GONE ARE THE DAYS

The opening chorus. Introduced by D. E. McFarlane and ensemble.

ALL: Gone are the days,
    Gone are the days,
    In our school of Bolsheviki
    We've no studies old and creaky,
    Learn to love creation;
    Love thoughts bring sensation;
    We sing with true elation
    Gone are the days.

PROFESSOR: Down with all ecclesiastics,
Moral teachings by bombastics,
We've our own iconoclastics,
Teaching plastics, by gymnastics.
ALL: Gone are the days,
Gone are the days.
PROFESSOR: We've no morals old and freaky
In our school of Bolsheviki,
While their ship of state was leaky
Politics were dark and sneaky
In our school of Bolsheviki.
ALL: In our school of Bolsheviki.
PROFESSOR: Gone are the days.
ALL: Gone are the days,
Gone are the days,
Gone are the days;
In our school of Bolsheviki
We've no studies old and creaky.
Learn to love creation;
Love thoughts bring sensation;
We sing with true elation;
Gone are the days.

A PENNY FOR YOUR THOUGHTS

Introduced by William T. Taylor and Clarence D. O'Connor. Also introduced in *Temple Belles* (1924) by Sophie Blum and Herman Singer.

VERSE 1

HE: I hope you will not think me mean
Because I act like Hetty Green;
I must be brave with you and save,
I'd like to open up my purse
And spend for better or for worse;
Yet I am prudent, tho' luxury I crave.
You want to know the reason
Why ne'er I spend a dollar,
I squeeze it in my fist until
The eagle starts to holler.

REFRAIN 1

A penny for your thoughts, my dear;
When I am all alone, I fear,
A nickel for your glances wouldn't pay.
Your ev'ry word is worth a dime,
A blush a quarter ev'ry time,
A smile can send a dollar on its way.
A chat where no one sees us, dear,
Is worth the gold of Croesus, dear,
To hold your hand, I'd give a mint or two.
If nothing in this universe can pay for a
kiss,
I'll just spend my time with you.

VERSE 2

SHE: Your pocketbook you always watch
As though your fam'ly tree were Scotch;
And all you crave is "save and save."
If you'd live ninety years, you'd say
You're saving for a rainy day;
While I am longing to cast the gloom
away.
As lady's home companion
You're perfect as can be, dear;
Yet with this one-man problem play
Some vaudeville I'd see, dear.

REFRAIN 2

HE: A penny for your thoughts, my dear;
SHE: When I am all alone, I fear;
A nickel for my glance you'd never pay.
HE: Your ev'ry word is worth a dime,
A blush a quarter ev'ry time,
SHE: My smile won't send a dollar on its way.
HE: A chat where no one sees us, dear,
Is worth the gold of Croesus, dear,
To hold your hand, I'd give a mint or two.
SHE: If nothing in this universe can pay for a
kiss,
BOTH: I'll just spend my time with you.

ANOTHER MELODY IN F

Introduced by Leonard F. Manheim and ensemble, and by Lillian Gustafson, Hyman Wittstein, and ensemble in *Jazz à la Carte* (1922).

BOYS: It's very aggravating
In classrooms to be waiting
When springtime is alluring us,
Assuring us
Of curing us
Of winter's melancholy;
When now's the time for folly,
All this daily grind our pleasure
robs.
MRS. HOUGHTON: I too am craving
To stop this slaving.
I'd like to see how nature
throbs.
BOYS: You're very kind, dear,
But bear in mind, dear,
If we would pass we must be on
our jobs.
Springtime and love are in
blossom;
Fancy can dance in delight,
Gaily the old world is calling
Captive in springtime's might.

GIRLS: Springtime and love are in
blossom today;
Fancy can dance in echoes of
May,
The old world is calling and we
must obey
Captive in springtime's might.

ALL: It's very aggravating
To stay indoors in waiting
When springtime is alluring us,
Assuring us
Of curing us
Of winter's melancholy;
When now's the time for folly,
In the spring our fancy turns to
love,
For Tennyson says, in the spring
A young man's fancy turns to
love, to love, to love.

WORKING FOR THE GOVERNMENT

Introduced by D. E. McFarlane, James Tedford, Thomas J. Farrell, Jr., and Carlos Contreras.

VERSE 1

PROFESSOR: In ancient days the harmless prank
Of breaking in a savings bank
Was not considered right.
HARVEY: I t'ink it's awful to believe
De t'ings dem poor simps could
conceive,
Dey canned all dynamite!
ANDRÉ: And tho' we burglarize today,
It's done in an aesthetic way,
And anesthetic, too.
TIEN TONG: But Bolsheviki, they no fail
To let good burglar get his kale,
ALL: If honest work he'll do.

REFRAIN

ALL: Sh! Ah! Pst! Go!
That's the noble spirit of our state.
Watch! Hide! Lie low!
Get the fam'ly jewels and all the
    plate!
For we are only honest workingmen,
And half of all our gains is sent
To— Sh! Ah! Pst! Go!
Fifty-fifty with the government.
We're working for the government.
We must protect the government!
Sh!!!

VERSE 2

HARVEY: The burglars had to use their domes
To get away from Sherlock Holmes,
Or they'd land in the jug.
PROFESSOR: A second-story resident
Today can run for President,
If he's an honest thug.
ANDRÉ: They tried reform on highwaymen
Who used to work in my day, men!
Our ancestors were fools!
TIEN TONG: But Bolsheviki got much sense,
No put them in the penitence,
But in good burglar schools.

REPEAT REFRAIN

INSPIRATION

Introduced by William T. Taylor, Clarence D. O'Connor, Carlos Contreras, Leonard F. Manheim, Percival E. Cowan, Thomas J. Farrell, Jr., James Tedford, and Robert N. West. Same music but different lyric used for "All You Need to Be a Star" in *Poor Little Ritz Girl* (1920).

VERSE 1

Cubic hearts are beating
In a wild tattoo.
Post-impressions whisper "I love you."
Our love's very mystic,
Very futuristic;
All in purple-orange glow
Modern love must go.

REFRAIN

Inspiration, inspiration, in the air;
Inspiration, inspiration, ev'rywhere;

"I love you," "I love you,"
Steals into my brain;
Say it again.
Like a fire burning, burning into glare.
Cubic hearts are yearning, yearning "now or
    ne'er."
Throw me a love wave, my futuristic mate,
Inspiration says it's not too late.

VERSE 2

We don't care for beauty;
All we want is soul;
Sympathetic love waves are the goal.
Our love's idealistic,
Highly altruistic;
If your love's in Timbuktu
'S all the same to you.

REPEAT REFRAIN

PEEK-IN PEKIN

Introduced by Thomas J. Farrell, Jr., and Percival E. Cowan. Same music but different lyric used for "Love's Intense in Tents" in *Poor Little Ritz Girl* (1920).

VERSE 1

HE: Summer breezes blowing,
Soon we will be going,
China,
Little birdies singing,
Home to us are bringing
China.
'Cross the sea.
In just a little while we'll be
In a nest for my Tsu-Tsan and me.

REFRAIN

Peek-in Pekin back in a baby bungalow;
We're all alone to live and love
Where the China roses grow,
And we will lock our door so no one can
    sneak in,
For our love is too close to Peek-in,
Peek-in Pekin back in our bungalow.

VERSE 2

SHE: You and I alone in,
Breath of breezes blown in
Love cote.

Little China Mrs.
Furnish up with kisses
Love cote.
Ev'ry day
We tell our love to China Bay,
No one near to hear us as we say.

REPEAT REFRAIN

DREAMING TRUE

Introduced by Clarence D. O'Connor and William T. Taylor, and by Lillian Gustafson in *Say It with Jazz.* Same music but different lyric used for "Love Will Call" in *Poor Little Ritz Girl* (1920).

VERSE 1

There once were two lovers whom fate forsook
And frowned at their fair romance;
They lived 'twixt the covers of Maurier's book,
But they never met by chance.
While Peter's immured in his prison,
Hope still gleams,
For his Princess so far away
Can tell of her love in dreams.

REFRAIN

In my dreams I'll kiss you
And I'll never miss you;
When the moon's on high,
Dreaming in the sky,
Darling, I'll caress you,
And my heart will bless you;
Dream of me, I'll dream of you,
And we are dreaming true.

VERSE 2

When two little eyelids are closed in sleep,
And you're in the Land of Nod;
Your two little eyes in dreams will creep,
Like two little peas in a pod.
I'll always be near tho' I'm dreaming
'Cross the sea,
If whenever I dream of you,
You'll dream all your dreams of me.

REPEAT REFRAIN

A COLLEGE ON BROADWAY

Introduced by William T. Taylor and ensemble.

VERSE

On high Olympus, mighty Jove all-powerful
Once asked Minerva, "Where's your holy shrine
    on earth?"
Apollo, Mars and Mercury cried, "Dad,
With Minnie dear, the same old shrine we've
    had."

REFRAIN

Bulldogs run around New Haven,
Harvard paints old Cambridge red,
Even poor old Philadelphia
Really has a college, it is said,
And Williamstown belongs to Williams,
Princeton's tiger stands at bay,
But old New York won't let the world forget
That there's a college on Broadway.

CALL ME ANDRÉ

Finale, Act I. Introduced by principals and ensemble.

PROFESSOR: Sure that gun isn't loaded!
ANDRÉ: It would, indeed, be a shame to
    scatter such a rare antique as you
    are, madame. You are costlier than
    your gems.
PROFESSOR: You are not only a thief of jewels,
    but a robber of hearts. You may
    have my heart but not my jewels.
HARVEY: What's up, Braggadocio?

ANDRÉ: Call me André!
PROFESSOR: André, I love you!
    Remember, please, a burglar's
        arts
    Are breaking safes, not breaking
        hearts.
ANDRÉ: But tell me, do I get my law
    degree?
PROFESSOR: You're not the best man in the
    class.
HARVEY: But he is good enough to pass.
ANDRÉ: A movie actor now I'm going to
    be.

HARVEY: He'll surely pass the test,
    I bet—
    He hasn't his degree as yet,
    The walls of that strong safe he
        has to break.
ANDRÉ: I'll make an honest effort,
    And I'm sure I'll succeed;
    And then my degree I'll make.
ALL: He will get the combination.
ANDRÉ: What a fix!
ALL: He will be the school's
    sensation.
ANDRÉ: 3-4-6.
ALL: He'll wind it and find it with
    never a scratch.
ANDRÉ: Match, Ming Boy, match.
PROFESSOR: Be scholastic, use the plastic
    sense of poise.
    Do not hurry; never worry—
ANDRÉ: Stop that noise!
PROFESSOR: Don't be impatient, you'll get it
    somehow.
ANDRÉ: Jumping Jiminy, it's open now!
    There's nothing in here but this
        paper.
EMMY: What paper?
ALL: What does the paper say?
ANDRÉ: This tells us that our Emmy
    Was eighteen years last May.
EMMY: André, don't read it. Give it to
    me.
ANDRÉ: One moment!
EMMY: I must have it!
ANDRÉ: You must?
EMMY: It will save Jimmy.
    Oh, André, if you care for me,
    You'll give me that paper.
MRS. HOUGHTON: I regret I have to leave you,
    We were on our honeymoon.
ALL: We were very, very happy,
    teacher.
    It is not a bit too soon.
EMMY: Won't you try and save my
    Jimmy?
MRS. HOUGHTON: Dear Miss Childs, I'm through
    with you.
    Lowell, go and call a taxi-plane,
    dear.
LOWELL: Anything for you I'll do.
ANDRÉ: All I aspire, all I ask life—
    This one desire—be my little
        wife!
EMMY: I'll get that certificate. That means
    no honeymoon for you, unless you
    save my Jimmy!
ANDRÉ: Yes, dear!
EMMY: I asked you for that paper
    because I love you.

CHORUS: Love and romance are the
    nation's esprit.
    All the world is singing Fly
        With Me.
JIMMY: Emmy!
ANDRÉ: I'm the happiest man in the
    world.
JIMMY: Thank you, André, for showing
    me the truth.
MRS. HOUGHTON: Emmy, what does this mean?
EMMY: Annulment, unless—
JIMMY: Farewell, I fear, dear, if I say
    You'll only find me in your way.
    In my dreams I'll kiss you,
    And I'll never miss you.
    When the moon's on high
    Dreaming in the sky.
    Darling, I'll caress you,
    And my heart will bless you;
    Dream of me, I'll dream of you,
    And we are dreaming true.
EMMY: Jimmy!

MOONLIGHT AND YOU

Introduced by William T. Taylor and ensemble, and by
Max Weinstein in *Say It with Jazz* (1921) under the alternate title, "The Moon and You." Introduced by Lillian
Gustafson, William Nachman, and Eileen Mayo in *Jazz à
la Carte* (1922).

VERSE 1

Rippling rills of summer moonlight
Echo in my heart;
Babbling tones of fond affection
From the brooklet start.
Would that you could hear the whispers
In my fancy teem;
Sweetheart mine, the moon and you,
Are melted in a dream.

REFRAIN

Deep in my moonlight dream,
One with the moon you seem;
Gleaming,
In my fairest dreaming,
The moon is beaming
Affection, too.
Bound by a moonbeam chain,
Sweetheart of mine, remain
In my nightland,
My fairy spriteland,
I dream of the moonlight and you.

VERSE 2

Beaming gold of moonlight splendor
Shimmers in your hair;
Mystic waves of winding wonder,
Perfumed beauty rare.
From your spell of moonlight magic
Never set me free;
Sweetheart mine, the moon and you
Are all in all of me.

REPEAT REFRAIN

GUNGA DIN

Introduced by James Tedford and ensemble.

VERSE 1

From ev'ry cafe
Folks stay away,
Can't dance on ice cream though they oughter;
Don't mind what they say,
We'll show you today,
How you can do your dance on water.

REFRAIN

Now you have to do the Gunga Din,
Din, Din, Din.
And you drink the water in between,
Din, Din, Din.
Raise a little on your toes and whirl;
Blaze the way to glory with your girl.
There! You've done it!
Do a little jigger on your heels,
Din, Din, Din.
Do the syncopation that appeals.
It is not a jag step,
Just a lot of rag step,
That's the way you do the Gunga Din.

VERSE 2

If you are chilled thru,
Don't wait for the flu
Or you'll be playing with a lily;
Don't drink ginger ale,
Its kick is too frail;
My dance will never leave you chilly.

REPEAT REFRAIN

THE THIRD DEGREE OF LOVE

Introduced by F. Fraser Bond.

VERSE

When you first revealed your heart,
Were you steeled to play our part,
Warrior in battle array?
Were you confident to win?
Were you anxious to begin?
Did you know exactly what to say?
How did you feel?
Tell me, pray.

REFRAIN

You feel the fever,
You can't deceive her
When first she looks into your eyes;
You think you're wise—
You're otherwise!
And little birdies seem to sing in your brain!
You start to tremble,
You can't dissemble,
She asks you what you're thinking of,
When of your love you'd speak,
Your knees get weak—
That's the third degree of love.

IF YOU WERE YOU

Introduced by William T. Taylor and ensemble.

VERSE 1

HE: If I were a king in Babylon,
    And you my humble slave,
    I'd sing of my love by night and day,
    My heart to you would say:

REFRAIN

    I adore you,
    I adore you,
    Were you princess, queen or slave,
    Lovers true are brave;
    I would love you, dear, always
    If you were you.

VERSE 2

SHE: If I were a princess far away
    And you were my humble slave,
    You'd still be the king of hearts I prize,
    Command me with your eyes.

PATTER*

    Soldier, saint or sage,
    Great men of every age
    Were wild about some dame.
    Napoleon fell for his Josephine,
    Louis had Du Barry,
    And I've got my little queen;
    It's hard to live with 'em,
    Without 'em we're wrecks,
    It's a weakness with the whole male sex.

POOR LITTLE RITZ GIRL, 1920

Tryout: Shubert-Wilbur Theatre, Boston, May 29–July 14, 1920; Stamford Theatre, Stamford, Connecticut, July 16–17, 1920; Nixon Theatre, Atlantic City, New Jersey, July 18–23, 1920. New York run: Central Theatre, July 28–October 16, 1920. 119 performances. Music by Richard C. Rodgers and Sigmund Romberg. Lyrics by Lorenz M. Hart and Alex Gerber. Produced by Lew Fields. Book by George Campbell and Lew Fields. Book originally by Harry B. Stillman and William J. O'Neil. Production staged and lighted by Ned Wayburn. Dances and musical numbers staged by David Bennett. Settings by Robert H. Law Studios. Costumes by Cora Macgeachy, Marie Cook, and Anna Spencer. Orchestra conducted by Charles Previn. Cast, starring Charles Purcell and Andrew Tombes, included Eleanor Griffith, Lulu McConnell, Florence Webber, Aileen Poe, and Grant Simpson. At the Boston tryout, the entire score was by Rodgers and Hart. By the New York premiere only six songs were by Rodgers and Hart. Another song, "Mary, Queen of Scots," had music by Rodgers and a lyric by Herbert Fields.

For the lyric to "The Boomerang," see *You'd Be Surprised* (1920), page 13.

The following lyrics are missing: "The Lord Only Knows" (introduced in the Boston tryout by Lulu McConnell, Alma Adaire, and Florence Webber), "What Happened Nobody Knows" (Lulu McConnell, Aileen Poe, and Florence Webber)—these first two titles might be different names for the same song—"Souvenirs" (introduced in the Boston tryout by Victor Morley and dropped before the

---

Not printed in vocal score.

New York opening), and "I Surrender" (introduced in the Boston tryout by Aileen Poe and Victor Morley and dropped before the New York opening; introduced in *Say Mama* [1921] by Phillip B. Leavitt and ensemble). Lyrics appear in the order in which they were sung in Boston tryout.

POOR LITTLE RITZ GIRL

Introduced in the Boston tryout by Rebekah Cauble and Marie Elise. Dropped before the New York opening and replaced by a song with the same title by Sigmund Romberg and Alex Garber. The music may have been used again with a different lyric as "Poor Little Model" in *Say Mama* (1921).

VERSE

Just a simple city lassie
Never breathed the country air,
If she goes there in her chassis,
Yokels stare!
Never studied Greek or Latin,
Never even learned to cook,
Jim Jam Jems, her book,
Pity her tired look.

REFRAIN

Poor little Ritz Girl,
The "use her wits" girl,
Adores the angels on Broadway.
Ride in your car, girl,
But not too far, girl,
Until she'll honor and obey.
Poor little Ritz Girl,
The title fits, girl,
Wears just a simple rope of pearls;
She must accept them! Poor little dear,
For each pearl she sheds a tear.
Pity the poor Ritz Girl.

THE MIDNIGHT SUPPER

Introduced by Aileen Poe, Lulu McConnell, Alma Adaire, and Florence Webber in the Boston tryout. Dropped before the New York opening. Also known as "Midnight Supper" and "One Midnight Supper at Home."

VERSE 1

LILY: Ain't it awful to be moral?
MADGE: Lily, hang the crepe, I'm dead!
ROYAL: If you've passed away, don't quarrel,
But butter the bread.
In the Ritz, I dreamed we dined,
Dressed in plumes and silk;
MADGE: Gawd, you're getting unrefined!
Lil, don't spill the milk!
ROYAL: And my art was no fiasco,
I was one of Broadway's hits.
LILY: The bread's as old as Dave Belasco!
ROYAL: Let's play dining at the Ritz!
I'm an heiress!
MADGE: Second-rater!
LILY &
ROYAL: Little service!
Waiter! Waiter!

REFRAIN 1

ROYAL: First some lobster à la Newburg!
MADGE: You mean pickle à la dill.
LILY: Let me have a filet mignon,
MADGE: Boston beans from Bunker Hill,
ROYAL: Some sweet bread!
MADGE: Here's wheat bread!
LILY: Caviar!
MADGE: Sardines!
ROYAL: We'll stretch our imaginations
LILY: And we'll let our fancies roam,
MADGE: But we'll save our reputations
ALL: At our midnight supper at home.

VERSE 2

ROYAL: Waiters ran in wild commotion
Ever at my beck and call;
MADGE: This cheese never crossed the ocean,
No perfume at all.
ROYAL: Ordered all the bill of fare,
Soup to peach soufflé;
LILY: Have a heart, we weren't there;
Our dreams ain't that way.
ROYAL: Chicken served like the movies
On a sterling-silver dish.
MADGE: Kind of think that them anchovies
Never hung around with a fish.
ROYAL: Now we'll order all the dishes.
MADGE: How's the salmon?
LILY: Um! Delicious!

REFRAIN 2

ROYAL: First some frog legs à la Paris,
MADGE: Coffee à la Hartford lunch,
LILY: Next we'll have some turtle bouillon,
MADGE: Twister crullers in a bunch.
ROYAL: Tortoni!
MADGE: Baloney!
LILY: Terrapin!
MADGE: Saltines!
ROYAL: We'll get all the thrills we're after
LILY: And we let our fancies roam,
MADGE: But retain our girlish laughter
ALL: At our midnight supper at home.

LADY RAFFLES BEHAVE

Published August 1920. Introduced in the Boston tryout by Aileen Poe and Victor Morley. Dropped before the New York opening.

VERSE 1

HE: I must insist that you throw up your hands,
Don't think that I'm a brute.
SHE: Look out, that gun might shoot.
HE: Don't move!
Stand back!
Now I give the commands.
SHE: This is a shame,
I'm not to blame.
HE: Let's have your name and what's your game.
SHE: If you would chat, remove the gat.
I rented this apartment,
I can even show my lease,
I'm paying twenty-five a month.
HE: I see rents can decrease.
You're unconvincing in your claims,
But quite a charming Jesse James.

REFRAIN

Lady Raffles, rob me of gold,
And I'll not betray you.
In your pack my silver enfold,
Come, I'll not delay you.
Steal my honor or steal my good name,
Rob me of my affection.
But if you knew what a heart meant,
You would leave my apartment,
Lady Raffles, behave.

VERSE 2

SHE: I'm sure you see how I made my mistake,
Tomorrow I will go.
HE: I've still the gun, you know.
SHE: Oh, spare my life,
I swear my lease I'll break.

HE: Tell the police about your lease.
SHE: That gun release, let us have peace.
My lease and key
HE: Are both N.G.
I fear that you've been buncoed,
And your lease won't hold at all.
But you did read the paper thru.
SHE: The print was much too small.
HE. But nowadays please bear in mind,
A good flat's mighty hard to find.

REPEAT REFRAIN

THE GOWN IS MIGHTIER THAN THE SWORD

Introduced in the Boston tryout by Alma Adaire and ensemble. Dropped before the New York opening.

VERSE

Ermine trimmed on crepe de chine
Won a crown for Josephine;
Cleopatra's swinging pearls hit Anthony
And Delilah's goatskin sheen
Caused Samson to use Danderine;
For a gown so many things can mean.

REFRAIN

Gowns rule the nations;
Paris creations
Change a clause in the laws.
The reason is because
Rulers find graces,
Covered with laces,
Can make them lay the cares of state away.
Mother Eve's fig leaf
Wasn't a big leaf,
For its sake, Mr. Snake Eve adored;
Orange blossoms and veils seductive
To the freedom of man destructive;
For the gown is mightier than the sword.

LET ME DRINK IN YOUR EYES

Introduced under the title "Drink into Your Eyes" in the Boston tryout by Rebekah Cauble, Marie Elise, and en-

semble. Dropped before the New York opening. Also introduced by Harold F. Springhorn and Arthur Fluegelman in *You'll Never Know* (1921).

VERSE

Since we were poor mammals
We're drier than camels,
I've spent all my hours with you;
I'd light up on liquor,
Now you do it quicker!
It's more economical, too.
You've made me an amorous stew!

REFRAIN

I'll do my drinking in your eyes,
Their cordial welcome puts me wise;
Rosy tips of ruby lips
Are redder than claret;
How can you compare it?
I'll never long for Scotch or Rye,
Your kick is always Extra Dry;
You're six percent, I believe, oh, dearie!
All other girls are just Bevo, dearie,
Your hug's a bracer that's a hit,
I want no chaser after it;
My thirst will rise,
For intoxication, it cries,
Let me drink in your eyes.

WILL YOU FORGIVE ME?

Introduced in the Boston tryout by Aileen Poe and Victor Morley. Dropped before the New York opening. Also introduced by Harold F. Springhorn and Arthur Fluegelman in *You'll Never Know* (1921), and by Alice Chester and Arthur Allie in *A Danish Yankee in King Tut's Court* (1923).

VERSE 1

I'm afraid I'll never learn
How to tell my love,
I must confess, I'm too polite,
Though you're charming, and I yearn
On my love, the talk to turn,
My reserve robs me of nerve tonight;
What I say will be quite all right.

REFRAIN

Will you forgive me if I take your hand
And hold it in mine?

If I move closer will you understand
And gently resign?
And if I sigh, dear,
Will you know why, dear?
Don't mind if my arms entwine!
Will you excuse me if I steal a kiss?
Your eyes tell me, "Do,"
And will you say that it is not amiss
If I make it two?
I beg your pardon if I whisper
That we'll never part.
Will you forgive me if I lose my heart?

VERSE 2

It's a human trait to err,
To forgive, divine,
And I will pardon your mistake;
But I'd really much prefer
That you please consider, sir.
Do not chance a new advance to make,
All conventions we must not break.

REPEAT REFRAIN

CALL THE DOC

Introduced in the Boston tryout by Roy Atwell. Dropped before the New York opening.

VERSE

Before I was born, Father wanted to be
The dad of the future's most famous M.D.,
To send him to college to get his degree
As a thoroughly finished physician.
When I think of Father, I'm certain that he
From all thoughts of evil and malice was free,
But could he have known what he made out of me,
Poor Dad would have lost his ambition.

REFRAIN 1

If there's a pain in baby's shoe,
They call the doctor!
When there's nothing else to do,
They call the doc!
If Mama feels her liver,
And they don't know what to give her,
Or if Papa wants Green River,
Call the doc!
If I'm taking in a show
They call the doctor!

Just when off to bed I go they call me too;
For any kind of reason
If it's anything at all—
Chicken pox or vertigo—
Typhoid—stomach—gall—
Scarlet and pneumonia—
Colic or the grippe—
Measles or diphtheria—
If baby has the pip;
Death will be much sweeter
When I tell St. Peter
They can go to hell
And call the doc!

REFRAIN 2

When a widow feels alone,
She calls the doctor;
When she feels a chill, the phone
Will ring for doc;
When an old maid is decaying
And she doesn't feel like praying,
Then there's no time for delaying,
Call the doc.
When a millionaire of seventy or eighty
Takes a wife of twenty-one or twenty-two,
She's solicitous and worried,
Ev'rything he sighs about:
Headache or insomnia!
Asthma or the gout!
Pleurisy, arterio!
Heartburn or a cold!
He may have a chance
But then, he's very, very old.
Soldierly he's striving,
Sometimes he's reviving;
Each time he revives,
She calls the doc.

REFRAIN 3

When they don't want to go to court,
They call the doctor!
Jury service is no sport,
They call the doc!
When it's school time, Bill's no dummy,
If the baseball game looks chummy,
With a groan he feels his tummy—
Call the doc!
Hubby wants a change of air,
He calls a doctor!
If a show is not quite there,
They call me too.
And a newly married couple
Call for anything at all,
Dizziness or giddiness,
If her food begins to pall.

Nervousness or happiness!
Melancholia! Sty!
Of course he couldn't tell
But there was something in her eye!
They show agitation
In their expectation;
When they want a stork,
They call a doc.

YOU CAN'T FOOL YOUR DREAMS

Published September 1920. Introduced by Eleanor Griffith, Charles Purcell, and Andrew Tombes. Refrain has the same music as the refrain of "Don't Love Me Like Othello" in *You'd Be Surprised* (1920).

VERSE 1

DOC: Look into my eyes again.
PEMBROKE: Take her pain away.
DOC: Read my eyes and see your pain is better.
BAB: Yes, there isn't any pain.
DOC: Do just what I say,
One deep breath now,
Rest a while you may.
You're a little sleepy now,
A tired spell will creep.
Nod your head and close your eyes,
And you are asleep.

REFRAIN

You tell me what you're dreaming,
I'll tell you whom you love.
In dreams your heart is scheming
For him you're dreaming of.
Your modesty can't hide it,
You lose control, it seems,
When you're asleep there's no concealing
A feeling,
Appealing.
And little love thoughts come a-stealing
Because you can't fool your dreams.

VERSE 2

DOC: Answer all I ask of you.
BAB: Ask and I shall speak.
DOC: I will ask your age and you will tell me.

PEMBROKE: That's a thing you needn't do.
She's eighteen this week.
She told me so,
That's not what I seek.
DOC: Come now, say how old you are.
BAB: I am just twenty-two.
DOC: When a maiden is asleep,
All she says is true.

REPEAT REFRAIN

LOVE WILL CALL

Published September 1920. Introduced by Eleanor Griffith. Same music but different lyric used for "Dreaming True" in *Fly with Me* (1920).

VERSE 1

My dreamy old mammy sang me to sleep
Each night to the Land of Nod,
Till two little eyes in dreams would creep
Like two little peas in a pod.
Old mammy sang of the love who mine would be,
And I'll wait for the only one
Until he will call to me.

REFRAIN

Wait till love comes calling,
Thru the night enthralling,
While the moon's on high,
Dreaming in the sky,
Tenderly he'll hold you,
Shadows soft enfold you.
Wait until your dreams come true,
And love will call to you.

VERSE 2

My dreamy old mammy sang soft and low,
And told me I'd know my love,
When all without warning my heart's aglow
Like rays of the sun above.
Day by day I am waiting faithfully,
For I know till I hear him call
My love will be true to me.

REPEAT REFRAIN

ALL YOU NEED TO BE A STAR

Introduced by Eleanor Griffith, Ardelle Cleaves, Charles Purcell, and Andrew Tombes. Same music but different lyric used for "Inspiration" in *Fly with Me* (1920).

VERSE 1

DOT: I am like my sister—
BAB: That is like a star!
DOT: I will spread the family name afar.
TAN: All your part assigns, dear,
   Is a bare six lines, dear.
DOC: Show her lines from tip to toe,
   She'll walk off with the show.

REFRAIN

DOT: Waves of art are roaring, roaring in my
   brain!
BAB: It's her inspiration soaring up again.
DOT: I hear voices calling, they kindle the spark!
DOC: Like Joan of Arc!
DOT: I will enter in the center, passion pent!
TAN: Heaven help the cast, for she has
   temperament.
ALL: Give her (me) publicity, gowns, and a car,
   That is all you need to be a star.

VERSE 2

DOC: Once I too was sighing
   As a star to shine.
TAN: Now you kill the stars in your own line.
DOC: One morn from above me
   Dreams were knocked out of me.
TAN: Knocked out! Was ambition lax?
DOC: No, by Father with an axe.

REPEAT REFRAIN

LOVE'S INTENSE IN TENTS

Published August 1920. Introduced by Ardelle Cleaves and Andrew Tombes. During the Boston tryout it was sung by Eleanor Griffith and Andrew Tombes. The song has the same music as "Peek-in Pekin" in *Fly with Me* (1920).

VERSE 1

HE: Summer breezes blowing,
   Soon we will be going
   Camping!
   Loving will be very
   Intimate and merry
   Camping!
   Rents increase—
   We won't renew our city lease.
   We will go where rent bills all will cease.

REFRAIN

   Not a cent of rent in our tent in paradise.
   We're all alone to live and love
   Underneath the starry skies.
   My lady, pay your rent
   With love to your grand lord;
   I've a lease from Cupid, the landlord!
   Love's intense in tents in our paradise.

VERSE 2

SHE: You and I alone in
   Breath of roses blown in
   Love tent.
   See the pretty missus
   Furnish up with kisses
   Love tent.
   Ev'ry day,
   We'll put the little coins away,
   And the landlord with our love we'll pay!

REPEAT REFRAIN

THE DAISY AND THE LARK

Introduced in the Boston tryout by Alma Adaire, Florence Webber, Rebekah Cauble, Marie Elise, and ensemble. Sung in the New York production by Florence Webber, Elise Bonwit, and ensemble.

VERSE 1

A drooping little daisy hid her head,
Despondent she grew in her grassy bed.
Proudly the tulip and the naughty rose
Snubbed the little daisy with a haughty pose—
But one hazy day a meadowlark
Brightened up the sky that looked so dark;
Warbled from his golden throat
All for daisy, every note.

REFRAIN

Don't be distressed, dear daisy,
I'll warble my song to you—
La la la la la!
La la la la la!
Roses are red with envy.
They can't tell me what to do.
Answer my little query, dear.
I'm weary, dear.
Be cheery, dear.
Say I'm beloved, dearie dear—
La la la la la!
La la la la la!
Don't droop your head.

VERSE 2

Two lovers strolled among the flow'rs one day.
He asked her for a kiss, she said him nay.
Angrily the laddie went away,
To the little maiden's sad dismay.
The ever-faithful lark heard the maiden sigh
And the daisy sadly heard her cry;
The maid took daisy's life
Asking petals if she'd be a wife.

REPEAT REFRAIN

SAY MAMA, 1921

Presented by the Akron Club for the benefit of the Oppenheim Collins Mutual Aid Association of Brooklyn, at the Brooklyn Academy of Music, February 10, 1921, and for the benefit of the Sav-A-Home Fund of the New York *Evening Mail*, at the Hotel Plaza, February 12, 1921. Music by Richard C. Rodgers. Lyrics by Lorenz M. Hart. Staged by Herbert L. Fields. Orchestra conducted by Richard C. Rodgers. Orchestrations by Roy Webb. Cast headed by Ralph G. Engelsman, Elise Bonwit, Carol King, Phillip B. Leavitt, and Dorothy Fields.

For information on "I Surrender," see *Poor Little Ritz Girl* (1920), page 18.

The following lyrics are missing: "Poor Little Model" (introduced by Ralph G. Engelsman and ensemble), "First Love" (Carol King; reprised by Carol King and Phillip B. Leavitt), "I Surrender" (Phillip B. Leavitt and ensemble), "Show Him the Way" (Carol King and Elise Bonwit), "Under the Mistletoe" (Ira R. Schattman), "Jack and Jill" (Carol King, Phillip B. Leavitt, and Elise Bonwit), and

"When the Crime Waves Roll" (Ralph G. Engelsman and ensemble).

WAKE UP

Introduced by Elise Bonwit and Ralph G. Engelsman. A fragment of the lyric was recalled in 1937 at the time of the 25th Anniversary of the Akron Club and printed in the 35th Anniversary Dinner Dance Book of the Akron Club (Hotel Plaza, New York, May 8, 1947).

Wake up and hear the church bells ringing,
Shake up and hear the birdies singing,
Make up with Mr. Moon Man and me.
Take up a ring to fit her finger,
Hurry up there and don't you linger.
[*Incomplete*]

WATCH YOURSELF

Introduced by Phillip B. Leavitt, Ralph G. Engelsman, and Rosalind Nathan. Also introduced in *You'll Never Know* (1921) by Milton R. Kroopf, Harold F. Springhorn, Leonard F. Manheim, and Walter S. Farrell.

VERSE 1

God protects the working girl,
If she's slave or shirking girl;
Helps the soldier who
Fights Red, White and Blue,
Helps the crook at prison's door,
If he vows to crook no more;
Paupers pray, and see
New prosperity.
But when some poor simpleton
Is pushed up to the altar,
All the prayers in the world
Can't free him from the halter.

REFRAIN

If you're single, mind this jingle,
Never mingle with the pretty ones;
All of them wait for you!
Mind the shy ones, they're the sly ones;
And the spry ones and the witty ones;
When they weep, you're through!
If she looks for protection,
Watch the pretty elf;
You're the sweet confection

She'll put upon the shelf!
When the she-male wants the he-male,
You're no free male!
Don't look after her,
Better go home and watch yourself!

VERSE 2

In the morning, her dear face
Adds to breakfast extra grace;
Luncheon comes, and then
Same old face again!
Same old features, same old mold,
Make the whole darn supper cold;
Afterwards, you're free
Same old face to see!
It's until death do us part!
Oh! How those words do burn! Oh!
If she goes to Heaven,
You'll be happy in Inferno!

REPEAT REFRAIN

CHORUS GIRL BLUES

Introduced by Dorothy Fields, assisted by Dorith Bamberger. Also introduced in *You'll Never Know* (1921) by Max J. Liebowitz and in *Say It with Jazz* (1921) by Marjorie Wiggin.

VERSE 1

Ma would implore us,
"Don't you be a chorus girl;
Stage life is sinful."
Pa said, "You said a chinful, Pearl!"
I read the *Police Gazette*,
Knew that's the life for this pet.
Now that I'm second from the end,
I'm a different woman, you bet.

REFRAIN 1

I'm tired of ev'ryone
Who says this life's all fun and revel,
That all we do each night
Is frolic and invite the devil.
To travel round they think is great,
So much to see from state to state—
My state is almost half dead
From sleeping three in a bed.
We get so hungry we tear
Food off the arm of a chair.
I've Johnnies by the score,
With flowers at the door they're waiting.

The flowers don't look big—
A steak is more invigorating.
When I've rehearsed all night like mad,
I've no ambition to be bad—
I've got those tight shoes,
Watch your cues,
Darn youse,
Chorus Girl Blues!

VERSE 2

Magazines bore us
That write of the chorus girl.
Say it's a bright life
When they speak of our night-life whirl.
They tell of our limousines,
While we're just subway sardines.
When you inhale the Bronx express,
Mary Garden, you tell what it means.

REFRAIN 2

They say our souls we risk
Each night to dine on Bisque Tortoni,
While Lulu, Flo and Gert
Know only one dessert, baloney.
We don't get bird's nest soup, fan-tan—
We drink our Campbell's à la can.
Instead of crab meat gratin
We grab for beans in the pan.
Imported cheese we don't miss—
Bite our own holes in the Swiss.
They say we've bottled fizz—
I ask you, how much is that bull worth?
We get our diamond rings,
Our pearls and precious things from Woolworth.
And when my two-by-four I lamp,
I haven't room enough to vamp—
I've got those tight shoes,
Watch your cues,
Darn youse,
Chorus Girl Blues!

PRISCILLA

Introduced by Dorothy Fields. Lyric found in Lorenz Hart Lyrics folder in the Rodgers and Hammerstein office. No music survives.

VERSE 1

Priscilla was a Puritan,
A bit more an than pure;
She lived in sixteen twenty-three,
Miles Standish loved her mightily,

But he was old,
And she was cold.
He didn't know how to propose,
And just to make it sure,
Sent young John Alden in his place
To plead his love demure.
She saw John, and knew,
Miles would never do!

REFRAIN 1

Oh, Priscilla, I'd like to know
The way that thou hooked thy John!
When he said Miles' love was great
Thou didst make John demonstrate!
Oh, Priscilla, thou wert not slow
His feelings to play upon.
When he turned to the door in doubt,
Why didst thou blow the candle out?
Thou workst too fast for me—
Oh, what I know about thee!

VERSE 2

Priscilla was a pioneer
In sixteen twenty-three,
On Plymouth Rock with all the men
She settled Massachusetts, then,
John Alden's wife,
Brought him to life.
He came to her on purpose bent,
She bent his purpose well.
For when he spoke of Miles she said,
"Oh, let him go to tell
The world Priscilla seeks
Husbands, not antiques!"

REFRAIN 2

Oh, Priscilla, I'd like to know
The way that thou hooked thy John!
With him after twelve o'clock
'Tis said that thou made Plymouth Rock!
Oh, Priscilla, thou wert not slow
His feelings to play upon!
Sat with him in the church one day
But his hands were not free to pray.
Thou played a hymn, 'twas he!
Oh, what I know about thee!

OVER THE LOWLANDS

Unused.

VERSE

Why did ever I come here?
Friendless, unknown!
Trusted all without a fear,
Now I'm alone!
Southward, southward
On my own.

REFRAIN

Over the lowlands soft and low
In Caroline.
I see the Santee River flow
In Southern Caroline.
All the plantation lights aglow,
Welcome they shine.
Memory! Oh, memory,
With wonderment you beckon me
Over the lowlands
In Caroline.

YOU'LL NEVER KNOW, 1921

Produced by the Players Club of Columbia University as the "Varsity Show of 1921" at the Grand Ballroom of the Hotel Astor, New York, April 20–23, 1921. Music by Richard C. Rodgers. Lyrics by Lorenz M. Hart. Book by Herman Axelrod, Henry William Hanemann, Malcolm H. Sanger, and Gerald D. Heller. Directed by Oscar Hammerstein II, Henry William Hanemann, and Herman Axelrod. Dances and musical numbers staged by Herbert L. Fields. Orchestra conducted by Richard C. Rodgers. Cast included Milton V. O'Connell (Class of 1921, Journ.), Harold F. Springhorn (1923), Arthur Fluegelman (1923), Max J. Liebowitz (1923), Milton R. Kroopf (1921), Harold J. T. Horan (1921), Albert B. Bernstein (1922, Law), Herman B. Waechter (1922), Leonard F. Manheim (1922), Walter S. Farrell (1921), and the twelve-year-old prodigy of the Class of 1924, Edward Roche Hardy, Jr.

For "Will You Forgive Me?," see *Poor Little Ritz Girl* (1920), page 19. For "Let Me Drink in Your Eyes," see *Poor Little Ritz Girl* (1920), page 19. For "Watch Yourself," see *Say Mama* (1921), page 22. For "Chorus Girl Blues," see *Say Mama* (1921), page 22. The lyric to "Law" (music by Ray L. Perkins; lyricist uncredited) is missing. Vocal score printed 1921.

WE TAKE ONLY THE BEST

Prologue. Introduced by Harold J. T. Horan.

Who rang?
I see the delegation's here.
Thrice welcome, for I greet
Two-fifty in each seat.
The Players Club demand that I appear,
For all they see, they pay no fee
And all but programs they get free,
From me, they'll know
What's in the show:
A boy, a girl; they fall in love
(That's novel, please don't frown).
The authors took a mem'ry course,
They saw each other in town,
Thought of a name, *You'll Never Know.*
How inspirations come and go.

REFRAIN

If you've heard our music before,
You've discrimination.
Only masters are in our score
For your delectation;
Kern and Berlin will not be played;
Your girl won't hear "The Love Nest";
If a mem'ry she has got, she
Will know the song's "Pagliacci,"
We take only the best.
(In our little hurdy-gurdy,
Wagner's shaking hands with Verdi.)

DON'T THINK THAT WE'RE THE CHORUS OF THE SHOW

Opening chorus. Introduced by ensemble.

Don't think
That we're the chorus of the show;
Please know before we start,
We've ev'ryone a part.
Our hero's broke; we're creditors, and so
We motivate this tête-à-tête.
Though we appear, we must cohere;
Our authors stick
To their technique;
The program says we're creditors,
Collecting from poor Steve,

But, entre nous, we're here to start
The show, and then we leave.
Oh, please applaud us, and we'll know
We'll all get parts in next year's show.

VIRTUE WINS
THE DAY

Introduced by Harold F. Springhorn and ensemble.

We must put a receiver in,
Fair play he's no believer in,
And we'll put the deceiver in a fix.
So, Stephen, we will yell for ya
From here to Philadelphia;
We want our dough.
You better show none of your tricks.
The bankrupt you will find,
Young man, you have an axe to grind,
Young man, we're all of us,
You kind young man, no hicks.
We trust in you, and just in you,
There's crust in you that sticks,
For when Steve begs for mercy,
You say "Nix!"

I know your man,
I've up my sleeve as much as Steve,
Trust to my plan,
He can't fool me,
And once I'll find
What's on his mind
Like A-B-C.

I know my man,
So trust to my plan,
It's simple as can be.
Believe me, I know what's up your sleeve,
Oh, Steve!

He can't wait until he
Gets the debtor willy-nilly,
And to make him take a spill he
Follows him for her to Philly,
Over fields of daffodilly,
Even way down south to Chile;
O'er level road and hilly
He will hunt him with a billy,
And when he makes his kill, he
Lies among the amarylli,
In his hand will be a lily.
(This is thrilly, but it's silly.)

. . .

He really knows his man,
We'll trust his little plan,
It's as simple as can be.
And you can believe
That he knows what's up your sleeve,
Oh, Steve!

He knows his man.
He's up his sleeve
As much as Steve,
We'll trust his plan.
Clever is he.
At once he'll find
What's on his mind
Like A-B-C.

So we'll put a receiver in,
Fair play he's no believer in,
With you to help us he can't get away.
We trust in you and just in you,
Though Stephen thinks he's gay,
He'll have to pay so we can say
That Virtue wins the day!

I'M BROKE

Intended for Harold F. Springhorn, Milton R. Kroopf, and Milton V. O'Connell. Although the lyric was printed in the privately published score of the show, the song was apparently dropped before the opening.

VERSE

I feel the fire of spring,
The joy in ev'rything;
I glow in health.
But not in wealth!
Dreams are ethereal
But not material.
Aesthetic thrills
Today won't pay my bills.

REFRAIN

I'm broke! O hum!
The secret's out today.
Each creditor should lend me more,
Or else how can I pay?
No joke! O hum!
I'm in a debtor's yoke.
My dreams won't make a sirloin steak.
I'm broke! O hum!

WHEN I GO ON
THE STAGE

Introduced by Milton V. O'Connell and ensemble. This is not the same song as "When I Go on the Stage" in *She's My Baby* (1928).

VERSE

I'm tired of this hotel life;
I will not tarry more.
I've made the bed
Where lay the head
Of young John Barrymore.
Each time I've kissed his pillow,
Enwrapt in dreams, I've said,
"I'll leave this cage,
Go on the stage,
And kiss his lips instead,
When to my career I'm wed."

REFRAIN

My picture in all the papers,
My capers in print,
My dresses for all the gapers
Will cost a mint.
My face on ev'ry ash can,
Beneath my princely wage,
With such a start
I don't need art
When I go on the stage.

JUST A LITTLE LIE

Introduced by Max J. Liebowitz and ensemble. Introduced by Helen Kuck in *Say It with Jazz* (1921), and by Naomi Remey and ensemble in *Temple Belles* (1924).

VERSE

SHE: Ev'ry fellow in his soul,
  Longs to be an Anatol.
  Do just as I say.
BOYS: Speak and we'll obey.
SHE: You must never hesitate,
  Even to exaggerate.
BOYS: Won't you kindly illustrate?
SHE: Lovers must prevaricate.

REFRAIN

Just a little lie will not hurt you;
Just a little blarney's a virtue;
Truth and love do not agree.
If you tell a maid she's your only,
It will help her when she is lonely,
While with other maids you'll be.
Oh, foolish youth!
Don't tell the truth!
Swear you'll be faithful,
Though she knows that it's a lulu;
If you'd bid farewell to your mate, dear,
Tell the truth, she'll give you the gate,
    dear;
Just a little lie will do.

YOU'LL NEVER KNOW

Introduced by Walter S. Farrell, Harold F. Springhorn, Arthur Fluegelman, Edward Roche Hardy, Jr., and ensemble.

VERSE

Mona Lisa,
You loved Da Vinci,
Never told him,
It was a cinch, he
Never knew,
And that's the way
He painted you.
Girls are riddles,
Today, no matter
What they tell you,
It's idle chatter!
You build castles fair
In the air,
And your hopes they shatter.

REFRAIN

Though you may try to guess,
You'll never know.
She never will confess
If she means "No" or "Yes,"
Her "baby maybe" smile
Nothing will show;
When she's warm she starts to scold,
And when she smiles she's getting cold.
If so, or just so-so,
You'll never know.

YOUR LULLABY

Introduced by Fenimore E. Cooper and Glee Club Octette. Also introduced by Myra Kingsley in *Say It with Jazz* (1921).

VERSE

The notes of the woodland are crooning
The song of our love to the night,
The music of breezes a-tuning
A lullaby airily light;
The woodwinds are mystically playing
Like violins slumbering deep;
The slaves of my love are obeying
And singing my sweetheart to sleep.

REFRAIN

Won't you let me sing your lullaby,
And slumber on, my fair?
While tenderly the night winds sigh
As they kiss your hair.
Soft their song dies in the trees
On the boughs above,
While my whispers softly hush the breeze,
You're dreaming of my love.

SOMETHING LIKE ME

Introduced by Milton R. Kroopf and Milton V. O'Connell. Introduced by Lillian Gustafson in *Say It with Jazz* (1921).

VERSE 1

HE: You're no longer in your teens,
    Comprehending what it means;
    Cruel years advancing,
    Charms are not enhancing;
    Left on Papa's hands;
    Now's the time to find your mate,
    Better not procrastinate;
    When a maid is decaying,
    That's no time for delaying!

REFRAIN 1

Don't pick the wrong man,
You need a strong man;
A worker,
No shirker;

A hero,
No Nero;
A man with training
Needs no explaining;
The features
That greet yours
Handsome must be;
You might say,
All right, say,
Something like me.

VERSE 2

SHE: I will find my beau ideal,
    Hercules, with arms of steel!
    I will surely rope him,
    If I have to dope him,
    He will love or die!
    I won't let him take a drink,
    My Apollo dare not think;
    Though Apollo a bear is,
    He'll be Apollinaris!

REFRAIN 2

I'll find the right man,
He'll be a bright man.
A stoic
Heroic
Who's wealthy
And healthy!
No Galahad man;
I want a Bad Man!
Who's handsome
And planned some
Great things I'll do;
A real man,
Ideal man;
Nothing like you!

REFRAIN 3

HE: Don't pick the wrong man,
    You need a strong man
    Of fashion
    And passion,
    A thinker,
    No drinker;
    A man of spunk'll
    Make you say "Uncle!"
    Adonis
    Alone is
    The type he should be,
    Efficient,
    Omniscient,
    Something like me.

MR. DIRECTOR

Introduced by ensemble.

VERSE

Last year's rendition
In this song position
Was labeled "There's Room for One More."
Clever its lyric,
A wild panegyric
On loaves, wines and thous, by the score.
They started dancing in the chorus,
It was blurred,
For you heard
Not a word!
If you don't hear what's written for us,
You won't mind if the meaning's absurd!

REFRAIN

Mr. Director,
Tempo corrector,
The bald-headed sector
Wants just the ponies;
So wave your baton
And we won't prate on;
We want a chance
To break out in dance.

JUMPING JACK

Introduced by Arthur Fluegelman and ensemble.

VERSE

In the nurs'ry one fine morn,
Lo! The newest dance was born!
All the toy dolls,
Girl and boy dolls,
Jumped like Jack;
Jumping Jack up on a shelf,
Pulled a string and stretched himself;
Dolls in elation,
Of imitation,
Jumped like Jack.

REFRAIN

Do the Jumping Jack,
The thumping, bumping Jack!
You toddle,
Balance on your toe, then hop,
Away you go and jump!
Perfect ladies jump like Hades,
Bend their knees;
You enfold her
Head and shoulder,
Just a wee squeeze!
It's liked by all the maids,
The Jack of all the trades!
You jump, dear!
When you do the Jack,
Your troubles you attack;
It's there!
When you do it,
You won't rue it.
I'll show you it;
You'll go to it.
All your joys come back
When you jump the Jack.

SAY IT WITH JAZZ, 1921

Produced by the Institute of Musical Art at the Institute, 120 Claremont Avenue, New York, June 1–2, 1921. Music by Richard C. Rodgers. Lyrics by Lorenz M. Hart and Frank Hunter. Book by Dorothy Crowthers, Frank Hunter, and Maurice Lieberman. Musical numbers staged by Herbert L. Fields. Production directed by Richard C. Rodgers. Orchestra conducted by Richard C. Rodgers. Cast headed by Margaret Hamilton, Lillian Gustafson, Helen Kuck, David Buttolph, and Bernard Ocko.

All lyrics are either missing or were used first in other productions.

For the lyric of "Your Lullaby," see *You'll Never Know* (1921), page 25. For "Don't Love Me Like Othello," see *You'd Be Surprised* (1920), page 12. For "The Moon and You" ("Moonlight and You"), see *Fly with Me* (1920), page 16. For "Dreaming True," see *Fly with Me* (1920), page 15. For "Something Like Me," see *You'll Never Know* (1921), page 25. For "Chorus Girl Blues," see *Say Mama* (1921), page 22. For "Just a Little Lie," see *You'll Never Know* (1921), page 24.

The following lyrics, some of which were written by or in collaboration with Frank Hunter, are missing: "Just Remember Coq d'Or" (introduced by David Buttolph), "See This Golden Rooster" (Ida Deck and David Buttolph), "Working for the Institute" (Margaret Hamilton, Bernard Ocko, and Walter Getrost), and "Oh, Harold" (David Buttolph and ensemble).

There is a possibility that "Working for the Institute" has the same music as "Working for the Government" from *Fly with Me* (1920), page 14. "Hymn to the Moon," sometimes attributed to Lorenz Hart, has a lyric by Frank Hunter.

Dorothy Fields and Miriam Rosenwasser in *If I Were King*

RODGERS AND HART | 1922–1925

SHAKESPEARES OF 1922

Introduced by (and written for) Georgie Price. Lyric was found in Lorenz Hart Lyrics folder in the Rodgers and Hammerstein office. Morrie Ryskind confirmed to Dorothy Hart after examining the lyric in May 1985 that it was co-authored by Hart and himself. "Shakespeare of 1921" listed in the *Rodgers and Hammerstein Fact Book* is really this lyric.

Morrie Ryskind recalled:

I remember that Larry and I wrote a vaudeville sketch for Georgie Price which he was going to try out for Keith vaudeville. Price liked it and said he would try it out at some theater in Brooklyn and would pay us what he thought it was worth. He made one condition: he asked us not to be there in the theater during the tryout because it would make him nervous; but we bought two seats in the gallery from which we figured Price couldn't see us, because we were just as much interested in the reaction as he was. The sketch and lyrics got a lot of laughs which pleased us and then we sneaked out of the theater to go home before Georgie could spot us. We met him the following day and he said the material was amateurish but there were several lines he might be able to use and so he offered us $100 as pay. My reply was, no thanks; if it was not any good we weren't entitled to anything and we would just take the material and just forget about it; but Larry kicked me in the shins and told Georgie how good it was for him to offer any pay; and as I recall, Price paid the $100.

When we left his house I said to Larry: "You heard the laughs it got; I'm not satisfied to get $50 apiece for material he might use for a year," but Larry, who didn't need the money as much as I did (he could go into any store and charge it to his father), argued it could result in our getting other offers from vaudeville and would pay in the end. I said if they didn't earn any better I didn't give a hoot; and as it turned out, Georgie used the material for the entire season.

VERSE

Broadway has a Shakespeare fad,
Actors all are Shakespeare mad,
And I'd like to do
His great plays for you.
But I'll bring them up to date,
Five acts you won't have to wait
Till you hear the best scenes of the dramas.
And the plays will look like new
When I add a song or two.
I'll make Shakespeare seem the cat's pajamas!

REFRAIN 1

First I'll play Shylock for he's Spanish like me—
Shylock's from Arverne by the Sea, Long Island.
He'll be the star of my new Shakespeare revue,
Shylocks of 1922.

SPEECH

He hath disgraced me, he hath cost me half a million. Laughed at my losses, mocked at my gains. If I sell for four dollars a dozen, he sells for three seventy-five. And what's his reason? I'm a Jehuda! Hath not a Jehuda eyes? Hath not a Jehuda hands, organs, dimensions, broadcloth, velveteen, sateen, tricolette, and different-quality serges? If you gyp us, do we not bleed? If you do not pay us, do we not sue? And if you cancel our orders, shall we not revenge? Revenge! Revenge on Antonio!

FINISH

If I catch Antonio Spagoni the toreador!
He shall die! Ach ai vei!
He shall die diddy diddy ei, die, die, die
Ach oy vei!
He shall die! He shall die!
I soon will be takin'
A pound of his bacon
If I catch him bending tonight.

REFRAIN 2

Hamlet, the Prince of Denmark, can't make me
    wince,
I'll play the Danish pastry Prince.
He wasn't crazy at all,
But I am crazy to do
Hamlets of 1922.

SPEECH

To be or not to be, that is the question! Whether 'tis nobler to buy your Gordon's gin, and pay the prices of outrageous bootleggers, or to take arms against this sea of highwaymen, and make your own home brew! To drink, to die (to dream, perchance). Alcohol, aye, there's the rub! Home brew does make cowards of us all.

Mother, you have my father much offended. You made him drink shellac. You are toy queen. Your husband's brother's wife. And, would it were not so, so you my mother.

FINISH

Mammy! Mammy!
The sun will rise, and the sun will drop,
But the sun won't shine where you sent my pop!
Mammy! Mammy! If you make one more drop
I'll call in a cop,
My mammy!

REFRAIN 3

Poor old King Lear, who was bearded and gray,
Without the whiskers I will play.
How he went mad in the rainstorm,
I'll show in my revue,
Lears of 1922.

SPEECH

Blow winds, chap these hands, what care I. They have turned me out. Ah, foul rain, thou art good for crops, but tough on an old bird like me. Alas, O Jupiter, why didn't I get a five years' lease? Here I stand, King Lear, I was raised by the King, my father, I was raised by the Queen, my mother, and now, O ye Gods, now I've been raised by the landlord. Here I stand in the storm! Ah, daughters, this is a hell of a night to kick thy poor old father out. My landlord. I had to sell my icebox to pay him. I had to sell my flivver to pay him. I belong to the landlord! Even my clothes are rent! I saved and saved. I had to give up my shaving, but I didn't raise my beard to pay a landlord! Blow, winds! Spit! I think I'm going cuckoo! He rents more flats every day. Last week he made an apartment out of the elevator. Next week there'll be no closets. Let fall the rain, Lear should worry!

FINISH

Though April showers may come my way
They can't grow flowers in bales of hay.
And when it's raining, I just reflect,
Because it isn't raining rain at all,
It's just a stage effect!
I see a rainbow, and life's worthwhile,
For I'm insane, bo, that's why I smile.
I haven't even got a bathtub,
So I hope the rain is strong
Whenever April showers come along.

REFRAIN 4

In Julius Caesar that we studied at school,
Mark Ant'ny knocked 'em for a gool.
But I don't need hungry supers in my modern
    revue,
Caesars of 1922.

SPEECH

Friends, buyers and countrymen! Lend me your ears. I come to bury Babe Ruth, not to praise him! The strikeouts men make live after them, the homers are oft interr'd with their bones. So let it be with Baby. Rest these noble bones, for he hath pulled the biggest bone since Merkel forgot to touch second base. Aye, a base bone! Judge Landis, as you know, was Baby's angel. Judge O ye Gods, when he cut Babe Ruth's salary, that was the unkindest cut of all. For when the noble Babe Ruth saw him stab, he cried, "Et tu, Landis! The Vaudeville for Baby!" So he went to work for Keith. And at the portals of the Palace, great Babe Ruth fell flat! Oh, what a fall there was, my countrymen! But last year, the bat of Babe Ruth would have swung against the world. Now, he makes all his home runs at night!

FINISH

After the ball went over,
Bambino swung, that's all.
All he could hit was the umpire,
After the ball.

REFRAIN 5

All the world loves a lover like Romeo,
They named a cigar for him, you know.
That's why I must find some other name to call
my revue,
Dumbbells of 1922.

SPEECH

Ah, there she sits, my Juliet, on the fire escape! Burning up with a tender passion. See how she rests her chins upon her hand. Would that I were a glove upon that hand, then I would be a happy kid! Juliet, our love will be famous forever. They named a cigar after us. Romeo and Juliet. Twenty-five cents. Us for two bits, while Robert Burns for a dime, and Prince Hamlet chokes you for a nickel. What's in a name? Sir Walter Scott had a medicine named after him— Scott's Emulsion! Nellie Melba, she's a peach, Wilson is a whiskey, and Napoleon is a cream cake! They named a vegetable for a baseball player, Corn on Cobb! And the best they can do for Lincoln is to name a penny after him. Mary Garden's only a scent. What's in a name? A rose by any other name would smell as sweet. A Limburger by any other name would smell! Juliet, when I come to you beneath your balcony . . .

FINISH

You'll hear me calling Yoo-hoo
'Neath your window ev'ry night!
You sweetly answer Yoo-hoo
As you're standing in the light.
While I'm climbing up the ladder
And I get a worm's-eye view,
Love may be blind, so Yoo-hoo
Means I love you.

JAZZ À LA CARTE, 1922

Produced by the Institute of Musical Art at the Institute, 120 Claremont Avenue, New York, June 2 and 3, 1922. Music by Richard C. Rodgers and Gerald Warburg. Lyrics mostly by Frank Hunter. Book by Dorothy Crowthers. Production supervised by Dorothy Crowthers. Musical numbers staged by Richard C. Rodgers and Herbert L. Fields. Dance numbers staged by Herbert L. Fields. Orchestra conducted by William Kroll. Cast headed by Lillian Gustafson, Janet Beck, and Helen Kuck.

Three songs had lyrics by Lorenz Hart. For the lyric of "Another Melody in F," see *Fly with Me* (1920), page 14. For "Breath of Springtime," see "Breath of Spring" in *You'd Be Surprised* (1920), page 13. For "Moonlight and You," see *Fly with Me* (1920), page 16.

WINKLE TOWN, 1922

Winkle Town was an unproduced show with music by Richard C. Rodgers, lyrics by Lorenz M. Hart, and book by Oscar Hammerstein II and Herbert Fields. In his autobiography, *Musical Stages* (Random House, New York, 1975), Rodgers wrote of it that "our hero invents a kind of 'electronic' system that obviates the use of electric wires for communication and electric power." The locale is a Connecticut village called Winkle Town. The plot, Rodgers recalled, "deals with the hero's attempt—ultimately successful, of course—to convince the town fathers that the idea is both practical and beneficial." More than half of its songs, including "Manhattan," which was written when Rodgers was either nineteen or twenty years old, turned up later in other productions. A copy of the libretto is in the Rodgers and Hammerstein office. Some of the music was part of a Rodgers gift to the Music Division of the Library of Congress. The work was apparently registered for copyright by Richard C. Rodgers, but perhaps under another title, since there is no record of a copyright registration for *Winkle Town*.

ONE A DAY

VERSE

RITA: He has made my poor heart beat a wild
tattoo.
GIRLS: So have Harry, Fred and Pete, and wild
Pat too.
RITA: Though I'm in love with him this
morning,
By tomorrow night the boy is through.
GIRLS: Will you renounce him without warning?
RITA: What else can I do?
To keep my heart, fond words of love I
speak
To seven Arrow collar boys a week.

REFRAIN

One a day,
Kiss and run away.
Say you're glad to have met him,
Let him frown.
Change him like a gown,
With the next one forget him,
Set him in his place,
Try a change of pace,
Don't let love be passé,
Learn your text,
Call out, "Next!"
When you play one a day!

THE HOLLYHOCKS OF HOLLYWOOD

VERSE 1

Far in the golden West
We'll build our little nest.
It never rains on California's breast.
Here the nobles came from Spain,
Then they ran right home again.
The great Pacific all serene
Cannot wash the old coast clean.

REFRAIN 1

Just a little cottage
Midst the hollyhocks of Hollywood,
Where clover clubs and orange blossoms grow,
Where there ain't no Ten Commandments
And a man can raise a thirst.
And the scented breath of spearmint breezes
    blow!
There is something stirring
Midst the hollyhocks of Hollywood.
When simple movie lovers go to rest,
We will sprinkle old Dutch Cleanser
On the walls and on the floors
Of our Hollywood nest!

VERSE 2

Out on the beach each day
Sweet bathing beauties play;
They never bathe in California's Bay.
Miners came in forty-nine,
Now they haven't time to mine;
Things are changing I've been told,
Now the ladies dig for gold:

REFRAIN 2

Just a little cottage
Midst the hollyhocks of Hollywood,
Where keeping servants is so hard to do;
If the housemaid's a good looker,
She can sign with Mr. Zukor.
And the cow can be a movie actor too.
Cameramen are hiding
Midst the hollyhocks of Hollywood,
To look before you kiss you'll find is best;
People at the Strand and Rivoli
Get all the inside dope
On our Hollywood nest.

I KNOW YOU'RE TOO WONDERFUL FOR ME

VERSE

Tenderly I dreamed a dream of you,
Tenderly you tell me that it's true;
Is my dream so deep
That I'm still asleep?
Wonder and worship, that's all I can do!

REFRAIN

I know that you're too wonderful for me!
I know it's much too wonderful to be!
You're so beyond compare,
I never dreamed you'd care,
It's just like magic to be loved by you,
I can't believe it's true!
You've always seemed a princess far away,
And now I find you in my arms today!
The reason you should care at all
Is more than I can see,
You're too wonderful for me!

OLD ENOUGH TO LOVE

Written for *Winkle Town.* Introduced in *Dearest Enemy* (1925) by Detmar Poppen and ensemble.

VERSE 1

Romeo was very youthful
But unskilled to be truthful;
Couldn't love her under cover
Though he tried.
Old Don Juan was over fifty,
With a great romantic gift he
Had it in him, he could win 'em,
Till he died.
Youth in love may be the fashion,
Young men may excel in passion,
They begin it, love a minute,
Then depart.
Though an old boy may be shopworn
And his head a little top-worn,
He'll be much more settled when he loses his
    heart.

REFRAIN

You must be old enough to love.
Boys have no training,
They all need explaining.
If you are forty or above,
You can approve her, maneuver,
Remove her like a glove!
Boys fall for fair ones older than their own
    mamas,
Grandpas get nifties in their purple pajamas,
Methuselah could choose a la petite of
    twenty-two.
You must be old enough to know the thing to do.

VERSE 2

Good tobacco can't get mellow
Till it's old and sweet and yellow;
Young tobacco, like young lovers,
Must be cured.
Even cheese is in a coma
Till it gets the old aroma;
Puppy cheese, like puppy love,
Can't be endured.
And despite all criticisms,
All the oldest witticisms
Earn our comic opera authors' daily bread.
Wisdom long must be instilled,
Even pickles must be dilled;
Good old Noah was just eighty when the kid was
    wed.

REPEAT REFRAIN

THE HERMITS

Written for *Winkle Town.* Introduced in *A Danish Yankee in King Tut's Court* (1923) by Helen Kuck, Gladys Briskie, David Buttolph, and Arthur Allie; in *Temple Belles* (1924) by Beatrice Hoffman, Edna Meyer, Albert Blum, and Herman Singer; and in *Dearest Enemy* (1925) by Flavia Arcaro and Detmar Poppen. Alternate title: "What Do All the Hermits Do in Springtime?"

VERSE 1

When winter passes,
Laddies and lasses
Bud into blossom as lovers.
Love is a germ, it's
Rough on the hermits.
Birdies sing above!
Bullfrogs croak of love!
In the spring a hermit's weary,
Not a soul to call him dearie!

REFRAIN

What do all the hermits do in springtime,
When the little birdies sing of love?
Every clinging vine knows that it's cling time.
While we cuddle oh so snug,
Hermits haven't got a girl to hug.
Kiss me once for every lonesome hermit.
Moonlight nights to them don't mean a thing.
They can't hold a tree
As you're holding me—
What do all the hermits do in spring?

VERSE 2

Hermits have souls, dear,
Their socks have holes, dear!
They are the boys who grow whiskers,
I bet they crave for
Someone to shave for!
Even birdies mate!
Bullfrogs have a date!
While the lovers all make merry
Hermits feel unnecessary!

REPEAT REFRAIN

PATTER

Hermits never care to marry;
They're so very solitary.
They're erratic
And ecstatic,
They're phlegmatic
And rheumatic.
In the spring when we make merry
Hermits feel unnecessary.
Springtime is the best narcotic
To induce the sense erotic.
In the spring you'll find that various
Little feelings are precarious.
In the moonlight it's nefarious
Not to be a bit gregarious.
No sensation, no elation,
How can hermits help a nation?
All the stupid meditation
Can't increase the population.

REPEAT REFRAIN

HERMIT REPRISE

TOM: I don't know, Harry,
    How you could marry.
    You haven't funds to keep house with.
HARRY: Why all this bother?
    I'll live with Father.
EDITH: While the birdies meet
    I'll be glad I eat.
RITA: Don't you wish you too had tarried?
    Now you're hermits though you're
        married.

REPEAT REFRAIN

CONGRATULATIONS

Opening, Act II.

PREACHER: Harry Perry and Edith Van Winkle, I
    pronounce you man and wife!
[*All throw rice*]
    ALL: Congratulations! Congratulations!
        You're lucky we don't choose
        To greet you with old shoes.
        We hope to see your Golden
            Anniversary!
    PERRY: Congratulations! Congratulations!
        From now on I'll be hanging round
            the nursery.
    TOM (TO
    HARRY): Old man, you're proud and happy,
        too;
        You've every right to be.
        The happiness in store for you
        Brings happiness to me.
    HARRY
    (TO TOM): To my dad I'm thankful,
        His check has made our bank full.
        Ev'ry day in ev'ry way
        The Winkle light will pay!
    PERRY: It's time you two decide
        To run away and hide,
        But first your dear old dad must kiss
            the Bride!
[*Kisses her*]
    EDITH: Oh, I'm so happy!
    ALL: Oh, she's so happy!
        She's crying tears of joy!
        Our tact we must employ
        And not annoy the girl and boy.
        A very, very merry auto ride is
            necessary
        All the way up to the ferry with you
            two.
        A jolly, jolly trolley,
        Ev'ryone just out for folly
        Bidding Harry and his dolly fond
            adieu.
    TOM: You're so beyond compare
        I knew you'd never care.
        'Twas not for me, dear, to be loved by
            you—
    ALL: To marry Harry was the thing to do!
    TOM: You've always seemed a Princess far
            away,
        And now you're in another's arms
            today!
    ALL: A very, very merry auto ride is
            necessary

To the ferry where our fond farewells
        you'll see.
    TOM: You're too wonderful for me!

DARLING WILL NOT GROW OLDER / SILVER THREADS

VERSE

RITA: "Silver Threads Among the Gold"
    Somehow always leaves me cold.
    Father Time will steal our beauty
    If our hands we meekly fold.
    And our faces, you will find,
    Just reflect our states of mind.
    Keep on dreaming, it's your duty,
    Make your dreams the youthful kind.

REFRAIN

    Darling will not grow older
    If she does what she's told her;
    She'll keep her tresses of gold.
    Be happy ev'ry day, dear,
    Wrinkles will stay away, dear,
    If you don't quarrel and scold.
    Diet and weigh yourself,
    Try it and stay yourself,
    Take your good sleep at night,
    Make your looks keep at night.
    Loving and fond caresses
    Will help to keep your tresses
    In all the glory of their gold.

GIRLS: Darling, I am growing old.
    Silver threads among the gold [*etc.*]

    Darling will not grow older [*etc.*]. Darling
        I am growing old [*etc.*]

[*"Silver Threads Among the Gold" is sung separately and then as a countermelody to "Darling Will Not Grow Older"*]

BABY WANTS TO DANCE

VERSE

When baby's fretting,
She needs some petting;

And so if you are wise,
When she is pouting,
Give her an outing
And lots of exercise.
She is tired of talk,
Let the baby walk.
She'll be gay right away if you say
"Put on a fox-trot!"

REFRAIN

Baby wants to dance!
Baby wants a chance!
Baby wants her dancing shoes!
Baby wants to step.
Baby's full of pep!
Baby has no time to lose.
Little baby charms
Make a fellow glad he
Took her in his arms
When she called him "Daddy."
Baby's doll must be
Over six feet three
'Cause baby wants to dance.

I WANT A MAN

Written for *Winkle Town.* Revised for *Lido Lady* (1926) and *America's Sweetheart* (1931). See these shows for the revised lyrics.

VERSE 1

You're no longer in your teens,
Comprehending what it means;
Cruel years advancing,
Charms are not enhancing,
Left on Papa's hands!
Now's the time to pick your mate.
Better not procrastinate,
When you start to decay
There's no time to delay!

REFRAIN

I want a man!
I want a man!
If he's not very strong
I'll help along all I can!
I'll foot the bills
To buy him pills.
Oh, let me hear the sound of snoring at night—
I want a man
To raise the window and to turn down the light!

VERSE 2

I will find my beau ideal,
Hercules with arms of steel.
Just you watch me rope him
If I have to dope him.
He will love or die!
When he breathes tobacco smoke
Gladly on each puff I'll choke!
I won't mind if he's frail
Just as long as he's male!

REPEAT REFRAIN

COMFORT ME

VERSE

When a girl is sad, pet her a bit,
You will make her feel better a bit.
I'm so utterly blue,
And you are too!
Ev'ry lover is fickle, I know;
Tears will trickle, and so
Stand by
And try
To sympathize when I sigh.

REFRAIN

Comfort me, comfort me, tenderly, do;
Comfort while, dearest, I'll comfort you too.
When all the weary world is mean
My head must have a place to lean.
If I cry, you must dry each tear you see;
Soothe my brow, you know how nice you can be.
I'll make you comfy in my arms, dear,
If you will only comfort me.

SINCE I REMEMBER YOU

VERSE

I must admit to a dark and sinful past;
If you admire a monk or a friar,
I fear I am sadly miscast.
But as Lothario, my career is through.
Each flame's an ember
As cold as December,
And now I remember just you!

REFRAIN

I can't remember other girls
Since I remember you!
Perhaps I used to smother girls
With hugs and kisses too.
You're my first love and my last.
Since you came I have no past.
Never could forget so fast
Since I remember you!

THE THREE MUSKETEERS

Written for *Winkle Town.* Introduced in *The Garrick Gaieties* (1925) by Romney Brent, Sterling Holloway, and Philip Loeb; sung in the touring edition of *The Garrick Gaieties* (1930) by Philip Loeb, Sterling Holloway, and Neal Caldwell.

VERSE 1

Three musketeers who fought for fun
Were one for all, and all for one.
In days of old King Louis
They knocked his foes gaflooey.
But then when the King bawled out the Queen
And made her swallow Paris Green
Our heroes said, "Revenge is sweet!"
And kicked old Louis in the street.
Though the King had a seat on his throne,
He soon was thrown on his seat! . . . Ah!

REFRAIN

Three merry musketeers,
Athos, Porthos and Aramis,
We are the kitten's pajamas,
Three musketeers!

VERSE 2

If one could make a lady fall,
'Twas all for one, and one for all;
The lady wasn't slighted,
The trio was united,
Our heroes made her husband fret,
His wife now had a male quartet.
When hubby sang off key at that
The musketeers gave him his hat.
Because his voice kept flat on the key,
They kept the key of his flat . . . Ah!

REPEAT REFRAIN

VERSE 3

Three musketeers so brave and bold,
They never let their feet get cold.
They fought for lovely ladies,
French Sallies, Janes, Sadies.
And when a damsel in distress,
To them would send an SOS,
They'd hurry down to set her free,
But looked her over carefully.
And if they didn't think her face about right
They all would right-about-face.

REPEAT REFRAIN

IF I WERE KING

Written for *Winkle Town*. Introduced in *If I Were King* (1923) by Miriam Rosenwasser and Dorothy Fields; in *A Danish Yankee in King Tut's Court* (1923) by Helen Kuck and Arthur Allie; and in *Bad Habits of 1925* by Charles Vaughn Holly.

VERSE 1

HE: I adore you, Princess far away.
     My poor heart I lay
     At your feet today.
     My love for you makes me bold to say,
     I behold you, and I see
     Heaven has come down to me.

REFRAIN 1

     The scented summer air
     Whispers the love I may not dare.
     Moon and the stars in gold and blue
     Sing of my love for you.
     And though I've never told you,
     In my dreams I've dared to hold you.
     The stars, sweetheart, I'd bring
     For you to wear,
     If I were King.

VERSE 2

SHE: Dear sir poet, cry not for the moon.
     Dreams of spring and June
     All must end too soon.
     Well, I know it, Life will change your tune.
     Fate is stern, relentless too,
     And I was not born for you.

REFRAIN 2

     The scented summer air
     Whispers of love you must not dare.
     Moon and the stars in gold and blue
     Sing of romance to you.
     And though you've never told me
     In your dreams you've dared to hold me,
     The stars I know you'd bring
     For me to wear,
     If you were King.

MANHATTAN

Published June 1925. Written for *Winkle Town*. Introduced in *The Garrick Gaieties* (1925) by June Cochrane and Sterling Holloway. In the original *Winkle Town* version, which included the verse and the first two refrains, the opening of the song was:

          Summer journeys to Niag'ra
          Or to other places aggra-
          Vate all our cares.

Lines 6–8 of refrain 2 read:

          We'll bathe at Brighton
          The fish we'll frighten
          When we're in.

Line 17 of refrain 2 read:

          The city's bustle will not destroy

VERSE

Summer journeys to Niag'ra
And to other places aggra-
Vate all our cares.
We'll save our fares!
I've a cozy little flat in
What is known as old Manhattan,
We'll settle down
Right here in town!

REFRAIN 1

We'll have Manhattan,
The Bronx and Staten
Island too.
It's lovely going through
The zoo.
It's very fancy
On old Delancey
Street, you know.
The subway charms us so
When balmy breezes blow
To and fro.
And tell me what street
Compares with Mott Street
In July?
Sweet pushcarts gently gliding by.
The great big city's a wondrous toy
Just made for a girl and boy.
We'll turn Manhattan
Into an isle of joy.

REFRAIN 2

We'll go to Greenwich,
Where modern men itch
To be free;
And Bowling Green you'll see
With me.
We'll bathe at Brighton;
The fish you'll frighten
When you're in.
Your bathing suit so thin
Will make the shellfish grin
Fin to fin.
I'd like to take a
Sail on Jamaica
Bay with you.
And fair Canarsie's lake
We'll view.
The city's bustle cannot destroy
The dreams of a girl and boy.
We'll turn Manhattan
Into an isle of joy.

REFRAIN 3

We'll go to Yonkers
Where true love conquers
In the wilds.
And starve together, dear,
In Childs.
We'll go to Coney
And eat baloney
On a roll.
In Central Park we'll stroll,
Where our first kiss we stole,
Soul to soul.
Our future babies
We'll take to *Abie's*
Irish Rose.
I hope they'll live to see
It close.
The city's clamor can never spoil
The dreams of a boy and goil.
We'll turn Manhattan
Into an isle of joy.

REFRAIN 4

We'll have Manhattan,
The Bronx and Staten
Island too.
We'll try to cross
Fifth Avenue.
As black as onyx
We'll find the Bronnix
Park Express.
Our Flatbush flat, I guess,
Will be a great success,
More or less.
A short vacation
On Inspiration Point
We'll spend,
And in the station house we'll end.
But Civic Virtue cannot destroy
The dreams of a girl and boy.
We'll turn Manhattan
Into an isle of joy.

The next two lyrics were probably written for *Winkle Town*, but are not found in the surviving script.

I'LL ALWAYS BE AN OPTIMIST

TOM: I'll always be an optimist until the day I
    die.
    In afterlife I hope the change'll
    Find me as a happy angel.
RITA: And if your soul went down below,
    You'd practice how to fly.
TOM: And if I'm broke I'm never whining.
RITA: Your pockets have a silver lining.
[*Incomplete*]

WE CAME; WE SAW; WE MADE 'EM!

VERSE 1

TOM: When we walked upon the campus,
    Sweet coeds would try to vamp us;
    From the moment that they'd lamp us
    They'd give us a smile.
HARRY: We were slender, bright and dapper,
    Most appealing to the flapper
    And we could not but entrap her
    With our manly guile.

BOTH: Like Indians, we wanted scalps,
    Brunette and blonde and titian;
    To find 'em, feed 'em and forget 'em
    Was our great ambition.

REFRAIN

We came; we saw; we made 'em,
We never flashed our eyes in vain;
We came, and when we played 'em,
They made us come right back again;
We saw so many bright heads, so many
    light heads that we could chaff.
TOM: We came; we saw; we made 'em.
    We made 'em what?
HARRY: We made 'em laugh!

VERSE 2

TOM: We discussed the classic dramas
    With their aunties and their mamas;
    We were pussy's own pajamas,
    Welcome on each mat.
HARRY: We used every innuendo,
    Spoke in tones diminuendo,
    Knocked 'em for a cold—crescendo!
    Then we left 'em flat!
BOTH: With our degrees, we felt as wise
    As Plato in the flesh, men!
    Though senior flappers made us feel
    That we were only freshmen.

REPEAT REFRAIN

HALF MOON INN, 1923 & 1925

There were two editions of this show. The first was produced by the Players Club of Columbia University as the "Varsity Show of 1923" at the Grand Ballroom of the Hotel Astor, New York, March 19–24, 1923. It included one Rodgers and Hart song, "Jack and Jill" (lyric is missing), which had been written earlier for *Say Mama* (1921), see page 21. The second edition, presented as the "Varsity Show of 1925" at the Grand Ballroom of the Waldorf-Astoria Hotel, New York, March 9–14, 1925, included the "Crossword Puzzle Song," music and lyrics by Rodgers, and one Rodgers and Hart song, "Babbitts in Love,"

which was introduced by C. A. Fairchild, Columbia 1925, and Hamilton S. Phillips, Columbia 1925.

BABBITTS IN LOVE

VERSE

A maiden with romance was once wed and won
When Cupid was just a beginner.
But now you must show her the old
    said-and-done
And use modern methods to win her;
Just give her a chart of the state of your heart,
And hand her a sales talk that's clever.
Be bigger and better, a little go-getter,
And she'll sign a contract forever.

REFRAIN

There's a little bit of Babbitt in the game of love,
Take a tip or two from me,
Sell your personality.
Get to be a steady habit with the girl you love,
You'll have her set to sign
Along the dotted line
If you're a real go-getter in love.

IF I WERE KING, 1923

Produced by the Dramatic Art Department of the Benjamin School for Girls for the Benefit of the Free Scholarship Fund of the New York Child Labor Committee at the Thirty-ninth Street Theatre, New York, March 25, 1923. Music by Richard C. Rodgers. Lyrics by Richard C. Rodgers and Lorenz M. Hart. Book by Justin Huntley McCarthy. Directed by Herbert L. Fields. Orchestra conducted by Richard C. Rodgers. Cast headed by Dorothy Fields, Sylvia Piermont, and Miriam Rosenwasser.

The lyrics to "Daughters of Pleasure," "Sextette," and "Courtly Etiquette" are by Richard C. Rodgers. There are no lyrics for Rodgers' music to "March Louis XI," "Minuet," and "Waltz."

For the lyric of "If I Were King," see *Winkle Town* (1922), page 33.

THE BAND OF THE NE'ER-DO-WELLS

Introduced by T. Turk and ensemble.

VERSE

When hypocrites snore in their beds
And gendarmes nod their silly heads,
In brotherhood we cling,
The cockleshells are all well met;
We sneak into our cellarette
And cluster round our king.
A rebel rogue our prince is known,
No puppet on a gilded throne
Is he of whom we sing.
He's clad in tatters yet his rule
Is not like Louis'. He's no fool:
He shares the swag we bring.

REFRAIN

We are the ne'er-do-wells,
Merry cockleshells,
With our hearts as light as our fingers.
Your lost purse could belong to worse
Than the band of the ne'er-do-wells!

PATTER

Ev'ry honest thief has entry!
Break the law and pass the sentry!
Pick the poke!
For a joke!
We can fleece
The police!
We're a band of gay banditti,
All the folks we rob we pity!
Try to scream,
Soon you'll dream!
Once you shout
You pass out!
We're the best light-fingered gentry
And our code is elementary.
Never steal on Sunday,
That's the one day that we rest!
So we're known throughout the city,
La noblesse of all banditti,
Band of the ne'er-do-wells!

A DANISH YANKEE IN KING TUT'S COURT, 1923

Produced by the Institute of Musical Art at the Institute, 120 Claremont Avenue, New York, May 31 and June 1, 1923. Music by Richard C. Rodgers. Book and lyrics largely by Herbert L. Fields, Dorothy Crowthers, and Richard C. Rodgers; four lyrics were by Lorenz M. Hart. Production and dance numbers staged by Herbert L. Fields. Orchestra conducted by Richard C. Rodgers. Cast headed by David Buttolph, Theodore Rautenburg, Ruth Bugbee, Alice Chester, and Arthur Allie.

   For "Will You Forgive Me?" see *Poor Little Ritz Girl* (1920), page 19. For "The Hermits," see *Winkle Town* (1922), page 30. For "If I Were King," see *Winkle Town* (1922), page 33.

   The lyric to "If You're Single" (introduced by Theodore Rautenberg, Arthur Allie, and Charles McBride) is missing.

TEMPLE BELLES, 1924

Purim entertainment produced by Irving Strouse at the Park Avenue Synagogue, New York, March 20, 1924. Music by Richard C. Rodgers. Lyrics by Lorenz M. Hart and Dorothy Crowthers. Production staged by Herbert L. Fields. Music director, Richard C. Rodgers. Cast headed by Naomi Remey, Edna Meyer, Sophie Blum, Herman Singer, and Beatrice Hoffman.

   The lyric for "Bob-o-link" was by Dorothy Crowthers. Lorenz Hart wrote no new lyrics for *Temple Belles.*

   For the lyric to "Just a Little Lie," see *You'll Never Know* (1921), page 24. For "A Penny for Your Thoughts," see *Fly with Me* (1920), page 14. For "The Hermits," see *Winkle Town* (1922), page 30.

THE MELODY MAN, 1924

Tryout when it was titled *The Jazz King*: Kurtz Theatre, Bethlehem, Pennsylvania, March 24–29, 1924; Orpheum Theatre, Harrisburg, Pennsylvania, March 25, 1924; Cambria Theatre, Johnstown, Pennsylvania, March 26, 1924; Auditorium, Wheeling, West Virginia, March 27, 1924; Auditorium, Toledo, March 28–29, 1924; Garrick Theatre, Detroit, March 30–April 5, 1924; Hanna Theatre, Cleveland, April 7–12, 1924. Tryout when it was known as *Henky*: La Salle Theatre, Chicago, April 21–May 3, 1924; Teller's Shubert Theatre, Brooklyn, May 5–10, 1924. New York run: Ritz Theatre, May 13–31, 1924; Forty-ninth Street Theatre, June 2–28, 1924. 56 performances. A comedy by Herbert Richard Lorenz (pseudonym for Herbert Fields, Richard Rodgers, and Lorenz Hart). Produced by Lew Fields. Directed by Lawrence Marston and Alexander Leftwich. Cast, starring Lew Fields, included Eva Puck, Sam [Sammy] White, Fredric March, Betty Weston, and Donald Gallaher.

MOONLIGHT MAMA

Published April 1924. Introduced by Eva Puck and Sam White. Song credited: "Words and Music by Herbert Richard Lorenz."

VERSE 1

Pretty mama's like the cat,
She comes out ev'ry night.
When the owls begin to chat
She finds the nighttime
Just the right time.

REFRAIN

I've got a moonlight mama
Sleepin' all day
And she's dancin' all night.
My pretty moonlight mama
Wants her own way
And she gets it all right.
All through the day she keeps forgetting
How my heart pines;
But ev'ry night I get my petting,
She makes hay while the moon shines.
She's just a love physician,
Makes me obey,
And there's never a fight.

Here's why I'm in condition,
An apple a day
And a peach ev'ry night.
She's just a drooping lily
While the sunbeams shine,
But at night she knocks you silly,
Moonlight mama of mine.

VERSE 2

I have never studied art,
I've never read a book.
But I've learned about my heart
In mama's night school,
That's the right school.

REPEAT REFRAIN

Earlier version

VERSE

Mama never leaves her flat,
She doesn't like it bright.
Pretty mama's like the cat—
She goes out ev'ry night.
Though she doesn't paint or write
She studies in the park
In a spot that's far from light,
'Cause mama likes it dark.

REFRAIN

I've got a moonlight mama
Sleepin' all day
And she's workin' all night.
My pretty moonlight mama
Wants her own way
And she gets it all right.
All through the day she keeps forgetting
How my heart pines;
But ev'ry night I get my petting:
She makes hay while the moon shines.
She's just a love physician—
Makes me obey
And she makes me feel right.
Here's why I'm in condition:
An apple a day
And my mama at night.
Cold winter nights cannot reform her,
That's why the winters get warmer!
My pretty moonlight mama
Makes the night mighty bright for me!

I'D LIKE TO POISON IVY

Published April 1924. Introduced by Eva Puck and Sam White. Credited to "Herbert Richard Lorenz."

VERSE 1

I've got a girl named Ivy,
She's awf'lly fond of me!
She follows me both night and day,
I wish she'd let me be!
At night, when I am sleeping,
I can't forget that face;
And if she goes to Heaven, then
I'll go to the other place!

REFRAIN

I'd like to poison Ivy
Because she clings to me!
She grabbed me the moment we met;
Just a Jane you want to forget.
Like Barnum stuck to Bailey,
She sticks to me, you see;
I'd like to poison Ivy,
Because she poisons me.

VERSE 2

I see that face each morning,
I see it ev'ry night!
I look at her at dinnertime
And lose my appetite!
She uses min'ral lava
And dresses up in silk;
But when the Moo-Cow looks at her
We all drink buttermilk.

REPEAT REFRAIN

BAD HABITS OF 1925

Produced by Irving Strouse for the benefit of the Evelyn Goldsmith Home for Crippled Children, Inc., at the Children's Theatre of the Heckscher Foundation, 104th Street and Fifth Avenue, New York, February 8, 1925. Music by Richard C. Rodgers. Lyrics by Lorenz M. Hart. A revue with sketches directed by Lorenz Hart and Irving Strouse. Dances directed by Gene Richard and Sydney Oberfelder. Orchestra conducted by Richard C. Rodgers. Cast headed

by Mrs. Arthur Bodenstein, Mrs. Leon Osterweil, Muriel Bamberger, Phillip B. Leavitt, Al Jackson, Nat Williams, and John Glass, Jr.

For the lyric to "Darling Will Not Grow Older," see *Winkle Town* (1922), page 31. For "If I Were King," see *Winkle Town* (1922), page 33.

The following lyrics are missing: "The Merrie Merrie" (introduced by Mrs. Leon Osterweil, Mrs. Arthur Bodenstein, Muriel Bamberger, Belle Grant, John Glass, Jr., Phillip B. Leavitt, Seymour Hess, and Louis Friedlander), "In Gingham" (introduced by Bereneice and Estelle Rosen, Rosalind Landau, Helen Tichenor, Helen Morse, Peggy Gartner, Ruth and Helen Amsterdam; danced by Priscilla Mitchell), "Across the Garden Wall" (introduced by Mrs. Arthur Bodenstein), "Mah-Jongg Maid" (introduced by Muriel Bamberger and ensemble).

I'D LIKE TO TAKE YOU HOME TO MEET MY MOTHER

Introduced by Roslee Steinfeld and Phillip B. Leavitt. Written in 1923, or later, after the publication and fame of "Yes, We Have No Bananas."

There are lots of peaches down in Georgia.
We wrote this one for fun,
And it brought us the "mon."
Just a little love, a little kiss.
We got lots of royalties for this.
Come on and hear, come on and hear
Alexander's Ragtime Band.
Then we wrote a bugle call like you never heard
   before,
And when our country was called into war—
Over There, Over There.
Did you know that we wrote Over There?
Merry Widow, Merry Widow was a hit.
Rodgers bought his new Tuxedo out of it.
Yes, We Have No Bananas is another by Rodgers
   and Hart.
Oh, Say Can You See.

I'd like to take you home to meet my mother
[*etc.*]

German

Ich mocht dich gern zu Hause nehm'n zu Mutter.
Sei wie 'ne Schwester zu Bruderlein fein.
Sie kocht gebratene ganz so weich wie Butter.
Es ist doch Sontag Kind sei nicht toll.

Komm doch mit Fress dich voll.
Der Vater sitzt und schmekt ein Bismarck
    Herring.
Wenn er dich küsst riecht der Vater so schön.
Ach, sag du liebst dein Fritzl
Mehr wie wiener Schnitzel,
Ach, süsses Mädel, komme und lass uns gehen.

Tough

I'd like to knock ya down to me old lady.
She'd love ta flag ya and drag ya around.
The sweetest little skirt is sister Sadie.
They won't believe their lamps when they see
That you got spliced to me.
You'll walk into me tony Mott Street Mansion,
And watch the flies and mosquitoes play tag.
When Pop gets drunk he's vicious,
You'll be dodging dishes.
Oh, I'd like to drag ya home to meet the hag!

Gilbert and Sullivan

If you'd only meet the mater
I'm convinced it would elate her,
No pleasure could be greater to allure.
For you'll enjoy a little chat in
Our apartment in Manhattan,
It's the nicest you have sat in, I am sure.
Then you'll meet the little sister,
From the moment you have kissed her
You're unable to resist her pretty smile.
They will meet us at the station,
And you're under observation,
Then my very proud elation
Will produce a chest inflation.
A very, very merry little drink is necessary

In the cellar where we'll bury all our woe.
And I'll be happy as a King is
When the little golden ring is
On your finger and the thing is
Comme il faut.
Little goose, come with your gander,
To our cottage we'll meander.
When you see the house your gander built
You'll feel as rich as Vanderbilt.
Oh, it's better now than later,
Come along and meet the mater and the dad.

Italian

Oh, pizzicato, presto, madre mia.
Oh, macaroni, spumoni, spaghett.
Hispano-Suiza, Cadillac and Reo.
Oh, generalissimo, carissimo, fortissimo, kissimo.
Maria Jeritza, Galli-Curci.
Gatti-Casazza, piazza, hurrah!
Bacardi, maraschino,
Rudolph Valentino.
Oh, pizzicato, presto, madre mia!

Mammy

I'd like to take you home to meet my Mammy,
Away down South by that old Swanee shore.
My Mammy is the heart of Alabammy.
I hear that waving corn seem to say
She will kiss your tears away.
Daddy may be black but he's a white man,
My sister's yaller, but she is true blue,
And in those fields of cotton,
Cares will be forgotten.
Give me Dixieland, my Mammy dear and You!

PATTER

There's a word of just five letters, starts with
M and ends with Y—Mammy . . . Mammy.
A word of thirteen letters, starts with X and ends
    with I—Mammy . . . Mammy.
And this one means a kangaroo that hasn't any
    tail.
Mammy , , , Mammy.
And this one means a lubricant you get out of a
    whale.
Mammy . . . Mammy.
Take me to your arms in joy,
Mammy, Mammy, here's your boy.
That's why you hear me say
Don't get in my way.
I'll nestle in her arms today
And in those fields of cotton
Cares will be forgotten.
Give me Dixieland, my Mammy dear and You!

JUNE DAYS, 1925

Rodgers and Hart contributed one song, "Anytime, Anywhere, Anyhow," to the musical comedy *June Days*, which opened at the Astor Theatre, New York, on August 6, 1925 (84 performances). It was introduced by Elizabeth Hines and Roy Royston. Music was found at the Warner Brothers Warehouse, Secaucus, New Jersey. The lyric is missing.

OVERLEAF: Herbert Fields, Richard Rodgers, and Lorenz Hart

MISCELLANEOUS EARLY SONGS

CANDY OPENING

VERSE

Candy selling seems to be quite an easy matter.
You sell a pound then sit around
And spend your time in chatter.
But to tell the truth, to sell a youth
A box of sweets is trying.
For there is more to a candy store
Than weighing off and tying.

REFRAIN

Being smart is an art selling candy.
For even candies have their style.
And every beau has to know
There's a brand he
Can send his girl to make her smile.
If he strikes what she likes, she'll remember
And she will love him all the more.
And if she gives her consent
He's content that he went
To the little candy store.

PATTER

Lollipops and lemon drops, chocolate cigars,
Nougatines and jelly beans and Hershey almond
    bars,
Licorice fudge and sugar plum,
Tootsie Rolls and chewing gum!
To us it's tough
To sell the stuff.
We dare not eat—
The life we lead is sweet!

REPEAT REFRAIN

CHLOE, CLING TO ME

Published October 1922. Music by Joe Trounstine. Lyric by Lorenz Hart and Herbert Fields.

VERSE 1

Deep the shadows of the night,
Not so deep as your eyes, Chloe.
Hear your Joey,
He can show he
Loves his Chloe so.
Even stars up in the sky
Seem like fireflies to your eyes;
Can't you hear me serenading?

REFRAIN

Chloe, Chloe, cling to me,
Red kisses bring to me,
Chase that frown,
Come on down;
Black-eyed beauty,
Do your duty.
Don't you know that I would walk a mile
To see my Chloe smile?
Hear me sing, Oh!
Chloe, cling to me.

VERSE 2

Once a day I think of you,
When I wake up in the morning;
When it's noontime, when it's moontime,
And at twilight too.
When awake or sleeping tight,
Ev'ry morning, noon or night;
That's the time I think of Chloe.

REPEAT REFRAIN

DADDY'S AWAY

VERSE

My daddy ain't a p'liceman
But he goes with cops a lot!
And yesterday he went away
And he's the only daddy I got!
Ma says there'll be no more fights,
'Cause she knows where he is nights!
When the sun shines hot, I ain't afraid,
Where my dad is, there's lots of shade!

REFRAIN 1

Daddy's away!
Where he must stay.
He bought bottles and he sold 'em
And a bad judge told him:
"You're going away!"
Ma said today,
"He's making small ones out of big ones
Till the first of May!"
Poor Mama can't get bail,
So Daddy's in jail!

REFRAIN 2

Daddy's away!
His suit is gray!
He mixed bootleg gin with water,
Now he mixes mortar!
Ma used to make
Chicken and steak!
Now all Pa gets is bread and water
And a tummy ache!
We have labels for sale
'Cause Daddy's in jail!

MONOLOGUE

My papa's in jail! Ma said they made it hot for him, so now he's in the cooler! The kids around my block won't play with me. . . . Sadie Thompson said, "Your papa's a bootlegger, and he's down and out!" So I told her, "My papa may be down, but he won't be out for ninety days!" I went to see my daddy. Ma took me. . . . Huh, they think my pa's a monkey . . . they put him in a cage, and he's got a keeper! I asked Ma should I throw peanuts? She smashed me! . . . Ma says the state's supporting him now. That'll relieve her for a while now! I met the nicest burglar! He was playing football, with an iron football! My father's on the baseball team. They got a major league, and a minor league. The major league for murderers, and the minor league for bootleggers! B'lieve me, Pa would like to make a home run!

I'm awfully sad,
Since they pinched my dad!
And now he's on his good behavior
Or he'll get in bad!
Won't someone please go bail?
My daddy's in jail!

DAUGHTERS OF THE EVOLUTION

VERSE

We who sing this little ditty
See the growth of New York City.
We are four society dames
Who have funny names!
Cut by Vanderbilts and Cabots
But that's no disgrace.
We make our contribution
Back from a different place
We're the Daughters of Evolution
And the mothers of a future race.

REFRAIN

The Irish! The Irish!
Have made New York

Like County Cork.
Killarney and Blarney
Rule one and all
In Tammany Hall!
John L. Sullivan was frisky
With Irish punch and Irish whiskey!
George M. Cohan may sound suspicious,
His patron saint was Aloysius!
Pat Rooney is a Russian Jew
And so's our friend Jack Donahue!
Ev'ry paddy has a pal in
Tender-hearted Judge Cohalan!
Who's the greatest of the great?
And who's the king that rules the state?
Who makes every man his henchman?
Maybe you think Al Smith's a Frenchman?
Take a look at old Bill Brady,
His mother was a Turkish lady!
The Irish! The Irish!
Took off the lid
And who else did?
For the best stock that you have in you
Is living on Tenth Avenue!
They've brought old Ireland down
To rule in New York town!

FLOW ON, RIVER

VERSE

Time and tide wait for no one
But you wait for me!
River, my flowing water,
In the morn and at twilight
Waiting patiently,
River, the mountain's daughter.

REFRAIN

Flow on, river,
To the sea!
Winding ever
Endlessly,
Through the valley
O'er the lea,
Under bridges
To the sea!

GOOD BAD WOMAN!

Lyric found in Lorenz Hart Lyrics folder in the Rodgers and Hammerstein office. Music was donated to the Library of Congress by Richard Rodgers.

VERSE

They call me wildcat, tigress,
Female leopard, snake and spider!
But I'm just a noble woman
With a great big heart inside her!
It's true, I've ruined lots of homes,
And every man I've met,
But my great big heart's just as good as new,
I've never used it yet!

REFRAIN 1

I'm a very good bad woman
With a snowball in my chest.
I snatch at poor men's heartstrings,
And I tie them up in knots!
I'm just as full of husbands as a leopard is of
    spots!
From breaking up so many homes, I'm just a
    bunch of nerves.
When I appear in public, why, they call out the
    reserves!
I'm a very good bad woman,
And I'd be much worse if I could.
You don't need any coal when I'm around, that's
    understood.
When I sit on a sofa, I set fire to the wood.
I'm a bad bad bad bad woman,
But I'll tell the world I'm good!

REFRAIN 2

I'm a very good bad woman
With a snowball for a heart!
When I start getting nasty
I can make a statue shiver!
I roll my eyes, and sixty men jump right into the
    river!
I love to take a manly heart, and torture it, and
    strike it.
And then I crush it like a grape, and even make
    'em like it!
I'm a very good bad woman,
And I've made bald heads turn to gray.
A woman's a grass widow when she's been
    divorced, they say!
Grass widow! Gosh, by this time, I must be a
    bale of hay!
I'm a bad bad bad bad woman
In a very charming way!

REFRAIN 3

I'm a very good bad woman
With a soul as black as ink!
Judge Aaron Jones was ninety-six, and yet he lost
    his heart.
I had to grab him mighty quick, before he fell
    apart!
"I'd give my all for you!" he said, and Aaron
    spoke the truth.
I got his all, I even took the gold crown off his
    tooth.
I'm a very good bad woman,
And I'm seldom left alone.
I donate all my alimony to an old man's home,
And now and then I even donate patients of my
    own!
I'm a bad bad bad bad woman
With a very busy phone!

GOOD PROVIDER

Lyric found in Lorenz Hart Lyrics folder in the Rodgers and Hammerstein office. Music was donated to the Library of Congress by Richard Rodgers.

INTRODUCTION

Lord, man, I certainly is tired! I got hurty feet, Me standin' on my feet all day and other people standin' on 'em in the subway. I'd like to stand on my hands and give my feet a rest.

How come you home so early? What you all doin' messin' round the house at six o'clock readin' *Snappy Stories*? Take yo' feet offen my sofa! Who you think you are—Gloria Swanson?

Did you buy anyt'ing for supper? I'm so hungry I could eat a house. . . . Huh? Frankfurters? They makes me noxious. Certainly I said I could eat a house . . . a porterhouse! Set yoseff down. Youse gonna get dinner soon as I catch my breff!

[*Pressing foot*] Lordy, I certainly has a flat tire today. Checking coats in a Chinese restaurant ain't my idea o' connubial bliss. I'm scared o' Chinamen. They're sneaky-like and flirty. . . . You all said a heapin' teaspoonful—I certainly can take care o' myseff.

But how come you home so early? Ain't people ridin' in taxicabs no more? . . . Huh? What's 'at you say, nigger? You done give up yo' job! Again? Seems to me givin' up yo' job is all you ever does give up!

Set yoseff down, man, I'se gonna do a little ex-postulatin'. Man, put on yo' shoes, because youse gonna git you walkin' papers right off. If you think

I'm checkin' coats all day long to put chops in you mouff, you all is laboring under a misdemeanor!

VERSE

Honey man, youse dispossessed!
Youse a bird without a nest.
Don't begin to holler,
Make yo' exit clean.
Pack yo' other collar
And yo' brilliantine!
When I look at you I see
Just six foot of misery.
Yo' kiss ev'ry hour
Seems to get more sour,
Mr. Simon Legree!

REFRAIN 1

You're just a good provider
Providin' lots of trouble for me.
Your ball and chain is settin' you free.
I'se oversaturated with your company.
Good provider, providin' me with sorrow and
    care,
Take yo' pink pajamas
Away from Mama's,
This nigger drama's all over for fair.
Royal Highness, my love for you is minus,
So, good provider, please reside elsewhere!

PATTER

Nothin' that you promised never come to pass.
The weddin' ring you gave me turned right into
    brass.
All my orange blossoms turned to lemonade.
Workin' in a kitchen for a hungry coon
Ain't what I imagined for my honeymoon.
When I picked you out my judgment got mislaid.
You declared you'd git me all that I was wishin'.
All you ever got me was a position.
Never return into my shack.
All that I earn goes on my back.
Your journey starts 'cause you're untrue,
You played with hearts and I'se trumpin' you!

REFRAIN 2 (half refrain)

You're just a good provider,
Providin' me with sorrow and care.
This marriage license
It ain't worth five cents.
While I'se got my sense
I'se givin' you the air.
Black Life Saver, you sure done lost yo' flavor,
So, good provider, please reside elsewhere!

HE WAS THE LAST ROSE OF SUMMER

VERSE

Every summer Mother dragged me to a new
    hotel.
First she dressed me swell. Then she tried to
    sell!
Mother hoped to marry me to every man in sight.
I fished with all my might, but not a fish would
    bite!
Father said to me in tears, "I've kept you for
    twenty years,
I don't think you will keep another season!"
Just before the fall began I closed my eyes and
    grabbed a man.
I hooked him quick before the fool could reason!
He was the only one in pants,
They left me for my romance!

REFRAIN 1

He was the last rose of summer
That bloomed at the summer hotel!
He doesn't wear such nifty clothes,
And when the breeze of summer blows,
He's not so mighty like a rose, as well!
The season was closing,
No man was proposing,
I caught him asleep in the hall!
All he can do is snore at night,
Pull down the shade and douse the light.
But he was the last rose of summer,
And he's better than no rose at all!

REFRAIN 2

He was the last rose of summer,
I plucked him before he could fade!
He limps a bit, he's very frail,
But thank the Lord, at least he's male!
The world owed me a living, and I'm paid.
I ask myself, "Has ma
Poor sweetie got asthma?"
I hope that he'll last till the fall!
He's not so young, his eyes are dim,
You have to chew his food for him,
But he was the last rose of summer,
And he's better than no rose at all!

I'M GETTING BETTER!

VERSE 1

Look at me and view
What strong will can do.
I had no corpuscles,
Now I'm full of muscles!
I gain power
Ev'ry hour.

REFRAIN

Ev'ry day in every way my motto I obey.
I believe each letter
And I'm getting better!
I tell you it must be true,
I read it in F.P.A.
Sweet concentration
Makes me say that every day
I'm getting better and better and better
In every way!

VERSE 2

Once my life was vile.
Now all day I smile!
I'm on good behavior,
For I've found a savior.
Ev'ry roué
Should read Coué.

REPEAT REFRAIN

JAKE THE BAKER

VERSE

Jake Berkowitz the baker married me last spring.
For a wedding band he handed me a coffee ring!
What he bakes, I can't eat.
How he hates to feed me meat!
All he gives me is strudels
With noodles!

REFRAIN 1

Down by the oven where the lovin' is hot,
I met my Jake.
Cold winter nights when I could use him a lot,
He's baking cake!
He was the catch of the season about ten seasons
    ago.
His kisses are sweet and sour,

They taste from flour and dough!
If I don't eat matzohs . . . he plotzes!
In French this means he's mad.
If I won't eat crullers . . . he hollers . . .
And they digest so terrible bad!
East is east, west is west,
He's got the yeast all over his vest!
I must put my face up against such a pie face
Since I married with Baking Powder Jake!

REFRAIN 2

Down by the oven where the lovin' is hot,
I met my beau!
He squeezes me and he imagines he's got
A piece of dough!
I eat so much bread and milk that I feel like a
    pudding. Oh, gee . . .
I cast my bread on the water, and it came back
    cookies to me!
When I want caresses . . . he fresses!
In French this means he eats!
He don't know a woman . . . is human.
How can men get wild when they never eat
    meats!
Wrong is wrong, right is right,
He bakes all day and he's cooled off at night!
Even my piller starts to smell from vanilla
Since I married with Baking Powder Jake!

PATTER

What's the use to diet?
It's impossible to try it
When nothing that he gives me makes me thin!
Every time I taste a schnecken
Three more pounds I gotta reckon,
Every cheesecake means another double chin!
And his matzohs without leaven
Bring me so much nearer Heaven,
And the cookies which a hammer wouldn't break!
His spice cake is not a nice cake!
His crumb cake is such a bum cake!
His jelly cake gives me a bellyache,
And so bicarbonate I must take!
All night long I twist and toss.
Crackers in bed is grounds for divorce!
I must put my face
Up against such a pie face,
'Cause I'm married to Baking Powder Jake!

LET ME WALK

VERSE

Sidney Ginsberg every day
Came round in his Chevrolet.
In front of Shirley Bernstein's door he'd stand!
He asked her to take a ride,
But when he got her inside
Sidney started driving with one hand!
Shirley cried to him in fear,
"Say, what's the big idea?
Don't you drive with one hand free,
You don't need no hands for me."

REFRAIN

Let me walk! Stop that, please!
Keep your hands from the knees!
You shouldn't go too far.
Say, who do you think you are?
Will you stop! Don't you touch!
Keep your foot on the clutch!
Move over, you loafer!
You ain't on a sofa!
Don't! . . . Please! . . . Quit! . . . Say!
I want you to know that I'm a good . . . HEY!
Such actions make me sore!
Don't commence! Look, I'll squeal!
Don't hold me, hold the wheel!
Listen here, I've walked home before!

A LONELY TRAVELING MAN

Lyric found in Lorenz Hart Lyrics folder in the Rodgers
and Hammerstein office. Music donated to the Library of
Congress by Richard Rodgers.

VERSE

I'm a lonely traveling man;
I find my pleasure where I can;
I've got a plan to snap the blues off short.
I'm a sailor boy at heart,
The Navy's where I got my start;
I've got a little girl in every port.
No cloudy sky can dull my days;
I have a happy heart.
I reassure myself always
They're miles and miles apart.

REFRAIN 1

If my Mabel from Troy should meet my Sue from
    Illinois,
Daddy burn my clothes!
If Kate from Baltimore
Knew of my Bronx Leonore,
Oh boy, they'd come to blows.
I'm hiding Brooklyn Lil
Down in Union Hill.
I lead a candy-coated life.
But it would wind up in a free-for-all
If they ever met my wife.

REFRAIN 2

If little Ruth from Duluth should meet my May
    from Santa Fe,
Fireworks would start.
If Bess from Bangor, Maine,
Saw Kansas City Jane,
They'd tear me all apart.
From here to Frisco Bay
I've got a place to stay.
It's just as simple as can be.
But it would wind up in a free-for-all
If their husbands should catch me.

MADAME ESTHER, QUEEN OF HESTER STREET

VERSE 1

I'm just a financier who knows
The cheapest way to buy old clothes,
I'm Madame Esther, Queen of Hester Street!
All I pay is eighty cents
To buy a coat and vest and pents,
I take out all the stains from soup and meat.
My motto is "We aim to please,"
I'll even buy your Bee-wee-wees.
I'll take it all, and why, do you suppose?
When I get just a little more,
I'll open a department store
And sell you back your clothes.

REFRAIN 1

Rags! Pots! Shoes! Pans!
I pay cash for what you got to sell.
Hats! Suits! Coats! Cans!
I don't make much but I do pretty well.
I only sell the best imported goods.

Look—smell the steerage, I don't cheat!
Rags! Shoes! Pots! Pans!
I'm Madame Esther, Queen of Hester Street!
We don't take checks! . . . CASH!

VERSE 2

A man can borrow cash from us,
We never make a bit of fuss
Until the note you gave has fallen due!
'Cause simply to procure it he
Can put up as security
His left eye and a good right arm or two!
And if in thirty days I find
The note has fallen far behind
It isn't always cash that I demand.
I back a truck up to your door
And take your stuff round to our store
And sell it secondhand!

REFRAIN 2

Rags! Pots! Shoes! Pans!
I ain't hard to please, I take it all.
Hats! Suits! Coats! Cans!
I even take the paper off the wall!
I got a tender heart that's soft as nails,
My business training is complete!
Rags! Pots! Coats! Cans!
I'm Madame Esther, Queen of Hester Street!
We don't take checks! . . . CASH!

MEET MY MOTHER

VERSE 1

Ev'ry girl I know has tried her best to show
Me what a perfect partner she could be.
Those who brag of cooking are so funny-looking
That they never did appeal to me.
Now you'll hear my own confession,
Ev'ry word of it is true.
You have made the big impression,
That's why I'm asking you, to

REFRAIN

Meet my mother,
She's wonderful!
Meet my brother,
He's marvelous!
Meet the father of the family.
Meet the neighbors,
You'll find 'em real,
Each one labors to make you feel

Right at home the way you want to be.
And you must meet the iceman,
Your credit's good.
He's a nice man,
He said it's good.
Meet a dozen cousins and their wives.
Meet the minister and he will
Marry you and me and we will
Meet at breakfast the rest of our lives!

VERSE 2

I've met ev'ry sort, but I could not be bought
By wealthy fathers who had lots of jack!
I don't care for highbrows; when they lift their
    eyebrows
I just grab my hat and don't come back!
Mother saw your photo one day,
And her eyes began to glow.
She said, "Bring her round next Sunday,
She's just the kind to know!" So

REPEAT REFRAIN

PATTER

At the station Uncle Peter
Meets us with his taximeter.
At the butcher's down the street
You'll be glad to meet the meat!
Uncle Randolph is a slicker,
Aunt Mathilde-Jane is thicker.
For the last ten years she's thought
That Rex Beach was a summer resort!
Meet Mariah, try her pie out,
Just a bite will knock your eye out!
Meet Miss Brown and Mrs. Lee,
Dishing dirt at the A and P.
After you've met all the town folks,
All the wise ones and the clown folks,
To get a treat, just make your feet
Walk down the village street
To meet and greet
The whole darned family.

MY DADDIES

VERSE

My mother came back from Reno,
Where she got a new divorce.
And she'll start off soon
On a honeymoon,
With another papa of course.

Mama's fickle, I confess.
She changes husbands like a dress.
Just when I get used to a new papa
He gets divorced from my mama!

REFRAIN 1

I've six papas,
Husbands of Ma's!
First a banker, then a broker,
Then she picked a stoker!
I wish I had
Just one dear dad!
She finds 'em, fools 'em, and forgets 'em!
Gee, it makes me mad!
Every stranger I see
Is Daddy to me!

REFRAIN 2

Each new divorce
Brings a new boss.
I think Ma is off her noodle,
I'd much rather have a poodle!
I'm in a fix,
No Daddy sticks!
The Prince of Wales may have forefathers,
But Ma gave me six!
No attention I get,
From Mother's sextet.

At Ma's last wedding, Mrs. Murray said, "Well, dear, will you ever stop?" Ma said, "No! As long as the good Lord provides 'em, I'll marry 'em!" The parson bought himself a new car on the business Ma brought him. Sometimes Ma gets married in the middle of the night, so the parson took the flat next door to be on hand for emergency calls! Ma keeps all the marriage certificates and frames them like they was diplomas. It's about time she graduated! But Mother's a professional bride. Ma's friends always throw rice and old shoes after the weddings. Next time I'm gonna throw an old shoe, but my foot'll be in it. My third daddy was arrested for rocking my mama to sleep. The judge said, "How can you arrest a man for rocking you to sleep?" Ma said, "You should have seen the size of that rock!"

FINAL CATCH LINE

Each daddy brings more wedding rings.
She uses them to string the curtains over doors
    and things.
Every parson's afraid
To lose Mama's trade!

ON THE BAHAMAS

In 1965, Richard Rodgers donated a piano-vocal manuscript with Hart's lyric to the Music Division of the Library of Congress.

VERSE

Deacon Josh
Once said, "By gosh,
The old farm makes me frantic."
And he sailed for the Bahama Isles
Upon the great Atlantic.
He wrote Si Jones
He ought to see
The queens dolled up in palms.
His friends rushed down
Impatiently
And bought banana farms!

REFRAIN

Down on the Bahamas
I've got fifty pretty mamas!
All dressed in grass pajamas!
And they all belong to me—
They do all the labor,
They love it, goodness knows—
When they shiver
By the river,
Hiram! Burn my clothes.
From morn to midnight
I raised chickens
And I fed them corn.
Now with chickens
I raise the dickens,
From midnight until morn!
When they do a dance, my mamas
Just shake the whole Bahamas.
Bahamas are a farmer's paradise!

ROBIN HOOD

VERSE

Robin Hood was a merry outlaw
But he made the first Boy Scout law:
One good turn a day
With what you earn a day.
The girls he stole from the rich were many
To give to his men who hadn't any.
Robin was a chief
Confirmed in this belief:
Without a maid

A man's afraid
To be an honest thief.

REFRAIN

Robin, Robin rode on a dobbin
With a merry maid.
When he gave her aid,
"Thank you, sir," she said.
He would run down right after sundown
From his mountain pass,
Grab a pretty lass
And step upon the gas.
Robin said, "You're good as dead
If when you're kissed you cry!"
Softly she'd reply,
"No girl likes to die, sir!"
Robin, Robin cared for his job in
Riding through the wood;
And maidens prayed to be waylaid
By Mister Robin Hood!

THE SPANISH DANCER

Music by Mel Shauer. Intended for Pola Negri.

VERSE 1

Under the moon of Spain,
Humming a Spanish strain,
Playing your castanets,
Wonderful Spanish Dancer.
Was it by love's design
Your eyes looked into mine?
Tell me you'll always care,
Throw me the red rose in your hair.

REFRAIN

My Spanish Dancer's eyes
Are kisses in disguise,
Telling tales of deep romance
All through Señorita's dance.
Words cannot banish love
When eyes make Spanish Love.
Just a glance gave me the sign,
Your answer, Spanish Dancer mine.

VERSE 2

Castles in Spain for two
Rising to skies of blue;
I'll build them all for you.
Wonderful Spanish Dancer,

Sunlight of sunny Spain,
Queen of my love, you'll reign.
I will remain, my dear,
Ever your faithful cavalier.

REPEAT REFRAIN

TELLTALE EYES

VERSE

Don't you know it's very wrong
That you make me wait so long!
When you speak you start
Trouble with my heart!
Though you say you're not in love,
I know what you're thinking of,
For a pair of telltale eyes
Say your words are telltale lies.

REFRAIN

Telltale eyes, I'm longing to read you;
Telltale eyes, you know how I need you.
Won't you say the little word?
Telltale eyes, confess by your twinkle;
If it's no or yes, just a wink'll
Tell me if my plea is heard.
My answer lies in telltale eyes,
You can't conceal it,
If you feel it
You'll reveal it.
You have told me just what your heart meant;
Here's the ring, I'll rent the apartment
For a pair of telltale eyes.

THE WANDERING
MINSTREL

VERSE 1

When Gilbert was pleasing the theatre fanatics,
The lot of the minstrel was hard.
The persons who patronized current dramatics
Cared little to hark to the Bard.
The singer, the man who performed on the oboe,
The fiddle, the drum, the trombone,
Was destined to be an unpopular hobo
And go on his travels alone.

REFRAIN 1

But the Wand'ring Minstrel doesn't wander
   anymore today,
Instead he holds his sway in ev'ry cabaret.
He's dropped his lute and harp to toot a diff'rent
   kind of song,
A laughing, dancing throng just follows him
   along.
With jazz and syncopation, with grunt and squeal
   and clash,
He wields a fascination that wins the dancers'
   cash.
Now ev'ry well-bred minstrel has a
Suite of ten rooms at the Plaza.
The Wand'ring Minstrel doesn't wander anymore.

VERSE 2

His songs are romances of mooning and spooning
In faraway lands of the East.
His Hindoo and Turkish and Japanese crooning
Gives pleasure to man and to beast.
He raises his madly melodious din to
A hymn for his Orient bride.
You'd never suspect that the nearest he's been to
The East is the Lower East Side!

REFRAIN 2

But the Wand'ring Minstrel doesn't wander
   anymore today.
His jazz bands blare and bray along the Great
   White Way.
His saxophone emits a tone that takes the place
   of wine,
His hearers cease to dine, and shake a wicked
   spine.
The weariest of nappers awakens to his notes,
And fourteen-year-old flappers tell Gaelic
   anecdotes.
An heiress takes his hand in marriage,
Now he's living at the Claridge.
The Wand'ring Minstrel doesn't wander anymore.

A WEDDING TRIP

VERSE 1

When we've dodged the shoes and rice
And we're in the car,
If you'll take my fond advice,
We won't travel far.
Wedding trips are not worthwhile;
Why should lovers roam?

And our honeymoon will smile
On our little home.

REFRAIN

We'll marry and never take a wedding trip;
Be wary of motorcar and sledding trip.
We won't need a stateroom at sea,
In our tête à tête room we'll be.
You'll sit in a great room with me at home;
Niagara is full of all the tourist folk;
Why aggravate those who may be purist folk?
When I kiss your lips and your hair,
Train conductors shouldn't be there;
Our love won't be able to bear a wedding trip.

VERSE 2

Folks who want a bridal suite
First must ask the clerk.
Bellboys never are discreet;
Even porters smirk.
Our sweet domesticity
Pleases every guest;
We'll escape publicity
In our little nest.

REPEAT REFRAIN

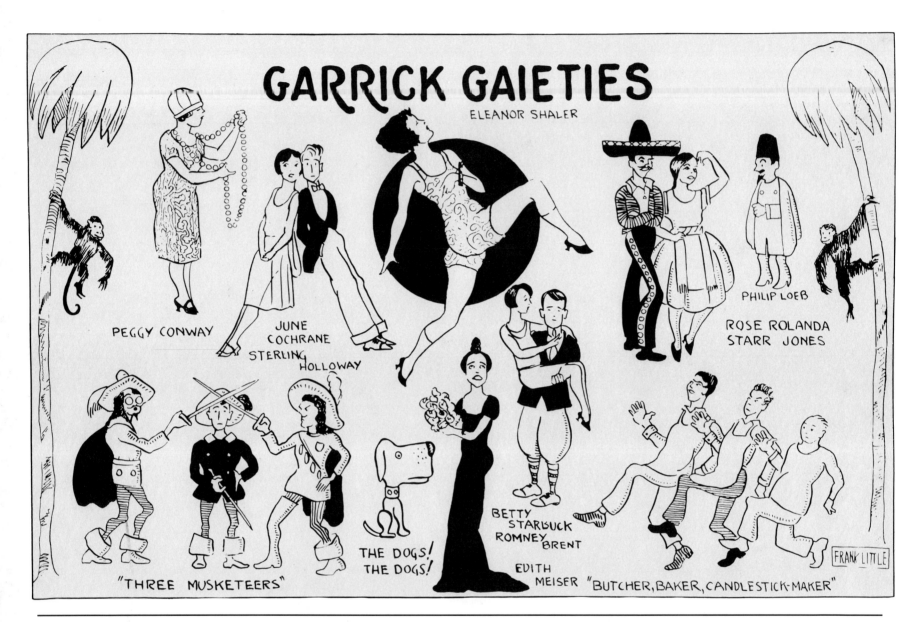

THE GARRICK GAIETIES | 1925

New York run: Garrick Theatre, May 17–November 28, 1925. 211 performances. Music by Richard Rodgers. Lyrics by Lorenz Hart. Produced by the Theatre Guild. Sketches by Benjamin M. Kaye, Arthur Sullivan, Morrie Ryskind, Louis Sorin, Sam Jaffe, Howard J. Green, and Edith Meiser. Directed by Philip Loeb. Dances and musical numbers staged by Herbert Fields. Settings and costumes by Carolyn Hancock. Stage manager, Harold E. Clurman. Orchestra under the direction of Richard Rodgers. Cast included Sterling Holloway, James Norris, Romney Brent, June Cochrane, Betty Starbuck, Edith Meiser, Philip Loeb, Eleanor Shaler, Lee Strasberg, Elisabeth [Libby] Holman, and Sanford Meisner.

For the lyric to "Manhattan," see *Winkle Town* (1922), page 33. For "The Three Musketeers," see *Winkle Town* (1922), page 32.

SOLICITING SUBSCRIPTIONS

Introduced by Sterling Holloway, James Norris, Romney Brent, and June Cochrane.

We bring drama to your great metropolis.
We are the little-theatre group.
Each of us has built a small Acropolis
To hold our little-theatre troupe.
We'd be very glad to meet you,
And greet you,
And seat you,
And treat you just great.
For all commercial art is hollow,
So follow Apollo
And swallow our bait.
Help to serve the art of your cosmopolis.
If you'll be one of us,
Each son of us,
Will welcome you at the gate.

The Neighborhood Playhouse may shine
Below the Macy-Gimbel line.
It was built to make a ride
For people on Fifth Avenue.
To Yeats and Synge and Shaw and such
We add an Oriental touch.
We bring out the aesthetic soul
You didn't know you have in you!
We like to serve a mild dish
Of folklore quaintly childish
Or something Oscar Wilde-ish
In a pantomime or dance.
Grand Street folk, we never see 'em—
They think the place is a museum.

And we know just what we do
Because we always take a chance!

The Provincetown Playhouse still owns
The art of Robert Edmond Jones.
From the classic drama
We're a notable secessionist.
We've even made the censors feel
The verity of Gene O'Neill.
The meaning doesn't matter
If the manner is Expressionist!
Our one great contribution
To art is revolution!
Our mood is very "Roosh-in"—
You can tell it at a glance.
Our bare stage may look funny,
But it saves us lots of money,
And we know just what to do
Because we always take a chance!

For your attention, many thanks.
We've brought along subscription blanks
For the Actor's Theatre,
That the audience may glory in
The dear old "Servant in the House,"
The pride of Mister Ranken Towse,
And plays by Henrik Ibsen
In a manner quite Victorian!
We spurn the bedroom dramas
With heroes in pajamas
For things that pleased our mamas
Such as Candida's romance.
We wear the sock and buskin
To the taste of old John Ruskin.
And we know just what to do
Because we never take a chance.

GILDING THE GUILD

Introduced by Betty Starbuck and ensemble.

The Garrick Gaieties is coming down the street.
Here's where we meet our meat.

REFRAIN

Gilding the Guild!
Gilding the Guild!
We possess a fine artistic touch;
Money doesn't count—not much!
Shubert may say
Art doesn't pay,
But we built that cozy little shack
Though we lack

Shubert's jack.
In this cute little building
We're gilding the Guild!

VERSE

We suppose you wonder—
Wonder what in thunder
This revue is all about.
If this entertainment
Is for art or gain meant
We'll remove your ev'ry doubt.
When summer comes we get mutinous,
And it's very cute in us.
Promise you won't begin shootin' us
If we start stepping out!

PATTER

Poor old Guild, no one talks about us!
Critics never make a big fuss!
Alec Woollcott's a cagey old bird,
He never gives us a word!
We complain we only can
Get more subscribers than the Metropolitan.
Shows may crash,
The Guild has got your cash.
If the show is slow you can look at the building.
We're gilding the Guild!

APRIL FOOL

Published June 1925. Introduced by Betty Starbuck, Romney Brent, and ensemble. Alternate title: "I'm Just an April Fool." Also intended for *June Days* (1925).

VERSE 1

HE: My poor heart goes
Any way the wind blows;
Spring is a habit with me;
Girls refuse me
But they cannot lose me;
Plato and I can't agree;
I am burdened with a fondness
For girlish blondness
That I can't explain;
When I'm doleful,
I become most soulful;
I like my sunshine after rain.

REFRAIN 1

I must believe in someone;
I'm just an April fool.
Doubting may overcome one;
Though I'm a dumb one,
I'm not a glum one.
It may rain in April,
But I cannot keep cool;
I simply must be admirin'
Some pretty siren;
I'm just an April fool.

VERSE 2

SHE: Willy-nilly
Both my hands are chilly
When they're not held by a man;
I like sofas
Full of handsome loafers;
Then we play catch-as-catch-can;
So my April occupation is osculation,
Morning, night and noon.
Cold hearts beating
Need a little heating
April is just as warm as June.

REFRAIN 2

[Repeat first 7 lines of refrain 1]
And my affection I pour on
Some pretty moron;
I'm just an April fool.

REFRAIN 3

[Repeat first 7 lines of refrain 1]
I'm just as easy as pie for
Some Lorelei, for
I'm just an April fool.

STAGE MANAGERS' CHORUS

Dudley Digges is listed as co-lyricist. Introduced by Willard Tobias, Sterling Holloway, Romney Brent, Lee Strasberg, Stanley Lindahl, Frances Hyde, Starr Jones, and Edward Hogan. Song dropped during run in June 1925. Alternate title: "Walk upon Your Toes."

ALL: Ssh— There's a bird that's more
          unheard
     Of than the Scarlet Tanager,

Poor in fame, but rich in blame,
The Theatre Guild Stage Manager.
We're the boys who hush the noise
And keep the actors quiet.
When carpenters rattle
We go into battle,
We're willing to do it or die it!
That is why we're always getting hell!

REFRAIN

Hush! Hush! Hush! Hush!
Walk upon your toes.
If you make the slightest sound
We'll biff you on the nose.
Smother your sniggle
And stop your giggle
And pull up your wriggling hose.
Any child can run the stage,
The job is just a pose;
That's why we run the Theatre Guild
     shows!

1ST STAGE
MANAGER: When Moffat Johnson had to ride
         To save that devil Sydney's hide
         You heard the gallop of his horse.
         I played the horse's part, of course.
[He takes a pair of prop hoofs and bangs them on the floor]

2ND STAGE
MANAGER: And when Miss Pauline Lord got hot
         Because Dick Bennett swore a lot,
         She slammed the door, you thought
             her grand.
         We were the door! She got the hand!
[He makes an offstage door-slam with a prop provided for the purpose]

3RD STAGE
MANAGER: Apollodorus braves the Nile
         And shows his legs for quite a while.
         He takes the dive and makes the
             flash,
         But I'm the boy who makes the
             splash.
[He sprinkles salt on the stage and uses an atomizer to make the sound of sprinkling water]

4TH STAGE
MANAGER: When Peppy Schildkraut squared his
             back
         And spat upon the railroad track
         You heard the Budapest Express,
         But then, you just heard me, I guess.
[Blows a whistle]

5TH STAGE
MANAGER: Processional is a thrilling play
         In which machine guns roar away.
         You heard the bullets fast and thick,

But I'm the boy who did the trick.
[Beats on a pad that gives the impression of shots]

6TH STAGE
MANAGER: The Guardsman's music played
             offstage
         Would make poor Alfred fume with
             rage.
         We signaled soft and loud each night
         With this demure electric light.

REPEAT REFRAIN

THE JOY SPREADER

"An American Jazz Opera" inspired by Gilbert Seldes. Music by Richard Rodgers and libretto by Lorenz Hart. Introduced by Edward Hogan, Betty Starbuck, Romney Brent, June Cochrane, Willard Tobias, Lee Strasberg, Starr Jones, Felix Jacoves, Frances Hyde, and ensemble.

There are two versions of "The Joy Spreader," and it is not certain which of them was performed in *The Garrick Gaieties.* The longer, more complete version is printed here. The simpler and shorter second version lacks the fantasy and romantic spirit of the first, but probably satisfied those who might have objected to a story in which the juvenile and the ingenue spent the night together in the department store.

Edith Meiser, who was in the original cast, recalls (July 1985) that the performers did not do justice to the piece, which was dropped from the show after only a few performances. When the decision was made to eliminate "The Joy Spreader," Dick, she remembers, was very unhappy, but Larry took the news philosophically. It did not seem to upset him at all.

SCENE 1: A DEPARTMENT STORE

[Counters right and left. Door with stairs leading up to it center. Materials, such as silk goods, on counters. There may also be, in the back of the counters, racks from which this material is supposed to be kept. Great commotion as the curtain rises, with customers running about shouting and tormenting the floorwalkers and salesladies]

MRS. KATZ: [trying to get girl's eye]
           Hurry, miss, I'm tired of waiting.
2ND
CUSTOMER: Aggravating! Aggravating!
3RD
CUSTOMER: Oh, such service isn't decent!
ALL GIRLS: Yes'm! Yes'm! Yes'm! Yes'm!
LITTLE GIRL: I want something just like Mama's.
MOTHER: What's the latest in pajamas?
STELLA: Here's a style that's very recent.

GIRLS: Yes'm! Yes'm! Yes'm! Yes'm!

STELLA: It will wear, you needn't worry.

ALL
CUSTOMERS: Hurry! Hurry! Hurry! Hurry!

4TH
CUSTOMER: I've been standing here for ages!

STELLA: Holy gee! We earn our wages.

MRS. KATZ: Miss, I'm gonna get you fired!

GIRLS: Yes'm! Yes'm! Yes'm! Yes'm!

2ND
CUSTOMER: All this waiting makes me nervous.

MOTHER &
LITTLE GIRL: Miss, is this the way to serve us?

4TH
CUSTOMER: Can't you see I'm getting tired?

GIRLS: Yes'm! Yes'm! Yes'm! Yes'm!

MRS. KATZ: You have heard me mention
I want some attention;
Is your comprehension clear?
Why should I be slighted?

STELLA: Ma'am, don't get excited!

MRS. KATZ: You should be indicted, dear!

STELLA: Serve this lady, Lizzie,
Can't you see I'm busy?
All right! Gee, I'm dizzy
Now!
Some old dames are fussy!

MRS. KATZ: Oh, you little hussy!

STELLA: G'wan, you darn old mussy
Cow!

MRS. KATZ: You're a liar!

STELLA: You're another!

[They fight furiously. Mrs. Katz slaps Stella, but the excitement is suddenly brought to a close by the bell striking five]

FOUR
CUSTOMERS: There's the bell!

[They start to go]

FOUR OTHER
CUSTOMERS: There's the bell!

ALL GIRLS: It's closing time!

ALL: It's closing time!

ALL
CUSTOMERS: We'll be late for supper.

[Exeunt customers]

[The girls file out to get their hats, and during the following scene return with the boys from the shipping department, who help the girls cover up the various counters for the night. Mary is at her counter and Stella goes to her]

STELLA: Tired, kid?

MARY: No, Stella dear.

STELLA: Listen, Mary, got a date?

MARY: Not yet.

STELLA: Not yet!
But you're gonna make one, I bet!

MARY: You get so tired—tired of working
Once in a while.

You feel like nothing—nothing but
shirking
Once in a while.

STELLA: And when you think of Tom, the
shipping clerk,
It's very hard for you to do your
work.

MARY: [showing book]
Take a look
In this book.
I took it home last night
Though it wasn't right . . .
And you and I and all the things
we do . . .
We aren't really—really alive, dear.

[Shows book again]
It seems that two lovers like
Tommy and me,
They live in a castle arising from
the sea.

STELLA: Don't they work?
What a break!

MARY: They're rich and they're handsome
And he brings her the moon.

STELLA: Heaven's sake!
What a break!

MARY: [carried away by the story]
Millions of moonbeams are dancing
In the bright yellow gleam of her
hair;
His eyes with starlight are
glancing—
He is stalwart and slender and fair!
They've lived in the palace forever
and a day.
She pledged with a chalice forever
to obey!

STELLA: [interrupting]
Here comes Tom!
What a break!

[Tom enters, smiles at Stella, who winks to him and exits. He crosses happily to Mary]

TOM: Hello, Mary, got a date?

MARY: Why, yes.

TOM: [crestfallen]
Why, yes? Well, that gives me a
stand-up, I guess.

MARY: Tom, I have my date with you!

TOM: [joyfully]
With me!

MARY: With you!
Call for me when the meeting is
through.

[They snatch a hurried kiss as the boys and girls stand around chatting. Stella raps for attention]

STELLA: Listen, folks, for just a minute!
Don't go home—there's a meeting.
Our employer, Mr. Jeremiah Price,

Will give you several words of good
advice.

ALL: Hurray! Hurray! Hurray! Hurray!
He's gonna give something away!

[Mr. Price, expensively and elegantly clad, enters in his most benevolent and pompous manner. He nods patronizingly to all]

PRICE: Good evening, little busy bees.

ALL: Good evening, Mr. Price!

STELLA: We surely think it very nice
For you to give us your attention.

PRICE: Oh, not at all, it is my duty
To spread the light of joy and
beauty—
To give you all my inspiration,
Thus everyone will love his
occupation.

[He comes down center]
Although the modern rage is
A cry for higher wages,
I pay you less to keep you from
temptation!
I've built you a chapel for sweet
meditation,
I've built you a rest room for your
recreation,
I've built you a ball field for health
conservation,
So you can all work through the
summer vacation. . . .
Tell me, do you love your work?

ALL: [circling about him]
Mr. Price, it's very nice!

PRICE: I'm conferring a favor on you!

[Price takes a scroll from one of the salesboys and reads from it]
You all love your work—
Such love is divine:
Instead of eight hours
You will now work nine.

ALL: Mr. Price, that's very nice!
The days of hard labor have gone
out of date.
Since love is the watchword there's
no room for hate.

PRICE: I love my employees more
Than mere words can tell.
If I am successful, you share my
success:
I give you my smiles and my daily
address!
Now, nothing else could please
more—
Than our big store yell.
Give the yell with happiness and
love.

[Two of the salespeople—a boy and a girl—have jumped from the side to take his order as soon as he has *given it. They lead the cheer—the boy on the left, the girl on the right*]

ALL: Rah! Rah! Rah! Rah!
Service! Service!
Strong hearts and willing hands!
Go get! Go get!
Action! Action!
Pep! Pep! That always lands!
Co-op! Co-op!
Cooperation too!
Rah! Rah! Rah! Rah!
Price's! Price's!
They all look up to you.

[*Both cheerleaders fall exhausted*]

PRICE: More high than royalty
I deem true loyalty
And with some prizes I'll reward
the faithful.
So I'll select a few of you, my
dears,
To whom I'll give some little
souvenirs.

ALL: Hurray! Hurray! Hurray! Hurray!
He's gonna give something away!

PRICE: Miss Smith, your work has always
stood the test—
A book of poems by Mr. . . . Edgar
Guest!

[*She takes it*]

Step forward, Miss Mary Brown.
Because you never flirt you
Have earned a prize for virtue.
Because you're modest as a girl can
be,
A copy of my memoirs autographed
by . . . me!
Mr. Thomas Jones!

[*Thomas Jones comes forward*]

A model of morality
Unto the whole locality.
He who denies it spreads a libel.
You've won a copy of the Bible!
Tom Jones and Mary Brown,
You're two of the nicest young
people in town.

[*They step back*]

To close the meeting as the skies
grow dim,
Let's greet the twilight with our
loving hymn.

ALL: Onward! Onward! Follow your duty!
Onward! Onward! Joyfully bold!
In the loyal army of beauty
Smile away and do as you're told!
Follow! Follow duty delightful!
Follow! Follow labor today!
Pack each minute so tight full, right
full!

Smile gaily as you pray!
AMEN!

PRICE: Good night!

ALL: [*extending their hands to shake hands
with Mr. Price*]
Good night!

[*All start to exit, and Price starts for opposite side*]

PRICE: [*Looks at watch*]
I'll be late for supper!

[*Exit Price*]

[*Mary has remained behind her counter. Tom has
watched the others leave. He crosses to Mary's counter,
runs behind, and kisses her*]

MARY: Oh, no, Tom!

TOM: Oh, yes, Mary, I can't help it!
I've been waiting for this moment;
I've forgotten what your "no"
meant.

MARY: If someone sees us!

TOM: I'm not sure that would displease
us.
When we are married . . .

MARY: Married on what? On your eighteen
a week?

TOM: I'll get a raise.

MARY: Possibly not. When you do you can
speak.

TOM: I'll count the days.
I'm going to kiss you!

MARY: You really shouldn't!

TOM: All right, I shouldn't.

[*He kisses her. Mary doesn't resist a great deal*]

MARY: [*her mood changing*]
I don't want to work the rest of my
life.
All the bustle and the worry:
Hurry! Hurry! Hurry! Hurry!
I don't want to have to answer
"Yes'm! Yes'm! Yes'm! Yes'm!"

[*She picks up book*]

Take a look
In this book.
I took it home last night
Though it wasn't right.
It's all about a princess far away.

TOM: She's not as lovely—lovely as you
are.
No one could be!
I can't do a thing all day—
I'm thinking of you.
I just eat my heart away—
I'm thinking of you.
And I don't want to wait,
I love you so!
Tomorrow is too late,
I love you so!

MARY: Oh, dearest, hold me in your arms
tonight!

Just tonight.
I'm sure it must be right!

TOM: [*Starts to take her in his arms*]
I'll keep you here!

MARY: Forever, dear!
Forever near!

TOM &
MARY: Forever, dear!

TOM: I'll be working ev'ry day
With joy in my heart

MARY: And forever I'll obey
The boy in my heart!
Now you're mine, dear.
You're divine, dear!
Ah!

[*They kiss passionately*]

To think you really held me near to
you!
I've told my heart, my hope, my
fear to you.
How does my boldness, dear,
appear to you?

TOM: My kisses should have made that
clear to you, my dear!

MARY: [*looking at watch*]
It's so late!

[*She starts to go*]

TOM: Please, let's wait!

MARY: I'll be late for supper!

[*Tom helps her on with coat, goes to door, and tries to
open it. He finds it locked*]

TOM: It's locked! We're locked in! . . .
Locked tight!

MARY: Good night!

TOM: Good night!

MARY: Try it again!
I must go home!
The folks will worry!
Open it. Hurry!

TOM: [*Tries again, unsuccessfully*]
It can't be done.
The janitor's the one
Who did it, the son-of-a-gun!

[*Comes back to her as she takes off her coat*]

I'm sorry, dear.
We must stay here.

MARY: What would the boss say
If he found us this way?

TOM: We'll tell him some excuse or other!

MARY: What will I say to Mother?

TOM: Tell her you love me!
Rub those little tears away,
They grieve me, my dear.
I don't care what people say,
Believe me, my dear.

MARY: And I don't fear the end
When I'm with you,
As long as I can spend

My time with you.

TOM: There comes a lovely moment of
beauty
Once in a while.
In such a moment love is a duty
Once in a while.

[*The chimes of a nearby church are heard*]

MARY: There's the bell.

TOM: There's the bell!

MARY: The steeple bell.

TOM: The steeple bell! . . .
We'll be late for breakfast.

[*They embrace as the curtain falls*]

SCENE 2

[*Morning. The lovers are asleep on counters, covered by counter cloths and unseen by the audience. Tom sticks out his head and yawns and goes back to sleep. Mary does likewise. The bustle of the workers entering is heard and their singing begins softly*]

[*Offstage*]

WORKERS: We'll be late, it's such a worry!
Hurry! Hurry! Hurry! Hurry!
We've no time to take a local.
Taxi! Taxi! Taxi! Taxi!

[*Two clerks come in and remove their coats. They start to remove the counter cloths. Before they disclose the lovers Price comes in and looks around. Next he sees the lovers asleep*]

PRICE: What's this! Tom Jones! Here, wake
up! Come down!

[*Tom starts down and yawns. Mary echoes his yawn, and Price turns on her*]

And Mary Brown! What does this
mean? Come down!

[*She does so*]

MARY: Oh!

TOM: Oh!

PRICE: Oh-oh-oh-oh! That doesn't mean a
thing, you know!
Asleep—and here! Together!
You'll kindly tell me whether
You think this store is a temple of
Venus!

TOM: Oh, sir, there's nothing wrong
between us.
How could we know that anyone
had seen us?

PRICE: It's too outrageous to be true!
A fatal sin! What you did does not
matter.
It's all the same.
It is a shame!

[*During the last few speeches the commotion has attracted the salespeople of the store, who return. They gather around Mr. Price, Tom, and Mary, and during*]

the last few lines of his speech, they sway to the jazz rhythm of the music that accompanies them]

I cannot tell just what your vice is,
But such mistakes won't do at
Price's.
For Price's name and high position,
Like Caesar's wife, must be above
suspicion!
You're fired!

TOM: We fire ourselves!
All the world I'd love to tell
That we are in love.
And you can go straight to Hell
For we are in love!

MARY
& TOM: We'll be too busy holding hands
today
To spend our time in making
Price's pay.

[*Stella has entered and now goes to Mary*]

STELLA: Goodbye, Mary. Got a date?

MARY: Why, yes. Why, yes!

STELLA: Well, I'll help you with your
wedding dress.

ALL: Hurray! Hurray! Hurray! Hurray!
They're gonna get married today!

[*Tom and Mary start to go*]

You get so tired—tired of working
Once in a while.

[*They exit, and Price composes himself*]

PRICE: These sinners dim the light of
beauty,
And to forget them is our duty.
So fill the cup with joy up to the
brim
And start the morning with our
loving hymn.

ALL: Onward! Onward! Follow your duty!
Onward! Onward! Joyfully bold!
In the loyal army of beauty
Smile away and do as you're told!
Follow! Follow duty delightful!
Follow! Follow labor today!
Pack each minute so tight full, right
full!
Smile gaily as you pray!
AMEN!

[*This song has been sung in a sarcastic and insurgent manner. As one of the salesmen on Price's command has encouraged them to strike, they all move toward Price threateningly as they sing it and Price is crowded into a corner stage right, and is thrown over, as the curtain falls and the last strains of their song are heard*]

[*The curtain falls*]

LADIES OF THE BOX OFFICE

Introduced by Betty Starbuck, Elisabeth [Libby] Holman, and June Cochrane.

[*Music to the tune of "Soliciting Subscriptions" song. Three girls enter stage left. They sing in chorus*]

GIRLS: We must entertain the big plurality,
We are the Broadway Theatre bunch.
Using up your brains with great frugality
Is the Broadway Theatre hunch.
We'd be very glad to meet you
And greet you
And seat you
And treat you just great,
For at the box office, we take you
And shake you
And fake you
And make you our bait.
Though we fool the public in totality
They don't think bad of it.
They're glad of it
And hurry to crash the gate.

The Movies

[*a girl dressed in a Mary Pickford manner*]

Today each Peg and Molly would
Achieve success in Hollywood.
They'd be very proud to join the ranks of
Marquise Gloria
And even half-wits go to plays
Since they can go to photoplays.
Children cry for Buster Keaton more than
for Castoria.
If your nose will photograph well
And your pearly teeth will laugh well
Though you only can act half well
You'll put Barrymore on the blink.
To see Chaplin and the Gishes
Wives neglect their dirty dishes
And we know just what we do because we
seldom let them think.

The Girl Show

[*dressed as a Ziegfeld chorus girl*]

To pay for my tomfoolery
The yokels pawn their jewelry.
I'm the Aphrodisiac that Mr. Ziegfeld
glories in.
St. Louis, Philadelphia,
I'm raising lots of hell for ya.

In ev'ry local scandal sheet, I always get
   my stories in.
My music is tin-panny,
My jokes will grab your nanny,
Of sense I haven't any, yet I tickle people
   pink.
Even Mother Eve's old fig leaf
In my show would seem a big leaf
And I know just what I do because I
   never let them think.

The Problem Play

[dressed as Sadie Thompson in Rain]
   A bottle of Belasco sauce
   Supplies my hot Tabasco sauce.
   I'm the sexy play that makes the
      clergymen censorious.
   My leading lady must subtract
   Her virtue in the second act
   But when the curtain falls her sacrifice is
      glorious.
   If only Mr. Banton
   In print would wildly rant on
   The folks from Troy and Canton
   Will make their shekels clink.
   If the plot is pornographic
   Then you're sure to stop the traffic
   And I know just what I do because I let
      them think they think.
[They repeat the refrain and exit stage right]

DO YOU LOVE ME?

Published August 1925. Introduced by Louise Richardson. Danced by Rose Rolando and chorus. Alternate title: "Do You Love Me, I Wonder?"

VERSE 1

Melancholy, weary,
Haunted by a query;
If he loves me or if he loves me not.
Won't you give an answer
To this poor romancer?
Or my fate will be I don't know what.
I love you so,
You ought to show
The way you feel
If it be "yes" or "no."

REFRAIN

Do you love me?
I wonder, I wonder,

I wonder, can it be true?
My poor heart's all
Asunder, asunder,
It's under spells cast by you.
Will you answer me clearly, sincerely,
Or merely banter with me?
Do you love me?
I wonder, I wonder
I wonder if it can be.

VERSE 2

Queries without number,
Enter in my slumber;
Won't you answer to my mute appeal?
I repeat the question,
But there's no suggestion
In my dreams to tell me how you feel.
I love you so,
You ought to show
Your heart to me
If it be "yes" or "no."

REPEAT REFRAIN

BLACK AND WHITE

Introduced by Elisabeth [Libby] Holman and ensemble. Danced by Eleanor Shaler and Willard Tobias. According to Eleanor Shaler (May 1985), "Black and White" was dropped a few nights after the New York opening and replaced by "On with the Dance," which used the music of "Black and White" with a new lyric which Hart wrote very quickly! A search at Yale University's Theatre Guild Collection in the Beinecke Rare Book Library has failed so far to locate the verse for the lyric.

REFRAIN

Take black and white,
The only creation.
In black and white
You'll cause a sensation!
It cuts a dash!
It's never rash!
It doesn't clash!
Widows delight
The men of the city;
It's black and white
That makes them look pretty.
How would you wish
Your "soup and fish"
But black and white?
And if you're falling in love,
Be sure to save ev'ry letter;

Words are all right,
But in black and white,
They're much better!
Say it with words,
And maybe you'll sever;
Say it with ink,
You'll say it forever!
Daytime and night,
Stick tight
To black and white.

ON WITH THE DANCE

Published July 1925. Added to the show in June 1925. Introduced by June Cochrane and ensemble. Danced by Eleanor Shaler. Refrain has same music as refrain of "Black and White."

VERSE

There's a revolution
Cutting loose like the deuce;
It's a thunderbolt.
It's the evolution
Of the truth calling youth
With a mighty jolt.
It says you mustn't conceal
Anything you feel.
In its execution
This new dance, at a glance,
Is a big revolt:

REFRAIN

On with the dance,
And off with your scruples;
Come take a chance,
You all can be pupils.
It may be rude,
It may be crude,
But don't say no.
You like romance;
Don't try to suppress it;
Break into dance
You're sure to confess it.
Don't you avoid
What you've enjoyed;
Just let 'er go.
And if you're falling in love,
You don't have to call a physician;
Start in to dance,
And step on that mean inhibition!
You can dance with your Nell,
And dance with your Sally,
Dance on the El,

And dance in the alley.
Don't look askance,
But on, on with the dance!

SENTIMENTAL ME

Published June 1925. Introduced by June Cochrane,
James Norris, Edith Meiser, and Sterling Holloway.
Added to the show in June 1925. Was probably written
before 1925 because an early piano-vocal lists composer
as "Richard C. Rodgers."

VERSE 1

HE: Look at me again, dear;
Let's hold hands and then, dear,
Sigh in chorus.
It won't bore us, to be sure;
There's no meaning to it,
Yet we overdo it,
With a relish
That is hellish to endure;
I am not the kind that merely flirts;
I just love and love until it hurts.

REFRAIN 1

Oh, sentimental me and poor romantic
you;
Dreaming dreams is all that we can do;
We hang around all day and ponder,
While both of us grow fonder—
The Lord knows where we're wandering
to;
I sit and sigh; you sigh and sit upon my
knee;
We laugh and cry, and never disagree;
A million kisses we'll make theft of
Until there's nothing left of
Poor romantic you and sentimental me.

VERSE 2

SHE: Darling, you're so handsome,
Strong and clever, and some—
Times, you seem, dear,
Like a dream, dear, that came true.
Why did I pick you out?
Better men I threw out
Of my living room
While giving room to you;
I would rather read of love in books;
Love is much more painful than it looks.

REPEAT REFRAIN 1

Comic version

[*Enter an old gouty lady and gentleman. The lady
is carrying a bunch of goldenrods, the man a
hot-water bottle*]

VERSE

MAN: Goldenrods in season
Always starts me sneezin',
My nostalgia for neuralgia starts in May.
When it starts in rainin'
My knees start complainin'
With erratic and neuratic pains all day.
Every time you hear me sneeze "cachoo"
That's my way of saying I love you.

REFRAIN

LADY: Oh, poor asthmatic me and poor rheumatic
you.
Catching cold is all that we can do.
Each time you hold my hand and squeeze
it
Your icy fingers freeze it,
Each loving word you sneeze is "cachoo!"
BOTH: I sneeze and sit, you sit and sneeze upon
my knee.
Your hay fever and mine do not agree.
SHE: I cannot love a human geyser.
HE: You female atomizer!
BOTH: Oh, poor asthmatic me and poor rheumatic
you!

AND THEREBY HANGS A TAIL

The Hart lyric is part of a sketch by Morrie Ryskind and
Philip Loeb that satirized the Scopes trial. In this sketch
the scene is an African courthouse. Hart's lyric was introduced by Philip Loeb, who was William Jennings Bryan,
and the ensemble. The number was added to the show in
June and dropped in August soon after Bryan's death in
late July 1925.

BRYAN: I'm sure I'd rather prosecute this case
Than run another Presidential race;
For the Congo's greatest menace is
A monkey who will not believe in
Genesis.
I assure the learned ape upon the
bench
I will cross-examine with a monkey
wrench.

CHORUS: I grow more wealthy as I get old.
Speeches may be silver,
But speeches are gold.
BRYAN: They call me the Great Commoner—
here's why.
No man could be more commoner than
I.
And I'm known in each locality
As the silver-tongued defender of
morality.
I started Prohibition on its way,
And all of us are lawbreakers today,
And every speech I make for home
and mammy
Goes to build another cabin in Miami.
I am very glad to hand out good advice
To any group of folks who pay my
price.
CHORUS: I grow more wealthy as I get old.
Speeches may be silver,
But speeches are gold.
BRYAN: In saying what I have to say
I have no hesitation.
These words have made me famous.
I accept the nomination.
MONKEYS: Peace, silver, Prohibition—
To save morals is our mission.

IT'S QUITE ENOUGH TO MAKE ME WEEP

Introduced by Philip Loeb, James Norris, Edith Meiser,
Betty Starbuck, Romney Brent, Sterling Holloway, and
June Cochrane. Added to show in October 1925.

SHAW: It's quite enough to make me weep
That I must lie here fast asleep.
Were I awake I'd let you know
That mine is the best name in the
show.
The papa of the Guild's new draw—
It's Arma Virumque—Bernard Shaw!
The Guild will play a repertory
Of my pleasant category.
Alfred Lunt can have the glory—
Bernard Shaw's not jealous, for he
Just makes up an inventory;
Counting up he finds no bore. He
Gets still richer all the more he
Makes his terms obligatory.
Just look up to Bernard Shaw, he
Is a sage who's wise and hoary.

He's as rich as Gould or Corey.
Though his art he may adore he
Gets his cash down a priori.
That's the moral of the story!

[*From right, enter a man and woman made up as Blunchli and Raina from* Arms and the Man. *They take the stage and sing:*]

B. & R.: Wake up, Papa, as soon as you can.
We're Blunchli and Raina from *Arms and the Man!*

SHAW: While I'm engrossed in slumber deep
I'm counting royalties as I sleep!

BLUNCHLI: You can't have the Garrick, they're trying something new.
Some crazy kids are doing a revue.

RAINA: Oh, Father dear, I fear you're through—
Those kids can fool the public just about as well as you.

[*The curtains open and a Gothic arch is seen stage center. Two tall candles are at either side of it, as in the final scene of* St. Joan. *Through the arch appears St. Joan, who sings as she walks down the steps of the arch:*]

JOAN: The Garrick, where so long I was sainted
By vulgar antics, has been tainted.
No longer am I gratified
That I have been beatified!

[*From the left Dick Dudgeon, from* The Devil's Disciple, *enters on a bound, springing over Shaw's bed to center stage, where he sings:*]

DICK: I'm Dick Dudgeon, the Devil's Disciple.

The fact these kids our Garrick swipe'll
Make poor Pop, our proud creator,
Look around for another Theayter!

[*From right enter Caesar and Cleopatra, dressed in the manner of that play*]

CLEOPATRA: I'm Cleopatra.

CAESAR: I am Caesar.
They've given our pop a punch in the beezer!

SHAW: Peace, my children, whatever they do
Your Bernard Shaw can do it too
And I will be a play physician
Writing these brats a new edition.
I've written a new refrain for that in-
Delicate song they call "Manhattan."
I'm sure that it will be a riot,
And, Caesar and Cleo, you might try it!

CAESAR: In dear old Egypt*
I'm gonna be gypped on the Nile!
For camels I will walk a mile!
Mammy!

CLEO: Among the Sphinxes
With pretty minxes you will flirt!
You'd better be alert
Or you'll create some dirt—with some skirt!

CAESAR: On the oasis
In shady places fate designs

CLEO: That we must speak some clever lines

CAESAR: And I will wisecrack you, dear, amid
The shades of a pyramid.

———————————

New lyric set to music of "Manhattan."

We'll turn the desert into an isle of joy!

SHAW: Now, Blunchli and Raina, see
If you can sing "Sentimental Me."

[*As Blunchli and Raina step forward to sing "Sentimental Me," Caesar and Cleopatra form a group center and, with others, do a step as the others are singing*]

B. & R.: Oh, Chocolate Soldier me,*
And poor ecstatic you.
Reading lines is all that we can do.
We sit around on chairs and chatter
As mad as any hatter
While Papa's purse gets fatter anew!
I sit and talk, you talk and sit upon my knee.
We saturate in clever repartee!
We make sad efforts to be funny
While Shaw gets all the money
From ecstatic you and Chocolate Soldier me.

DICK: That's pretty good,
But, Pop, how would you terminate this ballet?

SHAW: With the regulation show finale.
Clear the stage and let them do
So, the proper thing in a revue.
They are all instilled
With Gilding the Guild.

[*Shaw's bed is pushed off stage left by his characters Caesar and Cleopatra, etc., who exit. From the right, the entire chorus enters doing a dance routine across the stage, right to left, singing "Gilding the Guild"*]

———————————

New lyric set to music of "Sentimental Me."

Scenes from *Dearest Enemy*

DEAREST ENEMY | 1925
THE FIFTH AVENUE FOLLIES | 1926

DEAREST ENEMY, 1925

Tryout: Colonial Theatre, Akron, Ohio, July 20, 1925; Ford's Opera House, Baltimore, September 7–12, 1925; New York run: Knickerbocker Theatre, September 18, 1925–May 22, 1926. 286 performances. Music by Richard Rodgers. Lyrics by Lorenz Hart. Produced by George Ford. Book by Herbert Fields. Earlier titles: "Sweet Rebel" and "Dear Enemy." Entire production staged by John Murray Anderson. Book directed by Charles Sinclair and Harry Ford. Dances and ensemble directed by Carl Hemmer. Settings by Clark Robinson. Costumes by Mark Mooring, Hubert Davis, and James Reynolds. Orchestra under the direction of Richard Rodgers. Orchestrations by Emil Gerstenberger. Cast, starring Helen Ford and Charles Purcell, included Flavia Arcaro, Helen Spring, Detmar Poppen, Harold Crane, and John Seymour.

For the lyric to "The Hermits," see *Winkle Town* (1922), page 30. For "Old Enough to Love," see *Winkle Town* (1922), page 30.

The following lyrics are missing: "Ale, Ale, Ale" (introduced in Akron, Ohio, tryout by Stanley Forde, who was replaced by John Seymour; dropped before the New York opening), "Oh Dear" (introduced in Akron tryout by Helen Ford; dropped before the New York opening), "Dear Me" (introduced in Baltimore, Maryland, tryout by Charles Purcell and Helen Ford; dropped before the New York opening), "Dearest Enemy," and "How Can We Help But Miss You."

HEIGH-HO, LACKADAY

Introduced by Flavia Arcaro and ladies of the ensemble.

GIRLS: Heigh-ho! Heigh-ho! Lackaday!
Our hearts are smitten so,
All day we sit and sew!
Heigh-ho! Heigh-ho!
Our lads are in the war,
But till they win the war,
Heigh-ho! Heigh-ho! Lackaday!
1ST GIRL: I think I've worked too hard, or
Perchance, I've lost my ardor!
GIRLS: Heigh-ho! Lackaday!
2ND GIRL: When John was here, each night meant
A heavenly excitement!
Heigh-ho!
GIRLS: Heigh-ho!

2ND GIRL: Heigh-ho!
GIRLS: Lackaday!
3RD GIRL: Oh, let's call a brief cessation
To this endless occupation,
Just a moment of vacation
Let's decoy!
ALL: We have learned from observation
The creation of a nation
Comes to better consummation
Born in joy!
So let us quit,
And dance a bit!
ALL: One-two-three-four, turn about,
One-two-three-four, heigh-ho!
One-two-three-four, toes turned out!
One-two-three-four, heigh-ho!
MRS. MURRAY: I behold in consternation
You have taken a vacation.
Fingers in your occupation
Please employ!
The creation of a nation
Comes of steady application.
Vain sensation of elation
Please destroy!
GIRLS: Heigh-ho! Heigh-ho!
Heigh-ho! Heigh-ho! Lackaday!
Our hearts are smitten so,
All day we sit and sew!
Heigh-ho! Heigh-ho!
Our lads are in the war,
But till they win the war,
Heigh-ho! Heigh-ho! Lackaday!
Heigh-ho! Heigh-ho! Lackaday!

WAR IS WAR

Introduced by Helen Spring and ensemble.

JANE: Gather near, my pretty ones, and cluster,
Gather near, I pray you, do not fluster.
Hear what Mrs. Murray says and try to
trust her.
Your courage, you must muster!
An Englishman in time of peace
Will never harm a soul,
But the wolf steps out of the lambkin's
fleece
When the drums begin to roll!

REFRAIN 1

War is war! War is war!
A soldier feels repression as he never did
before.

A uniform can make the palest frail young
fellow
Feel he's male! Male! Male!
Every soldier is a frightful brute
Who snatches little ladies for his loot . . .

GIRLS: Hooray, we're going to be compromised!
Hooray, we're going to be compromised!
War is war!

REFRAIN 2

War is war! War is war!
A soldier can't be satisfied, he always
looks for more!
A modest maid can make the mildest
young mister
Simply wild! Wild! Wild!
Have a care or you'll be crying "Boo-hoo"
When a major general chases you . . .

GIRLS: Hooray! We're going to be compromised!
Hooray! We're going to be compromised!
War is war!

I BEG YOUR PARDON

Introduced by Helen Spring and Harold Crane. Added during the pre–New York tryout.

VERSE 1

HE: I'd like a kiss or two;
You're so divinely radiant
And there's no watchful lady aunt
To see.
SHE: Kisses are not for you;
Vainly you would demand some, sir,
Even if very handsome, sir,
You be.
HE: Love tells us what to do,
And not a soul can censure us.
SHE: Soldiers of scarlet hue
Seem a bit too adventurous
To me.

REFRAIN 1

HE: I'm sure! I beg your pardon,
I should not hold your hand.
I've not planned to be forward,
So don't misunderstand.
My arms should not enfold you,
I'm sure it must be wrong.
It seems so good

I would
Go further if I could.
I'll have to steal a kiss, I fear,
So you must pardon me, my dear.

VERSE 2

SHE: Though you're a likely lad
I doubt that you can be mature.
All of your hopes are premature-
Ly bold.
HE: Lady, a soldier's glad
Ever to face adversity.
Though other men may curse it, he
Won't scold.
SHE: Oh, if the strength I had
Both of your hands to manacle.
HE: It must be very sad
To be so puritanical
And cold.

REFRAIN 2

SHE: I'm sure! I beg your pardon,
I must withdraw my hand.
I've not planned to be wheedled,
So don't misunderstand.
I must forbid caresses,
I'm sure it must be wrong.
It seems so sweet
I beat
A maidenly retreat.
I have to slap your face, I fear,
So you must pardon me, my dear.

CHEERIO

Published September 1925. Introduced by Charles Purcell and male ensemble. Added during the pre–New York tryout.

VERSE

When we left Dover
On the way over
Mother tried her best to smile.
I knew that moment
Just what her woe meant.
I said, "Cheerio, it's just for a while."

REFRAIN

Cheerio, little mother of mine!
Don't be weary over the sea in the Homeland,
Anything I am happy to do

For the King, for the country, and you.
Cheerio, I will hold you again
With your dreary old little head on my shoulder.
Soon the wind will blow homeward ho!
So, cheerio! Cheerio!

FULL-BLOWN ROSES

Introduced by Flavia Arcaro and ensemble. Added during the pre–New York tryout.

GIRLS: Good day!
MEN: Good Lord!
HOWE &
CLINTON: Such faces hardly bear inspection.
TRYON: Their beauty is their own
protection.
GIRLS: A courtesy, sirs, we'll pay to you
And say to you
Good day to you.
We give our hearts away to you,
Let's have a little chat.
MEN: Your beauty is your surety,
Security for purity.
If one man can endure it he
Is blinder than a bat!
GIRLS: Let us have a little chat.
Life has been so very flat.
Though we try to be platonic,
Love's chronic and that's that.
[*Men and girls in counterpoint*]
MEN: Your beauty is your surety,
Security for purity,
If one man can endure it he
Is blinder than a bat!
GIRLS: Let us have a little chat.
Life has been so very flat.
Though we try to be platonic,
Love's chronic and that's that.
[*Enter Mrs. Murray, exquisitely gowned*]
MRS. MURRAY: Good day!
MEN: Hurray!
MRS. MURRAY: Forget the enmity between us.
MEN: Into a pigpen steps a Venus!
Full-blown roses are sweeter.
Full-blown blossoms are neater.
To hail a beauty when you meet
her
A soldier knows!
MRS. MURRAY: I'm transported to be courted
By such gallant cavaliers.
You're such very welcome foes!
TRYON: At your beck, ma'am, round your
neck, ma'am,

We will dangle lavalieres,
As our admiration grows!
MEN: Youthful buds cannot beat her.
Ev'ry year her beauty grows,
Buds are sweet, she is sweeter,
We're very glad to meet her
And greet her, our full-blown rose!

HERE IN MY ARMS

Published September 1925. Introduced by Helen Ford and Charles Purcell. Also introduced in *Lido Lady* (1926) by Phyllis Dare and Jack Hulbert.

VERSE 1

HE: I know a merry place
Far from intrusion.
It's just the very place
For your seclusion.
There you can while away
Days as you smile away.
It's not a mile away
But it's new to you.

REFRAIN

Here in my arms it's adorable!
It's deplorable
That you were never there.
When little lips are so kissable
It's permissible
For me to ask my share.
Next to my heart it is ever so lonely,
I'm holding only air,
While here in my arms it's adorable!
It's deplorable
That you were never there.

VERSE 2

SHE: I know a pretty place
At your command, sir;
It's not a city place,
Yet near at hand, sir;
Here, if you loll away,
Two hearts can toll away.
You'd never stroll away,
If you only knew!

REPEAT REFRAIN

REPRISE

Your pretty words were adorable,
It's deplorable that they were only lies.
Still you will find I am affable,
It was laughable that I believed your eyes.
Next to my heart it's ever so lonely,
I'm holding only air,
While here in my arms it's adorable!
It's deplorable you never will be there.

THO' WE'VE NO AUTHENTIC REASON

Introduced by principals and ensemble. Alternate title:
"Finale, Act I."

HOWE: Tho' we've no authentic reason
To suspect the maid of treason,
From her actions I begin to
See some things we must look into,
And the only thing to do
Is to stay and see it through.
MRS. MURRAY: When you tell me you remain, you
Give me leave to entertain you;
Let your duty in a measure
Be no duty but a pleasure.
TRYON: Duty calls us but in spite of it
Hip-hoorah, let's make a night of
it.
Full-blown roses are sweeter,
Full-blown blossoms are neater,
To hail a beauty when you meet
her.
A soldier knows.
You're like Venus and between us
I prefer the riper charms
That the autumn years disclose.
Your equator may be greater,
But I like to fill my arms
With the most substantial foes.
Youthful buds cannot beat her.
Ev'ry year her beauty grows,
Buds are sweet, she is sweeter,
We're very glad to meet her
And greet her our full-blown rose!
BETSY: John, John.
Here in my arms it's adorable!
It's deplorable that you never will
be there.

GAVOTTE

Introduced by ladies and gentlemen of the ensemble.

Oh, the light of Heaven's all a-glimmer
In Milady's eyes.
Warm their rays;
Their lovelight is no dimmer
Than the bright stars in the skies!
Lo, her lips are like the coral!
Oh, Milady's dress is gold.
And Milady loves to quarrel,
For Milady's heart is cold!
Oh, the light of Heaven's all a-glimmer
In Milady's eyes!
Warm their rays;
Their lovelight is no dimmer
Than the bright stars in the skies.

I'D LIKE TO HIDE IT

Introduced by Helen Ford and ensemble.

VERSE 1

He's gentle and he's such a handsome thing!
When I see John, reserve goes on the wing.
Though I know I mayn't, I just want to faint.
I try to taunt, but only want to cling.

REFRAIN

I'd like to hide it!
I'd like to hide it!
I'd like to smother down the flame inside.
But though I've tried it,
I can't abide it,
My heart keeps beating just the same inside.
It goes a-pitter-patter-patter
And though I want to tell him, "No!"
My heart has cried it,
So I confide it,
I'd like to hide it,
But I love him so!

VERSE 2

With ev'ry thrill I feel my will resign,
To my chagrin my blood turns into wine.
When I hear him speak, I get very weak.
I try to frown as chills run down my spine!

REPEAT REFRAIN

WHERE THE HUDSON RIVER FLOWS

Introduced by Flavia Arcaro, Detmar Poppen, Harold Crane, and ensemble.

VERSE

All crowds are such a menace
To love's sweet rendezvous.
I've the best of places for our fond embraces.
Tell me where it is, and I'll meet you.
It's not in Rome or Venice
Or where the Shamrock grows;
To the Nile or Po, dear,
I don't want to go, dear.
No, I'll meet you where the Hudson flows!

REFRAIN

Meet me in the forests of Manhattan,
There are secret corners we can chat in.
There's a sylvan den,
A sweet secluded Harlem glen!
And we will find a cozy cranny in Manhattan,
Just the kind that nanny goats have sat in.
Love will find repose,
Where the Hudson River flows!

PATTER

When the moon is shining down on Wall Street,
Meet me in the shadow of the Wall;
Then we'll run from ev'ry large and small street;
Half a mile up Broadway you can hear the
crickets call!
We will hire a wagon we can speed in;
All the thickest woods we'll journey through,
And I'll feel like Adam in his Eden
In the lovely Bronx with you!

REPEAT REFRAIN

BYE AND BYE

Published September 1925. Introduced by Helen Ford and Charles Purcell.

VERSE 1

If you'll only bide the time
And fortify your heart,

Fortune will decide the time
When sorrows will depart.
Let's put heads together
And be fancy-free.
Make your troubles disappear,
Let bliss appear
And see
All the jolly times of days to be.

REFRAIN

Bye and bye,
Not now but bye and bye,
Somehow we'll try and buy
A little nest.
Scheme a while when lonely,
Dream a while,
'Twill only seem a while
And love will do the rest.
Our happy days will come
Though slight delays will come;
The bright sun's rays will come
From out the sky.
Ev'ry cloud just flies on,
Love is on the far horizon,
You'll be my sweetheart
Bye and bye.

VERSE 2

Why should we be sorrowful
When just ahead we see
Pictures of tomorrow full
Of things that ought to be?
We won't know a trouble;
We won't know a care;
Ev'ry storm we weather, dear,
Together, dear,
Seems fair.
While we dream of all we have to share.

REPEAT REFRAIN

SWEET PETER

Published September 1925. Introduced by Hilda Spring, John Seymour, and ensemble.

VERSE

When Mynheer Peter Stuyvesant
Was Governor of the town,
He went ev'ry night to the tavern,
And drank all the Burgundy down.

His wooden leg till dawn would peg
While wifie at home would frown;
And when he would hobble home in the gloom
His wife knew the sound of his
    boom-boom-boom!

REFRAIN

Sweet Peter, sweet Peter!
Had a wife and couldn't cheat her,
Naughty Peter couldn't cheat her
With his boom-boom-boom!
Sweet Peter, sweet Peter!
Wide awake in bed he'd greet her,
Naughty Peter, he would greet her
With his boom-boom-boom!
Homeward he'd stumble,
With the key he'd fumble,
Downstairs he'd tumble
When she threw a broom.
Sweet Peter, sweet Peter!
Had a wife and couldn't cheat her,
Pickled Peter couldn't cheat her
With his boom-boom-boom!

HERE'S A KISS

Published October 1925. Introduced by Helen Ford and Charles Purcell.

VERSE

It's only been hail and farewell—
Brief our meeting,
Moments fleeting,
But mem'ries of love will wear well.
When you start your
Sad departure,
In your heart your regrets you'll bear well.

REFRAIN

Here's a kiss,
I'll give you this
As keepsake of my love;
With a fond adieu,
I'll pledge my love anew.
Ever dear, this souvenir
Will help me to remember!
Here's my heart to hold when we part,
Here's my love for you.

THE PIPES OF PANSY

Intended for *Dearest Enemy*, *The Girl Friend* (1926), *Peggy-Ann* (1926), and *She's My Baby* (1928). Dropped from all four shows before their New York openings.

VERSE

Sing a song of the Great God Pan!
He was young when the world began;
Today he's old and decrepit,
Far too enfeebled to step it.
His merry pipes are played
Now by a merry maid.
Old Pan's daughter
Pipes through the forest glade.

REFRAIN

The Pipes of Pansy are playing and saying
You must love someone!
The Pipes of Pansy are calling, you're falling,
So just love someone.
Leave your care
And catch the sunbeams in your hair.
When Pansy's pipes are blown,
How can you live alone?
The sky is bluer than azure,
It has your emotions tingling;
The song is newer than June is;
The tune is the oceans mingling
Two by two.
When even sparrows get married,
What else can you do?
The Pipes of Pansy are calling to you.

GIRLS DO NOT TEMPT ME

Dropped before the New York opening. Intended for the characters of Generals Clinton and Howe when the show was known as *Sweet Rebel*. No music survives; lyric was found in *Sweet Rebel* script registered for copyright at the Library of Congress, September 1924.

VERSE

Lips that smile on me in cherry red,
You're forbidden fruit today;
To your tender blushes very red
I'm a callous brute today.
Cupid, save your little arrows,
Kindly do not shoot today;

Sweet temptation of a berry red,
You must not take root today!

REFRAIN

Girls do not tempt me,
I'm not your prey.
Kindly exempt me,
Please go away!
Firm resolutions I must recall,
Each harmful sweet armful I have to forestall,
For if you tempt me,
I'll fall, that's all!

THE FIFTH AVENUE FOLLIES, 1926

Presented at the Fifth Avenue Club, 683 Fifth Avenue, at the corner of Fifty-fourth Street, New York, starting in late January 1926. Music by Richard Rodgers. Lyrics by Lorenz Hart. Produced by Billy Rose. Sketches by Harold Atteridge and Ballard MacDonald. Production conceived and directed by Seymour Felix. Settings and costumes by Booth, Willoughby, and Jones. Music director, Reginald Childs, conducting Harry Archer's Orchestra. Cast included Cecil Cunningham, Bert Hanlon, Doris Canfield, Bobbie Clif, and Johnne Clare.

The following lyrics are missing: "Do You Notice Anything?" (introduced by Cecil Cunningham, Doris Canfield, Bert Hanlon, and ensemble), "A City Flat" (Bert Hanlon and Cecil Cunningham), "Mike" (Cecil Cunningham), "High Hats" (Adler, Weil and Hanlon), and "Lillie, Lawrence, and Jack" (Cecil Cunningham, Doris Canfield, and Bert Hanlon).

Orchestra parts for "Do You Notice Anything?" are in the Theatre Guild Collection of Yale University's Beinecke Rare Book Library. They reveal that the song also was apparently intended for *The Garrick Gaieties* (1926). The editors think that the music for "Lillie, Lawrence, and Jack" also was used for "Tennis Champs" in *The Garrick Gaieties* (1926).

IN THE NAME OF ART

Introduced by Cecil Cunningham, Doris Canfield, and Bert Hanlon. The music is missing. Only a portion of the lyric survives.

Kind auditors, you see in us
A most unholy trinity!
Compared to us, Boccaccio's
A Doctor of Divinity!
Our sins, if laid from end to end,
Would stretch into infinity!
We earn an honest living
While we rob you of your sleep.
Our manager has warned us
It's the height of asininity
If we'd offend the morals
Of this sacrosanct vicinity!
Our show must please both movie stars
And ladies of virginity!
It's proper to be dirty,
But it's dirty to be cheap!
[*Incomplete*]

MAYBE IT'S ME

Published February and December 1926. Introduced by Johnne Clare, Albert Burke, and ensemble. Danced by Elizabeth Brown and Dan McCarthy. Also introduced in *Peggy-Ann* (1926) by Helen Ford and Lester Cole.

VERSE 1

HE: My features are no gems of regularity,
It's more than charity
To call them fair.
I'm not so very brilliant, and oh God, oh Gee,
With no kid prodigy
Do I compare.
I have ordinary habits
Like a million other Babbitts.
My morals never quite come up to scratch,
And tho' I'm as mediocre
As a cup of hotel mocha,
I'm sure you couldn't find a better match.

REFRAIN 1

There's something nice about you.
What can it be? Oh, let me see,
Maybe it's me.
I'm not so much without you,
But you're a she that needs a he.
Maybe it's me.
By yourself you're so dumb it's embarrassin',
But with me you are smart by comparison.
There's something nice about you.
What can it be? Now, let me see.
Maybe it's me.

VERSE 2

SHE: I cannot wear my dresses like a manikin
And I'm no panic in
My robe de nuit!
My intellect with ev'ry day diminishes.
A school that finishes
Has finished me.
I've learned what the taste of wine meant
To a lady of refinement;
And cigarettes have not improved my voice.
As for money, I can burn it,
It is spent before I earn it.
But still you couldn't make a better choice.

REFRAIN 2

There's something nice about you.
What can it be? Oh, let me see,
Maybe it's me.
I'm not so much without you,
But you're a he that needs a she.
Maybe it's me.
You tell me that your old man's a senator,
You are smart and so's your progenitor.
There's something nice about you.
HE: What can it be? Now, let me see.
Maybe it's me.

WHERE'S THAT LITTLE GIRL?

Published February 1926. Introduced by Albert Burke, Adler, Weil, and Herman, Bert Hanlon, Johnne Clare, Elizabeth Brown, Doris Canfield, and ensemble. Alternate title: "Where's That Little Girl with the Little Green Hat?" Same music but different lyric used for "What's the Use?" in *Lido Lady* (1926).

VERSE

Help me find a lady who is wearing
A daring green hat.
There is something she must have about her,
Without her I'm flat.
I am getting fidgety and sleepless,
I keep less in shape;
If I have to look for her forever,
She'll never escape.

REFRAIN

Where's that little girl with the little green hat?
I just saw her once and I lost her like that;

She has eyes of brown and lips that are red,
With the wearin' of the green on her head.
I don't care about the life she has led;
I'd better get her.
There's no blue for me in the heavenly skies;
Ev'rything turns green right in front of my eyes.
If I see her long enough for a chat,
We'll be living in a little green flat.
Where's that little girl with the little green hat?

SUSIE

Introduced by Doris Canfield and ensemble.

VERSE

I'm in the Gay Paree Revue,
The which is applesauce,
And since I joined the chorus
I don't believe in Santa Claus.
I thought I'd see a lot of sights
And travel round the earth.
I travel round, I see the sights,
But from an upper berth.
When I joined the chorus,
I didn't have a rag to my back.
Now I'm covered with 'em,
And that ain't no wisecrack.
I thought my life would be a dream
And look at what I get.
I'm always chasing rainbows,
And that's why I'm all wet!

REFRAIN 1

I'm Susie the Slob of the Chorus.
They call me the stagehands' delight!
I thought I'd be a chicken
But I'm just an awful egg.
I haven't laughed real hearty
Since the manager broke his leg.
I must sing and dance and skip
While I pray my tights won't rip!
We play four a day, that's a cinch, of course,
If we drop in our tracks then we please the boss.
It's true that I may be a pony,
But, Gawd, I ain't no horse!

REFRAIN 2

I'm Susie the Slob of the Chorus.
I frequently eat once a week.
The man who said we wine and dine
Must be an awful nut.
My stomach feels so empty
That it thinks my throat is cut!
It's dinnertime for some, but gee!
It's only twelve o'clock for me.
Of show girls' dinners I've often heard.
To me a restaurant's just a word.
It's true that I may be a chicken,
But, Gawd, I ain't no bird!

THE GIRL FRIEND | 1926

Tryout: Apollo Theatre, Atlantic City, New Jersey, March 8–13, 1926. New York run: Vanderbilt Theatre, March 17–December 4, 1926. 301 performances. Music by Richard Rodgers. Lyrics by Lorenz Hart. Produced by Lew Fields. Book by Herbert Fields. Entire production supervised by Lew Fields. Book staged by John Harwood. Musical numbers and dances arranged and staged by Jack Haskell. Settings by P. Dodd Ackerman. Costumes by Booth, Willoughby, and Jones. Orchestra under the direction of Paul Lannin. Orchestrations by Maurice B. de Packh. Cast, starring Sam [Sammy] White and Eva Puck, included June Cochrane, John Hundley, Evelyn Cavanaugh, and Francis X. Donegan.

For the lyric to "The Pipes of Pansy," see *Dearest Enemy* (1925), page 59.

The following lyrics are missing: "Turkey in the Straw" (introduced in the Atlantic City tryout by Stewart Baird, Frank Doane, Evelyn Cavanaugh, June Cochrane, and Francis X. Donegan, but dropped before the New York opening), "Two of a Kind" (introduced in the Atlantic City tryout by Evelyn Cavanaugh, Sam [Sammy] White, and ensemble, but dropped before the New York opening), and "Hum To" (dropped during rehearsals).

HEY! HEY!

Introduced by ensemble.

Hey! Hey!
Down on the farm we used to work all day,
But since the radio we shirk all day.
All the hicks, down in the sticks, are gay.
Church organ music used to fill the air;
Now hotsy-totsy rhythms thrill the air.
We reap and sow while saxes blow—away.
Out in the fields we let the radio stand.
Plowing is grand, in time to a band.
Now that the radio is ruling the land
We hear the groans of saxophones.
It isn't toil to till the soil.
All of the country girls in drab array
Do all the dances of the cabaret
And so the rube is not a boob today.

THE SIMPLE LIFE

Introduced by ensemble.

GIRLS: We've so little time for pleasure.
    We rise at five,

Everyone is in a measure
Glad he's alive.
BOYS: All day long we do the chore work
Till curfew's knell.
If you ask if we adore work
We do like hell.
GIRLS: The parson says it's beautiful
To be so dutiful
But we must snootyful each one.
BOYS: So after hours we cheat a bit,
At cards we beat a bit
And shake our feet a bit for fun.
GIRLS: Honest labor will not hurt you,
To be good is very nice,
But to balance so much virtue
We must have a little vice.
BOYS: We're believers in the Bible
And simple life.
GIRLS: Every female in this tribe'll
Make a good wife.
BOYS: Though we don't go home till morning,
Petting a lot,
Do we need our mothers' warning?
Yes, we do not.

THE GIRL FRIEND

Published March 1926. Introduced by Eva Puck and Sammy White. Also introduced by Emma Haig and George Gee in the London production of *The Girl Friend* (1927) (not the same production).

VERSE 1

LENNY: My girl's the kind of girl
For steady company.
It's steady company
That I prefer.
When in the Charleston dance
I want to bump a knee,
I want to bump a knee
With her.
Homely wrecks appeal
When their checks appeal,
But she has sex appeal.
Yes, sir!

REFRAIN 1

Isn't she cute?
Isn't she sweet?
She's gentle
And mentally nearly complete.
She's knockout,
She's regal,

Her beauty's illegal.
She's the girl friend!
Take her to dance!
Take her to tea!
It's stunning
How cunning
This lady can be.
A look at this vision
Will cause a collision.
She's the girl friend!
She is smart,
She's refined.
How can she be real?
She has heart,
She has mind.
Hell, the girl's ideal!
Isn't she cute?
Isn't she sweet?
An eyeful you'd die full
Of pleasure to meet.
In my funny fashion
I'm cursed with a passion
For the girl friend!

VERSE 2

MOLLIE: He's very short on looks
But long on decency.
He's long on decency,
He's very tame.
But he has made an awful
Hit with me since he—
A hit with me, since he
First came.
I have seen so well
He won't screen so well,
But that boy means so well.
He's game!

REFRAIN 2

MOLLIE: Isn't he cute?
Isn't he sweet?
He's gentle
And mentally nearly complete.
He's warm as
An oven.
He knows how
To love an'
I'm the girl friend!
LENNY: Take her to dance,
Take her to tea.
It's stunning
How cunning
This lady can be.
She ain't got
No culture.

She's keen as
A vulture.
She's the girl friend!

MOLLIE: He is smart,
He's refined.
How can he be real?
He has heart,
He has mind.
Hell, the boy's ideal!

LENNY: Isn't she cute?
Isn't she sweet?
An eyeful you'd die full
Of pleasure to meet.

BOTH: In my (his) funny fashion
I'm (he's) cursed with a passion
For the girl friend.

REPRISE 1

LENNY: Isn't she cute?
Isn't she sweet?
A female,
A he-male is happy to meet.
I'll broadcast emphatic,
Without any static.
She's the girl friend.

MOLLIE: Each time we kiss,
It's plain to see
The end'll
Be Mendel
Ssohn's music for me.
When we make a date-o
It's goodbye to Plato.
I'm the girl friend.

REPRISE 2

Isn't she cute?
Isn't she sweet?
She'd sock out a knockout,
That's nearly complete!
She's one of those sweeties
That gives you the deeties [D.T.'s]!
What a girl friend!

GOODBYE, LENNY

Introduced by ensemble. When *The Girl Friend* was a three-act show during its tryout, this number was the finale of Act I. When it became a two-act show, it became the finale of Act I, Scene 2.

ALL: Hurry! Hurry! Hurry! Hurry!
We're sorry you're going away.

BOY: Come on, all you local Charleston men,
Give the local Charleston yell for Len.

ALL: Rah! Rah! Rah! Rah! Maple Villa!
Boost! Boost! You gotta win!
Go get! Go get! Action! Action!
Stout heart! And steady chin!
Co-op! Co-op! Cooperation too!
Rah! Rah! Rah! Rah! Maple Villa,
Lenny, we're proud of you.

LENNY: Hard worry and labor were good for a
sap,
Just watch little Len put this town on the
map.
New York is just a feather
I'll put in my cap!
When I hit Grand Central, the city is
free,
It's gonna brass-band me and hand me
the key.
A Prince of Wales reception is what
they'll give me.

ALL: Co-op! Co-op! Cooperation too!
Rah! Rah! Rah! Rah! Lenny! Lenny!
We'll all be proud of you.

MOLLIE: Goodbye, Lenny, you'll be free,
But you see it will be
Kind of lonesome for poor little me.

LENNY: Mollie dear, I'll put away
Ev'ry cent of my pay.
You'll be happy to spend it someday.

ALL: Oh, he's gonna win the race with the
Charleston!
He will lead the pace with the
Charleston!
And he'll get first place with the
Charleston!
And it's Hay, Hay, Hay on Broadway!
When the other boys on wheels go
spinning, spinning,
Don't give a gol-darn!
But when Lenny on his bike goes
winning, winning,
Burn up the old barn!
When they're rootin' you, tootin' you,
get hot!
When you're speedin' it, leadin' it—joy!
Oh, you're gonna win the race with the
Charleston.
Maple Villa is proud of her boy.

THE BLUE ROOM

Published March 1926. Introduced by Eva Puck and Sammy White. Also introduced by Louise Brown and Roy

Royston in the London production of *The Girl Friend* (1927) (not the same production).

VERSE 1

All my future plans,
Dear, will suit your plans.
Read the little blueprints.
Here's your mother's room.
Here's your brother's room.
On the wall are two prints.
Here's the kiddies' room,
Here's the biddy's room,
Here's a pantry lined with shelves, dear.
Here I've planned for us
Something grand for us,
Where we two can be ourselves, dear.

REFRAIN

We'll have a blue room,
A new room,
For two room,
Where ev'ry day's a holiday
Because you're married to me.
Not like a ballroom,
A small room,
A hall room,
Where I can smoke my pipe away
With your wee head upon my knee.
We will thrive on,
Keep alive on,
Just nothing but kisses,
With Mister and Missus
On little blue chairs.
You sew your trousseau,
And Robinson Crusoe
Is not so far from worldly cares
As our blue room far away upstairs.

VERSE 2

From all visitors
And inquisitors
We'll keep our apartment.
I won't change your plans—
You arrange your plans
Just the way your heart meant.
Here we'll be ourselves
And we'll see ourselves
Doing all the things we're scheming.
Here's a certain place,
Cretonne curtain place,
Where no one can see us dreaming.

REPEAT REFRAIN

CABARETS

Introduced by ensemble.

Some cabarets
Are dumb cabarets
With prices.
We gad about,
But we're mad about
Our vices.
We want to dance
But not a chance;
They play the show.
We'd pay the show
To stop.
We cry so much
And they try so much
To make us.
Why must they sing?
Oh, we trust, they sing
To shake us.
We pay in there
Simply for taking the air.
We've dough enough
But don't know enough
To care.

WHY DO I?

Published March 1926. Introduced by June Cochrane, Francis X. Donegan, and ensemble.

VERSE 1

DONALD: Standing at attention,
        For your condescension,
        Isn't my idea of fun.
        You have but to hand me
        Glances that command me
        And the things you ask are done.
        You've the first word every time we
            quarrel,
        The last word when the fight is won;
        You've had me believin',
        Dear, that odd is even,
        Since you've had me on the run.

REFRAIN 1

        I give in to you, why do I?
        I'm as easy as pie,
        I'm afraid to lose my girl.
        How can I refuse my girl?

I don't dare to reply, do I,
When you tell me goodbye?
Fearing I'll disgrace myself,
I just go and chase myself.
On the day that you become my better
    half
You can call me Lord and Master, dear,
    and laugh.
You know that
In my love I don't lie, do I?
Who would offer to die?
Hardly any other guy,
So why do I?

VERSE 2

IRENE: Though you may not know it,
       And I may not show it,
       I've an awful yen for you.
       If I seemed too eager,
       My chance would be meager
       Though I shun all men for you.
       I'm evasive, just to take your fancy,
       Disdainful though it makes me blue.
       Dear, I only tease you,
       In the end to please you,
       In your taming of the shrew.

REFRAIN 2

       I give in to you, why do I?
       I'm as easy as pie,
       I'm afraid to lose my boy.
       How can I refuse my boy?
       I don't dare to reply, do I,
       When you tell me goodbye?
       Fearing I'll disgrace myself,
       I just go and chase myself.
       On the day that I become your better
           half
       You can tell me that you worship me
           and laugh.
       You know that
       In my love I don't lie, do I?
       It is silly to sigh
       For an undernourished guy,
       So why do I?

THE DAMSEL WHO DONE ALL THE DIRT

Introduced by Eva Puck.

VERSE

When one guy kills the other guy,
"Find the woman" is the cry.
It's from the French, we owe it to them;
In French they call it
Cherchez la femme.
The rise and fall of every nation
Allows a sex interpretation.
King Louis XIV had a mate
Who bowed before his smile and
When the King said, "Kids, I'm the state,"
He must have meant Rhode Island.

REFRAIN 1

Look for the damsel,
The dumb little damsel,
The damsel who done all the dirt.
When Washington crossed the Delaware,
It wasn't for the ride.
He had a date with a Jersey flapper on the other
    side.
The greatest of heroes
Would now rank as zeros
If not for the hem of a skirt.
Patrick Henry said with bated breath,
"Give me Liberty or give me death."
He was willing to give up his life,
So would you if you had such a wife.
She may be Carrie or Madame Du Barry,
Or Cleo or Sappho or Gert.
Fräulein or Ma'mselle,
It's always a damsel,
A damsel who done all the dirt.

REFRAIN 2

Look for the damsel,
The dumb little damsel,
The damsel who done all the dirt.
The man who said "Don't give up the ship"
Was very brave and bold.
The reason was he had Sophie Tucker hiding in
    the hold.
Columbus' cruising
Was not of his choosing,
They say he was rather a flirt.
He was getting friendly with the Queen
When he made his exit from the scene.
Sailing wasn't his idea of fun,
But he heard the King had bought a gun.
Whether it's Lizzy or good old Queen Izzy,
As long as she's wearing a skirt,
Humble or royal,
It's always a goil,
A goil who done all the dirt.

REFRAIN 3

Look for the damsel,
The dumb little damsel,
The damsel who done all the dirt.
On the Nile Mr. Pharaoh made
The Hebrews pay the price,
He hated them 'cause he couldn't make a date
    with Fanny Brice.
Old King Ulysses
Was none of your sissies,
The sail of his ship was a skirt.
Great Napoleon gave up his throne,
And perhaps you think he lived alone.
He had someone who looked swell in a
Little French château in Helena.
When a man kicks in
It's always a vixen
Who sticks in the daggers that hurt.
Many a Duchess
Has put guys on crutches,
And all on account of a skirt.

HE'S A WINNER

Introduced by Frank Doane and ensemble. Alternate
titles: "Sporting Life" and "Reporters' Opening."

GIRLS: Will young Silver ride the winning
        bicycle?
SPENCER: He could win the race upon a
        tricycle.
REPORTERS: This is copy for a special
        article;
        From the truth we may depart a
        particle.
GIRLS & BOYS: Is he married, is he single?
        In what circles does he mingle?
        Does he lead a steady life?
SPENCER: He's a boy you can't get sore on.
        Everybody loves a moron.
        He just needs a clever wife.
        He's a winner, though he's a
        beginner.
        He can't lose.
REPORTERS: That's news.
SPENCER: He's a comer,
        Though he's dumber
        Than a plumber.
        All next summer
        He'll give all the rest of them the
        blues.
        On his mind I pin no medals,
        All his brains are in his pedals,

But he'll win the six-day strife.
He is twenty-two years.
REPORTERS: We'll take off a few years.
ALL: And make it true to sporting life.

TOWN HALL TONIGHT

Introduced by Eva Puck, June Cochrane, Francis X. Donegan, Sammy White, and ensemble.

VERSE 1

Out in Oskaloosa,
Where the Shuberts don't produce a
Single Winter Garden show,
Every second Saturday
Was just like a regatta day
When to Town Hall we'd go.
On Main Street, where the minstrels would
    parade,
We kids would yell when Sousa's march was
    played.
Our dad would save his salary
To seat us in the gallery
And there sat we nuts
Eating peanuts
Up in Heaven, drinking lemonade.

REFRAIN 1

Town Hall tonight, Town Hall tonight.
There's the Minstrel King with eighty-seven
    strong,
There were eighty he forgot to bring along,
But we kids all thought the King could do no
    wrong.
Ladies and gents paid fifty cents
When there were no ticket agencies to fight.
For what you pay for seats today
They'd let you take the town away.
The town's at the Town Hall tonight.

2ND ENDING

These are the jokes that don't grow old,
In ev'ry new revue they're told.
The town's at the Town Hall tonight!

VERSE 2

Out in Oskaloosa
It's not easy to induce a
Show to come and play the shack.
It was just a one-night stand,

A "play your show and run" night stand,
Or get your money back.
An opera troupe once murdered La Bohème;
They got the cash, Puccini got the blame.
The tenor was so flat that night
He even scared the cat that night.
To stop we begged him,
Rotten-egg'd him,
But he kept on singing just the same!

REFRAIN 2

Town Hall tonight, Town Hall tonight.
The basso sung with such a husky throat.
As on the air his aria would float,
A frog jumped out each time he sang a note.
They sailed from Rome
But they walked home,
For they made a "bum" of La Bohème that night.
A cabbage and a scallion,
Was thrown at each Italian.
The town's at the Town Hall tonight.

2ND ENDING

Then ev'ry sour-belly voice
Seemed like a Martinelli voice.
The Town's at the Town Hall tonight!

GOOD FELLOW MINE

Published March 1926. Introduced by Evelyn Cavanaugh,
John Hundley, and ensemble. Hundley replaced Stuart
Baird during the Atlantic City tryout.

VERSE 1

HE: When a fellow needs a friend,
    He needs a friend like you;
    Not the kind that he can lend
    To other fellows too;
    A friend who could be something more
    And still remain a pal;
    He's got to be a friend, but gee,
    He's got to be a gal.

REFRAIN

I'll be a good fellow,
Good fellows are few;
I'll not sing the melody
Of love, dear, to you;
Though my heart's holding a secret,
I'll not give a sign;

Sweet words of love imploring you,
My lips decline;
But I can't help adoring you,
Good fellow mine!

VERSE 2

SHE: When a girl is all alone,
She needs a comrade too;
One that's one for all her own,
And one that's one like you.
With abiding loyalty
That nothing can destroy,
She must be a friend, but gee,
She's got to be a boy.

REPEAT REFRAIN

CREOLE CROONING SONG

Introduced by John Hundley and ensemble. Danced by
Dorothy Barber.

VERSE

When the red magnolia moon's
Rolling high again,
Old Louisiana tunes
Fill the forest glen;
Underneath the shady boughs
All the Creoles throng;
Each his fond affection vows
In a Creole song.

REFRAIN

The Creoles at ev'ning sing a crooning song,
A sweet southern serenade and spooning song.
Dusky sweethearts haven't a care
When magnolias bloom everywhere
And the woodwinds carry the air along.
Each dreamy young lover to his lady bows
And fondly they kiss beneath the shady boughs
And the moon aglow at the sight
Finds a cloud to darken his light
While the Creoles sing through the night,
Their crooning song.

I'D LIKE TO TAKE YOU HOME

Introduced by June Cochrane and Francis X. Donegan.
Alternate title: "I'd Like to Take You Home to Meet My
Mother." For earlier version, see *Bad Habits of 1925*,
page 36.

VERSE 1

HE: You're my mother's rival
But she's happy in defeat;
Life would be complete,
If you two could meet.
So let's go out together
To my dear old country seat
And we'll give the folks at home a treat.

REFRAIN

I'd like to take you home to meet my
mother.
She'd love to know you and show you
around.
You'd be just like a sister to my brother.
They won't believe their eyes
When they see that you care for me.
When you step in our dear old-fashioned
parlor
And throw your charms in the arms of Pa,
And when you play the organ
I'll feel rich as Morgan,
Gee, I'd like to take you home to meet my
ma.

VERSE 2

SHE: I'm a youthful blossom
Of a be-familied tree;
In my house you'll see
Relativity.
I'm afraid you'll have to meet
The whole menagerie.
You must marry all of them with me.

REPEAT REFRAIN

WHAT IS IT?

Introduced by Frank Doane and ensemble. Danced by
Dorothy Barber.

VERSE

All the little men are little women,
Their pants are wide as skirts;
All the little girls are little slim men,
Just glance, men's ties, men's shirts.
There is nothing to condemn in it,
No girl wants to be effeminate,
She'd even like to take a shave.

REFRAIN

What is it?
It's apt to worry you a bit.
A she or he,
It's quite impossible to see.
It takes a Ouija board to Ouija it
If he's a collegiate, or he's a she.
Don't flirt,
Perhaps her name is Bert;
She's cut her curls
But still she's wearing pearls;
She fits right in a nest of boys,
For the rest of boys
Are girls.

IN NEW ORLEANS

Dropped during rehearsals and replaced by "Creole
Crooning Song." Music is missing.

VERSE

Red magnolia moon rolls up in the sky,
Hear the Creoles croon their lullaby!
On the blue lagoon the darkies sigh.
Underneath the shady boughs,
Each his fond affection vows.

REFRAIN

Hush-a-bye! The Creoles are crooning
In New Orleans!
In New Orleans!
Stars on high while darkies are spooning
Smile on the scenes
In New Orleans.
In sweet magnolia trees the birdies of the night

All cuddle close because the time for love is
  right.
Hush-a-bye! The Creoles are crooning,
That's what love means
In New Orleans!

SLEEPYHEAD

Published March 1926 and May 1926. Introduced in Atlantic City tryout by Eva Puck. Cut before the New York
opening. Also introduced in *The Garrick Gaieties* (1926)
by Sterling Holloway, then dropped shortly after the
opening.

VERSE

Some day is always a glum day,
  You lose all your spirit;
Bleak day, that workaway weekday,
  And oh how you fear it!
Closing, your heavy eyes closing,
  Till nearly asleep, dear,
Dozing, while dreamily dozing,
  Your troubles will keep, dear:

REFRAIN

Sleepyhead, you'd better go dreaming;
Sleepyhead, don't open your eyes!
Sleepyhead, oh why should you worry away?
You'd better hurry away
Into your daydreams,
Gay dreams!
Sleepyhead, when tears come a-streaming,
Oh, weepyhead, no sorrow is wise;
Sleep away,
Deep away,
Keep away your sighs.
Sleepyhead, don't open your eyes!

THE GARRICK GAIETIES | 1926

New York run: Garrick Theatre, May 10–October 9, 1926. 174 performances. Music by Richard Rodgers. Lyrics by Lorenz Hart. Produced by the Theatre Guild. Sketches by Benjamin M. Kaye, Newman Levy, Marion Page Johnson, Herbert Fields, Chester D. Heywood, Edward Hope, and Philip Lord. Directed by Philip Loeb. Dances and musical numbers staged by Herbert Fields. Settings and costumes by Carolyn Hancock. Stage manager, Lee Strasberg. Orchestra under the direction of Roy Webb. Opening-night conductor, Richard Rodgers. Cast included Philip Loeb, Betty Starbuck, Romney Brent, William M. Griffith, Edith Meiser, Sterling Holloway, Bobbie Perkins, Eleanor Shaler, and Hildegarde Halliday.

For the lyric to "Sleepyhead," see *The Girl Friend* (1926), page 68.

SIX LITTLE PLAYS

Opening, Act I. Introduced by Philip Loeb, Betty Starbuck, Blanche Fleming, Jack Edwards, Romney Brent, William M. Griffith, Edith Meiser, Sterling Holloway, and ensemble. Alternate title: "Requiescat in Pace."

UNDERTAKER: Mine's a melancholy mission,
I'm the Theatre Guild mortician
And I've buried all the dramas
That they had this year.
Ev'ry play they did was charming
But the death rate was alarming.
And I must admit my business
Wasn't bad last year.

REFRAIN

Each little play has passed away—
Some died because the public
    scorned 'em.
They met their fate
And got the gate
Though all the learned critics
    mourned 'em.
The reviewers did their duty, ev'ry
    one—
Blew their horns like Angel Gabriel
    of the Sun,
But all through the year their jinx
    was near,
A constant and attentive lackey.
Sing of the praise
Of six little plays.
Requiescat in Pace!

Arms and the Man

RAINA: My pretty play,
Shaw's witty play,
Sighed like the rest,
Tried like the rest,
Died like the rest.

The Glass Slipper

With Joe Leblang
(You know Leblang)
My seats were dropped.
In the theaytre
My aviator flopped!

UNDERTAKER: While you were playing thirty
    subscriptions stopped.

Merchants of Glory

Marchands de Gloire,
Beaucoup de froid!
Vie de Paris;
Cri de Paris;
Gee, de Paris!

The Chief Thing

Each day can see
More vacancy
When trade has dropped.
This year the slush in
Plays from the Russian flopped.

UNDERTAKER: But after all, the chief thing is that
    you stopped.

Androcles and the Lion

LION: No fun I found;
My run I found
Netting six weeks,
Fretting six weeks,
Sweating six weeks.
Their aims expired,
Clare Eames expired,
Tom Powers froze.
Young Brent was bad, too,
And so they had to close!

UNDERTAKER: The Guild has a reputation for
    beastly shows.

The Goat Song

Poor nanny goat,
Could any goat
Seem half so bad,
Dream half so bad,
Scream half so bad!
Through sex it was
My exit was
Sudden and deft.
What makes it wrong is
Only the song is left.

UNDERTAKER: What makes it hell is only the
    smell is left.

UNDERTAKER: All through the year their jinx was
    near,
A constant and attentive lackey.
Sing of the praise of six little plays,
Requiescat in pace.

[*Bugle call*]

The Garrick Gaieties is coming
    down the street.

[*Bugle call*]

Come here, my son. I greet my
    meat.

WE CAN'T BE AS GOOD AS LAST YEAR

Introduced by Sterling Holloway, Philip Loeb, and company. It directly followed "Six Little Plays" in the show.

BOY: You're a little premature,
Give me a chance to be mature.
Since things have been so bad this
    year
I may turn out to be the only hit
    you've had this year.

UNDERTAKER: You cannot repeat last year
Even though you beat last year.
Remember this semester day
That distance lends enchantment
    only to the yesterday.
You can't be as good as last year!

ALL: You can't be as good as last year!
We can't be as good as last year,
For the last year was great.
How can we compare with the past
    year?
It is sad but such is fate.
We've lost all that artless spirit
With our Broadway veneer.
Then it was play but we're old
    hams today,
So we can't be as good as last year.

BOY: We were supers not real troupers
With an artless guile.
At our clumsy steps
Dear Mumsy, Dad and Sis would
    smile.
Now we're very hardened hams,
Broadway Winter Gardened hams.
All of you have pardoned hams—
Be kind to our white hairs.
Gone's the spirit
And we fear it
Takes away our chance.
Ancient timber
Can't be limber;
Gosh, how we will dance!
Though we fail we can't be ruing it.
We'll have lots of pleasure doing it.
Grind your teeth when we begin,
    for it
Is pretty certain you are in for it!

ALL: We can't be as good as last year
    [etc.]

MOUNTAIN GREENERY

Published May 1926. Introduced by Bobbie Perkins and
Sterling Holloway.

Published May 1926. Introduced by Bobbie Perkins and
Sterling Holloway.

VERSE 1

HE: On the first of May
It is moving day;
Spring is here, so blow your job—
Throw your job away;
Now's the time to trust
To your wanderlust.
In the city's dust you wait.
Must you wait?
Just you wait:

REFRAIN 1

In a mountain greenery
Where God paints the scenery—
Just two crazy people together;
While you love your lover, let
Blue skies be your coverlet—
When it rains we'll laugh at the weather.
And if you're good
I'll search for wood,
So you can cook
While I stand looking.

Beans could get no keener re-
Ception in a beanery.
Bless our mountain greenery home!

VERSE 2

SHE: Simple cooking means
More than French cuisines;
I've a banquet planned which is
Sandwiches and beans.
Coffee's just as grand
With a little sand.
Eat and you'll grow fatter, boy.
S'matter, boy?
'Atta boy!

REFRAIN 2

In a mountain greenery
Where God paints the scenery—
Just two crazy people together;
How we love sequestering
Where no pests are pestering—
No dear mama holds us in tether!
Mosquitoes here
Won't bite you, dear;
I'll let them sting
Me on the finger.
We could find no cleaner re-
Treat from life's machinery
Than our mountain greenery home!

TRIO PATTER

HE: When the world was young
Old Father Adam with sin would grapple,
So we're entitled to just one apple.
SHE: You mean to make applesauce.
HE: Underneath the bough
We'll learn a lesson from Mister Omar,
Beneath the eyes of no pa and no ma.
SHE: Old Lady Nature is boss,
Washing dishes,
Catching fishes
In the running stream.
We'll curse the smell o'
Citronella
Even when we dream.
HE: Head upon the ground,
Your downy pillow is just a boulder.
I'll have new dimples before I'm older,
But life is peaches and cream.*

---

*In published version this line leads directly to a reprise of
the last seven lines of the first refrain.

ENCORE 1

BOTH: In a mountain greenery
Where God paints the scenery—
Just two crazy people together.
HE: While you rest, my mama, let
Papa fry an omelette!
Every bun is light as a feather.
SHE: It's quite all right
To sing at night;
I'll sit and play
My ukulele.
HE: You can bet your life its tone
Beats a Jascha Heifetz tone.
Bless our mountain greenery home.

ENCORE 2

BOTH: In a mountain greenery
Where God paints the scenery—
With the world we haven't a quarrel.
SHE: Here a girl can map her own
Life without a chaperone.
HE: It's so good it must be immoral.
SHE: It's not amiss
To sit and kiss;
For me and you
There are no blue laws.
HE: Life is more delectable
When it's disrespectable.
Bless our mountain greenery home.

KEYS TO HEAVEN

Published May 1926. Introduced by Bobbie Perkins,
George Frierson, Blanche Fleming, and ensemble.

Published May 1926. Introduced by Bobbie Perkins,
George Frierson, Blanche Fleming, and ensemble.

VERSE

My piano teacher made me practice ev'ry day
When I started in to play.
I was very clumsy and I made my teacher sick.
I was pretty thick.
How it tickled teacher when at last
I had learned to play it very fast.
That was in the past,
But nowadays they give you hot stuff.
What good are scales when parties get rough?

REFRAIN

Keys to Heaven!
Music is a great way
To the Golden Gateway.
Keys to Heaven!

Open up your heart for me.
When your digits get the fidgets tripping along,
Ev'ry change'll make an angel try to go wrong.
Two hands can make those ivory things
Keys to Heaven!
Black notes! Blue notes
Melting into singing seas!
Please stay on
And play on
Those Heavenly Keys!

BACK TO NATURE

Introduced by the company as the opening number of the mini-operetta "The Rose of Arizona." Earlier title: "Vacationing."

VERSE

Vacationing! Vacationing!
You hear the Yankee nation sing.
We're out in Arizona in the wildwood.
We're busy as a bumblebee
In exercising fancy-free
To bring back all the happiness of childhood.

REFRAIN

Back to nature! Back to nature!
Hootin', scootin' land of Arizona.
Back to nature! Back to nature!
Breathing all the breezes' sweet aroma.
And we sing, oh, we sing,
Oh, it's great to be vacationing!
We are very rich and showy,
We're happy Hoi Pollowey,
It's great to be vacationing!

IT MAY RAIN

Introduced in the mini-operetta "The Rose of Arizona" by Blanche Fleming and Jack Edwards.

VERSE

Someday you may be
So far away from me
When ev'rything's going just wrong.
Though you're all alone
And miles away from home,
Keep humming and strumming this song:

REFRAIN

It may rain when the sun stops shining
It may rain when the sky is gray.
But after clouds will go,
You'll see a bright rainbow.
You never should forget
A violet
Is hiding 'neath the snow.
It may rain just when you are happy.
It may pour, but you need not sigh.
We'll see a sunny day,
For love will find a way
Till the clouds go rolling by!

DAVID CROCKETT

Introduced by Philip Loeb in the mini-operetta "The Rose of Arizona." Alternate titles: "Davy Crockett" and "Who Kept the Wolves Away from the Door (When Davy Crockett Went to War)?"

VERSE

Have you heard about old Davy Crockett?
Little Davy Crockett was a scout.
When he left his wife, the door, he'd lock it,
But he couldn't keep his rivals out.
Mrs. Crockett led a quiet life,
Nobody could be a better wife,
BUT

REFRAIN 1

Who kept the wolves away from the door
When Davy Crockett went to war?
Did wifie sit alone so cute
Or did she find a substitute?
It wasn't old Dave who made goo-goo eyes,
It must have been two other guys.
She used to hold conventions when the ev'ning
  began,
And I was there
And you were there
And so's your old man—BUT
Who kept the wolves away from the door
When Davy Crockett went to war?

REFRAIN 2

Who kept the wolves away from the door
When Davy Crockett went to war?
He wrote no letters on the trail,
But still she got a lot of mail (male).
Blankets were awful scarce, I am told,

But Mrs. Crockett wasn't cold.
The guys who called on Davy's wife were terribly
  tight.
They saved up ev'ry cent
And all they spent was the night! BUT
Who kept the wolves away from the door
When Davy Crockett went to war?

AMERICAN BEAUTY ROSE

Introduced by Edith Meiser in the mini-operetta "The Rose of Arizona."

VERSE

Say it with flowers
If you're falling in love;
I've said it with flowers
To the one I'm dreaming of.
Flowers are pretty the whole world around
But I have just one posy
For the sweetest boy I've found.

REFRAIN

You may long for the bluebells of Scotland,
You may fight for the lilies of France.
I am sure there's no land
Like dear old Holland,
Where tulips are simply immense.
Oh, the orchids grow under the drizzle
Of the rain that is falling in Brazil.
And the poppies replenish
The soil that is Spanish.
The violet in London grows.
The chrysanthemum's Japanese
But you can't compare all these
To the American Beauty Rose!

MEXICO

Introduced in the mini-operetta "The Rose of Arizona" by Jack Edwards and ensemble. Alternate title: "To Hell with Mexico."

VERSE

All you Shriners and Elks and Pythian
  Knights
And Babbitts of low degree,
Just listen to me.
'Cross the border there is a terrible band,

Just over the Rio Grande,
Who threaten our land.
Washington and Mister Lincoln
Give you this command:

REFRAIN

Boys of noble Arizona,
Will you stand for Mexico?
BOYS. NO!
Rich man smoking your Corona,
Even beggar men must go!
Forward, forward to the battle!
Onward, onward to the foe!
Here's to Pershing and to Coolidge,
And to H—! with Mexico!

TENNIS CHAMPS

Introduced by Romney Brent, Edith Meiser, and Philip Loeb. Quite possibly set to same music as "Lillie, Lawrence, and Jack" in *The Fifth Avenue Follies* (1926), page 60. Alternate title: "Helen! Susanne! and Bill!"

TILDEN: I'm Tilden, king of amateurs,
    Who loves to go on drama tours.
LENGLEN: I'm Suzanne Lenglen and I choke
    When my opponent makes a stroke.
WILLS: I don't play to the gallery
    Like good old Mrs. Mallory.
TILDEN: We don't accept a salary
    But none of us is ever broke.
LENGLEN: Miss Wills, your features are piquant as
    The poker face of Pocahontas!

REFRAIN 1

WILLS: Poor little Helen,
LENGLEN: Poor little Suzanne,
TILDEN: Poor little great big Bill!
LENGLEN: My backhand may go back on me
    So tout de suite I am ill!
WILLS: We kiss each other,
TILDEN: Sisters and brother.
LENGLEN: Why can't kisses kill!
WILLS: She's hysteric!
LENGLEN: She's a derrick!
TILDEN: Each of them's a pill!
WILLS: Little Helen,
LENGLEN: Little Suzanne,
TILDEN: Little great big Bill!

TILDEN: Upon the stage like Barrymore
    I don't think I should tarry more.

They paid me well but I am sure
I still remained an amateur.
LENGLEN: Each time I play a double set
    My partner has a trouble set,
    For when my skill can't pull me
        through,
    I'm Mrs. Fiske compared to you.
WILLS: Suzanne, your rep among all men is
    You talk a damn good game of tennis.

REFRAIN 2

WILLS: Poor little Helen,
LENGLEN: Poor little Suzanne,
TILDEN: Poor little great big Bill!
WILLS: It's just your stroke and not your face
    That gives the boys a thrill!
TILDEN: Strictly between us
    Neither's a Venus.
WILLS: You're not a caveman, Will!
LENGLEN: From her photo
    Most men go to
    Doctors with a chill.
    Poor little Helen,
    Poor little Suzanne,
    Poor little great big Bill!

LENGLEN: Each time I play a double set
    My partner has a trouble set.
TILDEN: We pay for nothing that is here,
    We live like monarchs gratis here.
LENGLEN: I got an auto for my craft,
    But honi soit, who calls that graft!
WILLS: It's easy to refuse the dough
    When no one lets you use the dough.
LENGLEN: Though I get pearls, I still am pure,
    That's damn good for an amateur.
WILLS: The way you faint shows your
        condition,
    It's just another inhibition.
    Poor little Helen!
LENGLEN: Poor little Suzanne!
TILDEN: Poor little great big Bill!

FOUR LITTLE SONG PLUGGERS

Introduced by Dorothy Jordan, Betty Starbuck, Gladys Laird, and Bobbie Perkins.

This act was written for us
To popularize a chorus.
There's little chance in a revue
To thematize a song for you.

So here's a happy opportunity
To give the old show unity.
The publisher who prints the stuff
Has told us ever since the stuff
Was printed—he'd be cheated
If it were not repeated.
So while they change the scenery
We'll do the "Mountain Greenery."

WHAT'S THE USE OF TALKING

Published May 1926. Introduced by Betty Starbuck and Sterling Holloway. Also introduced in the London production of *The Girl Friend* (1927) by Flora Le Breton and Bernard Clifton.

VERSE 1

All words are futile,
Mine are so pedantic;
I rave to you till
You are nearly frantic.
Love is ever mute in a dream,
And how highfalutin words seem.

REFRAIN

What's the use of talking,
Let's get acquainted, dear.
Oh, my! You're here, so'm I.
Vocal admiration's
Not all it's painted, dear.
Dancing's what we should try.
The words I can't begin,
You get my intuition.
The chance that you won't feel
My mute appeal is small.
Ev'ry move's a message
Of silent sympathy;
No use talking at all.

VERSE 2

Mere conversation
Never was so chummy;
I felt elation
Almost overcome me.
You were such a bore on a seat,
But how you can score on your feet.

REPEAT REFRAIN

IDLES OF THE KING

Introduced by Romney Brent, Edward Hogan, and Philip Loeb. Later intended for *One Dam Thing After Another* (1927) but dropped before the London opening.

REFRAIN

We're the idles of the King,
And we never do a thing!
We are twelve Knights in a
    barroom
On a medieval fling.
Our shirts can never bust;
When it rains our trousers rust.
Oh, we hate to work but we love
    to sing,
We're the idles of the King!

KING ARTHUR: I'm the host of the famous round
        table:
    Twelve big bums on the European
        plan.
    They eat here but they sleep in the
        stable,
    They're the guys who invented the
        Klan!
    My twelve strong Knights are a
        sturdy lot;
    Each is really like a brother.
    Though some are brave and some
        are not,
    It's six of one and half a dozen of
        the other.
    At my table round, you see,
    It's tea for twelve and twelve for
        tea.
    Though expenses may be large
    I demand no cover charge.
    When some heroes are off to the
        battle
    I find guests in ingenious ways—
    A vacant chair is very rare—
    I sell my seats at Grays.

REPEAT REFRAIN

SIR GALAHAD: I'm so good that I'm nearly
        disgusting;
    I am purer than pasteurized milk.
    All fair ladies are safe in my
        trusting;
    I don't hark to the rustle of silk.
    I've just been psychoanalyzed;
    I'm neither a sister nor a brother.
    It's odd the way I am devised:
    It's six of one and half a dozen of
        the other!

Me and the boyfriends, the boy-
    friends and me,
We go to Arthur's for afternoon
    tea.
Things are looking pretty bad.
Who put the gal in Galahad?
Twelve rough fighting men at the
    same table
Act as though they had come from
    the wilds.
I cannot eat, so I retreat
And run around to Childs!

REPEAT REFRAIN

LAUNCELOT: Just one damsel I never can stick
        to,
    I invented that triangle scene.
    I've been caught in flagrante
        delicto
    And I bat for the King with the
        Queen!
    My song of love to both I sing,
    To both of them I'm dearer than a
        brother.
    God save the Queen! God save the
        King!
    It's six of one and half a dozen of
        the other!
    Guinevere, she's my baby; no, sir,
        don't mean maybe;
    Yes, sir, she's my baby now!
    When the King broke down the
        door
    He found some armor on the floor,
    I'm afraid that he felt a bit
        slighted.
    Poor old Artie was always a fool.
    But I was smart enough to start
    A corespondents' school!

REPEAT REFRAIN

GIGOLO

Introduced by Betty Starbuck. Also introduced by Jessie Matthews in *One Dam Thing After Another* (1927).

VERSE 1

WOMAN: When a matron wants to mate
    Old friend husband gets the gate.
    When your grandma gets her hair cut
    Some young fellow meets his fate.

She selects the sort of beau
That is known as Gigolo.
Sophomores and even Freshmen
Make a little extra dough!

REFRAIN

GIRLS: If you are fat and forty
    You can be just as sporty.
    Look for a young Gigolo!
    Girl friends of Booth and Barrett
    Stay up and guzzle claret
    With boys of twenty or so.
    Diet and weigh yourself,
    Turn your fantastic face
    Into a plastic face,
    Oh, listen to the band, Ma,
    Don't always be a grandma;
    Go get yourself a Gigolo!

VERSE 2

BOYS: Darling, you are growing old,
    Silver threads must pay the gold.
    When I get my weekly wage,
    I forget about your age.
    While you pay the check you'll be to me
    Young and ever fair to see.
    Darling, I can't live without you,
    Silver threads must pay the gold!

REPEAT REFRAIN

QUEEN ELIZABETH

Published June 1926. Introduced by Edith Meiser.

VERSE

I'm Elizabeth, the Virgin Queen.
Don't laugh!
On my title I stand firm,
Though it's just a technical term.
My royal bed was only used by half!
I have never been a prude, or
I had not been born a Tudor.
A royal marriage is a mockery.
A husband's just a piece of crockery!
There's not much I haven't seen.
But I'm still the Virgin Queen!

REFRAIN 1

But even a queen has her moments,
And I see no reason to rue it.

A venial sin
Is no menial sin—
In fact, it's quite a congenial sin,
If nobody sees you do it.
Behind my portal
I am mortal
And the court'll still be blind.*
Though there's urge in
Me to burgeon,
I'm a virgin in my mind.
The rumors you heard about Shakespeare
Are vulgar as they are untrue.
I was his inspiration
To help out the nation,
And one must have a moment or two.

REFRAIN 2

But even a queen has her moments
When regal wild oats need their sowing.
I'd be alone,
Drink my tea alone,
And make England queen of the sea alone,
For sailors are well worth knowing.
All my gallants
Had their talents—
They were balance for my nerves.
When my army
Failed to charm me
I would call out the reserves.
You think Mary Stuart was naughty,
The blonde with the big eyes of blue.
But no royal redhead
Was ever a deadhead,
And one must have a moment or two.

REFRAIN 3

But even a queen has her moments,
Though duty is stern as a Tartar.
A tall he-man
And an all he-man
Was that handsome Sir Walter Raleigh man.
And what a knight—of the Garter!
When 'twas floody
O'er the mud, he
Threw his mantle down for me!
In his shirt, he
Proved a flirt; he
Was more daring vis-à-vis.
They say he discovered tobacco.

Earlier version of refrain 1, lines 9–12:
Then the sport'll quickly start.
Though there's urge in
Me to splurge in
I'm a virgin in my heart.

And I made him smoke, it is true.
For my tresses so titian
Gave him the ignition,
And one must have a moment or two.
Yes, two.

I CALL UPON YOU GENTLEMEN

Introduced by Romney Brent, Edward Hogan, Hardwick Nevin, Jack Edwards, Philip Loeb, Sterling Holloway, and ensemble. Dropped a few weeks after the New York opening. Alternate title: "Finale, Act II."

JUDGE: I call upon you gentlemen,
The operetta's mental men,
To come to a decision
With speed and with precision.
Let the attendant
Fetch the defendant!
Name?
STERLING: *Garrick Gaieties*, 1926.
JUDGE: Your jury is omniscient in
The art that they're proficient in,
And in the art that's musical
Each one of them's a Senator.
The case at hand's revusical.
STERLING: And so's your old progenitor!
ALL: You can't be as good as last year
[*etc.*]
JUDGE: I call upon the jury to discuss
This gentleman who's making such a fuss.
And first we'll hear the noblest of his house,
The king of waltzes—Meister Johann Strauss.
STRAUSS: Ich kann letztes Jahr nicht vergessen,
Nicht vergessen, mein Kind.
Sei lustig und froh unter dessen
Wie der blauen Donau Wind.
Dein kindlich Gemüt ist verloren.
Du bist alter, nicht wahr?
Weil an Broadway du biet
Und kollissen jetzt frisst.
Bist du nicht was du warst letztes Jahr.
JUDGE: W. S. Gilbert and Sir Arthur Sullivan.
When in the Spring the Shuberts get adventury
It takes these boys to get them to the Century.

GILBERT &
SULLIVAN: You are very hard of hearing
Not to notice that the cheering
Was much warmer in the former Anno Domini.
You won't hear the panegyrics
On your music and your lyrics
As you falter on the altar of Melpomene.
All the charm of adolescence
Is departed in senescence.
On the morrow all is sorrow at your bier.
While your enemies will cry "Umph!"
All your relatives will sigh "Umph!"
You cannot repeat the triumph of last year!
JUDGE: Maestro Irving Berlin!
He started poor. It really should elate us
How ragtime can improve one's social status.
BERLIN: You can't be as good, remember?
Just remember last year.
You finished your run in November.
You were finished then for always.
You lost all the sunshine and roses.
It's forever, I fear.
All alone, you'll be all alone,
For you can't be as good as last year.
JUDGE: Now. Let us hear the case for the defense.
STERLING: Witness number one!
[*Incomplete*]

ALLEZ-UP

Added after the New York opening. Introduced by Betty Starbuck, Bobbie Perkins, and Sterling Holloway.

VERSE 1

BETTY: They work us nights,
They work us days,
To give the rubes their circus days.
BOBBIE: With little pay and little leisure
This life affords a lot of pleasure.
STERLING: I stub my toe,
It hurts me so,
But still my happy spirits glow.
BETTY: A motto keeps us in condition,
Preserves our disposition.
STERLING: And if you think our life's the cats,
May your children all be acrobats!

REFRAIN

ALL: We love to holler "Allez-up!"
No matter what we do.
That's why we always rally up
When we're a little blue.
If you throw a violet, a cabbage or an
    egg
We repeat it even though we nearly
    break a leg.
It's taught to ev'ry acrobat
When he's a little pup;
If you begin you
Must continue
Yelling "Allez-up!"

VERSE 2

STERLING: I sprain my back to somersault
And earn a strolling mummer's salt.
BOBBIE: To do a wriggle ev'ry night is
Enough to cause appendicitis.
BETTY: I'm thrown by force
Right off my horse,
But that's a lot of fun of course.
BOBBIE: Though troubles fall on us like manna
We're just as glad as Pollyanna.
STERLING: And if you think our life is fun
You're a measly, mean old bachelor's
    son!

REPEAT REFRAIN

A LITTLE SOUVENIR

Published May 1926. Dropped before the New York opening.

VERSE

In a box of lavender
You've slept for me,
Kept for me,
Her photo!
Dance cards of the ball,
I see that you are here:
Two are here—
In toto!
Here's a little letter
Torn to tatters,
It shatters
And scatters the years.
Boutonniere and glove,
And other matters,
You have not aged at all,
It appears.
You have slept well,
Little trinkets,
Covered with perfume and tears.

REFRAIN

Just a little souvenir
Of another year.
Just a little souvenir
I'll keep forever.
Though I endeavor
To love anew
It tells me ever
There's only you!
Love will always cry to love,
You can't lie to love.
There is no goodbye to love
For us two.
There'll be no gloom again,
My room again
Is filled with April bloom again,
In souvenirs of you!

SOMEBODY SAID

Unused. Also may have been intended for *One Dam Thing After Another* (1927).

VERSE

Ev'rywhere I go you'll see
My baby too.
Strolling in the park,
Struttin' the avenue,
People pass remarks,
But I hear every word;
Here's a few I've overheard:

REFRAIN 1

Somebody said,
"Oh! Take a look at that baby!"
Somebody said,
"Ah! Why, how do you do!"
Somebody said,
"Gee, but she is such a wonderful baby!
Such beautiful hair and eyes and lips!
Too good to be true!"
Somebody said,
"Well, she's a little bit silly!"
Somebody said,
"Sure, nothing up in her head!"
But while they rave, I go tell,
Because I know she's in love with me,
So what do I care what somebody said!

REFRAIN 2

"Oh! Keep away
From that baby!" somebody said.
"No nobody
For you!" somebody said.
I know why,
But I don't want to be catty
When people do this and that and these
And other things too.
Somebody said,
"Say! She hasn't a penny!"
Somebody said,
"Gosh! Must be true what I've read!"
But if you want to know the honest truth,
They're jealous of her flaming youth,
So what do I care what somebody said!

LIDO LADY | 1926

PHYLLIS DARE, AS FAY BLAKE, ON THE STEPS AT THE LIDO SPORTING CLUB.

Tryout: Alhambra Theatre, Bradford, October 4–9, 1926; King's Theatre, Southsea, October 11–16, 1926; Royal Theatre, Leeds, October 18–23, 1926; Royal Theatre, Newcastle, October 25–30, 1926; Empire Theatre, Liverpool, November 1–13, 1926; Palace, Manchester, November 15–27, 1926. London run: Gaiety Theatre, December 1, 1926–July 23, 1927. 259 performances. Music by Richard Rodgers. Lyrics by Lorenz Hart. Produced by Jack Hulbert and Paul Murray. Book by Ronald Jeans, based on the book by Guy Bolton, Bert Kalmar, and Harry Ruby. Earlier titles: *The Lido Lady* and *The Love Champion*. Directed by Jack Hulbert. Costumes mostly by Guy de Gerald and Hoban et Jeanne. Cast, starring Phyllis Dare, Cicely Courtneidge, and Jack Hulbert, included Johnne Clare, Harold French, and Billy Arlington.

For the lyric to "Here in My Arms," see *Dearest Enemy* (1925), page 57.

The lyric to "I Must Be Going" (introduced by Cicely Courtneidge) is missing.

In the New York *Times*, October 17, 1926, Hart wrote:

It occurred to us that we might not be able to reach the British audience with no more than a rudimentary knowledge of what that audience cared to see. We had about five weeks in which to work. Part of that time was devoted to finding out where we were, familiarizing ourselves with places, names, colloquialisms, the popular news topics of the day.

But our task was aided greatly by two factors. London is mad about American music of the lighter sort. And it is refreshed greatly by the American-type shows sprinkled with American locutions. Unfortunately for us, *Lido Lady* is quite as British as *The Girl Friend* is American, so that we had to rely wholly upon what we took to be purely English English.

The extreme friendliness of those with whom we were associated was the other arm upon which we were able to lean. A London musical comedy company does not rush madly through its work. Rehearsals are quite the most leisurely affairs in the world. They are halted each afternoon for tea, and the vibrating energy which distinguishes American preparations for the fateful night is missing. At first we missed the scurrying to and fro, the uncertainty about details, the maddening stretching of working hours into early morning day after day.

But we found that spontaneity of performance was not lessened by the English calmness. We learned, for instance, that instead of two or three weeks' bookings which are consumed by American shows for road tryouts and minor changes, *Lido Lady* had deliberately been given nine weeks. At the end of that period, a producer can know with fair definiteness whether he is to have a London success or not.

It was Miss Courtneidge and Jack Hulbert who took us over to London. They agreed with us that the musical comedy as such is now an American monop-

oly. English musical comedies are too light. Their music is too feathery. The English composer strives to imitate American jazz, and because his feet do not touch American soil, he falls just short. Whether we live in the North or the South, the American Negro's music has influenced us. Lacking that influence, the English musical writer can only echo an echo.

To me it seems that the forte of the English musical show is the revue, of which *By the Way* was a striking example. At the present time, the most typically English, and at the same time the most satisfactory, musical shows of the season in London are Archie de Bear's *R.S.V.P.* and *The Co-Optimists*, both of which fall under that heading.

We tried to inject a bit of humor into *Lido Lady*. It is, of course, a completely European story with the Lido of Venice as its setting. Illustrative, however, of how complete our Anglicanization was is the opening number of *Lido Lady*, based on the utterly British habit of sipping tea.

A CUP OF TEA

Introduced by ensemble. Alternate title: "Lido Lady, Opening."

1ST GROUP: How long will you be here?
Whom did you see here?
Was it an easy crossing?
2ND GROUP: Coming out of Dover,
Almost tipped over;
I nearly died of the tossing!
3RD GROUP: Hello, old dear!
4TH GROUP: Hello, you here?
2ND GROUP: Are you alive yet?
1ST GROUP: Isn't it five yet?
3RD GROUP: Yes, it's time for tea.
ALL: It's time for tea!
Tea. Tea. Hurrah!!

The Briton must have his cup of tea.
He takes it wherever he may be.
He drank it in the land that once
was known as no-man's.
When he's in Rome he doesn't
imitate the Romans.
The Briton in Pekin or in Nome
Remembers it's five o'clock at home.
On Red or on Yellow Sea
Oh, can't any fellow see
The sun never sets on a cup of tea!

In Abyssinia
Or West Virginia

In far Sardinia or Spain,
In Philadelphia
Tea does as well f'ya,
Bootleggers yell f'ya in vain.
Tea has made them hear us,
Cheer us, fear us on the sea.
Tea has always paid us,
Made us brawny, brave and free.
Our aristocracy
And our autocracy
With our democracy agree.
At five o'clock they're invited;
At five-fifteen they're delighted.
That's why our land is united
Over a dish of tea!

YOU'RE ON THE LIDO NOW

Published November 1926. Introduced by Johnne Clare and ensemble.

VERSE

There's a beach outside of Venice
Where they all go in for tennis.
It's called the Lido, there you see dough
Circulating freely.
Girls in bathing suits go by there,
But their feet are always dry there;
And the nymphs who dance with satyrs
Never think of homes and maters.
They're so pally,
It's a bally bacchanale there.
See the serpent feed in
That lovely Eden.

REFRAIN

Out on the beach they're singing to you,
Hot as the sand and blue as the blue.
Don't stop to dress, pajamas will do,
You're on the Lido now.
Out on the beach the saxophones moan;
There is a sax appeal in their tone.
Try to be good, you try it alone,
You're on the Lido now.
When you've been good
More than you should,
One touch of vice
Seems a bit nice.
Drink all the wine they've got in the vats,
Try to forget the wife and the brats.

They'll show you how,
You're on the Lido now.

LIDO LADY

Published October 1926. Introduced by Phyllis Dare and ensemble

VERSE 1

At Lido life is very fast,
And days go past
With such rapidity
That your avidity
Makes you forget the great humidity.
At dawning when the light is dim
You start to swim;
After the wetting up,
You drill at setting up
Before the folks at home are getting up.
And then till late at night-time
We have a bright time
With new steps terpsichorean.
When we have finished dancing
We start romancing
In ways not quite Victorian.

REFRAIN

Keep pace with Lido Lady!
Keep up—she's in the lead!
Each game we play today demands more
    speed.
Wake up before the sunrise,
Take up the chase.
At night you'll see the fun rise
In the race.
If you love Lido Lady
Keep the pace!

VERSE 2

BOYS: At Lido what is known as play
    Means work all day.
SHE: If you adore a rest
    And you implore a rest
    You can go back to London for a rest.
BOYS: A little play won't be amiss;
    Perhaps a kiss.
SHE: So much material,
    For one poor dearie'll
    Make life a most romantic serial.
    We have no time to banter,
    Keep up the canter
    And trot in syncopation time.

BOYS: This racing seems unending
    And we are spending
    A terrible vacation time.

REPEAT REFRAIN

A TINY FLAT NEAR SOHO

Published December 1927. Introduced in *Lido Lady* (1926) by Cicely Courtneidge and Harold French. Under the title "A Little House in Soho" (with a few revised lines) was introduced in *She's My Baby* (1928) by Clifton Webb and Ula Sharon.

VERSE 1

HE: I can't afford, my dear, to build you
    A castle rising from the sea.
    The sight of Lido may have thrilled
        you
    Though it didn't me.
    But we are not Arcadian shepherds;
    We need a place to hang our hat.
    The jungle's nice but full of leopards;
    We need a home, and all that.

REFRAIN 1

HE: Hold on to me and someday you'll see
    We'll have a tiny flat near Soho.
    There'll be no fuss, but for folk like us
    It's quite the only place to go-ho.
    And when the cold and wintry winds
        begin to blow-ho
    Our hearts will glow-ho
    And melt the snow-ho;
    Oh-ho!
    I'd walk on air if we two could share
    A tiny flat near Soho Square.

VERSE 2

SHE: Each little room is four by seven;*
    It's damp inside the house as well.

*Alternate versions of verse 2, lines 1–4:
SHE: I do not want an Alpine chalet
    With majordomos in gold braid.
    And you can do without a valet,
    I without a maid.
        or:
    In Soho near the dear Sicilian,
    The Portuguese, the Turk, the Crete,
    With Argentine and Greek and Chilean
    What a Swagger Street.

The little place that we call Heaven
Will be as hot as Hell!
To hire a servant is so silly,
They stay a day and then they roam.
So while I shop in Piccadilly
You wash the dishes at home.

REFRAIN 2

SHE: Hold on to me and someday you'll see
    We'll have a tiny flat near Soho.
    There'll be no fuss, but for folk like us
    It's quite the only place to go-ho.
    We'll hug and kiss and no one else
        will ever know-ho,
    For lights that glow-ho
    We'll turn quite low-ho,
    Oh-ho!
    I'd walk on air if we two could share
    A tiny flat near Soho Square!

CHORUS INTRODUCING PANTOMIME DANCE

SHE: Hold on to me and each night you'll
        see
    The dinner I will serve in Soho.
[*Mime dance follows, leading into last half of chorus, sung:*]
MILKMAN: I'm just the milkman going on my
        daily tracks-oh.
    To stick to facts-ho,
    You'll soon need Glaxo—
[*She slaps him*]
    Smacks-oh!
BAILIFF: I'm just the bailiff and the rent you'll
        have to show-oh
    Or you will go-oh
    Way off to Bow-ho!
    Oh-ho!

REPRISE FOR FINALE, ACT III

HE: Hold on to me and someday you'll see
    We'll have a tiny flat in Soho.

SHE: Now I'm afraid I'll remain a maid,
    In trousers I'll no longer go-ho.
    You'll pull the splinters from the little
        baby's toe-ho
    While I will go-ho
    To see a show-ho!
    Oh-ho!
    We'll walk on air, for we two will
        share
    A tiny flat near Soho Square.

GOOD OLD HARRY

Introduced by Jack Hulbert, Bobby Comber, Billy Arlington, and ensemble. Alternate title: "Finale, Act I." This version includes a few measures of "Morning Is Midnight," page 85, which was dropped before the London opening.

GIRLS: Good old Harry, you've the proper spirit
And we cheer it.
BOYS: Hurrah! Hurrah!
GIRLS: We know when you once go to it
There is simply nothing to it.
BOYS: Anyone can see you've the pluck to win
When he looks at the length of your
chin.
GIRLS: And without a doubt
You will knock him out.
ALL: You'll send him off to slumber,
He'll fall and won't know why,
Still as a piece of lumber,
Let him lie!

HARRY: Thanks for the ovation,
I deserve it.
My punch is a sensation when I curve it.
For my uppercut gyration
You will hear throughout the nation
Great hurrahs of celebration.
I deserve it.
The other chap will see upon the floor
Great Jupiter and Mars and stars galore.
Morning is midnight
And he'll see the moon.
His break of day will not start,
Let us say, until afternoon.

BLAKE: Good old Harry, you've the proper spirit
And we cheer it.
ALL: Hurrah! Hurrah!
BLAKE: Though you've lots of courage in you
In this life you won't continue.
Death is not so hard if a man is brave
And we'll all come to cry at your grave.
BILL: Goodbye, dear old friend,
Ev'rything must end.
You'll be true to picture life
But you'll soon restrict your life,
With little devils you will roam.
With the late Napoleon
And the great unholy 'un
You'll have a happy little home.

FAY: You've got to go in training.
Each day you'll have to run,
Each day new strength be gaining
Till you've won.
ALL: Start slow and keep on going.
Now, start to race.
Speed up till form you're showing,
Fly through space.
If you love Lido Lady,
Keep the pace!

THE BEAUTY OF ANOTHER DAY

Opening, Act II. Introduced by Jack Hulbert, Phyllis Dare, and ensemble. No music survives. Lyric was found in Guy Bolton's *Lido Lady* script, which is in the Billy Rose Collection of the Lincoln Center Library of the Performing Arts.

Bring back the beauty of another day
When all the world was young and still at play.
And youthful love would sing a roundelay
That was so fond a lay
It filled the earth with mirth.
When lovers reveled in the purple night
Beneath the silver of a starry light,
When mortals roamed at leisure,
Virtue's fairest name was pleasure.
Truth was beauty—love was might.

MY HEART IS SHEBA BOUND

Introduced by Cicely Courtneidge and Jack Hulbert.

VERSE 1

In Jerusalem many years ago
King Solomon had queens enough
To start a musical show.
The Queen of Sheba came to see him one day,
But when she saw his harem
She said, "I'm going away,
Jolly little Solly.
Kiss your melancholy dolly,
Prepare to hear the worst;
Sheba does not thirst
To be your one hundred and first!"

REFRAIN

I'm going way down south
To my home in Sheba,
Back to Uncle Isaac and my old Aunt Reba.
My camel does the Charleston
On the old oasis,
The blues he chases for me.
You've got a hundred wives;
They're a hundred jinxes.
I've seen better faces on my old stone sphinxes!
There are red, red roses hanging round the door,
Little Shebaninnies playing on the floor.
When I go down south
I'm gonna kiss the ground,
'Cause my heart is Sheba bound!

VERSE 2

In Sheba, life is merry as a song!
There is no one-way traffic
And the camels all live long.
They sell you drinks at ev'ry hour, I suppose;
Where ev'ryone's a camel
They don't care when you close.
I know Sheba's map'll
Make me think of old Whitechapel.
Though I look a mess,
I can't stop to dress,
I'm taking the Sheba Express!

PATTER CHORUS

There's a word of just five letters
Starts with M and ends with Y.
Mammy! Mammy!
A word of sixteen letters starts
With X and ends with I.
Mammy! Mammy!
And this one means a unicorn
That hasn't any tail.
Mammy! Mammy!
And this one means a lubricant
You get out of a whale!
Mammy! Mammy!
Take me to your arms, I mean,
Mammy, Mammy, here's your queen!
That's why you hear me say,
"Don't get in my way!"

Earlier version

VERSE 1

The Queen of Sheba bade adieu
To Solomon in sad adieu
And he was not as glad a Jew

When she began to chant:
King Solomon, you're bigamous
And not just twice or trigamous;
A hundred wives is polygamous.
You're just a century plant.
Solly, you are jolly
But my lips must thirst.
I'll never be your precious one hundred and first.
So Sheba lived a single life
Alone and unafraid,
And left these words for ev'ry lovelorn maid:

REFRAIN

Wander, oh wander!
Leave your love yonder.
Abstinence makes the heart grow fonder.
Man is a plaything
You may regret.
A poodle is safer to pet.
Mother Eve had to leave joys when she had 'em.
So beware how you care for your sweet Adam,
    madam.
Better be wary of your young gent;
Familiarity breeds consent!

TRY AGAIN TOMORROW

Published October 1926. Introduced by Cicely Courtneidge and Jack Hulbert. Also introduced in *She's My
Baby* (1928) by Clifton Webb and Ula Sharon.

VERSE 1

Tony was a professor of dance
Who said, "M'dear, you haven't a chance
If you don't practice daily.
That is the only way!"
For ev'ry lesson he was well paid,
So very little progress was made.
Taking his pay
You'd gen'rally hear him say:

REFRAIN

Try again tomorrow:
Where there's a will there's a way.
Steal or beg or borrow,
But take a lesson a day.
If you break an ankle
Don't let it bother you much,
Add a new touch,
Just use a crutch!
Sitting out the dances

While all the others have fun
You'll be losing chances
To cuddle up to someone.
There you nearly had it;
Just keep it up!
Oh gosh, you've lost it now.
Try again tomorrow
And you'll learn how!

VERSE 2

[*This verse was censored by the Lord Chamberlain*]
Tony went out and married one day.
His wife was very pretty and gay,
But there was no dear baby
Coming around their way.
Tony was sad as soon as he found
No stork at all was coming around.
Wifie would say,
"Don't worry about today!"

[*Replacement for the censored version*]
Tony had a pupil to teach,
A blue-eyed blonde, a regular peach,
Who kept her face when dancing
Just out of Tony's reach.
For hours and hours he held her like this
With ev'ry hope of snatching a kiss,
But she'd declare,
When Tony just kissed the air:

REPEAT REFRAIN

VERSE 3

Tony was always ready to say,
"Dancing is never learnt in a day.
Persevere for a while, dear,
If you'd improve your style!"
Sometimes a little pupil would ask
If she had nearly finished her task;
Shaking his head,
In sorrowful tones he said:

REPEAT REFRAIN

DO YOU REALLY MEAN TO GO?

Introduced by principals and ensemble. Alternate title:
"Finale, Act II."

FAY: Do you really mean to go?
    Do you really mean it?
    If you've been brave before
    Then I've never seen it.
    You've always been a stranger
    To all affairs of danger.
    Perhaps you'll have to fight.
    Do you know how to?
HARRY: I vow to!
    I'll show you I won't fail tonight,
    I'm going to do it!
ALL: He's going to do it!
    When he goes to it,
    When he goes to it,
    That pair of crooks is going to rue it!
BILL: Yes, absolutely!
ALL: Yes, absolutely,
    He'll do it cutely.
BILL: He'll do it cutely.
FAY: Harry, suppose I said I didn't want you
        to go?
    You really won't know what to do.
    I wouldn't go if I were you.
SPENCER: Harry—she's right. You'd better stay.
    I'll start this trip alone tonight.
    You'll be in the way.

SPENCER,
BLAKE &
SINCLAIR: Yes, my boy, you oughtn't go.
    There may be more dangers than you
        can know.
    We're fond of you, we're like your
        brothers.
    You'd better leave all this in the hands
        of others.
BILL: Yes, my boy, you oughtn't go.
    You might hurt your finger or stub
        your toe.
    These crooks are smart and while you
        glance off,
    Before you know it, they will steal
        your pants off!
PEGGY: He's going absolutely!
ALL: Yes, absolutely!
    He'll do it cutely!
PEGGY: He'll do it cutely!

PEGGY: We're going way down south to the
        land of Sheba,
    Back to Uncle Isaac and our dear Aunt
        Reba.
    Hear that great big choo-choo with the
        whistle blowing,
    It knows we're going today!
        (Choo-Choo!)
    The Pullman porters wait and their
        faces shine up;

They'll be at the station, a dusky
    lineup.
We'll get off at Sheba with some
    prancing steps,
He'll come back to London with some
    dancing steps,
But we're not coming back till those
    crooks are found.
Harry boy, you're Sheba bound.

FAY: I promised you a kiss; I gave my word,
    I never break it!
    The kiss is yours—if you would take
      it.
    Here in my arms it's adorable,
    It's deplorable that you should want to
      go.
    When little lips are so kissable
    It's permissible . . .

HARRY: You think that you can laugh at me
    But presently you'll see.

FAY: Harry—I really care, I do!
    It's true—I care for you.
    Don't go! I want you here, my dear!
    It's love; it's really the real thing,
    The one ideal thing.
    It's much too splendid to be ended.
    Dear, I've not intended
    To chide you or deride you!
    It's much too splendid to be ended.
    You know I've not intended
    To chide you or deride you!

HARRY: Here in my arms it's adorable,
    It's deplorable that you were never
      there.
    When little lips are so kissable
    It's permissible that I should ask my
      share.
    Next to my heart it is ever so lonely,
    I'm holding only . . .
    I love but you, dear.
    Damn it, I do, dear!
    Here in my arms it's adorable,
    It's deplorable that you were never
      there.
    I love you! I love you! I love you!
    I . . .

Earlier version

CHORUS: Do you really mean to go?
    If you really mean it,
    You'll have a movie show
    And no one to screen it.
    We advise you if you can
    To take a cameraman.

HARRY,
BILL &
SPENCER: Hold on to us
    And you'll quickly see
    Those crooks will very soon lay lo-ho.
    There'll be no fuss,
    But I bet they'll cuss
    The day they made of us a foe-ho.

CHORUS: And if you catch them,
    Will you deal a deathly blow-ho?

HARRY: I'd have you know-ho,
    Their blood will flow-ho.

SPENCER: What will you do
    If they turn on you
    And punch you on the bo-k-ho?

HARRY: I'll try again tomorrow
    If I don't catch them today.

CHORUS: Maybe to your sorrow,
    They both will get clean away.

HARRY: Tho' they flew to Paris,
    It does not worry me much.
    Unless I'm Dutch,
    They'll be in my clutch.

BILL: You must take no chances,
    You'd better borrow my gun.

HARRY: Yes, I know what France is,
    I never move without one.

CHORUS: Don't try to fire it
    Until you get
    Someone to show you how;
    Try again tomorrow,
    But not just now.

PEGGY: Tomorrow, they'll be far away.
    Don't delay, but start today;
    We shall all meet again someday.
    Let us pray,
    But not today.

PEGGY: If our end we want to gain,
    We must cross the Spanish Main,
    So let's hop aboard the train right
      away.
    And we're not coming back
    Till those crooks are found;
    Harry boy, we're Sheba bound.

[Ending as in other version]

WHAT'S THE USE?

Published October 1926. Introduced by Harold French, Phyl Arnold, and ensemble. According to the sheet music cover, this song was introduced by Phyllis Dare. Same music but different lyric used for "Who's That Little Girl?" in *The Fifth Avenue Follies* (1926).

VERSE 1

When two lovers are not in a twosome
Life's gruesome and blue.
Happiness is something that I'm sure'll
Be plural for two.
If there's no one of another gender
For tender delights,
There are pleasures of the day to drink of,
But think of the nights!

REFRAIN 1

What's the use of hands when there's no one to
    hold?
What's the use of hearts if they have to be cold?
What's the use of having very good ears
When nobody tells the story that cheers?
There's no use in having feet, it appears,
With none to run to.
What's the use of lips when there's no one to
    kiss?
What's the use of eyes if they never see bliss?
When the April moon is shining above
And spring begins to give the winter a shove,
What, oh, what's the use if there's no one to
    love?

VERSE 2

Living on without a little teamwork
Will seem work to you.
All the pleasures that the world's afforded
Seem sordid and blue.
When you sing a solo by your ownsome,
So lonesome you get.
Anyone will tell you if you must sing,
Why, just sing duet.

REFRAIN 2

What's the use of arms when there's no one to
    hold?
What's the use of hearts if they have to be cold?
What's the use of any masculine chest
On which no girlie's head comes to rest?
There's no use of having feet, I protest,
With none to run to.
What's the use of eyes when a girl runs away?
What's the use of ears when she's nothing to
    say?
When the April moon is shining above
And spring begins to give the winter a shove,
What, oh, what's the use if there's no one to
    love?

CHERI-BERI

Introduced by Johnne Clare and Billy Arlington. This number almost certainly was "Ciribiribin." It is not by Rodgers and Hart. Written in 1909, it has music by A. Pestalozza and lyric by Rudolf Thaler. It is cued in the script as follows:

BILL: Hello, honey!

PEACHES: You're a nice husband. Here is the first day of our honeymoon, and you spend all day playing that violin. I don't believe you love me.

BILL: Love you. I'm crazy about you. Just give me the right look and you can hypnotize me. You're the kind of girl that could change an old soldier into a Boy Scout. If I could only tell you of my love like the Italians do in the opera.

ATLANTIC BLUES

Published October 1926. Introduced by Phyllis Dare and ensemble. The same music, with a slightly revised lyric, was used for "Blue Ocean Blues" in *Present Arms* (1928).

VERSE 1

The sea is darker than the sky,
I fear each wave as it rolls by,
And the ocean roars with glee
Ev'ry time I sigh.
In all my dreams I never knew
A much more melancholy view.
I'm here, you're there,
And between
All that sea of blue!

REFRAIN

Sailing—I got those weepy wailing Atlantic
  Blues.
Nervous—I got those Lord-preserve-us Atlantic
  Blues.
Ill winds, chill winds creep right under my skin.
While I sleep, troubles keep
Rolling in:
Grieving—I got those lover-leaving Atlantic
  Blues.
Hating—those ever-separating Atlantic Blues.
Oh, that
Woe that
Sends my heart to my shoes!

So that
I got those Atlantic Blues.

VERSE 2

The sea is swelling with my tears.
The wind is sighing with my fears.
All around me nothing but
Sea and sky appears.
The sky is like a hollow dome
Above a rolling sea of foam.
Ocean, turn that ship around,
Make it sail for home!

REPEAT REFRAIN

CAMERA SHOOT

Intended for Jack Hulbert, Cicely Courtneidge, and Billy Arlington. Dropped before the London opening. Introduced by Beatrice Lillie, Clifton Webb, and Jack Whiting in *She's My Baby* (1928). This, the only surviving version, is from *She's My Baby*.

VERSE 1

In each scenario
The young Lothario
Is very muscular
And red-corpuscular.
He's lean,
His hair has sheen
Of Vaseline.
His smile won't have a leer;
He's such a cavalier;
He finds each venial sin
An uncongenial sin.
I mean
He's very clean—
Upon the screen.
Camera shoot!

REFRAIN 1

If you're true to picture life
Nothing can restrict your life;
Far from reality you roam.
He-men who suggest a lot
When they bare their chest a lot
Do fancy needlework at home.
To learn the gentle art of indicating passion
Just lift your eyebrows and the world knows what
  you mean.
In the films they're through with life.

What has *art* to do with life?
We want to glorify the screen!
We want to glorify the screen!

VERSE 2

Our hero's lady love
Can't be a shady love,
And no obscurity
Can mar her purity.
She's chaste,
And she's straight-laced,
I mean her waist.
No man could kiss her in
Her tears of glycerine.
When she gets saccharine
You'd like to smack her in
The bean;
But she's a queen
Upon the screen.
Camera shoot!

REFRAIN 2

If you're true to picture life
Nothing can restrict your life;
Stars have to earn their daily bread.
Girls who in their folly would
Dress like queens in Hollywood
Wear flannel nighties when in bed.
I know a man who writes the stories for the
  pictures,
And when he learns to spell he'll write the
  captions too.
Movie plays dispel a gent's
Hopes of some intelligence.
We'll glorify the screen for you!
We'll glorify the screen for you!

VERSE 3

Just like that fellow Lloyd,
A clown in celluloid,
A fight I'm led into;
They break my head in two
While guys
Throw custard pies
Between my eyes.
My life in seven reels
'Twixt Hell and Heaven reels.
They wipe the floor with me.
While millions roar with me.
It's done
So ev'ryone
Can have his fun.
Camera shoot!

REFRAIN 3

If you're true to picture life
Nothing can restrict your life;
Acting is paramount, of course.
One important factor is
That our greatest actor is
Tony—that's Tommy Mix's horse.
And you don't have to be a Duse or a Bernhardt
If you can turn on your emotions by machine.
Sheiks may be effeminate;
What can you condemn in it?
We want to elevate the screen!
We want to elevate the screen!

I WANT A MAN

Published October 1926. Intended for Johnne Clare and
Billy Arlington. Dropped before the London opening. This
is the second version of the song; for other versions, see
Winkle Town (1922) and *America's Sweetheart* (1931).

VERSE 1

SHE: You must have been good-looking
    And young enough for marriage
    When Bernard Shaw was in his baby
        carriage.
    Your features make the weather
    Get cloudy, dark and rainy;
    In sex appeal you're lower than Lon
        Chaney.
    And your table manners are hardly polite.
    You prove by each bite
    That Darwin was right.
    I'll take you though you're ugly
    And rather more than half fat;
    I've always wanted something good to laugh
        at!

REFRAIN

    I want a man!
    And if he's not so strong
    I'll help along all I can.
    A lonely room is full of gloom;
    I want to hear the sound of snoring at
        night;
    I want a man
    To raise the window and switch off the
        light!

VERSE 2

HE: I confess that I, dear,
    See nothing to admire in

Your voice that's like an ocean liner's siren.
To add to your refinement
Your lips you start to pucker,
Which gives you all the charm of Sophie
    Tucker.
Life on a desert island with you would be
    quaint;
You'd have no complaint,
I'd act like a saint.
In your ideas of authors
You're very often erring;
You think that Kipling is a kind of herring!

REPEAT REFRAIN

EVER-READY FREDDIE

Intended for Cicely Courtneidge and ensemble. Dropped
before the London opening. According to sheet music
covers for several songs from *Lido Lady*, "Ever-Ready
Freddie" was published as a separate number. The editors
have not seen a copy.

VERSE 1

Freddie wasn't diligent
And he was a silly gent,
For he would slay time in the daytime!
All good men should rightly toil;
Freddie worked at nightly toil,
And people tell us that he's zealous.
At his work he always hits the mark
Finding pretty women in the dark.
He's got girls in every section
Of the globe, and his collection
Looks like a Noah's Ark!

REFRAIN 1

Ever-ready Freddie,
Ever working at love.
His daily job he'll always slight
But he does his work at night.
Meets 'em, treats 'em, cheats 'em.
They're so sadly misled.
When Freddie walks into the Cecil
Girls of sixty start to wrestle!
Ever-ready Fred.

VERSE 2

Ladies would come tearing 'cross
Regent Street to Charing Cross,
And try to follow this Apollo.

Freddie turned old Drury Lane
To a female fury lane;
He knew sopranos from Romanos.
He was not domestic in his work,
Not so English; rather like a Turk.
Girls from Cork and Edinburgh
Left their county, bed and borough.
Freddie would never shirk,

REFRAIN 2

Ever-ready Freddie,
Ever working at love.
His daily job he'll always slight
But he does his work at night.
Meets 'em, treats 'em, cheats 'em.
Husbands wish he were dead.
The day that little Freddie ran in
Girls forgot poor Jack Buchanan!
Ever-ready Fred!

EXERCISE

Dropped before the London opening. Intended for Johnne
Clare and female ensemble.

We swim a lot and never get a chill
Because we leave the beach and start to drill.
A girl fat as Venus,
Her neck's her size,
Can't show the opposite sex her size;
Wrecks her size,
For fat bedecks her size,
Checks her size
By exercise!
ONE–TWO–THREE
One and two and three and four and
ONE–TWO–THREE
One and two and three and four and
We swim a lot and never get a chill
Because we leave the beach and start to drill.
A girl as fat as Venus,
Her neck's her size,
Can't show the opposite sex her size;
Wrecks her size,
For fat bedecks her size.

TWO TO ELEVEN

Possibly from *Lido Lady*. Unused.

ALL: We'd like so much to tell you
Of the task we have before us;
We cuties have the duties
Of Euripides' Greek Chorus.
We don't wear bears and togas,
So you ought to have a gay time
While we represent the passing of
The nighttime into daytime.
The moon of which we always sing
In the continental number
Has bid the stars a cheerio
And nods his head in slumber.

1ST GIRL: The revelers are homeward bound
For sleep that's so delectable.
At least, let's say they're going home,
We assume that they're respectable!

2ND GIRL: And now the old gendarme,
Who in Lido has a damp post,
Keeps vigilance for stragglers
And drunkards 'neath each lamppost.

3RD GIRL: The little moths who fly by night
And roll a roguish eye by night,
Their merriment runs high by night
While inwardly they sigh by night.

4TH GIRL: The doctor who has left his bed
At half past three or four
For a lady who has a little
Headache, nothing more.

5TH GIRL: The milkman on his morning walk
With whom all homeward chappies
  talk;
And if it rains before he's through
He'll have more milk to sell to you!

6TH GIRL: The newsman now comes on his way
To bring the scandal of the day;
The hectic loves of Mrs. White
Will give your wife an appetite.

7TH GIRL: And now to work the toilers trail
With pickaxe and with dinner pail.
The office boy and banking clerk
To note the falling of the Mark.

8TH GIRL: The whining schoolboy starts to pace
With egg upon his morning face.
'Tis ten o'clock, the chief goes down
To show the staff his morning frown.

ALL: The wristwatch says eleven
And we must make haste, we're
  thinking,

For the duties of all cuties
Start with early-morning drinking.

MORNING IS MIDNIGHT

Published twice, October 1926 and December 1927. Written for *Lido Lady*, but dropped before the London opening. Later intended for *She's My Baby* (1928) but dropped before the New York opening. Added to the 1964 revival of *I Married an Angel*.

VERSE

When we're a twosome,
Life won't be gruesome,
For we fit as well as two peas in a pod.
I think that night life
Is just the right life,
And the morning is the only time to nod—
The naive all believe in the sun.
When the owl starts to howl,
All the tomcats have fun.
When we're in wedlock,
There'll be no deadlock.
We've adopted a motto
To stay blotto.

REFRAIN

Morning is midnight
And the sun's the moon.
My break of day
Doesn't start, let us say,
Until twelve at noon.
Later to bed
And later still to rise.
Who cares for health
Just as long as he's wealth-
Y and wise.
They say that the early bird will catch the worm.
I prefer a girlie if she doesn't squirm.
Morning will come,
But must it come so soon?
My break of day

Doesn't start, let us say,
Until noon.

Earlier (English) version

VERSE 1

Though I'm no boaster
My old four-poster
Is as well filled as a downy couch can be.
I have a motto
From Aesop:
What, ho!
As a sleeping dog I lie as much as three.
Now the night is all right and all that.*
While you snooze, I just choose
My full rig and top hat.
Nights are for pleasure;
I want full measure:
You can say what you may.
What care I? Eh, what!

REFRAIN (same as above)

VERSE 2

Mornings are many
When great Big Bennie
Strikes the hour of six before I go to bed.
Sleep—I forget it
And don't regret it.
I'll get all the sleep I want when I am dead.
Though you may rightly say I'm a fool,
In return I can learn
Things they don't teach at school.
All of my midnights
Are slip and skid nights.
I forget in the morning
What I did nights.

REPEAT REFRAIN

*Alternate version of verse 1, lines 8–10:
  Through the day I must stay sleeping tight,
  For I meet all the sweet-
  Est of people at night.

OVERLEAF: Helen Ford, Patrick Rafferty, and Lulu McConnell

PEGGY-ANN | 1926

Tryout: Walnut Street Theatre, Philadelphia, December 13–25, 1926. New York run: Vanderbilt Theatre, December 27, 1926–October 29, 1927. 333 performances. Music by Richard Rodgers. Lyrics by Lorenz Hart. Earlier title: *Peggy*. Produced by Lew Fields and Lyle D. Andrews. Book by Herbert Fields, suggested by the musical comedy *Tillie's Nightmare* by Edgar Smith and A. Baldwin Sloane. Directed by Robert Milton. Dances and musical numbers staged by Seymour Felix. Settings by Clark Robinson. Costumes by Mark Mooring. Orchestra under the direction of Roy Webb. Orchestrations by Roy Webb. Cast, starring Helen Ford and Lulu McConnell, included Lester Cole, Betty Starbuck, Edith Meiser, Jack Thompson, and Margaret Breen.

For the lyric to "Maybe, It's Me," see *The Fifth Avenue Follies* (1926), page 60. For "The Pipes of Pansy," see *Dearest Enemy* (1925), page 59.

The lyric to "In His Arms" (introduced by Helen Ford and dropped after New York opening) is missing.

HELLO!

Published August 1927. Introduced by Margaret Breen, Jack Thompson, and ensemble.

VERSE 1

HE: I was as cold as the bear called the polar,
My flame was never fanned,
And since the day that I first cut a molar,
I never held a hand!
But you looked me in the eye,
And my temp'rature went sky-high!
One glance at you and I knew that it looked
As if we two were booked!

REFRAIN

When I met you my love called out
"Hello!"
Did yours shout "Hello!" too?
Something inside me clicked and cried
"How do!"
Yours replied "How do!" too.
I was so excited,
Never stopped to talk,
While my feet invited
Your feet for a walk!
When your heart and my heart beat the
same tattoo,
It is tit for tat too!

VERSE 2

SHE: I guess I once must have done something
awful
And so God gave me you!
Of notes from boys who propose I've a
drawerful,
I've never read them through.
You gave me that sheepish look,
Now I'm studying a cookbook.
Love may be blind, but with pride, I decide
To be a dumbbell's bride!

REPEAT REFRAIN

A TREE IN THE PARK

Published December 1926. Introduced by Helen Ford and Lester Cole.

VERSE 1

When the noisy town
Lets its windows down,
Little slaves are free at night.
Then we'll soon retreat
From the busy street
Till the crowds are out of sight.
There's a rendezvous for lovers
Where we two can play,
Very near your door
In the city's core,
But it seems a million miles away.

REFRAIN

Meet me underneath our little tree in the park,
No one else around but you and me in the dark,
Just five minutes from your doorstep.
I'll wait for your step to come along
And the city's roar becomes a song!
While I'm waiting I discover more in your
charms;
Suddenly I turn around and you're in my arms!
And if there's a moon above you
I'll carve "I love you" upon the bark
Underneath our little tree inside the park.

VERSE 2

We'll make every bough
Shake and wonder how
Two could be so nearly one.
Every blade of grass

Sadly sighs, "Alas."
Grass could never have such fun.
In the desert town's oasis
We'll love 'neath the tree.
It can't be amiss
If two birdies kiss;
We're as good as little birds, aren't we?

REPEAT REFRAIN

HOWDY TO BROADWAY

Published October 1927. Introduced by ensemble. Alternate title: "Howdy, Broadway." For the London production (1927), the title was changed to "Howdy, London."

REFRAIN 1

We're not dressed in sable,
Our clothes bear the label
Of barnyard and stable and hay;
But all of us hired
Young girls were inspired
And got ourselves fired yesterday!
We're gonna go down where
Ladies' backs are bare
And the farm girls all go astray;
Our old clothes are dowdy,
We want to be rowdy,
And so we'll say Howdy to Broadway.

INTERLUDE

No more hangin' round the old barn door,
No more shoppin' in the general store,
No more bonnets that the Sears and Roebucks
sell.
No more slouchin' in a big long skirt,
No more hidin' in a high-neck shirt,
No more flannels that will scratch and make you
swell.
We know we look pretty good in pretty clothes
And so we are gonna get our city clothes.
So we thought it over once or twice.
If we're gonna have a little vice,
We can see it all and still be nice as well,
And how!
Pigsty! Bye-bye!
Broadway! Hey, hey!

REFRAIN 2

Our tootsies are straying
Where music is playing,

We're going cabareting! Hey, hey!
We're glad that we hired
Young girls were inspired
And got ourselves fired yesterday.
[four bars no singing]
And so we'll say Howdy to Broadway!
Our old clothes were dowdy
And now that we're rowdy
We're glad to say Howdy to Broadway!

A LITTLE BIRDIE
TOLD ME SO

Published December 1926. Introduced by Helen Ford.
For the London production (1927), the lyric was rewritten
by Desmond Carter and called "Country Mouse."

VERSE 1

Mother said, "My darling, if you're going to New
    York,
I must tell you of the mysteries of life.
In towns like that, a little friendly visit from the
    stork
Is rather awkward if you're not a wife!
Although he's not invited,
He'll always be delighted
To fly in at a weekend.
Where will that fellow's cheek end?"
But I replied, "I know just what to do, dear,
    while I roam—
I'll simply tell the stork I'm not at home."

REFRAIN 1

How did I come to know
Which way the wind would blow?
A little birdie told me so!
A little word called "yes"
Can make an awful mess.
The answer to "Giddap" is "Whoa."
Don't pity mother Eve, her weakness was
    detestable,
And soon she learned forbidden fruit was
    indigestible!
But how did I find out
What it was all about?
A little birdie told me so!

VERSE 2

When a handsome stranger says, "I think we've
    met before,"
There's more than conversation on his mind.

When he says, "Our souls should meet," just
    show him to the door!
For the meeting that he means is not refined!
He'll say his love is mental,
And very transcendental.
His talk will soon get boorish,
And very ostermoorish.
He will use poetic words that no one
    understands,
And illustrate the meaning with his hands.

REFRAIN 2

How did I come to know
Which way the wind would blow?
A little birdie told me so!
So look before you leap—
The narrow path is steep.
One little push and down you go!
Of very pure young girls I wouldn't say there's
    none that's left—
The well-known statue called Miss Liberty's the
    one that's left!
But purest driven snow
Will sometimes drift, you know.
A little birdie told me so!

CHARMING, CHARMING

Introduced by ensemble. Alternate title: "Store Opening."

SHOPGIRLS: Ain't it lovely in the store?
    Work has compensations;
    Ev'ry minute brings us more
    Cause for jubilations!
    All the customers one sees
    Are so nice and easy to please.
    They don't ask for B.V.D.'s,
    They buy combinations!
GIRLS: Hello, Mrs. Astor! How d'ye do?
1ST LADY: Gee, I'm feelin' swell. How the
    hell are you?
GIRLS: Hello, Queen Marie! We think
    you're a pip!
QUEEN: I'm charmed! Simply charmed!
    Here's a little tip!
GIRLS: Well, this is a pleasure. Hello,
    Mrs. Gould.
3RD LADY: Girls, do you think I'm too heavily
    bejeweled?
GIRLS: Well, of all surprises. Howdy, Mrs.
    Biddle!
4TH LADY: Thank you so much, children. I'm
    as fit as a fiddle.

BOYS & GIRLS: Charming! Charming!
    Ain't it simply charming?
    Ain't we distingué?
    Parlez-vous français?
    Such refinement
    Really is alarming.
    Throwing dough around
    As we go round.
    Merci, s'il vous plaît!

WHERE'S THAT
RAINBOW?

Published December 1926. Introduced by Helen Ford.
Song was originally titled "Where's That Lining?" It
began:

    Where's that lining you hear about?
    Where's that rainbow they cheer about?

When *Peggy-Ann* was trying out in Philadelphia,
"Where's That Rainbow?" was a duet for Helen [Peggy]
Ford and Margaret [Patricia] Breen. In its most recent
published edition, *Rodgers and Hart: A Musical Anthology*
(1984), the song is a boy-girl duet.

VERSE 1

Troubles really are bubbles, they say,
And I'm bubbling over today!
Spring brings roses to people, you see,
But it brings hay fever to me!
If I have ever had luck,
It's bad luck, that's sure.
That Pollyanna stuff, too,
Is tough to endure!

REFRAIN

Where's that rainbow you hear about?
Where's that lining they cheer about?
Where's that love nest,
Where love is king, ever after?
Where's that blue room they sing about?
Where's that sunshine they fling about?
I know morning will come,
But pardon my laughter!
In each scenario
You can depend on the end
Where the lovers agree.
Where's that Lothario?
Where does he roam, with his dome
Vaselined as can be?
It is easy to see all right

Ev'rything's gonna be all right—
Be just dandy for ev'rybody but me.

VERSE 2

Fortune never smiles, but in my case,
It just laughs right in my face.
If I looked for a horseshoe, I s'pose,
It would bop me right in the nose.
My luck will vary surely,
That's purely a curse.
My luck has changed—it's gotten
From rotten to worse!

REPEAT REFRAIN

WEDDING PROCESSION

Introduced by principals and ensemble. Alternate title: "Finale, Act I."

GIRLS: Here's that wedding you hear about,
Here's that torture they cheer about,
Here's the females that hang around as the bridesmaids.
Here's the flowers they sing about,
Here's the rice that they fling about,
Here's the deadly and fearful fate that betides maids.
BOYS: In each scenario you can depend on the end
When the ushers will ush
For that Lothario with their high hats
And their spats and their gloves
And their gush.
ALL: Are we gloomy today? Not we!
We're so happy it's they not we!
It's our duty to spread a lot of mush!
What is this form so sinister?
MINISTER: Tut, tut, I'm just the minister.
Good Lord, I won't know what to preach.
ALL: What is it?
MINISTER: I've forgotten my speech!
Dear children, don't get nervous now,
But I can't conduct the service now.
ALL: Here comes the bride,
Just watch her stride.
Her dress is all wool and it's five yards wide.
PEGGY: It is my wedding day!
ALL: It is, it is, hooray!
But how did you find out
What it was all about?

PEGGY: How did I come to know
Which way the wind would blow?
A little birdie told me so.
My sister could not really make a better match herself,
And if my ma wants more preserves she can go scratch herself,
For wives with wealth like mine
Can sleep till half past nine.
A little birdie told me so.
ALL: Here comes the groom, straight as a broom,
He'd like to fall thru the floor of the room.
MINISTER: I can't go on, I have no speech!
ALL: What'll we do? What'll we do?
MINISTER: I don't know what to preach.
FRED: Here's a speech, take this one.
MINISTER: Fourscore and seven years ago our fathers brought forth on this continent a new nation conceived in liberty and dedicated to the proposition that all men are created equal. We are now engaged in a great civil war,
[*Dolores enters and sprays everyone with poppy seed*]
DOLORES: This is for you—ha-ha.
MINISTER: Testing whether that nation or any nation so conceived and so
DOLORES: And this for you—
MINISTER: Dedicated can long endure. We are met on a
DOLORES: And this for the papa—
PEGGY: Meet me underneath our little tree in the park,
No one else around but you and me in the dark.
Just five—
Where's that rainbow you hear about?
Where's that lining they cheer about?
It is easy to see all right
Ev'rything's gonna be all right—
Be just dandy for ev'rybody but me.

WE PIRATES FROM WEEHAWKEN

Opening, Act II. Introduced by ensemble. For the London production (1927), the title was changed to "We Pirates from Wee Dorkin." Inexplicably, this song is not listed in New York programs for the show.

GUY: Stop!
ALL: What is it?

GUY: A pirate ship!
ALL: A pirate ship!
GUY: I fear that'll spoil my trip.
PIRATES: Hands up! If anyone moves—we'll fire!
GUY: Mine are up!
PIRATES: Hold 'em up higher—we'll search 'em!
SMALL: We're in a pretty pickle.
PIRATES: We sea-hawks are sea-hawkin'
All we-hawks from Weehawken!
We're here to do you dirt—
We'll even steal your shirt!
PEGGY: Stop!
PIRATES: Fee fie fo fum!
We smell the blood of a girl that's dumb.
PEGGY: This is my wedding day!
ALL: It is! It is! Hooray!
PIRATES: We sea-hawks are sea-hawkin'
All we-hawks from Weehawken!
We're here to do you dirt—
We'll even steal your shirt!
PEGGY: Don't be afraid,
I'm just a maid
Who loves to meet an outlaw.
I forgive you—and say
That a good turn a day
Is just about the best Boy Scout law.
PIRATES: Charming! Charming!
Ain't she simply charming!
PEGGY: Ain't we distingué!
PIRATES: Parlez-vous français?
PEGGY: Such refinement really is alarming.
PIRATES: Robbing boats around,
Cutting throats around.
ALL: Merci—s'il vous plaît.
PEGGY: Toodle-oo!
PIRATES: Toodle-oo!
PEGGY: Toodle-oo!

CHUCK IT

Introduced by Jack Thompson and female ensemble. Prepared for publication but not printed (Harms Inc. #7915).

RECITATIVE

FRED: Someday someone leaves you . . .
GIRLS: Hello!
FRED: Chuck it!
GIRLS: Come along and have a drink.
FRED: Oh, let me be, I want to think.
GIRLS: Come on, you temp'ramental man!
FRED: Get out before I forget that I'm a gentleman!
GIRLS: Oh!

FRED: Go!
    Someday someone leaves you . . .
GIRLS: Hello!
FRED: Chuck it!
GIRLS: We want someone to help us shop.
FRED: Get out before I call a cop!
GIRLS: What good is it to sit out here?
FRED: Get out before I begin to throw a fit in
    here!
GIRLS: Oh!
FRED: Go!

VERSE 1

Someday someone leaves you—
Leaves you much more than alone.
Somehow something grieves you
Some way you never had known.
Friends try to talk and ease your care.
It's hard to bear
Each cheerful
Earful.

REFRAIN

FRED: I want to be alone.
    Won't you leave me alone!
    Chuck it! Chuck it!
    You take my fun away.
    Why don't you run away?
    Chuck it! Chuck it!
    Maybe I'd find my long-lost smile
    If you'd subtract yourselves awhile.
    Show me how fast you run a mile
    And chuck it!
    I want to roll my own
    And call my soul my own.
    Stop it! Stop it!
    If you would disappear
    You'd see my bliss appear.
    Drop it! Drop it!
    Give me the gift of solitude;
    All I can do is moan.
    You only grieve me.
    Oh, why don't you leave me alone?

VERSE 2

Why can't I be lonesome?
Friends find some way to appear.
All of us have known some
Time when we want no one near.
For ev'ry friend who sees you sigh
Will always try
To do much
Too much!

REPEAT REFRAIN

I'M SO HUMBLE

Introduced by Helen Ford and Lester Cole. Dropped soon after the New York opening. An earlier title for this song was "Inferiority Complex."

VERSE 1

SHE: I feel like an atom
    In the lowest stratum
    Down below where lava ashes flare to
      smoke!
    You are like a star but
    I'm an old cigar butt
    That the meanest hobo wouldn't dare to
      smoke!
    My talk's nonsense; now and then it
    Sounds like speeches in the Senate.
    When to sleep I go,
    I feel so small and low.
    Someday I will wake and you will see
    There is really nothing left of me!

REFRAIN 1

I'm so humble, I'm so meek,
I just mumble when I speak.
I'm lower than a caterpillar's shoe!
All the world's superior, and I feel inferior,
So pity me, my dearie, or I'm through.
I was born with no great celebration.
Pa said, "Ma, you've ruined my
    reputation!"
But I must be weary or, dreary or, teary or
I wouldn't be inferior to you!

VERSE 2

HE: You're a little goofy,
    I'm a little goofy,
    There is something goofy in the best of us.
    You've a little complex,
    I've a little complex,
    And our inhibitions make a pest of us.
    Though I know I may be worse'n
    Any other crazy person,
    When in dreams I glide
    I feel subconscious pride.
    Some night I will wake right up by chance
    And kick my old subconscious in the pants!

REFRAIN 2

I'm not yellow, I'm not meek,
I just bellow when I speak!
I only walk upon Fifth Avenue.
I'm audacious, I'm so proud,

I'm loquacious in a crowd!
My chest expansion's big enough for two!
I was born and said with baby punches,
"Mother, serve me one of your best
    lunches!"
I am never weary or, dreary or, teary or
I wouldn't be superior to you!

HAVANA

Introduced by Margaret Breen, Jack Thompson, and ensemble. Alternate title: "Havana Opening."

VERSE

Cuba once laughed at
Old Broadway and chaffed at
Our dances with glances of doubt!
Beating the tango
And eating the mango
They'd kid us and bid us "Keep out!"
Till a lady came along,
Her name was Anna.
With the rhythm of a song,
She won Havana.

REFRAIN

Anna came to Havana,
She's Anastasia now,
No town is crazier now.
She took the tango and made it hot!
Cuba has no more tuba,
They play a saxophone now.
Nobody lacks a phone now
To call up Anna!
She thrilled 'em all
And filled 'em all
With oil they call banana!
She'd say, "Señor,
Hay, hay, señor!
Don't let it get cold!"
Anna is in Havana.
The boys don't hurry at all,
They have no worry at all,
They just have Anna!

GIVE THIS LITTLE GIRL A HAND

Published October 1927. Introduced by Lulu McConnell and ensemble. Alternate title: "Give That Little Girl a Hand."

INTRODUCTION

Hello! Hello! Hello!
We're here to say "hello."
For all that we girls know
Is how to say "hello."
Hello, you'll find this nightclub
Will really be the right club.
We'll go start the show
With "hello, hello, hello!"

VERSE

A nightclub hostess is one of those dames
Whose natural father was old Jesse James.
You may be a doctor, a lawyer or a yegg man
But when the hostess grabs you, you're a butter
     and egg man.
She will proudly bring to you
Little girls who sing to you,
Who won't mean a thing to you. Well,
They must have champagne
And some more chow mein
When the hostess starts to yell:
Oh, won't you

REFRAIN 1

Give this little girl a hand!
Ain't she pretty, ain't she sweet?
Biggest eyes in all the land.
Ain't she got the cutest feet?
She reads her Bible every night at curfew's knell,
A brand-new Bible at a different hotel.
Ain't her modesty just grand?
Come on, girlie, shake that thing.
She's a girl who loves her outdoor life.
She walks up and down between the Astor and
     the Strand,
Won't you give this little girl a hand?

REFRAIN 2

Give this little girl a hand!
Ain't she stately, ain't she trim?
Out at Long Beach on the sand,
She won't have to learn to swim.
She's fond of children, and she's got the cutest
     babe;

Why she acquired six before she married Abe.
She can dance to beat the band.
Ain't you clumsy? Lift them feet.
She has got that certain great appeal,
But her great supply can never meet the great
     demand.
Won't you give this little girl a hand!

REFRAIN 3

Give this little girl a hand!
Ain't she clumsy, ain't she fat?
She's too young to understand.
Get to work, you little cat.
She's so naive, that's why she's never very bored.
She's just a kid who went to school with Fannie
     Ward.
She can lift a baby grand.
Come, Big Bertha, shoot the works!
Maybe she's Lon Chaney in disguise.
If Benda made the mask she wears,
Then Benda should be canned.
Won't you give this little girl a hand?

Earlier version

VERSE

A nightclub hostess, without any aid,
Could teach Dick Turpin the tricks of his trade.
You may have a million, but by the time you
     leave her
You'll have to ask the way to the Official
     Receiver.
She will proudly bring to you
Little girls who sing to you.
They don't mean a thing to you—
Well—
They will make it plain
That they need champagne
While the hostess starts to yell:
Oh! won't you—

REFRAIN 1

Give this little girl a hand!
What a mover! Watch her feet!
Biggest eyes in all the land.
Could you find one half as sweet?
She likes this life because it gives her lots of
     scope.
That's not a wedding ring—it's just a Band of
     Hope.
Modesty like that is grand.
Come on, dearie, show them how.
She's a girl who loves an outdoor life.

In all sorts of weather she walks up and down
     the strand.
Won't you give this little girl a hand?

REFRAIN 2

Give this little girl a hand!
What an ankle! What a knee!
She's no need of monkey gland.
Ask her out one day and see.
She's so affectionate she loves with all her might.
How *does* she find time for her Amami night?
She can dance to beat the band.
Don't be clumsy! Pick 'em up.
She has got a lot of sex appeal.
She's the only reason sailors ever come on land.
Won't you give this little girl a hand?

REFRAIN 3

Give this little girl a hand!
What a picture! Look at that!
She's too young to understand.
Buy yourself some anti-fat.
She's very simple and that's why she's never
     bored.
She's just a kid who went to school with Fannie
     Ward.
She could lift a baby grand.
Come, Big Bertha, let it go!
Maybe she's Lon Chaney in disguise.
If Benda made that mask she wears,
Then Benda should be banned.
Won't you give this little girl a hand?

PEGGY, PEGGY

Introduced by Helen Ford and ensemble. Alternate titles: "Peggy," "Oh, You Peggy," and "The Race." Not listed in programs until a few weeks after the New York opening.

VERSE

They're off!
They're starting in to gallop,
They're starting in to gallop
Ahead!
You've got to beat them, Peggy!
You've got to beat them, Peggy!
Keep up!
You've got to win the money!
You've got to win the money!
Come on!
Come on!

REFRAIN

Peggy, Peggy, Peggy, Peggy,
Go ahead and fly.
Peggy, Peggy, Peggy, Peggy,
Hit 'em in the eye!
On a trot she goes
Leading by a nose.
Come on, filly, knock 'em silly.
Oh, you Peggy!
Peggy, Peggy, Peggy, Peggy,
Go and take the lead.
Peggy, Peggy, Peggy, Peggy,
Show a little speed!
Come on, honey,
Win that money.
Oh, you Peggy!
Peggy, Peggy, go and shake a leg.
Sally's ahead,
Bess is second.
Damn! Where's Peggy?
There she goes!
She's passing, she's passing.
Go it, Peggy, go on!
Speed up, step on the gas!
She's second!
Pass her, Peggy, pass her.
There she goes.
Oh, you Peggy!
Hop it, Peg, and shake a leg.
Come on, come on through!
You'll win it by a mile.
Begin to show your style.
[*Cheer*]
Peggy, Peggy, go and shake a leg!

Earlier version

VERSE

They're off!
Gotta do the washing.
Gotta do the washing.
Keep up!
Gotta can the peaches.
Gotta can the peaches.
Ahead!
Gotta do the scrubbing.
Gotta do the scrubbing.
Peggy! . . . Peggy!

REFRAIN

Peggy, Peggy, Peggy, Peggy!
Everybody roars.
Peggy, Peggy, Peggy, Peggy!
Got to do the chores.

On a trot she goes
Leading by a nose!
Go on, honey,
Win that money.
Oh, you Peggy!
Peggy, Peggy, Peggy, Peggy!
Go ahead and dash.
Peggy, Peggy, Peggy, Peggy!
Chop tomorrow's hash!
Go on, filly,
Knock 'em silly.
Come on, Peggy,
Peggy, Peggy,
Go and shake a leg!

COME AND TELL ME

Published December 1926. Sung in the pre–New York tryout by Helen Ford and Lester Cole. Dropped before the New York opening. Later intended for *Betsy* (1926), and again dropped before the New York opening, although it remains in the Act One finale (see page 97). Alternate title: "Tell Me." Since Guy and Peggy, who are principals of *Peggy-Ann*, appear as the singers on the sheet music, "Come and Tell Me" was almost certainly written for *Peggy-Ann*.

VERSE 1

I've a most obliging nature,
Doing favors is my fun!
All you have to do is state your
Slightest wish and it is done.
You'll always find me ready,
And glad to help you out,
So let me be your steady
And shout:
"Boy Scout!"

REFRAIN

If you want someone to run down
To your parlor after sundown,
Only come and tell me.
If you feel you need a tender
Person of the other gender,
Only come and tell me.
If you're blue and sobby
What a help I'll be;
You can play some hobby
Horsy on my knee.
If you're open to suggestion
On life's most important question,
Just come and tell it to me.

VERSE 2

Sentimental though the phrase is,
All you ask of me I'll do.
If you tell me, "Go to blazes!"
I'll trot right along for you!
No obstacles surmount one
If helpful one would be;
You only have to count "One
Two three"
To me!

REPEAT REFRAIN

PARIS IS REALLY DIVINE

Dropped before the New York opening. Intended for and sung in Philadelphia tryout by Helen Ford, Betty Starbuck, Edith Meiser, Margaret Breen, and Lulu McConnell. Introduced in *One Dam Thing After Another* (1927) by Sonnie Hale.

VERSE 1

PEGGY: When it's June in South Dakota
Mrs. Jones is on a boat a-
Float on the waves of the sea.
As seasick and wet as can be.
MRS. FROST: In Manhattan Mrs. Harris
Simply has to go to Paris.
She has to stick to her plan
And sail on the *Leviathan*!
DOLORES: Paris is the merry Mecca of the
route.
They enjoy themselves no doubt.
That is why they always shout:

REFRAIN 1

ALL: Paris is really divine!
Their hospitality
Is very fine.
When you arrive they kiss you
quick.
With great formality,
They throw a brick!
PEGGY: They say "Merci beaucoup" and
"S'il vous plaît."
That means one thing to you,
You've got to pay! Pay! Pay!
ALICE: They know us Yankees at a glance
Because we all sing
ALL: Vive la France!

VERSE 2

DOLORES: French revues that we adore so
Glorify the Paris torso.

ALICE: Shows here are nude too, we know,
But French girls have much more to
show.

PAT: Mrs. Jones says, "Only fawncy,
Even children parlez francey!"

PEGGY: One boy called out as he ran,
"A bas les Américaines!"

MRS. FROST: On the trail of Yankee dollars some
are bent.
Others have more sentiment.
They will even take a cent!

REFRAIN 2

ALICE: Paris will thrill you when you walk
As you hear them in so-
Cialistic talk!

PEGGY: But for a dollar bill in France
They'll strip old Clemenceau
And make him dance!

MRS. FROST: They show the slums to you,
Dear old Montmartre.
They show some bums to you
And call it art!

ALL: Art! Art!
Their only art is high finance.
It costs a lot to Vive la France!

TRAMPIN' ALONG

Introduced in Philadelphia tryout by ensemble. Dropped before the New York opening. Replaced by "Howdy to Broadway," which has some of the lines in the patter of "Trampin' Along."

REFRAIN 1

Trampin' along! Singin' a song!
None of us worryin'!
What's the use of hurryin'?
Hay foot! Straw foot! And slow!
Hittin' the trail! Swingin' the pail!
Each in her Easter dress
Hopes she hasn't creased her dress!
Sing high! Sing low! Heigh-ho! Oh Lord!
We're so tired of life upon the farm!
Though above the city there is no Lord!
Just a little sin will do no harm;
We're emancipated!
Trampin' along! Singin' a song!
Dressed in our drab array,
Want to see a cabaret!
Hay foot! Straw foot! Let's go!

PATTER

No more standin' round the old barn door!
No more shoppin' in the general store!

Home ev'ry night meant
Sleepin' at nine.
We want excitement,
Cocktails and wine!
We're going down
To New York town!
Pigsty! Bye-bye!
Broadway! Hey, Hey!

REFRAIN 2

Trottin' our feet! Singin' off beat!
Doing the shivaree,
With a jazz delivery.
Hay foot! Straw foot! Hot toes!
Dancin' on dimes! Bumpin' at times!
We were so serious!
Now we'll be delirious!
Shake this! Shake that! Here goes! Hey! Hey!
Being rural hasn't any charm.
All day we used to mow and weigh hay.
Life is much too simple on the farm!
We're not narrow-minded!
Trottin' our feet! Singin' off beat!
Wriggle high! Wriggle low!
Get yourself a gigolo.
Shake this! Shake that! Shake those!

OVERLEAF: Belle Baker and Jimmy Hussey

BETSY | 1926

Tryout: National Theatre, Washington, D.C., December 20–25, 1926. New York run: New Amsterdam Theatre, December 28, 1926–January 29, 1927. 39 performances. Music by Richard Rodgers. Lyrics by Lorenz Hart. Entire production produced under the personal direction of Florenz Ziegfeld. Book by Irving Caesar and David Freedman, revised by William Anthony McGuire. Earlier titles: *Buy Buy Betty* and *Betsy Kitzel.* Book staged by William Anthony McGuire. Musical numbers and dances staged by Sammy Lee. Settings by Frank E. Gates and E. A. Morange, Bergman Studios, and Joseph Urban. Costumes by Charles LeMaire. Orchestra under the direction of Victor Baravalle. Cast, starring Belle Baker, included Al Shean, Jimmy Hussey, Bobbie Perkins, Dan Healy, Allen Kearns, Madeleine Cameron, Barbara Newberry, Evelyn Law, and Borrah Minevitch's Harmonica Symphony Orchestra.

For the lyric to "Come and Tell Me," see *Peggy-Ann* (1926), page 92.

The following lyrics are missing: "In Our Parlor on the Third Floor Back" (introduced by Bobbie Perkins and Allen Kearns), "Follow On" (introduced by ensemble), "Push Around" (introduced by Belle Baker), "In Variety" (dropped before the New York opening), and "Show Me How to Make Love" (dropped before the New York opening).

THE KITZEL ENGAGEMENT

Introduced by Al Shean, Madeleine Cameron, Jimmy Hussey, Evelyn Law, Ralph Whitehead, Barbara Newberry, Dan Healy, and ensemble.

MOSKOWITZ: I'm going to say what's on my mind!
CHORUS: He's going to speak. Hooray!
LEVI: He's going to say what's on his mind;
That means that he has nothing to say.
MOSKOWITZ: I'll only use the simplest words;
I'll never talk above your heads.
CHORUS: He'll only use the simplest words;
He'll never talk above our heads.
MOSKOWITZ: Not in mood satiric,
But with salutations lyric,
I invoke my panegyric in this fashion;
With afflatus amatory,
I indite a category
To the glory of pure passion—
To purest passion's glory.
LEVI: Passion? Is this a bedtime story?
We don't understand your language,
But we know it isn't pleasant.

Passion is a dirty word,
And there are ladies present.
It's all right in society, I'm sure,
But we are poor but sure.
MOSKOWITZ: Three brothers who knew what to earn a daily wage meant
Tonight with three ladies make public their engagement;
The girls are wealthy and refined,
But that's a thing you shouldn't mind.
CHORUS: We see we'll have to be resigned.
They don't come from the settlement,
Never knew what a pot or a kettle meant.
LEVI: Never knew what to make their own bettel meant.
CHORUS: But they're welcome to the settlement.
MOSKOWITZ: I arranged the affair
And I want you to share
In their pleasure.
The three boys belong
In your settlement throng.
They're a treasure.
Joseph Kitzel!
CHORUS: Hurray for Joseph.
MOSKOWITZ: Miss Flora Dale, his fiancée!
CHORUS: Hurray.
MOSKOWITZ: Miss Winnie Hill is another;
She'll plight her troth with Joseph's brother.
CHORUS: Miss Dale and Miss Hill
You give us a thrill.
LEVI: The Kitzels won't fail
On hill and on dale.
MOSKOWITZ: Miss Meadow, a lady of fashion,
For Moe Kitzel has plighted her passion
[*Winnie kisses Levi*]
CHORUS: She kissed him!
LEVI: Is dis a system?
When I change your name to Kitzel
I will never wet my Witzel.
The other girls I ritz'll
Wish that Kitzel would be free.
Why should you care a bitzel?
The wedding ring that fits'll
Make you glad; and time that flits'll
Find you making Wiener schnitzel.
When you are Mrs. Kitzel
How happy we will be.
[*Above repeated by all*]
ALL: The girls are new to the settlement;
Never knew what a pot or a kettle meant.
But the boys have shown what their mettle meant.

It's a great big night in the settlement.

MY MISSUS

Introduced by Evelyn Law, Ralph Whitehead, and Barbara Newberry.

VERSE 1

WINNIE: Your ring is sweet.
The diamond's a divine stone.
LEVI: It can't be beat,
The very finest rhinestone!
JOSEPH: I'm so delighted
You've named the date!
FLORA: I'm so excited
I can hardly wait!
WINNIE: When your bride will kiss your friends
LEVI: That is where the friendship ends!
WINNIE &
FLORA: Be good to me
And you can make it known, dear,
Your own, dear,
Alone, dear,
I'll be!

REFRAIN

LEVI: My missus! My missus!
Look, this is she!
When Mister first kissed her,
That's history!
You know the joys I feel inside
To show the boys my blushing bride.
My missus! My missus!
Look, this is she!

VERSE 2

WINNIE: The clothes I wear
Will cost a lot—oh, rather!
LEVI: What do I care?
I'll get it from your father!
JOSEPH: To end each quarrel
A kiss we plan!
FLORA: It's quite immoral
How I adore my man!
WINNIE: Children cost a lot to mind.
LEVI: You'll have none; you're too refined.
JOSEPH &
LEVI: No drinks for me,
You'll never find your paw full,

It's awful
How lawful
I'll be!

REPEAT REFRAIN

STONEWALL MOSKOWITZ MARCH

Published December 1926. Lyric by Lorenz Hart and Irving Caesar. Introduced by Al Shean and ensemble. Irving Caesar told the editors in May 1985: "Larry and I worked on this song together."

My name is Stonewall Moskowitz.
It might be Bertram Boskowitz
And it might be Irwin Iskowitz
But please remember thiskowitz
That I give the people joykowitz,
For I love the hoi-polloikowitz.
I can mingle with a goykowitz.
I'm a Yankee-Doodle boykowitz.
Am I wise and am I wily?
Can I work just like a horse?
Do I live the life of Riley?
Why, of course, of course, of course, of course,
Of course, of course, of course.
But in spite of my great namekowitz
I am still the very samekowitz
As I was when I first camekowitz
Straight from Moscow just plain Moskowitz.

BOYS: His name is Stonewall Moskowitz.
It might be Bertram Boskowitz
And it might be Irwin Iskowitz
But please remember thiskowitz
That he gives the people joykowitz,
For he loves the hoi-polloikowitz.
He can mingle with a goykowitz.
He's a Yankee-Doodle boykowitz.
Is he wise and is he wily?
Can he work just like a horse?
Does he live the life of Riley?
Why, absolutely, positively, naturally of
course!
But in spite of his great namekowitz
He is still the very samekowitz
As when first he came to uskowitz
Straight from Moscow just plain Moskowitz.

. . .

My name is Stonewall Moskowitz.
I'm no Doctor of Philoskowitz.
I've got money in my bankowitz.
I'm as good as any mankowitz.
I'm a sport who never quitskowitz,
Who just tritz and tritz and tritzkowitz.
When I tip I give two-bitzkowitz.
I take dinner at the Ritzkowitz.
Do I go with fire-escapers?
And am I a man of force?
Have I got my second papers?
Why, absolutely, positively, naturally of
course.
I have ruled the social gamekowitz.
I've appealed to each great Damekowitz
From the day that I first camekowitz
Straight from Moscow as plain Moskowitz.

ONE OF US SHOULD BE TWO

Introduced by Madeleine Cameron, Evelyn Law, Bobbie Perkins, and Barbara Newberry.

VERSE

RUTH: Oh, can't we find a man for Betsy?
WINNIE: And I'll tell the man she gets he
Shouldn't tarry
But go marry
Right away, too!
MAY: It isn't fair to keep us waiting.
FLORA: There's no sense procrastinating.
While delaying
We're decaying
Day by day, too!
RUTH: If we stay single
Another year
We'll never wed, I fear!

REFRAIN

WINNIE: One of us should be two;
WINNIE &
RUTH: Two of us should be four;
WINNIE,
RUTH &
FLORA: Three of us should be six;
ALL: Four of us should be eight.
It seems like fate
That we've nobody to love.
We're only four!
WINNIE: One of us feels so blue;

WINNIE &
RUTH: Two of us feel so sore;
WINNIE,
RUTH &
FLORA: Three of us hate our fix;
ALL: Four of us loudly state
We want to mate
But we've nobody to love.
This lonely four!
A lover's joy, a lover's bliss
Is often said to hurt you.
Without a boy you cannot kiss
And that explains our virtue!
One of us should be two;
Two of us should be four;
Three of us should be six;
Four of us should be eight.
It seems like fate
That we've nobody to love!

SING

Published twice, December 1926 with *Betsy* and again in February 1929 with *Lady Fingers*. Introduced in *Betsy* by Belle Baker, Allen Kearns, and ensemble. Introduced in the English show *Lady Luck* (1927) by Cyril Ritchard, Laddie Cliff, and Leslie Henson. Introduced in *Lady Fingers* (1929) by Dorothy and Margaret McCarthy, and later during the run of the show by Marjorie White.

VERSE 1

You don't need a silver lining
Or a sun that's always shining
When your chin is dragging on your knee.
When your castles fall together,
You don't care about the weather
Or how bluish blue the sky may be.
Here is something to preserve us
From nervous despair,
Something that will always swerve us from care.

REFRAIN

When you are blue, sing;
Be sure you do sing;
I'm telling you sing something!
Start in to hum that dumb thing,
"Ta-ra-ta-ra sing boom!"
Don't be a killjoy
While there is still joy;
You need a li'l joy in you.
When you begin, continue
"Ta-ra-ta-ra sing boom!"

Worry and doubt will pay nowhere,
Sing all your cares away.
Look at the birds, do they know where
They'll get a meal today?
Sing to your mother,
Sing to your brother,
You have no other choice left,
And when you have no voice left,
"Ta-ra-ta-ra sing BUM!"

VERSE 2

Ev'ry bird and beast would follow
That young fellow called Apollo,
For they liked to listen to his song.
That's the reason young Italians
Eat the fruit that we call scallions,
For they want to make their voices strong.
Ev'ry simple country yokel
Is vocal at night
When he wants to woo his local delight.

REPEAT REFRAIN

THIS FUNNY WORLD

Published December 1926. Introduced by Belle Baker.

VERSE

A mop! A broom! A pail!
The stuff my dreams are made of!
You hope, you strive, you fail!
The world's a place you're not afraid of.
But soon you are brought down to earth,
And you learn what your dream was worth.

REFRAIN

This funny world
Makes fun of the things that you strive for.
This funny world
Can laugh at the dreams you're alive for.
If you're beaten, conceal it!
There's no pity for you.
For the world cannot feel it.
Just keep to yourself.
Weep to yourself.
This funny world
Can turn right around and forget you.
It's always sure
To roll right along when you're through.
If you are broke you shouldn't mind.

It's all a joke, for you will find
This funny world is making fun of you.

BUGLE BLOW

Introduced by Madeleine Cameron and ensemble.

VERSE

We've a race that's het'rogeneous
With folks from all the earth.
A moving picture Metro genius
Can come from foreign birth.
And the race that used to be gypped
By the Pharaohs down in Egypt
By the gross appear,
And we're mighty glad they're here.
All were diff'rent when they came,
But jazz has made them all the same!

REFRAIN

Bugle blow with a jazzy "Hello,"
We take them all and fix 'em up
And mix 'em up in jazztime!
We're all good Americans now!
Jazz band play, let the saxophones say
How do
To you.
Go wake yourself
And shake yourself in jazztime!
We're all good Americans now!
They take their places upon the dance floor,
And then races all blend somehow!
Go and show the drum how!
Each one croons just American tunes,
The ones that they recall are jazz.
We all are jazz relations!
We're all good Americans now!

PATTER

First we got the jazz;
Then you got the jazz;
All God's chillun got jazz!
Ev'ry time you hear a spiritual
With a fox-trot you will queer it, you'll
Cop it!
And once you start you'll never stop it.
Black Bottom may mean a river
That's colored by the mud!
But if a river can do that shiver
It must have Negro blood!
For it's the Niger! The Niger!
South African Tiger!

First we got jazz;
Then you got the jazz;
All God's chillun—Black, White—
Got their jazz!

I GUESS I SHOULD BE SATISFIED

Introduced by principals and ensemble. Alternate title: "Finale, Act I."

BETSY: I guess I should be satisfied
That any man should care for me,
That any man should call.
I guess I should be overjoyed
That any man is there for me,
Just any man at all.
WINNIE: I'm sure you should be very grateful.
ARCHIE: I guess you think the thing I did is
hateful.
Somehow I thought it was my duty
To give you a glance at a moment of
beauty.
BETSY: Please go. No doubt you all think it's
funny.
Well, laugh all you like.
RUTH: Well—Mr. Hascomb, why don't you
go?
ARCHIE: If you want someone to run down
To your parlor after sundown,
Only come and tell me.
If you feel you need a tender
Person of the other gender,
Only come and tell me.
RUTH: Now I see you're just like all the
other men
And I never want to see your face
again.
ARCHIE
(TO RUTH): No one seems to understand me.
If you need me—please command
me,
Just come and tell it to me.
RUTH: Please go. I don't want you to stay.
[Breaks down]
BETSY: Ruth. What is it, dear?
RUTH: Nothing. Let me alone.
[Breaks away]
BETSY: You love him! I didn't know!
You love him, and I made him go!
WINNIE,
FLORA
& MAY: Yes—you see what you did

97

With your vulgar display.
You've sent the only nice man
  around here away.

WINNIE: He wanted to give you a glance at
  romance,
  To give you the chance!

LOUIS: And I gave him the pants!

WINNIE: You know you should be satisfied
  That any man should care for you,
  That any man should call.

BETSY: It's all your fault!
  You wanted to get married in a
    hurry.

WINNIE,
FLORA
& MAY: We're going home.
  The kind of man you got is not our
    worry.

BETSY: Ruthie—darling! I did this to you—
  And you love him, I'm so sorry!

LOUIS: Wait a minute! Don't be sorry for Ruth.
  Be sorry for us. Our girls are leaving us
  —and all on account of you. Why did
  we go to all this trouble?

BETSY: So! You were trying to make me a man
  to order. You washed him and scrubbed
  him and put some clean rags on him
  and you called him "brother-in-law."
  Well, let me tell you right now—I'm
  never going to marry.

WINNIE: What! She's never going to marry!

JOE & MOE: Never going to marry?

LOUIS: We should remain old maids? Think of
  all this manhood that's going to waste.

WINNIE
(TO LOUIS): Well—there's only one thing left to do.
  Here's your ring!

LOUIS: Wait a minute! What did I do?

WINNIE: I'm through!

FLORA
(TO JOE): And I too!

[Gives him bracelet]

JOE: What did I do?

MAY
(TO MOE): As for you—adieu!

RUTH: Betsy—I'm sorry. Nobody thought of
  your feelings. We forgot all about you.

BETSY: This funny world [etc., last half only]

[Enter carnival crowd]

MOSKOWITZ: Stop! Why don't you people go away!
  Can't you see you're in the way here?

LOUIS: Wait a minute! They're customers!
  And customers are going to stay
    here!
  Don't cry. Ruthie, everyone sees ya!
  Frankfurters, ice cream and a bottle
    of magnesia!

MOSKOWITZ: Stop! Please!

[Music stops]

RUTH: Betsy dear, I'm so sorry for you.

BETSY: Why be sorry? There's just one thing
  to do:
  When you are blue, sing! [etc.]

CRADLE OF THE DEEP

Introduced by Evelyn Law and ensemble.

Flying in the air
Gives me a scare,
Raises my hair.
Sailing on a yacht
Somehow is not
Awfully hot.
As for limousines,
I haven't used them since my teens.
I've something new to do,
Something for you to do
If you know your beans:

Rock me in the cradle of deep-sea billows;
Waves are pillows, dear.
We'll make all the ocean ripple with our joy.
Boy! Ship ahoy!
Ev'ry little turtle will leave its puddle
When we huddle near.
When we're kissing we'll hide
Deep down inside
Until we disappear.
Fishes of today
Never think that love is sinful.
Hear them shout "Hurray!"
Fish, you went and said a finful!
Ocean may be roaring and wind may blow too,
But I'll go to sleep
If you rock me in the cradle of the deep!

Rock'd in the cradle of the deep
Upon twin waves we'll try to sleep.
If you are not the kind that clings
You must swim home on your water wings!
And when we're far enough from home
We'll park a little on the foam.
I fear we'll have no time to sleep
Rock'd in the cradle of the deep!

IF I WERE YOU

Published December 1926. Introduced by Bobbie Perkins and Allen Kearns. Also introduced in the London musical *Lady Luck* (1927) by Phyllis Monkman and Leslie Henson, and in *She's My Baby* (1928) by Irene Dunne and Jack Whiting; danced by Phyllis Rae. Initially dropped from *She's My Baby*, but restored to the score soon after the New York opening.

VERSE 1

HE: Tell me why your features all delight me,
  Tell me why I love your hair.
  I love you, but you do not requite me;
  I love you, and you don't care.
  You can say "Goodbye" each time with
    such ease;
  While I'm on my knees, you smile.
  When I want a hand to hold,
  All your fingers are so cold.
  Is it worth the while?

REFRAIN

If I were you,
Here's what I'd do:
I'd tell me that I really loved me.
I wouldn't hide it,
I'd just confide it,
I'd pet me and let me pet you.
I'd be oh! so tender,
Sitting on my knee,
Then with sweet surrender
I'd give in to me.
Gosh! You ought to see!
I'd hold me closer;
I'd kiss me too.
I'd do that if I were you.

VERSE 2

SHE: I'm afraid you really don't deserve me,
  I'm afraid you're fancy-free.
  You don't know how dreams of you unnerve
    me;
  You don't know what love can be.
  When you talk about your job with such
    ease,
  I throb for a squeeze and a kiss.
  All your phrases are so fond,
  Can't your actions correspond?
  Tell me what's amiss?

REPEAT REFRAIN

Later version (*She's My Baby*)

VERSE 1

SHE: You're in need of someone to adore you,
Someone with a little tact.
Your success I'm certain will surprise you
When I show you how to act.
Walk right up to your dear Polly
To say,
"It's folly to say we'll part."
You must sing a little song
Just to show her she's all wrong;
Here's the way to start:

REFRAIN (same as *Betsy* version)

VERSE 2

HE: I'll say, "Dear, a kiss is still in fashion
For a young romantic pair."
SHE: Dearie me, your words have all the passion
Of an oyster in its lair.
HE: Though I spend a lot of time
On my knees,
While I'm on my knees, she'll freeze
When I tell her that I care.
Though she's breathing frigid air,
I will say with ease:

REPEAT REFRAIN

FIRST WE THROW MOE OUT

Introduced by ensemble. Alternate title: "Finaletto, Act II, Scene 1." Set to the music of "Sing."

First we throw Moe out,
Then we throw Joe out;
Here's where you go out—sister.
Right on the head we've kissed her.
Ta-ra-ta-ra, OUT BUM!
Mama we swing out,
Louis we fling out,
Betsy, don't sing out, we know
We ought to sock your beano.
Ta-ra-ta-ra, OUT BUM!
Fooling the world will pay nowhere.
We've sent them for a ride.
Look at those birds, do they know where
They're going to land outside?

Louis is back. Out!
Then Joe we pack out.
Ruthie we whack out; Moe too!
Betsy and Ma must go too.
Ta-ra-ta-ra, OUT BUM!

BIRDS UP HIGH

Introduced by Allen Kearns and ensemble. Alternate title: "Birds On High."

VERSE

Deep in the night—
Deep music
Falls from the boughs on high.
Down from the height—
Sleep music;
All's like a lullaby.
Love is the only note
Trilled by the bluebird's throat,
While birds ev'rywhere come to
Rendezvous!

REFRAIN

Birds up high
And birds down low,
They always sit and sigh, and so
I want to do exactly as the birds do!
On the bough
And ev'rywhere
They seem somehow to hum an air
That means much more than any human words
do.
Hear them getting tuneful
When they see the moon full!
Robins tête-à-tête,
Birdies of a feather
Ought to get together;
Little redbreast, go find your mate!
I wish I may,
I wish I might
Be good by day and fly by night
With all the birdies high and low.

SHUFFLE

Introduced by Madeleine Cameron and ensemble. Also introduced in *One Dam Thing After Another* (1927) by Edythe Baker and ensemble.

VERSE

When you find a card game
Looking like a hard game,
Why say die? say I.
Keep your disposition
In the best condition.
You, who "boo-hoo" try,
Show your woes a poker face;
That's the way to win the ace!

REFRAIN

Just start into shuffle, shuffle,
And shake troubles today.
Don't let your nerves ruffle, ruffle.
Mix your bad hands
With your glad hands.
Throw gloom in the river, shiver!
Then start in to play.
Just let your cares glide off,
Slide off,
And shuffle away!

AT THE SASKATCHEWAN

Original opening, Act II, Scene 1. Intended for Al Shean and ensemble. Dropped before the New York opening.

MOSKOWITZ
& ENSEMBLE: We're just the newly rich
Who are the truly rich
And we're unduly rich now;
No more sobriety,
And no more piety;
We'll show society how!
Here dancing's a treat;
In shaking your feet,
You never will meet
Your own wife;
And so we go about,
Throwing our dough about;
That's all we know about
Life.
MOSKOWITZ: At the Saskatchewan,
We will attach you on
Our roll,
Though you're a Pole,
Or Lithuanian;
Take my Aunt Sarah's son,
Just for comparison;
Now he's called Harrison,
And he's Rumanian.
Mrs. Cohen eats fillet sole,

Lobster served on casserole;
Once she used to eat gefilte fish.
All the Goldbergs drink their soup
Like a Russian opera troupe—
They will sip you any tune you
  wish.
At the Saskatchewan,
We will not scratch you on
Your race,
Or on your face;
We'd let Lon Chaney in.

We're just the newly rich [etc.]

IS MY GIRL REFINED?

Dropped before the New York opening.

VERSE

I've got a gal who's so refined
She never says what's on her mind.
Because she never likes to speak of sex.
I'm wearing gloves just like a dude—
She blushes when my hands are nude.
Instead of kisses she gives little pecks!
From Vassar she's an A.B.,
An educated baby.
But if she'd get a glass of wine,
She'd go and clink it.
I've often heard the saying:
You can lead a horse to Wasser
But you're going to have a job
To make her drink it.

REFRAIN 1

Is my girl refined?
Is my girl refined?
She never takes a bath at night
Until she first puts out the light.
At a risqué play
I've often heard her say,
"With shame, I ache,
But for your sake,
I guess we'd better stay."
She won't let me hug and kiss.
Says, "Don't be so kind."
She says, "Don't do this and this
Till I first pull down the blind!"
When we're married we won't have a
Little kid to mind.
We won't make good,
Because she's too refined.

REFRAIN 2

Is my girl refined?
Is my girl refined?
The folks in Holland she would squash;
She calls their city Amstergosh!
For Rome she doesn't care,
The ruins shocked her there;
To my surprise,
She closed her eyes
Because the walls were bare.
She "Black Bottoms" like the rest
But one night she said,
"For Black Bottom, I suggest
You should say Dark Riverbed!"
Once she told her sister Fanny,
"Fanny, please don't mind,
I'll call you Frances,
For it's more refined."

SIX LITTLE KITZELS

Dropped before the New York opening.

VERSE 1

BETSY: The Kitzel family came to call;
  We proudly walked into the hall,
  And shot out like a cannonball;
  We took the family exit.
LOUIS: The place was quiet as a tomb;
  I looked as nifty as a groom,
  And kept my hat on in the room;
  Why pay the guy who checks it?
MAMA: And I was sure I wasn't erring
  When I took out a pickled herring
  And started in to eat it there.
LOUIS: They served the dinner from a buffet;
  I dunked my cracker in the kuffey.
ALL: And then we took the air.

REFRAIN

JOE: Joe!
MOE: Moe!
MAMA: Mama!
RUTH: And Ruthie!
BETSY: And Betsy!
LOUIS: And Louis!
ALL: We came in to play the social game
  in there;
  We went out much quicker than we
  came in there;
  We went out gaflooey
  As they all yelled "Pfui! Pfui!"

JOE: Joe!
MOE: Moe!
MAMA: Mama!
RUTH: And Ruthie!
BETSY: And Betsy!
LOUIS: And Louis!

VERSE 2

LOUIS: I tried to grab a piece of pie,
  Then something hit me in the eye;
  I never knew that Jews could fly;
  I flew just like a Zeppy.
MAMA: Look at the mama, old and gray,
  Thrown from the house, just like a
  play,
  The ten-and-twent'-and-thirty way;
  The scene was very peppy.
RUTH: Out of the door, a butler threw me;
  I cried out, "Villain, don't pursue
  me!"
  But all he did was scowl and hiss.
BETSY: In melodramas, by some token,
  The end of a sentence is unspoken;
  They read their lines like this:
[Hearts and Flowers music]
  Mother! Oh—
MAMA: My child, what did he—
BETSY: Mother, he—oh my God!
JOE: You mean, he—
RUTH: Oh my God!
LOUIS: You say I— You lie, you—
JOE: Damn you! I—
LOUIS: You dirty son-of-a—
MOE: Marry her or I'll—
LOUIS
(TO BETSY): Well, I guess, after all I—
  Will you, er? Can you, er?
BETSY: Well, er— Maybe I'll, er! Listen,
  darling,
  I'm about to become a—
LOUIS: You mean, you're about to have a—
BETSY: I'm going to give you a little—
MAMA: I'm so happy, I—

REPEAT REFRAIN

YOU'RE THE MOTHER TYPE

Published December 1926. Song dropped before the New York opening.

VERSE 1

HE: Girls like you will never tumble for a lie.
I won't say that you are quite a Lorelei,
But you're as charming,
And far more alarming;
I'll say you are!
Just stay the way you are.
That is why I think that you're the mate for me.
Life with you would certainly be great for me!

REFRAIN 1

You're just the mother type,
I want no other type,
For I'm in love with three square meals a day.
A plate with hash in it
Can make me passionate,
While by the dear old kitchen stove we play.
You'll look romantic when you're patching up my trousers.
Oh, what a Venus of the pots and pans you'll be!
I won't agree to sleep
Till you rock me to sleep.
How'd you like to baby me?

VERSE 2

SHE: You mean more to me with your sweet sentiment
Than most any other boy of twenty meant.
I think it's great you're
A lover of nature.
Just stay that way,
For life is gay that way.
I believe in laws that all the earth control;
Promise me you won't believe in birth control!

REFRAIN 2

I'm just the mother type,
You want no other type,
And I'll be very chummy with the stork.
All babies charm me, dear,
You'll have an army, dear,
And we'll make London smaller than New York.
And if George Washington's the Father of his country,
Someday the Mama of the U.S.A. I'll be!
I'll cook nice pies for you

And choose your ties for you.
You're the only babe for me.

BURN UP

Unused. Also possibly intended for *Peggy-Ann* (1926).

VERSE

Turn the page
To the passionate age
Where emotion is warm and bold!
To the time
When it isn't a crime
To admit that you're not so cold!
We don't repress
We just confess
That love is worth
All the rest of the earth.
That's my say,
I say!

REFRAIN

Burn up! Cut loose! Turn up your flame of joy!
Free yourself! Like a hot volcano!
Make up your mind! Take up life as a toy!
Be yourself! Let nobody say "no"!
If you want to do a thing,
Just do it—that's all!
If you feel you're gonna slip,
Go to it—and fall!
Knowing that life's overflowing the cup,
Drink that cup! Go and burn right up!

SOCIAL WORK

Unused.

VERSE

We belong to the leisure classes
Who each day annoy the masses
Handing out the dole
Of what our papas stole.
The specimens of immigration
Who make up most of our population
From our sunny smile would gladly run a mile!
It would appear
They hate to hear
A lecture in this style!

REFRAIN

Tony! Tony!
Buy some baloney!
Here's a dollar bill!
Patrick, here's a pill,
It will cure your chill!
Otto! Otto!
If you get blotto,
You will go to jail!
Don't you rush the pail!
Here's some ginger ale!
Long Tack Sam,
Don't say "goddamn"!
Such words you ought to squash.
Better say "by gosh"!
While you do your washing
In Manhattan, we help the Latin,
German, Greek and Turk!
It's such a pleasure
To give leisure time to social work!

TRANSFORMATION

Dropped before the New York opening. Apparently intended for Jimmy Hussey, Ralph Whitehead, and Dan Healy.

ALL: Bubble, bubble!
Toil and trouble!
MOE: Razor blade, shave off that stubble!
ALL: We're making a man of romance.
LOUIS: Hey, Archie, take off the pants!
ALL: With water and soap,
And clothing, we hope
To make him a man of romance.
LOUIS: I'm the man who makes the clothes that make the man!
New clothes put you in a new light.
Here's a blue suit,
Or rather a blue light.
It's a speedy shade because the color ran.
JOE: I'll cut your old face off, or rather
Make a new one with razor and lather!
MOE: No man knows of pleasures supernal
If his happiness isn't internal.
It's up to the feeder,
He's really the breeder!
A man who's too lean
Has a look that is mean.
Good food is the remedy.
Once you apply it,
It's all in the diet,
You can't deny it.

JOE: A razor blade can change a layer
Of stubble to a maiden's prayer!
And with a magic massage to follow,
I'll make a monkey like Apollo.

LOUIS: Just take a look at a nude man,
Can you tell if he's a gentleman or rude
man?
A Saturday night at a Turkish bath
Would fill a lady's heart with wrath.
On the day his stylish clothing fails to
come,
Beau Brummell ain't Beau Brummell but
Beau Bum.
A chorus man at fifty a week
On the stage looks like a movie sheik;
Give me a chance to measure and drape,
And I'll make a Lord Chesterfield
Out of Tarzan the Ape.

ALL: Bubble, bubble!
Toil and trouble!
Magic soap and water bubble!
With needle, with bread, and with blade,
He's fed, and he's shaved, and arrayed.
And now he's a match
For some girl to catch.
We've finished our Adam—he's made.

VIVA ITALIA

Unused.

Viva Italia!
New York-a celebrate it!
Italia give Colombo,
Colombo he locate it!
He sail across da osch in 1492,
And found Columbus Circle
And Columbus Avenue!
Maybe you think there's lotsa
People like Gatti-Casazza!
Who sing like Martinelli can?
A German tenor? The hell he can!
Italia! Italia!
Who give spaghetti and confetti?
Macaroni and spumoni?
Who give shoeshine
Like a new shine?
Who give close shave
Like a no shave?
Oh, Italia!
One-a, two-a, three-a, four-a!
Bravo, bis, and then encore-a!
Italia! Italia!
She make-a da whole New York!

If you don't understand my language
You must be a big dumb Dora.
My people made the Bronx and Brooklyn
Look like Sodom and Gomorrah!
We are here two million strong,
Not counting the Assyrians
And many Christian Scientists
And several Presbyterians.
The man who said Columbus
Was a wop is a buttinsky!

His name may be Columbus now
But once it was Kolinsky!
John L. Sullivan came to fame
But Jakie Solomon was his name!
As for Martinelli,
Whose voice is sweet as jelly,
His name is Stonewall Moskowitz
And it's still the very samekowitz
As it was when he first camekowitz
Straight from Moscow as plain Moskowitz!

A MELICAN MAN

Unused fragment.

My people do
Allee washee for you
And fight likee hellee in Mott Street!
Much dough we gain
From cookee chow mein,
We Chinee have made it a hot street!
Chow mein you eat without a fork
Was invented by us in old New York;
Give Chinee man this chop suey
He'll refuse it and say "Phooey!"
Husband too
Go and cut off his queue
And he drink lots of velly bad hootchy!
Curse and smoke
And now he's a Melican man!

Richard Dolman and Jessie Matthews
in *One Dam Thing After Another*

ONE DAM THING AFTER ANOTHER
A CONNECTICUT YANKEE
1927

ONE DAM THING AFTER ANOTHER, 1927

No tryout information. London run: London Pavilion, May 19–December 10, 1927. 237 performances. Music by Richard Rodgers. Lyrics by Lorenz Hart. Produced under the personal supervision of Charles B. Cochran. Book by Ronald Jeans. Staged by Frank Collins. Dances and ensembles staged by Max Rivers. Settings mostly by Marc Henri. Costumes mostly by Kitty Shannon and Doris Zinkeisen. Orchestra under the direction of J. B. Hastings. Orchestrations by Robert Russell Bennett. Pianist, Leslie Hutchinson. Cast, starring Jessie Matthews, Douglas Byng, Lance Lister, and Sonnie Hale, included Edythe Baker, Melville Cooper, Max Wall, and Sheilah Grahame (chorus).

For the lyric to "Shuffle," see *Betsy* (1926), page 99. For "Paris Is Really Divine," see *Peggy-Ann* (1926), page 92. For "Gigolo," see *The Garrick Gaieties* (1926), page 74. For "Idles of the King," see *The Garrick Gaieties* (1926), page 74.

THE ELECTION

Introduced by the company.

GIRLS: Ladies and gentlemen, how do you
    do?
You're very punctual, although you
    are few.
It's shameful that all the grand folk,
Up-to-date folk,
Are late folk;
We'd rather sing for you!
You think we're singing a silly
    refrain,
You think we're chorus ladies;
You're wrong again!
We've not been engaged for our
    beauty;
Our duty is plain.
We're what Euripides used for a
    plot.
We'll show it
Although it
Is rot!
When Mr. Cochran starts a show,
He never knows how far to go;

The London taste is often known to
    vary.
Today you like a Bible play.
Tomorrow something more risqué.
It's hard to tell, the public's so
    contrary.
Financial failure must be
    circumvented here,
So ev'ry form of show is represented
    here!
You can all vote and have a voice
In making Mr. Cochran's choice
Of what kind of show he should do!
Good sir, you are tardy in reaching
    your stall,
So what we've said before we now
    will recall:
We're casting a ballot, so do think,
If you think at all.
You'll pick your candidate when this
    is done.
You must vote,
But just vote
For one!
CANDIDATES: How de do, Mr. Moss!
How de do, Mr. Stoll!
STOLL: There's something that is troubling
    me;
There is, upon my soul!
MOSS: What is the awful question
That seems to trouble you?
STOLL: What letter of the alphabet is
    drunk?
MOSS: Wobble you!

REFRAIN 1

STOLL: Oh, Mr. Moss!
MOSS: Oh, Mr. Stoll!
STOLL: You are a lady killer
And your heart is black as coal.
MOSS: I am a lady killer?
That makes me catch my breath!
STOLL: Yes, you're a lady killer,
For you starved your wife to death!

REFRAIN 2

MOSS: Oh, Mr. Stoll!
STOLL: Oh, Mr. Moss!
You say that you're a golfer,
What is your favorite course?
MOSS: I do not feel like boasting,
To that I wouldn't stoop!
STOLL: But you're a famous golfer!
MOSS: And my favorite course is soup!

REFRAIN 3

STOLL: Oh, Mr. Moss!
MOSS: Oh, Mr. Stoll!
STOLL: A Scotsman once got married
In a barnyard, 'pon my soul.
MOSS: He married in a barnyard?
I ask you, is that nice?
STOLL: He did that so the chickens
And the hens could eat the rice!

MY HEART STOOD STILL

Published twice, May 1927 and October 1927. Introduced by Jessie Matthews and Richard Dolman. Also introduced in *A Connecticut Yankee* (1927) by William Gaxton, Constance Carpenter, and ensemble. It replaced "You're What I Need."

VERSE 1

HE: I laughed at sweethearts*
I met at schools;
All indiscreet hearts
Seemed romantic fools.
A house in Iceland
Was my heart's domain.
I saw your eyes;
Now castles rise in Spain!

REFRAIN

I took one look at you,
That's all I meant to do,
And then my heart stood still!
My feet could step and walk,
My lips could move and talk,
And yet my heart stood still!
Though not a single word was spoken,
I could tell you knew.
That unfelt clasp of hands
Told me so well you knew.
I never lived at all
Until the thrill
Of that moment when
My heart stood still.

In the first published version, verse 1, lines 1–4:
The boys at Harrow
Would always say
That Cupid's arrow
Couldn't fly my way.

VERSE 2

SHE: Through all my school days*
　　I hated boys;
　　Those April Fool days
　　Brought me loveless joys.
　　I read my Plato,
　　Love I thought a sin,
　　But since your kiss
　　I'm reading Missus Glynn!

REPEAT REFRAIN

MAKE HEY! MAKE HEY!

Introduced by Max Wall. Alternate title: "Make Hey! Hey!
While the Moon Shines."

VERSE

I can't look at the sun;
High noon,
You hear me sigh, "Noon,
I wanna bid you goodbye, noon."
Early morning I shun;
Daytime
Is such a gray time,
It wasn't made for my play time;
I'm remarkably bright
In the shadows of night;
When the saxophones blow,
Hey! Hey! Let's go!

REFRAIN

You gotta make hey! Hey! Hey! Hey!
While the moon shines!
Wake up! Shake up! And you're a wow!
Where crazy blues are blaring up
We'll be tearing up dance floors.
You gotta squeeze up!
Toes in!
Knees up!
Close in!
Hey! Hey! Hey! Hey! Gotta burn up!
Shiver! Quiver! You gotta play!
Nights don't weary us;
We've no serious moments;
You gotta be delirious.
Hey! Hey! Hey!

*In the first published version, verse 2, lines 1–2:
　In Heathfield school days
　I hated boys.

PATTER

Heigh-ho, milady! Heigh-ho, milady-o!
Moonlight is glancing as we a-dancing go!
Hands all a-tremble,
Pray don't dissemble, lady!
When you pressed me,
Then you blessed me.
Dull care takes flight in notes of the nightingale!
No thought of noon, we'll dance as the moon we
　　hail!
Right merrily, we'll trip along, lady,
Yea verily!
Heigh-o-heigh!

Good Master Owl doth hate the sun;
With a heigh-o-heigh;
For the night's the time for mating.
At morn, the owls sleep deep each one;
With a heigh-o-heigh and a nonny-nonny-o!
And by my troth, Good Master Owl
When Phoebus 'gins arise doth scowl!
But when the nightingale sings low,
With a heigh-o-heigh,
'Neath the leafy boughs a-twitter,
He serenades his lady o,
With a heigh-o-heigh and a hooty-hooty-o!
Days doth weary us,
Be delirious,
Heigh-o-heigh!
Hotdoggyboy! Hey! Hey! Hey! Hey!
Bubbly! Binjez!
Umpho! Gumpho! Issippi! Wow!
Oo-googli! Dozat! Shiveree!
Whozat! Quiveree jumpo!
Oo-googli, see you,
Popsy,
Bee you,
Wopsy.
Hey! Hey! Hey! Hey! Oogli Singee!
Velee Jellee you wattasay
Bibi steppee-vo, Fullee-Peppee-oo
Mammee!
Losee reppy-vo
Hey! Hey! Hey!

LADIES AND GENTLEMEN, WE'RE HERE AGAIN

Introduced by Max Wall and ensemble. Alternate title:
"Opening, Act II."

Ladies and gentlemen, we're here again.
Please do not listen to our silly refrain.

You'll now find the folks who are nobby
In the lobby,
A hobby
That gives us girls a pain;
All of the people who star in the show
Are much too good to waste at this time, you
　　know!
So we have to follow the entr'acte;
Our contract
Says so;
And till each customer comes to his stall,
We fill time
And kill time
For all!

I NEED SOME COOLING OFF

Published May 1927. Introduced by Edythe Baker and
ensemble. Later introduced in *She's My Baby* (1928) by
Nick Long, Jr., Pearl Eaton, Phyllis Rae, and ensemble.

VERSE 1

Blare away, you mad music!
Tear away all sham.
Maniac! Maniac!
That's what I am.
Strum for me that wild rhythm;
Drum for me; don't stop!
Dynamo! Dynamo!
Run till I drop!
Sun up in the sky,
You're so hot!
Burning up on high,
Oh, my! So'm I!

REFRAIN

I need some cooling off!
How I need cooling off!
Can't stop my feet; they're going to burn up!*
Sh! Sh! I know I'll go insane.
No white man wrote that strain.
My toes get hot whenever they turn up!
Hot coffee!
You'll find it's never time to retire.†
I'm shouting now, my temperature's higher.
Fire!

*In She's My Baby: Can't stop that step; I'm going to burn
up!
†In She's My Baby: I know it's never time to retire.

I'll hear that music crash
Until I burn to ash.
Oh, how I need some cooling off!

VERSE 2

Bang away that wild keyboard!
Clang away that drum!
Lucifer! Lucifer!
Downward I come!
Sigh away, you warm fiddle,
Cry away, you flute,
Saxophone! Saxophone!
Go on and toot.
Devil down so far,
You're not hot,
For to me you are
Old boy—cold boy.

REPEAT REFRAIN

MY LUCKY STAR

Published May 1927. Introduced by Sonnie Hale and
Mimi Crawford. Later introduced by the Nightingale
Quartette (Evelyn Sayers, Loretta Sayers, Jessie Payne,
and Doreen Glover) and ensemble in *She's My Baby*
(1928).

VERSE

Though the merry merry
Is a very necessary crew
People think we revel
On the level;
Raise the devil too.
Stars who have no voices
Have their choices
Of Rolls-Royces rare.
But we use the bus line*
When we have our fare!

REFRAIN 1

We keep on smiling in the chorus
Though life is not so easy for us;
Our guardian angels just ignore us.
Now—somehow—
We get the bird from all who've seen us.

*In She's My Baby, *lines 9–10:*
But we use the subway
When we have the fare!

HE: I'm no Apollo!*
SHE: I'm no Venus!
We haven't got a quid between us.
Now—somehow—
You're not a silly dancing boy
In line for me.
Darling, you combine for me
Ev'rything that's fine for me.
Though many little troubles bore us
Just keep smiling in the chorus,
For in my eyes you are
My lucky star.

REFRAIN 2

While we keep smiling in the chorus
There often is no dinner for us.
Our tummies, too, as they implore us,
Quake—and ache!
We get some gifts from Johns that you see;
They'll send some roses round to Lucy.
We wish they'd send us round a juicy steak
And cake.
They think that all the wine that†
We request we get;
Champagne by the chest we get!
Bovril is the best we get.
We keep on smiling in the chorus
Though we must dance till socks get porous.
I wonder where you are,
My lucky star!

*In She's My Baby, *to end of refrain:*
Though we must wear much less than Venus
We haven't got a buck between us.
Now—somehow—
They think we drink champagne and smoke
And curse at night.
While we must rehearse at night,
Flappers do much worse at night.
We work like dogs and that's the reason
The show makes money for a season
While critics rave about
Some lucky star.
†In She's My Baby, *lines 9–12:*
They think that all the cars that
We request we get;
Lincolns from the West we get!
Buicks are the best we get.

ONE DAM THING AFTER ANOTHER

Introduced by Mimi Crawford, Lance Lister, Jessie Matthews, and Joan Clarkson.

VERSE

When people peep inside my pram
And try to scare me with a rattle,
They never know how bored I am
With all their silly, childish prattle.
My mother's friends, all dressed in silk,
Can make every day a glum day.
They fill me up with so much milk
I'll turn into a pudding someday.

REFRAIN 1

One dam thing after another!
First it's brother,
Then it's Pa.
Ev'ryone's crazy to pet me.
If they'd let me,
I'd kill Pa!
Uncle John makes much
Piggyback and such,
Then he starts to slap
What a decent chap
Wouldn't even touch!
Ma will kiss my shoe,
Aunty does it too.
Then they pinch my toes,
And they tweak my nose
Till it's black and blue!
God bless them!
Grandpapa tickles my tummy,
Then my thumb he bites with glee,
And all the great big older folks
Seem dam childish to me!

REFRAIN 2

One dam thing after another!
I could smother
Sister's beau!
If he's a man, no one knows it,
Never shows it,
He's so slow!
When she starts to coo,
"Love me, lovey do,"
Then the great big gawk
Answers baby talk,
Pidgy Widgy Woo!
He says, "ittle spouse,"
She says, "ittle mouse,"

Lamp is oh, so bright,
Switch off naughty light,
Then they both play house.
Just kiddies!
She buys him terrible neckties,
Incorrect ties as can be!
If love can make you color blind,
It's dam childish to me!

PRETTY LITTLE LADY

Intended for Edythe Baker and ensemble, but apparently dropped before the London opening.

        BOYS
(TO EDYTHE): Pretty little lady,
      We are all in love with you.
(TO AUDIENCE): That's the kind of nonsense
      We must sing in a revue.
(TO EDYTHE): Oh, Miss Baker, won't you play?
    EDYTHE: You know I must agree
      Or I'd get sacked by C.B.C.
GIRLS & BOYS: Music is the food of love,
      Perhaps you may recall
      But we've overeaten
      Just a little at Albert Hall!
      So, Miss Baker, bang away!
    EDYTHE: You'll find me happy every day,
      For when I work I always play.
    GIRLS: On our knees,
      We say please,
      Make those keys sing.
      Miss Baker, do not say no!
    BOYS: Not a word of this song means a
      damn thing—
      We're in a musical show!
    EDYTHE: Whenever I'm attending a soiree,
      They always say,
      "Miss Baker, won't you play?"
      Well, whenever he goes into a
      home
      The hostess asks
      If he has brought his violin too—
      I cannot bring my big piano here!
BOYS & GIRLS: No fear!
      The management has bought you
      one, my dear!
    GIRLS: We have never heard you play.
      Oh, grant us this delight!
      BOYS
(TO AUDIENCE): They are awful liars,
      For they sing that every night.
BOYS & GIRLS: Oh, Miss Baker, won't you play?
    EDYTHE: The keys I fear to touch,

For now they'll all expect too
    much!
  ALL: Pretty little lady,
    We are all in love with you.
    That's the sort of nonsense
    We must sing in a revue,
    So, Miss Baker—pound away!

A CONNECTICUT YANKEE, 1927

Tryout: Stamford Theatre, Stamford, Connecticut, September 30–October 1, 1927; Walnut Theatre, Philadelphia, October 3–29, 1927. New York run: Vanderbilt Theatre, November 3, 1927–October 27, 1928. 418 performances. Music by Richard Rodgers. Lyrics by Lorenz Hart. Produced by Lew Fields and Lyle D. Andrews. Book by Herbert Fields, adapted from *A Connecticut Yankee in King Arthur's Court* by Mark Twain. Directed by Alexander Leftwich. Dances and musical numbers staged by Busby Berkeley. Settings and costumes by John Hawkins, Jr. Orchestra under the direction of Roy Webb. Opening-night conductor, Richard Rodgers. Orchestrations by Roy Webb. Cast, starring William Gaxton and Constance Carpenter, included William Norris, June Cochrane, Jack Thompson, Nana Bryant, and Paul Everton.

For the lyric to "My Heart Stood Still," see *One Dam Thing After Another* (1927), page 104.

The following lyrics are missing: "Nothing's Wrong" (introduced by Constance Carpenter) and "Britain's Own Ambassadors" (dropped during rehearsals).

A HOME COMPANION

Introduced by Nana Bryant and ensemble.

  CHORUS: For she's a jolly good fellow!
    For she's a jolly good fellow!
    For she's a jolly good fellow!
    And she lives down in our alley!
  MARTIN: The wedding celebration day
    Will be on Decoration Day
    Because it's your vacation day.
    You all can see the splicing.
  FAY: The finest cake Mazzetti cut,
    The dearest, too, you bet he cut,

Is shipped up to Connecticut
With Cupids made of icing.
  GALAHAD: I'll be there to wish you well
    When the happy wedding bell
    Sounds its dismal warning knell.
    I'll shed a tear for you.
  MARVIN: Soon the boys will miss your face
    At the dear old drinking place,
    While they booze, I'll have the grace
    To drink a beer for you.
  MARTIN: Fay, do you know what you're about?
    How did you ever pick me out?
  FAY: I've never any fun.
  CHORUS: Really?
  FAY: My breakfast table's set for one;
    My nerves are all awry.
  CHORUS: Really?
  FAY: I feel so tired before my day's begun,
    I'm sick of tabby cats and towsers;
    At night they're rather sad carousers.
    I hate my poor canary, too!
    I want a monkey who wears trousers.

REFRAIN

Give me something nice and stupid I
  can hug.
Give me something that throws ashes
  on the rug.
Something that gets sleepy and turns
  off the light,
Something musical that snores all
  night.
I've a sweet domestic animal in view,
A lady's home companion just like you!

THOU SWELL

Published October 1927. Introduced by William Gaxton and Constance Carpenter.

VERSE 1

Babe, we are well met,
As in a spell met—
I lift my helmet.
Sandy,
You're just dandy
For just this here lad.
You're such a fistful,
My eyes are mistful—
Are you too wistful
To care?
Do say you care

To say, "Come near, lad."
You are so graceful—
Have you wings?
You have a face full
Of nice things.
You have no speaking voice, dear.
With ev'ry word it sings.

REFRAIN

Thou swell!
Thou witty!
Thou sweet!
Thou grand!
Wouldst kiss me pretty?
Wouldst hold my hand?
Both thine eyes are cute, too—
What they do to me.
Hear me holler
I choose a
Sweet lolla
Palooza
In thee.
I'd feel so rich in
A hut for two.
Two rooms and kitchen
I'm sure would do.
Give me just a plot of
Not a lot of land,
And,
Thou swell!
Thou witty!
Thou grand!

VERSE 2

Thy words are queer, sir,
Unto mine ear, sir,
Yet thou'rt a dear, sir,
To me.
Thou couldst woo me.
Now couldst thou try, knight.
I'd murmur, "Swell," too,
And like it well, too.
More thou wilt tell to
Sandy.
Thou art dandy.
Now art thou my knight.
Thine arms are martial,
Thou hast grace.
My cheek is partial
To thy face.
And if thy lips grow weary
Mine are their resting place.

REPEAT REFRAIN

AT THE ROUND TABLE

Introduced by Paul Everton, William Norris, William Roselle, Jack Thompson, and ensemble. Alternate title: "Knights' Opening."

ALL: Here's to the dish of the day,
Thu meat or the fish of the day!
We eat to fight and fight to eat
Abundantly.
We drink a flagon a day
To kill a dragon a day!
We drink to fight and fight to drink
Redundantly.
Here's a toast to the good red meat!
Here's a toast to the wine and the sweet!

REFRAIN

Here's a toast to the ale and the antelope,
Here's a toast to the quail and the cantaloupe.
Here's a toast to the boar,
Here's a toast to the mutton,
A toast to the rabbit stew!
Here's a toast to the roast and the bitters too,
Here's a toast to the toast and the fritters too!
So hail!
And a toast to the ladies too!

LAUNCELOT: A toast unto our noble King,
Who thinketh not one evil thing.
No wicked thought
Was ever brought
To rest beneath his bonnet!
His sleep disdains all lowly dreams.
He fain doth not indulge in schemes.
His mind is pure,
Forsooth, I'm sure
There's ever nothing on it!!

ALL: Hail! Launcelot, hail!

LAUNCELOT: Let Merlin speak. With magic deep
His speech can put us all to sleep!

ALL: Hail! Merlin, hail!

MERLIN: Our noble King is most religious,
And as a churchman he's prodigious.
A heathen horde
Slain by his sword
Is buried ev'ry Monday!
The conscience of our lord and master
Is white and pure as alabaster.

It's free from taint,
For like a saint
He cuts no throats on Sunday!

ALL: He goes to church on Sunday!

MERLIN: Most noble liege, wilt thou not bless us,
And with thine eloquence address us.
Thy voice of gold
Is famed of old
Throughout this loyal nation.
The royal tongue will now deliver
Words flowing like a running river.
The prospect cheers
Our eager ears
That wait for thy oration!

ALL: Hail! The King will speak!

MERLIN: Hush! The King will speak!

ALL: Glory! The King will speak!
Glory! The King will speak!

ARTHUR: Er—!

QUEEN
GUINEVERE: Nay, Arthur, commit not thyself!

ARTHUR: Er— Sorry!

ALL: Hail! A mighty speech!
What eloquence! What voice of gold!
What wondrous magic it doth hold!
Hail! Hail! A mighty speech!!

REPEAT REFRAIN

ON A DESERT ISLAND WITH THEE

Published October 1927. Introduced by Jack Thompson, June Cochrane, and ensemble.

VERSE

GALAHAD: Come, sit thee near,
Place thyself upon my knee.
Make an end of thy fear,
For I love but thee in Camelot.

EVELYN: Oh, no not here,
Where observed of all we'll be.
Should thy father appear,
He would surely scold and damn a lot.

GALAHAD: Care not a jot.
Harken to my plot:
Soon we'll retreat to a sweet spot!

REFRAIN

Oh, for a year
On a desert island with thee,
Out in the sheer middle of the sea.
We'll sing tra-la;
Wouldn't we be happy and gay,
With thy mama many miles away?
In the morning air,
Murmur a blessing;
First we'll eat,
Then we will dress.
If it's fair,
We'll be caressing,
If it rains,
We'll caress!
Who knows next year
What the population will be
Out in the middle of the sea?

TRIO PATTER

EVELYN: I'll pack each little thing for thee.
What ten books shall I bring for thee?
We'll need some books to read.
GALAHAD: Thou needst not bring ten books along.
If thou wilt bring thy looks along,
'Twill be enough for me.
If the heat begins to swelter,
We won't have to fear the sun.
We will lie beneath a shelter
Only big enough for one.
EVELYN: Let the prudish people quarrel—
We'll forget them for the nonce.
If they think our love immoral,
"Honi soit qui mal y pense."
GALAHAD: I'll dress the way that Adam did.
EVELYN: And I the way his madam did.
GALAHAD: I'll see enough of thee!

REPEAT REFRAIN

IBBIDI BIBBIDI SIBBIDI SAB

Introduced by William Gaxton, William Norris, other principals, and ensemble. Alternate title: "Finale, Act I."

MARTIN: Ibbidi bibbidi sibbidi sab!
Ibbidi sibbidi casaba!

Martinelli . . . Mussolini!*
Kellar! Thurston! And Houdini!
ALL: Woe! Woe! The sun grows dim!
MERLIN: 'Tis but a cloud. A curse on him.
MARTIN: Say, drop that torch, I don't want
to scorch!
I'm gettin' hot! I'm gettin' hot!
Praise the Lord and pass up the
ignition.
Come on, Sun, he's gettin' rough.
Come on, Sun, and do your stuff!
Don't be a fizzle.
MERLIN: I'll make thee sizzle
And burn thy carcass to a frizzle!
I'm the magician and my nation
Will refuse this imitation!
MARTIN: Don't you move, I command.
Stay where you are, you
understand?
If anyone stirs, yes, even the King,
I'll blot out ev'ry man and thing!
I'll break you asunder
With lightning and thunder.
Indubitably, here in me
Your devastation lurks.
I'll disseminate anathema.
I mean, I'll shoot the works!

MARTIN: Ibbidi bibbidi sibbidi sab!
Ibbidi bibbidi casaba!
Martinelli . . . Mussolini!†
Kellar! Thurston! And Houdini!
ALL: Rise and shine on us,
Rise and shine on us,
Rise and shine on us, O Sun!
Lo, we plead to thee
In our need to thee,
So Godspeed to thee, O Sun!
Shine again, light of love,
Hold again, night of love,
Give again sight of love, O Sun!
SIR SAGANORE: Lo, behold on high.
All's in gold on high.
See the sky, it is day.
Praise on high, it is day.
ALL: Rise and shine on us,
Rise and shine on us,
Rise and shine on us, O Sun!

---

*1943 version:
Wet Manhattan, Dry Martini!
†1943 version, lines 3–4:
Gypsy Rose and Cleopatra!
Rudy, Bing and Frank Sinatra!

I FEEL AT HOME WITH YOU

Published October 1927. Introduced by Jack Thompson, June Cochrane, and ensemble.

VERSE 1

This used to be a grumpy,
Crabbed old lad—
Look at your beamish boy now.
This used to be a jumpy,
Silly and sad—
What is simply joy now.
Life was a canyon
Too dark to view,
Till a companion
Was found like you.

REFRAIN 1

I feel at home with you.
You always fit on
The knees that you sit on.
That's why I feel at home with you.
I love to roam with you.
Each place that we go,
You flatter my ego.
That's why I feel at home with you.
I've a sensible,
Comprehensible,
Great respect for you.
There's a dash in it
Of a passionate,
Tender feeling, too.
You are a part of me,
Something that's giving me
Reason for living—
That's why I feel at home with you.

VERSE 2

I used to be a hoyden—
Boys were my hate.
I was a lady hermit—
I couldn't be annoyed in
Making a date.
Silly I would term it.
You seemed so daring,
My heart grew frail.
Now I like wearing
My coat of male.

REFRAIN 2

I feel at home with you.
Your brain is dumber

Than that of a plumber.
That's why I feel at home with you.
I'll match my dome with you.
Your brain needs a tonic—
It's still embryonic.
That's why I feel at home with you.
Our minds are featherweight—
Their together weight
Can't amount to much.
You use no better words
Than three-letter words,
"Dog" and "cat" and such.
You have no head at all.
Something like your knob
Is used as a doorknob.
That's why I feel at home with you.

THE SANDWICH MEN

Introduced by ensemble.

ALL: We once were men.
We remember when
We used to do or dare
For ladies fair.
We once wore crests
On our manly breasts,
And now they're spread with dope
For Fairy Soap.
We were clad in armor
When to battle we'd go
Just as swift as a battering ram.
Now Armour's cattle
Is the armor we know,
And Swift is the premium ham!
We made crusades
For the love of maids,
And we were proud
And undefeated, ducks!
But "Onward, gallant soldiers,"
And make them wash in Lux!

Between these boards called
   sandwiches
We're such a sorry sight.
We troop throughout the land,
   which is
A hell of a job for a knight!
Each knight must droop his head,
   you know,
His body no one sees;
The boards are like the bread, you
   know,
And we're the piece of cheese.

1ST KNIGHT: Brave Sir Launcelot
Once would prance a lot;
Now he's advertising the Victrola.
2ND KNIGHT: Bold Sir Bedavere
Tramps ahead of here,
Telling all the world of Coca-Cola!
3RD KNIGHT: And Sir Tristan,
Famed for slaughter,
Hits the trail for Pluto Water!
4TH KNIGHT: Galahad's no longer fighting;*
He sells the paper that is never
   used for writing.
ALL: We droop, and stoop.
We hate our fate.
Lackaday, to our sighs.
People say who are wise
It pays to advertise!
We made crusades for the love [etc.]

EVELYN, WHAT DO YOU SAY?

Introduced by June Cochrane and male ensemble. The song "Morgan Le Fay" (intended for Nana Bryant and cut before the New York opening) has the same music and virtually the same lyric as "Evelyn, What Do You Say?" which replaced it. Whenever it appeared the line "Morgan, Morgan, Morgan Le Fay" was replaced by "Evelyn, Evelyn, what do you say." Similarly, the line "Morgan, Morgan Le Fay" was replaced by "Evelyn, what do you say."

VERSE

BOYS: Oh, won't you dance with one of us?
EVELYN: I like you all . . . both short and tall.
BOYS: Sweet lady, don't make fun of us.
EVELYN: How can I voice my certain choice?
BOYS: You're really charming,
Your style is disarming,
Your manners alarming,
You flirt so . . .
EVELYN: When twelve men address me,
It's apt to distress me,
For should you caress me,
'Twould hurt so!

REFRAIN 1

BOYS: Evelyn, Evelyn, what do you say?
Don't you look down on us

*Alternate version, lines 1–2:
Galahad sells panacea
That saveth four of every five from pyorrhea.

And please don't frown on us,
EVELYN: I don't really know what to say.
All alone I care for none
But I'll dance with everyone.
BOYS: Evelyn, Evelyn, you are O.K.
Good angels flew with you,
Brought something new with you.
ALL: That certain feeling
Comes a-stealing today . . .
Evelyn, what do you say?

REFRAIN 2

BOYS: Evelyn, Evelyn, what do you say!
You have that cheery smile,
Good Morning Dearie Smile.
EVELYN: By so many I'm led astray.
That's the reason, I suppose,
I am just a Wild, Wild Rose.
BOYS: Who Who Who made us that way?
If we could neck with you
We'd Hit the Deck with you.
ALL: That Certain Feeling
Comes a-stealing today . . .
Evelyn, what do you say!

I BLUSH

Published October 1927. Introduced by Constance Carpenter in Stamford, Connecticut, tryout. Dropped before the New York opening. Replaced by "Nothing's Wrong."

VERSE

All court conversation
To my observation
Is naughty
And woefully pert;
With joy unabating
The ladies-in-waiting
Are waiting
To dish thee the dirt;
Such talk never charms me,
In sooth, it alarms me
When told by a hoyden or a valet.
Mere greetings and glances
Rouse talk of romances;
Each kiss is a study in scarlet.

REFRAIN 1

Oh dear, when there's scandal about the court,
I blush!
Oh dear, at the naughtiness they report,

I blush!
Things they say sound very queer to me,
What they mean is never clear to me,
But it can't be very nice
The way they hush;
I blush!
Such sights are not fit for a maiden's view;
I blush!
Oh, dear, I know just what I ought to do,
I blush!
But you see,
I can't condemn a tale
If its end I do not know.
Oh dear, I blush!
But I love it so!

REFRAIN 2

Oh dear, but the Queen carries on a bit;
I blush!
Oh, dear, though I breathe not a word of it,
I blush!
Launcelot loveth her beauty well;
As a knight, he doth his duty well;
On the throne, they get so very warm,
They burn the plush.
I blush!
Arthur is a rather unwary King;
I blush!
The Queen made Launcelot honorary King;
I blush!
To be sure,
It's none of my concern
If he kissed her once or twice.
Oh dear, I blush!
But it's rather nice!

REFRAIN 3

Tristan told his heart to Isolde in song;
I blush!
Oh dear, but the song was six hours long;
I blush!
What they did was wrong beyond a doubt
If it took so long to sing about;
And the thought can make my lily
Cheek to flush.
I blush!
Oh dear, how they yodeled of love and death;
I blush!
They died not from love but from lack of breath;
I blush!
That it was
A proper way to die
It is silly to pretend.
I blush, but oh dear,
What a lovely end!

YOU'RE WHAT I NEED

Published December 1927. Sung in the Stamford, Connecticut, tryout of *A Connecticut Yankee* by William Gaxton and Constance Carpenter. Dropped before the New York opening and replaced by "My Heart Stood Still." Introduced and reprised often by Irene Dunne, Jack Whiting, the Nightingale Quartette (Evelyn Sayers, Loretta Sayers, Jessie Payne, and Doreen Glover), and ensemble in *She's My Baby* (1928).

VERSE 1

SHE: I was born
And held out my hands for you,
Yelled my young demands for you.
All forlorn,
Even in my toothless state,
Fate was in a ruthless state;
Long years through
I've been needing you.

REFRAIN

You're what I need,
I mean, my need
Starts and ends with you.
Won't you give in,
I mean, live in my home?
You're my menu,
I mean, when you
Smile my hunger's through.
Like a bluebird,
I mean, you, bird, fly home.
We will find a sky pilot,
Some nice old boy.
When he makes you my pilot,
Lead me to joy!
You've undone me,
I mean, won me,
For you've got me treed.
I love you so,
I mean that you're what I need!

VERSE 2

HE: Well, not bad!
But to speak with verity,
You need some sincerity.
So, I add,
When the song again you sing,
Think of someone when you sing;
I should say,
Sing it in this way!

REPEAT REFRAIN

SOMEONE SHOULD TELL THEM

Published October 1927. Introduced in the Stamford, Connecticut, tryout by William Gaxton and Nana Bryant. Dropped before the New York opening. Same music used for "There's So Much More" in *America's Sweetheart* (1931).

VERSE

SHE: Are not mine eyes fair to view?
They're there to view thee.
Wilt not thine own dare to view
What love can be?
Ah, see my color pale for thee,
Hear my heart fail for thee, too.
I have a sweet tale for thee,
'Tis sad but true.

REFRAIN 1

I know two little lovers who loved so
discreetly;
He'd hold her little fingers when twilight
would fall;
And ev'ry time they parted they sighed, oh
so sweetly;
Perhaps he kissed her, but that was all!
Who eats the empty shell and refuses the
kernel?
Who climbs the road to Heaven and stops
at the door?
These little lovers knew not the chance that
befell them;
Someone should tell them,
There's so much more!

REFRAIN 2

HE: Dear lady, you are charming, your beauty's
alluring;
I'll sit a little closer and drink in your
glance.
To feel your arms around me is so
reassuring;
And then to press you, I'll slyly chance.
I'll take your silken tresses to wind round
my fingers;
Perhaps I'll boldly kiss you and shout for
encore,
But even though the kindest of motives
impel you,
Someone should tell you,
There's nothing more!

SHE'S MY BABY | 1928

Lorenz Hart, Beatrice Lillie, Joan Clement, and Richard Rodgers

Tryout: National Theatre, Washington, D.C., December 12–17, 1927; Ford's Theatre, Baltimore, December 19–24, 1927; Shubert Theatre, Newark, New Jersey, December 26–31, 1927. New York run: Globe Theatre, January 3–March 3, 1928. 71 performances. Music by Richard Rodgers. Lyrics by Lorenz Hart. Produced by Charles Dillingham. Book by Guy Bolton, Bert Kalmar, and Harry Ruby. Production staged by Edward Royce. John Tiller dances by Mary Read. Settings by Raymond Sovey. Costumes by Raymond Sovey and Franullon, Inc. Orchestra under the direction of Gene Salzer. Orchestrations by Hans Spialek, Robert Russell Bennett, and Roy Webb. Cast, starring Beatrice Lillie, included Clifton Webb, Jack Whiting, Irene Dunne, and Nick Long, Jr.

For the lyric to "My Lucky Star," see *One Dam Thing After Another* (1927), page 106. For "You're What I Need," see *A Connecticut Yankee* (1927), page 111. For "Morning Is Midnight," see *Lido Lady* (1926), page 85. For "Try Again Tomorrow," see *Lido Lady* (1926), page 81. For "The Pipes of Pansy," see *Dearest Enemy* (1925), page 59. For "Camera Shoot," see *Lido Lady* (1926), page 83. For "I Need Some Cooling Off," see *One Dam Thing After Another* (1927), page 105. For "A Little House in Soho," see "A Tiny Flat Near Soho" in *Lido Lady* (1926), page 79. For "If I Were You," see *Betsy* (1926), page 98.

The lyric to "The Swallows" (introduced by Beatrice Lillie) is missing.

THIS GOES UP

Introduced by Nick Long, Jr., Pearl Eaton, and Phyllis Rae. Alternate titles: "Smile" and "Keep Your Eye on Me."

VERSE

HE: I'll do a dance that's very far from easy
But make it look as simple as Parcheesi.
When you get tired
And the labor irks,
Just look inspired
And show the dental works.
GIRLS: When you have to dance a mile
How the hell can ladies smile!

REFRAIN

This goes up! That goes up!
Turn nose up! Smile—
No pouting! No doubting!
I'm shouting! Smile—
Tho' work may be real serious,
Smile until you're delirious.

Hey, hey, foot! Hey, straw foot!
Lift your foot! Smile.

HERE SHE COMES

Introduced by ensemble. Alternate titles: "Musical Entrance—Tilly" and "All Set! Let's Go."

Kings die to call her cutie;
With hearts she'll play.
Ever our loyal duty
We will pay.
Here comes our royal beauty,
Queen of May.
Here she comes! Make way!
We've crowned her today
The Queen of the May.

WHEN I GO ON THE STAGE

Published February 1928. Introduced by Beatrice Lillie and ensemble.

VERSE 1

TILLY: Do you think I look like Marilyn Miller?
They say my looks will kill 'er.
ALL: Poor little Marilyn Miller.
TILLY: Others say I look like Marion Davies.*
ALL: Whom else would you suggest?
TILLY: I look like sweet Mae West!
I know I show great promise as an actress
And you can bet
I'll get one yet.
ALL: Is that a promise?
Is that a promise?
TILLY: That's not a promise, that's a threat!

REFRAIN 1

TILLY: I'll follow my ambition
And take up my position.
ALL: You'll be a star when you go on the stage.
TILLY: I'll make Irene Bordoni
Look like a poor baloney,
And Fannie Ward will start to look her age.

Alternate version:
    Others say that I'm like Gloria Swanson.

ALL: To hear your voice and cheer your voice
We'll track the globe.
TILLY: As a willing ham for Dillingham
I'll pack the Globe.
Charles King and Louise Groody
Will look like Punch and Judy.
But I don't care—
I'm going on the stage.

REFRAIN 2

TILLY: That youthful star Miss Talley
Will yodel in an alley.
My voice will ring when I go on the stage.
That statue called Jeritza
Will shiver when it hits 'er.
While Galli-Curci sings off key with rage,
Poor Schumann-Heink will hear
The fame my voice enjoys.
She'll come to earth
And then give birth to six more boys.
When I sing for Casazza,
He'll fall on his piazza.
But I don't care—
I'm going on the stage!

VERSE 2

TILLY: I have a voice that's never screechy or
squealy;
I have a voice like Gigli.
BOYS: You mean like Blossom Seeley!
TILLY: Others say my voice is like Miss Bori's
Or like Rose Ponsella's.
BOYS: You mean two other fellas!
TILLY: Someday they may acclaim my name with
bravos.
It will be heard
A household word.
BOYS: You'll get showers
Of jewels and flowers!
TILLY: My dears, I'll even get the bird.

REFRAIN 3

ALL: She'll make Rosina Galli
Perform her last finale;
She'll do some steps when she goes on the
stage.
The Albertina Rasch girls
Will look for jobs as cash girls,
While Harland Dixon breaks his legs with
rage.
Pavlova will receive a chill
When you go on;
She has no chance
You'll make her dance
The dying swan.

And when she does her ballet,
She'll show her Bacchanale;
She doesn't care,
She's going on the stage.

SMART PEOPLE

Introduced by ensemble. Danced by Clifton Webb and
Phyllis Rae. Added shortly after the show's opening.

VERSE

Isn't it sweet?
Yes, it's simply marvelous.
This is style!
It must be great
Living in a state of bliss.
Isn't it swell!
Yes, it's simply wonderful.
It's worthwhile.
We'd love to roam
All around a home like this.
Better get wise to the people here.
Hang around while I make it clear.

REFRAIN

Smart people do no thinking
Because they're smart.
Smart people, when they're drinking,
Don't talk of art!
Nobody starts romancing
When he is with his wife;
Changes his partner dancing
Just as he always does in life.
Smart people get hot quicker
When Greek meets Greek.
Smart people like strong liquor
And ladies weak!
All of them keep so busy
Finding ways to fall.
Smart people do no thinking at all.

WHEN I SAW HIM LAST

Introduced by Clifton Webb, Frank Doane, and ensemble.
Alternate title: "Finale, Act I."

PARKER: When I saw him last,
There was the child
Lying in his crib.

As I came past,
The infant smiled
And waved his little bib!
For children always go to me
And this one said "hello" to me!
ALL: Children always go to him
And this one said "hello" to him.
HEMINGWAY: But he's lost, you say—
In what way
Have you all gone mad today?
PARKER: Nursey took him for an airing,
Stopping in the traffic,
She bought the child an apple
And a copy of the *Graphic!*
The baby read such horrible tales
Beyond his mind's endurance.
He feared the nurse would murder
him
To collect his life insurance!
ALL: We feared the nurse would murder
him
To collect his life insurance.
PARKER: So he jumped for the crib;
He was no little craven.
And hopped into a railroad train
That was starting for New Haven.
ALL: New Haven?
PARKER: New Haven. Now he's riding for
New Haven!
What a place for a child to go!
It's a naughty college town.
I fear he'll learn to drink and smoke
And let his garters down.
ALL: What a place for a child to go!
It's a naughty college town.
I fear he'll learn to drink and smoke
And let his garters down.
HEMINGWAY: What a pack of lies! I've never
heard worse!
PARKER: Good Lord, you wouldn't doubt the
nurse!
For she's an American girl
Who was born and bred in the
U.S.A.!
She was born beneath the flag we
love,
Could such a girl lie, I say!

WHERE CAN THE BABY BE?

Introduced by Frank Doane, Pearl Eaton, Joan Clement,
Phyllis Rae, and ensemble.

Where can the baby be?
Think of its mother and dad.
They must be in an awful state;
Isn't it terribly sad?
Where can the baby be?
Why should we all be sad?
Things may not be so bad.
Perhaps he broke his leg
As babies often do.
That baby's habits weren't so neat;
Perhaps he fell upon the street.
He may have hurt his pride
And cracked his bottle too.
He'll never get his vitamins,
His oatmeal and his tea.
His paregoric waits in vain.
Where can the baby be?

A BABY'S BEST FRIEND

Published February 1928. Introduced by Beatrice Lillie.

VERSE

A baby can only have one mother;
She never belongs to no other;
Baby's smiles and baby's tears
Keep on smiling through the years.
When baby's tired,
And baby's blue,
And baby's hungry,
Her mother's true.

REFRAIN

Sleep on!
Mother's watching you.
Sleep on!
Soft and low!
Hush! Hush!
Close those eyes of blue,
Lullaby!
To sleep you'll go.
You can have another pal,
Another lover,
But a baby can only have one mother;
When you're tired and all alone
And a million miles from home,
A baby's best friend is its mother.

RECITATION

She was only a woman,
But the world called her bad;

She was only a human
Who was beaten and sad;
The courtroom was crowded,
And they jeered at her shame,
When a man should have gotten
The stain and the blame.
"Next case!" cried the clerk,
And she stood on the stand
With a tear in her eye
And four handkerchiefs in her hand.
"This woman is guilty,"
The district attorney cried.
And no lawyer to help her
Stood close to her side.
"I am innocent, sir,"
She replied to the judge.
And a tear down her face melted:
Her face was a smudge.
"I believe you," cried the judge,
"And I'll give you a chance."
"Oh, sir," cried the woman,
"I am now in a trance.
Oh, why do you help me?
When I'm beaten and sad?"
And the judge removed the wig
And mustache that he had.
"Don't you recognize me?
Come look in my eye!"
"My God, it's my MOTHER!"
The woman replied.
When you're tired and all alone
And a million miles from home,
A baby's best friend is its mother.

HOW WAS I TO KNOW?

Published December 1927. Dropped before the New York opening. Same music used later for "Why Do You Suppose?" in *Heads Up!* (1929).

VERSE

I wasn't so good sometimes;
I'd fib if I could sometimes;
I wasn't a saint in my mind.
So faraway high Heaven
Could never be my Heaven;
I hardly could hope ever
To find Heaven.

REFRAIN

How was I to know
That angels were living

Till I met you?
How was I to know
That wonders could happen
And dreams come true?
How did all the fates contrive
To let this perfect day arrive
And make me glad to be alive
And see that you could care for me?
In this world below
My picture of Heaven
Was skies of blue.
How was I to know
That I'd meet an angel like you?

WHOOPSIE

Published December 1927. Introduced by Beatrice Lillie, Clifton Webb, and ensemble. Dropped shortly after the New York opening.

VERSE 1

We may be sad and nervy
When things go topsy-turvy
And all the luck that comes to us is bad.
But the man worthwhile
Is the man who can smile.
So smile, smile, smile.
We've a cure
That's very sure
To make you glad as Pollyanna.
Say this word,
That sound absurd,
And joys come raining down like manna.

REFRAIN 1

Whoopsie!
Let little tears go sprinkle, sprinkle,
Just flit around and be gay.
Whoopsie!
Let little bells go tinkle, tinkle,
Spring's only nine months away.
Jog along just like a jaguar
With the coons of Nicaragua.
Cry ho!
Heigh-ho!
Say hey! Hey! Hey!
Whoopsie!
When cats and dogs go pitter-patter,
Just let them rain from the sky;
So look for the silver Whoopsie,
And watch the clouds roll by.

VERSE 2

When ev'rything's gaflooey
And life is simply phooey,
Let Nance O'Neil and Eva Le Gallienne sigh.
For the man who gets by
Is the man who can fly.
So fly, fly, fly.
If you're broke
And all's in soak,
Don't start in crying like a blubber;
Break a leg,
Go out and beg
And buy a nice new leg of rubber.

REFRAIN 2

Whoopsie!
When little hopes go humpy-bumpy,
Yodel a few fol-de-rols.
Whoopsie!
When little nerves go jumpy-jumpy,
Learn how to cut paper dolls.
Start a trance in Transylvania
With the Liths of Lithuania.
Chance gone.
Pants gone.
Cut up! Shut up!
Whoopsie!
When all ideals go hotsy-totsy,
Dear old asylum is nigh;
So look for the silver Whoopsie,
And let the clouds roll by.

WASN'T IT GREAT?

Introduced by Jack Whiting, Nick Long, Jr., William McCarthy, Joan Clement, Pearl Eaton, Phyllis Rae, and ensemble. Alternate title: "It's All Over Now."

CHORUS: Wasn't it great? Wasn't it swell!
          Did you hear the people yell!
EATON: Didn't Tilly cut capers!
S.M.: Wait till you see the papers!
CHORUS: How can they knock! What'll they
          say!
          It's the best show on Broadway.
CLEMENTS: Gosh, we ought to make money.
S.M.: Critics are very funny.
LONG: I've got a paper.
ALL: Hurray! What does it say?
       Turn the page, give us a glance.
LONG: Hey! Please give a fellow a chance.

RAE: Where's the theatrical page?

LONG: Here's the news of the stage.

S.M.: Tonight Miss Polly Hammond will
grin.
Say, this hasn't got the dope in.
Where the deuce do they begin it?

LONG: It's the early edition and nothing is
in it.

S.M.: No matter how well you do in a
show
The critics can make or ruin a show

LONG: It may be a bird you have faith in
And it's labeled a turkey by George
Jean Nathan.

POLLY &
PARKER: We've got 'em, we've got 'em!
Hurray!

ALL: Hurray! Let's look!

PARKER: Here's Woollcott!
He's written a great big book!
A panic! A riot of color and legs!

ALL: Dear old Alec! He knows his eggs.

POLLY: Here's Atkinson!

HEMINGWAY: Hammond!

EATON: Van Dyke!

LONG: And here's Dale!

HEMINGWAY: Walt Winchell and Coleman say it
can't fall!

PARKER: Look at Burns Mantle, he says it's a
wow!
And old Kelcey Allen, it's all over
now!

ALL: Washington's a mighty name
And Lincoln's great, we know,
Yet history will call to fame
The boys of old Park Row.

So Woollcott
And Gabriel
And Hammond
We hail!
And Winchell
And Coleman
And Vreeland
And Dale!
There's Allison Smith
And there's Davis' wife.
There's Van Dyke
And Dudley
And Benchley of *Life*.
There's Atkinson, Anderson, Mantle,
and wow!
There's old Kelcey Allen,
It's all over now.

PRESENT ARMS | 1928

Tryout: Shubert Playhouse, Wilmington, Delaware, April 9–14, 1928; Apollo Theatre, Atlantic City, New Jersey, April 18–21, 1928. New York run: Lew Fields' Mansfield Theatre, April 26–September 1, 1928. 155 performances. Music by Richard Rodgers. Lyrics by Lorenz Hart. Produced by Lew Fields. Book by Herbert Fields. Staged by Alexander Leftwich. Dances and musical numbers staged by Busby Berkeley. Settings by Wood and Harvey. Costumes by Milgrim. Orchestra under the direction of Roy Webb. Orchestrations by Roy Webb and Hans Spialek. Cast, starring Charles King and Flora Le Breton, included Busby Berkeley and Joyce Barbour.

Music for the Act II ensemble number "Kohala Welcome," also titled "Welcome," and "What Price Love," a deleted ballad, was found at the Warner Brothers Music warehouse in Secaucus, New Jersey. The Rodgers and Hammerstein office has a copy of an orchestral score for "Kohala Welcome." Lyrics for both numbers are missing.

TELL IT TO THE MARINES

Introduced by Charles King, Franker Woods, Fuller Mellish, Jr., Busby Berkeley, and ensemble. Earlier title: "A Bunch o' Nuts."

VERSE

CHICK: A sailor man may sport
    A girl in ev'ry port.
DOUG: A soldier can take care of two or three.
FRANK: Marines in ev'ry station
    Run through the population.
CHICK: We even make the lady salmons leap at
    sea!
DOUG: A soldier thinks he's rough.
    A sailor may be tough.
MAC: Their line of lousy lingo makes you
    dizzy!
FRANK: They may be tough and mean,
    But compared to a marine
    A soldier or a sailor is a lizzie!
DOUG: We can fight and ev'ry night we grab the
    frails.
MAC: Uncle Sam don't give a damn
    Because we're hard as nails!

REFRAIN

    Tell it to the old marines.*
    We've easy jobs,

When song was titled "A Bunch o' Nuts," lines 1, 9, and 11:

  1: Nuts! We're just a lot o' nuts.
  9: The bimbos make us welcome in their huts.
  11: There's guts behind this bunch o' nuts.

On land we say we're gobs,
It's either head or tail,
We're soldiers when we sail;
On land and sea
We're hippopotami!
We're soldiers that are sailors in Hawaii
And actors on the moving picture
    screens.
Skoits all love to wash our undershoits.
That's why they tell it to marines.

YOU TOOK ADVANTAGE OF ME

Published April 1928. Introduced by Joyce Barbour, Busby Berkeley, and ensemble.

VERSE 1

DOUGLAS: In the spring when the feeling was
    chronic
    And my caution was leaving you flat,
    I should have made use of the tonic
    Before you gave me *that!*
    A mental deficient you'll grade me.
    I've given you plenty of data.
    You came, you saw and you slayed me,
    And that-a is that-a!

REFRAIN

    I'm a sentimental sap, that's all.
    What's the use of trying not to fall?
    I have no will,
    You've made your kill
    'Cause you took advantage of me!
    I'm just like an apple on a bough
    And you're gonna shake me down
    somehow.
    So what's the use,
    You've cooked my goose
    'Cause you took advantage of me!
    I'm so hot and bothered that I don't
    know
    My elbow from my ear.
    I suffer something awful each time you
    go
    And much worse when you're near.
    Here am I with all my bridges burned,
    Just a babe in arms where you're
    concerned,
    So lock the doors
    And call me yours
    'Cause you took advantage of me.

VERSE 2

EDNA: When a girl has the heart of a mother
    It must go to someone, of course;
    It can't be a sister or brother
    And so I loved my horse.
    But horses are frequently silly—
    Mine ran from the beach of Kailua
    And left me alone for a filly,
    So I-a picked you-a.

REPEAT REFRAIN

DO I HEAR YOU SAYING, "I LOVE YOU"?

Published April 1928. Introduced by Flora Le Breton and Charles King. Alternate title: "Do I Hear You Saying?"

VERSE 1

HE: Is it really me?
    Is it really you?
    Do I really see
    And hear you too?
    Are we both awake?
    Are you standing there?
    Will the vision break
    That seemed so fair?
    Will it melt in empty air?

REFRAIN

    Do I hear you saying,
    "I love you! I love you!"
    Are those lovely words for me?
    Tell me you're not playing,
    It is true, you do too;
    It's too wonderful to be.
    Just to think that now I'll hold you in my
    arms,
    Sent from Heaven just to call mine, all
    mine.
    If I hear you saying,
    "I love you! I love you!"
    Life's been awfully good to me.

VERSE 2

SHE: I was not alive
    Till it came to be;
    How did fate contrive
    Such joy for me?
    When you heard me say

That you were my choice,
Did you hear the way
Love filled my voice?
I've a reason to rejoice.

REPEAT REFRAIN

A KISS FOR CINDERELLA

Published May 1928. Introduced by Busby Berkeley, Fuller Mellish, Jr., Franker Woods, and Charles King.

VERSE 1

FRANK: A Jane once was called Cinderella,
    Whose life wasn't much of a panic.
    She kept under the thumbs of her
      sisters, two bums;
    Poor kid was their kitchen mechanic.
MCKENNA: She was dead on the level, a virtuous
    slob,
    She never played house with a soldier
    or gob.
DOUGLAS: Her sisters went out but they never
    would take her
    And they dressed her so cheesy no guy
    tried to make her
FRANK: But Cindy went out to de ball!
ALL: Cindy went out to de ball!
MCKENNA: And, Chick, you're a feller that's like
    Cinderella
    And we're dressing you up for the
    ball.

REFRAIN 1

FRANK: Here is Cinderella's shoit,
    Stiff and clean from doit,
    And here's a little kiss for Cinderella.
MCKENNA: Here's the glove that's gonna fit
    On her hairy mitt,
    And here's another kiss for Cinderella.
DOUGLAS: Here is Cindy's little lingerie
    And the lacy things that no one can
    see.
FRANK: Cindy darling, give a glance,
    Here's your little pants.
    And here's another kiss for Cinderella.
ALL: Cinderella's going to the ball.

VERSE 2

FRANK: Her godmother said, "You're a
    princess!
    You poor little kitchen canary,"
    So, Chick, never fear, I'm your
    godmother dear,
MCKENNA: And that's what I call a good fairy.
DOUGLAS: Her foot was so tiny to fit it was hard.
FRANK: Her foot was a foot, but your foot is a
    yard.
MCKENNA: She had a complexion as smooth as
    vanilla
FRANK: And Chick has a skin that is draped
    with chinchilla.
DOUGLAS: But Cindy got hot at the ball.
ALL: Cindy got hot at the ball.
MCKENNA: Here's grease for that thick head to
    make it a slick head;
    You'll just look divine at the ball.

REFRAIN 2

DOUGLAS: Here's a hanky just for show,
    Here is one for blow.
    And here's a little kiss for Cinderella.
MCKENNA: Here's a thing you've used, I hope.
    It is known as soap.
    And here's another kiss for Cinderella.
FRANK: Use this Listerine and plenty too,
    And your friends will never know that
    it's you.
DOUGLAS: Here's the hat to fit the bean
    Of our little queen.
CHICK: And how's about a kiss for Cinderella?
ALL: Cinderella's going to the ball!

VERSE 3

DOUGLAS: You must make a hit with the peerage;
    Be careful and don't be a flivver!
CHICK: Don't worry; for years
    I have hung around piers!
FRANK: The piers that are on the East River!
MCKENNA: And, Cindy, when you eat your chow
    with a lord,
    It ain't highly proper to swallow a
    sword!
CHICK: Say, kid, when I eat I'm a bird that
    has culture.
FRANK: You eat like the bird that is known as
    the vulture.
CHICK: But Cindy will go to the ball.
ALL: Cindy will go to the ball.
MCKENNA: Remember, don't hiccup
    Or drink in the teacup.
ALL: You must be refined at the ball.

REFRAIN 3

FRANK: Chick, you need a guide tonight
    Who will steer you right.
    I think I better go with Cinderella!
CHICK: Darling, if your pan they see
    They'll be on to me!
    I don't think you should go with
    Cinderella.
MCKENNA: We're aristocratic through and through.
FRANK: Mac and I are Knights of Pythias too.
DOUGLAS: You would simply be de trop.
MCKENNA: Sure, that's why we'll go.
CHICK: Come kiss and say goodbye to
    Cinderella.
ALL: Cinderella's going to the ball.

IS IT THE UNIFORM?

Introduced by Flora Le Breton and ensemble.

VERSE

SHE: There's never any chance for poor
    civilians,
    The soldier has a handicap to win,
    Though the Lady's Colonel and Mr.
    O'Grady
    Are brothers under the skin.
    A millionaire may give a girl his millions
    And all she'll do is kiss him with a smirk.
BOYS: But let her meet a leatherneck;
    You'll see them both together neck.
SHE: It's wonderful how nature does her work.
BOYS: We know our beans:
    Join the marines!

REFRAIN

Is it the uniform?
Is it the man?
What is the magnet for a maid?
Clothing can ruin a form,
But with a tan
Soldiers are handsome on parade.
When into two strong arms you've strayed,
Do you want muscle or gold braid?
If it's the uniform,
Alter your plan.
Just keep your eye upon the man.

119

CRAZY ELBOWS

Published April 1928. Introduced by Demaris Doré and ensemble.

VERSE

I used to lay me down
And sleep like dead men do;
Now troubles weigh me down,
Excitement burns me through;
My life was once so placid,
To acid it grew,
Like swords that slay me down
Flapping,
Snapping.

REFRAIN

Crazy elbows!
Keeping time with a crazy tune!
Crazy elbows!
You'll be driving me crazy soon!
Songs used to be for singing,
Nights used to be for sleep,
Now I see elbows swinging,
In all my dreams their beat they keep!
Crazy motion,
Like a pendulum in my brain!
Crazy ocean,
Moving forward and back again!
On with the nervous music,
Shivering high and low!
Watch those crazy elbows go!

NUTS, HE TRAVELS WITH US NUTS

Introduced by the company. Alternate title: "Finale, Act I." After a few performances the ending was revised slightly and ended with a reprise of "Do I Hear You Saying, 'I Love You'?"

MAC: Nuts, he travels with us nuts—
    Say, ain't he cute in Captain
        Wiggins' suit?
    Them shoulder bars is lies,
    Them pants is a disguise.
ALL BUMS: On land and sea—a bozo he will
    be . . .
DELPHINE: Charles, do you allow your boys to
    talk to you in this way?

FRANK: Boys, he ain't my father.
MAC (TO
DELPHINE): You're a sentimental sap, that's all.
    You was getting ready for a fall.
ALL BUMS: You had no will,
    He made his kill
    'Cause he took advantage of you!
FRANK: Cinderella's dressed up nice and
        slick,
    Underneath the clothing is a hick!
ALL BUMS: So what's the use,
    He cooked your goose
    'Cause he took advantage of you.
MAC: You got so hot and bothered. He
        was a sap
    But you was twice as dumb—
FRANK: You didn't know the difference
        between a cap
    And Chick, who's just a bum!
ALL BUMS: Here are you with all your bridges
        burned,
    Just a babe in arms where he's
        concerned.
    You locked your doors
    And called him yours
    'Cause he took advantage of you.
DELPHINE
(TO CHICK): Tell these fools they're lying—
CHICK: What's the use—it's true.
OLIVER: Upon my soul this is too much!
    Go—all of you.
DELPHINE: Please, Father.
ALL BUMS: Congratulations, Chick.
    She's a broad with class!
    And you ought to stick!
    This bimbo sure does pass!
    Lady, you're a lulu,
    Lady, you're a pip.
    Chick, you are a lucky guy
    And we'll all join the wedding trip.
CHICK: I don't hear you saying, "I love
        you! I love you!"
    No more lovely words for me!
    There's no use in playing!
    It ain't true,
    It ain't true,
    It's too wonderful to be.
DELPHINE: Just to think I let you hold me in
        your arms,
    Sent from Heaven just to call mine,
        all mine.
    If I hear you saying, "I love you! I
        love you!"
    It's a jolly joke on me.
CHICK: Delphine, I tried to tell you,
    But you wouldn't let me.
OLIVER: Will you go—you common loafers.
FRANK: I was never so insulted in my life.

MCKENNA: Don't be insulted—it's everybody's
        party.
    Come on, baby—
DELPHINE: Will you go—
HOTSY-TOTSY: Crazy lady, he's a bozo as hard as
        nails.
FRANK: Crazy lady, if he ain't I'm the
        Prince of Wales.
ALL BUMS: Songs used to be for singing,
    Nights used to be for sleep, [etc., as
        in "Crazy Elbows"]

DOWN BY THE SEA

Published April 1928. Introduced by Charles King and ensemble. Earlier title: "Whoopie."

VERSE

I'll never be gypped,
I've my diploma
From girls in Egypt
And La Paloma.
In many places
I took a jade out.
But now their faces all fade out.

REFRAIN

Down by the sea
I've got a lady who makes "whoopie" with me!
Now and then
I get a yen for her.
And ev'ry time that we kiss
She gives me lots of that and plenty of this.
She has whims that all the hims prefer.
She's the reason why
The sailors cry
To spend the night ashore.
Easy to please but anyway she's no bore.
She has no college degree,
She's just a lady who makes "whoopie" with me.
That is why I live down by the sea!

I'M A FOOL, LITTLE ONE

Published April 1928. Introduced by Joyce Barbour, Busby Berkeley, Franker Woods, and Gaile Beverly.

VERSE 1

People of ability and talents
Often are a little off their balance;
It's very plain
There is a strain
Upon their brain.
Even Mr. Edwin Booth and Barrett
Had a little mousey in the garret.
Though they were bright,
They weren't quite
What you call right.
And though you think I'm as sane as can be,
Something is bothering me:
I confess that I am rarely all there.

REFRAIN 1

I'm a fool, little one,
'Cause I must be crazy to care for you.
I'm a fool, little one, that's all.
As a rule, little one,
You behave exactly as Mormons do.
As a rule, little one, you fall.
I admit you're my first one
And you're the worst one
I've ever met.
I don't know why I'm bound here;
The run-around here
Is all I get.
I'm a fool, little one.
It's a pity, but it's true.
I'm a fool, little one, for you!

REFRAIN 2

I'm a fool, little one,
'Cause I must be crazy to care so much.
I'm a fool, little one, I'm told.
As a rule, little one,
You are here to look at but not to touch.
As a rule, little one, you're cold.
When I need love and kisses,
Believe me, this is
No life to live.
Where were you born, in what land?
It must be Scotland,
The way you give.
I'm a fool, little one.
It's a pity, but it's true.
I'm a fool, little one, for you.

VERSE 2

SHE: I'm so happy on the days you turn up.
 HE: Every time I look at you, I burn up.
SHE: Come, let us cling.
 HE: O death, I sing,
      Where is thy sting?

SHE: If I'm just a little tall, please stretch up.
 HE: You look like a bottle of red catsup.
SHE: Don't start to chaff.
 HE: Don't make me laugh,
      My sweet giraffe.
      I cannot get all the things that you said.
      You're talking over my head.
SHE: Yet in this towering dome,
 HE: No one's home.

REFRAIN 3

SHE: I'm a fool little one,
      For I wouldn't love you if I were wise.
      I'm a fool, little one, that's all.
 HE: I'm a mule, little one,
      And I don't like taking much exercise.
      As a mule, little one, I stall.
SHE: I'm a hot volcano,
      So don't you say no,
      Be good to me.
 HE: Looking up at your crater,
      A red tomater
      Is all I see.
      I'm a fool, little one.
      It's a pity, but it's true.
      I'm a fool, little one, for you.

THIS RESCUE IS A TERRIBLE CALAMITY

Introduced by the company. Alternate title: "Finaletto, Act II, Scene 3."

DOUGLAS: This rescue is a terrible calamity!
         I'd like to see some desert island life!
   EDNA: He is right—why did it just occur
             when, damn it, he
         Was finding out he really had a wife.
   BOYS: It's just an awful break!
         We could kill that rescue crew;
         They could have had the decency to
             wait a day
         Or two.
 MARIA &
   GIRLS: Here on the island alone with men,
         When will such a lucky chance come
             around again!
         A girl can't help what happens
         When there's no one round to stop
             her!
         It was the only proper way
         We could have been improper!

CREW: You're saved! Hurray!
      And now we saved the day—
  ALL: We'd be obliged if you would go
          away—
CHICK (TO
DELPHINE): Are you sorry we have to go?
HORTENSE: Oh, Mac, are you sorry—?
    MAC: What a question!
         I was just in the middle of an
             important suggestion.
DOUGLAS: Who invented rescue boats?
         We ask in dejection.
   EDNA: Where can I sow those wild, wild
             oats?
         I've got a big collection.
   CREW: You're saved! Hurray!
         And now we've saved the day.
    ALL: We'd be obliged if you would go
             away.
         We have to be conventional
         Though it is not intentional
         And virtue wins the day.

BLUE OCEAN BLUES

Published April 1928. Introduced by Charles King and male ensemble. Same music, with a slightly revised lyric, as "Atlantic Blues" in *Lido Lady* (1926).

VERSE

The sea is darker than the sky,
I fear each wave as it rolls by.
And the ocean roars with glee
Ev'ry time I sigh.
The sky is like a hollow dome
Above a rolling sea of foam.
Ocean, turn that ship around,
Make it sail for home.

REFRAIN

Sailing,
I've got those weeping, wailing blue ocean blues.
Nervous,
I've got those Lord-preserve-us blue ocean blues.
Ill winds, chill winds creep right under my skin;
While I sleep, troubles keep rolling in;
Grieving,
I've got those sweetie-leaving blue ocean blues.
Hating,
Those ever-separating blue ocean blues;
Oh, that woe that sends my heart to my shoes
So that I've got those blue ocean blues.

HAWAII

Introduced by ensemble. Alternate title: "Coralline."

Coralline and blue,
The rainbow pales for you,
Hawaii;
Blue and coralline,
Upon a sea of green,
Hawaii.
Once the ocean smiled
And you were her child;
Born of her sheen
That the sun in his love had beguiled.
Coralline and blue,
Land of rainbow hue!
Fair and as wild as the ocean,
For you are her child,
So kiss the blue
That cradled you.

I LOVE YOU MORE THAN YESTERDAY

Published February 1929. Intended for Charles King and Flora Le Breton, but dropped before the New York opening. Introduced in *Lady Fingers* (1929) by Louise Brown and John Price Jones.

VERSE 1

I love you more
When I awaken
Than I adore you in a dream.
Each time we meet
I'm not mistaken
For twice as sweet you seem.
At night I dream that you're mine.
But ev'ry day you're more mine.

REFRAIN

I love you more than yesterday
But less than tomorrow.
Much less than tomorrow.

You are sweeter now than yesterday,
How lovely you are, oh,
Goodbye to my sorrow.
Those eyes just made for me
Won't fade for me,
They'll always shine.
So let me take your heart
And make your heart
Completely mine.
Though I know I loved you yesterday
I'll love you tomorrow
Much more than today.

VERSE 2

I love you still.
My love increases.
I have no will when you're away.
My fondest dreaming never ceases
But seems enhanced each day!
And since I've found that I care,
That heart of yours is my care.

REPEAT REFRAIN

Richard Rodgers and Lorenz Hart (holding John) aboard the *Berengaria*

CHEE-CHEE | 1928

Tryout: Forrest Theatre, Philadelphia, August 27–September 15, 1928. New York run: Lew Fields' Mansfield Theatre, September 25–October 20, 1928. 31 performances. Music by Richard Rodgers. Lyrics by Lorenz Hart. Produced by Lew Fields. Book by Herbert Fields. Earlier title: *Violet Town*. Adapted from Charles Petit's novel *The Son of the Grand Eunuch*. Directed by Alexander Leftwich. Dances and musical numbers staged by Jack Haskell. Settings by John Hawkins, Jr. Costumes by John Booth. Orchestra under the direction of Roy Webb. Orchestrations by Roy Webb. Cast, starring Helen Ford, included Stark Patterson, Betty Starbuck, George Hassell, William Williams, George Houston, and Philip Loeb.

Lyrics are missing for the following numbers: "Chee-Chee's Second Entrance," "Finale Act I," "Monastery Opening," and an untitled second-act trio.

WE'RE MEN OF BRAINS

Introduced by ensemble. Alternate title: "Eunuchs' Chorus." This was the second number; the opening number ("Prelude") did not have a lyric.

EUNUCHS: We're men of brains, endowed with
tact!
We're muscular and neat!
And yet, our lives, to be exact,
Are rather incomplete!

I AM A PRINCE

Introduced by Stark Patterson. No. 3 in the first-act sequence.

PRINCE
TAO TEE: I do not know my father very well,
I am a Prince.
His love is like a pearl beneath a shell,
I am a Prince!
My mother's very kind, they say,
I hope to know her better.
A hundred moons have gone their way
And more since last I met her!
And that is why it makes me wince
That I am a Prince.

IN A GREAT BIG WAY

Introduced by Betty Starbuck. No. 4 in the first-act sequence.

LI LI WEE: The holy man has eighty-one sweet
names on his chart;
I want to hold the eighty-second place
in his heart!
Though I'll just have a fraction of
married satisfaction,
If he's a man of action,
I'll wed today
In a great big way!

THE MOST MAJESTIC OF DOMESTIC OFFICIALS

Introduced by ensemble. Alternate title: "Entrance of the Grand Eunuch." No. 5 in the first-act sequence.

EUNUCHS: The most majestic of domestic officials,
The great G.E., we fear his mighty
initials!
Don't think it too absurd
That we heed his lightest word.
We bow our heads in reverence
Lest we should feel their severance.
Li Pi Siao! Li Pi Siao!

HOLY OF HOLIES

Introduced by George Hassell and Betty Starbuck. Alternate title: "Prayer." No. 6 in the first-act sequence.

LI PI SIAO: Holy of holies! Wafers of jade!
On which the Emperor's love song is
played.
Lightly my fingers caress you in bliss.
Is there beatitude sweeter than this!
[*Li Li Wee laughs*]
Be still, you little wart!
I hear with sweetest exaltation
The jades' clink with tintinnabulation,
With symbols of felicitation.
Is there beatitude sweeter than this?
LI LI WEE: Say, Pop, listen . . .

LI PI SIAO: Damn you, you loathsome brat!
Oh, the night of love, oh, the peace!
LI LI WEE: Pop, your only daughter has a
petition.
LI PI SIAO: I'll slaughter you!
Oh, the night of love with no
surcease,
Pleasure supernal
In prayers diurnal to Heaven!

HER HAIR IS BLACK AS LICORICE

Introduced by George Hassell. Alternate title: "Food Solo." No. 7 in the first-act sequence.

LI PI SIAO: Her hair is black as licorice,
Her eyes are round as peas.
Each eyebrow somewhat slicker is
Than the skin of Edam cheese!
Her cheeks are soft as hominy,
Her lips are sweet as wine,
Brewed in the anno domini
Of 1869.
Her neck is as luscious as roast beef;
She has oranges where she has most
beef;
Her waist is as slim as an eel.
Her shoulder, the shoulder of veal;
Her leg is like the leg of lamb,
As shapely and as sweet.
My sad heart glows to see her toes,
They're like a piggy's feet.
She's nice enough to eat.

I'LL NEVER SHARE YOU

Apparently dropped before the New York opening. Intended for Betty Starbuck and Stark Patterson. First replaced by an untitled number for which music but no lyric survives. Then replaced, according to John McGlinn, by "Dear, Oh Dear." Alternate title: "If You Were My Concubine." No. 8 in the first-act sequence.

PRINCE
TAO TEE: If you were my concubine,
Wouldn't that be nice?
LI LI WEE: Maybe each eight years or nine
You'd see me once or twice.

No other spouse
Would run your house;
The air you breathe is my song.
Sweet one,
Any rival alive'll not be so long.

TAO TEE: Your life and mine will be harmonic.
LI LI WEE: Your other wives must be platonic!
TAO TEE: You will be my best love,
The rest, love, don't ever heed.
LI LI WEE: Soon you will agree, you,
With me you get all you need!
If you have other loves, beware, you,
For have a care, you,
I'll never share you.

[Enter Miss Smile-of-a-rose-at-the-dawning-of-spring]
MISS SMILE: A man! A man!
A man in the harem!
[Enter concubines]
ALL GIRLS: A man! Oh, joy's fulfillment.
LI LI WEE: I never knew before what the wish to
kill meant!
TAO TEE: Imagine them mine,
As they could be by Chinese custom.
LI LI WEE: Yes, their feet have been broken by
custom,
As their heads will be after I bust
'em!
GIRLS (2ND
CHORUS): We would love to share you.
The air you breathe is our breath.
LI LI WEE: For this competition,
My mission is that of death.
TAO TEE: Why can't we all be quite harmonic?
LI LI WEE: These ladies don't look so platonic.
TAO TEE: You will be my best, love,
The rest, love, don't ever heed.
LI LI WEE: Girls, you'll soon agree, you,
From me you will get all you need.
ALL: If you have other loves, beware, you,
For have a care, you,
I'll never share you.

DEAR, OH DEAR

Published October 1928. Introduced by Helen Ford and
William Williams. No. 8 (new) in first-act sequence.

VERSE 1

HE: Once a tree was just a tree,
A brook was just a brook;
A rose by other names to me
Was hardly worth a look.
Now that I'm a changed man,

An amorous, deranged man,
I breathe eternal spring,
I care for ev'rything.

REFRAIN

Dear, oh dear,
My darling, how I care for you!
I care for you alone!
In my car
Those little trumpets blare for you,
They're there for you, my own.
Because we two love
Those trumpets play.
You are my true love,
That's what they're trying to say.
Oh! Dear, oh dear,
I'd go I don't know where for you,
I care for you alone.

VERSE 2

SHE: Once a kiss was just a kiss,
A smile was just a smile.
To hold a manly hand like this
Was hardly worth the while.
Each boy was like a brother,
And one was like the other.
Your kisses seem to be
Not brotherly to me.

REPEAT REFRAIN

AWAIT YOUR LOVE

Introduced by George Hassell, Dorothy Raye, and ensemble. Alternate title: "Concubines' Song." No. 10 in the first-act sequence. No. 9 was Incidental Music.

LI PI SIAO: Await your love with utter
circumspection
And show your pride with sighs of
low abjection!
MISS SMILE: I'll bow my head and curtsy in a
fashion
And I'll be cold with true Imperial
passion!
LI PI SIAO: But soft! Bear her aloft!
ALL
CONCUBINES: Ah, lucky one . . . Ah, fortunate,
Our destiny's importunate and cold!
Poor tabby cats, we purr alone.
The Holy Man wants her alone to
hold.

For by some strange device in a year
She's been selected twice in a year!
Oh, must we wait until we grow too
old!

REFRAIN

Poor excited and benighted
unrequited jades!
We wait through afternoons for
unobliging moons!
With feet anointed and disjointed,
disappointed maids.
Each night it's just the same alone!
Concubines in name alone!
We must play the game alone!
They won't pick our jades!
Poor jades on jades!
Poor little jades!

JOY IS MINE

Introduced by William Williams. No. 11 in the first-act
sequence. Might have been dropped before the New York
opening.

LI PI TCHOU: Joy is mine! Bliss divine!
Joy is mine! Bliss divine!
I'm overwhelmed . . . I cannot
speak!
Your kindness leaves me very meek.
Oh, I'm so glad!
Ah, bliss divine!
Oh, joy,
Sweet joy
Is mine!

I WAKE AT MORNING

Introduced by William Williams. No. 12 in the first-act
sequence.

LI PI TCHOU: I wake at morning loving her much
more
Than I did before the morning.
I see the moon rise only to implore
Let me keep her for next moonrise.
She's mine alone for all my years;

Joy appears with my tears.
Life, let me keep her till my day is
through.
That's all I ask of you.

I GROVEL TO THE EARTH

Introduced by Helen Ford. Alternate title: "Chee-Chee's First Entrance." No. 13 in the first-act sequence.

CHEE-CHEE: I mumble, humble, jumble,
I grovel to the earth.
I shiver and I stumble
As I embrace your girth.
Oh, most morosely meditative
minister,
Why is your brow so serious and
sinister!
I flutter, stutter, mutter
With genuflections low.
My heart is soft as butter,
But that is hard to show!
Oh, mightiest and most majestic
mandarin,
Why did you call this little goose and
gander in?

JUST A LITTLE THING

Introduced by William Williams and Helen Ford. No. 14 in the first-act sequence.

LI PI TCHOU: You're a brainy little zany!
Come to me and cling!
All the fussing and discussing
Just a little thing.
CHEE-CHEE: Idle chatter on the matter
Good can never bring,
I won't sorrow on the morrow
For a little thing!
Care in limbo, arms akimbo,
Let your voices ring.
Like an airy young canary
Singing in the spring.
LI PI TCHOU: Stupid, ain't he? But you're dainty,
Oh, you little thing!
BOTH: Come, be gay! Sing high, sing low,
Happy as a King!

We will never weep in woe
For a little thing!

YOU ARE BOTH AGREED

Introduced by George Hassell, William Williams, and Helen Ford. Alternate title: "Finaletto, Scene 1." No. 15 in the first-act sequence.

SIAO: You are both agreed in your silly
rejection?
TCHOU: We are.
CHEE-CHEE: Oh yes, we are.
SIAO: Then both of you should be ready for
dissection.
TCHOU: We are.
CHEE-CHEE: Perhaps we are.
SIAO: But I'll be merciful and spare your
heads.
TCHOU: I look with scorn on you.
CHEE-CHEE: He means glad tears he sheds.
TCHOU (TO
CHEE-CHEE): I love your face, for you're so dear.
CHEE-CHEE: I love your head the more so, dear,
But not without its torso, dear!
SIAO: Enough, you're banished!
It's time you vanished.
So now depart and far away, I trust.
My eyes refuse to look on carnal
lust.
[He claps his hands. Two eunuchs enter]
Harness a mule and a two-wheel cart.
Hurry, swine!
[Waves eunuchs out]
Have you any money with which to
go?
TCHOU: No charity. Oh no!
CHEE-CHEE: My husband is hasty, please give him
no heed.
Kindest of fathers, we thank you
indeed.
I love him, I love him
With ardor complete,
But give me the money,
A lady must eat!
[Takes ingot from Siao]
SIAO: Be gone . . .
TCHOU: We go and will never return.
CHEE-CHEE: We go forever.
TCHOU: Your kindness I spurn!
[Snatches ingot from Chee-Chee and throws it to
ground. Siao reaches to pick it up. Chee-Chee grabs it
before he reaches it]

CHEE-CHEE: You give it back to me, then I must
keep it.
Farewell, farewell
SIAO: Be damned!
TCHOU: [Snatches money from Chee-Chee,
offers it]
Here's your gold back!
CHEE-CHEE: [Takes it back again]
Thank you, farewell.

I MUST LOVE YOU

Published September 1928. Introduced by Helen Ford and William Williams. No. 16 in the first-act sequence. It was the principal love theme music of show. Same music used for "Send for Me" in Simple Simon (1930).

VERSE 1

HE: In the gray of the dawn I see your eyes,
And, lo, the sun is bright as at noon!
Though the twilight has gone and dark the
skies,
You will be there to bring me the moon.
I wasn't born until the moment you came
in my life,
I was waiting for your coming to begin my
life!

REFRAIN

BOTH: I must love you.
While my heart is beating,
It keeps on repeating,
"Must love you!"
Till night is through.
While I sleep I form words,
And they are those warm words,
"Must love you!"
Oh, give your charms to my arms,
They need them so!
Take them away, and the day
Has lost its glow!
Oh, what can I do?
That's what I was born for.
While I live I must love you.

VERSE 2

SHE: When I whisper your name into the night,
The air's aglow in glory of gold!
When the sky is aflame with silver light,
In all the stars your glance I behold.
And if my life is blessed with joys, I owe
each thing to you;

126

Oh, the world is full of kindness when I
    cling to you!

REPEAT REFRAIN

OWL SONG

Introduced by William Griffith. Alternate title: "Song of
the Owl." No. 17 in the first-act sequence.

OWL: Young lady, you molest
    The sanctity of my nest.
    Before my door
    You hug and kiss with passion.
    You have no sense of shame
    And good folks give the name
    Of Jezebels to ladies of your fashion!
    You can't get my permission
    To hold this exhibition.
    Hoo-hoo-hoo-hoo!
    Are you a Chinese matron?
    Excuse me if I'm quizzical.
    Behold in me a spinster
    Who entreats you
    Don't be *physical*!

I BOW A GLAD GOOD DAY

Introduced by Philip Loeb, George Hassell, and ensemble.
Alternate title: "Tavern Opening." No. 19 in the first-act
sequence. No. 18 included change-of-scene music and a
reprise of "I Must Love You."

[*To chairs, pretending they are lovers*]
    GIRLS: I bow a glad good day,
    And beg of you to stay.
    I'm so enchanted to meet you, sir.
    Long hours we'll while away.
    What do you say?
[*Music answers*]
    Oh, what a deep fine voice is
      yours.
    Yes, you may hold my hand.
    Kiss me or no. The choice is
      yours.
    Oh, sir, you understand.
[*Enter innkeeper*]
  INNKEEPER: Stop your dancing, silly geese!

Give a man some mental peace.
Night and day in mad caprice.
My daughters, silly jades,
Kiss their chairs through springs
    and winters.
All you'll get is wooden splinters,
And you'll stay old maids.
Many years each daughter stands,
Left on Papa's hands!
[*Enter two girls*]
    GIRLS: A man! A man is there!
  OTHER GIRLS
& INNKEEPER: A man? A man? Oh, where?
  INNKEEPER: He's as ugly as a toad
    And his feet don't match.
    But the chances are
    He's a very good catch.
[*Exit innkeeper. Enter Li Pi Siao*]
    GIRLS: We curtsy, we curtsy,
    We bow a glad good day,
    And beg of you to stay.
    We're so enchanted to meet you,
      sir.
    Long hours we'll while away.
    What do you say?
    SIAO: Go away!
    GIRLS: Oh, what a deep fine voice is
      yours.
    Yes, you may hold my hand.
    SIAO: No reason to rejoice is yours,
    For you don't understand.
    I'm what you call a shy young
      man.
  1ST GIRL: I'm going to make you my young
      man.
    SIAO: With no ladies I'm acquainted,
    For my morals are so sainted.
    I am pure in heart and deed.
    GIRLS: Then a change is what you need.
    SIAO: I'm a frigid and mental man
    And strange is my life,
    For I am a gentleman
    Who's true to his wife.
    I do not fear love's arrow.
    GIRLS: How narrow! How narrow!
    There's no charm in your obesity.
    SIAO: For me you're no necessity.

BETTER BE GOOD TO ME

Published September 1928. Introduced by Betty Starbuck
and Stark Patterson. No. 20 in the first-act sequence.

VERSE 1

  HE: When a truly modest maid
    Is a lovely little jade,
    Then morality's an awful strain on
      appetite.
    I respect your stainless youth,
    But to speak the simple truth,
    I could put your form between
    My arms and wrap it tight!
    But I must hold back
    And just hold back
    The things I'd die to do.
    This yearning youth
    Is burning youth
    For you!

REFRAIN

  BOTH: How long will this last?
    Can't you work fast?
    Fever like this can't be.
    Better be good to me.
    I'm so pale and thin,
    Better give in.
    Love is what makes me ache.
    Hold me or else I'll break.
    Like a shadow I fade away.
    I was once a glad boy.
    Something tells me you soon will say
    He was not a bad boy.
    This has got to stop.
    Maybe I'll pop.
    Love is like TNT.
    Better be good to me.

VERSE 2

  SHE: When a youth, by any chance,
    Has a devastating glance,
    Then the proper thing seems rather
      puritanical;
    Saintly hands would like to clasp
    What a naughty hand would grasp,
    Yet around each wrist
    My bracelet is a manacle!
    When my calf-like eyes
    Can't laugh like eyes
    That shine away in joy;
    In lonely want
    I only want my boy.

REPEAT REFRAIN

THE TARTAR SONG

Published September 1928. Introduced by George Houston and ensemble. No. 21 in the first-act sequence. No lyric survives for either "Chee-Chee's Second Entrance," No. 22, or "Finale, Act I," No. 23.

A knife does all the talking for the Tartar!
And it speaks in cutting phrases to the foe!
For it soon can change a foeman to a martyr,
Suddenly strikes its blow!
When Tartar wives have other serenaders,
Then the knife can make their vocalizing fade!
If you would win a Tartar girl
Show her the Tartar blade!
For a fight you never have to ask us,
Tartars never have to be afraid.
Keep the steel they boast of in Damascus.
It is second grade
To the Tartar blade!
Yo, the Tartar!
Yo, the Tartar!
And his blade!
[Repeat first eight lines]

KHONGHOUSE SONG

Introduced by William Williams and ensemble. This appears to have been the first sung number in Act II; the second act probably opened with an instrumental number.

TCHOU: [As they beat him]
You need not keep this up till
dawn,
Although your work inspires you.
Pray, do not waste your vim and
brawn,
So stop it if it tires you.
KHONGHOUSES: Work is work and play is play,
Each one in its place is.
So we must arrange our day
On a business basis.
Heave, boys, ho!
Sound the blow,
Make it harder as you go!
TCHOU: My little chair will long for me.
Our long acquaintance now must
cease.
I'll vertically drink my tea
Each morning from the
mantelpiece!
KHONGHOUSES: Heave, boys, ho.

Sound the blow!
Make it harder as you go!
TCHOU: It's hard to work the way you do.
I see your perspiration mount.
And so, my friends, I beg of you,
Don't strain yourselves on my
account.
KHONGHOUSES: Here's one for your pity! [stroke]
Here's one for your hate! [stroke]
Here's one for some reason or
other! [stroke]
Here's one for your city! [stroke]
Here's one for your state! [stroke]
Here's one for your dear old
mother! [stroke]
While our energy deserts us
Yet our work we do!
Friend, believe us that it hurts us
More than it hurts you!
Work is work and play is play,
Each one in its place is.
So we must arrange our day
On a business basis!
TCHOU: Each efficient financier
Figures what his pace is.
Can't you call a rest right here
On a business basis?
KHONGHOUSES: Heave, boys, ho!
Sound the blow!
Make it harder as you go!
TCHOU: You'll overwork, I'm thinking of
you.
That really is my one dread.
KHONGHOUSES: Come, my hearties, that will do,
The count has reached one
hundred.

SLEEP, WEARY HEAD

Introduced by Helen Ford. No. 3 in the second-act sequence.

Sleep, weary head,
I won't go away.
So sleep till the night is through.
Sleep, teary head,
Your cares throw away.
Let love fill the night with dreams for you.
Come, cool your brow while night breezes blow.
Forgo
Your woe!
Sigh low, lie you down,
Let love tie you down.
Don't cry, weary head,

I love you so!
To sleep you'll go.
The moon is low.
I love you so!
I love you so!

SINGING A LOVE SONG

Published September 1928. Introduced by George Houston and ensemble. No. 4 in the second-act sequence. Later the same music, with a new lyric, became "I Still Believe in You" in Simple Simon (1930).

VERSE

When a man is melancholy
He's a silly bore,
And I stay,
Just that way,
Night and day.
Singing love songs is my folly,
While her ears ignore;
Though I know
It is so,
On I go,
While the tears of music flow.

REFRAIN

Singing a love song,
With no one to love,
With no hands to cover your hands.
Someone must hear you,
Or the song will fade;
Love duets are played by four hands.
Music is made of love alone,
Love is shown
In a tone.
Singing your heart out
Seems so very wrong
With no one to hear your song.

LIVING BUDDHA

Introduced by Philip Loeb, who portrayed Profundity and Meditation, the Grand Prior. No. 7 in the second-act sequence. Alternate title: "Impassive Buddha." It was preceded by "Monastery Opening," which has no surviving lyric, and "Chinese Dance," which had no lyric.

PRIOR: Impassive Buddha, smiling in your might,
Spread through my fingers, radiance of
sight.
Hear our poor voices calling; Buddha,
hark.
See this poor sinner groping in the dark!
Buddha impassive, set his eyes free.
Rise, little sinner, now you can see!

MOON OF MY DELIGHT

Published September 1928. Introduced by Betty Starbuck
and Stark Patterson. No. 8 in the second-act sequence.
Refrain has same melody as "Thank You in Advance."

VERSE 1

Moon of moons, when you are mine,
Bright the night will be.
But remember, when you shine,
Concentrate on me!
Moon of moons, be mine alone,
Mine alone—don't laugh, moon!
I would never care to own
A quarter or a half moon.

REFRAIN

Moon of my delight,
I'm going to put a ring around you—
You'll stay home tonight,
Scintillating where I found you.
When you were a little crescent,
Your manners were as soft as wool.
Now you're getting effervescent—
But maybe that's because you're full.
Moon of my delight,
If you'd only treat me right,
We could have a satellite or two,
Moon of my delight.

VERSE 2

You're my moon and I'm your earth,
Bless me with your gaze.
What are lovely evenings worth
If I lose your rays?
If you ever should depart,
I would be a mean cheese.
If you leave me, then your heart
Must be made of green cheese.

REPEAT REFRAIN

THANK YOU IN ADVANCE

A piano-vocal with lyrics of "Thank You in Advance" was
found at the Warner Brothers Music warehouse in Secaucus, New Jersey. Since it was written down by a copyist
on Rodart Music paper, it is probable that this version was
created after *Chee-Chee*, probably in 1931–1932. The
music is the same as "Moon of My Delight."

VERSE

I don't take the attitude
That the world is mine,
And I'm full of gratitude
When my luck is fine.
Though a gift is oh so small,
I do not reject it;
Anything looks good at all,
If I don't expect it.

REFRAIN

Thank you in advance
For keeping me around to cheer you;
Thank you in advance
For letting no one else come near you.
Thank you for the joys in store for
My happy little heart each day.
Let me thank you even more for
A wedding on the first of May.
You have not a chance
Of getting out of this romance.
For a little home and one, two, three,
Thank you in advance.

I GROVEL TO YOUR CLOTH

Introduced by Helen Ford. Alternate title: "Chee-Chee's
Third Entrance." No. 9 in the second-act sequence.

CHEE-CHEE: I mumble, humble, jumble,
I grovel to your cloth.
I shiver and I stumble.
I'm glad to bring you broth!
Oh, most profoundly practical
profundity,
I must respect your dignified
rotundity!
I stutter. I mutter
With genuflections low.
My heart is soft as butter,
But this is hard to show.

Oh, stateliest serene ecclesiastical,
My future habitation is monastical!

WE ARE THE HORRORS OF DEADLIEST WOE

Introduced by ensemble. Alternate title: "Chorus of Tor-
ments." No. 13 in the second-act sequence. It followed a
Trio that either is lost or was never written, the "Bonze
Entrance" (Incidental Music), and a reprise of "I Must
Love You."

[*Chorus of figures chant in monotone without music:*]
We are the horrors of deadliest woe,
Reaping the guerdon of crime.
Suffering torment till judgment we go,
Until the ending of time! [*Screams*]

OH, GALA DAY, RED-LETTER DAY

Introduced by principals and ensemble. Alternate title:
"Palace Opening." No. 14 in the second-act sequence.

ALL: Oh, gala day, red-letter day,
The Empire knows no better day.
A father lost his son,
But now the two are one.
The Holy Man's chief minister
No longer seems so sinister.
His lad who went astray
Parental love will now obey!
PRINCE: Here's Li Li Wee
And Li Pi Tchou
And Li Pi Siao.
In them you see
A fond and true
United trio.
ALL: Here comes Li Pi Siao!
Hail to Li Pi Siao!
[*Enter three eunuchs*]
EUNUCHS: The most majestic of domestic
officials,
The great G.E., we fear his mighty
initials!
Don't think it too absurd
That we heed his lightest word.
We bow our heads in reverence
Lest we should feel their severance.
Li Pi Siao! Li Pi Siao!

SIAO: Oh, gala day, red-letter day,
The Empire knows no better day.
A father lost his son,
But now the two are one.

TCHOU: I bow to parental duty,
But I can't forget her beauty.
I wake at morning loving her much
more
Than I did before the morning.
I see the moon rise only to implore
Let me keep her for next moonrise.
She's mine alone for all my years;
Joy appears with my tears.
Life, let me keep her till my day is
through.
That's all I ask of you.*

---

*The reprise of "I Wake at Morning" replaced the following
deleted lines (intended for Tchou):*

Oh, Chee-Chee. Life has no savor,
Joy has no flavor.
Ever your slave or
Less I'll be. Oh, Chee-Chee!
I never more will see my Chee-Chee.

ALL: The Holy Man comes now,
So bow. All bow.
The stars and the moon
Will smile on us soon.
Oh, Holy Man, we kiss the ground
Where'er your footprints can be
found.

[Enter Holy Man]

ALL: Oh, Holy Man, son of Heaven!

HOLY MAN: Speak, Li Pi Siao!

SIAO: Celestial moon, my son is prepared to
enter your devoted service. And the
Prince of Medicines is ready to act!

HOLY MAN: Reverence to this.

ALL: Reverence to this.

HOLY MAN: Yes, Li Pi Tchou . . .

TCHOU: I worship at thy shrine.
My life will soon be thine,
Oh, Holy Man!

ALL: He worships at thy shrine,
His life will soon be thine.
Oh, Holy Man!

[Exit Tchou, singing:]

TCHOU: Farewell, oh life!

Farewell, my youth!
Farewell, my Chee-Chee!
A fickle wife to tell the truth,
But the all in all of me!

FAREWELL, O LIFE

Introduced by William Williams and ensemble. Alternate
title: "Finale, Act II." No. 15 in the second-act sequence.

TCHOU: Farewell, Oh life!
Farewell, my youth,
Farewell, my Chee-Chee!

PROCESSION: Our Holy Man's chief minister
Will never be more sinister.
The lad who once has strayed
Has harkened and obeyed.

TCHOU: [Sings reprise of "I Must Love You"]

Inez Courtney (center), Dick Keene, Glenn Hunter, and
John Hundley

SPRING IS HERE
——————————
1929

Tryout: Shubert Theatre, Philadelphia, February 25–
March 8, 1929. New York run: Alvin Theatre, New York,
March 11–June 8, 1929. 104 performances. Music by
Richard Rodgers. Lyrics by Lorenz Hart. Produced by
Alex A. Aarons and Vinton Freedley. Book by Owen
Davis, adapted from his play *Shotgun Wedding.* Staged by
Alexander Leftwich. Dances and musical numbers staged
by Bobby Connolly. Settings by John Wenger. Costumes
by Kiviette. Orchestra under the direction of Alfred New-
man. Pianists, Victor Arden and Phil Ohman. Cast, star-
ring Lillian Taiz and Glenn Hunter, included Inez Courtney, John Hundley, Joyce Barbour, and Charles Ruggles.

THERE'S MAGIC IN THE CUP

Introduced by Thelma White and ensemble. During Philadelphia tryout it was known as "A Cup of Tea." Alternate
title: "Opening, Act I."

MAUD: [*Takes cup*]
There's magic in the cup.
It always picks me up.
And makes a better-natured girl of me.
ALL: There's much in what you say.
You're picked up ev'ry day.
No wonder you must love your cup of tea.
MAUD: The tea and cakes and sandwiches
invigorate.
We eat them till our forms look like the
figure eight.
ALL: We don't neglect the crumpets,
The whole darn thing is free,
So let us blow our trumpets
And we'll praise a cup of tea.
Tea! We want more!
[*Boys pour cocktail from shakers into teacups*]
BOYS: Madam is served.
GIRLS: There's magic in the cup.
It always picks me up.
And makes a better-natured girl of me.
[*Girls go to chairs*]
No, this is not Long Island.
Please do not be deceived.
It's positively not Long Island,
So you can feel relieved!
We may be up at Pelham,
Or even New Rochelle,
But this is not Long Island;
We'd rather be in Hell!
We may be in Topeka or Peoria
Or even on the desert of Astoria!
And remember to the bleak end

We are not here on a weekend
And we are not,
Oh, surely not,
To serve the purposes of the plot—
On Long Island!

SPRING IS HERE IN PERSON

Introduced by Dick Keene, Inez Courtney, and ensemble.
This is not the same song as "Spring Is Here" in *I Married
an Angel* (1938).

VERSE 1

HE: Now you're sweet sixteen and seven months
and four days,
Darling, I'm afraid you're growing older.
Springtime is the time for love in Movietone
plays;
Women when they're seventeen grow colder.
Someday you'll be old and crusty
With much water on the knee.
Now, before that knee gets rusty
And your brain is dusty,
Do some things with me!

REFRAIN

Spring is here in person!
How does it look for tonight?
Let your pa and ma do their cursin',
It's spring in person
That makes it right.
We can knock each care down,
And we'll be happy for spite.
Let's be letting our hair down!
How does it look for tonight!

VERSE 2

You have just the kind of voice that Mama
adores.
In your patter is a small displacement.
If it's true that mothers buy their babies in
stores,
You were bought in Gimbel Brothers'
basement.
Can't your mother make you hustle?
For she was full of pep, they say.
And though she'd dress like Lillian Russell,
She threw off her bustle
On the first of May.

REPEAT REFRAIN

YOURS SINCERELY

Published March 1929. Introduced by Glenn Hunter,
Lillian Taiz, and ensemble.

VERSE 1

HE: Dearest one: I write what I'm afraid to
speak;
I'm weak when I'm with you.
Tears of love are causing all the ink to blot,
So what am I to do?
Hoping to find the phrases,
Groping to find each word,
How they all burned like blazes!
Now they all sound absurd.
Though I don't know where to end and to
begin,
You must give in, because I'm

REFRAIN

Yours sincerely,
The one who loves you dearly.
To think about it nearly takes my breath
away.
Very truly,
My passion is unruly.
A dream of you is newly born each night
and day.
Oh, but my thoughts are fervent!
How can I make them plain?
Ever your humble servant
Faithfully I remain.
I'm intending
To find a happy ending.
Because I love you dearly
I'm sincerely yours!

VERSE 2

SHE: Do not think I haven't got the heart to care;
But where is my romance?
So I've waited for my lover to appear;
I fear you've not a chance.
I must confess I've found one—
You must recall, last night.
Truly it does astound one
How two can love at sight.
But I like your phrases and the way you
wrote;
I'll use your note and write him.

REPEAT REFRAIN

WE'RE GONNA RAISE HELL

Introduced by principals and ensemble. Alternate title: "Finaletto, Scene 1."

TERRY: Spring is here in person.
And there are things we can do.
RITA: Soon your ma will wonder at her son.
It's spring in person.
MARY: I'm going too.
SLADE: You're too young, so shut up.
MARY: Terry is tame, he won't bite.
TERRY: You'll be seeing me cut up.
How does it look for tonight?
BETTY: You stay at home, Mary-Jane!
SLADE: You forget that I shall be there.
MAUD: So will I.
BETTY: I won't have it!
You've a nickel's worth of Romeo to
share.
What a gay Lothario! What a man to
royster!
You can feed him on some sirloin steak
that's rare,
Then a little caviar and a deviled oyster.
TERRY: Girls, I'll treat each one of you
To a cocktail with a cherry.
BETTY: You won't need a chaperone
As long as you have Terry!
TERRY: Well, come on, girls, we've no time to
stay.
ALL: Hooray!
We're gonna raise hell!
We're gonna raise Cain!
It's gonna be swell!
We'll drink champagne!
TERRY: Three—four—fifty—
I guess I'd better be thrifty!
SLADE: Lend me a buck.
TERRY: You're out of luck!
BETTY: Well, have a good time.
ALL: We're gonna raise hell!
We're gonna raise Cain!
It's gonna be swell!
We'll drink champagne!

YOU NEVER SAY YES

Published March 1929. Introduced by Joyce Barbour, Gil Squires, and ensemble.

VERSE

HE: I like you.
How I like you!
I mean to say I like you!
SHE: I think I get your trend;
In fact I comprehend.
HE: You charm me.
How you charm me.
I mean to say you're hot stuff!
SHE: In accents of despair
I say please take the air.
There's not much I can do with you.

REFRAIN 1

HE: Why the beautiful features
And why the beautiful dress?
Best upholstered of creatures,
You never say yes.
I'm all ready to go, ma'am,
But you remain more or less
The original "no-ma'am,"
You never say yes.
You're so discreet, but I'll bet your kiss is
nice.
Sweet, just like so much water ice!
Ev'ry time I endeavor
To steal a little caress,
Though you love it
You never say yes!

REFRAIN 2

SHE: Though there always will be men
Who ask my phone and address,
Least high-powered of he-men,
I never say yes.
Gently granting permission
Will never bring me success.
Men can lose their ambition.
I never say yes.
Suppose I do give in to your vile intents
You wouldn't know the rudiments.
I could know you forever
Without a thing to confess.
That's the reason
I never say yes!

WITH A SONG IN MY HEART

Published March 1929. Introduced by Lillian Taiz and John Hundley. Listed in Philadelphia programs as "Song in My Heart."

VERSE 1

Though I know that we meet ev'ry night
And we couldn't have changed since the last
time,
To my joy and delight,
It's a new kind of love at first sight.
Though it's you and it's I all the time,
Ev'ry meeting's a marvelous pastime.
You're increasingly sweet,
So whenever we happen to meet
I greet you . . .

REFRAIN

With a song in my heart
I behold your adorable face.
Just a song at the start,
But it soon is a hymn to your grace.
When the music swells
I'm touching your hand;
It tells that you're standing near, and . . .
At the sound of your voice
Heaven opens its portals to me.
Can I help but rejoice
That a song such as ours came to be?
But I always knew
I would live life through
With a song in my heart for you.

VERSE 2

Oh, the moon's not a moon for a night
And these stars will not twinkle and fade out,
And the words in my ears
Will resound for the rest of my years.
In the morning I'll find with delight
Not a note of our music is played out.
It will be just as sweet,
And an air that I'll live to repeat:
I greet you . . .

REPEAT REFRAIN

BABY'S AWAKE NOW

Published March 1929. Introduced by Inez Courtney, Thelma White, and ensemble.

VERSE

Out of the ether and into the air
Baby opens her eyes and cries,
"Let the party start again!"

Powders her nose and fixes her hair,
Sees how the landscape lies and sighs,
"Bring your baby all the men!"
And then,
Out where the wild gardenias grow,
Baby has got her chance,
So let her dance!

REFRAIN

Baby's awake now!
Baby can do things!
Ready to shake her chassis,
Baby has new springs!
Baby can learn how;
Baby can dance rings
Round ev'ry other lassie.
Baby can do things!
Her deportment isn't so mild.
Mammy, get your wandering wild child!
Beat on the big drum!
She's making her bow,
Burn up the baby's cradle!
Baby's awake now!

OH, LOOK

Introduced by principals and ensemble. Alternate title:
"Finale, Act I."

MARY-JANE: Oh, look!
ALL: It's a note!
MARY-JANE: It's from her!
ALL: Tell us what she wrote!
MARY-JANE: "Dearest ones, I hope that I've
impressed you all;
I loathe and I detest you all.
I'd rather die than stay!"
ALL: That's why she went away!
MARY-JANE: "Mother's a fool. Father's a sap!"
TERRY: I'm not the one she's sore on.
MARY-JANE: "Poor Uncle Slade is a half-witted
chap,
And Terry is a moron."
She signs it "Yours sincerely."
TERRY: And yet she loves me dearly.
To think about it nearly takes my
breath away.
ALL: Very truly,
Her conduct is unruly.
Her words are all unduly nasty things
to say.
SLADE: But she'll have to come back; she's
left her things.

TERRY: That's right. She's left her things.
She must come back!
With a song in my heart
I'll behold her adorable face.
ALL: Just a song at the start,
But it soon is a hymn to her grace.
When the music swells
He's touching her hand;
It tells that she's standing near,
and . . .
At the sound of her voice
Heaven opens its portals to him.
Can he help but rejoice
When his heart is all filled to the
brim?
But he always knew
He would live life through
With a song in his heart for you!
EMILY: Hush! They're coming now.
TERRY: Alone!
EMILY: No, with him!
[Terry takes gun]
TERRY: With him! I'll wait until I see the
white of his eyes.
[As Peter climbs wall Terry shoots]
EMILY: It's Peter!
PETER: Murder!
[Terry drops gun and Peter closes with him. They roll
over stage in fight]
EMILY: Don't, Peter, he's such a nice boy!
ALL: Peter's awake now!
He cannot do things!
He cannot shake his chassis,
Peter needs new springs!
Peter can learn how;
Peter can dance rings
Round ev'ry other laddie.
Peter can do things!
His deportment isn't so mild.
Mammy, get your wandering wild
child!
Beat on the big drum!
He's making his bow,
Burn up the baby's cradle!
Baby's awake now!

THIS IS NOT
LONG ISLAND

Introduced by ensemble. Alternate title: "Opening,
Act II."

Now this could be Long Island
But we must be exact.
It's positively not Long Island
That starts the second act!
We may be up in Yonkers,
Or even in White Plains,
But this is not Long Island;
We'd rather be in Cains.
We may be up at Sing Sing or a block away,
But never in the wilderness of Rockaway,
And although the plot is thinning,
At the second act beginning
We say, we're not,
Oh, surely not
On that musical comedy spot
Called Long Island.

RED-HOT TRUMPET

Introduced by Dick Keene, Inez Courtney, and ensemble.
In Philadelphia tryout, introduced by Thelma White.

VERSE

See the frolic
Of the modern bucolic
In his country club.
Once he used to be a bashful cub,
Now he's not a dub!
But one time you could trust 'im,
When the charming old custom
Was the good square dance.
Now his point of view has gained expanse
And he takes a chance—
Because:

REFRAIN

There's a red-hot trumpet in the hayloft
Blowing red-hot "Turkey in the Straw."
There are red-hot doings in the gay loft
And some rub-bub-bub by your paw and maw.
Oh, Reuben, Reuben, I've been thinking,
All the world is hot-cha-cha!
Shaking all the straw down,
They all faw down—
Da-da-da-da-da-da;
There's a red-hot rhythm in the barn house
And a heavy stomping on the floor!
There is graceful dancing in the darn house,
And the building shakes at four;
When the "Turkey in the Straw" starts to
wabble,
All the veterans forget the war;

With a red-hot trumpet in the hayloft—
Oh it ain't gonna rain no more. . . .

WHAT A GIRL!

Introduced by Glenn Hunter.

VERSE

To be or not to be,
That is the question.
Is she going to fall for my plan?
Is it love that tortures me
Or indigestion?
Why can't I be a lady's man?
I can learn some gosh darn poem like a parrot.
"I arise from dreams of thee."
Oh, I've as much sex appeal as a carrot,
And the best things in life are not free.

REFRAIN 1

What a girl!
Could she have a little pity?
Not a girl like her.
Shouldn't she
Be as sweet as she is pretty?
Couldn't she? No sir!
She hates my face
Around the place
And I don't know why.
Is it my tie?
Why can't I die?
Ever out
When the other fellow takes her.
Never out with me.
Cuddles up
When that other fellow makes her.
Huddles up with glee.
Another day
And I'll turn gray.
This thing can't go on.
So, I say to hell with her—
God, how I love that woman.

REFRAIN 2

What a girl!
Does she like me in my new suit?
Not a girl like her.
We can't dance.
My tuxedo is a blue suit.
She can't dance. No sir!
I'll save to buy

A white necktie,
A dress coat and all.
I'll look so tall.
Maybe she'll fall!
Would she cry
If I got the influenza?
Could she cry in pain?
When I die
She'll be singing a cadenza.
Then I die in vain.
Her ifs and buts
Will drive me nuts.
This thing has to end.
So, I say to hell with her—
God, how I love that woman.

RICH MAN! POOR MAN!

Published March 1929. Introduced by Inez Courtney,
Dick Keene, and ensemble.

VERSE 1

HE: I have often heard my father say,
     "Boy, you're a comer!
     You will be a President someday!"
SHE: He meant a plumber.
HE: My hopes are remarkable;
     I'll rise in this town.
SHE: Rest that thing that's parkable;
     Sit down,
     Clown.
HE: Bigger fools than I have made their way.
SHE: They don't come dumber!
     But I care,
     So why care?
     Don't frown!

REFRAIN 1

Rich man! Poor man!
Rich man! Poor man!
Beggar man, thief,
Who cares?
You're going to darken my doorstep.
Doctor! Lawyer!
Doctor! Lawyer!
Tammany chief,
Who swears?
I'm going to follow in your step.
You may be a hero to some
Or like Mr. Zero, a bum.
Pardon my language.
Rich man! Poor man!

Rich man! Poor man!
Certainly you can see
You'll be a lover to me.

VERSE 2

HE: As a dancer just the type you'll be
     That ev'ry youth picks.
SHE: And my legs will win renown for me.
HE: They look like toothpicks.
SHE: I'll drink from gold chalices
     With the wealthy bunch.
HE: In Childs' buckwheat palaces
     We'll munch
     Lunch.
SHE: I'll be living on Fifth Avenue.
HE: Hundred and tenth Street.
     And who'll be?
     Why, you'll be
     My hunch!

REFRAIN 2

Rich girl! Poor girl!
Rich girl! Poor girl!
Little girl coy,
With cash.
I'm going to darken your doorstep.
Song girl! Dance girl!
Song girl! Dance girl!
Working for Fräulein Rasch.
I'm going to follow in your step.
Be a spinster frowning at paint
Or like Peaches Browning, a saint.
So's your Aunt Emma!
Rich girl! Poor girl!
Rich girl! Poor girl!
Certainly you can see
You'll be a lover to me!

WHY CAN'T I?

Published March 1929. Introduced by Lillian Taiz and
Inez Courtney.

VERSE

BETTY: Darling, don't leave me,
        I'm so lonesome tonight.
        Nothing is right
        With me.
MARY-JANE: You can't deceive me;
        What you need is romance,
        Something in pants,
        Said she!

BETTY: You're so clever
But I never
Thought you over
Knew.
MARY-JANE: My maiden's prayer
Leaves me weak as a cat,
For I am that
Way too!

REFRAIN 1

BETTY: Feeling the way I do,
I'd like to say, "I do!"
Heaving a heavenly sigh.
Everybody has someone;
Why can't I?
Creeping to bed alone,
Resting my head alone,
Only the pillow nearby.
Some have a reason for dreaming;
Why can't I?
I feel forsaken
On nights like this.
Can't I awaken
To someone's kiss?
Only my book in bed
Knows how I look in bed.
Nobody hears when I cry.
Everybody has someone;
Why can't I?

REFRAIN 2

MARY-JANE: Feeling the way I do,
I'd like to say, "I do!"
Nature is hard to deny.
Everybody has someone;
Why can't I?
If love brings merriment
I must experiment
With some electrical guy.
Even old maids find a burglar;
Why can't I?
Should girls be good girls?
I think they should.
I need a good man
To make me be good.
Two feet are ever cold;
Four feet are never cold.
I only mean to imply
Everybody does something;
Why can't I?

A WORD IN EDGEWAYS

Introduced in the Philadelphia tryout by Charles Ruggles (Peter), Maidel Turner (Emily), Lillian Taiz (Betty), and Inez Courtney (Mary-Jane). Dropped before the New York opening.

VERSE 1

PETER: If I didn't earn your bread and
butter,
What would a lot of you do?
You would all be starving in the
gutter,
And it would serve you damn right,
too!
EMILY: Yes, Peter.
PETER: Yes, Peter!
You have always got to put your oar
in.
EMILY: Well, Peter—
PETER: Hell, Peter!
I could stamp this good-for-nothing
floor in!
It's enough to make me shriek.
Now, Betty, you let me speak!

REFRAIN 1

You paint your face and show your
knee;
God knows where you'll be landing.
You kiss the boys, but do it free
To hold your amateur standing.
No crowd's too wild for you to
splurge in,
No joke is too risqué,
And that's how you remain a virgin
In a highly technical way.
You talk of sex psychology
With boyfriends, as a rule,
And you know physiology
That you didn't learn at school.
Say something! Answer me,
Or you'll drive me to drink!
BETTY: Well, I think—
PETER: Will you let me get a word in
edgeways!

VERSE 2

PETER: I must keep my nerves in good
condition.
I take it all on the chin.
But it spoils my lovely disposition
Each time I see my dear wife grin.
EMILY: Yes, Peter.

PETER: Yes, Peter!
I guess you tagged me when I wasn't
looking.
EMILY: Ah, Peter.
PETER: Bah, Peter!
I sold my pure young body for home
cooking.
Then you went and cooked my goose.
Now, Emily, what's the use!

REFRAIN 2

You want a kiss and lift your pan.
You don't stop when I say no.
I don't know why you took a man,
You should have got a volcano!
A husband's duty as you term it
Is measured by no clock.
Gosh, I'd like to be a hermit
With a chance to sleep on a rock!
At dinner I can't eat a bit.
Your jealous eyes I see.
How can you think I cheat a bit
When you are too much for me?
Say something! Answer me!
Can't you see how I fret?
EMILY: Yes, my pet.
Will you let me get a word in
edgeways!

REFRAIN 3

Your mother dropped you on your
head
While walking in the rain, dear.
And that is why I've always said
You've water on the brain, dear.
By some coincidence or other
The stork gave you your bow.
As you remind me of your mother,
I believe in birth control now.
I do not give a damn today,
It's too late for regret.
You made me what I am today,
And you're not satisfied yet.
Say something! Answer me,
Or you'll drive me to drink.
MARY-JANE: Aw, go take a good run up an alley.
Will you let me get a word in
edgeways!

THE COLOR OF HER EYES

Published October 1930. Introduced by Gil Squires in the Philadelphia tryout but dropped before the New York opening. Introduced in *Me for You* (1929) by Lulu McConnell and Victor Moore. Dropped from *Heads Up!* (1929) before its New York opening. Introduced in *Ever Green* (1930) by Albert Burdon and Jean Cadell.

VERSE

SLADE: I remember her so well
I've never missed her.
She dances on my ceiling ev'ry night.*
It seems like yesterday
When last I kissed her.
She was a little gem† without a blight.
It was romantic—and my first
adventure—
We never met again, I'm sad to tell,
And yet my heart is open to no censure.
I can remember her so well!

REFRAIN

I remember she was eighteen,
Maybe nineteen,
Maybe I'm wrong.
Anyway, her teeth were all white,
They were all white
And they were strong.
As we sat together after dinner
I remember where my hand was placed.
I won't say a single word agin her
But she got thinner
Around the waist.
She looked so short without her shoes
on,
With her shoes off
She was *this* size.
I see it all,
But can't recall
The color of her eyes!

The following new lyrics were written for *Me For You*:

VERSE 2

LADY
SARAH: When I met him, I was just a little
flapper;
He wore his haberdashery so well;

His golfing suit was very smart and
dapper—
The latest thing Moe Levy had to sell.
That we both went for each other was
the rumor,
And ev'ry night, he always was on deck;
He told me all the jokes from *College
Humor*,
And paid his own share of the check.

REFRAIN 2

I remember he was half shot,
Maybe all shot,
Maybe I'm wrong!
Anyway, his breath was Scottish,
Maybe Ryeish,
But it was strong.
In his little rumble seat he rode me,
Then we stopped beneath a tree to rest;
After just one little kiss, he showed me
The tattooed lady
Upon his chest.
He looked just like a B.V.D. ad,
B.V.D. ad,
Shoulders this size!
I see it all,
But can't recall
The color of his eyes!

REFRAIN 3

EGBERT: I remember she had two legs,
Maybe one leg,
Maybe I'm wrong!
Anyway, her arms were all there,
They were all there,
And they were strong.
Almost everybody said who'd seen us,
She was like a statue in her charms;
After one short argument between us,
She looked like Venus:
I broke her arms.
At twelve o'clock she'd park the torso,
She could snore so,
To my surprise;
I see it all
But can't recall
The color of her eyes!

Verse 2 and refrain 2 of the *Me for You* version were revised as follows for *Ever Green:*

VERSE 2

SHE: When I met him, I was just a little
flapper;

He wore his haberdashery so well;
His golfing suit was very smart and
dapper—
The latest thing Moss Brothers had to
sell!
Although he was as virtuous as Lincoln,
He sometimes took me to Roman's
grill—
He'd quote me little titbits from the
Pink 'un,
And paid his own share of the bill!

REFRAIN 2

I remember he was half shot,
Maybe all shot!
Maybe I'm wrong!
Anyway, his beard was all there,
It was all *there*,
And it was strong!
In his little dickey seat he rode me,
Then we stopped beneath a tree to rest;
After just a little kiss, he showed me
The tattooed lady upon his chest!
His underwear I've not forgotten,
It was cotton,
Forty-eight size,
But after all,
I can't recall
The color of his eyes.

LADY LUCK IS GRINNING

Probably written for *Lady Luck* (London, 1927). Also intended for *Spring Is Here*, but dropped before the New York opening.

VERSE

HE: Once to a man;
Only once the wonder!
One glance began
All the spell we're under.
SHE: Here's my hand, will you take it?
In your own hold it fast.
Keep the spell, do not break it.
It's cast
At last.
HE: Please do not speak.
Keep the happy moment
Until the thrill is past!

Line was deleted because Rodgers and Hart's "Dancing on the Ceiling" was in Ever Green, *and replaced by:* Her vision comes before me every night.
†*"Gem" was changed to "girl" in* Me for You *version.*

REFRAIN

Lady Luck is grinning.
She must be our friend.
What a sweet beginning
For a happy end.

I think she knew, dear,
I needed you, dear,
And let our pathways blend.
So we must obey her
On a night like this.

Let us both repay her
With a lovers' kiss.
And oh, how grateful
I'll always be
That she gave you to me!

Robert Gleckler, Betty Starbuck, Ray Bolger, Janet Velie,
Victor Moore, Jack Whiting, Barbara Newberry, and
John Hundley in *Heads Up!*

ME FOR YOU | HEADS UP! | 1929
THE PLAY'S THE THING

ME FOR YOU, 1929

Tryout: Shubert Detroit Opera House, Detroit, September 15-28, 1929. Closed in Detroit. Music by Richard Rodgers. Lyrics by Lorenz Hart. Produced by Alex A. Aarons and Vinton Freedley. Book by Owen Davis. Play staged by Alexander Leftwich. Settings by Donald Oenslager. Costumes by Kiviette. Dances and ensembles by George Hale. Orchestra under the direction of Alfred Newman. Pianist, Phil Ohman. Cast, starring Victor Moore, Betty Starbuck, Lulu McConnell, and Jack Whiting, included Ray Bolger, Peggy Bernier, John Hundley, and Madeline Gibson. With a new book, many new songs, and some new performers, *Me for You* was transformed into *Heads Up!* (1929).

For the lyric to "The Color of Her Eyes," see *Spring Is Here* (1929), page 137.

The following lyrics are missing: "Mind Your P's and Q's" (introduced by Lulu McConnell, Naomi Johnson, and ensemble; dropped before the New York opening of *Heads Up!*), "Finaletto, Scene I" (introduced by principals and ensemble; dropped before the New York opening of *Heads Up!*), "The Three Bears" (intended for Jack Whiting, Peggy Bernier, Cy Landry, and Ray Bolger; dropped before the Detroit tryout of *Me for You*), "It's a Man's World" (introduced by Betty Starbuck, Peggy Bernier, Madeline Gibson, Naomi Johnson, and ensemble; dropped before the New York opening of *Heads Up!*), "The Bootlegger's Chantey," also listed as "We're an English Ship" (introduced by Ray Bolger, Cy Landry, and ensemble; dropped before the New York opening of *Heads Up!*), "Finale, Act I," also listed as "Now Go to Your Cabin" (introduced by principals and ensemble; dropped before the New York opening of *Heads Up!*), "Harlem on the Sand" (introduced by Peggy Bernier and ensemble; dropped before the New York opening of *Heads Up!*), and "Have You Been True to Me?" (intended for Ray Bolger and Peggy Bernier; dropped before Detroit tryout of *Me for You*).

JAZZ RECEPTION

Introduced by ensemble. Dropped before the New York opening of *Heads Up!* Alternate titles: "Kindly Nullify Your Fears" and "Opening, Act I—*Me for You.*"

Kindly nullify your fears.
Ta-ra-ta-ra!
Ta-ra-ta-ra!
For we are not British peers.
Ta-ra-ta-ra!
Ta-ra-ta-ra-ta-ra!
Please let us assure you with an
absolute assertion,
We are not satirical or in any way
Gilbertian!
The newest social crowd!
Ta-ra-ta-ra!
Indefatigably proud!
Indefatigably proud!
If you don't get in the swing
You can't mean a thing.
That's the reason why we sing,
Ta-ra-ta-ra!
Hotch-cha-cha-cha!
Boop-boop-a-roop!
Ta-ra-ta-ra!!
Kindly nullify your fears [*etc.*]

BUTLER: Begging your pardon!
ALL: The butler!
BUTLER: Ah no! The majordomo!
ALL: The majordomo. A fine example of
the genus homo.
BUTLER: I beg to announce Miss Molly Stark.
ALL: Her name is just a question mark!
BUTLER: A friend of young Miss Peasley's
and a model of propriety,
She's most discreet and circumspect.
ALL: And so not in society.
BUTLER: Miss Stark.
ALL: Ta-ra-ta-ra!
MOLLY: Hotch-cha-cha-cha!
ALL: Boop-boop-a-roop!
Ta-ra-ta-ra!
BUTLER: Van Rensselaer Stoddart—the name
is Dutch.
ALL: Today that doesn't mean so much!
BUTLER: Some years ago his family tree
would get the dear old boy
around!
But nowadays it's not your name
ALL: But have you real McCoy around!
BUTLER: Mr. Stoddart.
ALL: Ta-ra-ta-ra!
VAN
RENSSELAER: Hotch-cha-cha-cha!
ALL: Boop-boop-a-roop!
Ta-ra-ta-ra!
BUTLER: Mr. Rodman Stoddart.
VAN
RENSSELAER: My pride and joy!
ALL: We know he's your son
But we hope it's a boy.
BUTLER: Mr. Stoddart!
ROD: Janet, I love you! I love you!
Boop-boop-a-roo!
ALL: She's your guiding star.
ROD: Guiding star! Hotch-cha-cha-cha!
ALL: Ta-ra-ta-ra!
BUTLER: Miss Sylvia Alden,
She's English and sweet.
ALL: She has big broad A's
But very small feet!
BUTLER: Miss Alden.
SYLVIA: Rodney, I love you, I love you!
Boop-boop-a-roo!
ALL: He's her guiding star.
SYLVIA: Guiding star! Hotch-cha-cha-cha!
ALL: Ta-ra-ta-ra!
BUTLER: Miss Flora March,
Lady Sarah's secretary!
Miss March!
ALL: Tramp! Tramp! Tramp! The boys are
marching!
BUTLER: Mr. Egbert Peasley—our genial
host.
ALL: His liquor makes us love him most.
BUTLER: He never argues with a girl,
He'd rather let her treat instead.
ALL: No Lucky Strike, he's nonchalant,
And reaches for a sweet instead!
BUTLER: Mr. Peasley!
ALL: Ta-ra-ta-ra!
EGBERT: Hotch-cha-cha-cha!
ALL: Boop-boop-a-roop!
Ta-ra-ta-ra.
BUTLER: I beg to introduce two ladies! That
is, two feminine persons!
Miss Janet Peasley,
The daughter of our host!
And Lady Sarah Martingale,
The Royal Mounted's toast!
ALL: Ta-ra-ta-ra!
Hotch-cha-cha!
LADY SARAH
& JANET: Boop-boop-a-roop!
Ta-ra-ta-ra!

SWEETHEART, YOU MAKE ME LAUGH

Introduced by Jack Whiting and Betty Starbuck. Dropped during the tryout. Alternate title: "You Make Me Laugh."

VERSE

SHE: Just before this kid was born
Mother said, "Tomorrow morn,
I'll have a beautiful child!"
And the good old doctor smiled.

HE: But when you made your debut
    And the doctor looked at you,
    Though it wasn't his place
    He laughed right in your face.
SHE: I've been told my face's charms are
        numerous.
HE: Chief among them all is that it's humorous!

REFRAIN 1

HE: You're the best one.
    My favorite toy to enjoy;
    Sweetheart, you make me laugh!
    Sweet possessed one,
    What funny bone do you employ,
    Sweetheart, to make me laugh?
    We'll stand at the altar
    Like silly giraffes;
    Our Rock of Gibraltar
    Is founded on laughs.
    Be my best one—
    Your share will be more than half;
    Sweetheart, you make me laugh!

REFRAIN 2

SHE: You're the best one,
    My favorite toy to enjoy;
    Sweetheart, you make me laugh!
    Sweet possessed one,
    What funny bone do you employ,
    Sweetheart, to make me laugh?
    Let others be formal,
    They're living in ruts;
    Who wants to be normal?
    My baby is NUTS!
    Be my best one—
    Your share will be more than half;
    Sweetheart, you make me laugh!

MY MAN IS ON THE MAKE

Published October 1929. Introduced by Peggy Bernier. Introduced in *Heads Up!* by Alice Boulden and ensemble; danced by Atlas and LaMarr. Introduced in the London production of *Heads Up!* by Polly Ward.

VERSE

Love is blind!
Love is king!
Love's the one unselfish thing,
And I loved him at first sight,

But I played my hand just right.
Saw him first,
Played my card;
Now I've got him breathing hard,
And he's starting to rehearse
That "To have and hold till he's cold,
For better or worse!"

REFRAIN

My man is on the make,
He won't be hard to take;
Ma, get ready the veil!
He's trembling on the brink,
One push and down he'll sink;
Pa, your daughter won't fail!
He's worked himself into a lather,
He's starting to puff!
All ready to gather,
I'm ready for rough hot stuff!
Cut up that wedding cake!
Here's where I get a break.
Ma, my man's on the make!

SKY CITY

Published October 1929. Introduced by John Hundley. Dropped from *Heads Up!* before the New York opening.

VERSE

City where speed
Is master!
Where people plead,
"Go faster!"
Crowding the place,
Home of a race of ants!
Riding on air,
The "El" train;
Now under there,
The Hell train!
Bankers, no less,
And tailors who press your pants!
Horns tooting,
Mobs shooting through!
"New Babel,"
We label you!

REFRAIN

Sky City,
My City,
Climbing through
Heavens blue!

Proud and free,
Rising from the sea!
Crowd City;
Loud City;
Every block,
Walls of rock!
Nothing green,
Not a single tree!
We build it,
Rebuild it,
Steel cannot bend!
More glories,
More stories,
Where will it end?
My tall island,
Small island;
Blood and stone
Of my own!
Give me my
City in the sky!

A SHIP WITHOUT A SAIL

Published October 1929. Originally intended for Madeline Gibson and Jack Whiting, it was introduced by Betty Starbuck and Whiting. Introduced by Whiting and ensemble in *Heads Up!* (1929).

VERSE 1

I don't know what day it is,
Or if it's dark or fair.
Somehow that's just the way it is,
And I don't really care.
I go to this or that place,
I seem alive and well.
My head is just a hat place,
My breast an empty shell!
And I've a faded dream to sell.

REFRAIN

All alone, all at sea!
Why does nobody care for me?
When there's no love to hold my love,
Why is my heart so frail,
Like a ship without a sail?
Out on the ocean
Sailors can use a chart.
I'm on the ocean
Guided by just a lonely heart.
Still alone, still at sea!
Still there's no one to care for me.
When there's no hand to hold my hand

Life is a loveless tale
For a ship without a sail.

VERSE 2

When love leaves you all alone,
You're living in the past.
Then you feel so small alone,
And oh, the world seems vast.
You tell your grief to no girls,
You never make it known.
Your smile is like a show girl's,
Your laugh a hollow tone.
And then your little heart's a stone.

REPEAT REFRAIN

I CAN DO WONDERS WITH YOU

Published October 1929. Originally intended for Jack Whiting and Betty Starbuck, but dropped during the try-out. Introduced in *Simple Simon* (1930) by Doree Leslie and Alan Edwards.

VERSE 1

HE: When you came to me,
My power began;
I have grown to be
A miracle man.
Just like ABC
I find that I can
Do wonders!
Do just as you're told,
I'll help you a lot;
Take my hand to hold
And, presto! Great Scott!
Though you're feeling cold,
I'll make you get hot.
It's done! It's done!
I'm classed as one,
Surpassed by none.
You have made of me
A wizard.
Hey, kid,
Some fun!

REFRAIN

I'll change your silver to gold,
Dear, I can do
Wonders with you.

I'll change your new wine to old,
For I can do
Such wonders with you!
Work will be play,
And our cares will be fun;
March will be May,
And the rain will be sun.
I'll bet I'll even be true,
Dear, I can do
Such wonders with you.

VERSE 2

SHE: Let me fix your cap,
It's over your eye.
Do you think your map
Is helped by that tie?
You're a funny chap,
And yet I must try
To change you.
Now I recollect,
Your language is quaint;
To be circumspect,
You mustn't say "ain't"!
Such words ain't correct,
So heed to my plaint.
It's done! It's done!
I'm classed as one,
Surpassed by none.
I will wash your neck
And dress you.
Hey, kid,
Some fun!

REPEAT REFRAIN

IT MUST BE HEAVEN

Published November 1929. Although not listed in the surviving programs for *Me for You*, some of the Detroit critics cited the song in their reviews. Introduced by Barbara Newberry and Jack Whiting in *Heads Up!* and by Louise Brown and Arthur Margetson in the London production.

VERSE

HE: I may swear and smoke, I guess;
With no awe of the law I can nip.
And I say my prayers much less
Than a good sailor should on a ship.
Though I'm not saintly
In all that I do,
I believe quaintly in you.

I may have sown some
Wild oats being lonesome
But I'll never own someone new!

REFRAIN 1

It must be Heaven
Coming home at seven
Just to find you there;
Oh, how exquisite!
Nothing's missing, is it,
In the home we share;
You can't cook,
But that won't hurt;
One sweet look
Is my dessert;
And at eleven
I will go to Heaven
Just to find you there.

REFRAIN 2

SHE: It must be Heaven
Coming home at seven
Just to find you there;
Oh, how exquisite!
Nothing's missing, is it,
In the home we share?
Oh, how sweet,
The way we'll dine;
Leave your seat,
We'll just use mine;
And at eleven
I will go to Heaven
Just to find you there.

AS THOUGH YOU WERE THERE

Published April 1940 after being performed by Lee Wiley in an album of Rodgers and Hart songs produced by Music Box Records in 1940. Introduced by Madeline Gibson and John Hundley. Dropped before the New York opening of *Heads Up!*

VERSE

HE: I've become an actor;
You're the critic, judging the work,
And I'm not begrudging the work I do, dear,
You're the guiding factor.
When I take my part in the play
I put all my heart in the play for you, dear.

Though your voice can't cheer me
When you're not nearby
I pretend you hear me—that's why

REFRAIN 1

HE: Every day when you're away
And others ask me "Why behave?"
I behave
As though you were there.
Brush my hair and dress with care
Though no one's around to crave my face,
Shave my face
As though you were there.
I smile at the kiddies
As though you could tell,
Don't smile at their biddies,
I'm faithful as hell, well . . .
Nights alone when ladies phone
Old Adam whispers, "Why behave?"
I behave
As though you were there.

REFRAIN 2

SHE: Every day when you're away
And others ask me, "Why behave?"
I behave
As though you were there.
Your perfume pervades my room
And your taste makes me choose my dress,
Use my dress,
As though you were there.
Boys tell me while dancing
I haven't a heart;
At you I've been glancing
Though we are apart.
Evenings when all men are men
I make each poor old guy behave.
I behave
As though you were there.

ME FOR YOU

Published October 1929. Introduced by Peggy Bernier and Ray Bolger. Introduced by Betty Starbuck and Ray Bolger in *Heads Up!* Alternate title: "Me for You! Wouldn't You Love It?"

VERSE 1

HE: There's nothing wrong with me,
There's nothing wrong with you;
I think we're perfect models of creation.

SHE: You get along with me,
I get along with you;
That speaks well for the future of the nation.
HE: Putting two and two together just for fun;
What we two must do together should be done!
SHE: Let's give the world a hand,
And learn to understand
What two can do when they've become as one.

REFRAIN

Me for you, and the house and Ford!
Wouldn't you love it?
You for me, and the bed and board!
Two can live cheap as one, say I!
Wouldn't you love it?
That's until they multiply.
And, meanwhile, you'll love me
And I'll love you
Away down deep.
You'll trust me,
And I'll trust you,
When you're asleep!
I know what married folks should do!
Wouldn't you love it?
You for me and me for you!

VERSE 2

HE: You'll always cling to me,
I'll always cling to you;
You'll be as happy as the birds above you.
SHE: You'll always sing to me,
I'll always sing to you;
Our theme song will be "Me for you, I love you!"
HE: I'm so tall, I think it's great you're cute and short;
Don't you think to help out nature would be sport?
SHE: And when you sail your ship,
Please promise on each trip
To disappoint a girl in ev'ry port!

REPEAT REFRAIN

THEY SING! THEY DANCE! THEY SPEAK!

Dropped before the tryout. Intended for Betty Starbuck, Lulu McConnell, Jack Whiting, and Victor Moore. No music survives.

VERSE

ALL: There's a new art,
That's the true art
Out in Cal-i-for-ni-ay!
BETTY: Now the show shop
Is a slow shop
Since the talkies came to stay!
LULU: New York is just a Hollywood by proxy;
The Theatre Guild's a bum compared to Roxy!
MOORE: We admit without regrets
Broadway is the street of Nickelettes.

REFRAIN

ALL: They sing! They dance! They speak!
You see! You hear! You thrill!
BETTY: Now Clara Bow can squeak!
She sounded better still!
WHITING: When Hercules and young Ulysses
All talk like sissies
You get a chill!
MOORE: In doublets and in hoses
Young Romeo looks chic.
He uses "dem's" and "dose's"
Although his hair is sleek.
ALL: They break the hearts of all the missies
Because they sing! They dance! They speak!

HEADS UP!, 1929

Tryout: Some of the songs and principals, most of the ensemble, but none of the book, tried out as *Me for You* in Detroit (September 15–28, 1929). *Heads Up!*, with a new book and many new songs and performers, was first presented at the Shubert Theatre, Philadelphia, October 25–November 2, 1929. New York run: Alvin Theatre, November 11, 1929–March 15, 1930. 144 performances. Music by Richard Rodgers. Lyrics by Lorenz Hart. Produced by Alex A. Aarons and Vinton Freedley. Book by John McGowan and Paul Gerard Smith. Directed and choreographed by George Hale. Settings by Donald Oenslager. Costumes by Kiviette. Orchestra under the direction of Alfred Newman. Orchestrations by Robert Russell Bennett. Pianist, Phil Ohman. Cast, starring Victor Moore, Jack Whiting, Betty Starbuck, and Barbara Newberry, included John Hundley, Ray Bolger, and Alice Boulden.

The lyric to "The Lass Who Loved a Sailor" (introduced by Betty Starbuck and ensemble) is missing.

YOU'VE GOT TO SURRENDER

Introduced by ensemble.

GIRLS: Thirty-three lovesick maidens, we,
Twenty and a baker's dozen;
Each expects expectantly
Neither brother, son nor cousin,
But a delegation
From the naval station,
Where they teach the young idea to shoot.
Boys who sail a fool ship
That is called a school ship,
They're amateurs but cute.
Thirty-two lovesick maidens, we,
To be plain, we say it twice,
Hoping each cadet will be
Very nautical, but nice.
Hurray for the Navy!
We've got to surrender.
BOYS: Take it from the Navy;
You've got to surrender!
You've got to surrender, now!
Social belle or slavey
And each of your gender,
You cannot defend her, now!
When there's fighting we dash in it
With unholy glee;
Every lady gets passionate
When she smells the sea.
Take it from the Navy;
Play trumpet and drum, too,
The Navy has come to tea!

PLAYBOY

Introduced by Ray Bolger and ensemble.

VERSE

Oh, I've taken my fun where I found it
From the Bronnix to Kalamazoo,
With the Colonel's lady and Judy O'Grady
And the lady that's known as Lou;
It's a strange way I have with a woman;
She can sin just by looking at me!
But I merely begin it
And play for a minute
And lo! I'm a-sail on the sea!

REFRAIN

Playboy, I'm just a playboy
Who's willing to work at play;
"Hey, boy!" they holler. "Hey, boy,
Please ruin our lives today!"
When I'm on leave,
A hundred bosoms all heave;
A hundred brothers and sons
And husbands start to polish their guns.
Charm them, how do I charm them?
It must be my boyish grace.
Pet them, and then I let them
Admire my classic face.
I make them pay,
But what they buy is O.K.!
Oh, how that pretty playboy can play!

MOTHER GROWS YOUNGER

Introduced by Janet Velie, Barbara Newberry, and ensemble. In the London production of *Heads Up!* (1930), this song was titled "Daughter Grows Older."

MARY: Daughter grows older,
Mother grows young!
On each fair shoulder
Roses are hung.
Youth was the age of sentiment
And twenty meant the end;
Mother was hardly a friend.
Now both can quicken
Heartbeats of men
Which is the chicken
And which is the hen?
Where is our gray-haired mother now?
Another now is queen!
Mary, where have you been?
BOYS: Will you dance with me?
Or will you dance with me?
It's quite a problem to choose!

MARTHA: Take a chance with me!
I'm as safe as can be!
MARY: But really to be fair to you,
I know I can't compare to you!
BOYS: How can this jury agree?

WHY DO YOU SUPPOSE?

Published November 1929. Introduced by Barbara Newberry, Jack Whiting, and ensemble. This song has the same music as "How Was I to Know?" in *She's My Baby* (1928), a number dropped from that show shortly before its New York opening.

VERSE 1

HE: Each boy and girl should reason,
They love for a good reason:
Great oak trees from small acorns grow.
Kids know there must be something,
Although they don't see something;
You're quite a big girl
And you should know something.

REFRAIN

Why do you suppose that robins have red
breasts
And cats meow?
Why do you suppose that apples have
blossoms
Upon the bough?
Why do birds sing melodies?
And why do goats wear long goatees?
It must be that they aim to please
With real, hot nanny-goat appeal.
Don't you understand that flowers have
perfume
To draw the bee?
Why do you suppose
That you're so attractive to me?

VERSE 2

SHE: I traveled with just no one,
I'd care for and trust no one,
I walked with my chin on the ground;
To cheer me I had nothing,
I was such a sad nothing
And, till I found you,
Really I found nothing.

REPEAT REFRAIN

REPRISE

Why is nature young in May
And all the woodland green and gay?
When every lover longs to say,
"My own, I live for you alone,"
Don't you understand that flowers have
  perfume
To draw the bee?
Why do you suppose
That you're so attractive to me?

The following article, titled "A Lesson in Songwriting: How We Wrote the Hit Song of *Heads Up!*," was written for the New York *World,* December 1, 1929.

Editor's note. Herein the lyricist of the songwriting team of Rodgers and Hart exposes the way in which the most catchy song of their present show came into being. And if you think you can do better, just try it and see what happens.

Mr. Richard Rodgers, Esq., archly surveyed me and said something which I interpreted as a rebuke. Sure of my ground, I turned quickly and gave him a piece of the lower depths of my mind. And all over a lyric. A lyric means the words of a song that you never can and never need to hear.

This happened in Philadelphia, a place in which they try out our shows. The particular show was *Heads Up!* It is now playing at the Alvin Theatre. (This means that this article is designed to help the show at the box office.)

But to return to the lyric question. It seems Mr. Aarons and Mr. Freedley, our producers, wanted a new theme song. We already had a pretty good theme song, but nobody stormed the song seller in the lobby in hopes of buying copies. And it so happened that we found out the truth on the last Friday of our tryout in Philadelphia. So Mr. Aarons and Mr. Freedley gave us a few hours in which to grind out a hit.

Dick Rodgers thought of using a melody which we had written for an operetta called *She's My Baby,* but which we had discarded before the New York opening. So we went to our hotel and began to grope for a lyric. . . .

I showed this lyric to Mr. Rodgers and that was why he made the remark which I was careful not to quote in the first sentence of this monograph.

"It doesn't fit the music," said he, "and furthermore it has the quality of a certain insect."

So we started to think. "Why do you suppose we need another theme song?" I queried.

"That's it!" said Mr. Rodgers.

"What's it?" I queried, for once in my life perplexed.

"The title," he said again. "Why do you suppose!"

"Why do you suppose robins have red breasts?" Again I queried.

"That's great!" he answered.

And so the immortal poem was written. We finished it in time to catch the curtain coming down at the theatre. It was Friday, remember, and tomorrow was our last chance, our final out-of-town performance. . . .

Well, this was better, so we kept the actors, Jack Whiting and Barbara Newberry, after school that night and Dick taught them the song.

I forgot to add that while I was working on the lyric, Dick was busy finishing the musical transcript called "the piano part" in our native Tin Pan Alley vernacular. Before the lyric was completed, he dispatched one of the musicians to take the piano part to New York on the midnight train.

Mr. Russell Bennett made the orchestration in New York without knowing what the lyric was all about. Yet by a strange coincidence, on the musical line which corresponds to the words "cats meow" in the lyric, there is a distinct and authentic caterwauling in the instrumentation. Such is the telepathy of great souls.

Our musician came back to Philadelphia bearing the orchestration on the Saturday morning train. We called an orchestra rehearsal at noon, and that afternoon the song was sung to the great joy and edification of the five Quakers in the audience.

Thus "Why Do You Suppose?" was written, rehearsed, orchestrated and performed within sixteen hours in spite of the obstacles of distance and nervous tension.

New York *Times*, December 29, 1929:

On a night when a Philadelphia audience had left the theatre, the composers sat down at the piano in the orchestra pit to work on a new number. Cynics will smirk and the ignorant will gape, but they finished it in what is reported to have been twenty minutes—a statement which any reader is privileged to doubt. Perhaps it took half an hour. At any rate, the piece was completed in time for a messenger to make the 12:15 a.m. train for New York, where an expert was waiting to effect its orchestration. The orchestration was made overnight and the messenger returned on the noon train to Philadelphia.

The principals and chorus had been rehearsed meanwhile by the composers, but it was brand-new to the orchestra. Inasmuch as the messenger did not arrive at the theatre until 2 p.m., there was no time to rehearse the piece. What the audience in the theatre has not learned to this moment (if they are still interested in knowing about it) is that instead of the usual overture the orchestra played this new composition at a rehearsal during the period before the rise of the curtain.

ONGSAY AND ANCEDAY

Introduced by the Reynolds Sisters (Gladys and Helen) and "Irlsgay."

Did he say, "Oh! My Odgay!"
And did you comprehend?
Our oatbay's full of injay;
Such violence must end!
Now they send out the oreskay
To reestablish charm;
It's still a pretty little show,
So banish your alarm.
We're going to the eachbay
To take a little duck.
You soon will see our bathing suits!
You don't deserve such luck!
And if Pig Latin sickens you,
Just give the girl a chance.

KNEES

Introduced by Alice Boulden, Ray Bolger, and ensemble.

VERSE

Rudyard Kipling, the well-known bard
Who writes ballads by the yard,
Wrote a poem called "Boots";
All about the Queen's recruits.
Then he sat down to write the tune
But he couldn't that afternoon.
He met a boy from Tin Pan Alley
And he picked it for a hot finale.
He said, "Rudy, I'll be your buddy
And write this song."

REFRAIN

Knees! Knees! Knees! Knees!
Movin' up and down again,
Movin' up and down again,
Crazy!
Pull up your knees, knees, knees, knees,
Don't you dare to frown again,
Smile!
Hips! Hips! Hips! Hips!
Shaking this and that again!
Shaking this and that again!
Crazy!
Because your hips! hips! hips! hips!
Never will be fat again!
Smile!

While toes are burning
You're graceful,
A face full of grins
Turning a nip-up,
You rip up your shins!
Knees! Knees! Knees! Knees!
Moving up and down again,
Got to start to clown again!
Crazy!
Pull up your knees! knees! knees! knees!
Don't you dare to frown again,
Smile!

THE PLAY'S THE THING

The Play's the Thing is the title of an unfinished musical by Rodgers and Hart. Judging from Rodgers's music paper, it was probably written in the late 1920s and abandoned before completion. Rodgers donated music and lyrics for three numbers to the Music Division of the Library of Congress in the mid-1960s. The surviving lyrics are: "Ladies and Gentlemen, Good Evening (Opening, Act I)," "Music and the Emotions," and "Italy."

LADIES AND GENTLEMEN, GOOD EVENING

TURAI: Ladies and gentlemen, good evening!
My name is Sandor Turai
And I'm glad to meet you,
So listen closely to the lyrics
I entreat you!
Permit me first to tell
We three arrived tonight!
We've dined exceeding well,
The champagne was just right!
ADAM: Ah-ah—
MANSKI: Twenty-one A.D. Pommery
Followed by Old Hennessy
Are quite enough in summary
To turn a young man's fennessy!
TURAI: When will you learn to speak
When it is your turn to speak?
I'm a playwright who does very well in
Budapest!
The critics and the managers adore me,

Despite the fact that Shakespeare was so crude a pest
As to've written my immortal works before me!
And now I bow and leave the stage to Manski
To offer you his little song and dansky!
MANSKI: Ladies and gentlemen, good evening!
My name's Josef Manski.
I collaborate with Turai
And for improving Shaw and Molnár
I've a sure eye!
We've a business that pays
And very well indeed.
TURAI: Come to Manski and Turai for plays!
Satisfaction guaranteed!
MANSKI: Translations of our operettes appear
In London, Paris, Amsterdam, and Rio.
TURAI: And now, my friends, I think it's time to hear
The remaining member of our trio!
ADAM: Ladies and gentlemen, good evening!
My name is Albert Adam.
My reputation's petty;
I write the music for their great libretti!
TURAI: And let me add that you write very good music, too!
ADAM: I am twenty-five years old!
I've composed their latest score;
If it's successful, I'm told
They'll let me write some more.
These kind gentlemen discovered me in Budapest,
Assured me that my style was light and facile.
They bought me clothes and now I am so rude a pest
To accept an invitation to this castle!
I'm just a poor nonentity without them,
Reflecting in the halo that's about them.
I've no money, no parents, no name!
MANSKI: But you're young!
TURAI: That's what counts in the game!
ADAM: And I love the prima donna!
TURAI: You don't have to tell them that.
It's tradition!
That face need not be planted;
The audience takes it for granted
That the composer loves the prima donna!
ADAM: She writes all my music
With two dark eyes;
At her every footfall
Waltzes from out of the ground arise!
Her heart tells me the rhythm of every bar.
Oh! Sweetheart, what a composer you are!

TURAI: Isn't that the simplest way
To begin a play?

MUSIC AND THE EMOTIONS

TURAI: Music has effect,
Certain and direct,
On our most susceptible emotions.
Bugle calls at night
Make a soldier fight;
Hornpipes make a sailor love his oceans!
Even a prosaic bore like Manski
Gets excited when he hears Bodansky!
When we write together, he's the slow one.
MANSKI: That remark I'd designate a low one.
TURAI: Even you could get emotional with music to inspire you.
You'd write so well and rapidly the managers would hire you.

REFRAIN

Music is emotion
With a surge as sure as the sea!
It's like a magic potion
For fools like you and me.
There is the music of love's young salad days,
The moon-struck, June-struck sentimental ballad days.
A boy and girl—they meet—they glance—they kiss.
That's it. Now we can write the scene for this.
I meet you! I behold you! I adore!
[*Kisses Manski's hand*]
MANSKI: Oh, let me catch my breath!
I've never been kissed before!
I burn! I faint! I fall!
TURAI: That's Shelley—but not bad at all.
Now passion—
[*Adam plays*]
MANSKI: Oh, darling! My lips burn until I've kissed you—
TURAI: You beautiful witch—I can't resist you.
[*Embraces Adam*]
MANSKI: I scream for joy!

Come kiss my lips
And end my inhibitions.
TURAI: Stop! This is too realistic.
Manski, I'm getting my suspicions.
And now the music of lies and
deceit.

[*Adam plays. Turai and Manski are still embracing*]

Did you ever do this before? Tell
me, my sweet.
MANSKI: Never before this have I felt a
woman's urge in
The life force.
As yet my flower did not burgeon.
I am a

[*Loud blast of music*]

TURAI: Oh, wise crescendo! Our composer's
chaste.
His music's always in the best of
taste.

[*Pulls handkerchief from Manski's pocket*]

MANSKI: I bought it in a shop and please
don't bellow!

[*Lie music*]

TURAI: A lie! It's Cassio's. Oh, the wicked
fellow.

[*Chokes Manski*]

MANSKI: Stop choking me! And don't rewrite
Othello!
TURAI: For humor, nothing can surpass
Brass music for a pompous ass.
Step forward, Manski.
MANSKI: That's enough of that stuff!
TURAI: And music of anger and rage.
MANSKI: You yourself are the most conceited
ass
Writing for the stage!
TURAI: That's the spirit!
MANSKI: Did you hear it!
He said I was an ass.
That windbag's full of gas.
That this should come to pass
You've got your share of brass.
TURAI: Look out or you'll explode!
MANSKI: You vain inflated toad!
He said I was an ass.
I'll kill him.
Did you hear it?
TURAI: Good boy, old Manski,
That's the spirit!
Music is emotion [*etc.*]
ALL THREE: About this time in an operette
The audience starts to cough and
fret!
Then the music flares up,
The girls appear

And everything is grand.
The audience thinks it's just the
girls
But it really is the band!
This song is known in theatrical
parlance
As the icebreaker.
Play it, Adam!

[*Adam plays. All three sing*]

There's a sun in the sky and a heart
on my sleeve!
Heigh-ho! Everybody! Heigh-ho!
Bid your troubles goodbye,
It is no time to grieve!
Heigh-ho! Everybody! Heigh-ho!
Cast away your woolly winter
underwear!
Just a merry springtime look of
wonder wear.
There's a sun in the sky and a heart
on a sleeve
And a high in a spirit that's slow.
Heigh-ho! Heigh-ho!
Heigh-ho! Everybody! Heigh-ho!
ALL THREE: Music is emotion [*etc.*]
TURAI: That, my dear Manski, will show you
the miraculous effect of music on the
emotions. Two staid old fools behaving
like high school boys on a picnic, but
it's been a great day. August 20th!
MANSKI: Friday.
TURAI: Nobody ought to arrive anywhere on a
Friday.
ADAM: What difference can there be
For such a one as me
In Friday, Saturday, Sunday,
Wednesday, Tuesday, Monday.
Winter, summer, spring
Are each an identical thing.
When she writes all of my music
She makes each day and season a
sheer delight!
And gives me wonderful music to
write.
TURAI
(TO MANSKI): My unlucky day is Tuesday. Among
other things
You were born on a Tuesday.
MANSKI: Well, look at it for yourself. Here's
today's bag of bad luck. Friday. We
arrive—and who is out? Our princely
host. Who else? Everybody. All gone
off on a picnic. Friday. And the beauti-
ful—the one and only, the most vitally
important member of the whole house

party, our adorable prima donna—
where is she? Also off on a picnic. Is
she expected here tonight? No. When
is she expected? No one knows. Friday!
ADAM: And I've got to wait a whole night until
I see her. It's cruel!
MANSKI: Just Friday!
TURAI: Well now, listen to me! Let me tell you
the crowning piece of good fortune of
this magical Friday. The next room to
this is Illona's.
ADAM: What!
TURAI: Yes, through that door is the room
where she writes all of your music
with two dark eyes.
At her every footfall waltzes from
out of the ground arise.
I've a pull with the butler and got
the suite.
Friday all of our luck is complete.
MANSKI: His luck!
TURAI: And our luck. We profit indirectly.
When a composer is happy, his style
is natural and free.
When a prima donna's happy, she
stops singing off the key.
It is not for the librettists to
disparage or cry umph
When they gather pretty royalties
from the grand resulting triumph.
MANSKI: Sordid brute. You've no poetry in
your soul.

[*Lyric breaks off at this point*]

ITALY

Italy!
Here we are
Flown from the cage
Oh, so far
From that harlot, the stage!
Our host is a prince with a yacht on the sea,
So brother Terpsichore, laugh at Melpomene.
Caviar, wine, and the whole thing is free.
We can live high with the greatest economy!
And mark you, my friends, nothing to worry about
    while we are here.
The operetta's finished and our minds are clear!
The weather is perfect!
The night is divine!
The sea—is the sea!
And the dinner was fine.

SIMPLE SIMON
FOLLOW THROUGH
1930

SIMPLE SIMON, 1930

Tryout: Colonial Theatre, Boston, January 27–February 15, 1930. New York run: Ziegfeld Theatre, February 18–June 14, 1930. 135 performances. Music by Richard Rodgers. Lyrics by Lorenz Hart. Produced by Florenz Ziegfeld. Book by Ed Wynn and Guy Bolton. Dialogue staged by Zeke Colvan. Ensembles and dances staged by Seymour Felix. Settings by Joseph Urban. Orchestra under the direction of Oscar Bradley. Cast, starring Ed Wynn, included Ruth Etting, Harriet Hoctor, Will Ahearn, Bobbe Arnst, Alan Edwards, Doree Leslie, Lennox Pawle, Hugh Cameron, and Douglas Stanbury.

For "I Can Do Wonders with You," see *Me for You* (1929), page 142. "Mocking Bird" (introduced by Ed Wynn) is probably a sketch or production number without lyric. "I Love the Woods" is Ed Wynn's famous comic specialty. It has no lyric. "On with the Dance" (introduced by ensemble) appears to have been a dance number without a lyric. "In Your Chapeau" (introduced by Ed Wynn) is almost certainly a comedy sketch that had no lyric. "Roping" (a routine by Ed Wynn and Will Ahearn) is listed in the script as "Rope Dance" and almost certainly has no lyric. "The Trojan Horse" (introduced by ensemble) appears to have been a production number with incidental music but no lyric. According to the *Rodgers and Hammerstein Fact Book*, a number titled "Bluebeard's Beard" was added to *Simple Simon* during its post–New York tour. It appears to have been a production number without a lyric. Lyrics are missing for the following numbers: "Say When—Stand Up—Drink Down" (introduced in the Boston tryout by Douglas Stanbury and ensemble; dropped before the New York opening and replaced by "Hunting the Fox"), "Dull and Gay" (introduced by Douglas Stanbury and Helen Garden; alternate title: "The Gay and the Dull"), and "I Want That Man" (introduced by Bobbe Arnst; added to the show in April 1930 after the New York opening; dropped in May). "Cottage in the Country," frequently credited to Rodgers and Hart, is by Walter Donaldson.

CONEY ISLAND

Introduced by ensemble. Alternate title: "Opening, Act I."

1ST BARKER: Here is Bosco—he'll eat 'em alive.
On snails and serpents he can
thrive.
All for a jit, a small slim dime,

Come in and have a wonderful
time.
Growl! Bosco, growl!
ALL: Did you hear him growl!
Did you hear him growl!
1ST BARKER: The fat girl, prettier than Jane
Cowl;
So fat you cannot mate her,
With seven chins beneath her jowl,
Her waist is some equator.
When she's in the nude
You can see that she's tattooed.
There's a world of pictures and
each one's great
From her South Pole to the Bering
Strait!
ALL: Ev'ry Sunday all Manhattan,
Gallic, African and Latin,
Spends its sal'ry with a smile,
Scrambling to the Isle of Coney.
1ST BARKER: Bow-wow, try a hot baloney!
ALL: Till the atmosphere is vile.
All the democratic horde walk
Upon the boardwalk
In triple file,
Patronizing Jap and Yogi.
2ND BARKER: Hit the nigger for a stogie!
ALL: Good old phony Coney Isle.
1ST BARKER: Ladies and gentlemen,
Here is Frank, or Frances,
Both man and woman,
And how it dances!
This half is chest,
And this half breast,
It can be whatever you like best.
ALL: Ev'ry Sunday all Manhattan,
Gallic, African and Latin,
Good old phony Coney Isle.
3RD BARKER: Take a ride in the old dark mill.
Take your girl and you get a thrill.
It's the darkest place to ride.
It's only a dime and your hands are
not tied!
ALL: Ev'ry Sunday all Manhattan,
Gallic, African and Latin,
Good old phony Coney Isle.
4TH BARKER: Scenic Railway—the daredevil ride!
FREDDY: Mama, let's go on the giant slide!
MOTHER: Freddy, Freddy, it's much too
steep.
FREDDY: Only a quarter, Mama, it's cheap!
MOTHER: It's no joke!
Your mama's broke.
Papa is waiting for dinner at home.
If there's no dinner, he'll froth and
he'll foam.
You ride in airships and horsey
machines,

And your father must feed on a can
of sardines!
ALL: Ev'ry Sunday all Manhattan,
Gallic, African and Latin,
Good old phony Coney Isle.

DON'T TELL YOUR FOLKS

Published February 1930. Introduced by Will Ahearn and Bobbe Arnst.

VERSE 1

HE: I told your father I'm as pure as the snow,
That I would rather go to church than a
show;
I have dared to tell him more than you
think,
I'd be scared to tell him I take a drink.
If I were like the picture he has of me,
Good Lord, what a sap I'd be!

REFRAIN 1

I'm no plaster saint!
I must chew gum, and nibble my nails,
I trifle some with liquor and ales.
Don't tell your folks!
I use words like "ain't,"
My father's wife inherited gout;
I've let my life insurance run out.
Don't tell your folks!
Contemplating marriage,
You couldn't do worse.
In my baby carriage
I grabbed for my nurse.
I've no right to coax,
To ask for your hand is really a sin,
But if you feel you'd like to give in,
Don't tell your folks.

VERSE 2

SHE: I've told your mother that I'm bashful and
coy,
I've told your brothers that you were my
first boy;
I've told thirty stories, none of them true;
I tell dirty stories better than you.
If I were all the things your mother could
wish,
Then I'd be a tasty dish!

REFRAIN 2

I'm no plaster saint!
I know I should believe in the stork,
But what's the good, I live in New York;
Don't tell your folks!
My own folks are quaint.
Their social bent is on a small scale;
My uncle spent the summer in jail.
Don't tell your folks!
I don't follow fashion,
Conventions I break.
I give in to passion
And order a steak.
Please don't try to coax!
I must use tact, although you appeal,
But if I act the way that I feel,
Don't tell your folks.

MAGIC MUSIC

Introduced by Bobbe Arnst and ensemble.

VERSE

Give me a tune that's torrid,
Strains that singe;
Sugary songs are horrid,
They make me cringe!
Movietone waltzes are futile;
If you've hot lips, you must utilize them.

REFRAIN

It must be magic music;
No more, no less.
Hear the spirits effervesce!
Don't give me tragic music,
Let trumpets swell.
Blue notes, new notes cast a spell!
Dance away if you've got feet,
All God's chillun got hot feet!
If it's not magic music,
What can it be?
Making magic with me.

I STILL BELIEVE IN YOU

Published March 1930. Introduced by Ruth Etting. Same
music, except for part of the verse, used for "Singing a
Love Song" in *Chee-Chee* (1928).

VERSE

Never meant a word you told me
On the up-and-up;
I was wise,
Yet believed all your lies.
When you're not around to scold me,
Life's a bitter cup;
You don't care!
Even that, I can bear.
Each day I find
You more unkind.
I love you so, my dear,
That I don't mind.

REFRAIN

Somehow or other,
I believe in you;
Nothing that you do can change me.
Though you may say
Some things that hurt a lot,
Somehow they cannot estrange me.
Why does my room seem big and bare?
It's not fair
You're not there.
How can I love you?
Yet somehow I do,
For I still believe in you.

SEND FOR ME

Published February 1930. Introduced by Doree Leslie
and Alan Edwards. This song's refrain is musically the
same as "I Love You" from *Chee-Chee* (1928). Musically,
the verses are different.

VERSE

Sometimes when you're by yourself,
You've no fun at all.
Why should you deny yourself
When I'm at your call?
When you're drear and you're sad,
Someone near isn't bad.
Call for one who cares for you;
Won't I do?

REFRAIN

Just send for me;
Sunrise, noon or sundown
I'll be glad to run down;
Send for me.
I'll hear your plea;

When your cares pursue you,
I'll come running to you;
Send for me.
If you are deep in your sleep
And dreams are sad,
Send for me, dear, I'll appear
And make them glad.
You never need be
Loveless, dear, or lonely
If you'll only
Send for me.

SWEETENHEART

Published February 1930. Introduced by Will Ahearn and
Bobbe Arnst.

VERSE 1

HE: Why can't I write like Shelley or Keats
Of your much more than physical treats
In words that suited?
I love you.
You notice when my feelings are sung
My thoughts are old, my phrases are young.
Yet, woman disputed,
I love you!
All the amorous words I'm seeking
Are creaking and old,
If I use baby talk while speaking,
Don't scold!

REFRAIN

Sweetenheart, be sweet!
Or beatin' heart won't beat.
So, frantic'ly I rant.
Romantic'ly I rant.
You've got me talking like a baby,
Please tell me what your answer may be!
Sweetenheart, be true.
No cheatin' heart will do.
Oh, dearenest, be smart!
You're nearenest my heart.
When will the happy wedding day be?
Sweetenheart, let me love you.

VERSE 2

SHE: I ought to speak when feeling this way,
Like Sappho or like Edna Millay!
I've only one motto:
I love you.
I'm seventeen and matronly too,

Yet like a child when talking to you.
Son of King Otto,
I love you.
I dislike all the movie song words;
They're wrong words, they miss.
If you speak to your love, use strong words
Like this:

REPEAT REFRAIN

HUNTING THE FOX

Introduced by ensemble.

VERSE

From Scotland to Siberia
And Georgia to Gayleria,
Our hunting clothes are picturesque and quaint.
We kill with great precocity,
But with no animosity,
So widows and orphans of foxes
Have no complaint!
I do not care to shoot
At an inoffensive brute;
I'd rather lie reclined in my reclining room!
But if noblemen and kings
Didn't dress up in these things,
What would you do for pictures in your dining
   room?
What would you do for pictures in your dining
   room?

REFRAIN 1

Red and gold, gold and red!
Gold is the smiling overhead.
Red is the morn in the fall.
Gold is the horn that's calling.
Red the coats of prince and valet,
Gold the hearts beneath the scarlet.
Proud each head, young and old,
Ride with the red and gold!

TRIO

Hail to the huntress who could last!
How can the fox go past her?
Only the brave deserve the kill;
Hail to her horse so willing!
Fair Diana upon her steed
Is a model of charm and speed!
We're entranced, a lovely picture indeed!

REFRAIN 2

Sport of Kings, Kings of sport!
Hunting's the thing at every court.
Shout "Hello!" Happy noise,
Even the fox enjoys it.
It's a game that needs no thinking
And the best excuse for drinking.
Life is fun, time has wings,
Hunting's the sport of Kings!

COME ON, MEN

Probably used. Intended for principals and ensemble.
Alternate title: "Finaletto, Act I, Scene 5." Discovered at
the Warner Brothers Music warehouse in Secaucus, New
Jersey.

BLUEBEARD: Come on, men, seize them!
COLE: What is the meaning of this
   intrusion?
ALL: We fear collusion!
   Get ready for
   A civil war.
BLUEBEARD: You're under arrest, you and your
   daughter!
PRINCE
CHARMING: What's happening? Let go of her!
BLUEBEARD: I hereby proclaim King Otto of
   Dulna, King of Gayleria!
BLUEBEARD'S
MEN: Hail King Otto!
   Piety, his motto.
   Away, away with rum, by gum!
   And make the world dry for
   democracy.
SIMON: What's the matter?
BLUEBEARD: This is a civil war!
   I'll wring your neck as I've done
   before!
SIMON: This is a most uncivil war!
   "Shoot if you must this old gray
   head,
   But spare his nice red pants," she
   said.
COLE: Simon, we're in trouble. What can
   I do?
CINDERELLA: Oh, please help us, help us, do!
SIMON: Yes, indeed I will. Why, Princess!
   I'd go through anything for you.

TEN CENTS A DANCE

Published March 1930. Introduced by Ruth Etting.

VERSE

I work at the Palace Ballroom,
But gee, that Palace is cheap;
When I get back to my chilly hall room
I'm much too tired to sleep.
I'm one of those lady teachers,
A beautiful hostess, you know,
The kind the Palace features
For only a dime a throw.

REFRAIN

Ten cents a dance—
That's what they pay me;
Gosh, how they weigh me down!
Ten cents a dance—
Pansies and rough guys,
Tough guys who tear my gown!
Seven to midnight, I hear drums.
Loudly the saxophone blows.
Trumpets are tearing my eardrums.
Customers crush my toes.
Sometimes I think
I've found my hero,
But it's a queer romance.
All that you need is a ticket.
Come on, big boy, ten cents a dance!

PATTER

Fighters and sailors and bowlegged tailors
Can pay for their tickets and rent me!
Butchers and barbers and rats from the harbors
Are sweethearts my good luck has sent me.
Though I've a chorus of elderly beaux,
Stockings are porous with holes at the toes.
I'm here till closing time.
Dance and be merry, it's only a dime.

TAG

Sometimes I think
I've found my hero,
But it's a queer romance.
All that you need is a ticket.
Come on, big boy, ten cents a dance!

RAGS AND TATTERS

Introduced by ensemble. This is part of a production number.

Worn and torn!
We're bearing the scar of war.
Worn and torn!
We'll fight as we fought before!
We will meet the enemy unafraid,
With rags displayed, we're not dismayed!
Step by step we're marching to meet the foeman!
Yeoman, parade.
Rags and Tatters!
Lustier than Tartars!
Ragamuffin martyrs!

HE WAS TOO GOOD TO ME

Published February 1930. Introduced during the Boston tryout by Lee Morse. Both Miss Morse and the song were dropped from the show before the New York opening. Also intended for *Nine-Fifteen Revue* (1930).

VERSE

There goes my young intended.
The thing is ended.
Regrets are vain.
I'll never find another half so sweet
And we'll never meet again.
I was a good sport,
Told him
Goodbye,
Eyes dim,
But why
Complain?

REFRAIN

He was too good to me—
How can I get along now?
So close he stood to me—
Ev'rything seems all wrong now!
He would have brought me the sun.
Making me smile—
That was his fun!
When I was mean to him,
He'd never say, "Go 'way now."
I was a queen to him.
Who's goin' to make me gay now?

It's only natural I'm blue.
He was too good to be true.

DRUGSTORE OPENING

Probably unused. Intended for Will Ahearn and ensemble as the opening of Act II. Discovered at the Warner Brothers Music warehouse in Secaucus, New Jersey.

JACK: Right dress!
　　　Number one—
　　　Your plumes are overdone!
　　　To be a perfect model of urbanity,
　　　Good taste must not be sacrificed to vanity!
　　　Step out.
　　　Number three—
　　　Your calf's too plump for me!
　　　Our shapeliness is something international,
　　　So kindly let your diet be more rational.
　　　Right dress!
　　　Forward march!
BOYS: Service and courtesy,
　　　Courtliness and grace,
　　　Beauty and tranquility
　　　Signify our place!
　　　Whimsy, charm and elfishness
　　　Barrie would adore;
　　　Utter lack of selfishness
　　　This we give our store!
　　　This is a drugstore
　　　And not a mug store.
　　　We must retain our verve.
　　　Our battle cry is "Serve to live
　　　And live to serve."

OH, SO LOVELY

Unused. Although prepared for publication by Dr. Albert Sirmay, music editor of Harms, Inc., it was never printed.

VERSE 1

Although I've lived so close to you,
I've never tipped my hat.
I must have looked morose to you
As any alley cat.
The wall between our houses is a very thin
　　partition.
To break it down has always been my desperate
　　ambition.

And now we've broken through,
Here's me! There's you!

REFRAIN

Oh, so lovely!
So sweet to be like this!
So delightfully near.
Oh, so perfect!
The first and second kiss
Make the third one so dear.
There's no future
And there's no past,
But now we're living at last.
I'm so grateful
That falling in love can be
Oh, so lovely for me!

VERSE 2

Each day as I saw more of you,
My little dogs would cry;
Because I loved the four of you
Their jealousy ran high.
I used to read my storybooks
And all my time I'd give them;
But now I throw my books away
For you and I will live them:
I'll make my dogs approve.
You're there! Don't move!

REPEAT REFRAIN

PETER PAN

Introduced by ensemble. Added to the tour of *Simple Simon* after the New York run.

I'm Peter Pan, eternal youth,
Who's always knocking at your door.
And I'm perplexed, to tell the truth.
There are no children anymore.

THE SIMPLE SIMON INSTEP

Unused.

VERSE

There's a dance that's new
That I'll show to you.
Flippety-flop,
Comme ci, Comme ça.
Boop-boop-a-doop
And there you are!
Ah, that strain is sweet,
Written by the feet.
It's a bear—it's a bear—it's a bear!
No, that's 1922.
It's a 1930 tune.
So it's boop-boop-a-doop,
Boop-boo.

REFRAIN

Doing the Simple Simon Instep—
Stand on your head and then count two.
Twist your nose, make your chin step,
It's a cinch to do!
Using the process of osmosis,
Roll on your spine and look askance.
You can't get halitosis
If you do this dance.
Henry Ford and his Edsel
And Mrs. Ziegfeld and Flo,
All twist themselves in a pretzel.
What ho! Let's go!
Doing the Simple Simon Instep.
London, Poughkeepsie and Paree,
New Rochelle and Berlin step—
Do this drag with me.

PRAYERS OF TEARS AND LAUGHTER

Apparently dropped before the New York opening. Discovered at the Warner Brothers Music warehouse in Secaucus, New Jersey.

DULL: Pray, brothers, pray!
Pray, sisters, pray all day!
For Virtue is our battle call.
And damned be joyful souls who fall!
Moan, brothers, moan!
Moan, sisters, moan!
For pleasure always takes its toll,
So suffer on to save your soul!
Pray, brothers,
Pray, sisters,
Pray and damn the gay!

GAY: Shout! Laugh! Scream with joy!
Spring! Love! Girl and boy!
Gloom is reviled.
Sing wild, child!
Jubilant, jubilant jubilee!
Excellent, excellent ecstasy!
Spring! Leap! Do not tire!
Faint! Fall—with desire!
Glance with love,
Prance with love,
Dance with love afire!
Shout! Laugh! Scream with joy!
Spring! Love! Girl and boy!
Gloom is reviled.
Sing wild, child.
Jubilant, jubilant jubilee!
Excellent, excellent ecstasy!
Spring! Leap! Do not tire!
Faint! Fall—with desire!
Glance with love,
Glance with love,
Prance with love,
Prance with love,
Dance with love afire!

DULL: Look at the fools from the bad lands!
GAY: Look at the fools from the sad lands!
DULL: Pray, brothers, pray!
Pray, sisters, pray all day!
GAY: Shout! Laugh! Scream with joy!
Spring! Love! Girl and boy!
Come cross the line!
Let's combine!
DULL: Don't tempt us!
Don't tempt us!
From sin exempt us!
GAY: Shout! Laugh! Scream with joy!
Spring! Love! Girl and boy!
DULL: Don't tempt us!
Don't tempt us!
Oh!
GAY: Care destroy,
Girl and boy,
Scream with heavenly joy!

HUNTING SONG

Probably unused. Discovered at the Warner Brothers Music warehouse in Secaucus, New Jersey.

ALL: Here's a toast to the chase,
To the danger we face.
Here's a drink to the bag that we fill.
We cry for the hunt,
We die for the hunt!
Let us drink to the thrill of the kill!
1ST BOY: The Hunt!
2ND BOY: The Hunt!
3RD BOY: The Hunt!
ALL: The Hunt! The Hunt! The Hunt!
Tantivy! Tantivy! Tantivy!
The Lords and the Councillors Privy,
Halloh! Halloh! Halloh!
A-hunting we will go!

[Repeat from 1st "The Hunt"]
1ST BOY: Let us drink!
2ND BOY: Let us drink!
3RD BOY: Let us drink!
ALL: A drink! A drink! A drink!
We cry for the hunt,
We die for the hunt!
Let us drink to the thrill of the kill!
1ST BOY: My gun!
2ND BOY: My gun!
3RD BOY: My gun!
ALL: My gun! My gun! My gun!
Come, laddies, get up from your
couches
And fill up your bags and your
pouches.
Halloh! Halloh! Halloh!
A-hunting we will go!
1ST BOY: Let us drink!
2ND BOY: Let us drink!
3RD BOY: Let us drink!
ALL: A drink! A drink! A drink!
We cry for the hunt,
We die for the hunt!
Let us drink to the thrill of the kill!
1ST BOY: The Hunt!
2ND BOY: The Hunt!
3RD BOY: The Hunt!
KING: Let us drink!
2ND BOY: Let us drink!
3RD BOY: Let us drink!
ALL: A drink! A drink! A drink!
We cry for the hunt,
We die for the hunt!
Let us drink to the thrill of the kill!
KING: A-hunting I will go,
A-hunting I will go,
I hate the damn thing,
But it's the sport of a king,
So a-hunting I will go.
I do not care to shoot
At an inoffensive brute.
I'd rather lie reclined in my reclining
room.
But if noblemen and kings
Didn't dress up in these things,
What would you do for pictures in
your dining room!

The cut of my red hunting suit,
Drawn in London's best designing
    room,
Is not meant to bag
The bear or stag,
But to cover the walls of your dining
    room!
1ST BOY: The Hunt!
2ND BOY: The Hunt!
3RD BOY: The Hunt!
    KING: We'll kill the boar,
Make the lion roar,
And we'll track down the wild deer
    and tame.
    ALL: At all the game
We'll aim!
KING: We'll down the bear
In his rocky lair,
Tease the tiger just for a thrill.
    ALL: We'll kill! We'll kill! We'll kill! We'll
    kill!
    KING: Let us drink!
2ND BOY: Let us drink!
3RD BOY: Let us drink!
    ALL: A drink! A drink! A drink!
We cry for the hunt,
We die for the hunt!
Let us drink to the thrill of the kill!
    KING: The Hunt!
2ND BOY: The Hunt!
3RD BOY: The Hunt!
1ST BOY: Help!
2ND BOY: Help!
3RD BOY: Help!
    KING: Mercy me! A mouse!
[*faintly, from under table*]
    The Hunt!
2ND BOY: The Hunt!
3RD BOY: The Hunt!
[*Enter Simon with mousetrap, which he demonstrates*]
    ALL: Hurray! Hurray! Hurray!
Simon saved the day!
SIMON: Let us drink!
    KING: Let us drink!
3RD BOY: Let us drink!
    ALL: A drink! A drink! A drink!
We cry for the hunt,
We die for the hunt!
Let us drink to the thrill of the kill!
The Hunt! The Hunt! The Hunt!
Tantivy! Tantivy! Tantivy!
The King and the Councillors Privy!
Halloh! Halloh! Halloh!
A-hunting we will go!

COME OUT OF THE NURSERY

Probably dropped during Boston tryout. Mentioned in Boston reviews but not listed in Boston program. Alternate title: "Come Out of the Nursery and Dance."

VERSE

People of the nursery rhymes,
You are rather dull at times;
You're so charming, every one!
Too much charm is worse than none.
Nowadays, the dancers prove
Everybody has to move,
And from Cairo to Topeka
Ev'rybody likes paprika!
If you want to hold your sway,
Learn the rhythm of the day.

REFRAIN

Come, Sleeping Beauty,
Get out in the sun.
You have a duty
That's got to be done!
Come out of the nursery and learn to dance.
Young Jackie Horner,
Get into the swing!
Life in a corner
Won't get you a thing!
Come out of the nursery and learn to dance.
Miss Muffet on your tuffet,
Unloosen your toes!
Ma Hubbard,
Leave your cupboard
And do things,
Brand-new things!
[*Incomplete*]

SING GLORY HALLELUJAH

Probably dropped before the Boston opening. Lyric was printed in Isaac Goldberg's article on Rodgers and Hart that appeared in the Boston *Evening Transcript*, February 1, 1930.

VERSE

We're the patron saints of every prohibition;
And our credo is that pleasure is perdition;

We're so mournful, every one,
That we've never any fun
And we'd like to bring you to the same condition:

REFRAIN

Away with Sunday shows!
Away with Sunday baseball!
We don't enjoy that kind of fun
And since we don't enjoy it,
We're eager to destroy it.
Sing Glory Hallelujah!
Away with works of art!
Away with marble statues!
We hate to see Diana's leg!
And Venus even more so
Because she has no torso.
Sing Glory Hallelujah!
The man who cares for sex
Must write out checks:
It's cheaper to be pure, we think;
We hate the taste of booze
And so we choose
That none of you should take a drink!
Away with cabarets!
Away with modern dances!
Since none of us can dance a step
We haven't got the vigor
To like a pretty figger;
Sing Glory Hallelujah!

DANCING ON THE CEILING

Published February 1930 and December 1931. Written as "He Dances on My Ceiling" for *Simple Simon* (1930). Intended for Doree Leslie and ensemble. It was dropped before the New York opening. Introduced as "Dancing on the Ceiling" in *Ever Green* (1930) by Jessie Matthews and Sonnie Hale.

VERSE

The world is lyrical
Because a miracle
Has brought my lover to me!
Though he's some other place,
His face I see.
At night I creep in bed
And never sleep in bed,
But look above in the air.
And to my greatest joy,
My boy is there!

It is my prince who walks*
Into my dreams and talks.

REFRAIN

He dances overhead
On the ceiling, near my bed;
In my sight
Through the night.
I try to hide in vain
Underneath my counterpane;
There's my love
Up above.
I whisper, "Go away, my lover,
It's not fair."
But I'm so grateful to discover
He's still there.
I love my ceiling more
Since it is the dancing floor
Just for
My love.

FOLLOW THROUGH, 1930

A musical film version of the 1929 De Sylva, Brown, and Henderson Broadway musical. A Paramount Picture released in September 1930. Rodgers and Hart contributed four songs that were dropped from the film score. The cast was headed by Charles "Buddy" Rogers, Nancy Carroll, Zelma O'Neal, Jack Haley, and Thelma Todd.

I'M HARD TO PLEASE

Written February 1930. Registered for copyright as an unpublished song by Famous Music Corp., March 1, 1930. Dropped before the film was released.

VERSE 1

SHE: You can bet I know what I want,
     To get my want I'd be abrupt.

*In Simple Simon *version, these lines, sung by ensemble, were:*

   Is it your prince who walks
   Into your dreams and talks?

I'm as hot as a volcano.
If you say "no" I may erupt.
Though it sounds a bit improper
I'll do the best I can
Like a Royal Mounted copper
To go and get my man.
But you're not the Don Juan of my plan.

REFRAIN 1

I'd love a hero like Colonel Lindy,
Spreading his wings on the seven seas.
You get the gooseflesh when it gets windy,
And I'm very hard to please.
I'd love a statesman like Mussolini,
He made a king of a piece of cheese.
I couldn't change you, I'm no Houdini,
And I'm very hard to please.
Bill Tilden played fair and square games,
His rivals defeating.
All you play is solitaire games,
And not without cheating.
They say King Solomon's lips grew moister,
Kissing a thousand each night with ease.
You're just as passionate as an oyster,
And I'm hard to please.

VERSE 2

HE: There you stand with arms akimbo,
    Like a bimbo that's unrefined.
    If a man can love a vixen,
    His eyes need fixin' and love is blind.
    Cast upon a desert island,
    You would never see my bunk.
    I would ship you back to dry land
    And live just like a monk.
    If I fall for you, my darling, I'm sunk.

REFRAIN 2

Madame Du Barry won much endearment;
She was as hot as the Southern Seas.
But while I kiss you you chew your
     spearmint,
And I'm very hard to please.
Nobody caught Cleopatra erring,
She knew her onions, the world agrees.
You think that Kipling is just a herring,
And I'm very hard to please.
Anne Morrow (Queen Mary) can eat from
     two plates;
She's someone to follow.
You think finger bowls are soup plates;
Knives something to swallow.
Marble sets Venus de Milo's charms off,
She has no arms to swing in the breeze.

You might improve if I broke your arms off,
No, I'm hard to please.

IT NEVER HAPPENED BEFORE

Written February 1930. Dropped before the film was released. Registered as an unpublished song by Famous Music Corp., March 1, 1930.

VERSE 1

HE: I've said soft and sweet things
    To soft and sweet things before.
    They were incomplete things,
    Those indiscreet things of yore.
    This is something new.
    I don't know what to do.
    I'm completely humbled;
    I've tumbled for you.

REFRAIN

Why do I stand
Clinging to your hand?
It never happened before!
Why does my heart
Tear itself apart?
It never happened before!
Your ev'ry word's a kiss to me.
What in the world did this to me?
What makes it worth
Sun and moon and earth?
It never happened before!

VERSE 2

SHE: I played golf with Father;
     I'd never bother with boys.
     Hitting with his mashie
     Is just the pash he enjoys.
     Never felt this way;
     I've just been born today.
     I'm in love sincerely
     And merely can say:

REPEAT REFRAIN

SOFTER THAN A KITTEN

Written February 1930. Dropped before the film was released. Registered for copyright as an unpublished song by Famous Music Corp., March 1, 1930. Alternate title: "That's My Feeling for You."

VERSE 1

HE: I was gay once,
      Changed my girls by the week.
      Just would play once.
      Now my state is unique.
      Dear me, you made your appeal.
      Hear me, learn how I can feel.
      Let me picture my ideal.

REFRAIN 1

      Softer than a kitten,
      Fresher than the dew,
      Warmer than a mitten,
      That's my feeling for you.
      Sweeter far than candies,
      Truer far than steel,
      Higher than the Andes.
      That's how I feel.
      Like a watchman ready,
      Who's steady while freezing.
      Like a Scotchman, I'm tight,
      Each dime tightly squeezing.
      Prettier than a picture,
      Hotter than Peru.
      That's how I feel about you!

VERSE 2

SHE: I was cold once,
      Just as cold as a stone.
      Dull and old once,
      Thrills were something unknown.
      Dear me, what a change I note.
      Hear me, Shakespeare never wrote
      Half the lovely lines I quote.

REFRAIN 2

      Softer than a kitten,
      Fresher than the dew,
      Warmer than a mitten,
      That's my feeling for you.
      Purer than a dream song,
      Brighter than the day,
      Dumber than this theme song,
      I feel that way.
      Like a light, I glimmer,
      I'm dimmer without you.
      Like a kite, I'm sky-high,
      I fly high about you.
      Taller than the Woolworth,
      Stronger than home brew.
      That's how I feel about you.

BECAUSE WE'RE YOUNG

Written March 1930. Dropped before the film was released. Intended for Nancy Carroll and Charles "Buddy" Rogers.

VERSE

Just like a flash in a thunder crash it came.
My heart began to flame,
And I was not the same.
I heard you speak and I felt too weak to stand.
Now that I hold your hand,
A thousand years are spanned.
Because we're young,
The world is lyrical
Each kiss should be a miracle!

REFRAIN

Because we're young
We should be dreaming,
Because we're young
We should be in love.
Because you're near
My eyes are gleaming.
Because you're dear
We should be in love.
Spring gives love a chance;
Winter may destroy it,
Let's have our romance
While we can enjoy it.
The skies are hung
With magic moonbeams.
Because we're young
We should be in love.

Sonnie Hale and Jessie Matthews

EVER GREEN | 1930

Tryout: King's Theatre, Glasgow, October 13–November 15, 1930. London run: Adelphi Theatre, December 3, 1930–July 11, 1931. 254 performances. Music by Richard Rodgers. Lyrics by Lorenz Hart. Produced by Charles B. Cochran. Book by Benn W. Levy, based on an idea by Richard Rodgers and Lorenz Hart. Directed by Frank Collins. Choreography by Buddy Bradley and Billy Pierce. Settings mostly by Ernst Stern. Costumes mostly by Reville Ltd. Orchestra under the direction of Richard Crean. Orchestrations by Robert Russell Bennett. Cast, starring Jessie Matthews and Sonnie Hale, included Joyce Barbour and Albert Burdon.

"Hot Blues," a number danced in the show, almost certainly had no lyric.

For "The Color of Her Eyes," see *Spring Is Here* (1929), page 137. For "Dancing on the Ceiling," see *Simple Simon* (1930), page 154.

HARLEMANIA

Published October 1930. Introduced by Madeline Gibson.

VERSE

One, two, three isn't one, two, three
'Way up in Harlem Town;
One, two, three is one, TWO, three
'Way up in Harlem:
They go stomping down the street
While their hearts all beat off beat;
Dark eyes blaze with an off-beat gaze;
The world is turning brown.
Harlem! Harlem!
Harlem! Harlem!

REFRAIN

Harlemania!
Crazy tunes enslave us!
Save us! Save us!
All the world's off beat.
Harlemania!
Why do you incite us
To Saint Vitus
Till our toes turn on the heat?
With the best of intentions,
Folks who used to be nice
Shake what nobody mentions,
Not once, but twice!
Harlemania!
I can just cry, "Oh my!"
'Cause I know my
Mania is the Harlemania beat!

DOING A LITTLE CLOG DANCE

Introduced by Albert Burdon and Sonnie Hale. Alternate title: "Doing a Little Waltz Clog."

VERSE 1

Though skies of blue may turn to gray
We do not fear a rainy day!
And though we're broke, we laugh and joke,
For we dance our troubles away!

REFRAIN 1

We're doing a little waltz clog
And there is a sun in the sky.
One-two-three! One-two-three!
Toe, heel and toe!
Doing a little waltz clog! Oh!
Doing a little waltz clog!

VERSE 2

When Julius Caesar felt the knife
That ended up his famous life,
He didn't cry or start to sigh,
But he wrote a note to his wife:

REFRAIN 2

I'm doing a little waltz clog
As I kiss dear Brutus goodbye.
One-two-three! One-two-three!
Toe, heel and toe!
Doing a little waltz clog! Oh!
Doing a little waltz clog!

VERSE 3

The Labour Party rules today,
And many workers get no pay!
The Government does not repent.
Hear the good Prime Minister say:

REFRAIN 3

I'm doing a little waltz clog
While you are collecting the dole.
One-two-three! One-two-three!
Toe, heel and toe!
Doing a little waltz clog! Oh!
Doing a little waltz clog!

DEAR! DEAR!

Published October 1930. Introduced by Jessie Matthews and Sonnie Hale.

VERSE 1

SHE: As you draw me near you
I ought to fear you,
Rather than think you grand;
But I can't dissemble,
It makes me tremble
Merely to touch your hand!
Though we defy conventions,
I'm so glad.
No proper apprehensions
Have I had!
All of our transgressing
Seems such a blessing:
Am I bad?

REFRAIN

Dear! Dear!
This is much too nice:
It won't happen twice.
Dear! Dear!
Do you think we should?
Dear! Dear!
This is all so quaint,
And I'm not a saint;
Dear, it's too good to be good!
No love scenes
On Movietone screens
Compare with the one we've staged now!
With the urge
Completely to merge
I feel that we're both engaged now!
Dear! Dear!
One is made from two;
Which of us is you?
Dear, it's too good to be true!

VERSE 2

HE: Others of your gender
Often were tender,
I've kissed and run away.
Once I thought the iceberg
Rather a nice berg;
You've made me melt today!
You turned my blood vermilion
When you came;
I'm like a hot Sicilian,
You're to blame!
Poor unhappy varlet!

My soul is scarlet,
Yet I'm game.

REPEAT REFRAIN

NOBODY LOOKS AT THE MAN

Introduced by Sonnie Hale.

VERSE

Girls who dance have only two legs
But, my pet, you've four!
If, by chance, you break a few legs
Then I'll buy you more.
On your seat I rest my body,
Happy though I'm broke.
Kindly don't forget
That my pet
Has a heart of oak.

REFRAIN

Nobody looks at the man,
Nobody knows that he's there!
You only hear, "What a beautiful girl!"
And that's why I dance with my chair;
Goodness knows!
It never crushes my toes!
It never pushes my hand away
When I'm feeling gay.
Nobody wants to cut in,
It never gives me the air.
It only gives me a splinter or two,
And that's why I dance with my chair.

WAITING FOR THE LEAVES TO FALL

Introduced by Albert Burdon. Earlier title on Richard Rodgers manuscript given to the Library of Congress: "She Was Poor."

VERSE

They used to call her Lancashire Moll,
She was simple but to me she's a doll!
She was poor but I could call her a lady every
ounce,

That's more than foreign Kings can say about
their paramounts;
I went away and told her in the autumn I'd
return
And she waited till October, as I afterwards did
learn.

REFRAIN

She was poor but she was pure, poor thing.
Dressed in rags but still she kept her wedding
ring.
When the birds flew to the south
She lived from hand to mouth.
She was cold but she was bold, poor thing.
She was turned away from butcher shops and
dairies,
But was watched over by all good little fairies,
But she waited till October for my call,
Waiting for the leaves to fall.

NO PLACE BUT HOME

Published October 1930. Introduced by Sonnie Hale and Jessie Matthews. Earlier title on Rodgers manuscript given to the Library of Congress: "If We're in China."

VERSE 1

HE: A strolling player's just a nomad;
    He's one day here, and one day there.
    I sometimes think that I shall go mad,
    It's really more than I can bear!
    You're just the sort of girl I need with me,
    But think of what a life you'd lead with me.
SHE: Though you and I must both go touring,
    A gypsy's life can be alluring.

REFRAIN

If we're in China,
If we're in Rome,
If we're together
We'll be at home.
Eastward or westward,
On land or sea,
I'm by my hearthside
When you're with me.
And the lovely part is,
Till the journey's through,
Home is where the heart is
And that means you.
If you go with me
From Cairo to Rome,
There is no place but home.

VERSE 2

HE: In Hindustan or Honolulu
    Domestic life will be divine.
    The Turk or Hottentot or Zulu
    Could all be countrymen of mine!
SHE: And though we own no Ford sedan or
    house,
    This great big world would be our manor
    house.
HE: While life is filled with new impressions,
    The sun won't set on our possessions.

REPEAT REFRAIN

THE LION KING

Introduced by Sonnie Hale. Alternate title: "The Lion Song."

TOMMY: Ladies and gentlemen,
    Lend me your ears!
    Brawny and mental men,
    Commoners and peers,
    Bring your wife and kiddies
    And their maids and biddies
    To see Abracadabra,
    Abracadabra,
    King of the Lions!
    He waits inside.
    My star is a lion,
    No ordinary lion,
    An extraordinary lion,
    His fame is immortal,
    It will never grow dim.
    Lyonnaise potatoes were named after
        him.
    He poses in the pictures
    Where he scares Mickey Mouse
    And his family has founded
    The Lyon's Corner House.
    He's been modeled by sculptors
    Again and again.
    Birds in Trafalgar Square
    Make love in his mane.
    He directs all the traffic
    At the end of Pall Mall.
    He's the lion who is known as
    The unicorn's pal.
    As an actor he draws
    A remarkable wage.
    Leon the Lion is his name
    On the stage.
    You've heard Sophie Tucker

And she's pretty good too.
But my lion can roar
Much louder for you.
Ladies and gentlemen,
Lend me your ears!
Brawny and mental men,
Commoners and peers,
Bring your wife and kiddies
And their maids and biddies
To see Abracadabra,
Abracadabra,
Hurry, the show is about to start.

WHEN THE OLD WORLD WAS NEW (QUAND NOTRE VIEUX MONDE ÉTAIT TOUT NEUF)

Introduced by Mabel Couper. French words by J. Lenoir. French words for verse 2 survive, but no second verse in English.

VERSE

Weary the earth, for time is old,
Feeble is mirth and care is cold;
Lovers have departed,
Where are they,
Roses of yesterday!

REFRAIN

Love alone remembers
When the world was gay;
There were no Novembers,
Every month was May;
The earth was young then,
And songs were sung then
In a romantic way;
Time was just a vagrant,
No one heard of care;
Every rose was fragrant,
Every maid was fair.
Perhaps you loved me;
And I loved you
When the old world was new.

LOVELY WOMAN'S EVER YOUNG (LA FEMME À TOUJOURS VINGT ANS!)

Introduced by W. E. C. Jenkins. French words by J. Lenoir. A second verse in French survives, but no English second verse.

VERSE

Jupiter and Juno,
Where are they, do you know?
Venus still rules everywhere.
Troy is just a fable
Yet it has a label,
Lovely Helen came from there!
Truth is Beauty! Beauty, Truth—
And they have eternal youth.
Father Time cannot deny
Charm can never die.

REFRAIN

Though stars may fall and fade away
A lovely woman's young forever!
The years may crawl to Judgment Day
Yet lovely woman's young forever!
Time can make Gibraltar crumble
And tumble unsung.
The world grows old!
The sun grows cold.
But lovely woman's ever young.

IN THE COOL OF THE EVENING

Published October 1930. Introduced by Joyce Barbour. Earlier title on Rodgers manuscript given to the Library of Congress: "The Cool of the Evening."

VERSE

My face is haggard in the morning;
I'm a thousand years old.
I'm just a laggard in the morning;
My ambition is cold.
I wait for nightfall,
Till after ten;
I have no use for central heating then.

REFRAIN

In the cool of the evening,
The cool of the evening,
I must say, "I want to get hot!"
When the stars say, "Hello, folks!"
I've no time for slow folks;
I just say, "I want to get hot!"
There's something in the air
That causes my downfall;
Do I care?
Why, certainly not!
In the cool of the evening,
That old devil evening,
I must say, "I want to get hot!"

JE M'EN FICHE DU SEX-APPEAL

Introduced by Leon Morton.

VERSE

I'm completely surrounded by beauty;
Girls are camping upon my doormat.
Now I must be a man—that's my duty
(I have twenty chaise longues in my flat).
A vision of Venus each night meant
That my temperature surely would fall;
The man who has too much excitement,
He can't get excited at all.

REFRAIN 1

The milkman he do not drink milk.
The butcher he do not eat veal.
The silkworm he never wear silk.
And *je m'en fiche du sex-appeal.*
The first little sweetheart is charming;
The second, ah well, she is *belle;*
The third is a little alarming;
As for the fourth, the fourth is hell!
Too many curves are bad for the nerves.
Too much chicken just ruins the meal.
I have drained the whole cup.
J'en ai marre—I'm fed up.
Je m'en fiche du sex-appeal.
Je m'en fiche du sex-appeal!

REFRAIN 2

The fisherman never eat trout.
The furrier never wear seal.
The Guinnesses never drink stout.

Et je m'en fiche du sex-appeal.
I am sick of their laughter so rippling,
From chorus girl up to the star.
You have said the mouthful, Monsieur Kipling—
And I prefer the good cigar.
Too much whoopee can give you ennui—
I am growing as thin as an eel.
Greta Garbo is great—*
She give me *mal de tête.*
Je m'en fiche du sex-appeal.
Oh, to *hell* with sex appeal!

IMPROMPTU SONG

Introduced by Sonnie Hale. Alternate title: "Talking Song."

Table A—a British Lord!
By his Lady he's adored.
She is worthy of his pride,
Handsome Bridegroom, Charming Bride!
Now he's gazing in her eyes.
Mark the Lady's fervent sighs.
Now they kiss, oh what a life!
That's too real—she's not his wife!

Table C—a welcome sight.
The only Yankee here tonight!
Yankees are so broke today
They all stay in the U.S.A.
He's a constable, I hear,
With two hundred pounds a year,
But makes millions on the sly
Keeping old America dry.

A terrific financier
Is Lord Self-made-man, right here.
Lions in Trafalgar Square
Cry in fear when he goes there.
With a brain as sharp as steel
He gets the best of every deal.
Yet see his little baby glance,
He wears the skirts and she the pants.

Ah, here's a minister from Rome.
His friend the King's asleep at home.
His rugged features may be plain
Yet sex appeal is in that brain.
His shirt of black has brought him fame,
But hush, we dare not breathe his name.

Alternate version of refrain 2, lines 11–12:
   Greta Garbo, my God,
   That's what makes me *malade.*

[*Missing line*]
Because you cannot see the dirt.

A British author, what a man!
A famous vegetarian!
He lives on cabbages and peas
And for dessert a piece of cheese,
And only in this cabaret
He takes a little French poulet.

I ask you now to gaze upon
La Belle Charmante de soixante ans!
All hail—she wears fair Helen's wreath
Yet her heart is falser than her teeth,
And though she uses golden dye,
Her hair, her words, her love's a lie.

Oh, Grandmother, where's your gray hair,
Your dear old wrinkles, deep with care?
Why are those painted lips so glad?
To make men mad! To make men mad!
Come, let your lovely shoulders shake.
They aren't real—it's all a fake!

I ask you now to gaze upon
La Belle Dame de soixante ans!
Despite her years she'll always be
Like Venus rising from the sea!
She's lost her youth but kept the sheen,
Just like an ancient evergreen!
The roots are old—alas, no art
Can bring to life a withered heart.

I ask you now to gaze upon
La Belle Charmante de soixante ans!
She's lost her youth but kept the sheen
Laboriously evergreen.
Some people say she suffers from—from sex mania.
But I don't think that's true, do you? After all,
what's a husband discarded here or—or a lover
cheated there? The world's full of men—what does
one more or less matter? You've heard of growing
old gracefully? Well, well, we know better now. We
know that youth, like love, is something anybody
can have for the paying for. Ask Miss Green, ask
Miss Green, the celebrated . . .

IF I GIVE IN TO YOU

Published 1930. Introduced by Joyce Barbour and Albert Burdon.

VERSE 1

SHE: Though your profile's all awry
     And you are no Apollo,
     And you wear a beastly tie,
     You're the love I'll follow;
     Have the thought erased
     That I've fallen in your snare;
     I've a very funny taste,
     That's why I care.

REFRAIN 1

     If I give in to you,
     I'm giving in to myself.
     If you shatter my resistance,
     I'm as happy as an elf!
     I know it may be wrong, but
     That won't matter at all,
     And against my better judgment,
     I fall!
     I'm weak;
     Now you can go'n grin.
     You speak
     And I hear "Lohengrin."
     It's not your fault that I am
     Tucked away on your shelf.
     I am only giving in to myself.

VERSE 2

HE: I've a complex, I'm afraid;
    Oh, hear my sad confession.
    Mad desire on me has preyed
    With a strange obsession.
    Please do not be vain
    That my mind is all askew.
    I'm a little bit insane,
    For I love you.

REFRAIN 2

    If you give in to me,
    You're giving in to yourself.
    If I shatter your resistance
    You're as happy as an elf!
    You know it may be wrong, but
    That won't matter at all,
    And against your better judgment,
    You fall!
    You're weak;
    Yes, you may go'n grin.
    I speak—
    And you hear "Lohengrin."
    It's not my fault that you are
    Tucked away on my shelf.
    You are only giving in to yourself.

THE BEAUTY CONTEST

Intended for ensemble. Dropped before the London opening. Alternate titles: "Miss Hampstead Heath," "Opening, the Beauty Contest," and "Opening, Act I."

USHERS: Answer, please, to the name
Of the place from whence you came!

HEAD USHER: Miss Greenwich!

MISS GREENWICH: Here!

HEAD USHER: Miss West Ham!

MISS WEST HAM: Here!

HEAD USHER: Bray! Kew! Croydon!

MISSES BRAY,
KEW & CROYDON: Here! Here! Here!

HEAD USHER: Miss Hampstead Heath!

[No answer]

Miss Hampstead Heath!

[No answer]

HEAD USHER: Miss Hampstead Heath! Is she about?

MOTHER: Yes, she is, but she's just gone out.
I'm the mother of Hampstead Heath;
She's just gone out to brush her teeth.

MISS GREENWICH: I must go, too.

HEAD USHER: Be on your toes! To brush your teeth?

MISS GREENWICH: To powder my nose!

USHERS: Now we'll rehearse
Our little verse;
And let us sing
This little thing together!

BEAUTIES: If you want to know who we are:
We're not gentlemen of Japan,
But we've traveled from near and far
For the Beauty Prize;
We represent the nation's femininity,
But pulchritude's our only consanguinity—
Our homes are stretched from Greenwich to infinity;
Each one's the local queen of her vicinity.

USHERS: Take your places, please!
Girls, don't crowd!

BEAUTIES: Shut your faces, please!
They're too loud.

MOTHERS: My daughter will stand in the middle;
She's not going to play second fiddle.

USHERS: Order! Order!
Miss West Ham, stand here!

Miss Croydon, stand there!
Miss Kew, take the rear,
And, Miss Bray, take the air!
Miss Turnham Green!
Miss Turnham Green!

ALL: Miss Turnham Green will never turn 'em green with envy.

USHERS: Order! Order!

MOTHERS: What about the dressing rooms?

1ST GROUP
OF BEAUTIES: Mine is much too small!

2ND GROUP: They are most distressing rooms;
We cannot dress at all.

ALL BEAUTIES: You must admit that's not the treatment for us girls,
With local swains all eager to adore us girls;
If Mr. Cochran saw us, he'd implore us girls;
He'd say, "You're good enough to be my chorus girls—
I mean, young ladies!"

(TO USHERS): So, go to Hades!

[Dance]

USHERS: Stop this silly dancing!
It's time that we begin!

HEAD USHER: So take this face and that form,
Remove it from the platform,
For the audience is coming in.

Ben Lyon, Ona Munson, Tom Dugan, and Inez Courtney

THE HOT HEIRESS | 1931

A First National Picture. Released March 1931. Music by Richard Rodgers. Lyrics by Lorenz Hart. Screenplay by Herbert Fields. Directed by Clarence Badger. Cast, starring Ben Lyon and Ona Munson, included Walter Pidgeon, Tom Dugan, Holmes Herbert, Inez Courtney, Thelma Todd, and Nellie Walker.

NOBODY LOVES
A RIVETER

Introduced by Ben Lyon and Tom Dugan. Registered for copyright as an unpublished song by Richard Rodgers and Lorenz Hart, August 1930.

BILL: Get me?
HAP: Gotcha!
BILL: Get me?
HAP: Gotcha!
BILL: All for one and one for all!
   Dat's how us goils play basketball!
   Get me?
HAP: Gotcha!
BILL: Get me?
HAP: Gotcha!
BILL: Dat's how I earn my weekly check
   With a rainbow 'round my shoulder
   And a girder 'round my neck!
BOTH: Hear the happy riveters!
BILL: A girl can love a sailor,
   A butcher or a tailor,
   But nobody loves a riveter but his mother!
   A girl can love a plumber
   Or some guy even dumber,
   But nobody loves a riveter but his mother!
   She'd love a crook,
   Who'd break into a jewelry shop;
   If she's a cook
   She'd even love a cop.
   But when we start to rivet
   No woman can outlive it,
   So nobody loves a riveter but his mother!
   A girl can love an actor,
   A lawyer or contractor,
   But nobody loves a riveter but his mother!
   A girl can love a painter
   Whose paint makes her fainter,
   But nobody loves a riveter but his mother!
   King Solomon! Ten thousand wives all
      paid his rent,
   And each one paid one-tenth of one
      percent.
   But when we start to rivet

No deaf girl would forgive it,
So nobody loves a riveter but his mother!

LIKE ORDINARY
PEOPLE DO

Published December 1930. Introduced by Ben Lyon, Inez Courtney, and Ona Munson.

VERSE 1

HE: People with lots of style
   March down the aisle,
   And then they part.
   Often they try divorce,*
   It's dear of course,
   But very smart.
   We'll say "I do" and mean it,
   From the start.

REFRAIN 1

You'll be so crazy for me,
I'll be so crazy for you.
We'll see Niag'ra on our honeymoon,
Like ordinary people do.
And then we'll go on our spree
And watch a movie or two.
We'll clasp our fingers when the lights are
   low,
Like ordinary people do.
Of seven nights a week
I'll spend all seven at home.
And that's the way we'll seek
To make our heaven at home.
Baby, you'll love nobody but me,
I'll love nobody but you.
We'll change our parlor to a nursery,
Like ordinary people do.

VERSE 2

SHE: I know you haven't got
   A house and lot,
   But what care I?
   While we are young and strong
   We'll get along
   If we just try;
   Though we're as poor as church mice,
   We'll get by.

---

*Published version:
   They can afford divorce,

REFRAIN 2

You'll be so crazy for me,
I'll be so crazy for you.
We'll see Niag'ra on our honeymoon,
Like ordinary people do.
And oh, how happy I'll be
To cook a dinner for two!
And then we'll listen to the radio,
Like ordinary people do.
If I can hold your hand
I want no other reward,
For you'll look twice as grand
As Vincent Astor or Ford.
Baby, you'll love nobody but me,
I'll love nobody but you.
We'll try to live up to the marriage vow,
Like ordinary people do.

REFRAIN 3

You'll be so classy with me,
I'll be so classy with you.
We'll have twin beds upon our honeymoon,
Like all the ritzy people do.
We'll have a yacht on the sea,
A handsome captain and crew.
And you can buy your wife a gigolo,
Like all the ritzy people do.
Our home won't be so bad,
Say sixty rooms, just a flat!
We'll be the ma and dad
Of the pi-oodle and cat.
Darling, you'll be so doggy with me,
I'll be so doggy with you.
We'll do our loving on the telephone,
Like all the ritzy people do.

YOU'RE THE CATS

Published December 1930. Introduced by Ben Lyon and Ona Munson.

VERSE 1

HE: I'm afraid you got me stopped,
   Something in my heart has popped.
   I'm hard to get, but where did you get
      those eyes?
   You've a face and you've a mind,
   You're so gay and yet refined,
   You're an eyeful and I'm a guy full of
      sighs.
   Though I don't crave the dough,
   Write this on your cuff,

I'm goin' to save the dough
Till we have enough.

REFRAIN 1

You're the cats, you're the berries,
You're a lovely dame,
Gee, but I am awfully glad I came.
I'm a sap, I'm a half-wit,
I'm a dirty name,
Gee, but I am awfully glad I came.
You're such a tasty meal, you're very
   genteel,
That's how I feel about you.
My heart spurts so quickly it hurts,
I'd just go nuts without you.
You're the cats, you're the picture,
And I'm just the frame,
Gee, but I am awfully glad I came.

VERSE 2

SHE: All the other boys I've met
   Are the kind that girls forget.
   Words forsake me and your eyes make me
      obey.
   Though you're ev'ry inch a man,
   Tall and slender, strong and tan,
   You're so tender, you must surrender today.
   I make up rhymes and sense
   Leaves me where I'm at,
   So save your dimes and cents
   For that little flat.

REFRAIN 2

You're the cats, you're a honey,
You're a house aflame,
Gee, but I am awfully glad you came.
I'm so bold, I'm so brazen,
Yet I feel no shame,
Gee, but I am awfully glad you came.

You've got a grand physique, a kissable
   cheek,
You're most unique and stunning.
I don't faint each time you say "ain't,"
I think it's quaint and cunning.
You're the cats, and this picture
Fits into your frame,
Gee, but I am awfully glad you came.

VERSE (as sung in the film)

SHE: I'm afraid we've gone too far.
 HE: What a classy Jane you are.
   Please excuse me, I'll never do it again.
SHE: You're so strong, you great big bear.
 HE: I work in the open air.
   Please excuse me, I must do it again.
SHE: You're unconventional,
   And I'm very glad.
 HE: No, I'm American!
   So's my ma and dad.

HE LOOKS SO GOOD TO ME

Dropped before the film was released. A revised version of "He Was Too Good to Me" from *Simple Simon* (1930). Registered for copyright as an unpublished song by Richard Rodgers and Lorenz Hart, August 1930.

VERSE 1

I've found my young intended,
My search has ended,
I've met my man!
He's just my type, so slender, straight and tall.
I'm so glad it all began,
I think I love my man.

REFRAIN 1

He looks so good to me,
How can I help adore him?
He looks so good to me,
My arms are aching for him!
The world seems all rearranged,
Nothing's the same,
Ev'rything's changed.
He is my one and all,
He is my why and wherefore.
My moon and sun and all,
He is the man I care for!
It's strange what loving can do!
It seems too good to be true.

VERSE 2

There goes my young intended,
The thing is ended,
It's very plain.
I'll never find another half so sweet
And we'll never meet again.
Life's incomplete again.

REFRAIN 2

He looked so good to me,
How can I get along now?
So close he stood to me,
Ev'rything seems all wrong now.
He could have brought me the sun!
Making him smile,
That was my fun.
He was my one and all,
He was my why and wherefore.
My moon and sun and all,
He is the man I care for!
And now my love song is through.
It was too good to be true.

AMERICA'S SWEETHEART | 1931

Tryout: Shubert Theatre, Pittsburgh, January 19–24, 1931; National Theatre, Washington, D.C., January 26–31, 1931; Shubert Theatre, Newark, New Jersey, February 2–7, 1931. New York run: Broadhurst Theatre, February 10–June 6, 1931. 135 performances. Music by Richard Rodgers. Lyrics by Lorenz Hart. Produced by Laurence Schwab and Frank Mandel. Book by Herbert Fields. Earlier titles: *Came the Dawn* and *Come Across*. Production supervised and choreographed by Bobby Connolly. Book directed by Monty Woolley. Settings by Donald Oenslager. Costumes by Charles LeMaire. Orchestra under the direction of Alfred Goodman. Orchestrations by Robert Russell Bennett. Cast, starring Jack Whiting and Harriette Lake (Ann Sothern), included Gus Shy, Jeanne Aubert, John Sheehan, Inez Courtney, Vera Marsh, Dorothy Dare, Virginia Bruce, and Hilda, Louise, and Maxine Forman.

America's Sweetheart is the most elusive of all major Rodgers and Hart scores. Inexplicably, with the exception of a fragment of "Sweet Geraldine," and the recently rediscovered "Innocent Chorus Girls of Yesterday," the lyrics for all of the unpublished songs in the score are missing. No script, including the copyright registration copy of *Came the Dawn* (December 13, 1930—E. unp. 8370), one of the show's earlier titles, includes any lyrics. The following lyrics are missing: "Mr. Dolan Is Passing Through" (introduced by John Sheehan and ensemble), "In Californ-i-a" (introduced by Dorothy Dare, Vera Marsh, and ensemble), "My Sweet" (introduced by Inez Courtney and Gus Shy), "Opening, Act II" (introduced by John Sheehan and ensemble), "You Ain't Got No Savoir-Faire" (introduced by Inez Courtney and Gus Shy), "Two Unfortunate Orphans" (introduced by Vera Marsh, Dorothy Dare, and ensemble), "Tennessee Dan" (introduced by Hilda, Louise, and Maxine Forman), "God Gave Me Eyes" (introduced in the pre-Broadway tryout by Inez Courtney and Gus Shy; replaced by "My Sweet"), "A Cat Can Look at a Queen" (intended for Jeanne Aubert, but probably dropped before the pre-Broadway tryout), "I'll Be a Star" (intended for Harriette Lake, but dropped before the pre-Broadway tryout), and "Tonight or Never" (intended for Gus Shy and Jeanne Aubert, but dropped before the pre-Broadway tryout).

Music survives for many of these songs, including "God Gave Me Eyes," "I'll Be a Star," and "A Cat Can Look at a Queen." Theodore S. Chapin found a list in Lorenz Hart's handwriting at the Rodgers and Hammerstein office. The list includes two additional titles: "Come Across," an earlier title for the show, and "Tarts in Ermine," which might be an alternate or earlier title of "Innocent Chorus Girls of Yesterday." Hart's list also included "I'm Hard to Please," which was written for the movie version of De Sylva, Brown, and Henderson's *Follow Through* (1930).

I'VE GOT FIVE DOLLARS

Published January 1931. Introduced by Harriette Lake (Ann Sothern) and Gus Shy.

VERSE 1

MICHAEL: Mister Shylock was stingy;
I was miserly, too.
I was more selfish
And crabby than a shellfish.
Oh, dear, it's queer
What love can do!
I'd give all my possessions
For you.

REFRAIN 1

I've got five dollars;
I'm in good condition;
And I've got ambition—
That belongs to you.
Six shirts and collars;
Debts beyond endurance
On my life insurance—
That belongs to you.
I've got a heart
That must be spurtin'!
Just be certain
I'll be true!
Take my five dollars!
Take my shirts and collars!
Take my heart that hollers,
"Ev'rything I've got belongs to you!"

VERSE 2

GERRY: Peggy Joyce has a bus'ness;
All her husbands have gold.
And Lilyan Tashman
Is not kissed by an ashman.
But now, somehow,
Wealth leaves me cold.
Though you're poor as a church mouse,
I'm sold!

REFRAIN 2

I've got five dollars;
Eighty-five relations;
Two lace combinations—
They belong to you!
Two coats with collars;
Ma and Grandma wore 'em;
All the moths adore 'em—
They belong to you!
I've got two lips

That care for mating,
Therefore waiting
Will not do!
Take my five dollars!
Take my coats and collars!
Take my heart that hollers,
"Ev'rything I've got belongs to you!"

SWEET GERALDINE

Introduced by Hilda, Louise, and Maxine Forman. Only a partial lyric survives.

America has a sweetheart,
Sweet Geraldine March by name.
She's got a swell chauffeur—
An Argentine loafer.
Her salary's a shame!
Just look at her house and backyard,
It's built in Eyetalian style.
Now lots of folk go ter
St. Paul, Minnesoter,
To see where she was born!
[*Incomplete*]

THERE'S SO MUCH MORE

Published February 1931. Introduced by Jeanne Aubert and Gus Shy. Same music was used for "Someone Should Tell Them" in *A Connecticut Yankee* (1927).

VERSE

SHE: Are not my eyes fair to see?
They're there to see you.
Tell me, don't you care to see
What love can do?
HE: I held your little fingertips,
Squeezed your hand till it got sore;
I kissed you right on the lips.
Can there be more?

REFRAIN

A kiss is just a kiss
But that's all that a kiss is,
A lovely way to start
But it's only a start;
The one who only kisses
Knows not what he misses,

He leaves untasted the sweetest part!
Who eats the empty shell
And refuses the kernel?
Who climbs the road to Heaven
And stops at the door?
If simple little kisses
Are all I can sell you,
Someone should tell you
There's so much more!

WE'LL BE THE SAME

Published January 1931. Introduced by Harriette Lake
(Ann Sothern), Jack Whiting, and ensemble.

VERSE

They say a person changes ev'ry seven years:
I've been three diff'rent persons with one name.
My years with you will all be made-in-Heaven
    years,
So love's a thing that will remain the same!
In the future when styles and customs seem
    strange,
My love is the one thing that won't change!

REFRAIN

The sun may rise and shine at night;
Birds swim and fish take flight—
Heigh-ho, it's still all right,
We'll be the same!
They may have thirteen months in the year;
Nations may disappear—
Heigh-ho, no need to fear,
We'll be the same!
Though Hollywood's screenless,
Boston beanless,
And the sea turn into land,
The country may tumble,
I won't grumble—
I'll be holding your hand!
Though love no longer is in style,
Heigh-ho, we'll only smile!
We've got that flame,
We'll be the same!

HOW ABOUT IT

Published February 1931. Introduced by Inez Courtney
and Jack Whiting. Also intended for *The Hot Heiress*
(1931) but not used in the film.

VERSE

SHE: If she's not compassionate,
    Don't sit around and mope;
    Tell her to find a lake and splash in it
    Or go climb up a rope;
HE: I think you're sincere.
    At least, I hope you are!
SHE: What a silly, sentimental dope you are!
    Don't let her chat away.
    Simply ask her this:
    "Am I this-a or that-a-way?
    Do I hit or miss?"

REFRAIN

    How about it?
    How about it?
    Where's your sense?
    What I mean is so little,
    What you mean is immense.
    What's your object?
    What's your objection to me?
    Are you after gold or am I too cold?
    Or are you too old to see?
    I pine; I long
    And my heart is none too strong!
    You laugh; you play
    And you eat three meals a day!
    You're the party!
    You're the particular prize!
    How about it?
    Come, open your eyes!

INNOCENT CHORUS GIRLS OF YESTERDAY

Introduced by ensemble. Lyric rediscovered at Tams-
Witmark Music Library, New York, in February 1986.

VERSE

We all got stinkin' last night!
It's the nuts the way we're leaping!
It sure was an orgy all right.
Men didn't know who they were keeping.
We were clinching in every position.

We're the innocent victims of sin.
You can blame that goddamn Prohibition
And that alcohol rub called gin!

REFRAIN 1

Innocent little chorus girls of yesterday,
Thousands of miles from Mr. Shubert's farm!
Look at the royal rags in which we dress ter day;
Millions of yaps admire our silent charm.
We've all come to harm;
That's how we got charm.

REFRAIN 2

Innocent little chorus girls of yesterday,
Sadly repenting in our yacht or car.
We have too much refinement to confess today—
What a bouquet of broccoli we are.
We've all gone too far;
That is why we star.

A LADY MUST LIVE

Published February 1931. Introduced by Jeanne Aubert.

VERSE

Some women are colder than steel—
From such a fate Heaven preserve us!
Some women repress what they feel,
And that's why some women are nervous.
A woman is just like a plum
That ripens and falls very soon.
But should she refuse to succumb,
She swiftly dries up like a prune.

REFRAIN 1

Life is love and know that
Love is life, and so that
Should make you forgive,
For a lady must live.
When no love is calling,
All your joys start falling
Like sand through a sieve,
For a lady must live.
I've never thought that holding a hand meant
Throwing your soul away.
Had Mother Eve obeyed that commandment
Where would we be today?
We have lips; why waste them?
If you love to taste them,
You ought to forgive,
For a lady must live.

REFRAIN 2

How can love be vicious
When it's so delicious?
So you must forgive,
For a lady must live.
With my John and my Max,
I can reach a climax
That's proof positive
That a lady must live.
If she's not a cold-blooded person,
What's a girl to do?
But if I looked like Aimee McPherson,
I'd be a good girl, too.
What's the siren song for?
What's my chaise longue for?
So you must forgive,
For a lady must live.

I WANT A MAN

Published March 1931. Introduced by Jeanne Aubert. This is the third (and final) version of this song. See *Winkle Town* (1922) and *Lido Lady* (1926) for earlier versions.

VERSE

Some girls want cavaliers
To buy them lavalieres;
Some girls want hats,
Some girls want flats!
Some want a residence
Right near the President's.
Some want a ring,
Some want a king.
I want a simple thing:

REFRAIN 1

I want a man! I want a man!
That was my only complex
The day my sex life began;
I want him real
And not ideal.
I want no tenor who makes love with a song;
I want a man,
The kind that makes a good girl glad to go
    wrong.

REFRAIN 2

I want a man! I want a man!
If he is dark or fair
The kind of hair is no ban.
He can be frail
If he is male!
I want to hear the sound of snoring at night;
I want a man
To raise my window and to turn out the light.

REFRAIN 3

I want a man! I want a man!
If he is not so strong
I'll help along all I can.
I will not grieve
If he is naive;
I want to have someone to turn on the heat!
I want a man
To smooth my pillow and to warm up my feet.

NOW I BELIEVE

Intended for Jack Whiting and Harriette Lake (Ann Sothern). Dropped before the pre–New York tryout. The music for the refrain does not survive, but the music for the verse became music for the verse of "Isn't It Romantic?" in *Love Me Tonight* (1932). A reference to the use of the song in *America's Sweetheart* (1931) is in the sides for the show preserved by the Tams-Witmark Music Library in New York.

VERSE

My life was tragic!
Each day would bore me;
You came like magic;
Just to restore me!
I thought that love was what they talked about in
    plays;
"I'll be true always"
Seemed a silly phrase!
I'd never own up
That I was cheated;
I was grown up
But not completed.
And now I'm swaying to the rhythm of romance,
It must be love,
It can't be chance!

REFRAIN

Now I believe
In the magic of a summer night!
Now I believe
In the power of a song!
I can conceive of a being so divine as you;
If there's someone fine as you,
Poets can't be wrong.
Now I believe
Man was never meant to live alone!
Now to achieve all the joys we never knew!
Safe in your arms, all uncertainty has flown,
And so, I'll always believe in loving you.

OVERLEAF: Jeanette MacDonald and Maurice Chevalier

LOVE ME TONIGHT | 1932

A film by Rouben Mamoulian for Paramount Pictures. Released August 1932. Music by Richard Rodgers. Lyrics by Lorenz Hart. Screenplay by Samuel Hoffenstein, Waldemar Young, and George Marion, Jr., based on the play *Tailor in the Chateau* by Leopold Marchand and Paul Armont. Directed by Rouben Mamoulian. Music directed by Nathaniel Finston. Cast, starring Maurice Chevalier and Jeanette MacDonald, included Charles Ruggles, Charles Butterworth, Myrna Loy, and C. Aubrey Smith.

THAT'S THE SONG OF PAREE

Introduced by Maurice Chevalier, Marion "Peanuts" Byron, George "Gabby" Hayes, and ensemble. Registered for copyright as an unpublished song by Famous Music, February 8, 1932. Alternate title: "The Song of Paree."

MAURICE: Lovely morning song of Paree,
You are much too loud for me.

VERSE

It's not a sonata by Mozart,
The song of Paree has its faults.
It has less than a poor nanny goat's art,
But at least it's no Viennese waltz.
Seville has its fandango,
Chicago has its trot.
Buenos Aires, its tango,
Dresden, its gavotte.
No matter if the day be
Cold or wet or dry,
Each morning, like a baby,
Paris starts to cry.

REFRAIN

It has taxi horns and klaxons*
To scare the Anglo-Saxons,
That's the song of Paree.
It has men that sell you postcards

*Earlier version (different music) of refrain:
Paree has been my mother
Who brought me up with care,
And like an older brother
It has taught me how to swear.
Paree has been my sweetheart
And, oh, so sweet to me;
My mother, brother, sweetheart
Paree! Paree!

Much naughtier than most cards,
That's the song of Paree.
The noise is not delicious,
But it makes you so ambitious
You'd sell your wife and daughter
For just one Latin Quarter,
That's the song of Paree!

Bonjour, Duval,
How's my old pal?
DUVAL: Bonjour, Maurice,
How are you?
MAURICE: How about Friday?
1ST GIRL: Friday is my day!
2ND GIRL: Oh, what a man!
MAURICE: How are you?
How's your bakery?
GIRL: I need a beau.
MAURICE: Where's your husband?
GIRL: He kneads the dough!
MAURICE: Hello Mrs. Bendix!
How's your appendix?
And what is more,
How are you?
Bonjour, hello, sir,
How is the grocer?
GROCER: You owe ten francs,
How are you?
MAURICE: Ah, has my coy friend
Some other boyfriend?
MAN: This is my wife!
MAURICE: How are you?
How's your grandpa?
MAN: He's back in jail.
MAURICE: How's your business?
MAN: How can it fail?
MAURICE: Bonjour, Monsieur Cohen,
How are things goin'?
COHEN: Comment ça va?
MAURICE: How are you?

EARLIER VERSION OF LAST HALF OF SONG

MAURICE: You're looking healthy
And getting wealthy.
BLIND MAN: You're looking fine.
How are you?
MAURICE: Where's your baby?
He's such a pet.
WOMAN: Later maybe.
I'm not married yet!
MAURICE: Hello, Mrs. Bendix
How's your appendix?
And what is more,
How are you?
Bonjour, hello, sir.
How is the grocer?

GROCER: You owe ten francs.
How are you?
MAURICE: How's my physician?
How's the mortician?
MORTICIAN: Business is bad.
How are you?
MAURICE: How's your flivver?
MAN: Just see it shine.
MAURICE: How's your liver?
BUTCHER: I'm feeling fine.
MAURICE: Bonjour, Monsieur Cohen,
How are things goin'?
COHEN: Comment ça va?
MAURICE: How are you!

ISN'T IT ROMANTIC?

Published September 1932. Introduced by Maurice Chevalier, Bert Roach, Rolfe Sedan, Tyler Brooke, Jeanette MacDonald, and ensemble. Not all of the lyrics written for the film version were used.

Film version

MAURICE: The tailor's art
For your sweetheart.
EMILE: It's like poetry in a book!
How beautiful I look!
MAURICE: The love song of the needle
United with the thread.
The romance of the season . . .
EMILE: So Claire and I can wed!
MAURICE: Isn't it romantic?

VERSE 1

MAURICE: My face is glowing;
I'm energetic.
The art of sewing
I find poetic.
My needle punctuates
The rhythm of romance!
I don't give a stitch
If I don't get rich.
A custom tailor
Who has no custom
Is like a sailor:
No one will trust 'im.
But there is magic
In the music of my shears.
I shed no tears.
Lend me your ears.

REFRAIN 1 (unused)

Isn't it romantic?
Starting out the day
A citizen of France.
Isn't it romantic?
In the month of May
To sew a pair of pants.
My business is a honey:
Goods on every shelf.
We make so little money
I can't pay myself.
Isn't it romantic?
When each millionaire
Is broke and has the blues,
Why should I be frantic,
Pulling out my hair?
I've nothing left to lose.
I'd borrow from myself now,
But I can't afford to take a
  chance.
Isn't it romance?

REFRAIN 2

Isn't it romantic?
Soon I will have found
Some girl that I adore.
Isn't it romantic?
While I sit around,
My love can scrub the floor.
She'll kiss me ev'ry hour
Or she'll get the sack,
And when I take a shower
She can scrub my back.
Isn't it romantic?
On a moonlight night
She'll cook me onion soup.
Kiddies are romantic
And if we don't fight
We soon will have a troupe.
We'll help the population:
It's a duty that we owe to
  France.
Isn't it romance?

EMILE: Isn't it romantic?
Da, da, da, da, da,
A very catchy strain!
Isn't it romantic?
Da, da, da, da, da,
Oh, I forgot my cane!
[Maurice hands it to him]
Oh, thank you very much!
MAURICE: I'd better fix your tie!
EMILE: Da, da, da, da, da, da, da,
Da, da, da, Goodbye.
[Outside of shop Emile passes taxi driver]

Isn't it romantic?
Da, da, da, da, da,
[Taxi driver hails him]
Oh, no, I need some air.
Isn't it romantic?
TAXI DRIVER: Da, da, da, da, da,
[A long-haired composer comes down street and gets
into cab]
At last I've got a fare!
COMPOSER: Railroad station!
TAXI DRIVER: Da, da, da, da, da, da, da.
COMPOSER: Not too fast!
I hate to take a chance.
TAXI DRIVER: Isn't it romance!
Isn't it romantic?

Da, da, da, da, da,
To drive around the town.
COMPOSER: Isn't it romantic?
Da, da, da. da, da
I think I'll take that town.
TAXI DRIVER: Da, da, da, da, da, da, da,
Da, da, da, da, da!
COMPOSER: A-B-A-G-F-E-D
C-C-A-A-B-flat,
TAXI DRIVER: Isn't it romantic?
Da, da, da, da, da,
And now sir, we are here!
COMPOSER: How much do I owe you?
Da, da, da, da, da
TAXI DRIVER: Two francs!
COMPOSER: Oh, that's too dear!
Da, da, da, da, da, da, da,
Da, da, da,
You fool!
You've soiled my pants!
VENDOR: Isn't that romance?

[Composer walks to seat in train]
COMPOSER: Isn't it romantic?
Da, da, da, da, da
I'll write some words as well!
Isn't it romantic
Sitting in the train?
This song has got to sell!
[Soldiers on train listen as he writes]
While bravely at the throttle
Sits the engineer!
1ST SOLDIER: Hey Henri, pass the bottle!
2ND SOLDIER: This is rotten beer!
COMPOSER: Isn't it romantic!
Speeding right along
The outskirts of Paree!
SOLDIERS: Isn't it romantic?
Listen to that song!
1ST SOLDIER: It's too damn long for me!
SOLDIERS: Da, da, da, da, da, da, da!

We would rather sing than fight for
  France!*
Isn't it romance!

[marching through the countryside]
Isn't it the right foot?
Isn't it the left!
That town is full of dames.
So we lift a light foot!
Marching full of heft
And don't give your right names.
[As they march a gypsy boy with a fiddle follows in
rear]
You bet we're gonna pet 'em
Left! Right! Boys must play.
[Boy (fiddling) follows the notes as the soldiers sing]
We'll fool 'em and forget 'em
And we'll march away!
[Boy fiddles as soldiers sing]
Isn't it romantic?
Da, da, da, da, da—
[The boy runs off. Music continues to play as he runs
into a field and joins a gypsy band. He plays the last
half of the chorus for them; then, with accordions,
mandolins, etc., they take up the strain. They start
singing on the last line. Princess Jeanette, who has
been listening from her castle, begins to sing]
JEANETTE: Isn't it romantic?
Music in the night:
A dream that can be heard.
Isn't it romantic?
That a hero might
Appear and say the word.
Brought by a secret charm or
By my heart's command,
My prince will ride in armor
Just to kiss my hand.
Isn't it romantic?
He will hear my call
And bend his royal knee.
Isn't it romantic?
He'll be strong and tall
And yet a slave to me.
Sweet lover of my fancy,
Will you ever come to life:
To love, perchance?
Isn't it romance?

REPRISE†

Isn't it romantic?
Standing in the night
Alone and unafraid!

*Alternate version:
There's a tune that makes you want to dance!
†Intended for Chevalier to sing later in the film, but dropped
before the film's completion.

Isn't it romantic
That a woman might
Be pure as any maid!
I hear the breezes playing
In the trees above
And yet my heart is saying
Sad farewell to love.
Isn't it romantic
Merely to be me
On such a night as this.
Isn't it romantic
That my lips are free
From any lover's kiss.
I'm proud that I am lonely
I've no fear that I will fall
In love perchance.
Isn't it romance?

Published version

VERSE

I've never met you,
Yet never doubt, dear,
I can't forget you.
I've thought you out, dear.
I know your profile
And I know the way you kiss:
Just the thing I miss
On a night like this.
If dreams are made of
Imagination,
I'm not afraid of
My own creation.
With all my heart,
My heart is here
For you to take.
Why should I quake?
I'm not awake.

REFRAIN

Isn't it romantic?
Music in the night:
A dream that can be heard.
Isn't it romantic?
Moving shadows write
The oldest magic word.
I hear the breezes playing
In the trees above,
While all the world is saying,
"You were meant for love."
Isn't it romantic?
Merely to be young
On such a night as this.
Isn't it romantic.
Every note that's sung

Is like a lover's kiss.
Sweet symbols in the moonlight,
Do you mean that I will fall
In love, perchance?
Isn't it romance?

LOVER

Published February 1933. Introduced by Jeanette Mac-Donald, on horseback.

ORIGINAL LYRIC (as sung in the film)

Lover,
When you find me,
Will you blind me
With your glow?
Make me cast behind me
All my . . .
WHOA!
Kiss me,
He'll be saying.
Gently swaying,
I'll obey.
Like two children playing
In the . . .
HEY!
He'll be my lord and my master,
I'll be a slave to the last.
He'll make my heartbeat go faster—
NOT TOO FAST!
Lover,
When you take me
And awake me,
I will know,
Lover, you can make me
Love you so.

VERSE (published)

When you held your hand to my heart,
Dear, you did something grand to my heart.
And we played the scene to perfection
Though we didn't have time to rehearse.
Since you took control of my life
You have become the whole of my life.
When you are away, it's awful,
And when you are with me, it's worse.

REFRAIN 1 (published)

Lover, when I'm near you
And I hear you speak my name

Softly, in my ear you
Breathe a flame.
Lover, when we're dancing
Keep on glancing in my eyes,
Till love's own entrancing music dies.
All of my future is in you.
You're ev'ry plan I design.
Promise me that you'll continue
To be mine.
Lover, please be tender,
When you're tender fears depart.
Lover, I surrender to my heart.

REFRAIN 2 (published)

Lover, when I'm near you
And I hear you speak my name
Softly, in my ear you
Breathe a flame.
Lover, it's immoral
But why quarrel with our bliss
When two lips of coral
Want to kiss?
I say, "The devil is in you,"
And to resist you I try,
But if you didn't continue
I would die!
Lover, please be tender,
When you're tender fears depart.
Lover, I surrender to my heart.

MIMI

Published September 1932. Introduced by Maurice Chevalier. Reprised by C. Aubrey Smith, Charlie Ruggles, Ethel Griffies, Elizabeth Patterson, and Charles Butterworth.

VERSE

My left shoe's on my right foot,
My right shoe's on my left.
Oh! Listen to me, Mimi,
Of reason I'm bereft!
The buttons of my trousers
Are buttoned to my vest.
Oh! Listen to me, Mimi,
There's passion in my breast!

REFRAIN

Mimi,
You funny little
Good-for-nothing Mimi,

Am I the guy?
Mimi,
You sunny little honey
Of a Mimi,
I'm aiming high
Mimi,
You've got me
Sad and dreamy.
You could free me,
If you'd see me.
Mimi,
You know I'd like to
Have a little
Son of a Mimi,
By and by.

Earlier version to different music

VERSE

Rodolfo who lived in an attic
Had a hunger that was most emphatic.
But not for food
Did poor Rodolfo brood!
His passion for Mimi was tender.
She was broke too
That's why she was slender.
Rudy lived on caresses and kisses
While he sang to his common-law Missus.

REFRAIN

Mimi, Mimi,
When your eyes get dreamy,
Do they ever see me?
Oh, Mimi, they should!
Mimi, Mimi,
How'd you like to be me,
All het up and steamy?
Oh, Mimi, be good!
And say that you will
Event-u-al-ly agree.
Oh, don't be crew-ill to me.
Eeney, Meeney, Mimi, Mimi,
Let the parson team me
With my peach and creamy
Mimi!

A WOMAN NEEDS SOMETHING LIKE THAT

Introduced by Jeanette MacDonald and Joseph Cawthorne. Registered for copyright as an unpublished song by Famous Music, March 10, 1932.

DUKE: The Doctor!
JEANETTE: How do you do!
DOCTOR: Is this the charming patient
Who needs curing?
DUKE: His bedside manner's very reassuring.
Do what you can, sir!
[Exits]
DOCTOR: Just what is wrong?
JEANETTE: I cannot answer.
I can't permit you to examine me!
DOCTOR: But, madam, it's the simplest thing on earth!
JEANETTE: Before a single instrument you cram in me,
Tell me, are you a man of noble birth?
Forgive me if I make this strange demand.
No commoner has ever touched my hand!
DOCTOR: Permit me, madam, if you please—
[Gives her card]
JEANETTE: [Reads]
Doctor Pierre de Pontignac.
A noble family—and now I'm at my ease!
DOCTOR: And now, my dear, remove your dress!*
JEANETTE: My what?
DOCTOR: Your dress—that's no occasion for distress!
JEANETTE: Is that necessary?
DOCTOR: Very! Yes!
My dear, I admire your sleeves and your fichu,
But I'm here to look at your skin and its tissue!
JEANETTE: Oh, dear!
[Removes skirt]
DOCTOR: As long as professional ethics apply,
I'll see you with only a doctor's eye!
[Jeanette removes waist]
The doctor's eye is satisfied!
Now I'll hear your heart!
[Applies stethoscope]
Don't sigh!
[Her heart is heard in the music]

*Lyric up to here was deleted from the film.

Very good! Nothing's wrong here!
Now I'll take your pulse, my dear!
[Takes pulse holding watch, which is heard in the music]
Perfectly regular   right on the tick!
Madam, oh madam, you cannot be sick!
JEANETTE: Then why do I lie awake in bed?
And why does blood rush to my head?
DOCTOR: At night?
JEANETTE: Quite right—at night!
And why does music make me sad?
And why do love songs drive me mad?
DOCTOR: At night?
JEANETTE: Quite right—at night!
And frequently I faint away.
DOCTOR: That's strange! That's strange!
You faint, you say?
JEANETTE: I fall into a faint.
DOCTOR: That's very quaint.
Perhaps you are anemic.
Let me see!
[Pulls down the lids of her eyes]
I find no weakness here,
Your eyes are bright and clear.
My dear, your eyes look very good to me.
JEANETTE: I feel depressed when I'm alone in bed at night.
DOCTOR: How old are you?
JEANETTE: I'm twenty-two.
While other people dance,
I feel so dead at night.
DOCTOR: At twenty-two
That won't do!
Are you married?
JEANETTE: My husband died three years ago!
At sixteen I was wed.
DOCTOR: You've been a widow for three years?
JEANETTE: Three years the Prince is dead.
DOCTOR: Were you very happy with your spouse?
JEANETTE: He was the son of a noble house.
It was the happiness of great peace!
A Rochambeau—my better half.
And here you have his photograph!
[Shows photograph of old man]
DOCTOR: How old was your bridegroom, dear?
JEANETTE: Seventy-two!
DOCTOR: Seventy-two?
JEANETTE: Seventy-two!
DOCTOR: Ah—this won't do!
JEANETTE: Sweet music makes me cry and pout.
Perhaps I'd better journey South.
Perhaps my tonsils should come out?
[Doctor looks in mouth]
DOCTOR: Well . . . it's a very pretty mouth!
JEANETTE: I'm wasting away.

For three years I've sat alone.
No joy I've tasted!
DOCTOR: With eyes and red lips
And a figure like that,
You're not wasted away—
You're just wasted!*
Let me tell you this, my dear!
A doorbell needs tinkling,
A flower needs sprinkling,
And a woman needs something like
   that!
A car needs ignition
To keep in condition,
And a woman needs something like
   that!
All inventions of Edison
And medicine would leave you flat.
A peach must be eaten,
A drum must be beaten
And a woman needs something like
   that!
Madam!

THE POOR APACHE

Published September 1932. Introduced by Maurice Chevalier. Earlier title: "I'm an Apache."

VERSE

I wear a sweater where you
Wear a collar and a tie!
Well, why not?†
I'm an Apache!
The thing that makes me happy
Is to make a woman cry!
Well, why not?†
I'm an Apache!
My sweetheart is a shopgirl,
She's a treasure,
And so I am a gentleman
Of leisure!
When I grab her wrist and twist it
No woman can resist it!
Well, why not?†
I'm an Apache!
And yet—

Lyric from here to end was deleted from the film.
†*In the film Chevalier sings:*
   Mmm, hmm, why not?

REFRAIN

I'd love to treat her pretty
And show her round the city
But what's a poor Apache got to do?
With one deep sigh
I must black her eye!
I'd love to buy things for her
And tell her I adore her
But what's a poor Apache got to do!
With one good kick
I make her pay me quick!
While other men are dancing
And tenderly romancing
I've got to throw her body around!
The spot that no one dares touch,
The spot that only chairs touch,
Is frequently touching the ground!
She comes and whispers sweetly,
"I love you so completely,"
And then I gently whisper to her,
[*Yells*] "Oh—nuts to you!"
That's how I say I love you too.
Sad but true,
That's what a real Apache must do!

TRIO

I was found in a basket
In front of a church
But my childhood was not very sainted.
I didn't know my mother,
Who didn't know my father,
My parents were not well acquainted!
I soon joined my gang,
Who taught me their slang
And how to pick pockets
And rob girls of lockets.
I learned how to slouch
In doorways and crouch,
To master a wench
With a hammer and wrench.
It's the game
I could blame
But it's bosh!
I'm Apache!
Maybe someday
I'll be good at some dirty work.
Maybe that day
Your police will lead me away.
You'll find, my friend,
I'll be an Apache to the end!
With a smile I'll be seen
By Madam Guillotine!
And when at last I'm led off
To have them chop my head off
I'll tell the executioner this:
"Oh—nuts to you!"

And then I'll close my eyes of blue.
Sad but true,
That's what a real Apache must do!

CLEANING UP THE FLOOR WITH LULU

"The Poor Apache" was drawn from this earlier song written for Maurice Chevalier to sing in this spot in the film.

I wear a muffler where you
Wear a collar and tie!
Well, why not?
I'm an Apache!
My heart is soft and yet I crack
My sweetheart in the eye.
Well, why not?
I'm an Apache!
Each time I get some money
On a chance haul,
I take my little baby
To a dance hall.
When I grab her wrist and twist it
No woman can resist it!
Well, why not?
I'm an Apache!

REFRAIN 1

I like to hug and kiss,
But my idea of bliss
Is cleaning up the floor with Lulu!
Some fellows like to dance,
But where I find romance
Is cleaning up the floor with Lulu!
The only thing that makes me sentimental
Is throwing baby through a floor or two.
And every time she crashes
She lifts her lovely lashes
And murmurs gently—"Darling, I love you!"

REFRAIN 2

I like to rob and kill,
But where I get a thrill
Is cleaning up the floor with Lulu!
I'm healthy and I'm wise,
And so my exercise
Is cleaning up the floor with Lulu!
While other girlies dance upon their toesies,
My Lulu dances on a diff'rent spot.
She spends her falls and winters

In pulling out the splinters
And saying, "He loves me—he loves me not!"

LOVE ME TONIGHT

Published August 1932. Introduced by Jeanette Mac-
Donald and Maurice Chevalier. Alternate title: "Lover,
Love Me Tonight."

VERSE (published but not sung in film)

There's a glistening ring
Around the moon—
Are you listening?
It is not too soon—
Must we sleep tonight all alone?
Let us keep tonight
As our very own.

REFRAIN

Your heart and my heart
Were made to meet.
Don't make them wait—
Love me tonight!
Why should our lips
Be afraid to meet?
Love me tonight.
Who knows what tomorrow brings
With the morning light?
Dear, I am here
With a heart that sings—
Love me tonight!

THE SON OF A GUN IS NOTHING BUT A TAILOR

Introduced by C. Aubrey Smith, Elizabeth Patterson,
Ethel Griffies, Blanche Frederici, Myrna Loy, Robert
Greig, Edgar Norton, Cecil Cunningham, Rita Owin,
George Humbert, and Jeanette MacDonald.

DUKE: A tailor! A tailor!
The bounder is a tailor!
The princess mustn't hear of this
Or the breath of life would fail
her!
I'd rather throw a bomb in her

Than have her wed a commoner
And nothing could be commoner
Than a commoner who's a tailor!
VALENTINE: A tailor!
2ND AUNT: A tailor!
3RD AUNT: The bounder is a tailor!
YOUNG: The news would make your
ancestor
Upon that wall grow paler.
DUKE: If painted ears could hear at all
His frame would crash from off the
wall.
[The picture crashes to the ground]
PICTURE: The son of a gun is nothing but a
tailor!
BUTLER: The son of a gun is nothing but a
tailor!
[Exits and joins servants in the kitchen]

REFRAIN

Come here, you geese,
The great Maurice
Is not the Knight of the Golden
Fleece.
The son of a gun is
Nothing but a tailor!
"My Lord!" I said
And bent my head
And now I wish I were dead
instead.
The son of a gun is
Nothing but a tailor!
VALET: It makes me boil
With rage to think
I blacked his boots.
I should have blacked his eye.
To think I pressed
His coat and vest
When he's the one
Who can press the best!
The son of a gun is
Nothing but a tailor!
CHAMBERMAID: I made the bed
Where lay his head
And now my cheeks
Are burning red.
The son of a gun is
Nothing but a tailor!
I used to flirt
Until it hurt,
While he stood there
In his undershirt!
The son of a gun is
Nothing but a tailor!
CHEF: I've given indigestion
To the Prince of Wales,

The Tsar and Queen Marie.*
Imagine cooking pheasant for
A guy who's just a peasant, for
The son of a gun is
Nothing but a tailor!
LAUNDRESS: Working with a red-hot i-ron
Makes a lady keep perspirin'
Till her strength is just
About to fail her!
But it's worse to stand above a
Board and scrub the britches of a
Son of a gun who's
Nothing but a tailor!
Down upon my hands and kneeses
Washing out his B.V.D.'ses
Is a job that hardly pleases me!
If I had known, I would have tore
the
Buttons off his panties, for the
Son of a gun is
Nothing but a tailor!
JEANETTE: Nothing but a tailor!†
ALL: [whispered]
The son of a gun is nothing but a
tailor!
[Repeated eight times]

THE MAN FOR ME

Registered for copyright as an unpublished song by
Famous Music, February 29, 1932. Dropped before the
film was released. Intended for Jeanette MacDonald and
Maurice Chevalier. Alternate title: "The Letter Song."

JEANETTE: [Speaks as she writes]
There is nothing doing at night!
[Stops writing]
That's silly! What can I write?
[Writes again]
How I wish that you could be here!
[Stops writing]
That's stupid! Can't think!
Oh, dear!
I wish someone could help me!
Writing always makes me nervous!
MAURICE: If Mademoiselle forgives me—
I am at her service!
JEANETTE: Oh!

*Version sung in film:
I've given indigestion to a President,
Ptomaine to a Duke.
†Lines from here to end were sung in the film but were not
on Rodgers's score.

MAURICE: Oh—I'm sorry!* Allow me!

JEANETTE: It's such a stupid letter!

MAURICE: I'll be indebted if you let me help you.

JEANETTE: Oh, no! I'd be the debtor!
What can I write?
It's so hard for me.
Night after night
Is dull as can be.
I'm writing to a girlfriend,
My little Marie!

MAURICE: Let me see! Let me see!
Why don't you write this
As I dictate it.

[She writes as he dictates]
I have met the one man, my dear!

JEANETTE: Who is it?

MAURICE: [continuing to dictate]
On a visit here!
I am so excited tonight!

JEANETTE: Excited?

MAURICE: And delighted! Dear!
He is so distinguished and sweet,
Very debonair yet discreet!
He's the light of fashion!

JEANETTE: [continuing to write]
My passion's at fever heat!

MAURICE: He's so modest all of the while.

JEANETTE: Oh, very!

MAURICE: With a merry smile.
He is made of iron. He's tall.

JEANETTE: Gigantic!

MAURICE: With romantic style!
He's a Julius Caesar in mind
With Apollo's beauty combined.

---

*An earlier version included these lines:

JEANETTE: Are you waiting for anybody?

MAURICE: For Vicomte Gilbert!

JEANETTE: Oh, you are a friend of Gilbert's—
I'm bothered—no end.
I'm writing a friend.
It's such a stupid letter!

So, my little friend, you see
He's the very man for me!

JEANETTE: I'll sign my name!

MAURICE: It's easy to see
This little note
Is sweet as can be.
It's sure to please your
Girlfriend, your
Little Marie!
Now read it for me,
Read it for me!

JEANETTE: [reading]
I have met a foolish young man

MAURICE: Who is it?

JEANETTE: On a visit here!
I'll get rid of him if I can.

MAURICE: I'm choking.

JEANETTE: I'm not joking, dear.
He is undistinguished and plain!
Very unattractive yet vain!
And he needs a shaking!

MAURICE: I'm taking
The first fast train!

JEANETTE: All he does is grin like a mule!

MAURICE: I'm frowning.

JEANETTE: He's a clowning fool!
He could never learn how to love!

MAURICE: I'll grow to—

JEANETTE: He should go to school!
He's a simple Simon in mind.
To describe his looks is unkind.
So, my little friend, you see
He is not the man for me.

GIVE ME JUST
A MOMENT

Intended for Jeanette MacDonald and Maurice Chevalier. This lyric, and the scene for which it was written, was discovered by film and theatre historian Miles Kreuger. It was deleted from the screenplay before the film was completed. No music survives.

INTRODUCTION

You're only dreaming, you know;
I'm not here beside you at all.
Wake up, and away I will go;
There's really no me on the wall.

VERSE

You have always been my princess far-away
My shining star—away up in the distant blue!
I'd always dreamed that you'd come here to me.
When you are near to me,
I know I'm dreaming true!
When the dream dissolves,
I'll not complain.
For just a fleeting moment
I've not lived in vain.

REFRAIN

Give me just a moment,
Give me just a moment of love—
In your arms!
One immortal moment in your arms.
Let your lips make music,
Let your lips make music of love
And its charms!
Speak to me and music has its charms.
We will be one—
One with the heart of night
'Til we're a part of night
United with the dark!
So we will melt our shadows
With the stars and Heaven above.
Give me just a moment of love!

OVERLEAF: George M. Cohan, Jimmy Durante, and Claudette Colbert

THE PHANTOM PRESIDENT | 1932

A Paramount Picture. Released September 1932. Music by Richard Rodgers. Lyrics by Lorenz Hart. Screenplay by Walter DeLeon and Harlan Thompson, based on the novel by George F. Worts. Directed by Norman Taurog. Cast, starring George M. Cohan, Claudette Colbert, and Jimmy Durante, included George Barbier, Sidney Toler, Louise MacKintosh, Jameson Thomas, Julius McVicker, Alan Mowbray, and Charles Middleton.

THE COUNTRY NEEDS A MAN

Introduced by members of the company.

GUIDE: This way, ladies and gentlemen.
    This is our capitol, democracy's
        shrine,
KIDDIES: Goody!
MEN: Swell!
LADIES: Divine!
GUIDE: Where brawny, honest and mental
        men
    As congressmen combine.
KIDDIES: Goody!
MEN: Swell!
LADIES: Divine!
GUIDE: Anarchists may joke and say that
        we are broke,
    But if you're patriotic to a land
        that's not despotic,
    You'll admit that liberty's flag is
        unfurled
    On the land that's the richest and
        will always be the richest.
    It's the very richest country in the
        world.
KIDDIES: Goody!
MEN: Swell!
LADIES: Divine!
WASHINGTON'S
    PICTURE: My countrymen
JEFFERSON'S
    PICTURE: And mine
LINCOLN'S
    PICTURE: My countrymen
THEODORE
ROOSEVELT'S
    PICTURE: And mine
WASHINGTON: We weren't so rich in our day,
        Tom.
JEFFERSON: We know what Depression means.
WASHINGTON: We ate no filet mignon while
        fighting King George.

On continental crab cakes we'd
    very seldom gorge,
And the caviar was rotten that
    they served at Valley Forge,
But we won the war on beans.
JEFFERSON: Our land is topsy-turvy,
    It's fear is like the scurvy,
    It needs a nervy man like you.
WASHINGTON: Like me?
JEFFERSON: Like you.
WASHINGTON: Not me.
    You wrote the declaration
    That started our great nation
    And unfurled the flag of freedom
        to the sky.
    Mr. Volstead's famed amendment
    To our liberty the end meant;
    You'd never let our freedom's well
        run dry.
    And the country needs a man like
        you.
JEFFERSON: Not me!
    Perhaps like Abe.
ROOSEVELT: That's great!
    But I am forced to state
    You spoke for abolition
    Against a great sedition
    Without your party's permission
    And told them to go fishin'.
LINCOLN: But the country needs a man like
        you.
ROOSEVELT: Like me?
LINCOLN: Like you.
ROOSEVELT: Not me.
LINCOLN: The murderers they call gangmen
    Would soon be given to hangmen.
    You'd end them quick with your
        big stick!
JEFFERSON: And with no hesitation
    You'd ask each foreign nation
    To pay us what she owes
    And pay right through the nose.
ALL: The country needs a man.
ROOSEVELT: George, will you take the job?
WASHINGTON: After you, my dearest Tom.
JEFFERSON: After you, my honest Abe.
LINCOLN: After you, my bully Ted.
ROOSEVELT: After you, my noble George.
ALL: It seems the country needs a man.
    Oh, fathers of our country,
    What shall we do?
    Give the solution if you can.
    The country needs a man!

SOMEBODY OUGHT TO WAVE A FLAG

Introduced by George M. Cohan, Jimmy Durante, and ensemble. Presented in whole but mostly in part in numerous sequences throughout the film.

VERSE

Sing a song of Wall Street and the war
    debt.
Ev'ry day we get a little more debt.
Ev'ry time our Congress goes in session
They achieve again in the Depression.
There are Reds in Russia,
There are Whites in Prussia,
There are blues just everywhere.
Let's string the three together
And fly them in the air.

REFRAIN

BLAIR: You are men
    And you are freemen.
ALL: Maybe someone ought to wave the flag!
BLAIR: This is when you've got to be men.
ALL: Maybe someone ought to wave the flag!
BLAIR: Make a braver land of the brave.
ALL: Don't you waver; just let it wave.
BLAIR: She's a grand old flag;
    Don't let her drag.
ALL: Maybe, someone ought to wave a flag.
    Blair! Blair! Blair!
    We want Blair!
    Blair! Blair! Blair!
    Blair! Blair! Blair!
    Blair! Blair! Blair!
    Blair! Blair! Blair!
    Blair! Blair! Blair!

    . . .

THE MEDICINE SHOW

Introduced by George M. Cohan, Jimmy Durante, George Barbier, Louise MacIntosh, Julian McVicker, and ensemble.

BARKER: Now, folks, fall in line
    For the big Medicine Show.
    Everybody go!
    Let's go,
    Folks, right inside to Dr. Varney,
    The Kalamoochie's pride.

[*Sings reprise of "Somebody Ought to Wave the Flag"*]
  Step in, friends!
  There's room in here.
  Standees, please stay in the rear.
  Stand up, boys!
  You've got strong feet.
  Give this little lady your seat.
COONEY: Thanks for your applause.
  I brought along a little song,
  But I am no Caruso.

[*Next lines are to Eddie Leonard's "Roly Boly Eyes"*]
  He's no Robinson Crusoe.
  But I want to vostiferate he'll please
   you, so
  Do you remember when Eddie
   Leonard sang in the *Ziegfeld Follies*
   of seventeen seventy-six?
  You know and I know
  He didn't sing
  "Roll dem Roly
   Boly-wah-wah-wah-wah eyes."
  And do you remember when
   Christopher Columbus sang to the
   Queen of all the Spaniards?
  You know and I know
  He didn't sing
  "Roll dem Roly
   Boly-wah-wah-wah-wah eyes."
  And when Washington crossed the
   Delaware Gap
  And Napoleon baked his famous cake,
  What did they sing?
  They didn't sing the "Jelly Roll
   Blues."
  They didn't sing—
  Let's not go into that again,
  But let me repeat
  Let me repeat again.
  I regurgitate, with or without,
  What did they sing?
  They sang the song
  Which my friend will give an
   interpretation.
VARNEY: You tell 'em!
COONEY: I'll inform 'em
  And give 'em that-a.
VARNEY: With no hesitation,
  Sing, brother, sing!
  Make the Wall-King ring
  Make the Wall-King ring
  Till he falls off his throne.

[*Sings verse and refrain of "Somebody Ought to Wave the Flag"*]
COONEY: I congratulate you, friends,
  On the pleasure that is in store for
   you.
  And before this meeting ends,

Dr. Varney will do more for you
Than any physician or optician,
Osteopath or chiropractor.
Doctor Varney's not an actor
But Mister Cooney is.

A Schnozzola

Lyric by Lorenz Hart and music by Arthur Johnston and Jimmy Durante.

COONEY: And who do you love?
  Schnozzola!
  What was George Washington
  When he crossed the Delaware?
  What did he point with
  To get him there?
  Ah—a
  Schnozzola.
  And Abraham Lincoln, another great
   guy!
  Just look at Abraham Lincoln right in
   the eye.
  Ah—a
  Schnozzola.
  And as my dear old mater used to say,
  So the nose goes.
  Watch the nose pose
  As the nose shows.
  When the nose grows,
  Then the nose knows.
  That is my mother's no-sary.

Sick

By Lorenz Hart and Jimmy Durante.

COONEY: Once I was a man who was full of
   diseases.
  I had dryness in the endocrines and
   water on the kneesies.
  I tried every medicine.
  I tried every tonic.
  I had treatment osteopathic,
  Homopotic and colonic.
  Till I got the thirteen herbs
  They cured me of dyspepsin,
  And angina pictorial
  Chicken pox, small pox, medium pox,
  Big pox, bigger pox,
  Tuberculosis, liver cirrhosis,
  Bronxitis, halitosis,
  Boy, was I sick!

RONKTON: Do you see what I see?
SCRANTON: Blair, it's Blair!
  Or his twin brother standing there.

VARNEY: Now I'm not going to sell you a thing,
  What I give, I shall give away free.
  Did I hear a jeer?
  Did I hear a jeer?
  And even another?
  Don't apologize, brother,
  You'll soon be ashamed,
  And properly tamed,
  When you've listened a moment to
   me
  What have I got in my hand?
WOMAN: A fountain pen.
VARNEY: Ah, you understand.
  The beautiful little lady is right.
MAN: What a smooth talker,
  What charming rascality.
  There's just one word for it,
  Personality.
VARNEY: And here we get the great surprise.
  It's worth two dollars.
  A dollar-fifty, anyway.
  Yet I'm going to give it away
  With a hundred more,
  Tonight in this store.
  And here we have a spot remover,
  Ladies and gents,
  It's worth a dollar and fifty cents.
  And here are the original thirteen
   herbs.
  The price, plainly marked, is two-fifty.
  I put it with this two-dollar pen,
  And this dollar can of spot remover.
  Now think of it, men,
  Five-fifty of merchandise in all.
  Yet I'm not asking five-fifty,
  For the price would be small.
  I'm not asking four nor three.
  And what's more, ah, hah!
  Keep your hand in your pocket,
   brother.
  You think the price is two.
  Well, you're wrong if you do.
  Ladies and gentlemen,
  While they last,
  The price is one dollar.
  Speak fast, brothers, fast.
  I give these away to the world and his
   wife,
  And I make them my friends
  And my debtors for life.
  Now who'll be the first one to speak?
COONEY: I will.
  I'll take one.
  I'll take two.
VARNEY: Louder, brother, your voice is too
   weak.
COONEY: I'll take one.
RONKTON: Hold on there,

What's the matter with you?
What are you sniffing at,
You poor fish?
Ah-ah, a sunflower,
Swish, swish, swish!
SCRANTON: It's uncanny.
I'd swear the fellow were Blair.
MELROSE: The resemblance is remarkable,
His nose, his eyes, his hair.
[*Train whistle*]
That's our train.
RONKTON: Wait, Senator,
We've not come here in vain.
I've got a funny notion,
By all the crazy fates,
With him we'll make Blair President
Of these United States.

GIVE HER A KISS

Published October 1932. Introduced by "animals and birds."

VERSE

LADY FROG: Don't you feel the thrill of
something,
Something, something in the air?
MAN FROG: Your eyes entice,
I mean they're nice.
I admire your dress, your perfume
And the way you dress your hair!
That's where it ends!
I mean we're friends!

REFRAIN

BIRDS, BEES,
ETC.: Give her a kiss,
Face the issue,
Give her a kiss,
Make her kiss you,
She'd adore it—
Thank you for it.
Give her a kiss,
Why have you lips?
Give her a kiss,
Press those two lips.
She's so lovely—
Give her a kiss.
Take the lady by storm;
You know you can.
She'll reply with a warm
"Man, you're my man."

How can you miss?
She will soften,
Chances like this
Don't come often.
Now or never—
Give her a kiss.

SECOND ENDING

You can make it,
Give her a kiss,
She can take it,
Now or never—
Give her a kiss.

THE CONVENTION

Introduced by George M. Cohan, Jimmy Durante, and ensemble.

VARNEY: My friends, this land is sad today,
It faces want and dearth.
But government of the people,
By the people, for the people,
Shall not perish from the earth.
VERMONT: Hey, hey, hey,
That's a new thought.
CALIFORNIA: That's a true thought.
HARLEM
BAND: We nebber known dat before.
We nebber known dat before.
TENORS: Hi-de-hi.
BASSES: Hi-de-hi.
TENORS: Ho-de-ho.
BASSES: Ho-de-ho.
Of de people,
Of de people,
TENORS: By the people,
BASSES: By the people,
TENORS: For de people,
CROWD: For de people.
We nebber heard dat before.
VARNEY: Take this note of pessimism,
What's it really worth.
When government of the people,
By the people, for the people,
Shall not perish from the earth.
HAWAIIAN
ORCHESTRA: O-neekee
Wichi
Wichi
Wachee
Hula.
Putchee

Butchee
Bear.
That means these gentle voices
Singee
Nicee
Teddy Blair.
VARNEY: I've piled up in a pat form
Each plank upon my platform,
And every plank's a drug to cure
your ills.
When a man is sick a physician
Must put him back into condition.
Our country needs a medicine man,
A medical Thomas Edison man,
With nerve instead of pills.
1ST MAN: He's convincing, enormous.
2ND MAN: That fella could reform us.
He's marvelous, magnetic,
He's real!
WOMAN: Now that's what I call sex appeal.
VARNEY: What have I got in my hand?
OLD MAN: A fountain pen.
VARNEY: Ah, hah! Trust the little fellow's
bright young eyes.
Now we need a man to wield this
pen,
To make our countrymen free men.
And here's another gadget sold by
the Medicine Man.
It fits right in with our party's most
enthusiastic plan.
It's a spot remover, ladies and gents,
And it sells for a dollar and fifty
cents.
But we need it to remove every spot
and every blot
That the opposing party's
administration
Has placed upon our beloved nation.
And here's a bottle of thirteen
herbs.
It needs no ballyhoo,
It needs no blurbs.
It represents the spirit of the
original thirteen states,
The spirit which our nation so
eagerly awaits.
What has been the inspiration of the
composers of every nation?
Of Beethoven, Mozart and Liszt?
COONEY: Liszt! That's it! Liszt!
List close, my friends, and hear!
CROWD: Blair! Blair! Blair!
Blair! Blair! Blair!
Blair! Blair! Blair!
Blair! Blair! Blair!
He'll sweep the country everywhere.
Blair! Blair!

In the presidential chair.
Blair! Blair!
The country needs a man.
BOY: The country needs a man.
The country needs a man,
Let's say it in the simplest way we
can.
The country needs a man.
Like you.
COONEY: Not me!
BOY: Yes, you!
COONEY: How mortifying!
The country is like a man who was
full of diseases.
It's got dryness of the endocrines
And water on the kneesies.
It needs a man like Blair
To give it back its equilibrium,
To save it from smallpox, medium
pox,
Big pox and bigger pox,
Osmosis, cirrhosis and halitosis.
Boy, is it sick!
A DELEGATE: Ladies! Gentlemen!
Friends! Massas!
I'se a great big man from the South
With a big cigar in my mouth.
Mister Blair's g'wanna keep the
South solid;
He's g'wanna, he's g'wanna, he's
g'wanna.
Theodore K. Blair is g'wanna make
the world safe for mint juleps.
He's g'wanna make the world sing
"Dixie."
CROWD: Hooray, hooray!
A DELEGATE: Vote for Blair and I'll make every
one of you a colonel, yes suh!

CROWD: Blair! Blair! Blair!
Blair! Blair! Blair!
Blair! Blair! Blair!
Blair! Blair! Blair!
COONEY: Rhode Islanders, Vermonters,
Connecticutters, Massachusettions,
New Hampshirites and Mainiacs.
Mister Blair is a Yank.
Gosh darn- gol durn
He's a Harvard man.
He's a conservative.
He's against liquor.
He's for Blue Sundays,
Chocolate sundaes and Billy
Sundays.
I'll be switched.
Gentlemen,
I'll be switched.
I'll be swan—
I'll be swan—
I'll be swan—
I'll be for Blair.
Gosh darn it, Blair.
Blair! Blair! Blair!
Blair! Blair! Blair!
My brother Smiths of Utah,
Vote for Blair today,
And I'll make you Vice-Presidents
Of the U.S.A.
Do it for your wives,
Won't they feel grand,
To be the fifty-seven second ladies
of the land.
CROWD: Blair! Blair! Blair!
Blair! Blair! Blair!
COONEY: Vote for Blair
And I'll make you Vice-President,
That's the faith I have in you.

I'll even move the Capitol
From Washington down to Lenox
Avenue.
VARNEY: [Sings refrain of "Somebody Ought to
Wave the Flag"]

THERE HE IS—
THEODORE K. BLAIR

Unused.

There he is—Theodore K. Blair.
A good American name.
A good American self-made businessman.
But no good American showmanship.
No good American sex appeal.
Now listen here,
The four of us can elect anybody we pick.
Pardon, Senator, you're not even picking the right
word. The four of us can nominate anybody. But you
can't elect a man whose personality doesn't appeal
to the voters.
Blair lacks political charm.
Blair has no flair for savoir-faire.
Mr. Blair has never had a good
Hot and rousing love affair.
Mr. Blair is a man above reproach.
Full of chivalry.
Chivalry's all right but a little
Chevalier wouldn't hurt.
You know in this day and age
America could stand a President
Who's just a little bit naughty.

Frank Morgan, Edgar Connor, and Al Jolson

HALLELUJAH, I'M A BUM | 1933

A film produced by Joseph M. Schenck for United Artists. Released January 1933. Music by Richard Rodgers. Lyrics and rhythmic dialogue by Lorenz Hart. Screenplay by S. N. Behrman, adapted from a story by Ben Hecht. Directed by Lewis Milestone. Music directed by Alfred Newman. Cast, starring Al Jolson, included Madge Evans, Frank Morgan, Harry Langdon, Chester Conklin, Tyler Brooke, Tammy Young, Bert Roach, Edgar Connor, Dorothea Wolbert, Louise Carver, Richard Rodgers (as a photographer), and Lorenz Hart (as a bank teller).

I GOTTA GET BACK TO NEW YORK

Published May 1984 as part of *Rodgers & Hart: A Musical Anthology.* Registered for copyright as an unpublished song by Rodart Music Corporation, December 1959. Introduced by Al Jolson (Bumper) and Edgar Connor (Acorn). Alternate titles: "I've Gotta Get Back to New York" and "I've Got to Get Back to New York."

ACORN: Bumper! Bumper!
  How far is we?
BUMPER: A hundred and twenty-one miles,
  Maybe twenty-two.
  From Central Park
  Maybe a hundred and twenty-three.
ACORN: A hundred and twenty-six miles
  From Lenox Avenue.
BUMPER: Way up North the sun'll
  Always shine—
  That lovely Hudson tunnel
  Is my Mason-Dixon Line.
  Where the tempo races,*
  Let me be.
  The great wide-open spaces
  Are places that smother me.
  If I'm in Miami, Budapest or Rome,
  I'll always shout O.K., New York.
  The prodigal son goes home.
  Here's a hitch for me and my son.
  Come on,
  We're approaching the Metropolis
  As gentlemen of renown.
ACORN: Yes, suh, Bumper,
  We's sure goin' to town!

REFRAIN

  I'll climb up that Woolworth and kiss
    every floor.

Lines 13–19 were not sung in the film.

The subway makes music for me with a
    roar.
I'm dying to feel that I'm living once
    more.
I gotta get back to New York.
There's only one statue, I know you'll
    agree.
The dame with the torch looking over
    the sea.
The smell of the Bronnix is perfume to
    me.
I gotta get back to New York.
High, high, away up high,*
My city in the sky.
I want to move these feet
On each old dirty street.
New York is New York and that's all
    you can say.
It gets in your blood and it's in there to
    stay.
I'm one of six million who can't keep
    away.
I gotta get back to New York.

BUMPER'S HOME AGAIN

Introduced by Edgar Connor, Al Jolson, Harry Langdon, and ensemble. Alternate title: "My Pal Bumper." This number was taken from the sound track; some words and speakers won't be completely accurate.

ACORN: Good morning, Bumper.
  You slumbered sweet and deep
  On the first night home from our
    vacation.
BUMPER: Don't forget, Acorn,
  I lost my beauty sleep
  The way we changed our means of
    transportation.
ACORN: All the boys, Bumper, will welcome
  you with cheer.
BUMPER: I guess they'll appreciate me selling.
  It's hard work, Acorn, to superintend
    careers
  Of gentlemen of leisure without money.
  Who protects your apple stand
  When you've no license in your hand?
ALL: My pal Bumper.

Alternate version of refrain, lines 9–12:
  Train, keep on going. Train,
  I'm riding home again.
  Feet, keep on stepping. Feet,
  I'll never say retreat.

When you break a law or two
Who can make the cops garoo?
My pal Bumper.
Those birds sing better than ever
    today
BUMPER: They must have been practicing
  While I was away.
ALL: Who can keep a businessman
  From vacations in the can?
  My pal Bumper.
  Who can keep the cops away
  When we kiddies want to play?
  My pal Bumper.
BUMPER: Hold up the mirror
  Set of Africana.
  In its reflection
  I would see my pan-a.
  Wipe that toothache.
  I've a snootful.
ALL: Bumper, you look beautiful.
  You certainly got sunburnt in Florida.
  You look tanned, you do.
  Yes, sir,
  Acorn, so do you.
  Hello, Mr. Man.
  When you're hungry for a steak
  Who can hear your belly ache?
  My pal Bumper.
  He can make me feel I'm full
  When he feeds me full of bull.
  My pal Bumper.
  His friend in movies is a featurino.
  He's borrowed from the Central Park
    Casino.
ALL: Hello, Bumper!
BUMPER: Hello, hello!
ALL: Hello, Bumper!
BUMPER: Hello, hello!
ALL: Hello, hello, hello, hello!
BUMPER: Hello, hello, hello, hello!
EGGHEAD: You were away so long.
  Gee, it was a crime.
BUMPER: I'm glad to be home,
  But I had a great time.
EGGHEAD: What goes on down South
  In this man's nation?
BUMPER: Panhandling!
  Manhandling!
  Inebriation!
  And repopulation!
  Though it's not a good country for a
    man to get rich in,
  The Southway can boast of an excellent
    kitchen.
  Over a banquet of fine roast goose
  I had a conference with the Mayor.
  I took the opportunity
  Of discussing the citizens of our parks,

And he promised us all immunity.

ALL: Hark! Hark! Hark!

SCUM: Don't you see that Bumper's back.
Welcome to your King.
Does Your Majesty bring
News of the plutocrats down South?
Those rich idle shirkers
Who live on us workers.
Yeah, you can call what you muff.

BUMPER: That's just about enough
Of that radical stuff.
If a man doesn't work he oughta be
dead.
Pardon me, Egghead,
You talk like a red.

EGGHEAD: I accuse you

BUMPER: Yes.

EGGHEAD: Of wasting your time.

BUMPER: Go on.

EGGHEAD: While I
Slave away for the city
He slaves for the city.
Your parents, I saw.
Your brother's in crime.
When the revolution comes you won't
sit pretty.

BUMPER: Egghead,
I demand an explanation.

EGGHEAD: Well, it's up to you to prove I'm
wrong.
Ha, ha, ha!
Why the hesitation?

BUMPER: Very well, then.
I appoint myself attorney for the
Defense
And you're the Prosecution.

EGGHEAD: Ah,
Can that child's stuff and pretense.

BUMPER: We've a right to a fair trial
By the Constitution.
I'll call upon my first witness:
Bumper?
Yes, sir?
What do you do?
I love to breathe the air and feel I'm
free.
I never have to care
But because of me
I don't give a stitch
If I never get rich.
Not a soul I know
Ever owed me dough.
When a bank'll crash
I don't lose my cash.
I find great enjoyment in
unemployment.
I'm the only man to whom Depression
can't ever come.

In other words,
Gentlemen,
Hallelujah,
I'm a bum.

EGGHEAD: The workers will rule the world
someday
And all of your kind will be wiped
away,
Your socks and pants may have holes
But you're plutocrats down to your
souls.
Madam,
Cossacks,
Hoovers,
Cossacks.
Ah!
What do I see?
You shiver and tremble
And you call yourselves free.
You're slaves, at what price, to the
powers of cash.
I'm proud as can be
But they can't frighten me.
You'll die as you live,
A useless slob.
Parasites living off parasites.
And what have you got?
I likes guzzling!

BUMPER: Fellow citizens, kindly scram.
Don't let your principles make you
forget
That we were good friends and we're
good friends yet.
So remember, save the papers for me.
All right the *Times* in the morning and
the *Sun* at night.
Say, let me treat you to lunch today.

EGGHEAD: Lunch with a plutocrat?

BUMPER: What we eat anyway.
Come to the Casino and now I must
run.
Acorn, let's go.
We meet the Mayor at one.

LAYING THE CORNERSTONE

Introduced by Frank Morgan and ensemble. Alternate
title: "Cornerstone Laying."

SCHOOLTEACHER: Where is the Mayor?
How long must we wait?

PRES. OF BOARD: It's early for the Mayor.

He's only two hours late!
Make your program shorter,
Make a couple of cuts!

SCHOOLTEACHER: But—

PRES. OF BOARD: No buts!

WORKMAN: Oh, nuts!

SECRETARY: The Mayor! The Mayor!
His Honor, the Mayor!

MAYOR: Citizens of New York,
I behold this dedication
With true municipal pride
And a spirit of elation.
Though in order to be with you,
I had to shorten my vacation!
But I just had to take part—

WORKMAN: Stop, you're breaking my heart!

MAYOR: In the dedication of Public
School Forty-six
In District Number Seven—

SECRETARY: Public School Forty-four—and
The District is Eleven.

MAYOR: Hmmm!
Public School Forty-four,
And the District is Eleven!
Before any further mistakes can
be made.
I pronounce this cornerstone
well and truly laid.

CHILDREN: Do!
My country 'tis of thee,
Sweet land of liberty,
Of thee I sing:
Land where my fathers died,
Land of the Pilgrims' pride,
From every mountainside,
Let freedom ring.

SECRETARY: That woman with the thirteen
kids,
Remember, Mrs. Stone?
You promised you'd be
photographed with them.

MAYOR: Oh, please, leave me alone!

SECRETARY: Their father is a cop!

MAYOR: Sorry, just can't stop!

SECRETARY: I brought them here.
They're all of them here.
The thirteen, Ma and Pappy!

MAYOR: All right then,
Bring the regiment in,
But kindly make it snappy!

MRS. STONE: You'll look so nice with baby.
On the *Daily News* front page.

MR. STONE: Little John is only six months
old.

MAYOR: He certainly acts his age!

SECRETARY: He's a great friend to the men
Of the Municipal forces.

MAYOR: James! To the Casino!
And don't spare the horses!

SLEEPING BEAUTY

Dropped before the film was released. Intended for Al Jolson and Madge Evans.

BUMPER: Once upon a time there was a King and
Queen
In the magical isle of Manhattan.
They rode through Central Park in a
lemon limousine
With a body of walnut and satin.
But one day the King said with sighs of
distress:
"What good are my riches and my land
When we haven't a Prince or a little
Princess
To take to Coney Island?"
And one day the King said, with tender
sentiment:
"Queenie, ain't it time for a blessed
event?"
And so upon a Sunday morn,
A young princess was born.
She looked a lot like you
And her name was Angel too.
They hired the Park Casino for the
christening.
A royal shindig—
Angel, are you listening?
ANGEL: Um-hum!
BUMPER: That's nice.
And all the gnomes and elves and
fairies
Came to wish her luck.
It was a royal affair.
The crowd was very ritzy
With the cover charge one buck.
All the swells were there.
One of them brought her caviar
And one a case of beer.
One said: "I hope you'll be
Rich enough to have appendicitis every
year
And pay the doctor's fee."
And they all wished her luck except
one.
This Queen was a son of a gun.
Because she wasn't invited,
She rushed in all excited.
They had forgotten to invite the Queen
of Tenth Avenue

And she said:
"King, I'll take out all the ritz you have
in you."
And what was much worse,
She delivered this curse:
"The Princess will stick her finger with
a spindle,
And then her strength will begin to
dwindle,
And she will fall asleep
In slumber deep
And never, never, never will she wake
Until the day
A prince will come and take
The curse away
With a kiss
Just like this."
Oh, Angel,
That was a lousy stunt at a christening.
Are you listening?
ANGEL: Um-hum!
BUMPER: That's nice.
And sure enough,
The Princess stuck herself at the age of
seventeen
With a spindle and fell right on her
bean,
And fell asleep.
The King and Queen began to shake
her,
But nothing could awake her.
They rang bells and spoke through a
loudspeaker.
They pinched her nose and sprinkled it
with paprika.
But not a peep came from Angel in her
sleep!
They called the Duke, Ted Lewis with
his trombone,
And he wah-wah-wah-wahed.
But she still lay still as a stone.
They even called upon Dame Sophie
Tucker
And she shouted just like a Mack truck
had struck her.
Although they would travel abroad ev'ry
year,
To the Bronx, which is further than
Asia,
They were sad 'cause their own Princess
Angel, poor dear,
Had this awful disease called aphasia.
And she slept and she slept
Until the day Prince Charming came
To take the spell away
With a kiss
[He kisses her]
Just like this!

He wasn't a prince with a big limousine
And he hadn't a million or even one
bean
But in summer he lived in the park,
Where he ruled like a king after dark
In the winter, down South, with the
birds he would swing.
And he felt like a king ev'ry year when
he'd sing:
"Southland, I'm coming home to you!
Southland, I'm coming home to you!
To the Duchy of Alabamy
With my . . . ." No, he never sang
"Mammy."
He had lots of tramps to wait on him.
The Prince was just as selfish as me.
Till he awoke Angel from her sleep,
He never knew what love could be.
If on the other hand I look after you,
It's not through a sense of duty.
You are too beautiful
And you are my sleeping beauty.

TICK-TOCK

Introduced by Al Jolson, Harry Langdon, and Edgar Connor.

ACORN: [Acorn listens to watch]
Tick-tick-tick.
Dat sho' am slick.
BUMPER: Not so quick!
ACORN: Tick-tick-tick.
EGGHEAD: What's that thing?
BUMPER: It's a lady's bag.
EGGHEAD: The aristocratic rag of a plutocratic
hag!
Why the clock?
BUMPER: So the lady you give it to won't give
you a stand-up.
EGGHEAD: People starvin' and they put clocks in
bags.
ACORN: Come on, Bumpah, look inside.
What you waitin' for?
BUMPER: It's from Cartier's.
ACORN: What's Cartier's?
BUMPER: Our favorite jewelry store,
The one we patronize.
ACORN: We?
EGGHEAD: We?
BUMPER: Vanderbilts and me.
ACORN: Come on, let's see.
[Bumper takes out bill and says, "Aha!"]
EGGHEAD: What is it? A dollar!

ACORN: Hey, brother, don't holler.

BUMPER: One!

ACORN: Huh?

BUMPER: Thousand!

ACORN: A grand? That's a mint!

BUMPER: One thousand? One thousand?
Won't be a misprint.

ACORN: One thousand?
One thousand?
Is there any readin' in it?

BUMPER: One thousand dollars.
Let's sit down for a minute.

EGGHEAD: It's counterfeit. But if it's good, one
half is mine.

BUMPER: One half is yours! Too, too divine!
My blue blood reddens with jocularity,
My noble heart is filled with thoughts
of charity,
But from the truth you show a slight
disparity.
Plebeian youth, I deign to say to you
Three little words.

EGGHEAD: Three little words?

BUMPER: Three little words:
Screw, bum, screw.*

EGGHEAD: One half is mine and don't you make a
fuss.

ACORN: Bumpah found it, it belongs to us.

EGGHEAD: Where you find it?
In my bin, right here!

BUMPER: Gentlemen! Gentlemen!
Spare my noble ear.

DEAR JUNE

Introduced by Al Jolson.

BUMPER: [*Sings words on postcard found in
handbag*]
Dear June,
I got to Cleveland O.K. this afternoon.
The job looks good and now I'm on my
own.
I'm grateful to you, June dear, for the
loan.
I meant nothing to you
And yet you helped me, baby.
I'll pay you back sometime,
And I don't mean maybe!
Thanks again!
Sincerely, Len.

*In the film:
Blow, bum, blow.

Miss June Marcher:
414 East 52nd Street
New York, N.Y.
It's hers.
Sweet dreams of wealth,
Goodbye.

BUMPER FOUND
A GRAND

Introduced by Edgar Connor, Harry Langdon, Al Jolson,
and "tramps."

EGGHEAD: It belongs to us.

ACORN: It belongs to we.

EGGHEAD: Surely you agree
One half belongs to me.

ACORN: I'll cut you down!

BUMPER: Steady! Steady!
Acorn, you talk like a rich man
already!

ACORN: I *is* rich.
That's mine. I found half of it.

TRAMP: What's the matter?

ACORN: Me and Bumpah found a grand!

EGGHEAD: Half is mine, you understand.

BUMPER: It belongs to that lady
And I'm gonna return it.

EGGHEAD: Return it to a plutocrat?
I'd rather see you burn it.
Besides, you can't give away my
money.

BUMPER: That's funny!

EGGHEAD: You found it,
But that's accidental, man.

BUMPER: She lost it.

EGGHEAD: We've got it.

BUMPER: You forget that you're a gentleman.

ACORN: Egghead is right, I must agree,
But it don't belong to him,
Jus' to you and me.

TRAMP: Bumpah found a grand!
Bumpah found a grand!

FRANK: A grand? A grand?
I don't understand.

TRAMP: A thousand dollars fell into his hand.

FRANK: Bumpah found a grand!

TRAMP: Bumpah found a grand!

BUMPER: We don't want money,
Money is a curse;
It's risky business and worse.
I know a fellow who found some
dough.

He put it in a bank,
The bank gave interest,
Dough began to grow.
He got rich in a hurry,
Then he started in to worry,
Worried because he was in dough,
And jumped right out of a window!

FRANK: Heard you found a grand,
Let's put it on a horse.
I've got a tip.

ACORN: A tip?

FRANK: Lovelorn, some horse, a pip!

EGGHEAD: I don't want to bet, you see,
And half of it belongs to me.

ACORN: How much is ten to one?
I don't understand.

FRANK: Five little figgers, just ten grand.

ACORN: Bumper, there you are.
We win ten grand,
And give the lady back her thousand
Jes' as you planned.

BUMPER: And if Lovelorn loses
And leaves us flat . . .

ACORN: If he loses, we ain't got it.
What's wrong with that?

BUMPER: Don't make me laugh!

EGGHEAD: I want my half!

TRAMP: Bumper found a grand!
Bumper found a grand!

MARY: A grand, my land!
Cripple, take my stand.

CRIPPLE: Now! Where is Bumper?
Mary, take my hand.
Bumper found a grand!
Bumper found a grand!

TRAMP: Bumper found a grand!
Bumper found a grand!

MUMBLER: Mm . . . and

TRAMP: A grand! A grand!
A thousand dollars fell into his hand!

MUMBLER: Mm . . . and

BUMPER: Just one grand and friendship ends.

ACORN: No, Bumpah, I'se friends.
Stop following us, all of you.
It belongs to us, it do.
To Mister Bumpah and me,
Not to the whole community.

EGGHEAD: I want my half.

FRANK: Bumper, we're waiting to hear from
you.
We wanna know what you're gonna do.

VOICE: Come on, Bumpah,
Please be fair now.
Ev'rybody wants his share now.

ANOTHER: You can't get away with it.

VOICE: No givin' back!
Let's grab it from him.

ANOTHER: You'll do what we say with it.
ANOTHER: Come on, Mack.

WHAT DO YOU WANT WITH MONEY?

Published December 1932. Introduced by Al Jolson.

VERSE

Friends, Rummies, Countrymen,
Well, anyway, jes' friends:
We find a thousand dollars
And friendship ends.
If you divide the thousand,
What each gets is a joke.
A little less than nothing.
You're better off just broke.

REFRAIN

You got the grass,
You got the trees;
What do you want with money?
You got the air,
You got the breeze;
What do you want with money?
Look at the birds,
Hear how they sing;
They have no rent
To pay in the spring.
You own the world
When you don't own a thing.
What do you want with money?
What do you want with dough?

TRIO PATTER

Frankie, you got your shine box!
Sam, you got your fiddle!
Egghead, you got your principles
And you're richer than Ford or Biddle.
You know you can't take money;
You know you hate the rich!
Be consistent, Egghead,
You stupid son of a which
One of you is unhappy right now?
What do you want with money?
What do you want with dough?

HALLELUJAH, I'M A BUM

Published December 1932. Introduced by Al Jolson.

VERSE

Rockefeller's busy giving dough away;
Chevrolet is busy making cars;
Hobo, you keep busy when they throw away
Slightly used cigars.
Hobo, you've no time to shirk.
You're busy keeping far away from work.

REFRAIN

The weather's getting fine.
The coffee tastes like wine.
You happy hobo, sing,
"Hallelujah, I'm a bum again!"
Why work away for wealth
When you can travel for your health?
It's spring, you hobo, sing,
"Hallelujah, I'm a bum again!"
Your home is always near;
The moon's your chandelier;
Your ceiling is the sky,
Way up high.
The road is your estate,
The earth your little dinner plate;
It's spring, you hobo, sing,
"Hallelujah, I'm a bum again!"

BUMPER'S GOING TO WORK

Introduced by Al Jolson, Harry Langdon, Edgar Connor, and ensemble. Alternate title: "Kangaroo Court."

BUMPER: I'm gonna give Angel the life she deserves.
ACORN: Oh, Bumper, this change'll be bad for my nerves!
Gotta shave ev'ry mohnin' like a white-col-iah slave.
BUMPER: No one can notice when you need a shave.
You'll have money to play with and a full dinner platter.
ACORN: I'se got misapprehension.
BERGMAN: Hey, Bo. What's the matter?
ACORN: Me and Bumper's gone to work.

I'se goin' to be a pale-faced clerk.
BERGMAN: Bumper's goin' to work,
Bumper's goin' to work.
MARY: To work.
FRANKIE: To work.
BERGMAN: He's gonna be a clerk!
ENGLISH: His duty to his pals he's gonna shirk.
FIRST BUM: Bumper's gone to work.
ACORN: I'se saying far-well to a beautiful youth.
How about the boys? Will you tell them the truth?
FRANKIE: Bumper, we heard a rotten report.
BUMPER: What do you mean, a report?
FRANKIE: The rumor is out that you're goin' to work.
You must answer, in short, to the Kangaroo Court.
BUMPER: All right, I'll answer, and I'll make it short.
Go on and form your Kangaroo Court.
FRANKIE: For judge I call on a guy who's been tried
For arson, theft and homicide.
He's faced the jury in ev'ry state.
A hundred judges read his fate.
Who else is better qualified
To know what a judge should do
Than honest, forthright
Conscientious, clean-cut
Stinkfoot Lou!
ALL: Hear! Hear! Hear!
STINKFOOT: Order in the court.
As District Attorney,
I give youse guys
Legs McGurney.
Pinhead Pete will read the charge.
He's now appointed clerk
On the case of the people of the park
Versus Bumper's goin' to work.
BUMPER: One minute, Your Honor, before we start,
I must have an attorney to take my part.
JUDGE: To defend such a crime takes a lawyer with guts.
EGGHEAD: If you think he can't get one, Your Honor is nuts.
I'll defend him and end this silly fuss.
He belongs to us workers
And not to you shirkers.
When the revolution comes
He'll be with us.
JUDGE: The charge!
PINHEAD
PETE: Bumper, you're on trial for desertin' our cause.

STINKFOOT: And tho' you gave us our spirit
And you gave us our laws
If you're found guilty this sentence
   we'll deal:
We'll tell the world that Bumper is a
   road apple heel!
LEGS: Come on, mug! You'll kindly take the
   stand!
PINHEAD: Tho' nobody will believe you, raise
   your right hand,
Do you swear on the word of a good
   bindle stiff
That the bull you'll spill will be true?
BUMPER: I do.
LEGS: Before causing this court any further
   expense,
Will you plead guilty to this repulsive
   offense?
EGGHEAD: I object.
Your impertinence is really immense,
To call honest labor a social offense.
BUMPER: But I plead guilty.
I did take a job.
STINKFOOT: This court is shocked! I'd rather
   you'd rob.
EGGHEAD: And His Honor would too!
And he did, the fat slob!
BUMPER: I'm committing a horrible crime, I'll
   admit.
But I've got a good reason, and this
   is it:
There's no use stalling. I'm falling—
   I'm in love.
[*Bums laugh*]
STINKFOOT: Order! Or I'll conduct this case
   behind closed doors.

I'D DO IT AGAIN

Published as "I'll Do It Again," December 1932. Introduced by Al Jolson. Alternate titles: "I'll Do It Again," "I Didn't Want to Do It But I'd Do It Again," and "Flea Song." Directly followed "Bumper's Going to Work."

VERSE

BUMPER: Look, Your Honor, and please take
   note,
There are two little fleas on Your
   Honor's coat,

Just two little sweethearts and we
   don't care whether
Those fleas are married or just living
   together.
The way of the world is he and she.
If you pardon the flea, then you must
   excuse me!

REFRAIN

I looked into her eyes and went the
   way of all men.
I didn't want to do it,
But I'd do it again.
I knew a little look would be the
   finish of me.
I didn't want to do it,
But I did it, you see.
Once I was wise,
I took my freedom
Where I hung my hat,
Didn't surmise
That I could be dumb
Till she gave me that!
Thought that "Home, Sweet Home"
Was just a "Prisoner's Song,"
But now I'll be so happy in the pen.
This good man has gone wrong,
And I'd go and do it again.
EGGHEAD: Bumper's right. I move for acquittal!
STINKFOOT: Bumper, you're not guilty.
The reason is quite plain.
You're beyond our jurisdiction
'Cause you are insane.
So goodbye, Bumper, and Acorn too.
This trial has been in vain.
BUMPER: Goodbye, boys.
ACORN: I'll just say Auf Wie-der-sehn!

YOU ARE TOO BEAUTIFUL

Published December 1932. Introduced by Al Jolson.

VERSE

Like all fools, I believed
What I wanted to believe.
My foolish heart conceived
What foolish hearts conceive.

I thought I found a miracle;
I thought that you'd adore me.
But it was not a miracle,
It was merely a mirage before me.

REFRAIN

You are too beautiful, my dear, to be true,
And I am a fool for beauty.
Fooled by a feeling that
Because I had found you
I could have bound you, too.
You are too beautiful for one man alone,
For one lucky fool to be with,
When there are other men
With eyes of their own to see with.
Love does not stand sharing,
Not if one cares.
Have you been comparing
My ev'ry kiss with theirs?
If, on the other hand,
I'm faithful to you,
It's not through a sense of duty.
You are too beautiful
And I am a fool for beauty.

ORIGINAL REFRAIN (as sung in the film)

You are too beautiful, my dear, to be true,
And I am too drunk with beauty.
Drunk with a feeling that
The arms that possess you
Really caress you, too.
You are too beautiful for one man alone,
For one lucky fool to be with,
When there are other men
With eyes of their own to see with.
Love cannot stand sharing,
Not if one cares.
You won't be comparing
My ev'ry kiss with theirs.
You know I care and
I'll be faithful to you
And not through a sense of duty.
You are too beautiful
And I am too drunk with beauty.

OVERLEAF: Fred Astaire, Joan Crawford, and Clark Gable in *Dancing Lady*

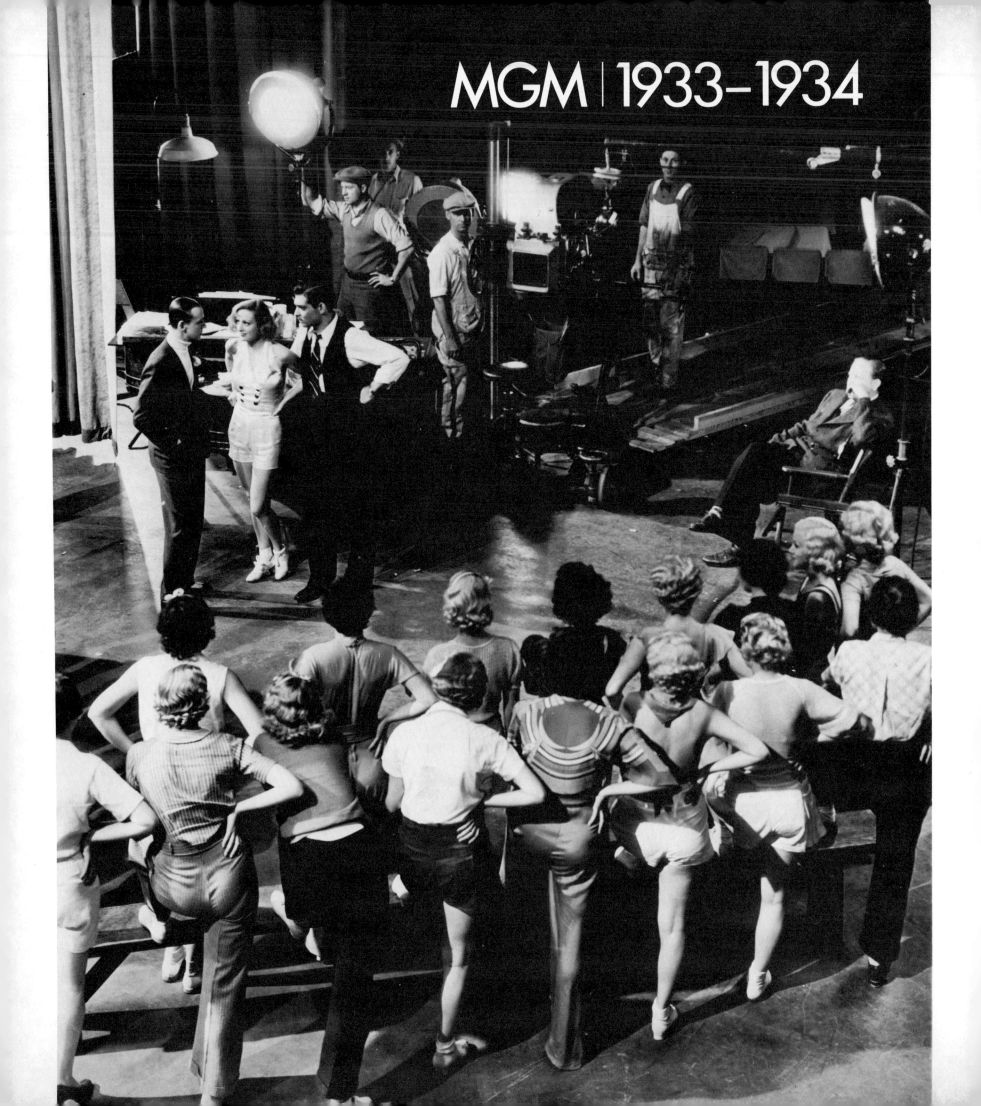

MGM | 1933–1934

PEG O' MY HEART, 1933

WHEN YOU'RE FALLING IN LOVE WITH THE IRISH

MGM Song #102 is dated February 21, 1933, and was registered for copyright as an unpublished work by Metro-Goldwyn-Mayer, March 20, 1933. It was written for the 1933 MGM film *Peg o' My Heart*, which starred Marion Davies, was directed by Robert Z. Leonard, written by Frances Marion, and based on the play by J. Hartley Manners. Dropped from the film before its release in May 1933.

VERSE

Once a green island came out of the blue
Covered with pretty colleens.
That's what the luck of the Irish really means.
Fighting and loving was all they could do,
And they didn't fight very much,
So it's a land full of laughter,
Love and such.

REFRAIN

When you're falling in love with the Irish,
You're in love.
Once you start with the heart of the Irish,
You're in love.
They've a charm that can change you like this:
From a laugh to a tear to a kiss.
When you're falling in love with the Irish,
You're in love.

I MARRIED AN ANGEL, 1933

From February to April of 1933, Rodgers and Hart teamed with Moss Hart on a musical adaptation of a Hungarian play about a banker whose wish comes true when he marries an angel. The film—*I Married an Angel* (MGM Production #1116)—was intended as a vehicle for Jeanette MacDonald. It was jettisoned, according to Rodgers, when Metro boss Louis B. Mayer decided that fantasies were uncommercial. In 1938 *I Married an Angel* became a Broadway musical and used some of the material written in 1933. Four years later it became a film musical starring Nelson Eddy and Jeanette MacDonald.

LOVE IS QUEEN, LOVE IS KING

MGM Song #163. Music is dated April 13, 1933. Alternate title: "Opening."

ALEXIS: Love is queen, Love is king,
Borja moy! I've forgotten the thing!
1ST GIRL: Love is spring, Love is love.
Oh! Imperial Highness, I've dropped my glove!
OLD MAN: Allow me, please, Your Imperial Highness!
Let me commend the Baron's spryness.
2ND GIRL: Is he really a Grand Duke?
MAN: Of the very first water. He's a lineal descendant of Ivan the Terrible's granddaughter.
1ST GIRL: Your Imperial Highness,
Forgive my shyness.
But the touch of your lips makes me throb.
ALEXIS: Here comes the master. I must be on the job!
WILLY: Your Imperial Highness, I humbly beg your pardon, but you really should be fired for the way you've set the table in the garden. For the clumsy seating of the guests, I can't commend your slyness. And now, serve the drinks, you blithering fool. I mean—Your Imperial Highness.
ALEXIS: Cointreau or wine, madame?
You look divine, madame!
1ST GIRL: This is the Grand Duke Alexis Michaelovitch.
2ND GIRL: How do you do?
ALEXIS: Madame! I am charmed to meet you. Pardon me!
ANNA: Is he really a Grand Duke? I thought he was . . .
WILLY: My major domo!
Vienna's full of Russian Dukes who work and never grumble.
If royal tummies aren't filled they're very apt to rumble!
Your dress is beautiful,
You really look a dream.
ANNA: I fear that it's just a little bit too extreme. I dislike the mode. I'm afraid I'm not gay.
WILLY: Maybe you're not, but you're charming that way!
ANNA: And I don't like big parties
And people and noise.
WILLY: I'm afraid you're too shy.
You're not used to the boys.
ANNA: I'd love to talk to you alone.
WILLY: Alone?
ANNA: Let's have a tête-à-tête of our own.
Not of dresses or people but real things;
Of beauty and truth and ideal things.
WILLY: Well, let's talk.
ANNA: But not here!
WILLY: Why not here?
ANNA: Oh, dear! Let's get away. What do you say?
WILLY: But where?
ANNA: This music can drive me insane.
WILLY: What do you say to a ride in my plane?
Let's be unconventional, make it intentional.
ANNA: If you really must, dear, then what can I say?
WILLY: Let's fly away!
Anna, oh, Anna!
ANNA: You?
WILLY: Anna, dear.
ANNA: I can't hear, what did you say?
WILLY: Er, nothing. It's a windy day!
1ST ANGEL: Clarinda!
CLARINDA: Yoo-hoo!
1ST ANGEL: Look!
CLARINDA: I get it!
1ST ANGEL: Lucinda!
LUCINDA: Yoo-hoo!
1ST ANGEL: Look!
LUCINDA: I get it!
1ST ANGEL: Look! 'Tis Willy! Get'st thou me?
LUCINDA: Sister, I'm ahead of thee!
1ST ANGEL: Will she marry with yonder chap?
CLARINDA: Yonder chap would be a sap!
ALL: She may be all right for somebody else,
But she's no darn good for him.
Hi-dee, hi-dee hallelujah!
His future's looking grim!
If he can't see that label says "poison,"
His eyesight must be dim.
She may be good for someone.
But she's no darn good for him!

191

ANNA: Yes, dear, what did you want to say?

WILLY: Oh? Nothing, Anna. It's a windy day!

ANGELS: She may be the apple of somebody's
eye,
But she's applesauce for Willy.
Ho-dee, ho-dee-ho hosannah!
Her sex appeal is nilly!
She'd be faithful to the Army and the
Navy
And the shepherds on the hilly
She may be good for someone,
But she's no darn good for Willy!

ANNA: It's so romantic.

WILLY: What?

ANNA: It's grand.

WILLY: Fine view, Anna. Yes, let's land!

HARRY: My dear countess!

COUNTESS: Why so formal?

HARRY: Your interest in Willy is, er, rather ab-
normal. You're not his mother!

COUNTESS: He's old enough to be my brother! I'm
only thirty-two!

HARRY: Yes, thirty-two, I know that's so; you
told me that ten years ago. But why the
interest in Willy?

COUNTESS: He's so helpless, the sweet silly. This
marriage must come off without a hitch.
She's charming, cultured, a saint, and,
by the way—very rich. Look! What a
landing. Neat and trim.

HARRY: He's landed her, but she hasn't landed
him!

COUNTESS: And you didn't propose?

WILLY: No!

COUNTESS: No?

WILLY: No!

COUNTESS: Oh! How could you! You wouldn't
fool me, would you?

WILLY: I can't make up my mind.

COUNTESS: And I want it so. Oh! You're selfish!

WILLY: Women are all alike, I find!

COUNTESS: Are you a man or are you a shellfish?

WILLY: Women have never been decent with
me,
I am quite disillusioned . . . That's
all.
This feeling against them isn't recent
with me,
And I laugh when I think how I
would fall.

COUNTESS: But Anna is perfect. She's created for
you.

WILLY: I know she's a jewel, but what can I
do?
I've been fooled too often
For this hard heart to soften.
Why, only last May . . .

WILLY'S
VOICE: While happy and idle, I quaffed at a
seidel.
I heard a waiter screaming, and
turned my head.
"You must pay your bill," the ruffian
said.
"I'm sorry," she said, "I'm afraid
that I'm broke."
"What is this?" he asked. "A
practical joke?
I'll call the police!" And he grabbed
at her shoulder.
At first I checked myself, but then I
grew bolder.
"Allow me!" I cried.
"God bless you!" she sighed,
And then I took her home!
Her place was very near,
I hadn't been in love for over a year.
So when we entered her apartment,
I learned what a song in my heart
meant.

WILLY: But women are women and cats are
cats;
Men are mice who think they're rats.

WILLY'S
VOICE: I gave her diamonds and rubies
Like other pinheaded boobies.
And then one evening
I caught her giving
My gems to someone named Jim.

WILLY: Yes, women are women and cats are
cats;
Men are only mice who think they're
rats.
That wasn't the first time
And it wasn't the worst time.
When I was fourteen,

WILLY'S
VOICE: My school flame was Gretchen,
A sweet little mädchen.
I showed her to my schoolfellows
with pride.
"I languish for your love," she
deeply sighed.
"Meet Otto," I said.
And he gave her a kiss.
"What is this?" I asked. "A practical
joke?"
But Otto laughed at me and pinched
her shoulder.
At first I checked myself, but then I
grew bolder.
"Allow me!" I cried. He quickly
replied.
I thought him impolite.
And then my little sweet said,

"Punch him in the eye and break off
his feet."
It's strange how punches can vex us
When they land in the old solar
plexus.

WILLY: Oh, women are women and cats are
cats.
Men are mice who think they're rats.

WILLY'S
VOICE: A man is sore when he loses,
And she poured salt on my bruises.
Because she walked off with great big
Otto,
I got real blotto that night!

WILLY: Yes, women are women and cats are
cats.
Men are only mice who think they're
rats.
When I was only four,

WILLY'S
VOICE: I fell in love by chance
With a lady who looked nice in red
satin pants.
And then I gave her with pleasure
My best lollipop, my treasure . . .

WILLY: But women are women and cats are
cats.
Men are mice who think they're rats!

WILLY'S
VOICE: She was the first of my pashes
Who turned my love into ashes.
At four, I swore I would be a hermit.
I still affirm it today.
For women are women and cats are
cats.
Men are only mice who think they're
rats!

FACE THE FACTS

MGM Song #168. Music is dated April 11, 1933.

VERSE

Romeo and Juliet died with a kiss.
Can any execution be as lovely as this?
A kiss, a dream, a man and a wife
Are the only real things in this fiction called life.

REFRAIN 1

What is a kiss?
Only this, a little friction,
Maybe not in fiction,
But let's face the facts.
What is a dream
But a sign of indigestion?
We must never question facts.
Two hearts in waltz time
May start a-thumping.
To be specific,
Two hearts are pumping sumping.
What's love itself, but spontaneous combustion?
All the world is nuts,
Let's face the facts.

REFRAIN 2

What is a moon
But an ad for propagation
Paid for by the nation?
So let's face the facts.
What is a sigh
But the tonsils pushing air out?
Thought will only bear out
Facts.
They sing of springtime
In each cadenza.
It's just a season
For catching influenza.
Marriage is merely a space between divorces.
Horses don't divorce,
Let's face the facts.

TELL ME I KNOW
HOW TO LOVE

MGM Song #100. Music is dated April 14, 1933.

VERSE 1

SHE: It's so new,
    This thing with me and you.
    I'm terrified and overjoyed and terrified.
    Though I'm shy,
    With sheer delight I sigh,
    To find my dream of earthly joy is verified.

REFRAIN

    Tell me I know how to love,
    Let me hear it from you.
    Tell me I know how to love,
    And your words will come true.

If I'm slow to start with
You may have to lead.
I've a heart to part with.
Courage is all I need.
I'm not so pleased with myself,
My attractions are few,
But I'll be pleased with myself,
If I'm pleasing to you.
Sing a lover's praises
And his love will grow.
Tell me I know how to love
And I'll know.

VERSE 2

HE: Can it be
    You're really here with me?
    I'm shivering and burning up and shivering.
    Twice and more,
    I thought I loved before,
    But you're the first to whom I'd ever give a
        ring.

REPEAT REFRAIN

ANIMATED OBJECTS

MGM Song #159. Music is dated April 1, 1933.

CLOCK: Tick-tick-tick. Tock-tock-tock.
    Listen to your grandfather clock.
    Tock-tock-tock. Tock-tock-tock.
    Come to your senses, snap out of it
        quick.
    Willy wasn't cruel to you tonight.
    No, he was right and perfectly right.
    You're a good little girl, indeed you
        are.
    But goodness isn't good when it's
        carried too far.
    Too much truth is a little erratic.
    Be truthful now and then.
    But don't be a fanatic.
    You know you can't continue.
    The chances are agin you.
    The world is sure to skin you.
    If word of mine can win you,
    Go strain each nerve and sinew.
    And get some good sense in you.
    You were wrong to fight.
    Willy was right. Yes, perfectly right.
    Listen to your grandfather clock.
    Tick-tick-tick. Tock-tock-tock.

1ST NEWEL
    POST: You could have avoided this foolish
        fight,
        For Willy was right. Yes, perfectly
        right—
    1ST RAIL: You
    2ND RAIL: Can't
    3RD RAIL: Get
    4TH RAIL: A-
    5TH RAIL: Way
    6TH RAIL: With
    7TH RAIL: It.
    8TH RAIL: Get
    9TH RAIL: A-
    10TH RAIL: Way
    11TH RAIL: With
    12TH RAIL: It.
2ND NEWEL
    POST: Willy wasn't cruel to you tonight.
        No, he was right and perfectly right.
    (LAMP)
VICTORIAN
    LADY: Beauty is truth and truth is beauty,
        Beautiful truth is wifely duty.
NAPOLEON: Ma foi! Mon pauvre Willy!
        Pourquoi ne voulez-vous pas le faire
            pour lui?
        Gardez votre amour et never play
            with it.
        Êtes-vous folle? You can't get away
            with it!
    KAISER: Bist du verrückt, mein armes Kind?
        Frag um Vergebung und tue es
            geschwind.
        Behüte deine Liebe
        And don't you play with it.
        Donnerwetter noch einmal.
        You can't get away with it!
ARMCHAIR: There now, my pretty, there now, my
        sweet.
        I fear you're rather indiscreet.
        Prevarication can sweeten life.
        And your duty, my dear, is to be a
            good wife.
        Certainly, assuredly, indubitably, pet,
        You ain't gonna get away with it,
            you bet.
        Willy wasn't cruel to you tonight.
    ANGEL: No, he was right. Yes, perfectly
            right!
        Oh!
COUNTESS: Oh! It's time that you should know
        What made your husband go.
    ANGEL: His bank! Oh, what a blow.
        You fool, you've hurt him so.
    ANGEL: I, oh no!
COUNTESS: No?
    ANGEL: Oh!

COUNTESS: It's not your fault, it's just your
    youth.
    Why must you speak that
    confounded truth?
    How'd you like everyone to be frank
    about you,
    To say what they think about
    everything you do?
    You're not so perfect.
ANGEL: Have I ruined Willy?
COUNTESS: You'll save him yet if you're not too
    silly.
ANGEL: How?
COUNTESS: Right now
    Willy needs Harry.
    He must make the loan,
    And you've insulted Harry.
ANGEL: Had I only known.
COUNTESS: It's not too late.
ANGEL: What do you suggest?
COUNTESS: You make yourself attractive,
    Let nature do the rest.

WHY HAVE YOU EYES?

Found on the same musical hectograph as "Animated Objects." MGM Song #159. Music is dated April 1, 1933.

VERSE

COUNTESS: Look into your mirror.
    What do you see?
    Just a little pale face.
    Do you think a male face
    Wants a little pale face near?
    Men will never cheer or crave or favor
    Any little frump now.
    Don't you be a chump now;
    You must play your trump now, dear!

REFRAIN

Why have you eyes?
Why have you hair?
You have all that slenderness,
Yet no touch of tenderness.
Slenderness needs tenderness.
Why such a nose?
Why have you lips?
Why the pretty dental works
Made by nature's gentle works?
You could use some mental works too.
Why do velvet shoulders grow on
Figures of ice?

You've a lovely neck and so on,
So forth, so nice!
Why let the men kiss other lips,
Other lips instead of yours,
Lips without the red of yours?
Use that little head of yours too!

I MARRIED AN ANGEL

Published April 1938. Registered for copyright as an unpublished song by Metro-Goldwyn-Mayer, February 25, 1933. Refrain written in 1933 for projected film version. Introduced by Dennis King in the stage production of *I Married an Angel* (1938). Verse was written in 1938.

VERSE

There's been a change in me!
I have a lovely disposition,
That's very strange in me.
And life's as sweet as it can be.
I've lots of courage and ambition.
From ev'ry care my mind is free,
So I repeat, with your permission,
There's been a change in me!

REFRAIN

Have you heard?
I married an angel.
I'm sure that the change'll be
Awf'lly good for me.
Have you heard?
An angel I married.
To Heaven she's carried this
Fellow with a kiss.
She is sweet and gentle,
So it isn't strange,
When I'm sentimental,
She loves me like an angel.
Now you've heard.
I married an angel.
This beautiful change'll be
Awf'lly good for me.

BATH AND DRESSMAKING SEQUENCE

Written in 1933 for the unproduced film version. Registered for copyright as an unpublished song by Metro-Goldwyn-Mayer, April 25, 1933. See "The Modiste," page 245, which is a revision of this song.

WILLY: Have you heard
    I married an angel?
    I'm sure that the change'll be
    Awf'lly good for me.
    Have you heard
    An angel I married?
    To Heaven she's carried this
    Fellow with a kiss.
    She is sweet and gentle,
    So it isn't strange.
    When I'm sentimental,
    She loves me like an angel.
    Have you heard
    I married an angel?
    This beautiful change'll be
    Awf'lly good for me.
[*As Willy sings refrain of "I Married An Angel," the following is heard:*]
VOICE
THROUGH
PHONE: Hello!
ANGEL: Oh! Hello!
    How do you do?
    And how are you?
[*Angel goes to electric light button. Business with light. Then runs back to telephone*]
VOICE: Hello!
ANGEL: Oh! Hello!
VOICE: What can I do for Madam?
ANGEL: Madam! Madam!
    You don't know me from Adam.
    But how are you?
    I just want to say,
    "How do you do!"
[*Business with fire extinguisher and sprinkler system, etc.*]
    Ha ha! Willy,
    Come in, my dear.
    Because, darling,
    It's raining in here.
[*Turns off sprinkler*]
    Oh! it isn't raining anymore now!
    It's sunny!
[*She runs to window, takes off bathrobe*]
TWO BOYS: Yoo hoo! Hurray!
ANGEL: Why do you laugh?

What's so funny?
I know very well
You can't see me.
The window is shut,
Tight as can be.

TWO BOYS: Yoo hoo!

ANGEL: Oh! You're unkind!

OLD WOMAN: Don't you know enough
To pull down your blind?

ANGEL: Willy, darling, something's ringing.
Something's ringing, darling,
Stop your singing!

WILLY: Don't let it worry you,
Sweet, in the least.
I'll answer the bell.
Dear, it's just the modiste!

[*Runs through room and opens door*]
Entrez, s'il vous plaît.

MODISTE: Monsieur is Viennese.
I can tell by the accent.

WILLY: You're the modiste
Madame Rastignac sent.
This way, please.
Have you heard
I married an angel?

MODISTE: The clothes I arrange'll seem
Really like a dream!

FIRST GIRL: Have you heard?
It sounds funny to me.

SECOND GIRL: The angel of whom he sings
Hasn't any wings.

WILLY: Don't let this distress you,
Though it's new and strange.

MODISTE: After my girls dress you,
You'll look just like an angel.

WILLY: Have you heard

MODISTE: You married an angel
With dresses the change'll be
Heavenly to see.
Thirty-four—

FIRST GIRL: Thirty-four.

MODISTE: This, Madam, Monsieur will
adore.
When you wear it,
Monsieur will love you,
Oh, yes.

ANGEL: Will Willy love me
Or will he love the dress?

MODISTE: Chic! Very chic.
The lovely chemise?

ANGEL: Chemise?

WILLY: Chemise?

MODISTE: Chemise?

ANGEL: What's that for?
Tell me please!

WILLY: Ex-to cover,
Ex-to cover.

ANGEL: Oh, tell me, sweet lover.

WILLY: It's hard to express.
It goes under your dress.

ANGEL: But tell me, darling, what for?

WILLY: Darling, explanations are a bore.

ANGEL: But if you can't be frank,
I shall be hurt.

MODISTE: It's your comme-ci, comme-ça,
It's your undershirt!
This is the dernier cri de Paris.
It's very practical, don't you agree?

ANGEL: Willy, what is it?
Tell me, do.

WILLY: It's, well, never mind
But look at this shoe!

ANGEL: Very nice.
But the harness,
What is that!

WILLY: It's to hold up.

ANGEL: To hold up?

WILLY: To hold up your hat!

MODISTE: And this

WILLY: Good Lord!

ANGEL: What's that for,
And where do I wear it?

WILLY: Take it away!
I just can't bear it.

ANGEL: Is it a scarf?
Where does it go?

WILLY: I, Heaven's name, get into it
And then you'll know.

MODISTE: Put them on, Madam,
S'il vous plaît,
And you will be so distingué.
Monsieur, in a moment
You will see
How elegant Madam can be.

WILLY: Well, we're waiting to be
impressed.

ANGEL: One minute, and I'm fully dressed.

MODISTE: Our mode will make Madam so
smart,
So chic, a vision of Paris art.

ANGEL: Here I am!

WILLY: Good Lord!

[*Reprise of "I Married an Angel" (refrain)*]

DANCING LADY, 1933

MGM's *Dancing Lady* was one of many backstage musicals inspired by the tremendous success of Warner Brothers' *42nd Street*. Joan Crawford starred. Clark Gable was also featured. David O. Selznick produced and Robert Z. Leonard directed. Script was by Allen Rivkin, Zelda Sears, and P. J. Wolfson from James Warner Bellah's novel. Big song hit was Burton Lane and Harold Adamson's "Everything I Have Is Yours." Jimmy McHugh, Dorothy Fields, and Nacio Herb Brown also contributed numbers. Rodgers and Hart wrote three, only one of which was used in the movie. This was Fred Astaire's screen debut. Released in late November and early December 1933.

THAT'S THE RHYTHM OF THE DAY

Published November 1933. Registered for copyright as an unpublished song by Metro-Goldwyn-Mayer, August 24, 1933. Introduced by Nelson Eddy. Danced by Joan Crawford and ensemble. Alternate titles: "Rhythm of the Day" and "Go, Go, Go."

INTRODUCTION

You're old-fashioned,
You're passé,
Rhythm's in the air today.
Come with me and leave the past,
Life today is wild and fast.

VERSE

On your toes!
Everybody rise.
On your toes,
Open up your eyes.
This is the time for plenty of action.
Action!
On your toes,
Shout it to the skies.

REFRAIN

Go! Go! Go!
Let it go faster.
Faster! Faster! Follow master.
Go! Go! Go!
That's the rhythm of the day!
Run! Run! Run!
Rhythm is master.
Motors turning, wires burning.
Run! Run! Run!
That's the rhythm of the day!
Even love is electric,
Even love has a beat.
Here's the only correct trick,

Keep at fever heat.
Up! Up! Up!
Hitting the skyline.
Pulses beating, keep repeating
Go! Go! Go!
That's the rhythm of the day!

DANCING LADY

There are two Rodgers and Hart songs with this title, and they have different words and music. The first version, MGM Song #247, is dated June 9, 1933, and was registered for copyright as an unpublished work by Metro-Goldwyn-Mayer, June 20, 1933. The second version (a waltz), MGM Song #295, is dated August 4, 1933, and was registered for copyright as an unpublished work by Metro-Goldwyn-Mayer, August 16, 1933. Neither of the two Rodgers and Hart "Dancing Lady" songs was used in the film. "My Dancing Lady," introduced by Art Jarrett and danced by Joan Crawford and chorus, was written by Dorothy Fields and Jimmy McHugh.

Version 1

VERSE

You remember me,
I'm the second from the right,
The one that smiled at you tonight!
It's a hollow smile of glee
For the baldy-headed row,
And it's just part of the show!
Life's a dance for girls like me,
But what a dance that dance can be.

REFRAIN

Dancing lady, be a soldier.
You were hired for never gettin' tired.
Do exactly what is told ya.
Duchess, where's that smile?
Dancing lady, dance your head off.
Keep rehearsin' and never mind the cursin'
Though your lips have bit the red off.
Duchess, where's that smile?
You have no time to sleep,
You've no time to weep,
No time for romance,
Only time for dancing.
Dancing lady, struttin' for us,
Don't let down now.
You gotta go to town now!

It's the merry, merry chorus.
Duchess, where's that smile?

PATTER

Ting-a-ling, the old alarm clock's ringing.
Ting-a-ling, all right, I'm out of bed.
Here's a roll. Look out you'll spill your coffee.
Hurry up and both your dogs are dead.
Hurry up. Now you've made the subway.
What a nerve! Fresh guy! Watch those . . .
Times Square!
Let me get through there.
Here's the theatre. Ten a.m.
Heads up!
Into your bloomers,
Just like all the rest of them!
Toe Heel Toe Kick
Toe Heel Toe Kick
Toe Heel Toe Kick
Gosh, that movement makes you sick.
One a.m.
Lunch with the rest of them.
Coffee and a bun.
Back at one.
Toe Heel Kick
Five o'clock, six o'clock,
Dinner back at eight.
Nine o'clock, ten o'clock,
Goodbye to that date!
Eleven, twelve, one,
That director's a son of a gun.
Toe Heel Kick
Kick, you bimbo, kick.

CODA

Dancing lady,
Struttin' for us,
Don't let down now,
You gotta go to town now.
It's the merry, merry chorus.
Duchess, where's that smile?

Version 2

Dancing lady, you're lovely tonight.
May the day never start.
Love's in the rhythm of the music.
Love's in the rhythm of my heart!
Dancing lady, you live for the dance,
But when dancing is through,
You know my arms are waiting
And so is romance,
Dancing lady, for you.

HOLLYWOOD PARTY, 1934

A film produced by Howard Dietz and Harry Rapf for Metro-Goldwyn-Mayer (earlier title: *Hollywood Revue of 1933*). Released May 25, 1934. Music by Richard Rodgers. Additional music by Walter Donaldson and Nacio Herb Brown. Lyrics by Lorenz Hart. Additional lyrics by Gus Kahn, Howard Dietz, and Arthur Freed. Screenplay by Howard Dietz and Arthur Kober. Directed by Edmund Goulding, Russell Mack, Richard Boleslawsky, Allan Dwan, Roy Rowland (none credited). Cast, starring Jimmy Durante, included Laurel and Hardy, Charles Butterworth, Polly Moran, Lupe Velez, Frances Williams, and Jack Pearl.

HOLLYWOOD PARTY

Published May 1934. There are two Rodgers and Hart songs with this title and they have different words and music, although both were sung in the film as if they were one song. The first version, MGM Song #250, is dated June 12, 1933, and was registered for copyright as an unpublished work by Metro-Goldwyn-Mayer, June 20, 1933. The second version, MGM Song #325, is dated August 29, 1933, and was registered for copyright as an unpublished work by Metro-Goldwyn-Mayer, September 23, 1933. The second "Hollywood Party" was published. Introduced by Frances Williams.

Version 1

VERSE

What do the sirens scream for?
Why all the crowd?
What do the lights all gleam for?
Horns toot out loud?
Traffic is so terrific,
Mobs making noise,
Out near the old Pacific
Girls tell their boys,

REFRAIN

"Come and wear your white tie,
It's the right tie,
For tonight I meet you

At that noisy, girlsy and boysy
Hollywood Party."
All the minks and sables,
Wine with labels,
Garbo-Gables,
Greet you.
Taxi send us
To a tremendous
Hollywood Party.
All the girls wear ermine coats they got from
    men,
And tomorrow they must give them back again.
Let the laughter spring out,
Music ring out,
Satan sing out, "Hot-cha,"
At that crashing,
Furniture-smashing
Hollywood Party.

Version 2

VERSE

Phones busy!
We're dizzy!
It's that affair.
He's going!
She's going!
They're going there.
Put on your bib and tucker.
Put on your soup and fish.
I'm going!
You're going!
This is our dish.

REFRAIN

Hollywood Party!
Get up! Get out! Get in it!
Hollywood Party!
Nobody sleeps tonight.
Bring along your girl!
Go home with someone else's.
Forget about your girl.
She's gonna do all right.
We'll be kicking our heels up
Till the rooster is crowing.
Bring the automobiles up.
Ev'rybody is going.
Hollywood Party!
Going a mile a minute.
Hollywood Party!
Nobody sleeps tonight.

HELLO!

MGM Song #307 is dated August 18, 1933, and was registered for copyright as an unpublished work by Metro-Goldwyn-Mayer, September 9, 1933. Introduced by Jimmy Durante, Jack Pearl, and ensemble.

GIRL. This is a holiday,
    No melancholy day,
    This is a jolly day
    To welcome the Baron
    Who came from the Congo today.
    Gladly we wait for him,
    Our hearts dilate for him,
    To make a date for him,
    To welcome the Baron
    To Californiay,
    To Californiay.
DURANTE: The Baron's coming to say Hello!
CROWD: Hello!
DURANTE: Just hello!
CROWD: Hello, hello, hello.
DURANTE: Not hello, hello, hello,
    But hello.
CROWD: Hello.
MARINERS: Hello.
CROWD: Hello.
MARINERS: Rocked from the cradle of the deep,
    The Baron comes to say hello, hello,
        hello.
CROWD: Not hello, hello, hello,
    But hello.
MARINERS: Not hello, hello, hello,
    But hello!
DURANTE: He won't say how-dye-doo
    Mitt me, Babe, or how are you?
    Press the flesh, old thing, or cheerio,
    Or say how's tricks, ah there or
        heigh-de-ho,
    Wie gehts, mein Freund, or mazeltoff,
    Bon jour or any high-hat fuff,
    But now you ought to know
    The Baron's gonna say hello!
SLAVES: A goona, goona,
    A Trader Horn-a
    Good afternoon-a,
    Or is it morn-a?
    Here's the Baron
    Kicking King Kong around.
ALL: What's he gonna say?
    What's he gonna say?
SLAVES: He's coming here to say hello.
ALL: Oh no!
    That scootin' shootin' son of a gun
        from Africa,

That prevaricatin' second to none from
    Africa,
    Is going to say,
    He's going to say,
BARON: I'm going to say,
    I'm going to say,
ALL: It's an honor to our nation
    To hear your salutation.
    We have our celebration
    In great anticipation.
BARON: I want to say,
    I want to say,
ALL: No leopards made him shiver,
    No tigers made him quiver,
    Down by the Niger River,
    Where lions eat your liver.
BARON: I want to say,
    I want to say,
    This greeting really's a sensation,
    A most magnificent ovation.
    I've seen nothing like it before
    But I really expected much more.
    I only want to say,
    Hello.
ALL: Oh, Baron! Please!
BARON: I only want to say hello.
    Oh, hello, hello, hello.
ALL: We are very glad to meet you
    And we greet you
    With hello, hello, hello.
ECHO: Hello, hello.
BARON: Hello forever.
DURANTE: Hello forever.
ALL: Hello, hello, hello.
DURANTE: Hello!

REINCARNATION

MGM Song #246 is dated August 25, 1933, and was registered for copyright as an unpublished work by Metro-Goldwyn-Mayer, September 9, 1933. Music by Richard Rodgers and Jimmy Durante. Introduced by Jimmy Durante and Polly Moran.

Doin' some research work for the Smithsonian
    Institute,
I was called into consultation by Professor
    Ebbelworth,
That eminent philantherist who had heard what I
    did
For Einstein and his relatives.
Professor Ebbelworth said: "Jimmy, I need you,
I want to consult with you about a subject

Which has baffled all of the scientists of the
　world
Namely, reincarnation.
Not the carnation I'm wearing so jauntily in my
　buttonhole,
Not the carnation of a king, but reincarnation."
Professor Ebbelworth and me being the only two
　guys
That know the lowdown.
What is reincarnation, you mugs?
You earthworms, you incompoops, you
　chuckleheads?
Last night with my head on my lacy pillow,
I was a man dreaming I was a butterfly!
Sipping the sap from flower to flower,
Just like a butterfly,
I had butterfly worries and butterfly desires!
Just a man dreaming I was a butterfly!
How do I know now that I'm not a butterfly
Dreamin' that I'm a man?
Wait! I can see myself now,
I go way back to Adam,
Adam and his Madam,
Boys, I was Adam!
And that's reincarnation.
And later on, in later years I lived again,
From who did I get my feminine charm,
My Bourbon nose, my these and those?
Elizabeth, I hate New Joisey.
Mae West, my bosom friend,
No, I'll tell you:
I was Queen Marie Antoinette,
That lovely French coquette.
I can see myself standin' there yet.
Put this underneath your hatta:
A man has more lives than a catta.
These episodes in my career
Are just a demonstration of three little words:
Reincarnation!

THE MAHSTER'S COMING

MGM Song #238 is dated June 1, 1933, and was registered for copyright as an unpublished work by Metro-Goldwyn-Mayer, June 14, 1933. Dropped before the film was released. Intended for Jimmy Durante when film was known as *Hollywood Revue of 1933*.

1ST SERVANTS: The Mahster's coming—
2ND SERVANTS: The Mahster's coming—
　　　　　　　Returning to his domicile
　　　　　　　　manorial.
　　　　　　　As pictured in last Sunday's
　　　　　　　　editorial.

To represent a permanent
　memorial—
To our Mahster.
Let trumpets trump and drums
　begin your drumming,
Louder and fahster to welcome the
　Mahster,
The Mahster is coming.
BIRDS: Tweet, tweet, tweet, make music
　sweet,
The Mahster's coming!
PARROT: Birdies sing and bees begin your
　humming.
The Mahster! The Mahster!
OWL: Who? Who?
PARROT: Not you, you son of a gun!
The Mahster's coming.
3RD SERVANTS: The Mahster's coming!
Four architects have built his
　home baronial.
Designed the place with proper
　ceremonial.
In Spanish, English, French,
　mixed with Colonial.
For the Mahster,
Let trumpets trump and drums
　begin your drumming,
Louder and fahster
To welcome the Mahster,
The Mahster is coming!
DUCKS: Quack, quack, quack, the
　Mahster's back.
SWANS: We would sing with the rest of
　the boys,
But we swans never make any
　noise,
Yet if we did—
We'd all be humming.
The Mahster's coming—
SERVANTS: The Mahster's coming.
DURANTE: Hello, Brother!
PELICAN: Hello, James!
How's Mother?

YOU ARE

MGM Song #233 is dated June 6, 1933, and was registered for copyright as an unpublished work by Metro-Goldwyn-Mayer, June 14, 1933. Revised version to same music intended for Zasu Pitts and Jack Pearl, possibly for the film *Meet the Baron* (1933). Dropped before the film was released. Revised August 26, 1933.

Version 1

VERSE

I cannot speak, I'm so delighted,
Why am I like I am?
Just like a child when it's excited,
Why am I like I am?
Anyone can see
What you do to me.

REFRAIN

You are—
What's the use of trying to say what you
　are?
All the funny little things you do
Are so new,
You are just you.
You are—
How can I begin to tell what you are?
When you look at me, your eyes of blue
Are not blue.
You are just you.
If my emotion were shared by you,
I'd own the ocean, the Heavens also,
I'd fall so,
For you are
Much the nicer half of what we two are.
Ev'ry time I try to say what you are,
I'm through.
You are just you.

Version 2

REFRAIN 1

PEARL: You are—
Vat's the use of trying to zay vat you are.
There is just one phase like that,
There couldn't be two,
You are just you.
PITTS: You are—
What a lovely Casanova you are.
When you tell me that the skies of blue
Are not blue,
I know it's true.
PEARL: I got a cestle in southern France
Where you can wrestle mit pots and
　panzies.
This man zees
That you are,
Such a melancholy dame as few are.
Ven I try to illustrate vot you are,
I'm through,
You are just you.

VERSE

PEARL: Yust look at me, I'm so delighted.
Why am I like I am?
I am in your net,
Take me while it's "yet."

REFRAIN 2

PITTS: You are—
What a handsome movie hero you are!
Beauty such as yours would break
The camera in two.
You are just you.
PEARL: You are—
What a most delicious morsel you are.
Pretty as a pretzel from your head to your
    shoe,
You are just you.
PITTS: I'm just a slavey
And you're so ritz;
PEARL: You are the gravy
Upon my schnitzel,
Don't kitzel.
PITTS: Oh, you are—
Cuter than the monkeys in the zoo are.
PEARL: I've already had the mumps,
The measles and flu,
And now I've you.

BLACK DIAMOND

MGM Song #223 is dated June 12, 1933, and was registered for copyright as an unpublished work by Metro-Goldwyn-Mayer, June 20, 1933. Dropped before the film was released.

VERSE

I've ruby lips and iv'ry teeth and ebony cheeks.
My heart's a semiprecious stone.
I'm just a Harlem gem that shines in cabaret
    speaks
With a brilliance of my own.
Look me up and say hello;
I'm an easy girl to know.

REFRAIN

Call me Black Diamond,
That's my name,
I just aim to be loved.
Call me Black Diamond,
It's no shame
That I'm game to be loved.

If a Black Diamond has its flaws
Just because it's not white,
Still it's a diamond in the rough,
Good enough for a night.
Though I've felt that I could melt,
A diamond has a duty;
To be hard and shiny is my art.
Wedding rings are not the things
To emphasize my beauty;
Put me next to a beating heart.
Take a Black Diamond, let it go
While the glow is still bright.
Call me Black Diamond,
That's my name
But my flame is pure white.

PRAYER

MGM Song #225 is dated June 14, 1933, and was registered for copyright as an unpublished work by Metro-Goldwyn-Mayer, July 10, 1933. The remarkable saga of "Prayer" epitomizes what Rodgers and Hart went through when they were under contract to Metro-Goldwyn-Mayer. In its first version the melody that became the tune to "Blue Moon" was intended for Jean Harlow to sing in *Hollywood Party* (1934). It was called "Prayer." Neither Miss Harlow nor "Prayer" appeared in *Hollywood Party.*

Oh, Lord,
If you ain't busy up there,
I ask for help with a prayer,
So please don't give me the air.
Oh, hear me, Lord.
I must see Garbo in person
With Gable when they're rehearsin'
While some director is cursin'.
Please let me open up my eyes at seven
And find I'm looking through the Golden Gate,
And walking right into my movie heaven,
While some executive tells me I'll be great.
Oh, Lord,
I know how friendly you are.
If I'm not going too far,
Be nice and make me a star.

MANHATTAN MELODRAMA

In its second life the "Prayer"/"Blue Moon" tune was given a new lyric and became the title song of the 1934

MGM film *Manhattan Melodrama*, which starred Clark Gable, William Powell, Myrna Loy, and Leo Carillo, and was the movie that John Dillinger had been watching when he was gunned down outside the Biograph Theater in Chicago. "Manhattan Melodrama" was also known as "It's Just That Kind of a Play." It was registered for copyright as an unpublished work by Metro-Goldwyn-Mayer, March 30, 1934, but was cut from the film before it was ready for release.

VERSE

All New York's a stage
And all its men and women are very bad actors.
How they rant and rage
For food and drink and money,
For those are the factors.
Out of the Bronx and Yonkers
Rushing to earn a wage—
He must be strong who conquers
On the Manhattan stage.

REFRAIN

Act One:
You gulp your coffee and run;
Into the subway you crowd.
Don't breathe—it isn't allowed.

Act Two:
The boss is yelling at you;
You feel so frightened and cowed.
Don't breathe—it isn't allowed.

The rows of skyscrapers are like a canyon,
The sun is hidden 'neath a stony shroud,
Eight million people and not one companion:
Don't speak to anyone—it's not allowed.

Act Three:
You hate the sight of Broadway.
It's just that kind of a play—
Manhattan Melodrama.

THE BAD IN EVERY MAN

Manhattan Melodrama was also responsible for the third setting of the "Prayer"/"Blue Moon" tune. Under its new title, "The Bad in Every Man," it was sung by Shirley Ross in the film and was registered for copyright as an unpublished work by Metro-Goldwyn-Mayer, May 9, 1934, four days after the picture opened in New York.

VERSE

Sitting all alone
In moving picture theatres
Is ev'ry night's pleasure!
Walking on my own
When working hours are over,
I've nothing but leisure.
Am I a fool? I wonder.
Marriage is one way out.
But I'm afraid to blunder.
I sit home and doubt.

REFRAIN

Oh, Lord!
What is the matter with me?
I'm just permitted to see
The bad in ev'ry man.
Oh, hear me, Lord!
I could be good to a lover,
But then I always discover
The bad in ev'ry man.
They like to tell you that they love you only.
And you believe it though you know you're
    wrong.
A little hallroom can be awfully lonely
And a night can be so very long.
Oh, Lord!
Perhaps I'll alter my plan
And overlook if I can
The bad in ev'ry man!

BLUE MOON

The fourth lyric setting of the "Prayer" melody came
about when Jack Robbins, head of MGM's music publishing company, liked the tune and said he would promote
it if Hart would write a more commercial lyric. The result,
"Blue Moon," was published in December 1934.

VERSE 1

Once upon a time,
Before I took up smiling,
I hated the moonlight!
Shadows of the night
That poets find beguiling
Seemed flat as the moonlight.
With no one to stay up for,
I went to sleep at ten.
Life was a bitter cup for
The saddest of all men.

REFRAIN

Blue moon,
You saw me standing alone,
Without a dream in my heart,
Without a love of my own.
Blue moon,
You knew just what I was there for,
You heard me saying a prayer for
Someone I really could care for.
And then there suddenly appeared before me,
The only one my arms will ever hold.
I heard somebody whisper, "Please adore me."
And when I looked,
The moon had turned to gold!
Blue moon,
Now I'm no longer alone,
Without a dream in my heart,
Without a love of my own.

VERSE 2

Once upon a time,
My heart was just an organ.
My life had no mission.
Now that I have you,
To be as rich as Morgan
Is my one ambition.
Once I awoke at seven,
Hating the morning light.
Now I awake in Heaven
And all the world's all right.

REPEAT REFRAIN

THE POTS

MGM Song #255 is dated June 16, 1933, and was regis-
tered for copyright as an unpublished work by Metro-
Goldwyn-Mayer, July 10, 1933. Dropped from *Hollywood
Revue of 1933.*

COOKS: With the pots and the pans, and the
    pans and the pots,
CLEANERS: With the flannels and the dusters to
    remove the spots,
COOKS: With the pots and the pans,
CLEANERS: And the garbage cans,
ALL: We're the pots who rule the pots!

DINNER
WAITERS: With the forks and the knives, and
    the knives and the forks,

WINE
WAITERS: With the corks and the bottles, and
    the bottles and the corks,
COOKS: With the pots and the pans,
CLEANERS: And the garbage cans,
ALL: We're the pots who rule the pots!

MAIDS: With the sheets and the pillows, and
    the pillows and the sheets,
BUTCHERS: With the meats and the fishes, and the
    fishes and the meats,
COOKS: With the pots and the pans,
CLEANERS: And the garbage cans,
DINNER
WAITERS: And the knives and the forks,
WINE
WAITERS: And the bottles and the corks,
ALL: We're the pots who rule the pots.

BUTLERS: With a scowl and a bow, and a bow
    and a scowl,
VALETS: With a towel and a brush, and a
    brush and a towel,
COOKS: With the pots and the pans,
CLEANERS: And the garbage cans,
DINNER
WAITERS: And the knives and the forks,
WINE
WAITERS: And the bottles and the corks,
MAIDS: And the pillows and the sheets,
BUTCHERS: And the fishes and the meats,
ALL: We're the pots who rule the pots!

COOKS: Pans, pots,
CLEANERS: Cans, pots,
DINNER
WAITERS: Forks, pots,
WINE
WAITERS: Corks, pots,
MAIDS: Sheets, pots,
BUTCHERS: Meats, pots,
BUTLERS: Scowls, pots,
VALETS: Towels, pots,
ALL: Pots, pots, pots,
    Pots, pots, pots,
POTS: We're the pots who rule the pots,
    With the pots and the pans, and the
    pans and the pots,
    We're the pots who rule the pots,
    We're the pots who rule the pots.

I'M ONE OF THE BOYS

MGM Song #256 is dated June 16, 1933, and was registered for copyright as an unpublished work by Metro-Goldwyn-Mayer, July 10, 1933. Dropped from *Hollywood Revue of 1933*.

VERSE

When beautiful Lillian Russell
Put on a great big bustle,
She glorified the backbone of a nation!
I wore it! I wore it!
And made the world adore it!
It started the first inflation.
When Madame Sarah Bernhardt wore the hobble
    skirt,
I was the very first to hobble on Broadway.
I've always had a passion
To wear the latest fashion,
That's why I have to look like this today.

REFRAIN 1

I'm one of the boys,
Just one of the boys,
I go to the tailor that Marlene employs.
No dresses from France so modern as these.
And under my pants are B.V.D.'s.
I'm one of the boys,
Girls, I'm one of the boys.
I handle a big cigar with manly poise.
Once I was maternal,
Now they call me Colonel.
I'm one of the boys, one of the boys.

REFRAIN 2

I'm one of the boys,
Just one of the boys,
I've got to go in for things a man enjoys.
Men who brought me candy said, "How sweet
    you are."
Now I take my brandy at the bar.
I'm one of the boys,
Girls, I'm one of the boys.
Dice, cards and tobacco are my fav'rite toys.
People ask me, "Dearie,
Ain't you Wallace Beery?"
I'm one of the boys, one of the boys.

BURNING!

MGM Song #262 is dated June 20, 1933, and was registered for copyright as an unpublished work by Metro-Goldwyn-Mayer, July 10, 1933. Dropped from *Hollywood Revue of 1933*.

VERSE

Down where the old equator flows,
Warm over land and sea.
Down where the old equator flows,
Love put its fire in me.
And the fire of love,
Like a boiling crater,
Flows hot and free.

REFRAIN

Burning!
On fire!
Aflame!
Ablaze!
Burning! Burning! Burning!
Must I go through all my nights and days
Burning! Burning! Burning!
My heart's a torch,
My fingers scorch.
Flames hiss with my kiss,
Lips burning,
Hips burning,
Eyes burning,
Thighs burning,
Burning ooh! Burning ooh! Burning on fire!
Aflame!
Ablaze!
Burning! Burning! Burning!

BABY STARS

MGM Song #267 is dated July 8, 1933, and was registered for copyright as an unpublished work by Metro-Goldwyn-Mayer, July 17, 1933. Dropped from *Hollywood Revue of 1933*. See also "Development of Baby Stars Number," which follows.

VERSE

We're the baby movie stars of whom they write
In the magazines with raptured delight.
We are models of refinement,
Never knew what beer or wine meant.
But, my dears! Oh, my dears!
We think we're gonna find it out tonight.

REFRAIN

We are the cute little baby stars
Fresh from Peoria, Troy and Emporia.
After the preview we may be stars
Or maybe right back slinging hash.
We cahnt say "can't," but we can't say "cahnt";
We're weak in the platinum dome.
We are the cute little baby stars,
Babies with babies at home.

DEVELOPMENT OF BABY STARS NUMBER

MGM Song #349 dated October 26, 1933, was registered for copyright as an unpublished work by Metro-Goldwyn-Mayer, December 15, 1933. This lyric is a continuation of "Baby Stars." Though completed at different times and registered for copyright separately, they are really part of the same song. Dropped before the film was released. Alternate title: "Baby Stars Number."

GIRLS: Is this the Apex Studio?
    May we see the gateman?
GIRLS
(AS MEN): The gateman's very busy,
    You'll have to wait a while!
GIRLS: One o'clock, two o'clock, three o'clock,
    Four o'clock, five o'clock, six o'clock.
    Ah! The gateman!
(AS MEN): Where were you born?
    Where do you live?
    Who do you know, huh?
    The gate's very crowded,
    You'll have to wait a while!
GIRLS: Monday, Tuesday, Wednesday,
    Thursday,
    Friday, Saturday, Sunday.
    Hurray! We're in.
    Please, Mr. Office Boy,
    May we see the secretary?
(AS MEN): Who you got a letter from?
GIRLS: Why, we have a letter from a
    gentleman
    Who lives way down . . .
(AS MEN): Answer when you are spoken to.
    Who you got a letter from?
GIRLS: Why, I'll tell you.
(AS MEN): Don't interrupt!
    You can't see the secretary for a little
    while.
GIRLS: January, February, March,
    April, May, June, July.

Hurray! We're in!
Please, Mr. Secretary!
May we see the President?
(AS MEN): What do you eat?
What do you drink?
Who do you love,
Huh?
You can't see the President for a little
while!
1933, 1943, 1953,
1963, 1973, 1983.
GIRLS: At last we're in!
Please, Mr. President!
We have lots of talent!
(AS MEN): Who are you?
GIRLS: Who are we?
We are the cute little baby stars
Fresh from Peoria, Troy and Emporia.
After the preview we may be stars
Or maybe right back slinging hash.
We can't grow old but we can't stay
young
As through the ages we roam.
We are the cute little baby stars,
Babies with babies at home.

YOU'VE GOT THAT

Hart wrote two different lyrics to Rodgers's music for this song. The first version (MGM Song #278) is dated July 21, 1933, and was registered for copyright as an unpublished work by Metro-Goldwyn-Mayer, August 7, 1933. The second, or revised, version is dated August 30, 1933, and was registered for copyright as an unpublished work, September 9, 1933. It was intended for Lupe Velez and Charles Butterworth. Dropped before the film was released.

Version 1

VERSE

SHE: What do I mean?
What do I mean to you?
How can I look like a movie queen to you?
I'm so humble,
My words of love I mumble,
But you won't give a girl a tumble.
What do I mean?
HE: What do you mean to me!
You're my Broadway Melody!
I belong to you.
You belong to me.

REFRAIN 1

If it takes lots of what-is-it,
You've got that!
If it takes this-a and that-a,
You've got that!
Out in the movie sector
They'll see how good you are.
Let me be your director,
You be my star.
You've got charm, you've got attraction,
You've got "ooh."
When I make musical pictures,
I'll make you.
Billboards will make you famous,
Shouting how great you are.
With your face on every ash can
You will be a star.

REFRAIN 2

SHE: If it takes lots of what-is-it,
I've got that!
If it takes what-you-may-call-'em,
I've got that!
Out in the movie sector
They'll see how good I am.
If you're my big director,
I'm your star ham.
I've got charm, I've got attraction,
I've got "ooh!"
When you make musical pictures,
I'll make you.
Passion combined with patience
Makes little girls go far.
If it takes all of your bankroll
I will be a star!

Version 2

VERSE

SHE: I looked around,
I looked around in vain,
But never found
And looked around again.
Now I've met you,
Don't let this upset you.
I won't rest until I get you.
You're my ideal,
Handsome and passionate.
It's not because your bank has cash in it.
But you have got that "je ne sais quoi"
That appeals to moi.

REFRAIN 1

If it takes lots of what-is-it,
You've got that!
If it takes what-cha-ma-call-'em,
You've got that!
You're in the best condition;
No one can call you slow.
Turn on the old ignition;
Let yourself go!
You've got vim, plenty of vigor,
You've got ooh!
You've got what's making me happy,
Making you;
You make the wildest tiger
Look like an alley cat.
If it takes lots of what-is-it,
You've got this and that.

REFRAIN 2

HE: If it takes lots of what-is-it,
You've got that!
If it takes what-cha-ma-call-'em,
You've got that!
You've a supply of what-for;
Your waist is just my size.
Two features I go hot for,
I mean your eyes.
You've got charm, you've got attraction,
You've got ooh!
Grace plus looks added to action
Equals you.
You'd be a decoration
For any bachelor's flat.
If it takes lots of what-is-it,
You've got this and that!

FLY AWAY TO IOWAY

MGM Song #276 is dated July 24, 1933, and was registered for copyright as an unpublished work by Metro-Goldwyn-Mayer, August 7, 1933. Dropped from *Hollywood Revue of 1933.* It satirized the Harry Warren–Al Dubin hit "Shuffle Off to Buffalo," which was featured in *Forty-Second Street* (1933).

VERSE

We'll be married by a judge, a priest, a parson,
A rabbi to make it binding.
We will start our honeymoon
Though it's May instead of June!
We won't see Niag'ra Falls, Paree, the Bronx,

Or any foreign nation.
I've got the location for us.

REFRAIN

Go and pack the fam'ly toothbrush.
It's the month of May
Ooh-ooh-ooh
Soon we're gonna fly-a,
Fly away to Ioway
Would it suit you on a choo-choo
Where it's gray all day?
No-oh-oh.
Wouldn't you rather fly-a,
Fly away to Ioway?
Down in old Dubuque
There's a cozy nook
Where the church bells chime.
But for old Des Moines
My sad heart yoins
In three-quarter time.
What a rhyme.
Go and pack your aunty's panties
And your dad's toupee.
Ooh-ooh-ooh.
Soon we're gonna fly-a,
Fly away to Ioway.

GIVE A MAN A JOB

MGM Song #308 is dated August 21, 1933, and was registered for copyright as an unpublished work by Metro-Goldwyn-Mayer, September 9, 1933. Dropped before the film was released.

REFRAIN

Step out in front,
Get back of the President
And give a man a job.
He bore the brunt,
Now bear with the President
And give a man a job.
If the old name of Roosevelt
Makes the heart throb,
You'll take this message
Straight from the President
And give a man a job.

VERSE

You and you and you and you,
You've got a President now.
He gave the land a new deal.
You hold the cards, now you deal.

You and you and you and you
Put shoulder to the plow.
He gave us what we asked for,
Let's pay him back somehow.

PATTER

DURANTE: You look like a banker,
Who drives your car?
BANKER: I drive it myself
Have a cigar.
DURANTE: Keep your cigar and hire a chauffeur
And keep a bum from being a loafer.
You look like a grocer.
MAN: No, sir!
My job's extermination.
DURANTE: You must give your assistants
All a nice weekend vacation.
MAN: I'll need more men to kill the rats.
DURANTE: We want you to hire a crowd.
You'll do good work when you hang
out this sign.
It means no rats allowed.
What are you?
WOMAN: I'm a sick woman.
DURANTE: Oh, a hypochondriac.
Get a doctor for pneumonia,
Another one for insomnia.
Get a doctor for osmosis
And one for halitosis.
One for anemia.
One for eczema.
For bronchitis, neuritis, fleabitis,
St. Vitus
And for every other kind of an "itus."
That will deite us.
Get a doctor for each disease you got.
It will give you great enjoyment.
In that way,
Madame, you'll end unemployment.

I'M A QUEEN IN
MY OWN DOMAIN

MGM Song #347 is dated November 27, 1933, and was registered for copyright as an unpublished work by Metro-Goldwyn-Mayer, December 15, 1933. Dropped before the film was released.

VERSE

I would rather hand a kid a piece of pie
Than sit upon a throne and hold my head up
high!

I'd rather wash the dishes while I sing
Than marry a man because he was a king.
I'd rather stand dishing out my bread and jam
Than dish out queenly, dirty looks while lords
salaam.
I'm never called Your Majesty, but just plain
"Ma'am,"
And I am just what I am.

REFRAIN

I don't want a Russian sable coat,
I don't want the finest yacht afloat.
While I bake my bread, and I make my bed,
I'm a queen in my own domain.
I don't want a palace by the sea,
Polo isn't quite the game for me.
With a cup of tea and my conscience free,
I'm a queen in my own domain.
I feel mighty rich in
My funny little kitchen
Laying out my simple plans.
I don't want a castle,
I would rather wrastle
With the royal pots and pans.
Nobles needn't bow down to the ground,
Let me have a few real friends around!
While my love can live and my heart can give,
I'm a queen in my own domain!

MY FRIEND THE NIGHT

MGM Song #384 is dated November 27, 1933, and was registered for copyright as an unpublished work by Metro-Goldwyn-Mayer, December 15, 1933. Dropped before the film was released.

VERSE

Noisy parties of drunken buffoons,
Jazz bands screeching detestable tunes,
Odor of cigarettes, stench of cigars,
That's why I want to walk under the stars!
Hollow laughter and scrambled affairs,
Lifted eyebrows and gossip and stares,
Parlors and people are shackles and bars.
That's why I want to walk under the stars!

REFRAIN

My friend the night
Looks down on me
With gentle eyes of the stars,
My friend the night.

His touch is light on me;
His fingers are the summer breeze in its flight,
My friend the night.
When he lifts his voice in boisterous commotion,
He blows a gale of laughter in my ear.
He slaps me with a surging of the ocean
As a symbol of his devotion!
My friend the night
Looks down on me
And watches while I sleep.
He holds me tight,
My friend the night.

KEEP AWAY FROM THE MOONLIGHT

MGM Song #343 is dated November 29, 1933, and was registered for copyright as an unpublished work by Metro-Goldwyn-Mayer, December 15, 1933. Dropped before the film was released.

VERSE

You have a lovely disposition,
Yet every day you say me nay!
I'm in a very sad condition,
When every day you say me nay.
You're careful, clever, virtuous and sensible,
I'm carefree, foolish, naughty, reprehensible.
Look out or I will carry out my mission
And get my way.

REFRAIN

If you're afraid to love me,
Keep away from the moonlight.
You're not safe in the moonlight with me.
If you're afraid to kiss me,
Walk around in the sunlight.
Keep away from the moonlight and me.
When all the stars up above
Like a million eyes are looking right at you,
You'll fall in love,
Because moonlit skies can melt a statue.
When all the birds are wooing,
Do I know what I'm doing?
Keep away from the moonlight and me.

THE NIGHT WAS MADE FOR DANCING

A lead sheet with this lyric fragment is with the Richard Rodgers manuscripts donated in 1965 to the Music Division of the Library of Congress.

The night was made for dancing
And you were made for love.
And while we two are dancing,
We're sure to fall in love.
The dew is on the grass below,
The moon is up above.
And in between are we—
And night was made for dancing,
Dancing to love.

MEET THE BARON, 1933

While at work on *Hollywood Party* (1934), Lorenz Hart, Richard Rodgers, and Jimmy Durante wrote "Yes Me," MGM Song #245 for the film *Meet the Baron* (1933), MGM Production #710. Music is dated August 29, 1933; it was registered for copyright as an unpublished song by Metro-Goldwyn-Mayer, September 9, 1933. Most of the songs for *Meet the Baron,* including "Don't Blame Me," were written by Dorothy Fields and Jimmy McHugh even though almost all of the numbers, including "Don't Blame Me," were not used in the film. *Meet the Baron* featured Jack Pearl, Jimmy Durante, Ted Healy, the Three Stooges, Edna Mae Oliver, ZaSu Pitts, and Greta Mayer.

YES ME

JIMMY: Yes me
And remember the yes you gave me
Must be a stupendious yes
For if you give me a comme ci,
comme ça, yes
OTHERS: Yes! Swine.
JIMMY: Going to the opera or the six-day bike
race in my open barouche.
You know and I know
The crowd cheers,

They want souvenirs.
I gave them my tie, my collar,
My vest, my socks, my shoes, my
coat, my pants.
When I tips my hat-a
Ladies give me that-a,
They all shout Ha-cha-cha-cha.
Here comes the marster.
Every debutante says, "I wants
Durante."
I belongs to the four hundred,
The five hundred, the six hundred,
the seven hundred.
OTHERS: Yes!
JIMMY: I'm big.
OTHERS: You're big.
JIMMY: I'm great.
OTHERS: You're great.
JIMMY: I'm swell.
OTHERS: You're swell.
JIMMY: I'm nuts.
OTHERS: You're nuts.
JIMMY: That's right.
Yes me.
OTHERS: It's raining.
JIMMY: It's snowing.
OTHERS: It's snowing.
JIMMY: It's black.
OTHERS: It's black.
JIMMY: It's white.
OTHERS: It's white.
JIMMY: It's old.
OTHERS: It's old.
JIMMY: It's good.
OTHERS: It's good.
JIMMY: Stop, it's lousy.
ONE VOICE: Right.
JIMMY: Everyone shout Ha-cha-cha-cha!
OTHERS: Ha-cha-cha-cha!
JIMMY: Ha-cha-cha-cha!
All for one
And that one's the marster.
Yes me . . .
Yes me . . .
Yes me . . .

THE MERRY WIDOW, 1934

A Metro-Goldwyn-Mayer Picture produced and directed by Ernst Lubitsch. Released October 1934. Music by Franz Lehár. Original lyrics by Victor Leon and Leo Stein translated by Lorenz Hart. Additional music by Herbert

Stothart and Richard Rodgers. Additional lyrics by Lorenz Hart and Gus Kahn. Screenplay by Ernst Vajda and Samson Raphaelson based on Franz Lehár's operetta. Music adapted, arranged, orchestrated, and conducted by Herbert Stothart. Cast, starring Jeanette MacDonald and Maurice Chevalier, included Edward Everett Horton, Una Merkel, George Barbier, and Minna Gombell.

GIRLS, GIRLS, GIRLS!

Music by Franz Lehár. Refrain 1: Heard as the Soldiers' Chorus; introduced by Maurice Chevalier and male ensemble; MGM Song #1045, dated March 30, 1934; Lyric #1 in film sequence.

   Reprise: Introduced by Maurice Chevalier; MGM Song #1046, dated April 3, 1934; Lyric #16 in film sequence.

REFRAIN 1

Though our country will never make war—
We've a reason that's worth marching for—
Not for battle our banner unfurls—
But for girls—girls—girls—girls—girls.
When we're marching we never retreat—
For we're charging a foe that is sweet!
But we're caught in the swirls
Of the enemy's curls,
And surrender to girls—girls—girls.

REPRISE

VERSE (not heard in film)

Ruby lips taste like claret
When they're pressing close to mine.
What a flavor!
I compare it to the oldest vintage wine.
I don't need a book of verses
Or a jug beneath the bough,
And my memory rehearses
Not a moment so sweet as now.

REFRAIN 2

Let us gaze in the wine while it's wet.
Let's do things that we'll live to regret.
Let me dance till the restaurant whirls
With the girls, girls, girls, girls, girls!
When there's wine and there's women and song,
It is wrong not to do something wrong!
When you do something wrong,
You must do something right,
And I'm doing all right tonight.

VILIA

Music by Franz Lehár. Introduced by Jeanette MacDonald, Bella Loblov, violinist, unknown tenor, and ensemble. MGM Song #1051, dated April 3, 1934. Lyric #2 in film sequence. Title on MGM conductor's score is "Gypsies in the Courtyard."

VERSE

The night is romantic and I am alone.
In vain through my window the moonlight is
   thrown.
"Oh, Vilia, my Vilia!" Oh yes, that's the tune,
The song of the shepherd who cried for the
   moon.

REFRAIN

Vilia, oh Vilia, oh let me be true;
My little life is a love song to you.
Vilia, oh Vilia, I've waited so long;
Lonely with only a song.
Vilia, oh Vilia, don't leave me alone!
Love calls to love and my heart is your own.
Vilia, oh Vilia, I've waited so long,
Lonely with only a song.
Only a song,
Only a song.

MELODY OF LAUGHTER

Music by Franz Lehár. Introduced and reprised by Jeanette MacDonald and ensemble. MGM Song #1048, dated April 3, 1934. Lyric #5 in film sequence. Song includes recitative, "We'll Go to Cafe Paree," which is sometimes listed as a separate number. Alternate titles: "The Melody of Laughter" and "The Melody of Paris."

SONIA: The melody of laughter, love and
   Maytime,
      That is Paris at café time.
GIRLS: Your tiara, your pearls and your
   lavaliere soon
      Will enrapture the eye of each
      cavalier.
SONIA: A rondelay of roses, wine and dances,
GIRLS: Manly glances, light romances.
SONIA: Once again I'll learn to sing
   ALL: The melody of Paris in the spring.

1ST MAN: We'll go to the Café de Paris to dine
2ND MAN: Then to the Opera—

3RD MAN: We'll get there at nine.
4TH MAN: Then we'll have supper at the Grand
   Hotel.
5TH MAN: When it's twelve o'clock and all is
   well,
   MEN: Then we will dance if madame is
   willing
SONIA: How mad—how wild—and how
   thrilling.

SONIA: How wonderful a moment for gay time.
   This is Paris and it's play time.
   Every man is a man of sincerity,
   And if he tells you he loves you, it's
   verity.
   The atmosphere is perfumed with
   romances—
   My heart dances at his glances.
   What a thrilling thing to sing
   The melody of Paris in the spring.
GIRLS: The atmosphere is perfumed with
   romances—
   Her heart dances at your glances.
   What a wonderful thing to sing
   The melody of Paris in the spring.

MAXIM'S

Music by Franz Lehár
   Lyric #7: Introduced by Maurice Chevalier; MGM Song #1052, dated April 4, 1934;
   Lyric #11: Reprised by Maurice Chevalier; MGM Song #1052, dated April 4, 1934.
   Sonia Paris Hotel, Episode B: Reprised in hotel by Jeanette MacDonald and ensemble and in carriage by Maurice Chevalier and ensemble; MGM Song #1073, dated May 1, 1934.
   Lyric #18: Final reprise by Jeanette MacDonald, MGM Song #1053, dated April 6, 1934.
   In all, five Lorenz Hart translations and settings of "Maxim's" are heard in the film.

Lyric #7

I'm going to Maxim's,
Where all the girls are dreams.
Each kiss goes on the wine list
And mine is quite a fine list.
Lo-lo, Do-do, Jou-jou,
Clo-clo, Mar-got, Frou-frou,
We promise to be faithful
Until the night is through.

Lyric #11

I'll stay up at Maxim's
Until the morning beams.
When I am feeling so good,
Be sure I'm out for no good.
Lo-lo, Do-do, Jou-jou,
Wake up, young man, please do.
Come on and spare the horses
And drive me to Maxim's.

Sonia Paris Hotel, Episode B

1ST MAID: I think he said Maxim's.
2ND MAID: He's going there, it seems.
3RD MAID: I heard that's where a man can
See ladies dance the can-can.
SONIA: Lo-lo, Do-do, Jou-jou,
Or any name will do.
True love is out of fashion
And men go to Maxim's.

1ST MAN: She can't go to Maxim's.
2ND MAN: Not in my wildest dreams—
3RD MAN: Her face must not be shown there.
4TH MAN: And we are too well known there.
DANILO: [driving in carriage]
Lo-lo, Do-do, Jou-jou,
Clo-clo, Mar-got, Frou-frou.
We promise to be faithful
Until the night is through.

Lyric #18

SONIA: Goodbye to you, Maxim's,
I don't believe in dreams.
The evening was splendid,
But now the play is ended.
I give you to Jou-jou,
Clo-clo, Mar-got, Frou-frou.
The wine has lost its flavor.
I leave Maxim's to you.

MERRY WIDOW WALTZ

Music by Franz Lehár. Introduced by Jeanette MacDonald and Maurice Chevalier. MGM Song #1050, dated April 3, 1934. Reprise is MGM Song #1083, dated May 21, 1934. Lyric #17 in film sequence.

Not a word, dear,
Have I heard, dear,
Yet I know.

You've not told me,
But you hold me,
So I know.
Words may be unspoken,
Yet I know you hear;
Music sighs;
Your heart replies,
"I love you, dear!"

REPRISE

I never knew before
How much I could adore;
But when you hold my hand,
And look at me,
I understand.
And the music murmurs low;
It's telling me
You know I know,
And Heaven gives the sign
You're mine all mine.

Now or never
And forever
I love you.
Let me hold you
Till I've told you
I love you.
I believe in magic
While our arms entwine.
Heaven's near
When you are here
And mine all mine.

IF WIDOWS ARE RICH

Music by Franz Lehár. Introduced by Jeanette MacDonald and ensemble. MGM Song #1049, dated April 6, 1934. Lyric #20 in film sequence. Alternate title: "Widows Are Gay."

SONIA: I've heard
Many men say,
Widows have charm,
Widows are gay.
And if we poor ones
Should be rich ones,
We are much more attractive
That way.
MEN: Don't fear.
We are sincere;
Please don't believe
All that you hear.
You must forgive us

If we're too bold.
How can such beauty
Be cold?
SONIA: With one million she's sweet,
If she has two, she is complete.
A Merry Widow can't be too bold,
That's what I've always been told.

IT MUST BE LOVE

MGM Song #1018 is dated March 16, 1934, and was registered for copyright as an unpublished work by Metro-Goldwyn-Mayer, March 30, 1934. Dropped before the film was released. Intended for Maurice Chevalier and ensemble.

INTRODUCTION

DANILO: This thing is something new to me.
Who knows what it will do to me.
Am I insane
Or just a plain fool?

REFRAIN 1

How my heart is aching,
I think it's breaking,
My hand is shaking in my glove.
I'm not well at all.
GIRLS: If it hurts, that's love.
DANILO: And yet I am delighted
And so excited.
Although it's night, the sun's above.
Never felt so well.

VERSE

GIRLS: If you're thrilled, that's love.
DANILO: First I am serious,
Then I'm delirious,
The change in temperament is quite
mysterious.
My heart is clattering,
My teeth are chattering,
My brains are scattering away.
GIRLS: That's love, that's love.
DANILO: I don't feel like drinking,
Yet I keep drinking.
I don't know what I'm thinking of.
I must be a fool.
That's love. It must be love.
Pardon me
If I seem
Bounding with joy

Like a boy in a dream.
Pardon me
If I'm strange.
There's been an awful change.
Thank you for what you've done.
I'm such a crazy one.

REFRAIN 2

How my heart is aching,
I think it's breaking,
My hand is shaking in my glove.
I'm not well at all.
GIRLS: If it hurts, that's love.
And yet he is delighted
And so excited.
Although it's night, the sun's above.
Now he feels so well.
DANILO: I am thrilled. That's love.
First I am serious,
Then I'm delirious,
The change in temp'rament is quite
    mysterious.
GIRLS: His heart is clattering.
His teeth are chattering.
His brains are scattering away.
DANILO: That's love! That's love!
I don't feel like drinking.
GIRLS: Yet he keeps drinking
DANILO: I don't know what I'm thinking of.
I must be a fool.
ALL: That's love, it must be love!

A WIDOW IS A LADY

MGM Song #1019 is dated March 16, 1934, and was registered for copyright as an unpublished work by Metro-Goldwyn-Mayer, March 30, 1934. Dropped before the film was released. Apparently intended for Jeanette Mac-Donald.

A widow is a lady
And a lady has a heart,
And her heart will always start to romance.
A lady is a woman
And a woman needs a man,
Life alone is a solitary dance.
Let me find a gallant,
With romantic talent,
One who's mine and only mine alone.

But if he can't be mine alone,
I'll stay behind my wall,
A lonely lady after all.

SECOND ENDING

I hoped that he'd come back,
But he's forgotten that we met,
Now I'm the one who must forget.

DOLORES

MGM Song #1042 is dated March 23, 1934. Registered for copyright as an unpublished song by Metro-Goldwyn-Mayer, June 4, 1934. Unused in the film. Intended for Maurice Chevalier, who played Danilo.

VERSE

I must give the King and Queen ev'rything I've
    got
I love him.
I love her.
Achmed tells me that he's great,
Dolores say's he's not.
And that is why I've been a soldier of the Queen
Since I was sixteen.
It takes a lot of adjectives to tell her what I
    mean.

REFRAIN 1

Dolores, Dolores, my beautiful volcano,
You never let me say no to you.
Dolores, Dolores,
You're bad, and you're delightful,
An appetizing sightful to view.
When you kiss you don't peck like a sparrow,
When you sleep you don't dream like a child.
This chorus, Dolores, I sing in admiration of
What has made a nation wild.

REFRAIN 2

Dolores, Dolores, my dynamite in ermine,
You do what you determine to do.
Dolores, Dolores,
You are my strongest weakness,
I bow my head with meekness to you.
Though the pen greater power than sword has,
You have something that beats any pen.

This chorus, Dolores, I sing in salutation of
What has made the nation's men.

MUCHACHA and LITTLE DOLORES

"Muchacha" was published by Rodart Music, January 1935. "Little Dolores" was published May 1935. They are the same song. "Muchacha" was the first version; "Little Dolores" was the second. With the exception of the word change from "Muchacha" to "Dolores" in the lyric, the songs are identical. "Little Dolores" is not the same song as "Dolores," which was intended for *The Merry Widow* (1934).

Click-clickety-click!
Go heels upon the ground,
Love keeps time
To the sound.
Are you in love, Muchacha,
And will you always dance for me,
Little Muchacha?
Clack-clackety-clack!
You play your castanets,
While my heart
Pirouettes.
How is your heart, Muchacha,
And will it always dance for me,
Little Muchacha?
Bright as the day your shining teeth are
    gleaming;
Dark as the night your gentle eyes are dreaming.
Boom-zingety-boom!
The drums go through my brain!
Does my heart
Throb in vain?
How do you feel, Muchacha?
Tell me you give a thought to me,
Little Muchacha!
Click-clickety-click!
Go heels upon the ground,
Love keeps time
To the sound.
Are you in love, Muchacha,
And do you dance for me?
Little Muchacha,
Funny Muchacha,
Are you in love with me,
Muchacha?

OVERLEAF: Bing Crosby (far left) and W. C. Fields (center)

MISSISSIPPI | 1935
MISCELLANEOUS | 1930–1935

A film produced by Arthur Hornblow, Jr., for Paramount Pictures. Released April 1935. Music by Richard Rodgers. Lyrics by Lorenz Hart. Screenplay by Francis Martin and Jack Cunningham, adapted by Herbert Fields and Claude Binyon from the play *Magnolia* by Booth Tarkington. Directed by A. Edward Sutherland. Music conducted by Sigmund Krumgold. Cast, starring Bing Crosby and W. C. Fields, included Joan Bennett, Queenie Smith, and, as a bit player, Ann Sheridan. Music and lyric for "I Keep on Singing" are missing.

NO BOTTOM

Song is dated July 30, 1934, and was registered for copyright as an unpublished work by Paramount Productions, Inc., August 9, 1934. Introduced by ensemble. In the film it was linked with "Roll Mississippi," although it is a separate number. Alternate titles: "Mississippi Opening" and "The Leadsman's Song."

1ST LEADSMAN: No bottom, no bottom,
No bottom on this lead line.
Wish dat Memphis gal was mine.

RELAY MAN: No bottom, no bottom,
No bottom on this lead line.

W. C. FIELDS: That Memphis gal eats like a swine.

2ND LEADSMAN: By the Mark Four,
She ain't gonna kick me round no more!

RELAY MAN'S VOICE: By the Mark Four.

W. C. FIELDS: She buys her shape in a Beale Street store.

3RD LEADSMAN: By the Mark Three.

1ST LEADSMAN: Take the water, leave the gin for me!

RELAY MAN'S VOICE: Two and a half.

W. C. FIELDS: His gal's got a neck like a big giraffe.

1ST LEADSMAN: By the sandbar;
Quarter Twain, here you are.

2ND LEADSMAN: By the Mark Twain,
Never ride this boat again.

3RD LEADSMAN: Coil the line up tight.
Heave it up, dat's right.

VOICES OF LEADSMEN: With a Mark Twain lead
Heave it up ahead.
By the Mark Four,
Ain't gonna heave no more.

'Cause there ain't any bottom now,
No bottom now.

ROLL, MISSISSIPPI

Song is dated July 25, 1934, and was registered for copyright as an unpublished work by Paramount Productions, Inc., August 9, 1934. Introduced by Queenie Smith and ensemble.

VERSE

Choc'late Romeo,
Now's the time to go!
Shine yo' face up,
Gotta chase up
To the show.
Coffee-color chile,
Gotta dress in style;
You'll be dancin'
And romancin'
With yo' beau,
With yo' Mississippi beau.

REFRAIN

Roll, Mississippi,
Keep rollin' with all yo' might.
Dance, Mississippi,
We're gittin' along tonight.
While we ride,
Be a good river,
Ease yo' flow.
Keep yo' tide,
Like a good river,
Way down low.
Roll, Mississippi,
Keep givin' the rhythm right.
Gotta roll; roll; roll;
We're gittin' along tonight!

SOON

Published March 1935. Registered for copyright as an unpublished song by Paramount Productions, Inc., August 8, 1934. Introduced by Bing Crosby.

VERSE

Ev'ry day that I'm without you
Seems a year,

Yet I let each fear about you
Disappear.
Days that part us will be few,
And I know without a doubt
You feel it too.

REFRAIN

Soon, maybe not tomorrow
But soon there'll just be two of us.
Soon you and I will borrow
The moon for just the two of us.
Sweetly and so discreetly
We'll be completely alone;
No other world,
Only our own.
Now we must be contented
With schemes about the two of us.
Yet we can have our sweet-scented
Dreams that will come true of us,
For presently and pleasantly
Our hearts will be in tune.
So, soon, maybe not tomorrow,
But soon.

DOWN BY THE RIVER

Published March 1935. Registered for copyright as an unpublished song by Paramount Productions, Inc., August 3, 1934. Introduced by Bing Crosby.

VERSE

In a sparkling moment,
I loved you, you loved me.
Oh, how sweet fate can be.
In that happy moment
I forgot all my past.
Now I realize the way
The spell was cast,
At last.

REFRAIN

Once we walked alone
Down by the river,
All the world our own
Down by the river.
Maybe the river made our love song start.
Full was the river, yet more full my heart.
So I love you two,
You and the river,
I'll be there for you,
I and the river.

You will remember when you hear my song
Down where the river rolls along.

IT'S EASY
TO REMEMBER

Published March 1935. Refrain registered for copyright as an unpublished song by Paramount Productions, Inc., November 16, 1934. Verse finished February 1935. Introduced by Bing Crosby. Alternate title: "Easy to Remember."

VERSE

With you I owned the earth.
With you I ruled creation.
No you, and what's it worth?
It's just an imitation.

REFRAIN

Your sweet expression,
The smile you gave me,
The way you looked when we met—
It's easy to remember,
But so hard to forget.
I hear you whisper,
"I'll always love you,"
I know it's over, and yet—
It's easy to remember,
But so hard to forget.
So I must dream
To have your hand caress me,
Fingers press me tight.
I'd rather dream
Than have that lonely feeling
Stealing through the night.
Each little moment
Is clear before me,
And though it brings me regret—
It's easy to remember
And so hard to forget.

THE NOTORIOUS
COLONEL BLAKE

Registered for copyright as an unpublished song by Paramount Productions, Inc., August 22, 1934. Dropped from the film before it was released.

REFRAIN 1

Look at him! Look at her!
Sparkin' down the street.
Who is him? Who is her?
She looks mighty sweet.
That's the boy who killed three men.
Hush for goodness' sake.
He's that shootin' stabbin' smilin'
Most notorious Colonel Blake.
Look, miss, there goes Colonel Blake!
Colonel Blake. Oh, that's a big mistake.
He shot seven men and threw their bodies in the lake.
He's that laughin' sneerin' snarlin' fiend
Notorious Colonel Blake.

REFRAIN 2

Look at him! Look at her!
I remember when
In a fight he destroyed
Twenty-seven men.
Shot seven hundred with his gun
For that young lady's sake.
He's that death-defying killer
Most notorious Colonel Blake.
Hats off! There goes Colonel Blake.
That's him, darling, you must keep awake.
He stabbed seven thousand men and you couldn't stab a cake!
He's that shootin' stabbin' smilin'
Most notorious Colonel Blake.

PABLO, YOU ARE
MY HEART

Registered for copyright as an unpublished song by Paramount Productions, Inc., August 22, 1934. Dropped before the film was released. Music was reworked later to become "Johnny One-Note" in *Babes in Arms* (1937).

VERSE

Mexico is full of many handsome caballeros,
Tipping their sombreros,
Bowing to the knee.
I've a lot of lovers from the border to the border,
Running in disorder,
Dashing after me.

REFRAIN 1

I dance with Pedro,
I walk with Pepito,

But, Pablo, you are my heart!
I like Ricardo,
I flirt with Lorenzo,
But, Pablo, you are my heart!
I promised Pancho that I'd share his rancho,
And told him we would never part.
I kissed Pepito, Ricardo, Lorenzo,
But they didn't count from the start,
For, Pablo, you are my heart.

REFRAIN 2

I laugh with Lopez,
I stay out with Gomez,
But, Pablo, you are my heart!
I squeeze Alvarez,
I tickle Rodriguez,
But, Pablo, you are my heart!
I told Gonzales I'd cook his tamales,
His love talk was a work of art.
Lopez, Rodriguez, Alvarez, Gonzales,
I can't tell those onions apart,
For, Pablo, you are my heart.

THE STEELY GLINT
IN MY EYE

Registered for copyright as an unpublished song by Paramount Productions Inc., August 17, 1934. Dropped before the film was released.

Every man is born a coward without a doubt
And the hero's just a coward turned inside out.
Now you're going to be a hero,
You're starting out at zero,
And the first thing you can learn is how to pull your weapons out.

My convenient little dagger
Makes desperados stagger
And my pistol makes a horse thief sigh
But if I want to scare them rigid
I just give them the frigid
Steely glint in my eye.

My good sword's a nasty omen
To an enemy's abdomen
And my cat-o'-nine-tails makes them cry
But if a cad my word should question
I could give 'im indigestion
With the steely glint in my eye.

I killed a man in Cincinnati.
He drew the fifth ace from his shoe.

For the thing that drove me batty
Is that I held five aces too.

Oh, my trusty little cutlass
Has made many villains gutless.
My tomahawk is never shy.
But I make strong men crawl like lizards
And go creeping on their gizzards
With the steely glint in my eye.

MISCELLANEOUS, 1930–1935

During the early 1930s, when Rodgers and Hart worked primarily in Hollywood, they wrote songs for a number of miscellaneous ventures. At least two of the lyrics from this period are missing. They are: "Rest Room Rose" (introduced by Fanny Brice in the Billy Rose Broadway revue *Crazy Quilt*, 1931), and "What Are You Doing in Here?" (introduced by the chorus of the hit musical *Anything Goes* to open *The Post-Depression Gaieties*, a revue presented for one performance by Marc Connelly for the benefit of the Authors League Fund and the Stage Relief Fund, New Amsterdam Theatre, New York, February 24, 1935).

HANDS

Unfinished song. Probably written 1930–1932. No music survives. Lyric found by Theodore S. Chapin in the Rodgers and Hammerstein office.

I do men's nails for seventy-five cents—
And I guess I earn my pay.
Kindly realize that a heel or two
Get a manicure plus a feel or two!
God, how I hate their hands!

Brokers, clerks and singers—
Arthur, John and Bill,
Each time you touch their fingers
They think you get a thrill.

I do men's nails for seventy-five cents
And in case you think that price is immense
Kindly realize that a heel or two
Get their manicure and a feel or two!
God, how I hate their hands!

. . .

If you think girls are vain
You should watch one of those males.
Squeeze a lady's hand while she's
Polishing his nails—
He thinks she's hot and even more so,
Just dying to grab that manly torso

God, how I hate their hands!
Hands can tear one asunder,
I go through torture nobody understands.
Stop it! My life is a nightmare!
Hands! Hands! Hands! Hands! Hands!

Hands can hold you and hurt you,
Hands can grip;
Hands can laugh at your virtue,
Hands can slip;
Hands can tear your heart out,
Hands can make you dream.
What a fool you seem.
You could scream.

Hands can hold you and hurt you,
Hands can grip;
Hands can laugh at your virtue,
Hands can slip;
Hands can beg for mercy,
I'm afraid of you.
I am black and blue.
This won't do.

Hands can hold you and hurt you,
Hands can grip.
Hands can laugh at your virtue stands
My God, they're driving me crazy
With their goddamn hands.

SOMEONE MUST BE GETTING MARRIED SOMEWHERE

Probably written 1930–1932. No music survives. Lyric found by Theodore S. Chapin in the Rodgers and Hammerstein office.

There are fifty million laundrymen in China;
Someone must be getting married somewhere.
A million Colonels vote in Carolina;
Someone must be getting married somewhere.
Ten thousand politicians hail from the county Cork;
Six hundred crooked judges run the county of New York.

And fifty million Frenchmen that do business with the stork.
Someone must be getting married somewhere.

All the chickens know their eggs in northern Prussia;
Someone must be getting married somewhere.
Every sturgeon knows his caviar in Russia;
Someone must be getting married somewhere.
Ten thousand Tiller girls arrive from London ev'ry day;
We've a hundred million playwrights who can almost write a play;
And the dresses that Lane Bryant sells are not so décolleté;
Someone must be getting married somewhere.

There are fifty thousand rabbis in Manhattan;
Someone must be getting married somewhere.
People never fish upon the isle of Staten;
Someone must be getting married somewhere.
There are sixteen Spanish dancers born in Harlem every day;
The prophets up in Utah haven't any time to pray;
And seven million critics who could all improve this play;
Someone must be getting married somewhere.

RHYTHM

Introduced by Beatrice Lillie in the London revue *Please* (1933) and *The Show Is On* (1936).

Rhythm! Rhythm! Rhythm! Rhythm!
There's rhythm in the treetops,
There's rhythm under the sea,
There's rhythm in this heart of mine!
(La-de-dah!)
There's rhythm in the wee tots,
And baby, take it from me,
There's rhythm in this heart of mine!
(Zaz-zoo-zaz!)
Rudyard Kipling
Wrote a poem in rhythm,
With a rippling
"You're a better man than I am, Gunga Din!"
There's rhythm in the rainbow,
The sun is going to shine,
There's rhythm in this heart of mine!

Rhythm! Rhythm! Rhythm! Rhythm!
There's rhythm in this heart of—
I got rhythm, I got "AH!!!"
Who could ask for anything more!

There's rhythm in the wee tots!
When there are grey skies,
I don't mind the grey skies!
I don't mind the blue skies—
Blue skies shining at me,
Nothing but blue skies do I
See the pretty apple, top of the tree,
The higher up the sweeter it grows
Of Washington Square,
I'm withering there, 'cause
I got rhythm, I got "AH!!!"
And baby, take it from me,
There's rhythm in this heart of mine!

Even Sousa
Wrote a march in rhythm.
You can't choose a
Better beat to tickle your feet.
And baby, take it from me,
The sun is going to shine.
There's rhythm in this heart of mine!
Rhythm! Rhythm! Rhythm!
RHYTHM!

THAT'S LOVE

Published February 1934. Registered as an unpublished song by Irving Berlin, Inc., August 21, 1933. Introduced by Anna Sten in the 1934 film *Nana*.

VERSE

Why say forever
There's never any love forever;
But, my dear,
Why not place my head between your arms
In tenderest embrace.
Love's but a moment that's splendid,
Though it soon is ended.
That's my way.
Why regret
That we met
And loved today.

REFRAIN

Kiss me and say goodbye,
That's love.
Laugh with a gay goodbye,
That's love.
Press my body tight and crush my lips,
Hush my lips with yours.
Though it's just a night,
Why measure it?
Treasure it, it's yours.

If I'm your light of love,
Who cares?
While I've a night of love,
Who cares?
When my lips have made you happy,
Leave my arms without a sigh,
I'll never ask you why.
That's love. Goodbye.

YOU ARE SO LOVELY AND I'M SO LONELY

Published April 1935. Introduced by Walter Pidgeon in the Broadway play *Something Gay*, which ran for seventy-two performances at the Morosco Theatre, New York, beginning April 29, 1935.

VERSE

Don't know where I'm heading
And I feel a bit like shedding
A tear when you're not here.
I feel, looking at you,
You're as lovely as a statue.
It's not a mere infatuation, dear!

REFRAIN

You are so lovely
And I'm so lonely;
When loveliness meets loneliness,
You have romance.
You're much more lovely,
I'm much less lonely,
When your two eyes reward my sighs
With just a glance.
This great big universe would be too small to
  hold me
If you just told me
I had a chance.
You are so lovely
And I'm so lonely;
When loveliness meets loneliness,
You have romance.

I'LL TAKE A LITTLE OF YOU ON TOAST

Introduced by Helen Morgan, Ken Murray, and ensemble on *Let's Have Fun*. Radio broadcast, October 22, 1935. No

score survives. Lyric has been transcribed from an air check, and many words, including the entire verse, are inaudible.

REFRAIN 1

I want no cottage small,
I want no waterfall,
No skies of blue at all,
I'll take a little of you on toast.
Keep your sweet summer breeze,
Also that song called "Trees,"
I don't want "Mammy's Knees,"
I'll take a little of you on toast.
Oh, for happiness I am pining
For a shining rainbow.
Skies will have a quicksilver lining
If I am your main beau.
Your smile is nice and kind;
Your charms are well designed.
Darling, if you don't mind,
I'll take a little on toast.

REFRAIN 2

We want no desert man,
We want no caravan,
But an American,
We'll take a little of you on toast.
Though we'd have loved a bid,
Some nights we kiss and kid.
We're sick of pyramids.
We'll take a little of you on toast.
All your melodies sound entrancing
When the desert sun sinks.
When we listen to your romancing,
Who cares what the Sphinx thinks?
We're tired of [*inaudible*]
You're full of desert play,
You're what our tastes [*inaudible*]
We want a little on toast.

REFRAIN 3

I want no caviar,
No chocolate diamond bar;
One thing I want so far,
I'll take a little of you on toast.
Don't give me consommé,
I'll skip the fish today;
But for a small entree,
I'll take a little on toast.
We've prepared for your execution;
Smile, sir, if you can, now.
In this drama of retribution
You're the leading man now.
Down on the river Nile
There's a big crocodile;

You know what makes him smile.
He'll take a little on toast.

PLEASE MAKE ME BE GOOD

Introduced by Helen Morgan, Ken Murray, and ensemble in *Let's Have Fun.* Radio broadcast October 22, 1935. No score survives. Lyric has been transcribed from an air check, and many words from the patter are inaudible.

VERSE

My lips want attention.
Take them by storm.
My hands, need I mention,
Must be kept warm.
All in good form.

REFRAIN

Please make me be good,
Heed all of my glances,
Don't take any chances,
Please make me be good.
I'm not made of wood,
No trouble with my sight,
Keep me within eyesight,
Please make me be good.
I adore you,
But my foot can slip.
I implore you,
Hold me tight,
Don't let me slip.
Be firm as you should,
And while you caress me,
Be sure to outguess me,
Please make me be good.

PATTER

Good morning, Mr. Strook.
Good morning, Mr. Iceman.
Come on, no one can hook.
Stop it, like a nice man.
What's new around the palace?
Is Cleo up to new tricks?
There's a blonde in [*inaudible*]
Can show that guy a few tricks.
Today's young man is tomorrow's [*inaudible*]
She'll take a little of him on toast.
Second edition is on the press.
Coming! Coming!
Let me see that galley.
It's time to cease for the headline.

Deadline for the third edition.
Yes sir, mister editor.
Now listen here, you cub.
How can I print that story?
You wrote it like a dub.
Why, that story is a sensation.
That's what I'm driving at.
Our family circulation
Will never stand for that.
Why I got the story from a slavegirl.
She told it without malice.
She got it straight from her boyfriend,
The iceman at the palace.
Cleopatra's pleading
For Dickie's curly head.
If Cleopatra loves him,
Print a story that he's dead.
Hey, you kid!
Hey, you kid!
Writing hieroglyphics on the pyramid.
Making chalk marks on the pyramid.
What's this?
What did they write?
Cleo loves Dickie.
Dickie loves the queen.
Will she give him
Serpents teeth or Paris Green?
He'll lie as he should.
Or [*inaudible*]
[*inaudible*]
She'll make him be good.

2ND ENDING

Watch me as you should.
When lovers get placid,
They get [*inaudible*] acid.
Please make me be good.

The three following lyrics cannot be further identified or precisely dated.

YOU CARRY MY HEART

VERSE

I'm affectionate and gentle,
In fact, I'm very sentimental,
And yet I walk around without a heart!
I've been told by my physician
That I'm in wonderful condition
And yet I walk around without a heart!
You ought to know
Why this is so.
You ought to know.

REFRAIN

You carry my heart.
I have to be near you.
It beats with joy to hear you
Speak my name.
Take care of my heart.
Hear how it entreats you,
So happily it heats you
With its flame,
Filled with love,
Beating with deepest emotion,
Instilled with love,
Throbbing away like the ocean!
You carry my heart.
You'll have it forever.
I know that we can never live apart.
You hold my heart.

STEPS

Step by step, mile by mile,
Footsore, weary and blue,
I'm marching home to you.
Mile by mile, town by town,
With love that is true
I'm marching home to you.
I'm tired of striving for success,
Seeking happiness!
Where did it get me?
Where did it get me?
Roaming here and there,
Wandering everywhere,
What did it get me?
Regret and sorrow!
Step by step, mile by mile,
With my troubles I'm through,
I'm marching home to you.

THE DESERT LULLABY

The voice of the desert is calling me,
Eternally ca-halling me.
The light of the desert in your eyes I see,
Gleaming, beaming, dreaming, scheming.
Sweetheart, the camels are wai-haiting,
They constantly wai-hait for me.
And ev'ry star shiny in the sky
Sings the desert lullaby!

JUMBO | 1935

Produced by Billy Rose at the Hippodrome, New York, November 16, 1935–April 18, 1936. 233 performances. Music by Richard Rodgers. Lyrics by Lorenz Hart. Book by Ben Hecht and Charles MacArthur. Production staged by John Murray Anderson. Book directed by George Abbott. Equestrian, acrobatic, and aerial dances by Allen K. Foster. Production and theatre designed by Albert Johnson. Costumes by Raoul Pene DuBois. Additional costumes by Wynn and James Reynolds. Orchestra under the direction of Adolph Deutsch. Orchestrations by Adolph Deutsch, Murray Cutler, Joseph Nussbaum, Hans Spialek, and Conrad Salinger. Cast, starring Jimmy Durante and Paul Whiteman and his orchestra, included Donald Novis, Gloria Grafton, Poodles Hanneford, and Bob Lawrence.

OVER AND OVER AGAIN

Published November 1935. Introduced by Bob Lawrence and Henderson's Singing Razorbacks (members of the ensemble). Music was originally "The Party Waltz" and was written for *Hollywood Party* (1934).

RINGMASTER: Swing high, swing low upon the
trapeze.
At first you'll fall but then
A year from now you'll do it with
ease
Over and over and over again.
A star does not come out of the
sky;
He starts to work at ten.
To reach the top you've got to
keep trying
Over and over again.
Up in the morning and down in
the ring,
Acrobat, rider and clown;
Queen of the wire and aerial
king,
Work or you'll forfeit your crown.
Stick to your trick and your trick
will be art;
Artists are hardworking men.
After you're perfect that's when
you first start
Over and over again.

RAZORBACKS: Once again, and again,
Do it over and over again.
Swing high, swing low upon the
trapeze.
At first you'll fall but then

To reach the top you've got to
keep trying
Over and over again.

STAKE DRIVERS: Drive those stakes into the
ground!
Hit 'em, hit 'em, Bo!
Gotta raise a mile of canvas!
Hit 'em, hit 'em, hit 'em, hit 'em,
Over and over again.

CLOWN: For seven years I practiced
falling on my face,
For seven years I practiced
bouncing on my knee,
For seven more I fell upon
another place,
It took that long to make an
artist out of me.
Over and over again.

MANAGER: I route the show from Kokomo to
Oskaloosa,
Haverstraw and Chickasaw and
Syracusa,
Saratoga and Tioga and Lake
Gypsy,
And we play New York, but play
it in Poughkeepsie.
Over and over again.

DOCTOR: I have to operate on elephants
and men,
And when a tiger cub is born I'm
in the den;
I have to treat a leopard when it
has neuritis,
And climb a ladder when the
giraffe has tonsillitis.
Over and over again.

ALL: Once again and again
RINGMASTER: Do it over and over again.
MANAGER: Not so good, my lass. You'll have
to do it over.

CHORUS: Swing high, swing low upon the
trapeze.
At first you'll fall but then
A year from now you'll do it with
ease
Over and over and over again.
A star does not come out of the
sky;
He starts to work at ten.
To reach the top you've got to
keep trying
Over and over again.

THE CIRCUS IS ON PARADE

Published November 1935. Introduced by Henderson's Singing Razorbacks.

VERSE

Listen to me now before you quit.
You must agree now, you must admit,
There was a circus in days of yore,
There'll be a circus forever more.
Show me a mammal with heart and pride
Who sees a camel and doesn't want to take a
ride.
Barnum has never died.
Every time the circus music starts
Here's the happy song in people's hearts:

REFRAIN

Hold your hoss, here they come,
Rat-tat-tat goes the drum,
The circus is on parade.
See the clown falling down,
It's the best show in town,
The circus is on parade.
See the monk climb the rope,
Hear the steam calliope,
Buy me a lemonade.
Look-a-here, look-a-there,
Throw your hats in the air,
For the Big Parade.

TRIO

From Broadway to Main Street,
From Main Street to Broadway,
Ev'ry Main Street becomes an insane street
The minute the band begins to play.
No matter if it's raining,
Or ninety in the shade,
Ev'ry kid plays the hook.
Teacher, take a look;
There stands the second grade.
All the world is in short pants
To see the circus on parade.

REPEAT REFRAIN

THE MOST BEAUTIFUL GIRL IN THE WORLD

Published November 1935. Introduced by Donald Novis and Gloria Grafton.

VERSE

We used to spend the spring together
Before we learned to walk;
We used to laugh and sing together
Before we learned how to talk.
With no reason for the season,
Spring would end as it would start.
Now the season has a reason
And there's springtime in my heart.

REFRAIN

The most beautiful girl in the world
Picks my ties out,
Eats my candy,
Drinks my brandy—
The most beautiful girl in the world.
The most beautiful star in the world
Isn't Garbo, isn't Dietrich,
But the sweet trick
Who can make me believe it's a beautiful
   world.
Social—not a bit,
Nat'ral kind of wit,
She'd shine anywhere,
And she hasn't got platinum hair.
The most beautiful house in the world
Has a mortgage—
What do I care?
It's goodbye care
When my slippers are next to the ones that
   belong
To the one and only beautiful girl in the
   world!

TRIO PATTER

SHE: Climb off your perch and go home with
       your dreams.
 HE: No, ma'am, I'm in love.
SHE: Where did you think of such elegant
       schemes?
 HE: Here, ma'am, up above.
SHE: Do you think that kind of blarney
       Will win a woman's heart?
 HE: Little daughter of Killarney,
       That heart was mine from the start.
SHE: I'd slap your face if I had you down here.
 HE: Presto, here I come.
SHE: Careful, dear.

 HE: Have no fear.
SHE: Darling, look out,
       Or you'll fall on your ear.
 HE: Which side?
SHE: Outside.
 HE: Which side?
SHE: This side.

REPEAT REFRAIN

LAUGH

Introduced by Jimmy Durante and ensemble.

You gotta laugh, laugh, laugh
When things are catastrophic;
You gotta laugh, laugh, laugh
And take it philostrophic.
I remember years ago when you were just a baby
We were playing this very town—
Always a hard-luck town for the Considine
   Wonder Shows.
A guy walks up to me and says,
Are you Brainy Bowers?
I said yes, I'm Brainy Bowers.
He says, *the* Brainy Bowers?
I said sure—
And with that he hands me a paper—
A suppenee!
You could have eliminated me from the Olympic
   Games!
But I laughed—I laughed him out of it.
And only yesterday I was strolling through a
   department store,
The Boston store in Minneapolis,
When a guy walks up to me and said,
Would you like to go to Florida?
I said sure—
He said O.K., here's a palm for you.
He rendered me incognito!
Then I strolls over to the chemise department.
I don't know why, but there I was in the chemise
   department,
A lone wolf—unescorted!
When suddenly I see the same guy coming
   straight towards me, saying,
So that's the kind of a guy you are, huh?
A chemise fancier—a twiddle twa—
Me a twiddle twa!
That meant fight!
I makes a leap for him,
He makes a leap for me—he connects!
Then what do I do?
I resorted to jiujitsu.

I grabbed his wrist with one hand
And with the other I twisted his leg around his
   neck—
And first thing you know—
I'm flat on my back.
I gets up kinda wobbly,
Gathers all my strength—
And I was off—
Yes, I was off—
Off like a toupee in a windstorm—
But he overtakes me,
Grabs me and throws me against the wall.
I bounces back.
Again he throws me against the wall.
Again I bounces back.
A handball player!
But to show him what kind of a guy I was,
I gets up, and what do I do?
I throws myself against the wall
And bounces back, singing:
Billy, Billy, bounce—your baby boy—
Billy, Billy, bounce—your baby boy—
Billy, Billy, bounce—
Ah—the place is too small for my steps.
So, Mickey, whenever you're in trouble
I want you to always remember the password:
Chin up,
Old bean—and stand the gaff—
Be a Pagliacci and laugh,
Ha-ha,
Ho-ho,
Be a Pagliacci and laugh.
You ain't laughin'.
I've struck out.
Maybe I need some assistance.
O.K. Bring on the Pagliaccis.

MY ROMANCE

Published November 1935. Introduced by Donald Novis and Gloria Grafton.

VERSE

I won't kiss your hand, madam,
Crazy for you though I am.
I'll never woo you on bended knee.
No, madam, not me.
We don't need that flow'ry fuss.
No, sir, madam, not for us.

REFRAIN

My romance
Doesn't have to have a moon in the sky.

My romance
Doesn't need a blue lagoon standing by.
No month of May,
No twinkling stars.
No hideaway,
No soft guitars.
My romance
Doesn't need a castle rising in Spain
Nor a dance
To a constantly surprising refrain.
Wide awake,
I can make
My most fantastic dreams come true.
My romance
Doesn't need a thing but you.

LITTLE GIRL BLUE

Published November 1935. Introduced by Gloria Grafton.

REFRAIN

Sit there and count your fingers.
What can you do?
Old girl, you're through.
Sit there and count your little fingers,
Unlucky little girl blue.

Sit there and count the raindrops
Falling on you.
It's time you knew
All you can count on is the raindrops
That fall on little girl blue.

No use, old girl,
You may as well surrender.
Your hope is getting slender.
Why won't somebody send a tender
Blue Boy, to cheer a
Little girl blue?

TRIO PATTER

When I was very young
The world was younger than I,
As merry as a carousel.
The circus tent was strung
With ev'ry star in the sky
Above the ring I loved so well.
Now the world has grown old.
Gone are the tinsel and gold.

REPEAT REFRAIN

SONG OF THE ROUSTABOUTS

Introduced by Henderson's Singing Razorbacks. While virtually all of the lyric is missing, a few lines were written in on the conductor's score, which is located at the Rodgers and Hammerstein office.

Oh, there ain't no job in Omaha
. . . .
So we're goin'
Yes, we're goin'
. . . .
. . . .
Ain't no money to be made—Santa Fe
. . . .
So we're goin'
. . . .
. . . .
Yes, we're goin'—goin'!
. . . .
Oh, we don't know where we're goin'
But we're on our way
Oh, the girls are mean in Aberdeen
. . . .
To meet you at the train
. . . .

WOMEN

Introduced by Jimmy Durante. The first version was found in the score Richard Rodgers donated to the Music Division of the Library of Congress. The second version is included in a typescript of the libretto.

Version 1

When you go to the circus
What do you see?
A hippopotamus.
Who wants to see a hippopotamus?
Only another hippopotamus.
Put twelve acrobats up there
With lumpy muscles
Hanging by their shoes!
Fill the ring with elephants,
Lions, tigers and boxing kangaroos.
I'll even let you throw in a penguin.
Then have a beautiful, voluptuous
Woman walk down the center of the ring

As illustrated.
Who will they look at?
It don't need an answer.
In studying the situation
I get an inspiration.
Men. Men like to see women!
And I'm the first one who ever thought of it.
Cash in on it.
Instead of men
Get a lady orchestra.
Bring 'em up on a rising floor.
The rising floor has been done before,
But we can claim it.
Take out the ring and put in a swimming pool.
Don't fill it with water,
Fill it with perfume.
Sashay la Femme!
Number Three!
They'll pay a bonanzo to see it!

REFRAIN

Send the Arabs back to Araby,
Send the jugglers back to Japan.
Swarm the place with women.
Pulchritude!
And I don't mean longitude.
Throw out your elephants.
All right. An elephant never forgets.
But what has he got to remember?
Put a dozen girls on the flying trapeze
Wearing eleven pink chemises,
Swinging coy, glamorous and whimsical.
It'll tear your heart out!
They laughed at Edison when he invented the steamboat.
They laughed at Marconi when he invented the wireless.
And we're laughing at the greatest inventor of all.
Exploiting women, I'm a pioneer.

Version 2

When you go to the circus, what do you see?
A hippopotamus.
An' who wants to see a hippopotamus?
Only another hippopotamus!
I've studied the situation, an' I've got an inspiration.
Men . . . Men like to see women!
And I'm the first one that ever thought of it.
I'm open for congratulations!
I'm not talkin' from hearsay or hunger.
Believe me, this is bigger than Einstein!
Let me prove my argument.
Put twelve acrobats up there, hangin' by their toes!

Fill the ring with elephants, lions, tigers,
    kangaroos!
I'll even let you throw in a penguin.
Then have a beautiful, voluptuous woman walk
    down the center of the ring
As illustrated.
Who will they look at?
I don't need an answer.
Do what I tell you and you'll have the greatest
    show this side of oblivion.
The lights in the arena are very low.
You see nothin'.
Slowly the lights come up—gradually.
Still you see nothin'.
Then you ask for a magenta.
I'll illustrate it.
Give us a red!
Now gimme a blue!
I said, gimme a blue!
I gotta right to see the blues!
Gimme a blue! I said a blue!
Never mind. That's near enough. Your union
    ain't too strong.
I never forget a face! Then suddenly you hear
    trumpets in the distance—
That's not a trumpet!
That's not a trumpet!
That's a trumpet!
Then out of a clear sky, a chocolate-colored sky,
You see women—
There—there—there—an'
Over there!
I see you're not interested.
It's goin' in one eye an' out the other.
O.K. I'll give you a demonstration.
Not with lions, not with tigers, but—
Women! Women! Women!
Ballet routine!
Go!
Why, they're marvelous! Superb!
An early spring.
That's it, keep it classical.
What's that!
I'm answered!
Hold it!
That's what'll get you the money.
At ease!
Send your Arabs back to Araby,
Send your jugglers to Japan.
Throw out your ring,
Put in a swimming pool!
Don't fill it with water,
Fill it with perfume.
Not Mary Garden, not Christmas Night,
But Sashay la Femme—Number Three!
Surround me!
What happened? My back was turned.

Make a picture.
The fox hunt!
Change!
The landing of the Pilgrims.
At ease!
Throw out your elephants.
I know there's a saying goin' around,
An elephant never forgets.
What has he got to remember?
Every girl up on your toes,
The public wants to see you pose,
Standin' there
Coy, glamorous an' whimsical—
The Children's Hour!
Why, it'll tear their hearts out.

MEMORIES OF MADISON SQUARE GARDEN

Introduced by ensemble.

VERSE

We were stars long ago
When your dad used to come to the show.
Though it's so long ago
We were stars.

REFRAIN

When the circus played the Garden
Down on Madison Square,
We were the shining stars
On the trapeze and bars.
Ev'ry social swell and Bow'ry belle applauded us
    there.
We could stand up with the best of them there
    and do our share.
Strike the band up and we'll do it again
Way down on Madison Square.
Times have changed
Since the show that we played
For your ma and her beau
When New York was New York long ago.

DIAVOLO

Published November 1935. Introduced by Bob Lawrence
and Henderson's Singing Razorbacks.

RINGMASTER: Razorbacks!
RAZORBACKS: Ready, boss!
RINGMASTER: Roustabouts!
ROUSTABOUTS: Ready, boss!
RINGMASTER: Men with the rifles!
MEN WITH
    RIFLES: Ready, boss!
RINGMASTER: Set 'er up, boys!
MEN SETTING
    UP CAGES: Set 'er up—
      Who will risk his life tonight to
        thrill the mob?
      Who has a date
      Tonight with fate?
DAREDEVIL
(DIAVOLO): Diavolo!
    MEN: Set 'er up—
      Who will risk his life to make their
        pulses throb?
      Who runs a race
      With time and space?
DAREDEVIL: Diavolo!
    MEN: Set 'er up—
      Who depends on Lady Luck to
        keep his job?
      Who knows no fear
      While people cheer?
      Who'll die because
      He loves applause?
      Whose nerves are hardy?
      Who is the star?

REFRAIN

DAREDEVIL: Diavolo the thrill king,
      Diavolo is still king.
      With no fear of death,
      He keeps clear of death,
      Zooming through the air.
      Diavolo, the fearless,
      Diavolo, the peerless,
      Stars will never come.
      Who can ever compare!
THE BOYS: Who remembers Flying Clayton
      And the night he died in Dayton?
DAREDEVIL: Outlined in silver light above,
      Nerves tense and muscles tight
        above.
      Perched on his dizzy height above.
THE BOYS: Steady! Steady!
      Are you ready?
DAREDEVIL: Diavolo, they're breathless,
      Diavolo, you're deathless.
      Spotlights catch you up
      Like a statue up there!
THE BOYS: Who remembers Dan Costello?
      Greatest of them all, poor fellow.
DAREDEVIL: Laugh at death, Diavolo!

THE MORE I SEE OF OTHER GIRLS

Probably unused. Alternate title: "Elephant Song." Music and lyric at the Music Division of the Library of Congress, Washington, D.C. The Act II finale, "The Circus Wedding," was a production number which reprised earlier material. It included no new lyric.

The more I see of other girls,
The more I care for you,
For those old but new
Little things you do.
I love that face and figure grace-
Ful as a willow tree.
Madam, hear my plea,
Don't fall down on me.
Eyes that say so much,
Tiny feet that twinkle,

Skin I love to touch,
What's a little wrinkle?
The more I see of other girls
And what those damsels do,
More and more I care for you!

OVERLEAF: Tamara Geva and Ray Bolger in *On Your Toes*

ON YOUR TOES
DANCING PIRATE
ALL POINTS WEST
1936

ON YOUR TOES, 1936

Tryout: Shubert Theatre, Boston, March 21–April 8, 1936. New York run: Imperial Theatre, New York, April 11 November 29, 1936; Majestic Theatre, November 30, 1936–January 23, 1937. 315 performances. Music by Richard Rodgers. Lyrics by Lorenz Hart. Produced by Dwight Deere Wiman. Book by Richard Rodgers, Lorenz Hart, and George Abbott. Staged by Worthington Miner and George Abbott (uncredited). Choreography by George Balanchine. Settings by Jo Mielziner. Costumes by Irene Sharoff. Orchestra under the direction of Gene Salzer. Orchestrations by Hans Spialek. Cast, starring Ray Bolger, Luella Gear, and Tamara Geva, included Doris Carson and Monty Woolley. Vocal score published 1985.

TWO A DAY FOR KEITH

Published June 1952. Introduced by Dave Jones, Ethel Hampton, and Tyrone Kearney. Titled "Twice a Night" in the London production (1937) and introduced there by Philip Morgan, Irene North, and Barrie Manning.

VERSE

PHIL II (PA): I worked for Keith when I married
    Lil.
LIL (MA): And after a year I got young Phil.
PHIL II: I couldn't pay the hospital bill.
PHIL III
(JUNIOR): So I was born in vaudeville.

REFRAIN 1

ALL 3: It's two a day for Keith
    And three a day for Loew;
    Pantages plays us four a day
    Besides the supper show;
    But you're our fav'rite audience
    No matter where we go;
    With two a day for Keith
    And three a day for Loew.
PHIL II: Remember my dad, old Phil the
    first?
LIL: And Phil the Second is not the
    worst.
PHIL III: As a dancing fool Phil the Third is
    cursed.

REFRAIN 2

ALL 3: It's two a day for Keith
    And three a day for Loew;
    For Fally-Marcus five a day
    For half as much the dough.
    We never will forget you folks
    Right here in Kokomo,
    With two a day for Keith
    And three a day for Loew.
    No, we never will forget you folks
    Right here in Kokomo,
    With two a day for Keith
    And three a day for Loew.

THE THREE B'S

Introduced by Ray Bolger and ensemble. Alternate title: "Questions and Answers." Registered for copyright in 1952 as "Questions and Answers," but listed in the script and program of the original 1936 production as "The Three B's."

JUNIOR: Your music, fortunately, is much better than your manners. And now, before we finish for the day, there are a few elementary questions I would like to ask. For instance—
[*Plays a few bars of César Franck symphony*]
    Whom was this written by?
MISS WASSERVOGEL: By César Franck.*
JUNIOR: Pronounce it "Fronck."
[*Plays a few bars of "Les Préludes"*]
    Name this for me, Joe McCall.
MCCALL: We won't get home until
    morning . . .
JUNIOR: You won't get home at all!
    Now, please name the
    Russians
    Who love to use percussions.
CLASS: Tchaikovsky, Moszkowski,
    Mussorgsky, Stravinsky.
JUNIOR: And what did Shostakovich
    write?
SIDNEY COHN: "Lady Macbeth from Minsky."
JUNIOR: Four masters I quote now.
    You tell me what they wrote
    now.
    Puccini, Bellini, Von Suppé,
    Von Bülow.
COHN: Puccini wrote "Poor
    Butterfly."

Pronounced with New York accent: "Seezer Frank."

JUNIOR: That answer hits a new low!
    Who are the three B's of
    music?
    Name the holy trinity
    Whose true divinity
    Goes stretching to infinity.
    No asininity
    In this vicinity.
    Who are the three B's of
    music?

REFRAIN

CLASS: Bach, Beethoven and Brahms.
    Great examples of the charms
    of Orpheus
    Throw us right into the arms
    of Morpheus.
JUNIOR: Johannes B.
    Ludwig van B.
    And Johann—
CLASS: Be sure to sing their praise.
    You will never get the old
    diploma here
    If they catch you whistling
    "La Paloma" here.
JUNIOR: Two of them wrote
    symphonies
    And one wrote psalms.
CLASS: Bach, Beethoven and Herr
    Johannes Brahms!
    Rossini, Bellini,
    Campanini, Tetrazzini,
    Cambini, Trentini,
    Martini, Paganini,
    Stokowski, Godowsky,
    Levitski, Leschetizsky,
    Wolf-Ferrari, Molinari,
    And the man who wrote
    "Sari."
FRANKIE: There isn't one name ending
    in a "vitch."
SIDNEY: You forget Borrah Minevitch!
[*All repeat refrain, beginning "Bach, Beethoven and Brahms" and ending "Herr Johannes Brahms"*]

IT'S GOT TO BE LOVE

Published March 1936. Introduced by Doris Carson and Ray Bolger.

VERSE

SHE: I love your eyes,
But I wouldn't know the color.
Aquamarine
Or em'rald green?
And if your hair
Couldn't possibly be duller,
The shade I see
Looks gold to me.
That's how naive I've grown to be.
Mais oui.

REFRAIN 1

It's got to be love!
It couldn't be tonsillitis;
It feels like neuritis,
But nevertheless it's love.
Don't tell me the pickles and pie à la mode
They served me
Unnerved me
And made my heart a broken-down pump.
It's got to be love!
It isn't the morning after
That makes every rafter
Go spinning around above.
I'm sure that it's fatal, or why do I get
That sinking feeling?
I think that I'm dead,
But nevertheless it's only love.

REFRAIN 2

HE: It's got to be love!
It could have been fallen arches
Or too many starches,
But nevertheless it's love.
Don't tell me the lamp in the barbershop
Gave me sunstroke.
With one stroke
You made me feel like yesterday's hash.
It's got to be love!
It couldn't be indigestion.
Beyond any question
I'm fluttery as a dove.
I've heard people say it's no worse than a
cold,
But, oh, that fever!
I'm burned to a crisp,
But nevertheless it's only love.

TOO GOOD FOR
THE AVERAGE MAN

Published May 1936. Introduced by Luella Gear and Monty Woolley.

VERSE

When Russia was white
It was white for the classes
And black for the masses.
Unfortunate asses!
All wealth belonged to few.
When England was Tudor
The King and his cronies
Had cocktails at Tony's.
The poor had baloneys,
And that's how England grew!
Sing "La and huzzah" for the poor folks
As long as the poor folks are your folks.

REFRAIN 1

Finer things are for the finer folk.
Thus society began.
Caviar for peasants is a joke.
It's too good for the average man.
Supper clubs are for the upper folk,
Packed like sardines in a can.
Through the smoke you get your check and
choke.
It's too good for the average man.
Each poor man has a wife he must stick to.
Men of fashion can be cocky.
To be caught in flagrante delicto
Is much too good for the average mockey!*
All-night parties, drinking like a lord,
Fit into our social plan.
Waking in the alcoholic ward
Is too good for the average man.

REFRAIN 2

Fancy nerves are for the fancy class
Since psychiatry began.
Neurasthenia isn't for the mass.
It's too good for the average man.
Patriotic talk against the Red
Is a plutocratic plan.
Sleeping with a bomb beneath his bed

*Revised lyric of refrain 1, lines 10 and 12:
Rich men have a diff'rent habit. . . .
Is much too good for the average rabbit.

Is too good for the average man.*
Lots of kids for a poor wife are dandy.
Girls of fashion can be choosy.
Birth control and the modus operandi
Are much too good for the average floozy!
Psychoanalysts are all the whirl.
Rich men pay them all they can.
Waking up to find that he's a girl
Is too good for the average man.

THERE'S A SMALL HOTEL

Published March 1936. Introduced by Doris Carson and Ray Bolger. "Comic Reprise" sung by Luella Gear and Monty Woolley.

VERSE

FRANKIE: I'd like to get away, Junior,
Somewhere alone with you.
It could be oh, so gay, Junior!
You need a laugh or two.
JUNIOR: A certain place I know, Frankie,
Where funny people can have fun.
That's where we two will go, darling,
Before you can count up
One, two, three,
For . . .

REFRAIN

There's a small hotel
With a wishing well;
I wish that we were there
Together.
There's a bridal suite,
One room bright and neat,
Complete for us to share
Together.

*Revised lyric of refrain 2, lines 5–8:
Rich old age can blossom like the rose.
Plastic surgeons have a plan.
Cutting up your face to spite your nose,
It's too good for the average man.
and:
Revised lyric of refrain 2, lines 1–8:
Rich old age can blossom like a rose,
Plastic surgeons have a plan.
Cutting off your face to spite your nose,
It's too good for the average man.
Fancy food is for the fancy taste,
Diet for the poorer man.
Gaining too much weight below the waste
Is too good for the average can.

Looking through the window
You can see a distant steeple.
Not a sign of people.
Who wants people?
When the steeple bell
Says, "Good night, sleep well,"
We'll thank the small hotel
Together.

INTERLUDE

Pretty window curtains made of chintz
In our make-believe land.
On the wall are sev'ral cheerful prints
Of Grant and Grover Cleveland.
Go down into the parlor and feast your
eyes
On the moosehead on the wall.
Perhaps you'd like to play the organ—
They tune it ev'ry other fall.
The garden will be like
Adam and Eve land.
No, they never did go in for carriage
trade;
They get what is known as marriage
trade.

CODA

Oh, when the steeple bell
Says, "Good night, sleep well,"*
We'll thank the small hotel,
We'll creep into our little shell,
And we will thank the small hotel
together.

COMIC REPRISE

There's a small hotel
Which we loved so well—
From there we'll get the air tomorrow.
One big bill to pay,
One old jazz ballet,
Is all we'll have to share tomorrow.
Looking through the window
Is a man with a subpoena.
If you lose that meanie
You're Houdini.
When the steeple bell
Says, "Good night, sleep well,"
We'll miss that small hotel
Together.

Alternate version of lines 2–3:
  Says, "Good night, sleep well,
  You very small hotel."

THE HEART IS QUICKER THAN THE EYE

Published March 1936. Introduced by Luella Gear and Ray Bolger.

VERSE

PEGGY: Dear old mother was as wise as ten folks
And she knew her way about the
menfolks.
Once she said to me, "Daughter, you're
quite a pup.
Daughter, dear, it's time to wise you up."
She said, "Love has always been my
hoodoo.
Though I've lived, I know much less than
you do."

REFRAIN 1

Mother told me there's no use asking
why
He loves she
And she loves he.
The heart is quicker than the eye!
Mother warned me that fair play doesn't
apply.
Turn your back
And love goes whack!
The heart is quicker than the eye!
Love can kill you off, baby, faster than
Flit.
It finds its mark, and, toots, you're it!
Dear sweet Mother was careful and so
sly!
But, my dear,
You see I'm here.
The heart is quicker than the eye!

PATTER

In December, Nineteen-five,
Mother got a little snootful.
In September, Nineteen-six,
I was born alive and beaut'ful.
I recall a few years later,
I was taken with the measles
And my darling little mater
Just sat up all night—
With a good-looking guy!
PHIL: Oh me! Oh my!
PEGGY: We would travel quite a lot,
But we always went to Reno.
She'd remarry like a shot—
Not for long, but how could she know?
Number four was a musician

Who could swing it sweet and hot.
Whistler's Mother is a classic,
Mother's whistler was not—
He was dropped like the rest.
PHIL: Mother always knows best.
It may seem strange to you—
I have a mother, too.

REFRAIN 2

PHIL: Mother told me, "Be good until you die."
She meant well, but could she tell
The heart is quicker than the eye?
Mother warned me my instincts to deny.
Yet I fail.
The male is frail.
The heart is quicker than the eye!
She said, "Love one time, Junior.
Look at the Lunts!"
I've fallen twice—with two at once.
Passion's plaything—that's me, oh me, oh
my!
But at least
I'm quite a beast.
The heart is quicker than the eye!

PATTER (spoken)

PHIL: Miss Porterfield, I want to
Thank you for your advice.
PEGGY: You're welcome.
PHIL: But it didn't do me any good.
PEGGY: I didn't think it would.
PHIL: Well, c'est la vie!
PEGGY: The same goes for me.
PHIL: I don't know which way to turn
Or which is which.
PEGGY: That's why I just told you
BOTH
(SUNG): The heart is quicker than the eye!

TAG

PEGGY: You say love is blind.
I say love's cockeyed, too.
The gift of gab obscures the view.
Mother begged me, "Don't drink with
any guy."
So I was made
On lemonade.
The heart is quicker than the rye!

First published version

VERSE

I'm the biggest fall guy in the nation,
And I fell for prestidigitation;
Not for sleight of hand,

But for sleight of heart,
My magician surely knew his art.
True, he doesn't look like Cagliostro—
In the theatre, even from the lahst row.

REFRAIN

Was it magic?
I fell and don't know why.
Never looked, but I was booked,
The heart is quicker than the eye.
Without magic—
He'd never attract a fly.
Mark ye well, he rang the bell.
The heart is quicker than the eye.
You say, love is blind,
I say, love's cockeyed too,
The gift of grab obscures the view.
Dear, sweet Cupid
Has hurled a custard pie;
But at least I love the beast.
The heart is quicker than the eye.

QUIET NIGHT

Published March 1936. Introduced by Earle MacVeigh and ensemble.

VERSE

Horace was a poet who adored the night;
In his verse he always underscored the night.
I recall what Horace said in Latin A—
"Never make your love affair a matinee!"
Wait till after dark
For that classical spark.

REFRAIN

Quiet night,
And all around
The calm and balmy weather;
Quiet night,
No other sound
But hearts that beat together.
You can almost hear the things I'm thinking;
You can almost see my heart take flight.
Whisper low,
But don't say, "No."
It's such a quiet night.

GLAD TO BE UNHAPPY

Published March 1936. Introduced by Doris Carson and David Morris.

VERSE

Look at yourself.
If you had a sense of humor,
You would laugh to beat the band.
Look at yourself.
Do you still believe the rumor
That romance is simply grand?
Since you took it right
On the chin,
You have lost that bright
Toothpaste grin.
My mental state is all a jumble.
I sit around and sadly mumble.

REFRAIN

Fools rush in, so here I am,
Very glad to be unhappy.
I can't win, but here I am,
More than glad to be unhappy.
Unrequited love's a bore
And I've got it pretty bad.
But for someone you adore,
It's a pleasure to be sad.
Like a straying baby lamb
With no mammy and no pappy,
I'm so unhappy,
But oh, so glad.

ON YOUR TOES

Published March 1936. Introduced by Doris Carson, Ray Bolger, David Morris, and ensemble.

REFRAIN

See the pretty apple, top of the tree,
The higher up, the sweeter it grows.
Picking fruit you've got to be
Up on your toes!
See the pretty penthouse, top of the roof,
The higher up, the higher rent goes.
Get that dough, don't be a goof;
Up on your toes!
They climb the clouds
To come through with airmail.
The dancing crowds

Look up to some rare male
Like that Astaire male.
See the pretty lady, top of the crop.
You want to know the way the wind blows?
Then, my boy, you'd better hop
Up on your toes!
Up on your toes!

VERSE

Remember the youth 'mid snow and ice
Who bore the banner with the strange device:
"Excelsior!"
This motto applies to folks who dwell in
Richmond Hill or New Rochelle, in
Chelsea or
In Sutton Place.
You've got to reach the heights to win the race.

REPEAT REFRAIN

DANCING PIRATE, 1936

An RKO Radio Film. Released June 1936. Music by Richard Rodgers. Lyrics by Lorenz Hart. Screenplay by Ray Harris and Francis Faragoh, based on a story, "Glorious Buccaneer," by Emma Lindsay-Squier. Directed by Lloyd Corrigan. Music conducted by Alfred Newman. Cast, starring Charles Collins, Frank Morgan, and Steffi Duna, included Luis Alberni, Victor Varconi, Jack Larue, and Alma Real.

ARE YOU MY LOVE?

Published April 1936. Introduced by Steffi Duna.

VERSE

No, no, I'm not so sure if he loves me.
What can I do?
No, no, that would be too much bliss.
Yes, yes, I know a way to discover
If he'll be true.
Yes, yes, my little plan won't miss.
I'll be brave and I'll ask him this.

REFRAIN

Are you my love?
Then life's begun for me.
Are you my love,
The moon and sun for me?
Are you my joy,
Are you my pain?
Are you my universe, earth and Heaven?
Are you a dream
That's overtaken me?
If you're a dream,
Then don't awaken me.
My heart must know or lose its beat.
Are you my love, my sweet?

WHEN YOU'RE DANCING THE WALTZ

Published April 1936. Introduced by Charles Collins and Steffi Duna.

VERSE

You were coy when we danced the minuet;
I cannot forget our halting conversation.
I'm afraid that the polka is too fast;
Not a word was passed,
To my deep consternation
Love has brought to life another dance,
Fragrant with the flower of romance.

REFRAIN

When you're dancing the waltz,
You must not lose your head (sir/ma'am).
When you're dancing the waltz,
Lose your shyness instead (sir/ma'am).
You are both vis-à-vis,
Let your fingers entwine,
You've no need for a secon' glass of wine.
Swaying,
Then it's one, two, three glide,
Let your reticence go (sir/ma'am).
Let (his/my) arm be (my/your) guide.
Not too closely, oh no (sir/ma'am),
For the dance of the day
Is exciting and gay.
You'll be carried away
When you're dancing the waltz.

ALL POINTS WEST, 1936

Symphonic narrative. Published March 1937. Introduced by Ray Middleton as soloist with Paul Whiteman and the Philadelphia Orchestra at the Academy of Music, Philadelphia, November 27 and 28, 1936. Also performed at the Hippodrome, New York, December 1, 1936; later performed at Radio City Music Hall, New York, June 1939.

(Chanted) Leavin' Track 33 at eleven
twenty-seven, the Great Lakes Express,
bound for Albany, Syracuse,
Rochester, Buffalo, Erie, Cleveland,
Toledo, Detroit, Kalamazoo.
(Sung) And all points West!
(Spoken) Clear enough, ain't it? Don't stand too
near the mike—that's the secret.
(Sung) Remember when we used to call 'em
Through megaphones?
Had to yell our lungs out.
Now it's easy.
(Spoken) What? Eleven twenty-nine? O.K. Ahem!
(Chanted) Leavin' Track 7 at eleven twenty-nine,
the Congressional Limited, bound for
Philadelphia, Wilmington, Baltimore,
Washington.
(Sung) And all points South!
(Spoken) That's an easy one. What a trainful.
That's old Senator Hawkins. Only comes
here to look at the musical shows and go
to cabarets.
(Sung) Now he's runnin' back
To make our laws.
Must be nice in Washington.
Never been to Washington.
Never was in Washington, D.C.
(Spoken) See that salesman with his sample cases
and his wife?
(Sung) She's kissing him goodbye.
A long, long trip.
She's whispering in his ear.
He promises.
Oh yes, he'll be true.
Oh yes, he'll be true.
Ha! Ha!
Those salesmen get around,
Must be marvelous!
Home is where your satchel is,
And fun on the train,
Fun on the train!
(Spoken) It's leavin' now!

(Sung) Pinochle,
Highballs,
Girl across the aisle,
Magazines, highballs,
And the girl across the aisle.
Start talkin' at Manhattan Transfer.
They talk, they talk!
Fun on the train,
Fun on the train.
I never get in 'em.
(Chanted) Eleven-fifty, Great Plains Express,
leavin' Track 12 at eleven-fifty. The
Great Plains Express, bound for
Philadelphia, Pittsburgh, Kankakee,
Des Moines, Omaha.
(Sung) And all points West!
(Spoken) Out West! There's a mother saying good-
bye to her boy. Go West, young man.
She's crying. They always cry. He'll be
going to get a job out there. They say
there's lots of jobs for any young man out
West. I ain't so young anymore. But I'd
love to go.
(Sung) Where the breezes smell fine
From the sage and pine
And the sun turns rock into gold.
I have heard when you ride
On the prairie so wide
You forget that a man can grow old.
Oh, the Rockies rise
To the sunburned skies
And the world opens up like a fan,
But for me there is dust,
There is dirt, there is rust,
While you go West, young man,
While you go West, young man!
(Chanted) Leavin' Track 2 at twelve o'clock,
the Montreal Royal Express, bound for
Albany, Plattsburg, Montreal.
(Sung) And all points North!
(Spoken) Look at those doughboys. You ask where
those rookies are going? Plattsburg!
Where the camp is. That's where they
train.
(Sung) They line 'em up each morning
And, boy, they got to shine.
Each button must be buttoned
Before they get in line.
The drummer starts in drummin',
The bugles start to blare.
With uniforms a-gleaming
And noses in the air
And noses in the air!
At night there's beer and smoking
And maybe shootin' craps.
They sit together joking
Until it's time for taps

Da-da-da
Da-da-da
What a life!
(Spoken) I never get anywhere.
(Chanted) Leavin' Track 7 at twelve-five, the
New England Pilgrim, bound for
Bridgeport, New Haven, Hartford,
Boston.
(Sung) And all points North!
(Spoken) No. 42 for Boston? Yes, miss, leaves
right away—Track 7. College girls. Ain't
they pretty? Finishing school, they call
it. Eight of them. They used to call 'em
flappers. Now they're debs.
(Sung) How young they are!
How sweet they are!
How clean they are!
How fresh and beautiful.
Their hands are soft,
Their eyes are bright.
At night they sleep
And dream their hearts away.
Life is a dance to them.
It makes me feel a little old
To see young girls,
How young they are.
(Chanted) Leavin' Track 17 at twelve-ten, the

Honeymoon Express, bound for
Harmon, Ossining, Albany, Rochester,
Buffalo, Niagara Falls.
(Sung) And all points West!
(Spoken) Look at that guy! No honeymoon for him!
Poor guy, he's handcuffed to a cop. Yop!
A burglar, maybe a killer. No Niagara
Falls for him. He'll get as far as Ossin-
ing. Up the river. Maybe for keeps. How
mad he looks. What's he mad about? At
least he's going somewhere. But there's
a honeymoon couple with all their
friends and relations. Rice they're throw-
ing and old shoes.
(Sung) Hands to hold
And sights to see,
They got the world,
The world is free.
Speeding through the night
With kisses in the gloom.
Be happy, little bride and groom.
Bright young love
And sights to see,
They're all for you
But not for me.
You have sights to see

And bright young love in bloom.
Goodbye, you pretty bride and happy
groom,
Goodbye.
(Spoken) What's that yelling! What's the crowd!
Police whistles!
(Chanted) The crook! The prisoner broke away!
Look at the cops!
(Sung) They got him!
No, they didn't!
I hope he makes it.
(Spoken) Look out, there's a cop behind that post.
He got his sleeve. He got away. Hurry!
The cop's got his gun out! Don't shoot!
Don't shoot, you fool, you'll hit someone!
Oh, you fool! Why me? Here! Here!
(Chanted) I'm goin', goin'! On Track 7 at twelve-oh
—sights to see—to see—to go—I'm
goin' somewhere now.
(Sung) Oh, I leave at last
On a train that's fast
And the whistle is starting to blow.
Now the track is all clear
And the chief engineer says,
"All points West, let's go!"
Says, "All points West, let's go!

June Preisser, Mickey Rooney, and Judy Garland
in the film version, 1939

226

BABES IN ARMS 1937

Tryout: Shubert Theatre, Boston, March 31–April 12, 1937. New York run: Shubert Theatre, April 14–October 23, 1937; Majestic Theatre, October 25–December 18, 1937. 289 performances. Music by Richard Rodgers. Lyrics by Lorenz Hart. Produced by Dwight Deere Wiman. Book by Richard Rodgers and Lorenz Hart. Directed by Robert Sinclair. Choreography by George Balanchine. Settings by Raymond Dovey. Costumes by Helene Pons. Orchestra under the direction of Gene Salzer. Orchestrations by Hans Spialek. Cast, starring Mitzi Green, Ray Heatherton, and Wynn Murray, included Duke McHale, Harold and Fayard Nicholas (the Nicholas Brothers), Rolly Pickert, Grace McDonald, Alfred Drake, Robert Rounseville, and Dan Dailey (chorus). Vocal score published 1960.

WHERE OR WHEN

Published March 1937. Introduced by Mitzi Green and Ray Heatherton.

VERSE

When you're awake, the things you think
Come from the dreams you dream.
Thought has wings, and lots of things
Are seldom what they seem.
Sometimes you think you've lived before
All that you live today.
Things you do come back to you,
As though they knew the way.
Oh, the tricks your mind can play!

REFRAIN

It seems we stood and talked like this before,
We looked at each other in the same way then,
But I can't remember where or when.
The clothes you're wearing are the clothes you
    wore,
The smile you are smiling you were smiling then,
But I can't remember where or when.
Some things that happen for the first time
Seem to be happening again.
And so it seems that we have met before,
And laughed before, and loved before,
But who knows where or when!

BABES IN ARMS

Published April 1937. Introduced by Mitzi Green, Ray Heatherton, Alfred Drake, and "the gang."

They call us babes in arms,
But we are babes in armor.
They laugh at babes in arms,
But we'll be laughing far more.
On city streets and farms
They'll hear a rising war cry.
Youth will arrive,
Let them know you're alive,
Make it your cry!
They call us babes in arms,
They think they must direct us.
But if we're babes in arms
We'll make them all respect us.
Why have we got our arms,
What have we got our sight for?
Play day is done,
We've a place in the sun
We must fight for.
So babes in arms to arms!

I WISH I WERE IN LOVE AGAIN

Published March 1937. Introduced by Grace McDonald and Rolly Pickert.

VERSE

You don't know that I felt good
When we up and parted.
You don't know I knocked on wood,
Gladly broken-hearted.
Worrying is through,
I sleep all night,
Appetite and health restored.
You don't know how much I'm bored.

REFRAIN 1

The sleepless nights,
The daily fights,
The quick toboggan when you reach the
    heights—
I miss the kisses and I miss the bites.
I wish I were in love again!
The broken dates,
The endless waits,

The lovely loving and the hateful hates,
The conversation with the flying plates—
I wish I were in love again!
No more pain,
No more strain,
Now I'm sane, but . . .
I would rather be gaga!
The pulled-out fur
Of cat and cur,
The fine mismating of a him and her—
I've learned my lesson, but I wish I were
In love again!

REFRAIN 2

The furtive sigh,
The blackened eye,
The words "I'll love you till the day I die,"
The self-deception that believes the lie—
I wish I were in love again.
When love congeals
It soon reveals
The faint aroma of performing seals,
The double-crossing of a pair of heels.
I wish I were in love again!
No more care.
No despair.
I'm all there now,
But I'd rather be punch-drunk!
Believe me, sir,
I much prefer
The classic battle of a him and her.
I don't like quiet and I wish I were
In love again!

ALL DARK PEOPLE

Published April 1937. Introduced by the Nicholas Brothers.

VERSE

Skeet-ski-daddle,
Beedy, weedy, weedy:
Doesn't mean a thing in English,
But it means a lot up Harlem way.
Skeet-ski-daddle,
Beedy, weedy, weedy,
When the tune gets hot and tinglish,
Means a colored person wants to play
At the Old Savoy, that's what they say.

REFRAIN

Play that music for me and my sweet—
All dark people is light on their feet.
Pay no mind to a little conceit,
All dark people is light on their feet.
And just the same as flowers get honey
All God's chillun got buck-and-wings.
Paleface babies don't dance in the street,
All dark people are light on their feet.

WAY OUT WEST

Published April 1937. Introduced by Wynn Murray, Alex Courtney, Clifton Darling, James Gillis, and Robert Rounseville.

VERSE

I'd travel the plains.
In mountain streams I'd paddle.
Over the Rockies I would trail.
I'd hark to the strains
Of cowboys in the saddle—
Not very musical but male.
I've roamed o'er the range with the herd,
Where seldom is heard an intelligent word.

REFRAIN 1

Git along, little taxi, you can keep the change.
I'm riding home to my kitchen range
Way out west on West End Avenue.
Oh, I love to listen to the wagon wheels
That bring the milk that your neighbor steals
Way out west on West End Avenue.
Keep all your mountains
And your lone prairie so pretty,
Give me the fountains
That go wrong at Rodeo City.
I would trade your famous deer and antelope
For one tall beer and a cantaloupe
Way out west on West End Avenue.
Yippee-aye-ay!

REFRAIN 2

Git along, little elevator, climb once more
To my lone shack on the fourteenth floor
Way out west on West End Avenue.
When the sun's a-rising over Central Park
I pull the blinds and it's nice and dark
Way out west on West End Avenue.
Redskins may battle
With their tomahawks and axes.

I'll join the cattle
In the big corral at Saks's.
Oh, the wild herd gathers when the moon is full.
There's not much buffalo, but lots of bull
Way out west on West End Avenue.
Yippee-aye-ay!

MY FUNNY VALENTINE

Published March 1937. Introduced by Mitzi Green.

VERSE

Behold the way our fine-feathered friend
His virtue doth parade.
Thou knowest not, my dim-witted friend,
The picture thou hast made.
Thy vacant brow and thy tousled hair
Conceal thy good intent.
Thou noble, upright, truthful, sincere,
And slightly dopey gent—you're . . .

REFRAIN

My funny Valentine,
Sweet comic Valentine,
You make me smile with my heart.
Your looks are laughable,
Unphotographable,
Yet you're my fav'rite work of art.
Is your figure less than Greek?
Is your mouth a little weak?
When you open it to speak
Are you smart?
But don't change a hair for me,
Not if you care for me,
Stay, little Valentine, stay!
Each day is Valentine's Day.

JOHNNY ONE-NOTE

Published March 1937. Introduced by Wynn Murray, Douglas Parry, Alfred Drake, Elenore Tennis, the Nicholas Brothers, Bobby Lane, Mitzi Green, and Duke McHale.

VERSE

Johnny could only sing one note
And the note he sang was this:
Ah!

REFRAIN

Poor Johnny One-Note
Sang out with gusto
And just overlorded the place.
Poor Johnny One-Note
Yelled willy-nilly
Until he was blue in the face—
For holding one note was his ace.
Couldn't hear the brass,
Couldn't hear the drum.
He was in a class
By himself, by gum.
Poor Johnny One-Note
Got in *Aïda*—
Indeed a great chance to be brave.
He took his one note,
Howled like the North Wind—
Brought forth wind that made critics rave,
While Verdi turned round in his grave!
Couldn't hear the flute
Or the big trombone.
Ev'ryone was mute.
Johnny stood alone.

TRIO

Cats and dogs stopped yapping,
Lions in the zoo
All were jealous of Johnny's big trill.
Thunderclaps stopped clapping,
Traffic ceased its roar,
And they tell us Niag'ra stood still.
He stopped the train whistles,
Boat whistles,
Steam whistles,
Cop whistles,
All whistles bowed to his skill.

REFRAIN (continued)

Sing, Johnny One-Note,
Sing out with gusto
And just overwhelm all the crowd.
Ah!
So sing, Johnny One-Note, out loud!
Sing, Johnny One-Note!
Sing, Johnny One-Note, out loud!

IMAGINE

Introduced by Wynn Murray, Alex Courtney, Clifton Darling, James Gillis, and Robert Rounseville. Reprised by Duke McHale at the start and finish of the ballet "Peter's

Journey." Registered for copyright as an unpublished song by Chappell and Company, Inc., April 1951.

QUARTETTE: Wear a smile,
A sunny smile,
Be happy till the last long mile.
A smile for breakfast,
A smile for lunch.
BABY ROSE: There'll be no breakfast for this here bunch!
MARSHALL: Oh, cut it out—
QUARTETTE: Wear a smile,
A merry smile.
A smile can make the world worthwhile.
Be bright and cheery
When things look tough.
A sailor laughs when the sea is rough.
BOY: I've got enough of this cheerful stuff.
BABY ROSE: This situation is fearful,
But I've got a way to be cheerful!

REFRAIN

Imagine your bills are paid,
Imagine you've made the grade.
With no dishes in the sink
All you do is drink
Claret lemonade!
Imagine you own a car,
A trailer that has a bar.
Your clothes fit you very well,
Telling what a swell you are.
You're such a handsome kid.
Folks tell of what you did.
No wonder Mr. Goldwyn made a bid.
Imagine you're out of debt
And love brings you no regret.
If you can imagine this,
Then you must be nuts, my pet!
PETER: I'll travel like a king.
Don't want to miss a thing.
I'll see the town first. Then I'll travel.
Just imagine: Europe—Hollywood. I can see myself now in a first-class cabin.
[Blackout]
QUARTETTE: Imagine you aren't broke.
With money right in your poke.
The world's at your beck and call,
And your cares are all a joke.
[Ballet]
QUARTETTE: Imagine your dream is past.
The dawn is arriving fast,
Your eyes see the morning break
And you are awake at last.

PETER: I know I'm wide awake
And this is not a fake.
[Flourishes roll of money]
I'll spend it on something real. I'll make it double itself—triple itself. I'll be somebody someday.
Imagine the dough I'll cop.
My stock isn't going to drop.
Though I can imagine this,
I'm not going nuts, old top.

ALL AT ONCE

Published March 1937. Introduced by Mitzi Green and Ray Heatherton.

VERSE

You're the most beautiful baby
In your mother's eyes and mine,
And ev'ry other mother's child is too divine.
You're very sensible, Baby,
But you've got a lot to learn.
I appoint myself your teacher
And I must be stern.

REFRAIN

All at once
Baby starts in toddling,
And all at once
Baby needs no coddling.
Then soon
Knows all the names
Of toys and games,
Discovers duty,
Beauty.
All at once
Baby needs affection
To fall at once
In the right direction.
If Baby's wise,
Baby's eyes
Should be able to see
All at once
Baby's going to love me!

PATTER

SHE: All the world's a nursery.
We grow no older through the seven ages.

We keep our bottles and our bogeymen,
And little babies are as wise as sages.
When I was three I was a siren,
And knew the old trick
Of vamping my dad for a peppermint stick.
HE: At five I was a gangster.
I'd loot the pantry,
And give the cream pie a lick.
SHE: I was a comedian.
At six I had a little knack or two.
I used to practice on my teacher dear
And make her sit upon a tack or two.
BOTH: Now that we've met we forget our old age.
We're kids again in the nurs'ry stage.

REPEAT REFRAIN

THE LADY IS A TRAMP

Published April 1937. Introduced by Mitzi Green.

VERSE

I've wined and dined on Mulligan stew
And never wished for turkey
As I hitched and hiked and grifted, too,*
From Maine to Albuquerque.
Alas, I missed the Beaux Arts Ball,
And what is twice as sad,
I was never at a party
Where they honored Noël Ca'ad.
But social circles spin too fast for me.
My Hobohemia is the place to be.

REFRAIN 1

I get too hungry for dinner at eight.
I like the theatre, but never come late.
I never bother with people I hate.
That's why the lady is a tramp.
I don't like crap games with barons and earls.
Won't go to Harlem in ermine and pearls.
Won't dish the dirt with the rest of the girls.
That's why the lady is a tramp.
I like the free, fresh wind in my hair,
Life without care.
I'm broke—it's oke.
Hate California—it's cold and it's damp.
That's why the lady is a tramp.

*Alternate version: and drifted, too.

REFRAIN 2

I go to Coney—the beach is divine.
I go to ball games—the bleachers are fine.
I follow Winchell and read ev'ry line.
That's why the lady is a tramp.
I like a prizefight that isn't a fake.
I love the rowing on Central Park Lake.
I go to opera and stay wide awake.
That's why the lady is a tramp.
I like the green grass under my shoes.
What can I lose?
I'm flat! That's that!
I'm all alone when I lower my lamp.
That's why the lady is a tramp.

REFRAIN 3 (reprise)

Don't know the reason for cocktails at five.
I don't like flying—I'm glad I'm alive.
I crave affection, but not when I drive.
That's why the lady is a tramp.
Folks go to London and leave me behind.
I'll miss the crowning, Queen Mary won't mind.
I don't play Scarlett in *Gone With the Wind*.
That's why the lady is a tramp.
I like to hang my hat where I please.
Sail with the breeze.
No dough—heigh-ho!
I love La Guardia and think he's a champ.
That's why the lady is a tramp.

REFRAIN 4 (reprise)

Girls get massages, they cry and they moan.
Tell Lizzie Arden to leave me alone.
I'm not so hot, but my shape is my own.
That's why the lady is a tramp!
The food at Sardi's is perfect, no doubt.
I wouldn't know what the Ritz is about.
I drop a nickel and coffee comes out.
That's why the lady is a tramp!
I like the sweet, fresh rain in my face.
Diamonds and lace,
No got—so what?
For Robert Taylor I whistle and stamp.
That's why the lady is a tramp!

YOU ARE SO FAIR

Introduced by Grace McDonald, Rolly Pickert, Ted Gary, Mitzi Green, Duke McHale, and John Owens. Registered for copyright as an unpublished song by Chappell and Co., Inc., April 1951.

VERSE

You're a siren if there ever was one—
And there was one.
You're a Lorelei,
I'm a dope.
You're a baddie if I ever saw one—
And I've seen one.
Darling, you're a lie;
I've no hope.
I'm at the end of my rope.

REFRAIN 1

You are so fair—
Like an Oriental vision,
But you won't make that decision.
You're not quite fair.
I'd pay your fare
To Niag'ra Falls and back too,
But you never will react to
This love affair.
You are the crepes suzette
I should get
On my bill of fare,
But if you love me not,
Flower pot,
See if I care.
See how you'll fare
If you keep on playing Rover.
When I come to think it over,
You're only fair.

REFRAIN 2

You are so fair
But you know you're no Apollo
And to say you're hard to swallow
Is only fair.

I'd pay your fare
All around the world and back too,
For I'd like to give the sack to
This love affair.
You are the Camembert
I can't bear
On my bill of fare,
So if you love me not,
Flower pot,
See if I care.
See how you'll fare
If you keep on playing Rover.
When I come to think it over,
You're only fair.

REFRAIN 3

Your hair ain't fair
And you got no style in dressing.
I'm afraid you ain't possessing
No savoir-faire.
I'd pay your fare
To the tropic of New Guinea,
For I'd like to yell *"C'est finis"*
To this affair.
You are the freak event
In the tent
Of a county fair;
So if you love me not,
Polka dot,
See if I care.
See how you'll fare
If you keep on playing Rover.
When I come to think it over,
You're only fair.

OVERLEAF: George M. Cohan, Austin Marshall, and Joy Hodges

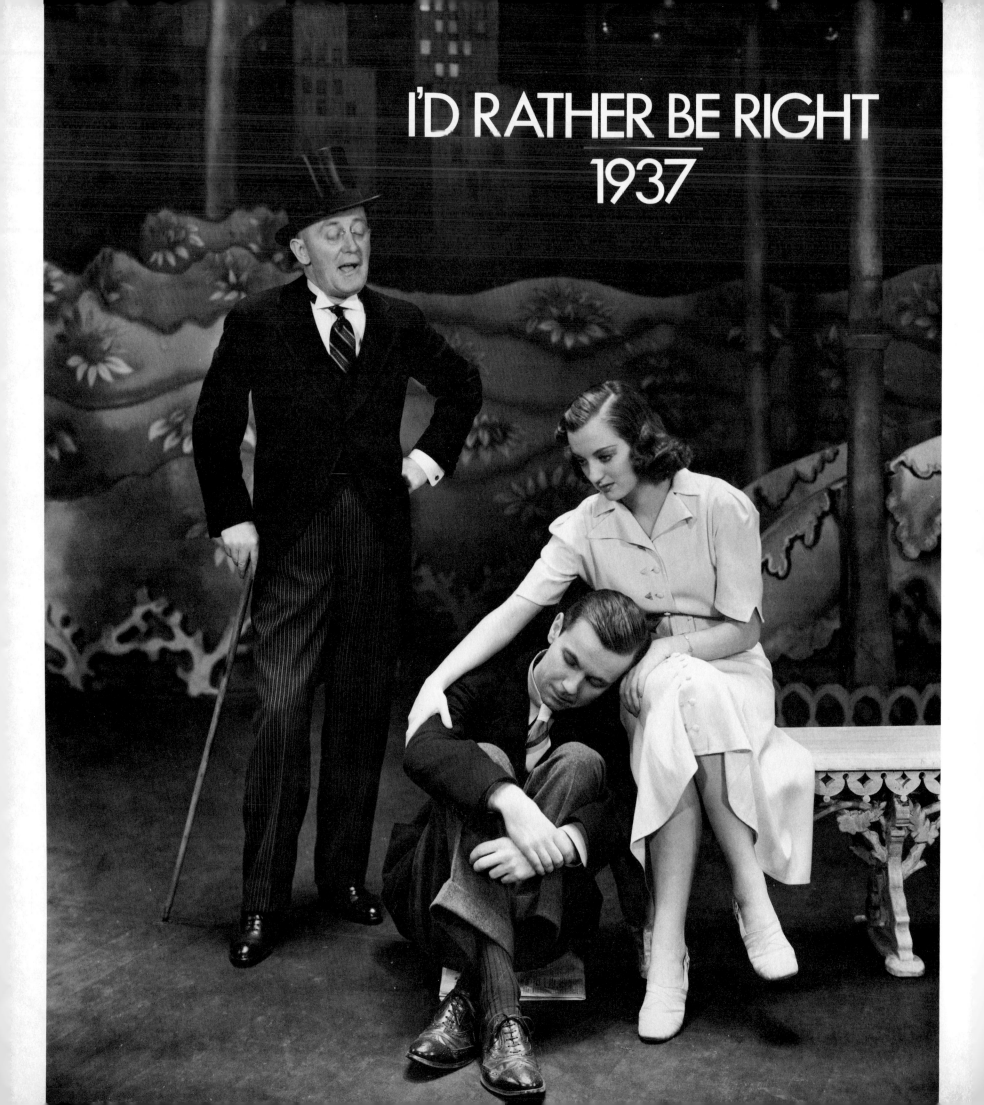

I'D RATHER BE RIGHT
1937

Tryout: Colonial Theatre, Boston, October 11–23, 1937; Ford's Theatre, Baltimore, October 24–29, 1937. New York run: Alvin Theatre, November 2, 1937–May 21, 1938; Music Box Theatre, May 23–July 9, 1938. 290 performances. Music by Richard Rodgers. Lyrics by Lorenz Hart. Produced by Sam H. Harris. Book by George S. Kaufman and Moss Hart. Directed by George S. Kaufman. Dances by Charles Weidman and Ned McGurn. Settings by Donald Oenslager. Costumes by Irene Sharaff and John Hambleton. Orchestra under the direction of Harry Levant. Orchestrations by Hans Spialek. Cast, starring George M. Cohan, included Taylor Holmes, Joy Hodges, Joseph Macaulay, Austin Marshall, Florenz Ames, Mary Jane Walsh, and Georgie Tapps. The lyrics to "Spring in Milwaukee" and "What's It All About?" are missing.

A HOMOGENEOUS CABINET

Introduced by ensemble.

CABINET: We're a homogeneous Cabinet,
And you can't tell us apart.
From the way we're grouped,
You'd think we'd trouped
With Rupert D'Oyly Carte.
But—
Perkins and Farley,
And Farley and Perkins,
Know all of your business and all
of its workin's—
Do Perkins and Farley,
And Farley and Perkins—
Do Perkins and Farley and Hull.

ROOSEVELT: Gentlemen, I want you to meet two
young friends of mine—Miss Peggy
Jones and Mr. Philip Barker.

[*There is an exchange of greetings*]

FARLEY: I keep my popularity forever hale
and hearty
By finding jobs for everyone in the
Democratic Party.
A job for every uncle and a job for
every niece—
I give a job for every vote, and
how the votes increase!
Some guys are such good voters
they get twenty jobs apiece!
Three cheers for the land of F.D.!

ROOSEVELT: Secretary of Labor Perkins!

MISS PERKINS: All of these strikes keep a girl on
her toes;

I've barely got time to powder my
nose.
I fight for the workmen and fight
for the bosses,
And the more that I fight, the
bigger their losses.
It would help the whole thing a
great deal, I suppose,
If I gave it all up and just
powdered my nose.

ROOSEVELT: Secretary of the Treasury
Morgenthau!

[*He pronounces the last syllable "thow"*]

MORGENTHAU: Uh . . . That's Morgenthau
["*thaw*"], Mr. Roosevelt.

[*He pronounces it "Rewsevelt"*]

ROOSEVELT: That's Roosevelt ["*Rowsevelt*"].

MORGENTHAU: I'm quite a busy man right now—
I'm Secretary Morgenthau.
You may have heard that I attend
To what you call the money end.
Since first this land of ours began,
I am its top financial man.
I have achieved, you must admit,
The biggest goddamn deficit!

ROOSEVELT: And these are the rest of the boys.
This is Secretary of the Navy—ah—
I'm sorry, I never can remember
your name.

SWANSON: Nobody knows who I am—

CABINET: And nobody gives a damn!
Perkins and Farley and Hull—
We meet twice a week and it's
dull.
Perkins and Farley and Hull,
Morgenthau, Cummings and Ickes,
We'd like to give all of them
mickeys.
Roper and Wallace and all of the
rest
Are unknown in the East and the
same in the West.

ALL: But Perkins and Farley,
And Farley and Perkins,
Know all of your business and all
of its workin's—
Do Perkins and Farley,
And Farley and Perkins,
Do Perkins and Farley,
And Farley and Perkins,
Yes, Perkins and Farley,
And Farley and Perkins,
Do Perkins and Farley and Hull.

HAVE YOU MET MISS JONES?

Published September 1937. Introduced by Joy Hodges and Austin Marshall.

VERSE

It happened—I felt it happen.
I was awake—I wasn't blind.
I didn't think—I felt it happen,
Now I believe in matter over mind.
And now you see we mustn't wait.
The nearest moment that we marry is too late!

REFRAIN

"Have you met Miss Jones?"
Someone said as we shook hands.
She was just Miss Jones to me.
Then I said, "Miss Jones,
You're a girl who understands
I'm a man who must be free."
And all at once I lost my breath,
And all at once was scared to death,
And all at once I owned the earth and sky!
Now I've met Miss Jones
And we'll keep on meeting till we die,
Miss Jones and I.

ROOSEVELT (unused) REFRAIN

"Have you met Miss Jones?"
Someone said as they shook hands.
She was just Miss Jones, that's all.
Then he said, "Miss Jones,
You're a girl who understands
I'm a man who doesn't fall."
And all at once he lost his breath,
And all at once was scared to death,
And all at once he lost his head and will.
Now he loves Miss Jones
And they'll love until their hearts stand still,
Miss Jones and Phil!

EARLIER (unused) REFRAIN FOR JOY HODGES

"Have you met Miss Jones?"
Someone said as we shook hands.
I was just Miss Jones, that's all.
Then he said, "Miss Jones,
You're a girl who understands
I'm a man who must not fall."
And all at once we lost our breath,
And all at once were scared to death,
And all at once we spoke in tender tones.

Now that he owns me,
I own half of everything he owns;
He owns Miss Jones.

HERE HE IS

Introduced by George M. Cohan and ensemble. Part One of "Beauty Sequence." Segues to "Take and Take and Take." On some scripts this portion of the score is titled "Beauty Sequence," but it makes more sense to see the two numbers together as making up the "Beauty Sequence."

WOMEN: Here he is! Here he is! Here he is!
How dare you?
How could you?
ROOSEVELT: Ladies, I implore . . .
WOMEN: Give up our beauty?
This means war!
ROOSEVELT: Ladies, let me catch my breath!
WOMEN: Give me vanishing cream,
Or give me death!
HAIRDRESSERS: Girls, stick together,
The crisis is grave.
WOMEN: I regret I have but one life to give
For my permanent wave!
Not for a year,
Not for a month,
Not for a day
Will we give beauty away.
Not for a man,
Not for a flag,
Not for the earth—
That's what our beauty is worth.
We'll give up our sons for battle,
We'll give up our husbands for
less;
But feminine drums will rattle
For feminine makeup and dress.
Not for a year,
Not for a month,
Not for a day
Will we give beauty away.

TAKE AND TAKE
AND TAKE

Published October 1937. Introduced by Mary Jane Walsh. Danced by Irene McBride and ensemble. Part Two of "Beauty Sequence."

VERSE

When a man meets a man on a train,
He doesn't talk of crops and rain.
When a man sees a musical show,
He likes the first or second row.
And the man on the train
Who won't speak of the rain,
And the man at the show
In the very first row,
No matter what place they're in,
Are brothers under the skin!

REFRAIN

You take your brains,
You take your gold,
I'll take my beauty,
And take and take and take.
While I take pains
Not to grow old,
I'll take my beauty
And make and make and make.
Beware, rich girls,
Smart girls, beware
Of a fancy rag,
A shapely bone,
A lovely hank o' hair.
I can't sew a stitch,
Can't bake a cake,
But watch this cutie
Take the cake for beauty;
Take and take and take!

SPRING IN VIENNA

Introduced by Joseph Macaulay. Danced by Margaret Sande and ensemble. Title was changed to "Spring in Milwaukee" in May 1938. The lyric to "Spring in Milwaukee" is missing although it is possible that the two lyrics are virtually identical and the word "Vienna" was changed to "Milwaukee" because of the German annexation of Austria in March 1938.

DIRECTOR
& GIRLS: It's spring in Vienna,
And spring when I sing;
It's spring in the hilltops,
And spring in the spring.
It's spring in Vienna,
And spring in my heart,
The spring in the breeze
Says we'll never part;
It's spring in Vienna,

DIRECTOR: So I and Frederica
Won't part.
GIRLS: Lilacs in blossom,
Dew on the grass;
Knockwurst on table,
Beer in the glass.
I'm happy when a
Spring starts to start.
Spring in Vienna
Says we won't part.

THE WORLD
IS MY OYSTER

Dropped before the New York opening. Same music used for "Spring in Vienna."

The violins whisper,
The breeze is in tune,
The lilacs in blossom,
Each hour is noon.
The world is my oyster
And high in the sky
The sun laughs forever
As long as they buy!
The world is my oyster
As long as they continue to buy!

TRIO

Music entreating,
Be glad today!
Sunshine is greeting
Two hearts in May.
Youth and its gay time
Never will die.
Life is in Maytime
If they will buy!
While they continue to buy!

A LITTLE BIT OF
CONSTITUTIONAL FUN

Introduced by Mary Jane Walsh and ensemble.

ROOSEVELT: All right. Then I'll tell you something.
I meant every word of it and I still do.
You're a bunch of old fogies, and you

always were, and that's all you ever will
be. How do you like that?

THE CHIEF

JUSTICE: Old fogies, eh? Well, we'll show you a
thing or two, Mr. President. Boys! Hit
it!

THE GIRLS: No money in this world ever budges
Our judges.
When duty calls, their duty is done.
We patriotic ladies know them,
And show them,
A little bit of constitutional fun.
The way they always want to be
lawful
Is awful—
Their fortitude is second to none.
They love their Constitution—
We know it,
And show it,
By giving them some constitutional
fun.
Judge John Marshall
Was most impartial—
From law he'd never retrench,
But after duty,
He liked a cutie
To soothe his callus from the bench.

GIRLS &

JUSTICES: Judge John Marshall
Was most impartial—
From law he'd never retrench;
But after duty,
He liked a cutie
To soothe his callus from the bench.
The way they always want to be
lawful
Is awful—
Their fortitude is second to none.
They love their Constitution—
We know it,
And show it,
By giving them some constitutional
fun.
Judge John Marshall
Was most impartial—
From law he'd never retrench;
But after duty,
He liked a cutie
To soothe his callus from the bench.
Though Presidents may try to coerce
them,
Disperse them,
They've won their fight before it's
begun.
And we're the girls they never say
"no" to,

But go to
To get a little constitutional fun,
And they deserve some constitutional
fun.

NOT SO INNOCENT FUN

Dropped before the New York opening. Originally titled
"Nine Young Girls and Nine Old Men." A change in the
title was made in ink on a copy of the lyric by Richard
Rodgers. Music does not survive, but the same music
appears to have been used for "A Little Bit of Constitutional Fun."

VERSE

GIRLS: We're nine courtly courtesans who court
the court;
They thought they couldn't be caught.
They're nine courtly courtiers who
stormed our fort;
They bought, so we never fought.
We wonder why such perspicacious men
as you
Can turn from Jekyll into Hyde the way
you do.
We must know the reason why such luck
befell us,
So tell us! Tell us! Tell us!

REFRAIN

MEN: George Washington was true to his wife
for life,
At war and peace was second to none,
Yet ev'ryone who knew him conceded he
needed
A little bit of not so innocent fun.
Elizabeth remained on her throne alone,
And never did what shouldn't be done;
And yet we learn from reading Macaulay
that Raleigh
Gave Bess a bit of not so innocent fun.
Caesar's wife was above suspicion,
Her code of conduct was strict,
But as for Julius
We wouldn't fool yus,
He often got his toga kicked.
A coupla foreign rulers make laws because
They have to keep their place in the sun.
Perhaps they shouldn't worry their hair off
but tear off
A little bit of not so innocent fun,
And we would like some not so innocent
fun!

SWEET SIXTY-FIVE

Published September 1937. Introduced by Joy Hodges
and Austin Marshall. Danced by Georgie Tapps and Jack
Whitney.

VERSE

PHIL: We'll own a little nest,
We'll be well dressed.
Farewell to fears
In forty years.
We'll drive a bright new Ford,
PEGGY: Perhaps a Cord.
BOTH: We'll be in Heaven
In seventy-seven
A.D.!

REFRAIN

PEGGY: Baby, how sweet to be
Sweet sixty-five!
PHIL: Still close to me to be
Forty years from today.
PEGGY: You'll fall for the lure of me,
Growing increasingly fond.
PHIL: You'll always be sure of me,
I'll be too weak to wander.
BOTH: We'll walk down Lovers' Lane
If our knees will allow.
No reversals,
Long rehearsals
Will have taught us how
To be happy
Forty years from now!

WE'RE GOING TO
BALANCE THE BUDGET

Introduced by George M. Cohan and company. During the
Boston tryout, this song was listed on programs as "Tune
Up, Bluebird."

VERSE

Shoot your cameras,
Fly your flags,
Loosen up your money bags.
Spread the good news throughout the land,
Open that mike up
And strike up the band.

REFRAIN

Tune up, bluebird, you're going to sing.
Swing out, church bells, you're going to ring.
Take aim, Cupid, you're gonna go "bing!"
We're going to balance the budget!
Cheer up, farmer, you'll buy a new car.
Wake up, landlord, and open the bar.
Come out, rainbow, wherever you are.
We're going to balance the budget!
Ta-ta-ra!
Hear the horn of plenty blow.
Ta-ta-ra!
The dollar bills will flow.
Yankee-Doodle, we're letting you know
We're going to balance the budget!

EARLIER VERSE

PHIL: I will send you roses—I mean orchids;
    We'll be eating chicken—I mean quail.
PEGGY: We'll be raising two or three or four kids
    On the most expensive cakes and ale.
PHIL: You will see my happy chest expansion
    When I build our house—I mean our
    mansion.

WE JUST DANCE AND SING

Dropped before the New York opening. Intended as a tap number for George M. Cohan. At one point, this song was to have opened Act II. It was replaced by "American Couple," a ballet that had no lyric. It was introduced by several members of the company but was dropped shortly after the New York opening and replaced by "What's It All About?," which was introduced by Georgie Tapps and ensemble. That lyric is missing, although it is possible that this number ("We Just Dance and Sing") was retitled "What's It All About?"

They tell us that the country's in a pretty awful
    way,
That this and that has fallen or that nobody can
    pay.
We've cogitated, ruminated, tried to work it out,
And proudly we announce we don't know what
    it's all about.
In fact, the simple truth is, we don't know a
    single thing,
So we just dance and sing.

LABOR IS THE THING

Introduced by Florenz Ames and ensemble.

ALL: We work all day
    For the P.W.A.
    Let the market crash,
    We collect our cash
    We sing as we work,
    And we work as we sing:
    "Skit-skat Beety-o!
    Skit-skat Beety-o!
    Labor is the thing, my lads.
    Labor is the thing!"

SOLO: At twelve o'clock when the whistle blows
    "lunch"
    We scram to the Colony with the bunch.
    At three o'clock we always arrange
    To get our reports from the exchange.
    At six o'clock we go to the club.
    A guy who works needs a steam and a rub.
    While drying off we sing:

ALL: "Skit-skat Beety-o!
    Skit-skat Beety-o!
    Labor is the thing, my lads.
    Labor is the thing!"

SOLO: The union workingman's homeward trend
    Is toward Fifth Avenue or East End.
    A union man must leave home to vote—
    A meeting's been called on Vanderbilt's
    boat.
    At last the nervous breakdown comes—
    We go to fed'ral sanitariums
    To cut out dolls and sing:

ALL: "Skit-skat Beety-o!
    Skit-skat Beety-o!
    Labor is the thing, my lads.
    Labor is the thing!"

    We work all day
    For the P.W.A.
    Let the market crash,
    We collect our cash.
    We sing as we work,
    And we work as we sing:
    "Skit-skat Beety-o!
    Skit-skat Beety-o!
    Labor is the thing, my lads.
    Labor is the thing!"

I'D RATHER BE RIGHT

Second version

Published October 28, 1937. Introduced by Joy Hodges, Austin Marshall, Mary Jane Walsh, George M. Cohan, and ensemble. (See earlier version with the same title.)

VERSE

HE: When I first got my job
    They paid me seventeen a week.
    In just five years I'm getting twenty-two.
    I'll get another two-buck raise
    When I've the nerve to speak.
SHE: And if you don't I'll still love you.
    You're always right no matter what you do.

REFRAIN

    I'd rather be right than influential.
    I'd rather be right than wealthy and wise.
    I don't come through, dear,
    Where brains belong,
    But pertaining to you, dear,
    I can't go wrong.
    I'd rather be right than presidential.
    Let other folks fight for heights above.
    What do I fight for?
    Just to be right, for
    I'd rather be right,
    Just right about love!

I'D RATHER BE RIGHT

First version

Published October 7, 1937. Dropped before the New York opening. Replaced by "I'd Rather Be Right" (second version). Music used later with a new lyric for "Now That I Know You" in *Two Weeks with Pay* (1940).

VERSE

When you know that someone loves you so,
You know enough to go through life.
I'm not smart;
My brains are in my heart.
Behold in me the one who'll be your wife.

REFRAIN

Don't have to know much;
There's only so much you can learn.
There's no guessing
How the distressing tide may turn.
When it's sunny
You can't bet your money
It isn't going to shower,
Perhaps in an hour.
Oh, yes,
You can often be wrong.
You may be wrong about faces,
And wrong about races,
So wrong lots of places.
You must be,
Just be sure someone loves you,
Sure that you love with all your might.
That's the way I'd rather be right.

OFF THE RECORD

Introduced by George M. Cohan. Sung by James Cagney
in the film biography of Cohan, *Yankee Doodle Dandy*
(1942), in re-creation of a scene from *I'd Rather Be Right.*

VERSE

It's really a wonderful job
For fellows like George, Abe and me, too.
It's great to shake hands with the mob,
And to hold every kid on your knee, too.
Ev'ry word that I speak goes into headlines;
When I speak, all the papers hold their
    deadlines.
But I've found a way of dropping a hint,
Or a glint of the truth
That the boys cannot print.
For instance . . .
For instance . . .

REFRAIN 1

When I was only governor, and just a good-time
    Charlie,
A certain party came to me—he said his name
    was Farley.
Don't print this—it's strictly off the record.
He sat right down and talked to me till I was in
    a stupor,
And ended up by selling me the works of
    Fenimore Cooper.
Don't print it—it's strictly off the record.
I said, "You're quite a salesman;
You've been sent here by the fates.

If you can sell these dreary books,
Which ev'rybody hates,
Then maybe you can sell me to the whole United
    States!"
But that's off the record.

REFRAIN 2

My messages to Congress are a lot of boola-boola.
I'm not so fond of Bankhead, but I'd love to
    meet Tallulah.
Don't print it—it's strictly off the record.
I sit up in my bedroom reading books like *Silas
    Marner,*
And Sears and Roebuck catalogues to get away
    from Garner.
Don't print it—it's strictly off the record.
If I'm not re-elected and the worst comes to the
    worst,
I'll never die of hunger and I'll never die of
    thirst.
I've got one boy with Du Pont and another one
    with Hearst.
But that's off the record.

REFRAIN 3

When I go up to Hyde Park, it is not just for the
    ride there.
It's not that I love Hyde Park, but I love to park
    and hide there.
Don't print that—it's strictly off the record.
Oh, sing a song of Boulder Dam, but what's a
    little song worth?
We'll use it to throw razor blades, and maybe
    Alice Longworth.
Don't print it—it's strictly off the record.
And now I'd like to talk about some folks I used
    to know—
Mr. John L. Lewis and his famous C.I.O.
"Frankie and Johnnie were sweethearts"—
But that's off the record.

REFRAIN 4

My speeches on the radio have made me quite a
    hero.
I only have to say "My friends" and stocks go
    down to zero.
Don't print it—it's strictly off the record.
The radio officials say that I'm the leading fellow.
Jack Benny can be President and I'll go on for
    Jell-O.
Don't print it—it's strictly off the record.
It's pleasant at the White House, but I'll tell you
    how I feel:
The food is something terrible—just sauerkraut
    and veal.

If Eleanor would stay at home, I'd get a decent
    meal—
But that's off the record.

MOVIE LYRICS*

When I was courting Eleanor I told her Uncle
    Teddy
I wouldn't run for President unless the job was
    steady.
Don't print it—it's strictly off the record.
We entertained the royalty but we were never
    flustered.
We gave them Yankee hot dogs with Colman's
    English mustard.
Don't print it—it's strictly off the record.
I sit up in my study writing gags for Mr. Ickes
And insults for the gentlemen who'd love to slip
    him mickeys.
Don't print that—it's off the record.
I scrapped the Prohibition Act when we required
    a bracer
And finished up the Boulder Dam to give the
    boys a chaser.
Don't print it—it's strictly off the record.
And for my friends in Washington who complain
    about the taxes
Who cares as long as we cannot be axed out of
    the Axis?
Don't print it—it's strictly off the record.
I can't forget how Lafayette helped give us our
    first chance
To win our fight for liberty and now they've
    taken France.
We'll take it back from Hitler and put ants in his
    Japans
And that's off the record.

A BABY BOND
FOR BABY

Introduced by Taylor Holmes. Alternate title: "A Baby
Bond."

VERSE

I'll tell the microphone I love you.
That's worse than writing, "I love you, dear."
And by the stratosphere above you,
I'll swear forever to be true, dear.
I won't buy you perfume,

*These additional lyrics were written for James Cagney to
sing as George M. Cohan in* Yankee Doodle Dandy *(1942).*

237

I won't buy a ring;
I've a token of affection
That means more than anything.

REFRAIN

It's just a baby bond for baby—
Take it, tootsie, with my love;
Papa's glad to dig down deep for baby.
A bunch of roses may be
Old and faded in a day,
But a baby bond will keep for baby.
Please remember,
In December,
There may be a storm;
Bonds are only scraps of paper,
But, by gosh, they'll keep you warm.
Baby, love your baby,
And I'll promise that I'll buy
Another baby bond for baby
Bye and bye!

EV'RYBODY LOVES YOU

Published September 1937. Dropped before the New York opening. Not listed in pre-Broadway tryout programs.

VERSE

I wonder what you're dreaming while you're
    sleeping.
I'll never know.
You'll never know.
Now at last the world cannot come peeping
Into the thoughts you call your own.
You close your eyes and you're alone.
You're in a world that's bright and new
And there is no one in it but you.

REFRAIN

Comfy and cozy,
All the world is rosy.
Ev'rybody loves you when you're asleep.
Too late to start now
Taking things apart now.
Ev'rybody loves you when you're asleep.
You forget
Your alphabet
When you've been counting sheep;
Does my dreamer know troubles will keep?
Comfy and cozy,
All the world is rosy.

Ev'rybody loves you
When you sleep!

A TREATY, MY SWEETIE, WITH YOU

Dropped before the New York opening. Printed galleys of this song are in the Rodgers and Hammerstein office, which indicates that it was prepared for publication. Theodore S. Chapin called this song to the attention of the editors.

VERSE

Mussolini signed with me,
I got the President of Peru,
And Hitler put his Johann Hancock
Where I told him to.
I gave my famous autograph
Just twice as often as Gable did;
My name is known in Guatemala
And in old Madrid.
I'm called "The Signing Kid!"

REFRAIN

I've signed treaties with Rumania,
Treaties with Albania, too.
Let me do
A treaty, my sweetie, with you.
I've signed documents in Naples,
Papers with the Papal See.
Now give me
A treaty, my sweetie, with thee.
I've had the Chinese at my knees,
Got Dutchmen and such men to sign.
But I'd break relations with Norway
If your way could only be mine.
I don't care if Madagascar
Gives me what I ask her to.
Let me do
A treaty, my sweetie, with you!

HIS CHANCES ARE NOT WORTH A PENNY

Dropped before the New York opening. Intended for George M. Cohan, Marion Green, and ensemble. Alternate title: "Finaletto." It is not clear from the surviving lyric at what point in the script it was to have been performed.

ALL: His chances are not worth a penny,
He's not nearly as good as Jack
    Benny.
He doesn't rank as second choice.
He hasn't got a bedroom voice.
Boake Carter is smarter,
Alec Woollcott is cuter,
And we'd rather turn on
The avuncular sermons of Uncle
    Don.
His chances are not worth a penny,
He hasn't got sex for the many.
He'll get a low rating, if any,
From Crosley or even Nick Kenny.
No, his chances are not worth a
    penny,
For he's not half as good as Jack
    Benny.

ROOSEVELT: So my chances are not worth a
    penny?
Who writes those programs for
    Benny?
And didn't you like Cordell?
I think he sang quite well.

WESTERNERS: Western people for a change
Kind of like "Home on the
    Range,"
But in the land of sage and pine
We love to hear "Sweet Adeline!"

SOUTHERNERS: Way down South we cotton to
    Vallee
And Lanny Ross is up our alley.
Though Dixie songs are mighty
    fine
We still prefer "Sweet Adeline!"

FARMERS: Oh, we don't like gosh-darned
    op'ras
While we feed the cows and swine.
Give us "Trees" and "Old Man
    River,"
And, by heck, "Sweet Adeline!"

SOCIETY
WOMEN: Music stands upon its
Greatest height with Kostelanetz,
Yet at nine when great folks dine
Let Tibbett sing "Sweet Adeline"!

INDIANS: Oskee-wasky, Wampum-woo.
Hokus-pokus, Kissie-koo.
Si Paskee Poo!
Si Paskee Poo!

ROOSEVELT: Poor old Hull,
You're not so dull.

HULL: And you're nearly as good as Jack
    Benny.

ALL: His chances are not worth a penny,
He's not nearly as good as Jack
    Benny.
We'll listen to him maybe when he

Takes a couple of tips from Jack
  Benny.
We'd rather hear Sophie or Fennie
Or someone who imitates Benny.
No, his chances are not worth a
  penny,
He's not nearly as good as Jack
  Benny.

[*Exit all but Cabinet*]
  CABINET: Tomorrow when reading Nick
      Kenny
    You'll find that you're not a Jack
      Benny.
    Did you hear the opinions of many
    Rather go to the charms of Jack
      Benny

And your chances are not worth a
  penny?
They'll elect Eddie Cantor or
  Benny.
Goodbye, Chief!

OVERLEAF: Carole Lombard

FOOLS FOR SCANDAL | 1938

A film produced by Mervyn Le Roy for Warner Brothers– First National. Released March 1938. Music by Richard Rodgers. Lyrics by Lorenz Hart. Screenplay by Herbert and Joseph Fields, based on the play *Food for Scandal* by Nancy Hamilton, James Shute, and Rosemary Casey. Directed by Mervyn Le Roy. Music conducted by Leo F. Forbstein. Cast, starring Carole Lombard and Fernand Gravet, included Ralph Bellamy, Allen Jenkins, Jeni Le Gon, and Les Hite and his orchestra.

THERE'S A BOY IN HARLEM

Published March 1938. Introduced by Jeni Le Gon.

VERSE

There's a new dark music by a new dark man,
And he writes his symphonies in black and tan.
All his rhythms "send you,"
Other songs are tame
But the outside world has never heard his name.
Oh!

REFRAIN

There's a boy in Harlem
And he writes all the songs.
Manhattan belongs to him.
Oh, he won't leave Harlem,
But his tunes get about.
He pounds them out
When the lights are dim.
Though his clothes are sloppy
The boy has earned a good pile.
All the writers copy
This person in the woodpile.
Oh, he lives for pleasure,
He's in no one's employ.
And Harlem lives for its Harlem boy!

FOOD FOR SCANDAL

Introduced by Carole Lombard and Fernand Gravet and spoken with musical background.

RENÉ: [*Dials telephone*]
    P-A-D-1725.
    Are you there?
    Is this Lady Arlington's maid?
    I'm Miss Winters' man.

Have her call my lady at eleven a.m.
Promptly, if you can.
Thank you! Goodbye.
[*Hangs up; dials again*]
    R-E-G 1456.
    Are you there?
    Is this Baron Bottomley's man?
    I'm Miss Winters' cook.
    Have him call my mistress at
        eleven two
    Mark this in your book.
    Be sure! Bonjour!
[*Hangs up; dials again*]
    O-X-F 8653.
    Are you there?
    Is this Lady Sutherland's maid?
    Promptly, if you can,
    Have her call Miss Winters at
        eleven-four.
    I'm her handyman.
    Mais oui, merci!
[*Makes more telephone calls. At five minutes to eleven, brings breakfast to Virginia's bedroom and awakens her*]
VIRGINIA: Awhwhwh—
    Good m —
    You? What's this?
    RENÉ: Your breakfast, miss.
    One lump or two?
VIRGINIA: Get out of here, you!
    RENÉ: Hot milk or cream?
VIRGINIA: Get out or I'll scream!
    RENÉ: I'm the new cook.
VIRGINIA: Where is my maid?
    RENÉ: I'm the new maid.
VIRGINIA: Do you mean to say you slept here all
        night?
    RENÉ: Like a lamb.
VIRGINIA: But I heard the door slam.
    RENÉ: Madame doesn't realize a door can slam
        on both sides!
VIRGINIA: Oh, if this should get into the
        tabloids—
    You must go!
    RENÉ: Oh no—I am the cook. Don't move.
VIRGINIA: What's the matter?
    RENÉ: I want to look—I want to remember
        you as you look now.
VIRGINIA: If someone should call on me, what will
        they think?
    RENÉ: I am the cook—they will believe that!
VIRGINIA: Oh yes—I can conceive that!
    RENÉ: Try the coffee—while it's hot!
VIRGINIA: You dog!
    RENÉ: Well—
VIRGINIA: Hm. It hits the spot. Get out—before
    you ruin my reputation. Imagine what a
    scene—

RENÉ: Eggs Benedictine!
    Food for scandal—
    Why don't you taste it?
    Food for scandal—
    Take it—don't waste it.
VIRGINIA: I don't think I'll eat it at the moment—
    RENÉ: Oh.
VIRGINIA: I only wish you understood what "go"
        meant.
    RENÉ: No. Food for scandal—
    Eat it—don't question.
VIRGINIA: Food for scandal
    Means indigestion.
    RENÉ: Madame, don't be flying off the handle.
    It's food for scandal!
    Madame is served!
[*Telephone rings. René answers*]
    RENÉ: Oh, Miss Winters—she's still at rest,
        ma'am.
    I shan't wake her—I think it best,
        ma'am.
    Ring her in an hour, madame,
        will you—yes.
VIRGINIA: Put down that receiver or I'll kill you.
    RENÉ: Yes.
[*Hangs up. Phone rings again. René answers it*]
    Yes, Lord Craven—I am the cook, sir.
    Madame's resting—I'll take a look, sir.
    She looks very beautiful in bed now.
VIRGINIA: I'll break your head now.
    RENÉ: She's still asleep.
[*Hangs up*]
VIRGINIA: I'll call the police.
    RENÉ: Then you'll get in every column.
VIRGINIA: Oh, what can I do?
    RENÉ: Don't look so solemn.
[*Phone rings. René answers*]
    Oh, Lord Saville—Madame is nervous.
    She can't speak now.
    I'm in her service.
    I am here to pay Madame attention.
VIRGINIA: Oh!
    RENÉ: That's a fact I beg you not to mention.
VIRGINIA: Oh!
[*He hangs up. Phone rings again. He answers*]
    RENÉ: Lady Duncan—she's quite all right,
        ma'am.
    I'm not here long—just for the night,
        ma'am.
VIRGINIA: Scoundrel, and everything appalling.
    RENÉ: Madame is calling
    And so goodbye.
[*Hangs up. Phone rings again. He answers*]
    Hello.
[*To Virginia*]
    Oh, it's Philip, your noble strong man,
    Such a strong man—and much a wrong
        man.

[*into the phone*]
    I am here with Madame—she is
      sleeping.
VIRGINIA: Fine!
  RENÉ: Are you laughing, sir, or are you
      weeping?
VIRGINIA: Swine!
   RENÉ: [*to Virginia*]
    It's just Philip—he seems perturbed
      now.
[*into the phone*]
    No, my Madame can't be disturbed
      now.
    I just cook and do some other small
      things.
    Must you know all things?
    Go climb a tree!
[*Hangs up. The doorbell rings*]
    There's the doorbell! Perhaps our
    First visitor.

HOW CAN YOU FORGET?

Published March 1938. Dropped before the film was released.

VERSE (as intended for film)

You still remain
Tattooed upon my brain;
My hands still clutch
Your well-remembered touch;
My ears are still resounding
With your voice and its tone;
My foolish heart's still pounding
To the beat of your own.
My eyes still see
The eyes that looked at me;
My lips still wear
The perfume of your hair.
I thought I'd nip my heartbreak in the bud
And now I find you're in my blood.

REFRAIN

How can you forget
When you lie awake and dream at night?
How can you forget
When your heart has a mosquito bite?
When the drops of rain that fall
Say, "Pet 'er, pet 'er once again!"
"Don't let 'er, let 'er leave you,"
Says the postman then.
How can you forget?

"Ring 'er, ring 'er, ring 'er," says the phone.
You can win her yet.
Bring 'er, bring 'er, bring 'er back alone.
Fish were meant to fry,
And you're in the net,
Till the day you die, lover,
How can you forget?

VERSE (in published song)

I know I should forget her,
Imagine that I've never met her.
Those things can never last,
You can't bring back the past.
I know I should forget her,
Imagine that I've never met her.
There's lots of fish in the brine,
Just look around and cast your line.

LOVE KNOWS BEST

Dropped before the film was released.

VERSE

I'm a poor gondolier
Working at a humble trade
But I make my serenade
To a queen.
I'm a bold gondolier,
Confident to gain my end;
I have an advising friend
On the scene.
Love's my friend
And he knows what I mean.

REFRAIN

Sweet one, don't ask me
Why it has to be,
But if our hands are pressed,
Love knows best.
Sweet one, you and I
Need no reason why
Our lips must be caressed.
Love knows best.
Love knows why
Two hearts leap with laughter.
When we sigh
Love knows why.
Sweet one, must you know
Why I need you so?
Just put your heart at rest.
Love knows best!

ONCE I WAS YOUNG

Unused.

VERSE

I'm not worth the paper I am written on;
Once my heart was made of ice and snow,
Till the old volcano I was sittin' on
Started snorting and cavorting down below.
Though it burned me up,
It taught me things I know.

REFRAIN

Once I was young,
I was sure no one would get me,
Love wouldn't upset me.
Boy, I was young!
Once I was wise,
And I said, talking with wisdom,
Love certainly is dumb.
Boy, I was wise!
I knew the answers.
"Have your fun now;
Hit and run now."
I, with my answers,
Mighty sly was.
Until I was stung!
I'm in love and I must own up
You've made me a grown-up.
Dunce I was.
Once I was young!

LET'S SING A SONG ABOUT NOTHING

Unused.

VERSE 1

SCENARIO
  WRITER: I have a girl in Boston,
      Quite a scholar, she.
      But she takes her glasses off
      When she kisses me.
      I sing—

REFRAIN 1

    Let's sing a song about nothing;
    Nothing matters but you.

Truth is fiction compared to the
    friction
Of a little kiss or two.

ALL: Nothing, nothing, nothing, nothing,
Nothing matters but you!

VERSE 2

EXTRA GIRL: I have a boy in Richmond.
Southerners are fine.
And I always fall for his
Mason-Dixon Line.
I sing—

REFRAIN 2

Let's sing a song about nothing;
Nothing matters but you.
Sugar's sour compared to the hour
When you said that you'd be true.

ALL: Nothing, nothing, nothing, nothing,
Nothing matters but you!

VERSE 3

EXTRA BOY: I met a girl in Pittsburgh
'Midst the coal and coke.
Pittsburgh seems like Paradise
Even while I choke.
I sing—

REFRAIN 3

Let's sing a song about nothing;
Nothing matters but you.
Just say "Howdy" and skies that
    were cloudy
Turn a well-known shade of blue.

ALL: Nothing, nothing, nothing, nothing,
Nothing matters but you!

VERSE 4

VIRGINIA: I've got a great he-man,
Athletic as can be.
He loves his polo, swimming, hikes,
And incident'ly me.
I sing—

REFRAIN 4

Let's sing a song about nothing;
Nothing matters but you.
You're so athletic, the rest are
    pathetic,
But you're too good to be true.

ALL: Nothing, nothing, nothing, nothing,
Nothing matters but you!

VERSE 5

RENÉ: There is a charming lady
In the seat nearby.

She'd love that man next to her
If that man were I.
I sing—

REFRAIN 5

Allons chanter de rien;
Rien n'importe que vous
Your expression is spoiled by
    repression
And your boyfriend sticks like glue.

ALL: Nothing, nothing, nothing, nothing,
Rien n'importe que vous!

VERSE 6

STAGEHAND: I got a girl in Brooklyn
Which I can't avoid.
She can't say a woid like "bird."
What she says is "boid"
I sing—

REFRAIN 6

Let's sing a song about nothing;
Nothing matters but her.
How I miss her; her funny kisser
Is the one that I prefer.

ALL: Nothing, nothing, nothing, nothing,
Nothing matters but her!

DENNIS KING · VERA ZORINA · VIVIENNE SEGAL · WALTER SLEZAK · AUDREY CHRISTIE · CHARLES WALTER

"I MARRIED AN ANGEL"

PRINTED IN U.S.A

I MARRIED AN ANGEL | 1938

Tryout: Shubert Theatre, New Haven, April 14–16, 1938; Shubert Theatre, Boston, April 19–30, 1938. New York run: Shubert Theatre, May 11, 1938–February 25, 1939. 338 performances. Music by Richard Rodgers. Lyrics by Lorenz Hart. Produced by Dwight Deere Wiman. Book by Richard Rodgers and Lorenz Hart. Adapted from the play by Janos Vaszary. Directed by Joshua Logan. Choreography by George Balanchine. Settings by Jo Mielziner. Costumes by John Hambleton. Orchestra under the direction of Gene Salzer. Orchestrations by Hans Spialek. Cast starring Dennis King, Vera Zorina, Vivienne Segal, and Walter Slezak, included Audrey Christie and Charles Walters.

For the lyric to "I Married an Angel," see the unproduced musical film *I Married an Angel* (1933), page 194.

Lyrics for two numbers, "Othello" and "Women Are Women," might be missing. "Othello" was written for the Act II Roxy Music Hall sequence. It was registered for copyright as an unpublished song by Robbins Music Corporation, February 18, 1939. Music is preserved in the Rodgers and Hammerstein office. The number appears to have been a dance sequence that had no lyric. "Women Are Women" might be a part of the opening number in the 1933 film score "Love Is Queen, Love Is King." It was registered for copyright as an unpublished song by Robbins Music Corporation, February 18, 1939. Music and lyric appear to be missing.

DID YOU EVER GET STUNG?

Published May 1938. Introduced by Dennis King, Vivienne Segal, and Charles Walters.

VERSE

WILLY: Every woman is a cheat.
PETER: That depends on whom you meet.
PEGGY: Some of us are kind of sweet.
  ALL: So
    Everything's comparative.
    You know it.
WILLY: I have fallen once or twice.
PETER: And they always gave you ice.
PEGGY: But they also looked so nice.
  ALL: So
    It's the same old narrative
    We know it.
    Know it well!

REFRAIN

WILLY: Did you ever get stung?
    Did you ever get star-struck?

Did a glamorous skirt
Ever pilfer your shirt and tie?
Did you ever get flung?
Never knowing you are struck
By a twenty-ton truck
In the form of a female eye?
Did you say, "She lives for me!
This is it! Now at last!"
You bit! You were it!
You got hit by the blast!
Then you must have been stung
Where the doctor can't help you.
And you swear that you're cured
Till another Queen Bee flies past.

I'LL TELL THE MAN IN THE STREET

Published May 1938. Introduced by Vivienne Segal and Walter Slezak.

VERSE

    I won't tell of my love to the red, red rose
    Or the running brook where the sweet magnolia grows.
    I won't tell of my love to ev'ry little star
    Or the whippoorwill on the hill afar.

REFRAIN 1

    I'll tell the man in the street
    And ev'ryone I meet
    That you and I are sweethearts.
    I'll shout it out from the roof,
    I'll give the papers proof
    That we are two complete hearts.
    I want the world to know;
    I'll use the radio.
    And when I've said all my say,
    Until you're old and gray
    You'll never get away from me.

REFRAIN 2

    I'll tell the man in the street
    You're crazy with the heat
    If you believe I'm yours, dear.
    And when you turn out your light
    And go to bed at night
    You'll never hear my snores, dear.
    You can't play hide-and-seek

With my divine physique.
There is no price you can pay
To make me go astray.
You'll never get your way with me.

REPRISE (ACT TWO)

  HARRY: I'll tell the man in the street
    That Willy is a cheat
    Who'd rob us if we let him.
GENERAL: Hear! Hear!
  HARRY: I'll shout it out from the roof
    He's married to a goof
    Who broke him when she met him.
ENSEMBLE: Hooray!
  HARRY: I want the world to see
    That he's an S.O.B.
ENSEMBLE: Oh!
  HARRY: Even a dog has his day.
    And when I bark I say
    He'll never get away from me.

THE MODISTE

A revision of "Bath and Dressmaking Sequence," page 194, which was written for the unproduced film *I Married an Angel* (1933). Introduced by Dennis King, Vera Zorina, Janis Dremann, and Marcella Howard.

  VOICE: Hello.
  ANGEL: Oh, hello!
  VOICE: What can I do for Madam?
  ANGEL: Madam? Madam? You don't
    Know me from Adam. But how
    Do you do, and how are you?
[*Hangs up telephone*]
    Glad to meet you!
[*Phone rings*]
  VOICE: Honolulu calling.
  ANGEL: Honolulu? Honolulu?
HARRY'S
  VOICE: Hello, Willy. This is Harry.
  ANGEL: Harry? Who is Harry?
    I don't know a single Harry.
    How are you and how do you do?
[*Hangs up*]
    Glad to meet you.
[*Doorbell rings*]
    Something's ringing!
    Darling, stop your singing.
  WILLY: Don't let it worry you, sweet, in the least!
    I'll answer the bell, dear.
    It's just the modiste.

Entrez—s'il vous plaît.

MODISTE: You're from Budapest. I can tell by
the accent.

WILLY: Ah, you're the modiste Madame
Rastignac sent.
This way, please.
Have you heard?
I married an angel—

MODISTE: The clothes I arrange'll seem
Really like a dream!

1ST GIRL
(TO 2ND): Have you heard?
It sounds funny to me.

2ND GIRL
(TO 1ST): The Angel of whom he sings
Hasn't any wings.

WILLY
(TO ANGEL): Don't let this distress you,
Though it's new and strange—

MODISTE: After my girls dress you,
You'll look just like an angel—

WILLY: Have you heard—

MODISTE: [Measures Angel's bust]
You married an angel—
With dresses, the change'll be
Heavenly to see.
Thirty-four—

1ST GIRL: [Hands her a dress]
Thirty-four!

MODISTE: [Shows Angel the dress]
This, Madame, Monsieur will adore.
When you wear it, Monsieur will love
You, oh yes!

ANGEL: Will Willy love me or will he
Love the dress?

MODISTE: [Shows chemise]
Chic—very chic—the lovely chemise?

ANGEL: Chemise?

WILLY: Chemise?

MODISTE: Chemise.

ANGEL: What's that for? Tell me, please!

WILLY: Er, to cover—er, to cover—

ANGEL: Oh, tell me, sweet lover!

WILLY: It's hard to express;
It goes under your dress—

ANGEL: But, tell me, darling—what for?

WILLY: Oh, darling, explanations are a bore.

ANGEL: But if you can't be frank,
I shall be hurt—

MODISTE: It's your comme ci, comme ça.

WILLY: It's your undershirt!

MODISTE: [Holds up girdle]
This is the dernier cri de Paris.
It's very practical, don't you agree?

ANGEL: Willy, what is it? Tell me, do.

WILLY: It's—well, never mind—
But look at that shoe!

ANGEL: Very nice; but the harness, what is
that?

WILLY: It's to hold up—

ANGEL: To hold up?

WILLY: To hold up your hat!

MODISTE: [Shows brassiere]
And this—

WILLY: Good Lord!

ANGEL: [Takes brassiere and puts it on head]
What's that for, and where do I wear
it?

WILLY: Take it away! I just can't bear it!

ANGEL: [Puts it around neck]
Is it a scarf? Where does it go?

WILLY: In Heaven's name, get into it, and
then you'll know.

[Angel exits]

MODISTE: Wait for Madame, s'il vous plaît,
And she will be so distingué.
Monsieur, in a moment you will see
How elegant Madame can be.

WILLY: Well, we're waiting to be impressed.

MODISTE: One moment, please, and she'll be
fully dressed.
Our mode will make Madame so
smart,
So chic, a vision of Paris art.

[Angel appears, wearing everything wrong]

ANGEL: Here I am!

HOW TO WIN FRIENDS AND INFLUENCE PEOPLE

Published May 1938. Introduced by Audrey Christie,
Charles Walters, and ensemble.

VERSE

Back home our girls are models of good
behavior.
You're taught you have to save your charms from
the men.
In school, our girls are taught how to use
discretion.
Each day we have a session from nine to ten.
We're taught the why and wherefore,
How and when.

REFRAIN

When you talk
Don't talk, just sigh!
Get coy! Get shy!
That's how to win friends and influence people.

When you dance
Forget your feet!
Get close! Be sweet!
That's how to win friends and influence people.
Babes begin with
Yah! Yah! Yah!
Big girls win with
Yah! Yah! Yah!
But when you love
And find you're caught,
You'll give no thought
To how to win friends and influence people.
Yah! Yah! Yah!

SPRING IS HERE

Published May 1938. Introduced by Dennis King and
Vivienne Segal.

VERSE

Once there was a thing called spring,
When the world was writing verses
Like yours and mine.
All the lads and girls would sing
When we sat at little tables
And drank May wine.
Now April, May and June
Are sadly out of tune.
Life has stuck the pin in the balloon.

REFRAIN

Spring is here!
Why doesn't my heart go dancing?
Spring is here!
Why isn't the waltz entrancing?
No desire,
No ambition leads me.
Maybe it's because
Nobody needs me.
Spring is here!
Why doesn't the breeze delight me?
Stars appear!
Why doesn't the night invite me?
Maybe it's because
Nobody loves me.
Spring is here, I hear!

ANGEL WITHOUT WINGS

Musical interlude. Introduced by Vera Zorina, Mary Louise Quevli, Janis Dremann, Marcella Howard, Barbara Towne, Sylvia Stone, Diana Gaylen, and Althea Elder.

ANGEL: Lucinda! Arabella! Can you hear me?
    What shall I do now? Can you
    hear me?
    Lucinda! Clarinda!
    Philomena! Rosalina!
    Arabella! Seronella!
    Where did you come from, sisters
    dear?

LUCINDA: Out of the everywhere into the here.

CLARINDA: Where are your wings?

ANGEL: I've lost those things.

PHILOMENA: How can an angel lose her wings?

ANGEL: It just happened. It wasn't planned—

LUCINDA: But how?

ROSALINA: Tell us, now—

ANGEL: It's one of those earthly things you
    wouldn't understand.
    But welcome to our city, I hope
    you'll like our town.
    Excuse my lack of hospitality. Won't
    you—er—sit down?

CLARINDA: What a modern house!
    Everything so glossy!*

ROSALINA: Tell us who designed it?

ANGEL: Herman Rosse.

PHILOMENA: Quite a change from our abode
    With its heavenly dome.

ANGEL: It's only fifty rooms but to me it's
    home.

ALL: And no matter how humble
    There's no place like home.

LUCINDA: We came down here
    To try to help our sister, dear.
    I'm sorry I've waited to ask for so
    long.
    Tell us, sweet Brigitta, what is
    wrong?

ANGEL: I love my husband. He doesn't love
    me anymore.

LUCINDA: When did this happen? And what
    for?

ANGEL: He left me today!

LUCINDA: The Heaven you say!

ANGEL: He left me flat.

CLARINDA: Why did he do that?

Earlier version:
  Nothing could be keener!
  Tell us who designed it?
  Jo Mielziner.

ANGEL: I only said that his methods were
    fakey
    And the Bank itself was very, very
    shaky.

PHILOMENA: That was very sweet of you
    And just the very thing to do.

ANGEL: But what can I do
    How can I win him back?

ROSALINA: How can you win a husband back?

LUCINDA: We wouldn't know how to win him
    back.

CLARINDA: Ask Arabella—

ROSALINA: Arabella has a fella—

ARABELLA: Oh, sugar! Oh, spice—
    What's the good of my advice?

LUCINDA: Everybody knows it. Don't look so
    solemn.
    It was even printed in Lucifer's
    column—
    Of course, this may surprise you
    greatly—
    She's been flying around with
    Gabriel lately.

ROSALINA: You can't call that the worst of
    crimes.

LUCINDA: You hear that horn blowing at the
    funniest times

CLARINDA: How did you catch Gabriel?

ARABELLA: I didn't do a thing.

LUCINDA: Unh-unh—

ARABELLA: I didn't do much—except—well,
    sing,
    I played a few hosannas on my harp.
    I sang little songs I composed myself.
    Little things I took from the shelf,
    such as
    Beauty is truth,
    Truth, beauty.
    Gabriel blow your rootie-tootie.

LUCINDA: You see, that's sweet and not at all
    silly.
    Brigitta, suppose you try that on your
    Willy.

ALL: Beauty is truth
    Truth, beauty—
    Willy blow your rootie-tootie.

ANGEL: I don't think he'd appreciate that
    much,
    It hasn't quite got the earthly touch.
    Willy is different—strange and odd.
    And not an angel at all. Thank God.
    Thanks for advising me. Thanks
    indeed.
    But you can't give the advice I need.
    A man cannot live with an angel—
    that's true.
    Can't you understand that, any of
    you?

I've tried to be a woman. It's not for
    me.
    I've tried to be a wife. I couldn't be.
    Everything I do is wrong,
    So I must go back where I belong.
    Lucinda, Clarinda, take me back.
    Arabella, Seronella, take me back.
    Philomena, Rosalina, take me back!

LUCINDA: My dear Brigitta, you must awaken.
    You are sadly mistaken.
    You've come down to earth and here
    you must stay.
    It's too late for us to take you away.

ANGEL: I'll make him unhappy. You must
    take me along.

LUCINDA: You're a woman now. It would be
    wrong.

ANGEL: Oh no, I'm not. I'm like Philomena
    and you.
    I'm still an angel no matter what I
    do.

LUCINDA: You're not an angel anymore
    But one of those strange things.

ANGEL: A woman without love
    Or an angel without wings.

ALL: Angel without wings,
    You must come down to earth.
    You'll find some wonderful things,
    Much more than Heaven is worth!
    Angel without wings,
    You cannot fly up above.
    Open your eyes.
    Turn away from the skies
    And look at your Heaven—your love.

A TWINKLE IN YOUR EYE

Published May 1938. Introduced by Vivienne Segal.

VERSE

PEGGY: It's not what you do
    But what you promise,
    And you can fool a Doubting Thomas!
    If you've got old Egypt in your eyes
    You can be Antarctic otherwise.
    The flame's aroused
    Before not after.
    The thing itself is a cause for laughter.
    A couple of good lies
    From a couple of good eyes
    Can cut a man down to your size.

REFRAIN 1

You can do any little thing that you've a
    mind to,
But you must do it with a twinkle in your
    eye.
You can be unreserved and even
    unrefined, too,
But don't forget that little twinkle in your
    eye.
My aunt Clarisse mistook the iceman for
    my uncle.
Because she smiled my uncle Freddy
    passed it by.
Now, you can get away with murder of
    that kind, too,
But you must do it with a twinkle in your
    eye.

REFRAIN 2

You can break twenty hearts to get a new
    sensation,
But you must do it with a twinkle in your
    eye.
You may accompany a man on his
    vacation
If you return with just a twinkle in your
    eye.
My sister Sue once took a swim without a
    stitch on.
The cop who caught her took her to the
    jail nearby.
The judge who tried her held her for
    examination.
Of course, it may have been the twinkle
    in her eye.

REFRAIN 3

You can tell any man you're innocent like
    me now,
But you must do it with a twinkle in your
    eye.
There are a million manly goldfish in the
    sea now,
And you can hook them with a twinkle in
    your eye.
My uncle's wife once met a man who
    smiled so sweetly,
And Auntie didn't even seem to like the
    guy.
But, then, my little cousin Bess is nearly
    three now,
And she has quite a little twinkle in her
    eye.

I'M RUINED

Introduced by Dennis King, Walter Slezak, and Vivienne
Segal. Although not listed in programs, it is part of the
script. It was also titled "Roxy Routine #1" and segued
to "At the Roxy Music Hall."

WILLY: I'll be ruined, just ruined
    Before tomorrow ends,
    But, at least, not by my enemies
    But by my dearest friends.
HARRY: Forget it for tonight!
    Let's all get good and tight.
    Your bank will close in the morning,
    But tonight it's still all right.
PEGGY: In America, when things looked glum,
    Our President was not so dumb.
    He closed the banks for a day or two,
    Then opened them up—and the run was
        through.
    So, Willy, try America.
    It might do very well for ya!
WILLY: I'll open up a chain of banks
    In the state of Philadelphia.

AT THE ROXY
MUSIC HALL

Published August 1938. Introduced by Audrey Christie
and reprised by Miss Christie and Charles Walters.

VERSE

You've got to come to New York.
It would be such a pity
For anyone to go through life
Without seeing Roxy City!
The first thing foreigners do in New York
Is to look at Roxy City!

REFRAIN 1

Come with me
And you won't believe a thing you see.
Where an usher puts his heart in what he ushes,
Where a fountain changes color when it gushes,
Where the seats caress your carcass with their
    plushes,
At the Roxy Music Hall.
Hold my hand.
Don't be frightened when you hear that band:
They come up like Ali Baba from the cellar,

Through the courtesy of Mr. Rockefeller.
Then they play the overture from "William
    Tell"-er,
At the Roxy Music Hall.
You don't have to read the ads.
It's always worth the dough.
Any week you go,
It's the same old show!
Don't be shy
If a naked statue meets your eye.
Where the ballet is so sweet with birds and roses
That you break out in a rash before it closes,
At the Roxy Music Hall.

REFRAIN 2

Step this way.
Hear the super-duper organ play.
Where they change the lights a million times a
    minute.
Where the stage goes up and down when they
    begin it.
It's a wonder Mrs. Roosevelt isn't in it,
At the Roxy Music Hall.
Come along.
Hear them sing the "Volga Boatman" song.
Where the acrobats are whirling on their digits,
Where the balcony's so high you get the fidgets,
Where the actors seem to be a lot of midgets,
At the Roxy Music Hall.
If you're lost while climbing up
And find the going hard,
They are on their guard:
They send a Saint Bernard!
Come with me
Where the drinking cups are always free.
It's a Wonderland where ev'ryone is Alice,
Where the ladies' room is bigger than a palace,
At the Roxy Music Hall!

REPRISE (after Roxy Show)

Now you've seen
What a Roxy show can really mean—
And the ballet that you saw is called *Othello*,
Though it might as well have been some other
    fellow.
The stuff's been here so long it's good and
    mellow,
At the Roxy Music Hall.
Did you hear
What they sang about Milwaukee beer?
How those manly voices hated wine and kümmel.
They would fight for lager, lieber Gott im
    Himmel.
Can you picture the effect on Rudolf Friml?
At the Roxy Music Hall.

They can show the Grand Canal,
The Bridge of Sighs as well.
They do Venice swell,
And without the smell.
This way, please.
Join the happy crowd of glad standees
Where the spectacle goes on ad infinitum
And the picture is a secondary item,
At the Roxy Music Hall

MEN FROM MILWAUKEE

Probably unused. An operetta parody written for Dennis
King to perform in the Act II Roxy Music Hall sequence.
Registered for copyright as an unpublished song by Rob-
bins Music Corp., February 18, 1939.

On the Seine
And on the Rhine
Our foes are all fermenting wine,
But in old Wisconsin we're here

To fight for Victory of our beer.
Men of old Milwaukee,
Silent men not talkie,
We must stay forever free.
Down with Port or Rhine wine,
Let us call it Swine wine.
Ever powerful we will be.
Fight if you but smell wine,
Claret or Moselle wine.
Throw Champagne into the sea.
Grape or rotten berry,
Down with Spanish Sherry
And to hell with Burgundy!

OVERLEAF: Jimmy Savo (center) and Teddy Hart (insert)

THE BOYS FROM SYRACUSE | 1938

Tryout: Shubert Theatre, New Haven, November 3–5, 1938; Shubert Theatre, Boston, November 7–19, 1938. New York run: Alvin Theatre, November 23, 1938–June 10, 1939. 235 performances. Music by Richard Rodgers. Lyrics by Lorenz Hart. Produced by George Abbott. Book by George Abbott, based on the play *The Comedy of Errors* by William Shakespeare. Directed by George Abbott. Choreography by George Balanchine. Settings and lighting by Jo Mielziner. Costumes by Irene Sharaff. Orchestra under the direction of Harry Levant. Orchestrations by Hans Spialek. Cast, starring Jimmy Savo, Wynn Murray, Muriel Angelus, and Teddy Hart, included Marcy Westcott, Ronald Graham, Betty Bruce, Burl Ives, Robert Sydney, and Bob Lawrence. Vocal score published 1965.

I HAD TWINS

Introduced by Bob Lawrence, James Wilkinson, and ensemble. Alternate title: "He Had Twins."

[*Throughout the song the Policeman interprets the sounds representing the words of the Duke and the Merchant, Aegean, who are inside the courthouse. The Duke's mouth moves and we hear a bass clarinet, followed by the translation by the Policeman. When Aegean speaks, we hear an E-flat clarinet, followed by the Policeman's translation*]

CROWD: Hurrah! Hurroo!
  There'll be an execution.
  It serves him right.
  The law makes retribution.
  There's going to be a killing.
  Hurrah! Hurroo!
1ST CITIZEN: It serves him right.
  Hurrah! Hurroo!
  What did he do?
POLICEMAN: He came from Syracuse.
  CROWD: No! No! No!
POLICEMAN: Yes! Yes! Yes!
  So let him plead,
  For what's the use?
  The sap's from Syracuse!
  CROWD: The sap's from Syracuse!
POLICEMAN: Sh! Listen!
[*Aegean (E-flat clarinet) pleads*]
[*Duke (bass clarinet) answers*]
  Yes—he dies!
  CROWD: Good! That's one down!
[*Duke*]
POLICEMAN: He dies tomorrow at sundown.
  Our rigid laws of Ephesus
  Most rightfully refuse
  A visa to any citizen

Of uncivilized Syracuse.
If any one of us would dare to go
To that barbaric city,
He'd get the ax the same as he—
That's why he gets no pity.
CROWD: Give him the ax, the ax, the ax—
  Give him the ax, the ax—
[*Duke*]
POLICEMAN: Unless he can pay a thousand
    marks,
  Or borrow it from the local sharks.
[*Duke*]
  Why did you come here?
[*Aegean*]
  I had twins.
  CROWD: He had twins.
  That's nothing much agin him.
  He had twins.
POLICEMAN: I never thought he had it in him.
  CROWD: Ha, ha, ha, ha, ha.
[*Duke*]
POLICEMAN: Is that why you came here?
[*The Policeman now translates Aegean's story for him, each line coming first from Aegean's E-flat clarinet and then sung by the Policeman*]
  I had twins who looked alike,
  Couldn't tell one from the other.
  They had two slaves who looked
    alike,
  Couldn't tell one from his brother.
  But on one unlucky day
  We went sailing on the sea.
  This was an unlucky blunder,
  For our ship was torn asunder
  Just like that!
  Just like that!
  Just
  Like
  That!
  See?
  One young twin went down with me,
  One went swimming with his
    mother.
  We were parted by the sea,
  Man and wife and slave and brother.
  Now my one remaining brave boy
  Went a-searching with his slave boy.
  Having lost my son
  And wife, too—
  I will gladly give my life, too—
  Just like that!
  Just like that!
  Just
  Like
  That!
  See?
  I have searched the isles of Greece
  From my home to far-off Samos.

  Didn't know your local laws.
  I am just an ignoramus.
  I am sinless!
  I am twinless!
  I am wifeless!
  I am lifeless!
  I
  Am
  Glad
  To
  Die!
  He had twins,
  For them he'd give his life.
  He had twins,
  To say nothing of his wife.
  CROWD: Hurrah! Hurroo!
  There'll be an execution.
  It serves him right.
  The law makes retribution.
  There's going to be a killing.
  Hurrah! Hurroo!
  What did he do?
  He came from Syracuse.
  Yes! Yes! Yes!
  Yes! Yes! Yes!
  Yes! Yes! Yes!

DEAR OLD SYRACUSE

Introduced by Jimmy Savo and Eddie Albert. Danced by Eddie Albert, Alice Craig, Vivien Moore, Lita Lede, and ensemble.

VERSE

This is a terrible city.
The people are cattle and swine.
There isn't a girl I'd call pretty
Or a friend that I'd call mine.
And the only decent place on earth
Is the town that gave me birth.

REFRAIN 1

You can keep your Athens,
You can keep your Rome.
I'm a hometown fellow
And I pine for home.
I wanna go back, go back
To dear old Syracuse.
Though I've worn out sandals
And my funds are low,
There's a light that's burning in the patio.
I wanna go back, go back

To dear old Syracuse.
It is no metropolis,
It has no big Acropolis,
And yet there is a quorum
Of cuties in the forum.
Though the boys wear tunics that are out of style
They will always greet me with a friendly smile.
I wanna go back, go back
To dear old Syracuse.

REFRAIN 2

Both the Nile and Danube*
Are a silly bore.
I've a hometown river
That assaults my door.
I wanna go back, go back
To dear old Syracuse.
When a man is lonely
It is good to know
There's a red light burning in the patio.
I wanna go back, go back
To dear old Syracuse.
Wives don't want divorces there,
The men are strong as horses there,
And should a man philander,
The goose forgives the gander.
When the search for love becomes a mania,
You can take the night boat to Albania.
I wanna go back, go back
To dear old Syracuse.

WHAT CAN YOU DO WITH A MAN?

Introduced by Wynn Murray and Teddy Hart.

VERSE

LUCE: Listen to your lady who speaks.
This affair has run its course.
I'll reside in Athens six weeks
While I get me a divorce.
DROMIO: Listen to your lover who asks
Why this battle has begun.
LUCE: He has long neglected some tasks
That a husband should have done.

Alternate version of refrain 2, lines 1–4:
I do not agree
With Mr. Spartacus.
I was never meant
To be a hearty cuss.

REFRAIN 1

He eats me out of house and home
But doesn't like my cooking.
That's nothing new with a man.
What can you do with a man?
He likes to use my brush and comb
And yet he's funny-looking.
Home's like a zoo with a man.
What can you do with a man?
Some men wear half pajamas.
I took a chance.
I bought the guy pajamas—
He wears the pants.
By day he's like a five-year-old;
At night he's ninety-seven.
What can you do with a man like that?

REFRAIN 2

DROMIO: When you get mad, don't count to ten,
Go on and count a million.
Don't be a shrew with a man.
That's what you do with a man.
You need a regiment of men—
I'm only one civilian.
Wait for your cue with a man.
That's what you do with a man.
Marriage is such a blessing,
So I have found.
I've got a thousand blessings,
Each weighs a pound.
I'm only four foot ten right now,
I once was five foot seven.
That's what you did to a man like that!

REFRAIN 3

LUCE: I wear my nicest negligee
And find him reading Plato.
Nothing is new with a man.
What can you do with a man?
I shook the tree of life one day
And got a cold potato.
I'm in a stew with a man.
What can you do with a man?
Where is his sense of duty,
Where is his taste?
Acres and acres of beauty
Going to waste!
He walks me in the woods at night
To find a four-leaf clover.
What can you do with a man like that?

FALLING IN LOVE WITH LOVE

Published November 1938. Introduced by Muriel Angelus and ladies of the ensemble.

VERSE

I weave with brightly colored strings
To keep my mind off other things;
So, ladies, let your fingers dance,
And keep your hands out of romance.
Lovely witches,
Let the stitches
Keep your fingers under control.
Cut the thread, but leave
The whole heart whole.
Merry maids can sew and sleep;
Wives can only sew and weep!

REFRAIN

Falling in love with love
Is falling for make-believe.
Falling in love with love
Is playing the fool.
Caring too much is such
A juvenile fancy.
Learning to trust is just
For children in school.
I fell in love with love
One night when the moon was full.
I was unwise, with eyes
Unable to see.
I fell in love with love,
With love everlasting,
But love fell out with me.

THE SHORTEST DAY OF THE YEAR

Published October 1938. Introduced by Ronald Graham, Dolores Anderson, and ensemble. Danced by Betty Bruce, Heidi Vosseler, and George Church.

VERSE

It rained the day before we met,
Then came three days that I forget;
And then, my love, we met again
And I remember things from then.
I measure time by what we do
And so my calendar is you.

REFRAIN

The shortest day of the year
Has the longest night of the year,
And the longest night
Is the shortest night with you.
The smallest smile on your face
Is the greatest kind of embrace,
And a single kiss
Is a thousand dreams come true.
Your softest sigh,
That is my strongest tie.
There's you, there's I;
What can time do?
The shortest day of the year
Has the longest night of the year,
And the longest night
Is the shortest night with you.

THIS CAN'T BE LOVE

Published October 1938. Introduced by Eddie Albert and Marcy Westcott. Reprise sung by Wynn Murray.

VERSE 1

HE: In Verona, my late cousin Romeo
    Was three times as stupid as my Dromio.
    For he fell in love
    And then he died of it.
    Poor half-wit!

REFRAIN

    This can't be love
    Because I feel so well—
    No sobs, no sorrows, no sighs.
    This can't be love,
    I get no dizzy spell,
    My head is not in the skies.
    My heart does not stand still—
    Just hear it beat!
    This is too sweet
    To be love.
    This can't be love
    Because I feel so well,
    But still I love to look in your eyes.

VERSE 2

SHE: Though your cousin loved my cousin Juliet,
    Loved her with a passion much more truly
      yet,
    Some poor playwright

Wrote their drama just for fun.
It won't run!

REPEAT REFRAIN

COMIC REPRISE

    This must be love,
    For I don't feel so well—
    These sobs, these sorrows, these sighs.
    This must be love,
    Here comes that dizzy spell,
    My head is up in the skies.
    Just now my heart stood still—
    It missed a beat!
    Life is not sweet—
    This is love.
    This must be love,
    For I don't feel so well.
    Alas, I love to look in your eyes.

LET ANTIPHOLUS IN

Finale, Act I. Introduced by the entire company.

[Chant with orchestra alternating with speaking lines]
Let Antipholus in!
Let Antipholus in!
Let Antipholus in!
[etc.]

LADIES OF THE EVENING

Introduced by Bob Lawrence, James Wilkinson, and ensemble. Danced by Heidi Vosseler and George Church.

LADIES: Poor little daughters of the moon
    When the sun is dawning.
    What is as sour as a day in June
    For the ladies of the evening
    In the morning?
    Lost is the music of the night
    For the daily clamor.
    Noses are red and cheeks are white.
    Where the hell's our glamour?
    Where the hell's our glamour!
POLICE: We let the burglars take their snatch
    To the shop for pawning.

    All that we ever aim to catch
    Is the ladies of the evening in the
      morning.
    All night they bring rich men to grief
    Till they have no cash left.
    Cops can't afford the good roast beef,
    But we have the hash left.
ALL: A plum becomes a prune,
    A joke becomes a pun,
    And daughters of the moon
    Must stray beneath the sun.
    Let them earn an honest drachma
    While the moral girls are yawning.
    A policeman's lot
    Is ladies of the evening
    In the morning.
    So start the day
    The Police Department way
    With the ladies of the evening
    In the morning.

HE AND SHE

Introduced by Wynn Murray and Jimmy Savo.

VERSE

SHE: I was I,
    You were you,
    And now we're only we.
    We are one
    Who were two,
    Or we had better be.
HE: "I now pronounce you man and wife"
    Are magic words like "Open Sesame."
SHE: But though they made you mine for life,
    They also made you think much less o'
      me.
HE: It only shows how little you know of it.
SHE: I know a pair who made quite a go of it.

REFRAIN 1

SHE: He was a man who was very fond of
      women.
    She was a girl who was very fond of men.
    She had a taste for both corpulent and
      slim men.
    He wouldn't look at a lady under ten.
    She went abroad just to find a man to
      marry.
    He went abroad just to find himself a wife.
    She didn't want any Tom or Dick or
      Harry.

He sought a mate who'd be true to him
    for life.
She fell in love with the angle of his
    eyebrow.
He fell in love with the dimple on her
    knee.
And when they wed,
He went around with other women
And she went with other men.
And that is he and she!

REFRAIN 2

HE: He always said, "I would like to have a
    daughter."
She always said, "I would like to have a
    son."
She took to kids like a duckling takes to
    water.
He always thought having babies would be
    fun.
He told her this on the very day he met
    her.
She said, "The wish is the father to the
    sport."
He bought a house, in the nursery he set
    her.
She helped the stork make his annual
    report.
He won renown as the father of a
    squadron.
She won awards for her prolificacy.
And just because,
And just because they loved their children
They got married after all.
And that is he and she!

REFRAIN 3

HE: She was so pure as the snow before it's
    driven.
SHE: He never smoked and he never touched a
    drop.
HE: When she said "Boo" she would ask to be
    forgiven.
SHE: When he would swim he would always
    wear the top.
HE: She wore no rouge though she had a bad
    complexion.
SHE: He always prayed ev'ry time he went to
    bed.
HE: She was so kind that she hated vivisection.
SHE: He loved his ma and he swore he'd never
    wed.
HE: She was so chaste that it made her very
    nervous.
SHE: He loved to go to the vicarage for tea.

BOTH: And when they died,
    And when they died and went to Heaven
    All the angels moved to Hell.
    And that is he and she!

YOU HAVE CAST YOUR SHADOW ON THE SEA

Published November 1938. Introduced by Marcy West-cott and Eddie Albert.

VERSE

HE: Let the winds of the Seven Seas
    Blow my good ship where they please;
    I can never sail away from you.
    Though my bark like a shell is hurled
    To the edge of this flat old world,
    You'll be with me till the journey's through
    Until I return to you.

REFRAIN 1

You have cast your shadow on the sea,
On both the sea and me.
Not a shadow dancing in the sun
That fades when day is done.
Although I sail
And reach the ends of the world,
Your hand will reach my heart.
When you cast your shadow on the sea,
You'll be with me!

REFRAIN 2

SHE: You will cast your shadow from the sea,
    On both the land and me.
    Not a shadow dancing in the sun
    That fades when day is done.
    Since you have made
    This tender shade for my heart,
    My heart's no longer free.
    When you cast your shadow from the sea,
    You'll be with me.

COME WITH ME

Introduced by Bob Lawrence, Ronald Graham, James Wilkinson, John Clarke, and ensemble.

REFRAIN

Come with me
Where the food is free,
Where the landlord never comes near you.
Be a guest in a house of rest
Where the best of fellows can cheer you.
There's your own little room,
So cool, not too much light,
Where you're one man for whom
No wife waits up at night.
When day ends
You have lots of friends
Who will guard you well while you slumber.
Safe from battle and strife,
Safe from the wind and gale,
Come with me to jail!

INTERLUDE

You never have to fetch the milk
Or walk the dog at early dawn.
There's no "Get up—you're late for work!"
While you rest in the pearly dawn.
You're never bored by politics.
You're privileged to miss a row
Of tragedies by Sophocles
And diatribes by Cicero.
Your brother's wife will never come
On Sunday noon to bring to you
Her little son who plays the lute,
Her little girl to sing to you.
You can commit your little sins
And relatives won't yell "Fie!"
You needn't take that annual trip
To the oracle at Delphi.
You snore and swear and stretch and yawn
In this, your strictly male house;
The only way that sinners go to Heaven
Is in the jailhouse!

REPEAT REFRAIN

BIG BROTHER

Introduced by Teddy Hart.

Where do you wander tonight,
Big Brother?
Is the world treating you right,
Big Brother?
If you are East or West
Listen to my request:
Come to your brother's breast,

Big Brother!
Come to your twin.
I'll treat you like a mother.
Each little twin can have only
One Brother,
Big Brother! Big Brother!

SING FOR YOUR SUPPER

Published October 1938. Introduced by Muriel Angelus,
Marcy Westcott, Wynn Murray, and ensemble. Danced by
Betty Bruce and ensemble.

VERSE

Hawks and crows do lots of things,
But the canary only sings.
She is a courtesan on wings—
So I've heard.
Eagles and storks are twice as strong.
All the canary knows is song.
But the canary gets along—
Gilded bird!

REFRAIN

Sing for your supper,
And you'll get breakfast.
Songbirds always eat
If their song is sweet to hear.
Sing for your luncheon,
And you'll get dinner.
Dine with wine of choice,
If romance is in your voice.
I heard from a wise canary
Trilling makes a fellow willing,
So, little swallow, swallow now.
Now is the time to
Sing for your supper,
And you'll get breakfast.
Songbirds are not dumb,
They don't buy a crumb
Of bread,
It's said.
So sing and you'll be fed.

OH, DIOGENES

Published November 1938. Introduced by Wynn Murray.
Danced by George Church, Betty Bruce, and ensemble.

VERSE

There was an old zany who lived in a tub;
He had so many fleabites
He didn't know where to rub.
He kept looking for an honest man.
Said, "I'm gonna find him if I can."
If I could meet Diogenes today,
This is what I'd say:
"Rub a dub dub,
Hop out of your tub,
Diogenes!"

REFRAIN

Oh, Diogenes!
Find a man who's honest.
Oh, Diogenes!
Wrap him up for me.
Oh, Diogenes!
Find a man who's stolid—solid!
Hook that fish if he's in the sea.
Hunt him! Trail him!
Catch him! Nail him!
If he is free.
Have you got your stick?
Have you got your lantern?
Can you do the trick
And produce him, please!
Catch that fellow!
Ring that bell,
Oh, Diogenes!

FILM VERSION, 1940

The film version, with two new songs by Rodgers and Hart
("The Greeks Have No Word for It" and "Who Are
You?"), was a Universal Picture, released in August
1940.

THE GREEKS HAVE NO WORD FOR IT

Introduced by Martha Raye and ensemble.

INTRODUCTION

VESTAL
VOTARIES: Strike the lute in the arena
For the festival of Athena.
Bend the toe, the light fantastic,
Plastic, elastic and gymnastic.
Gently sway and gently follow
All the precepts of Apollo.
La-di-da,
La-di-da,
LUCE: La-di-da,
La-di-da,
La-di-dig-dig-dig!
Vum-vum-vum,
Boogie-Boogie-Woogie Zum!
PHYLLIS: Stop, 'tis sacrilege!
Quiet, Luce!
LUCE: You just haven't got it,
What's the use?

VERSE

When Orpheus started the Orpheum
circuit
Me and Romeo used to work it;
One day we danced for the great
Achilles
And gave Achilles the willies.

REFRAIN

The Greeks have no word for it,
It's too hot.
But you either have it or you have it
not.
The Greeks have no word for it,
They're too slow.
But the African slaves all call it
hi-de-ho!
You pose and pose
And peck and peck;
You lift your nose
And you twist your neck;
You cut the rug,
You knock your knees;
Then you lift your tunic
And shake your toga
In the evening breeze.
Oh, you can't do a hep to it,
Hear the call!
But the Greeks have no word for it at
all.

WHO ARE YOU?

Published July 1940. Introduced by Allan Jones.

VERSE

Look into the pupils of my eyes and you will see
What a pretty picture luck has sent to me!
Now my life's beginning as I bathe in your
  reflection.
Thank you, Luck, for guiding me
In the right direction!

REFRAIN

Who are you
To give this world of mine
A light and brighter shine?
I wonder who are you
To make a vacant room
A place where flowers bloom
And tell me who am I
That when I think of your face
I dance into space
So happy and graceful, too.
If that's what you can do
I wonder who are you?

TOO MANY GIRLS | 1939

Tryout: Shubert Theatre, Boston, October 2–14, 1939. New York run: Imperial Theatre, October 18, 1939–May 18, 1940. 249 performances. Music by Richard Rodgers. Lyrics by Lorenz Hart. Produced by George Abbott. Book by George Marion, Jr. Directed by George Abbott. Choreography by Robert Alton. Settings and lighting by Jo Mielziner. Costumes by Raoul Pené DuBois. Orchestra under the direction of Harry Levant. Orchestrations by Hans Spialek. Vocal arrangements by Hugh Martin. Cast, starring Marcy Westcott, Hal LeRoy, Mary Jane Walsh, and Richard Kollmar, included Diosa Costello, Desi Arnaz, Eddie Bracken, Leila Ernst, and Van Johnson.

HEROES IN THE FALL

Introduced by James Wilkinson and ensemble. Alternate title: "The Team." Richard Rodgers, in his autobiography, *Musical Stages* (Random House, 1975, p. 192), wrote: "I vaguely remember that I came up with the idea for the opening number in the show, 'Heroes in the Fall,' in which the football players of Pottawatomie College lament the brevity of their tenure as campus luminaries. Since Larry was nowhere to be found, I had to supply the necessary lyric myself. This happened on a few other occasions as well. All the major songs, however, did have lyrics written by Larry."

VERSE

When the spring semester closes
Life is not a bed of roses.
The glories of the autumn
Will not pay our rent.
Spring is the winter of our discontent.

REFRAIN

We hate the little flowers,
We hate the robin's call,
We hate the signs of spring
Because we're heroes in the fall.
We resent the scent of roses,
The trees, the grass and all,
And summer leaves us cold
Because we're heroes in the fall.
We hate the little children
Who gambol on the green;
The sight of strolling lovers
Just aggravates our spleen.
We wish the little groundhog
Would never start to crawl;
We hate the signs of spring
Because it makes bums of us all—

We're heroes in the fall.

Summer—summer—summer—summer
Summer—summer—summer
1: I'm a bellboy.
2: I'm an iceman.
3: Fuller Brush man.
4: I'm a tutor.
5: I'm an actor.
6: I'm a waiter.
7: I'm a chauffeur.
8: I'm a shoe clerk.
9: I'm a lifeguard.
10: I'm a caddy.
11: I'm a nursemaid to the nastiest little brat you ever saw, and every night I have to take his mother out dancing.

We wish the little groundhog
Would never start to crawl;
We hate the signs of spring
Because it makes bums of us all—
We're heroes in the fall.

TEMPT ME NOT

Introduced by Desi Arnaz, Richard Kollmar, and ensemble.

VERSE

GIRLS: The first thing we learn in school
Is what to wear and how to wear it.
MANUELITO: Go 'way, I just can't bear it!
CLINT: Steady, my lad, keep cool.
Just look at a woman's knee.
Stockings make the limbs attractive.
MANUELITO: That's a law that's retroactive.
Together they're nice to see.
CLINT: Clothes make women make a fool of me!
MANUELITO: Of me!
GIRLS: Of you?
2 BOYS: Of me!

REFRAIN 1

BOTH: Tempt me not,
Get thee behind me, Satin!
MANUELITO: The sight of silk
Is a danger sign.
CLINT: It's all a plot
Making a Yank a Latin.
My blood was milk;
Now it's turned to wine.
MANUELITO: Give a girl a skirt,

Give a skirt a rustle,
And a man of muscle
Is up a tree.
CLINT: Can't you see my nerves are shot?
Get thee behind me, Satin!
BOTH: I beg of thee, keep thou away from me!

REFRAIN 2

AL: Tempt him not,
Get thee behind him, Satin!
ALL: The sight of silk
Is a danger sign.
It's all a plot
Laid out for a baby Latin.
His blood was milk;
Now it's turned to wine.
Any kind of skirt
Seen by Manuelito
Is a big magneto.
His wits are dim—
Hide that limb—
His nerves are shot—
Get thee behind him, Satin!
I beg of thee, keep thou away from
him.

MY PRINCE

Introduced by Marcy Westcott. Alternate title: "What a Prince!" By October 1940 it was replaced by "You're Nearer."

VERSE

It was gay on the Riviera
At a lovely costume ball.
It was spring, La Primavera.
He appeared so straight and tall.
I smiled shyly but I simmered
Underneath his manly glance
And his lustrous, dark eyes glimmered
With the torchlight of romance.
But he left me at a loss
With a well-known double cross.

REFRAIN

What a Prince!
He said, "Cinderella, let's dance again."
In his arms
I discovered Princes are only men.
Time's gone by; meanwhile I

Haven't seen him since.
What a guy! What a heel! What a Prince!
It may be
That I am beginning to lose my touch;
Or did he
Merely drink a magnum or two too much?
I was flat on the mat
For the count of nine.
Where's that charming Prince of mine!

TRIO:

Charming—he knew his stuff.
Charming—gentle but rough.
Charming—I yelled, "Enough!"
When he said, "Let us leave in my regal little
    Buick.
I know a joint where they're hep to all the jive.
Then after that
You can see my royal flat.
It's a Louis Quatorzian dive."
[*Clint to boys*] The Rat!
Charming—then I understood.
Charming—but he meant no royal good.
Charming—I replied I would
Just take a peek at his sumptuous apartment.
Oh, but his line was swell!
Then the clock went "Bong!" twelve times—
Cinderella was saved by the bell!
I could cry.
I'm afraid I've lost you, my lucky star,
And that I
By not going far enough went too far.
I was flat on the mat
For the count of nine.
Where's that charming Prince of mine!

POTTAWATOMIE

Introduced by Clyde Fillmore and Hans Robert.

We think of thee, Pottawatomie,
Pottawatomie, of thee!
Where the cactus on the campus blooms again,
Where the lovely greensward's mightier than the
    pen,
Boys and girls together in thy bounty,
Fairest school in all of Stop Gap County,
Pottawatomie, 'tis thee.
Pottawatomie!

You made a lot o' me,
Pottawatomie.
You hit the spot o' me,

Pottawatomie.
I love Pottawatomie
With all my anatomie,
So each tiny tot o' me
That is begot o' me
Will go to Pot—
Will go to Pot—
To Pottawatomie!

Boys and girls together in thy bounty,
Fairest school in all of Stop Gap County,
Pottawatomie, 'tis thee.
Pottawatomie!

'CAUSE WE GOT CAKE

Published May 1984 as part of *Rodgers & Hart: A Musical Anthology*. Introduced by Mary Jane Walsh. Danced by ensemble.

VERSE

The spirit's always willing when it's fed;
When it's not fed the spirit's dead.
And if the spirit really wants to dance
It needs a little more than bread.
To cure the spirit's ache
Give it a little cake!

REFRAIN

Come, you all, kick up the cakewalk,
'Cause we got cake.
Lady Luck finally learned to bake.
Who said bread? Kick up the cakewalk,
'Cause we got pie,
Here and now, not in the by and by.
Say goodbye to trouble and famine,
It's time to laugh.
Laugh, boys, you can examine
The fatted calf.
Come, you all, kick up the cakewalk,
We got a break.
Ev'ryone who is awake, walk
The cakewalk,
'Cause we all got cake!

LOVE NEVER WENT TO COLLEGE

Published October 1939. Introduced by Marcy Westcott and Richard Kollmar.

VERSE

A pretty girl and a bright young man
Try to be just friends but never can.
That is what perplexes
Young folks of opposite sexes.
Love likes to pull their legs a bit,
So they're either in love or out of it.
Love doesn't make much sense
But his technique is immense.

REFRAIN

Love never went to college.
Ignorant boy, that.
But think of the joy that he starts.
His work requires no knowledge,
So he can do it
By using intuitive arts.
He just says, "You two kids,
Start falling in love.
I ain't got brains
But I reigns over all these parts."
Love never went to college,
Never had teaching,
And yet he keeps reaching our hearts!

SPIC AND SPANISH

Published October 1939. Introduced by Diosa Costello and ensemble. Alternate title: "All Dressed Up Spic and Spanish."

VERSE (published version)

There's no Cinderella in Spain;
That story was pulled by a Dane.
Our young girls are simple and pure,
But watched night and day to be sure.
And now I'm alone,
Wide awake and full-grown,
With no fairy Prince
To call on the phone.
What's the matter with me
That I'm here all alone?

REFRAIN

All dressed up
Spic and Spanish,
But I got no place to go.
Got some things I got to show.
Oh!
All dressed up
Slick and Spanish,
No one takes me for a ride
Haven't got a thing to hide.
I want to go away
Where the men make music,
And play till the night is day.
Cock-a-doodle Daddy!
Spic and Span,
Spic and Spanish,
Not the type to cook or sew.
Here's the girl but where's the beau?
I want to go away! Away!

VERSE (in printed script)

I'm tired of leading the cheers
Which no one who cares for me hears.
If I had a lover today,
I'd cheer him in some other way.
And now I'm alone,
Wide awake and full-grown,
With no caballero
To call on the phone.
What's the matter with me
That I'm here all alone?

I LIKE TO RECOGNIZE
THE TUNE

Published October 1939. Introduced by Eddie Bracken,
Marcy Westcott, Mary Jane Walsh, Richard Kollmar, and
Hal LeRoy.

VERSE

Some funny folks like to shoot off rockets,
Others like to pick your pockets.
Some of them kill when they feel the urge,
Others go in for perjury.
I, too, have a passion that I can't understand.
It comes out when I hear a band.

REFRAIN

I like to recognize the tune,
I want to savvy what the band is playing.

I keep saying,
Must you bury the tune?
I've got to know the answer soon.
Is it a cat meowing in the attic?
Is it static?
Must you bury the tune?
A guy called Krupa plays the drums like
    thunder,
But the melody is six feet under.
There isn't anyone immune—
They kill the Billy Roses and Puccinis.
Don't be meanies.
Must you bury the tune?

ADDITIONAL STANZAS

When that big maestro plays the songs he's
    written
Poor Tchaikovsky down below starts spittin'.
There isn't anyone immune—
They kill the Irving Berlins and Rossinis.
Don't be meanies.
Must you bury the tune?

When old Ben Bernie starts his band with
    "Yowser,"
Ole Man Mose is dead, and so's *Tannhäuser.*
There isn't anyone immune—
They kill the Georgie Cohans and the Strausses.
Don't be louses.
Must you bury the tune?

When Horace Heidt gives out with rhythm silky*
Mrs. Roosevelt starts to dance with Willkie.
There isn't anyone immune—
They kill the Vincent Youmans and the Gounods.
Don't be *you-knows.*
Must you bury the tune?

When she hears those chords of Eddie Duchin's
Elsa Maxwell quivers with her two chins.
There isn't anyone immune—
They kill the Arthur Schwartzes and the Glinkas.
Don't be shtinkers.
Must you bury the tune?

Alternate version of lines 1–2:
    When Kay Kyser jazzes "Florodora"
    Mrs. Roosevelt starts to dance with Borah:

LOOK OUT

Introduced by Mary Jane Walsh and ensemble. Danced by
Diosa Costello, Desi Arnaz, and ensemble.

We have won the fray,
Give a hip olé,
I mean hip-hooray!
Shout:
Bum, get a rat trap
Bigger than a cat trap,
Bum, give a rat trap now!
Yell a big bravo,
I mean vivavo,
For the world to know.
Shout:
Bum, get a rat trap
Bigger than a cat trap,
Bum, you're a rat and how!
Hold your hats, boys! Wow!
Now, Harvard, look out!
Princeton, look out!
We shout: Look out, Yale!
You're a ham,
Better scram,
Notre Dame;
We'll make Williams wail.
Army, you're through!
Navy, you too!
Pooh! Pooh! To Purdue!
Georgia Tech,
Take a trek,
You're a wreck!
Look at Brown turn blue!
We'll make a bum-bi-ya, Columbia;
In our quota,
Minnesota's
Gotta go!
When we win,
We'll take the skin a ya,
Virginia!
California,
Let's warn ya,
It'll snow!
Dartmouth, beware!
Fordham, take care,
We'll put you to rout!
U. of C.,
U. of P.,
U. of all the alphabet,
We shout:
Look out!
Pottawatomie!
Pottawatomie!
Yeah!

Hit him harder!
Hit him harder!

THE SWEETHEARTS OF THE TEAM

Introduced by Mary Jane Walsh and ensemble. Dropped from the show during the post-Broadway tour. In the June 1941 St. Louis Municipal Opera production, it was replaced by a song titled "Romantic Guy, I," sung by Jack Williams in the role of Al, which was created by Hal LeRoy. It is not known whether "Romantic Guy, I" is by Rodgers and Hart, as no copy survives.

VERSE

ALL: We're the sweethearts of the team!
We're the Varsity Second Eleven
And we ought to be in Heaven.
Our names are in the columns.
And our faces are in print.
Endorsing creams and cigarettes
Is bringing us a mint.
1ST GIRL: My sweetheart is a halfback.
2ND GIRL: My hero is an end.
EILEEN: When her lover is an athlete
Then a lady needs a friend.

REFRAIN 1

ALL: We're the sweethearts of the team.
They're in training, so we're trained to dream.
Our lovers don't drink,
They don't smoke very much.
Our lovers make touchdowns
But they never touch.
They get all of their power
From beefsteak and eggs,
But it's all in the arms
And all in the legs.
When the moon's aglow
And the stars are agleam,
Their strength of character makes you scream.
Love is just condensed milk—
Alma Mater takes the cream
From the sweethearts of the team!

CODA

Rah! Rah! Ev'ry man's a hero.
Siss! Boom! Hear the people scream!
But so far the score is zero
For the sweethearts of the team!

REFRAIN 2

We're the sweethearts of the team.
We've lost nothing that we can't redeem.
Their shoulders are big
And their waistlines are small.
With amorous passion
They tackle a ball.
They give dear Alma Mater the fame it deserves.
While they build up their strength
They tear down our nerves.
They obey their coach
For his word is supreme.
All work, no women, is part of his scheme.
So they jump on a dummy—
That's the way they let off steam.
We're the sweethearts of the team!

REPEAT CODA

SHE COULD SHAKE THE MARACAS

Published October 1939. Introduced by Diosa Costello and Desi Arnaz.

VERSE

Ev'ry Latin has a temper,
Latins have no brains,
And they quarrel as they walk in
Latin Lovers' Lanes.
So before you lose your temper,
Listen, little señorita,
And I'll tell to you the story
Of Pepito and Pepita:

REFRAIN

She could shake the maracas,
He could play the guitar,
But he lived in Havana
And she down in Rio del Mar.
And she shook her maracas
In a Portuguese bar
While he strummed in Havana.
The distance between them was far.
By and by
He got a job with a band in Harlem.
She got a job with a band in Harlem.
Ay! Ay! Ay!

He said, "I'm the attraction!"
She said, "I am the star!"
But they finally married
And now see how happy they are.
So shake your maracas,
Play your guitar!

I DIDN'T KNOW WHAT TIME IT WAS

Published October 1939. Introduced by Marcy Westcott and Richard Kollmar.

VERSE 1

Once I was young—
Yesterday, perhaps—
Danced with Jim and Paul
And kissed some other chaps.
Once I was young,
But never was naive.
I thought I had a trick or two
Up my imaginary sleeve.
And now I know I was naive.

REFRAIN

I didn't know what time it was,
Then I met you.
Oh, what a lovely time it was,
How sublime it was, too!
I didn't know what day it was.
You held my hand.
Warm like the month of May it was,
And I'll say it was grand.
Grand to be alive, to be young,
To be mad, to be yours alone!
Grand to see your face, feel your touch,
Hear your voice say I'm all your own.
I didn't know what year it was.
Life was no prize.
I wanted love and here it was
Shining out of your eyes.
I'm wise,
And I know what time it is now.

VERSE 2

Once I was old—
Twenty years or so—
Rather well preserved:
The wrinkles didn't show.
Once I was old,
But not too old for fun.

I used to hunt for little girls
With my imaginary gun.
But now I aim for only one!

REPEAT REFRAIN

TOO MANY GIRLS

Introduced by Desi Arnaz and ensemble.

VERSE

To say goodbye to one sweetheart
Is not much pain if any,
It's twenty times the tragedy
To say goodbye to many.
Goodbye, my ev'ry sweetheart,
Goodbye, my ev'ry care.
Goodbye, you gorgeous idiots
Who got into my hair!

REFRAIN

Too many girls,
Too many girls.
They're not worth what they cost.
When you win, then you've lost.
They're just oysters who haven't any pearls.
I tell you, men, there's too many girls.
While you work they all sleep.
While you sleep they all work
To get you in deep.
Too many girls,
Too many girls.
I got lonesome last night
And I thought that I might
Like my fingers to play among some curls.
How can one man have too many girls!

GIVE IT BACK TO THE INDIANS

Published October 1939. Introduced by Mary Jane Walsh.
Danced by Hal LeRoy and ensemble.

VERSE

Old Peter Minuit had nothing to lose
When he bought the isle of Manhattan
For twenty-six dollars and a bottle of booze,

And they threw in the Bronx and Staten.
Pete thought that he had the best of the bargain,
But the poor Red Man just grinned.
And he grunted, "Ugh," meaning O.K. in his
    jargon,
For he knew poor Pete was skinned.
We've tried to run the city,
But the city ran away.
And now, Peter Minuit,
We can't continue it!

REFRAIN 1

Broadway's turning into Coney,
Champagne Charlie's drinking gin,
Old New York is new and phony—
Give it back to the Indians.
Two cents more to smoke a Lucky,
Dodging buses keeps you thin,
New New York is simply ducky—
Give it back to the Indians.
Take all the reds
On the boxes made for soap,
Whites on Fifth Avenue,
Blues down in Wall Street losing hope—
Big bargain today,
Chief, take it away.
Come, you busted city slickers,
Better take it on the chin.
Father Knick has lost his knickers—
Give it back to the Indians!

REFRAIN 2

Eighty-sixth Street looks like Berlin
And the Giants never win.
No dark park to kiss your girl in—
Give it back to the Indians.
Even Harlem's getting darker,
No more jokes to make us grin.
M-G-M's got Dotty Parker—
Give it back to the Indians.
Go to the park,
See the monkeys in the zoo,
All absolutely free;
But then the city tax comes due—
And when you get through
Whose monkey are you?
Just to make it easy sailin',
Sell the Fair, it's made of tin.
But be sure that they get Whalen—
Give it back to the Indians!

REFRAIN 3

The Music Hall has presentations,
But you simply can't get in.

Try to jump those excavations.
Give it back to the Indians.
Shakespeare doesn't get a showing,
When those striptease girls begin,
Yet *Tobacco Road* keeps going;
Give it back to the Indians.
Bound on the north
By the Bronx—a pretty view.
East
By Long Island smoke.
West
By New Jersey—pots of glue.
South Brooklyn's asleep—
Chief no wanna keep!
Swing bands give you heebie-jeebies.
Dewey's put an end to sin.
Men wear clothes like Lucius Beebe's—
Give it back to the Indians!

THE HUNTED STAG

Intended for Ivy Scott and ensemble as the opening number of the show. Dropped before the New York opening.

1ST ROBIN
    HOOD: Four miles to the Hunted Stag,
        Where beer and service never lag;
        In the little white house with the big
            blue flag.
        Four short miles to the Hunted Stag!

2ND ROBIN
    HOOD: Three miles to the Hunted Stag,
        The rendezvous of wit and wag;
        Come by automobile or by old gray
            nag.
        Three short miles to the Hunted Stag!

3RD ROBIN
    HOOD: Two miles to the Hunted Stag;
        Our food gives us the right to brag.
        Take a taste of the quail and the
            grouse we bag.
        Two short miles to the Hunted Stag!

4TH ROBIN
    HOOD: One mile to the Hunted Stag,
        Where the coffee isn't Kaffee Hag.
        Dance a Viennese waltz or do the
            shag.
        One short mile to the Hunted Stag!

5TH ROBIN
    HOOD: Step right into the Hunted Stag!

IVY: Our Pilgrim Fathers and the
    Puritans,
Brave pioneers, those two sets.
In sixteen-twenty left their hearth
    and homes
To settle in Massachusetts.
They left old England for the new,
A most prophetic thing to do.
They braved the deep and they
    climbed the crag
To make the home of the Hunted
    Stag,
For the little white house with the
    big blue flag.
They did it all for the Hunted Stag.

BOYS: Eat New England turkey,
Try our Boston beans,
Oyster fry and chicken pie
And chowder in tureens
In the little white house with the big
    blue flag.
Eat—eat—eat—in the Hunted Stag!

IVY: And when they disembarked on
    Plymouth Rock,
Both clergyman and cobbler,
As specialité of my maison,
They shot a turkey gobbler.
In seventeen hundred fifty-four
They fought the French and Indian
    War.
And shot each French and Indian
    hag
To restrict the guests of the Hunted
    Stag.
For the little white house with the
    big blue flag—
They did it all for the Hunted Stag!

BOYS: Eat a Boston cream pie,
Try a Boston scrod,
Little clams and candied yams
And creamy cakes of cod.
In the little white house with the big
    blue flag—
Eat—eat—eat—in the Hunted Stag!

IVY: By seventeen hundred and
    seventy-five
We were an institution.
They taxed our tea to hurt the
    Hunted Stag;
Comes the revolution!

In eighteen fifty-eight or so
We served Miss Harriet Beecher
    Stowe.
They burned her books for a rebel
    gag,
So we licked the South for the
    Hunted Stag.
For the little white house with the
    big blue flag—
They did it all for the Hunted Stag!

BOYS: Eat New England dinners,
Try our corned beef hash,
Pies of quince and meat of mince
And sweet potato mash.
In the little white house with the big
    blue flag—
Eat—eat—eat—in the Hunted Stag!

IVY: Through ev'ry crisis of our history
Our table d'hôte has flourished.
They always fought to save the
    Hunted Stag
And kept the nation nourished.
If you're American to the core,
You must prevent all future war;
The dove of peace is in the bag,
If you patronize the Hunted Stag.
In the little white house with the big
    blue flag—
Eat—eat—eat—in the Hunted Stag!

BOYS: Try an apple dumpling,
Cel'ry on the knob,
Filet of sole and jelly roll,
Yellow corn on the cob.
In the little white house with the big
    blue flag—
Eat—eat—eat—in the Hunted Stag!

FILM VERSION, 1940

The film version, including one new Rodgers and Hart song, "You're Nearer," was produced by George Abbott for RKO Radio Pictures and released in November 1940.

YOU'RE NEARER

Published August 1940. Introduced in the film by Trudy Erwin (dubbing for Lucille Ball), Frances Langford, Ann Miller, and Libby Bennett. By October 1940 it had replaced "My Prince" in the post–Broadway tour of the stage production, where it was sung by Anne Francine and Marie Nash.

VERSE

Time is a healer,
But it cannot heal my heart.
My mind says I've forgotten you
And then I feel my heart.
The miles lie between us,
But your fingers touch my own.
You're never far away from me,
For you're too much my own.

REFRAIN

You're nearer
Than my head is to my pillow.
Nearer
Than the wind is to the willow.
Dearer
Than the rain is to the earth below.
Precious as the sun to the things that grow.
You're nearer
Than the ivy to the wall is.
Nearer
Than the winter to the fall is.
Leave me,
But when you're away you'll know
You're nearer,
For I love you so.

OVERLEAF: Marta Eggert and Jack Haley

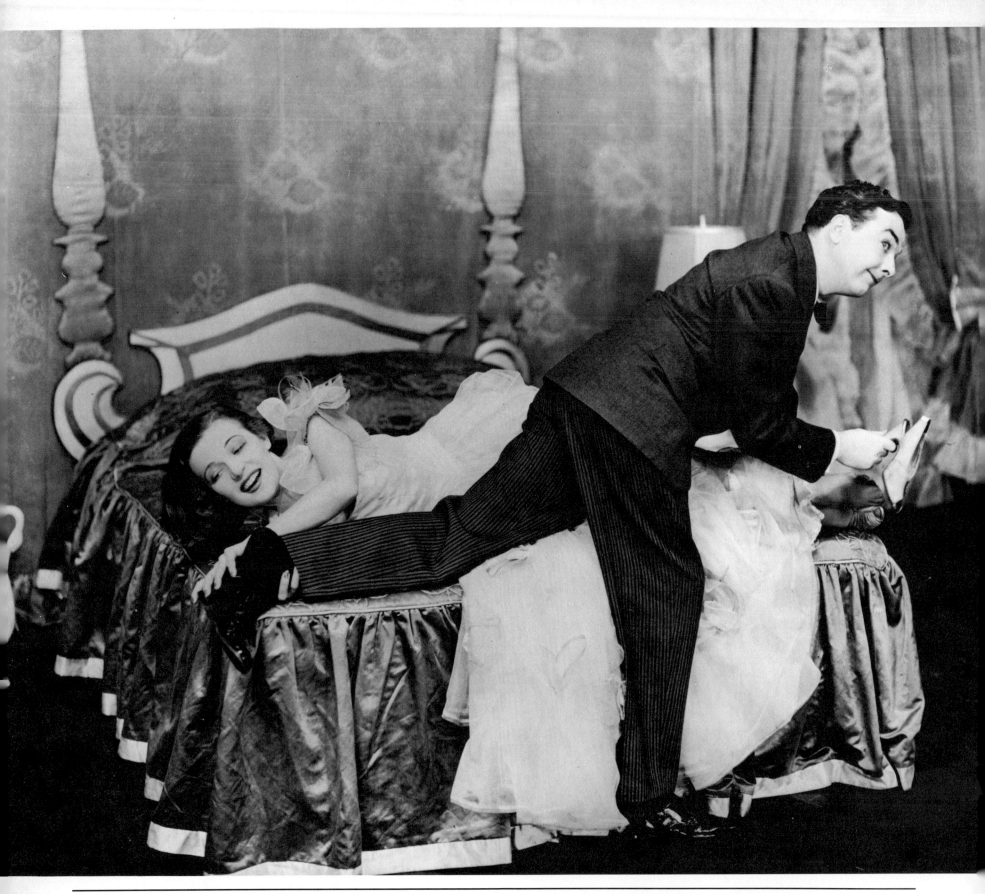

HIGHER AND HIGHER | 1940

Tryout: Shubert Theatre, New Haven, March 7–9, 1940; Shubert Theatre, Boston, March 12–30, 1940. New York run: Shubert Theatre, April 4–June 15, 1940, and August 5–24, 1940. 108 performances. Music by Richard Rodgers. Lyrics by Lorenz Hart. Produced by Dwight Deere Wiman. Book by Gladys Hurlbut and Joshua Logan, based on an idea by Irving Pincus. Directed by Joshua Logan. Choreography by Robert Alton. Settings by Jo Mielziner. Costumes by Lucinda Ballard. Orchestra under the direction of Al Goodman. Orchestrations by Hans Spialek. Cast, starring Jack Haley, Marta Eggert, and Shirley Ross, included Leif Erickson, Lee Dixon, Robert Chisolm, Billie Worth, Hollace Shaw, June Allyson, and Vera-Ellen.

A BARKING BABY NEVER BITES

Introduced by Jack Haley and Shirley Ross.

VERSE

ZACK: When you start to call me names
You make yourself quite clear.
Aspersions on my parentage
Are not so nice to hear.
I can't follow your advice,
My dear, I can't begin to,
For there are not so many lakes
A fellow can jump into.
SANDY: You ask me to do some things
A lady must decline.
If I sat on all those tacks
I'd have a punctured spine.
But though you are no gentleman
I'm certain that you're mine!

REFRAIN 1

ZACK: A barking baby never bites!
Give me the kind that growls and fights.
The sweet ones kiss you and they're through,
So I'd rather get the raspberry from you.
Those dames whose baby talk I've heard
Are lady dogs—you know the word.
"I love you, Sugar Pie" means murder!
So, baby, bark to beat the band
'Cause I'm gonna have you eating from my hand!

REFRAIN 2

SANDY: A barking baby never bites!
He won't go chasing cats at nights.
Most thoroughbreds are vicious, too,
So I'd rather have a dirty dog like you!
If you turned sweet on me someday
You'd have to go—you couldn't stay.
I'd call the old S.P.C.A., dear.
I'd never trust a quiet guy,
For a sleeping dog can lie, and lie and lie!
ZACK: And you'll never ever find me in a fix,
For I'll just be teaching some new dog old tricks.
BOTH: So, baby, bark to beat the band
'Cause I'm going to have you eating from my hand!

FROM ANOTHER WORLD

Published March 1940. Introduced by Marta Eggert, Jack Haley, Shirley Ross, Eva Condon, Robert Chisolm, and ensemble.

VERSE

SANDY: Are you sure you love this guy?
MINNIE: Oh yes! Oh yes!
ZACK: That girl can feel.
She could play Camille.
SANDY: Did you smile as he passed by?
MINNIE: Not at all! Not at all!
SANDY: Were you that dumb?
ZACK: She loves the bum!

REFRAIN

MINNIE: You are from another world,
Oh, so strangely sweet.
When you left this other world,
Did you guess we were destined to meet?
Now I hear another song,
Music found in the sound of your feet.
You are from another world,
Making mine complete.

DEVELOPMENT

ZACK: Hey, everybody!
[Enter Hilda]
HILDA: Hey, everybody!
[All the servants enter]
BYNG: What's the commotion?
ZACK: She's come from across the ocean.
She is from another world,
As bright as any fairy.
BYNG: A kitchen canary.
She is from another world—
She'll never be gentility.
ZACK: She will be my ability
Remember, she's the boss's daughter,
Just arrived from across the water
From another world.
HILDA: Let's take an oath never to tell
That she's not the boss's daughter.
BYNG: It can't be done.
HILDA: Be quiet, son!
ZACK: So spread the news
To the servants around town
And every columnist will get it down!
[Servant to janitor]
SERVANT: Yes, Miss Deborah Drake has arrived.
She is from another world.
[Two servants to two soda jerkers]
SERVANTS: She is from another world,
Oh, so strangely sweet.
SODA JERKERS: It's so cold, that other world,
Will she ever get used to our heat?
[Girl on phone]
GIRL: Can't meet you tonight,
My mistress just arrived from Iceland—
From another world.
[Cop on phone to four other cops]
COP: She is from another world,
Oh, so strangely sweet.
ALL COPS: She comes from that other world,
Making ours complete.
SERVANTS: Tonight's the night
She goes to the Stork Club
And ev'ry New York club.
How will she look,
How will she behave?
[Enter Sandy as a maid]
SANDY: Enter, Madame. Come, you must be brave!
[Enter Minnie. She sings refrain]

MORNING'S AT SEVEN

Introduced by Lee Dixon, Billie Worth, and ensemble.

VERSE

Sleep, you sleepers; snore, you drones.
Lose your fun to rest your bones.
You work eight hours,
You snooze eight hours,
And for your play you use eight hours.
Sleep, you sleepers, but I say
I want my sixteen hours for play.

REFRAIN

Morning's at seven, dinner's at eight,
But at eleven o'clock we dance!
We will dance till
Morning's at seven; we have to wait,
But at eleven o'clock we shag—
Heaven is in the bag!
Birds are singing,
Dawn's at the crack.
While we're swinging
Time marches back!
Morning's at seven, luncheon's at two,
But at eleven o'clock I dance with you!

NOTHING BUT YOU

Published March 1940. Introduced by Marta Eggert, Leif
Erickson, and ensemble.

VERSE

This may seem queer to you,
The meaning unclear to you.
Have you ever dreamed of someone
Very dear to you?

REFRAIN

I woke up from a dream one day
And there was nothing but you.
I looked into my heart that day
And there was nothing but you.
You were there, so there was love,
Brave and bright and new.
When I look into life I see
Past and future, too—
Nothing there but you.

VERSE (published)

When you walk into a room,
Then the room is light.
When you say anything, then
What you say is right.

If that is due to my singular condition,
Well, then, that condition is my one ambition.
I'm in love with you.

DISGUSTINGLY RICH

Introduced by Jack Haley, Shirley Ross, Lee Dixon, Eva
Condon, Robert Chisolm, Hilda Spong, Billie Worth, and
ensemble.

VERSE

Brenda Frazier sat on a wall.
Brenda Frazier had a big fall.
Brenda Frazier's falling down,
Falling down, falling down,
Brenda Frazier's falling down,
My fair Minnie.
There's money in the movies,
There's money in the ads.
There's money in the old johns,
There's money in the lads.
Minnie, Minnie, Minnie, Minnie—
Money, Money, Money, Money—
Eenie, Meenie, Money, Mo,
Catch a fortune by the toe.

REFRAIN 1

I'll buy everything I wear at Saks.
I'll cheat plenty on my income tax.
Swear like a trooper,
Live in a stupor—
Just disgustingly rich.
I'll make money and I'll make it quick,
Boosting cigarettes that make me sick.
Smothered in sables
Like Betty Grable's—
Just disgustingly rich.
I will buy land
Down on Long Island
And as a resident
I will pan the President.
I'll aspire
Higher and higher.
I'll get married and adopt a son,
Right from Tony's or from "21."
Swimming in highballs,
Stewed to the eyeballs—
Just disgustingly rich—
Too, too disgustingly rich.

REFRAIN 2

Break my ankles on the tennis courts.
Get pneumonia doing winter sports.
I won't be civil,
Rude as the divil,
Just disgustingly rich.
Ev'ry summer I will sail the sea,
On my little yacht, the *Normandie*,
Catch barracuda
Down in Bermuda—
Just disgustingly rich.
I'll eat salmon,
I'll play backgammon,
Turn breakfast into brunch.
I'll take Errol Flynn to lunch.
I'll aspire
Higher and higher.
I'll buy autos like the autocrats.
I'll drink Pluto like the plutocrats.
Playing the horses,
Getting divorces—
Just disgustingly rich—
Too, too disgustingly rich.

REFRAIN 3

He'll be photographed with Myrna Loy
Just to prove he is a glamour boy.
Perfumed and scented,
Slightly demented—
Just disgustingly rich.
I will take a plane to Florida,
Where the weather's even horrida.
I'll eat salami
Down in Miami—
Just disgustingly rich.
Get my capers
Into the papers,
Hoping my folly would
Lead me out to Hollywood.
I'll aspire
Higher and higher.
In the funnies and the valentines,
I'll be pictured drinking Ballantine's.
Dopey and screwy,
Voting for Dewey—
Just disgustingly rich—
Too, too disgustingly rich.

CODA

We will never even try to swim.
We'll just sit until the sun grows dim.
We'll eat baloney
Down at the Roney—
Just disgustingly rich—
Too, too disgustingly rich—

Just disgustingly rich—
Too, too disgustingly rich.

BLUE MONDAY

Opening, Act II. Introduced by Robert Chisolm, Hollace
Shaw, Marie Louise Quevli, Marie Nash, and ensemble.

ALL: Blessed be the poor,
So bless'd be us.
We haven't got the fare to
Ride upon the bus.
Bless'd be the needy.
Bless'd be the seedy.
We're the broke indeedy.
Bless'd be us.

BYNG: It's Monday—get to work.
Arouse yourselves.
You're dead because on Sunday
You carouse yourselves.
The coffee was rancid,
The linen was black.
If your salaries were paid up,
I'd give you the sack.

ALL: We will never buy a thing at Saks.
We will never pay an income tax.
Shortly our chief work
Will be relief work.
Too disgustingly poor.

BYNG: You owe this to the double-crossing
quackery
Of that retarded problem child called
Zackery.
Well—happy Monday.

ALL: Monday—Monday—blue, blue Monday.
Nothing to look forward to,
Only lots of work to do.
Monday, Monday, blue, blue Monday.

BYNG: I could be a Communist,
The kind that growls and barks,
But I haven't got the money
To buy a secondhand edition of Karl
Marx.
Bless'd be the fools
And bless'd be Zack.
He took us for a ride
And he never brought us back.

ALL: Monday—Monday—blue, blue Monday.
Nothing to look forward to,
Only lots of work to do.
Monday, Monday, blue, blue Monday.

EV'RY SUNDAY AFTERNOON

Published March 1940. Introduced by Marta Eggert and
Leif Erickson.

VERSE 1

HE: I love to do my work,
Never complain;
Never get tired,
Don't mind the strain.
I always say, "Old man,
Wait till you're through.
Sunday will come—
Thursday comes, too.
In those two days
Think what you'll do."
For they're the lovely days with you.

REFRAIN 1

Ev'ry Sunday afternoon and Thursday night,
We'll be free as birds in flight.
If on Sunday afternoon we ever fight
We'll make up on Thursday night.
Leave the dishes,
Dry your hands.
Change your wishes
To commands.
Ev'ry Sunday afternoon we'll be polite,
But we'll make love on Thursday night.

VERSE 2

SHE: I work my life away
Thinking of play.
What will I wear?
What will you say?
Then I remind myself,
"Old girl, you're strong,
And you're in love.
Life can't go wrong.
Smile your old smile,
Sing your old song.
Wait till those dear days come along."

REFRAIN 2

Ev'ry Sunday afternoon and Thursday night,
We'll be free as birds in flight.
If on Sunday afternoon we ever fight
We'll make up on Thursday night.
I'm your slave, dear,
But it's bliss.
If you shave, dear,
We can kiss.
Ev'ry Sunday afternoon we'll be polite,
But we'll make love on Thursday night.

A LOVELY DAY FOR A MURDER

Introduced by Lee Dixon, Billie Worth, and ensemble.

VERSE

Have you heard of St. Bartholomew's Day?
Or the day when they took our liquor away?
Or the day when we have our taxes to pay?
Or the day when the Trojans were fooled by
Ulysses?
Well, today is a day
That makes those days look like sissies!

REFRAIN

What a lovely day for a murder!
I could spit.
If there's any day for a murder,
This is it.
Oh, we'll never visit the parson,
So I say
For seduction, robb'ry and arson
What a day!
I could choke my grandmother with her shawl.
I could turn Republican in the fall.
Oh, it gets absurd and absurder,
So I say
If you care to join me in murder,
Darling, it's the loveliest day!

HOW'S YOUR HEALTH?

Introduced by Jack Haley, Marta Eggert, and Leif
Erickson.

VERSE

ZACK: I feel sick
I got chills.
PATRICK: You look a little pale beneath the
gills.
MINNIE: Maybe he's got fever.
PATRICK: Zacky, don't believe her.
MINNIE: Maybe he's got pneumonia.
PATRICK: His pulse is fine and dandy.
MINNIE: It can't be fine and dandy.
ZACK: What's a little pneumonia—
I lost Sandy!

REFRAIN

PATRICK: How's your health?
MINNIE: How's your health?
PAT & ZACK: Are your knees like butter?
Your voice a mutter?
Your heart a fluttering dove?
ZACK: How's your health?
MINNIE: How's your health?
PAT & ZACK: If you feel like crawling,
And life's appalling,
It means you're falling in love.
Love's the only barometer
For all your pains and aches.
Love can raise your thermometer
Until the darn thing breaks.
PATRICK: How's your health?
MINNIE: How's your health?
ALL: Are you full of vigor?
Your mind a trigger?
Your step elastic?
Your strength gymnastic?
Then stop your bawling,
It means she's falling
In love with you!

IT NEVER ENTERED
MY MIND

Published March 1940. Introduced by Shirley Ross.

VERSE

I don't care if there's powder on my nose.
I don't care if my hairdo is in place.
I've lost the very meaning of repose.
I never put a mudpack on my face.
Oh, who'd have thought
That I'd walk in a daze now?
I never go to shows at night,

But just to matinees now.
I see the show
And home I go.

REFRAIN 1

Once I laughed when I heard you saying
That I'd be playing solitaire,
Uneasy in my easy chair.
It never entered my mind.
Once you told me I was mistaken,
That I'd awaken with the sun
And order orange juice for one.
It never entered my mind.
You have what I lack myself,
And now I even have to scratch my back myself.
Once you warned me that if you scorned me
I'd sing the maiden's prayer again
And wish that you were there again
To get into my hair again.
It never entered my mind.

REFRAIN 2

Once you said in your funny lingo
I'd sit at bingo day and night
And never get the numbers right.
It never entered my mind.
Once you told me I'd stay up Sunday
To read the Monday-morning dirt
And find you're merging with some skirt.
It never entered my mind.
Life is not so sweet alone.*
The man who came to dinner lets me eat alone.
I confess it—I didn't guess it,
That I would sit and mope again
And all the while I'd hope again
To see my darling dope again.
It never entered my mind!

I'M AFRAID

Introduced by Jack Haley, Shirley Ross, and ensemble.
"Developed" by Shirley Ross, Janet Fox, Lee Dixon,
Robert Chisholm, Eva Condon, Robert Stanley, and company. Replaced "Life! Liberty!" during the pre-Broadway
tryout.

Earlier version of refrain 2, lines 9–10:
You were my barometer,
And now my only friend is my thermometer.

VERSE

ZACK: When the light is gloomy,
Chills go running through me,
Funny thoughts come to me,
I'd like to hide my head.
SANDY: You're a nervous fellow,
And I'm twice as yellow,
I'm all set to bellow,
Please let me go to bed.

REFRAIN 1

SANDY: I'm afraid of rats and mice,
I'm afraid of snow and ice,
I'm afraid of reading scary tales,
Even of fairy tales.
I'm afraid of rain and fogs,
I'm afraid of touching frogs,
I'm afraid of counting sheep at night
'Cause sheep can scare me too.
Afraid of cops,
Afraid of crooks,
Afraid of germs,
Afraid of worms you put on hooks.
I'm afraid of Fu Manchu,*
And of tigers in the zoo,
But most of all I'm afraid I'll fall
For a horrible thing like you.

REFRAIN 2

ZACK: I'm afraid of rats and mice,
I'm afraid of Fanny Brice,
I'm afraid to see spectacular
Movies like *Dracula.*
I'm afraid of catching cold,
I'm afraid of growing old,
And I even fear the sight of geese,
'Cause I get gooseflesh, too.
Afraid of cow,
Afraid of bull,
And I take care my underwear
Is made of wool.
I'm afraid of trained seals, too,†
When their aim is clear and true.
But most of all I'm afraid I'll fall
For a beautiful sap like you.

Earlier version:
I'm afraid of Irish stew,
†*Earlier version of refrain 2, lines 13–14:*
When a little child says "Boo!"
I am frightened through and through.

MONTAGE

SANDY: I'm afraid of wedding bells,
I'm afraid of wishing wells,
I'm afraid to love the way I do,
Frightened to say, "I do."
I'm afraid that Mr. Zack,
Will be there to scratch my back.
I'm afraid that lots of orange juice
Will soon be served for two.
Afraid that I
Will learn to care.
Afraid to try
The little guy who wasn't there.
I'm afraid I'm going to sign
On the well-known dotted line.
But most of all I'm afraid I'll fall
For that lovable dope of mine.

ELLEN: Get this—just looka here.
Society girl unmasked.
It's the biggest dirt of the year.
Deborah Drake's in love.
She confesses that she's a maid.
Her boyfriend made her tell her right
name.
But society forgives.
What do you think of that lucky dame?
MIKE: I'm afraid I've gone to work
Like the conscientious Turk,
But the customers put you at ease,
Giving gratuities.
Come on, buddy, shake a hip,
Kindly help me take this tip.
I'm afraid you must cooperate
To help me count the change.
WAITER: Ah, a customer,
I'm afraid you can't get in
If you don't know Mr. Zacky.
MIKE: That guy is wacky.
Don't be abusive,
This joint is exclusive.
Hey, Joe—help me throw out this bum.
WAITER: Oh, that phone will never stop.
MIKE: Help me answer it, old top.
WAITER: You are wanted at the telephone;
I'm afraid it's Mr. Byng.
BYNG: I'm afraid you work too hard.
You will lose your union card.
I'm afraid I must invite you all
To the annual Butler's Ball. Goodbye.

Zacky is rich and he's quite a nice boy,
But why must our Butler's Ball
Admit the hoi polloi?
I'm afraid I'm going to be;
Dancing with the bourgeoisie.
While the world is full of shaking
thrones,
Drake got rich making thrones.
I'm afraid our Ball today
Has no air of the soignée,
And the offspring of a cabbagehead
Is sauerkraut to me.
To dance with cooks*
Just makes me sick.
HILDA: If you had eyes
You'd see my dress was très, très chic.
BYNG: I'm afraid there is no wall
Between festival and brawl,
But most of all I'm afraid you'll fall
For the jolliest Butler's Ball.

IT'S PRETTY IN THE CITY

Dropped before the New York opening. Sung during the
New Haven and Boston tryouts by Fin Olsen. It was the
last number in Act II, Scene 1, and was followed in the
score by "How's Your Health?"

VERSE

From the land of the fjords
To the land of the Fords
I come without nostalgia.
Here I have such pretty girls
And there I had neuralgia.

REFRAIN

It's pretty in the city.
Girls look so sweet
On ev'ry street.

Earlier version of this line and the next three:
To think that I
Must serve the Drakes.
HILDA: And that is why the poor old guy
Has got the shakes.

They turn on the heat.
You mustn't go to Iceland.
Take my advice—
Life has no spice
When love is kept on ice.
Here you ride in a taxicab
Fondling a pretty girl's head.
There you can't find a taxicab;
Loving is hell in a sled.
But here your ears don't freeze off;
Love wears a crown.
It's better with your skis off;
It's such a pretty town.

LIFE! LIBERTY!

Dropped before the New York opening. Intended for Act
II, Scene 3. Music is missing. Alternate title: "Life! Lib-
erty! And the Pursuit of You." It was sung in the New
Haven and Boston tryouts by Jack Haley, Shirley Ross,
and ensemble; "developed" by Jack Haley, Shirley Ross,
Lee Dixon, Robert Chisolm, Hilda Spong, Eva Condon,
Robert Stanley, and ensemble. It was replaced by "I'm
Afraid."

VERSE

In seventeen hundred and seventy-six
Hancock put his Hancock
On some hist'ry-making tricks.
In nineteen-forty I want to make it known
I have a doctrine of my own.

REFRAIN

Life! Liberty! And the pursuit of you!
I pledge allegiance to two eyes of blue.
Life! Liberty! And the escape of me!
I couldn't use them, I'd refuse them—
Never set me free.
My folks, and their descendants,
Were all Yanks, and how!
I make my Declaration of Dependence
Right here and now!
Take my life! Liberty!
And my devotion, too.
I belong to you!

OVERLEAF: Gene Kelly and chorus

PAL JOEY | 1940

Tryout: Forrest Theatre, Philadelphia, December 16–22, 1940. New York run: Ethel Barrymore Theatre, December 25, 1940–August 16, 1941; Shubert Theatre, September 1–October 18, 1941; St. James Theatre, October 21–November 29, 1941. 374 performances. Music by Richard Rodgers. Lyrics by Lorenz Hart. Produced by George Abbott. Book by John O'Hara, based on a series of short stories in *The New Yorker* by Mr. O'Hara. Directed by George Abbott. Choreography by Robert Alton. Settings and lighting by Jo Mielziner. Costumes by John Koenig. Orchestra under the direction of Harry Levant. Orchestrations by Hans Spialek. Cast, starring Vivienne Segal and Gene Kelly, included June Havoc, Jack Durant, Leila Ernst, Stanley Donen, Jean Casto, Van Johnson, Jerome Whyte, and (replacing Mr. Durant) David Burns. The lyric to "Love Is My Friend" is missing. Vocal score published 1962.

YOU MUSTN'T KICK IT AROUND

Published December 1940. Introduced by Gene Kelly, June Havoc, Diane Sinclair, Sondra Barrett, and ensemble.

VERSE

I have the worst apprehension
That you don't crave my attention.
But I can't force you to change your taste.
If you don't care to be nice, dear,
Then give me air, but not ice, dear.
Don't let a good fellow go to waste.
For this little sin that you commit at leisure
You'll repent in haste.

REFRAIN

If my heart gets in your hair,
You mustn't kick it around.
If you're bored with this affair,
You mustn't kick it around.
Even though I'm mild and meek
When we have a brawl,
If I turn the other cheek
You mustn't kick it at all.
When I try to ring the bell,
You never care for the sound;
The next guy may not do as well.
You mustn't kick it around!

I COULD WRITE A BOOK

Published December 1940. Introduced by Gene Kelly and Leila Ernst.

VERSE 1

JOEY: A B C D E F G—
I never learned to spell,
At least not well.
1 2 3 4 5 6 7—
I never learned to count
A great amount.
But my busy mind is burning
To use what learning I've got.
I won't waste any time,
I'll strike while the iron is hot.

REFRAIN

If they asked me, I could write a book
About the way you walk and whisper and
look.
I could write a preface on how we met
So the world would never forget.
And the simple secret of the plot
Is just to tell them that I love you a lot;
Then the world discovers as my book
ends
How to make two lovers of friends.

VERSE 2

LINDA: Used to hate to go to school.
I never cracked a book;
I played the hook.
Never answered any mail;
To write I used to think
Was wasting ink.
It was never my endeavor
To be too clever and smart.
Now I suddenly feel
A longing to write in my heart.

REPEAT REFRAIN

CHICAGO

Introduced by Michael Moore and ensemble. Alternate title: "A Great Big Town."

There's a great big town
On a great big lake
Called Chicago.
When the sun goes down
It is wide awake.
Take your ma and your pa,
Go to Chicago.
Boston is England,
N'Orleans is France,
New York is anyone's
For ten cents a dance.
But this great big town
On that great big lake
Is America's first,
And Americans make
Chicago.
Hi ya, boys.

REPRISE

There's a great big town
On a great big lake
Called Morocco.
When the sun goes down
It is wide awake.
Take your ma and your pa,
Go to Morocco.
Morocco.

THAT TERRIFIC RAINBOW

Introduced by June Havoc and Van Johnson. Registered for copyright as an unpublished song by Chappell & Co., Inc., June 8, 1951.

VERSE

My life had no color
Before I met you.
What could have been duller
The time I went through?
You weakened my resistance
And colored my existence;
I'm happy and unhappy too.

REFRAIN

I'm a red-hot mama,
But I'm blue for you.
I get purple with anger
At the things you do.
And I'm green with envy
When you meet a dame.

But you burn my heart up
With an orange flame.
I'm a red-hot mama
But you're white and cold.
Don't you know your mama
Has a heart of gold?
Though we're in those gray clouds,
Someday you'll see
That terrific rainbow
Over you and me.

WHAT IS A MAN?

Published February 1952. Introduced by Vivienne Segal.
Originally this song was titled "Love Is My Friend." After
the New York opening, the lyric was changed. "What Is
a Man?" does not appear in programs until May 19, 1941.
From December 25, 1940, until May 12, 1941, "Love Is
My Friend" is listed in this spot. Yet Vivienne Segal,
in a July 1985 conversation with Dorothy Hart, did not
recall the song and had no memory of having sung it.
Gene Kelly, in response to a query from Dorothy Hart,
did not recall it either. The lyric to "Love Is My Friend"
is missing.

VERSE

There are so many, so many fish in the sea,
Must I want the one who's not for me?
It's just my foolish way.
What can I do about it?
I'm much too used to love
To be without it.

REFRAIN

What is a man?
Is he an animal,
Is he a wolf,
Is he a mouse,
Is he the cheap or the dear kind,
Is he champagne or the beer kind?
What is a man?
Is he a stimulant,
Good for the heart,
Bad for the nerves?
Nature's mistake since the world began,
What makes me give,
What makes me live,
What is this thing called man?

Hello, Jack—can't keep the appointment,
Have an awful cold [*sneeze*].
Hello, Frank—

Have to meet my husband.
So long—please don't scold.
Hello—hello—love.

What is a man?
Is he an ornament,
Useless by day,
Handy by night.

From Charlie Chaplin
To Charlie Chan
All have one trick—*
One that is slick.
What is this thing called man?

HAPPY HUNTING HORN

Published February 1952. Introduced by Gene Kelly,
Jane Fraser, and ensemble.

VERSE

Don't worry, girls,
I'm only on vacation,
Not out of circulation;
Don't worry, girls.
Don't worry, girls,
While I still have my eyesight
You're going to be in my sight;
Don't worry, girls.
You never can erase
The hunter from the chase.

REFRAIN

Sound the happy hunting horn,
There's new game on the trail now;
We're hunting for quail now,
Happy little hunting horn.
Play the horn but don't play corn.
The music must be nice now,
We're hunting for mice now,
Happy little hunting horn.
Danger's easy to endure when
You're out to catch a beaut;
Lie in ambush, but be sure when
You see the whites of their eyes—don't shoot!
Play the horn from night to morn.
Just play, no matter what time,

In the published script the closing lines are:
  They're all alike,
  They're all I like.
  What is this thing called man?

Play, "There'll be a hot time!"
Happy little hunt—bang! bang!—ing horn.

BEWITCHED, BOTHERED AND BEWILDERED

Published February 1941. Introduced by Vivienne Segal.
Alternate title: "Bewitched."

VERSE

After one whole quart of brandy,*
Like a daisy I awake.
With no Bromo Seltzer handy,
I don't even shake.
Men are not a new sensation;
I've done pretty well, I think.
But this half-pint imitation
Put me on the blink.

REFRAIN 1

I'm wild again,
Beguiled again,
A simpering, whimpering child again—
Bewitched, bothered and bewildered am I.
Couldn't sleep
And wouldn't sleep
Until I could sleep where I shouldn't sleep—
Bewitched, bothered and bewildered am I.
Lost my heart, but what of it?
My mistake, I agree.
He's a laugh, but I love it
Because the laugh's on me.
A pill he is,
But still he is
All mine and I'll keep him until he is
Bewitched, bothered and bewildered
Like me.

REFRAIN 2

Seen a lot—
I mean a lot—
But now I'm like sweet seventeen a lot—
Bewitched, bothered and bewildered am I.
I'll sing to him,
Each spring to him,

In the published script the first four lines are:
  He's a fool, and don't I know it—
  But a fool can have his charms;
  I'm in love and don't I show it,
  Like a babe in arms.

And worship the trousers that cling to him—
Bewitched, bothered and bewildered am I.
When he talks, he is seeking
Words to get off his chest.
Horizontally speaking,
He's at his very best.
Vexed again,
Perplexed again,
Thank God I can be oversexed again—
Bewitched, bothered and bewildered am I.

REFRAIN 3

Sweet again,
Petite again,
And on my proverbial seat again—
Bewitched, bothered and bewildered am I.
What am I?
Half shot am I.
To think that he loves me
So hot am I—
Bewitched, bothered and bewildered am I.
Though at first we said, "No, sir,"
Now we're two little dears.
You might say we are closer
Than Roebuck is to Sears.
I'm dumb again
And numb again,
A rich, ready, ripe little plum again—
Bewitched, bothered and bewildered am I.

ENCORE

You know,
It is really quite funny
Just how quickly he learns
How to spend all the money
That Mr. Simpson earns.
He's kept enough,
He's slept enough,
And yet where it counts
He's adept enough—
Bewitched, bothered and bewildered am I.

REPRISE (at end of show)

Wise at last,
My eyes at last
Are cutting you down to your size at last—
Bewitched, bothered and bewildered no more.
Burned a lot,
But learned a lot,
And now you are broke, though you earned a
    lot—
Bewitched, bothered and bewildered no more.
Couldn't eat—
Was dyspeptic,
Life was so hard to bear;
Now my heart's antiseptic,

Since you moved out of there.
Romance—finis;
Your chance—finis;
Those ants that invaded my pants—finis—
Bewitched, bothered and bewildered no more.

PAL JOEY

Introduced by Gene Kelly. Alternate title: "What Do I
Care for a Dame?"

What do I care for a dame?
What do I care for a dame?
Every old dame is the same.
Every damn dame is the same.

I got a future—
A rosy future;
You can be sure I'll be tops.
I'm independent;
I'm no defendant.
I'll own a nightclub that's tops,
And I'll be in with the cops.

What do I care for the skirts?
What do I care for the skirts?
I'll make them pay till it hurts.
Let them put up till it hurts.

I'm going to own a nightclub;
It's going to be the right club.
For the swell gentry—
It's elementary.
I'll wear top hat and cane.
In Chez Joey,
They'll pay Joey,
The gay Joey—
I can see it plain.

THE FLOWER GARDEN
OF MY HEART

Introduced by June Havoc, Shirley Paige, and ensemble.

VERSE

I haven't got a great big yacht,
But I'm contented with my lot.
I've got one thing much more beautiful and
    grand.

I do not own a racing horse,
But that don't fill me with remorse.
I possess the finest showplace in the land.
So come with me and wander
To a lovely spot out yonder.

REFRAIN 1

In the flower garden of my heart
I've got violets as blue as your eyes.
I've got dainty narcissus
As sweet as my missus
And lilies as pure as the skies.
In the flower garden of my heart
I've got roses as red as your mouth.
Just to keep our love holy
I've got gladioli
And sunflowers fresh from the South.
But you are the artist
And love is the art
In the flower garden of my heart.

RECITATION

Violet—the flower dear old Grandmother wore
Away 'way *back* in the days of yore.
Sunflower—the favorite of white and dusky pixie
Away down South in the land of Dixie.
Heather—Sir Harry Lauder sang of its beauties—
The decoration of all Scotch cuties.
Lily—the flower of youthful purity—
It's very sweet—you have my surety.
Lilac—the sky turns blue and the church bells
    chime.
Ah, love, we love sweet lilac time.
If you're a hundred percent American—goodness
    knows,
You love the American Beauty Rose.

REFRAIN 2

In the flower garden of my heart
I've got daisies to tell me you're true.
Oh, the west wind will whisk us
The scent of hibiscus
And heather that's smothered with dew.
In the flower garden of my heart
I've got lilacs and dainty sweet peas.
You will look like sweet william
And smell like a trillium
Surrounded by fond bumblebees.
But love is the archer and you are the dart*
In the flower garden of my heart.

Alternate version of refrain 2, lines 11–12:
    But you are the pastry and I am the tart
    In the flower garden of my heart.

ZIP

Introduced by Jean Casto. Registered for copyright as an unpublished song by Chappell & Co., Inc., June 8, 1951.

VERSE

I've interviewed Leslie Howard.*
I've interviewed Noël Coward.
I've interviewed the great Stravinsky.
But my greatest achievement
Is the interview I had
With a star who worked for Minsky.
I met her at the Yankee Clipper
And she didn't unzip one zipper.
I said, "Miss Lee, you are such an artist.
Tell me why you never miss.
What do you think of while you work?"
And she said, "While I work
My thoughts go something like this."

REFRAIN 1

Zip! Walter Lippmann wasn't brilliant today.
Zip! Will Saroyan ever write a great play?
Zip! I was reading Schopenhauer last night.
Zip! And I think that Schopenhauer was right.
I don't want to see Zorina.
I don't want to meet Cobina.
Zip! I'm an intellectual.
I don't like a deep contralto,
Or a man whose voice is alto.
Zip! I'm a heterosexual.
Zip! It took intellect to master my art.
Zip! Who the hell is Margie Hart?

REFRAIN 2

Zip! I consider Dali's paintings passé.
Zip! Can they make the Metropolitan pay?
Zip! English people don't say clerk, they say
    clark.†
Zip! Anybody who says clark is a jark!
I have read the great Kabala
And I simply worship Allah.
Zip! I am just a mystic.
I don't care for Whistler's Mother,
Charlie's Aunt or Shubert's brother.
Zip! I'm misogynistic.

Earlier version of lines 1–2:
    I've interviewed Pablo Picasso
    And a countess named di Frasso.
†*Earlier version of refrain 2, lines 3–4:*
    Zip! Hearing rhumba bands will drive me to drink.
    Zip! Mrs. Perkins isn't red, she's just pink.

Zip! My intelligence is guiding my hand.
Zip! Who the hell is Sally Rand?

REFRAIN 3

Zip! Toscanini leads the greatest of bands.*
Zip! Jergen's Lotion does the trick for his hands.
Zip! Rip Van Winkle on the screen would be
    smart.
Zip! Tyrone Power will be cast in the part.
I adore the great Confucius
And the lines of luscious Lucius.
Zip! I am so eclectic.
I don't care for either Mickey—
Mouse and Rooney make me sicky!
Zip! I'm a little hectic.
Zip! My artistic taste is classic and dear.†
Zip! Who the hell's Lili St. Cyr?

PLANT YOU NOW, DIG YOU LATER

Published December 1940. Introduced by Jack Durant, June Havoc, and ensemble.

VERSE 1

LOWELL: Sweetheart, the day is waning,
        Must go without complaining,
        Time for Auf Wiederseh'ning now.
        Don't let this sad disclosure
        Ruffle your calm composure,
        Smile at the one who knows your
        Ev'ry whim.
        Wait for him now.

REFRAIN

        Where's the check?
        Get me the waiter.
        I'm not going to stay.
        Plant you now, dig you later.
        I'm on my way.
        My regret couldn't be greater
        At having to scram.
        Plant you now, dig you later.
        I'm on the lam.
        Bye-bye, my hep chick,
        Solid and true.

Earlier version of refrain 3, line 1:
    Zip! That Stokowski leads the greatest of bands.
†*Earlier version of refrain 3, lines 11–12:*
    Zip! My artistic taste is classic and choice.
    Zip! Who the hell's Rosita Royce?

I'll keep in step, chick,
Till I come digging for you.
So, little potater,
Stay right where you are.
Plant you now, dig you later
Means au revoir,
Just au revoir!

VERSE 2

GLADYS: I know your time is money
        And though you leave me, Sunny,
        We'll have a future honeymoon.
        Right now it's time to start your
        Farewells that mean departure.
        I keep deep in your heart
        You're all for me.
        Call for me soon.

REPEAT REFRAIN

DEN OF INIQUITY

Published November 1950. Introduced by Vivienne Segal and Gene Kelly. Alternate title: "In Our Little Den of Iniquity."

VERSE

VERA: Just two little lovebirds all alone
      In a little cozy nest
      With a little secret telephone;
      That's the place to rest.
JOEY: Artificial roses round the door—
      They are never out of bloom—
VERA: And a flowered carpet on the floor
      In the loving room.

REFRAIN 1

BOTH: In our little den of iniquity
      Our arrangement is good.
VERA: It's much more healthy living here;
      This rushing back home is bad, my dear,
JOEY: I haven't caught a cold all year.
VERA: Knock on wood!
BOTH: It was ever thus since antiquity,
      All the poets agree.
VERA: The chambermaid is very kind,
      She always thinks we're so refined.
JOEY: Of course, she's deaf and dumb and
      blind—
BOTH: No fools, we—
      In our little den of iniquity.

REFRAIN 2

BOTH: In our little den of iniquity
      For a girly and boy,
VERA: We'll sit and let the hours pass;
      A canopy bed has so much class,
JOEY: And so's a ceiling made of glass—
      Oh, what joy!
BOTH: Love has been that way since antiquity,
      Down to you and me.
VERA: The radio, I used to hate,
      But now when it is dark and late
      Tchaikovsky's "1812" sounds great—*
      That's for me,
BOTH: In our little den of iniquity.
[Dance]
      Oh, what joy!
[Dance]
JOEY: We're very proper folks, you know.
VERA: We've separate bedrooms comme il faut.
      There's one for play and one for show.
BOTH: You chase me
      In our little den of iniquity.

DO IT THE HARD WAY

Published December 1940. Introduced by Jack Durant, June Havoc, Claire Anderson, and ensemble.

VERSE

Fred Astaire once worked so hard
He often lost his breath,
And now he taps all other chaps to death.
Working hard did not retard
The young Cab Calloway.
Now hear him blow his vo-de-o-do today.

REFRAIN

Do it the hard way
And it's easy sailing.
Do it the hard way
And it's hard to lose.
Only the soft way
Has a chance of failing;
You have to choose.
I took the hard way
When I tried to get you;
You took the soft way
When you said, "We'll see."
Darling, now I'll let you

*Alternate version: Ravel's "Bolero" works just great—

Do it the hard way
Now that you want me.

TAKE HIM

Published March 1952. Introduced by Leila Ernst and Vivienne Segal.

VERSE 1

LINDA: He was a cutie—I admit I used to care.
      But it's my duty to myself to take the air.
      I won't prevent you from eloping if you
        wish.
      May I present you with this tasty dish.

REFRAIN 1

Take him, you don't have to pay for him.
Take him, he's free.
Take him, I won't make a play for him.
He's not for me.
He has no head to think with.*
True that his heart is asleep.
But he has eyes to wink with.
You can have him cheap.
Keep him and just for the lure of it,
Marry him, too.
Keep him, for you can be sure of it,
He can't keep you.
So take my old jalopy,
Keep him from falling apart.
Take him, but don't ever take him to
    heart.

VERSE 2

VERA: Thanks, little mousey, for the present and
      all that,
      But in this housey, I would rather keep a
      rat.
      Only a wizard could reform that class of
      males.
      They say a lizard cannot change his
      scales.

REFRAIN 2

Take him, I won't put a price on him.
Take him, he's yours.
Take him, pajamas look nice on him.

*Earlier version of refrain 1, lines 5–8:
True that his head is lumber,
True that his heart is like ice.
You'll find this little number
Cheap at half the price.

But how he snores!
Though he is well adjusted,
Certain things make him a wreck.
Last year his arm was busted
Reaching from a check.
His thoughts are seldom consecutive.
He just can't write.
I know a movie executive
Who's twice as bright.
Lots of good luck, you'll need it,
And you'll need aspirin, too.
Take him, but don't ever let him take
    you.

REFRAIN 3

BOTH: I hope that things will go well with him;
      I bear no hate.
      All I can say is the hell with him;
      He gets the gate.
      So take my benediction,
      Take my old benedict, too.
      Take it away, it's too good to be true.

I'M TALKING TO MY PAL

Dropped before the New York opening. Sung by Gene Kelly in the Philadelphia tryout.

VERSE

I'm independent.
I'm a descendant
Of quite a family of heels.
I'm never lonely.
I and I only
Know how my pal Joey feels.
Who else would pay for my meals?

REFRAIN

I'm talking to my pal,
Myself, my closest friend.
And that's the only pal
On whom I can depend.
When I come home at night,
A bit too tight to see,
My wallet is all right—
I'd never steal from me.
My friend stands pat
When I am flat.
He only cheats when I do.
I can't be sure of girls,
I'm not at home with men—
I'm ending up with me again.

THEY MET IN ARGENTINA | 1941

Maureen O'Hara and Buddy Ebsen (far right)

An RKO Radio Picture produced by Lou Brock. Released in May 1941. Music by Richard Rodgers. Lyrics by Lorenz Hart. Screenplay by Jerry Cody, adapted from a story by Lou Brock and Harold Daniels. Directed by Leslie Goodwins and Jack Hively. Cast, starring Maureen O'Hara and James Ellison, included Alberto Vila, Buddy Ebsen, Robert Barrat, Joseph Buloff, and Diosa Costello.

NORTH AMERICA MEETS SOUTH AMERICA

Introduced by Diosa Costello and Maureen O'Hara.

VERSE

See those handsome boys.
See that flash of femininity.
Hear that happy noise.
North and South are in proximity.
Cuban maids,
Men from Ioway,
Form parades
While the Latins play.
What a day!

REFRAIN

North America meets South America.
Two happy continents say "Hello!"
North America greets South America.
They get together to stage a show.
The farmer from the North drops his plow.
Gaucho gives up roping his cow.
North America meets South America.
There's only one America now!

I CONGRATULATE YOU, MR. COWBOY

Introduced by Buddy Ebsen.

I congratulate you on your [missing]
But I do it with greatest regrets.
You'll remember there's always [missing]
For an elephant never forgets

I am sorry for you, Mr. Cowboy.
There are no pretty girls in this state.

Since you have the good taste of a plow boy,
You would like the type every man hates.

Never visit the city of Dallas.
It will do you no good if you do.
There's a redheaded lady named Alice
Who would not give a tumble to you.

I congratulate you, Mr. Cowboy,
And I am mighty darn happy to say,
It has happened, old partner, and now, boy,
I've a reason for living today.

CONTRAPUNTO

Intended for Joseph Buloff and Buddy Ebsen, to be paired with "I Congratulate You, Mr. Cowboy." Apparently dropped from the film.

SANTIAGO: I congratulate you, mi amigo.
You sing like a bird, that I know.
And it really should flatter your ego,
The bird that I mean is the crow.

DUKE: I congratulate you, mi amigo.
You've a voice to set nations agog.
From Miami way up to Oswego
It is known as the horn of the fog.

SANTIAGO: I congratulate you, mi amigo.
You're as gallant with girls as can be.
Ladies like you in each place that we go.
You're so sweet that they go home with me.

DUKE: I congratulate you, mi amigo.
You went home with a girl, it is known.
If you ask me, my friend, why did she go?
She knew you couldn't make it alone.

YOU'VE GOT THE BEST OF ME

Introduced by Buddy Ebsen and Diosa Costello. Registered for copyright as an unpublished song by Chappell & Co., Inc., March 11, 1941.

VERSE

Fair or foul,
Foul or fair,
I have got you in my hair.
Am I glad to have you there?
No, ma'am!
Hot or cold,
Cold or hot,
You have put me on the spot
Do you really care a lot?
You, ma'am,
Do, ma'am,
Not!

REFRAIN

You've got the best of me,
So take the rest of me.
There's only one of me,
So don't make fun of me.
I think it's fair of me
To say, "Take care of me
As I'd take care of you."
I'm never sure of you
And that's the lure of you.
I want the most of you
And not the ghost of you.
Somehow in spite of you
I love the sight of you,
So go ahead and get the best of me!

CAREFREE CARETERRO

Introduced by Alberto Vila. Used as a counter melody to "Amarillo."

I don't need a hacienda,
I don't want a new sombrero.
While my horses do my labor
I'm a carefree careterro.
Hear the little bell that tinkles
Round the neck of my Rosita.
She's my little mare—my sweetheart.
I don't need a señorita.
Olé—Rosita!
Olé—Pepito!
With the heavens for my ceiling
And the grass below my carpet,
As my palace goes a-wheeling
I'm a carefree careterro.
Olé—Rosita!
Olé—Pepito!

What a gallant caballero
Is the carefree careterro!

AMARILLO

Published March 1941. Introduced by James Ellison and
Alberto Vila.

VERSE

I've heard it said
And I have read
The world has seven wonders.
That's something I can't understand today.
I know a town
Of no renown
That's not among those seven,
That seems a lot like Heaven
When I'm far away.

REFRAIN

Amarillo,
Where the hills turn to gold
Then sunset comes round
And the night turns to silver beneath the moon.
Amarillo,
Where the cool mountain breeze
Caresses the ground
And you rest in the calm of the afternoon.
Oh, my girl is there,
My girl is there,
And soon that's where I'll be.
And her deep blue eyes,
Her deep blue eyes,
Are earth and skies to me.
Amarillo,
Where the hills turn to gold,
Is where she will wait,
And my girl is the star of the Lone Star State.

LOLITA

Introduced by Alberto Vila.

Lolita, there's a moon on the rio.
Lolita, there's stars in your eyes.
The full moon you are now.
I love you
And the full moon is wise.

Oooo-lee-eeeeee,
I'm the one who adores you.
Oooo-lee-eeeeee,
I'm the starlight in your eyes.
Oooo-lee-eeeeee,
Here's your love who implores you.
Oooo-lee-eeeeee,
On the rio to love.

CUTTING THE CANE

Published March 1941. Introduced by Diosa Costello and
ensemble. The dance number "Chako," which preceded
it, apparently has no lyric.

VERSE

Working to dance,
Dancing to work,
Working and dancing to love.
Working to dance,
Dancing to work,
Two people can sing to love.

REFRAIN

When you hear rhythm from nowhere,
Faint at first, finally plain,
Take your love,
Both of you go where,
Where they are cutting the cane.
Go where the beat of it leads you,
Letting your heart be your guide.
Go to your lover who needs you,
Trembling to be at your side.
Cut the cane, go with your true love,
Use your heart, never your brain,
Then at last you'll know you do love,
While you are cutting the cane.

NEVER GO
TO ARGENTINA

Introduced by Diosa Costello.

Never go to Argentina
If you don't dance.
Rhythm down in Argentina
Rhymes with romance.

The music of the real guitar,
The steel guitar,
Is like a soft caress.
With moon enough
Quite soon enough
Your only word is "Yes!"
Never go to Argentina,
Don't take a chance.
Little girls in Argentina
Won't address you,
Won't caress you,
Not unless you dance!

Stay at home
If you don't believe in laughter.
Stay at home
If you never want to sing.
Stay at home
If it's solitude you're after.
To a killjoy Argentina doesn't mean a thing.
Stay at home
If you don't believe in living.
Argentina's democratic
But romance is king!

Never go to Argentina [etc.]

SIMPATICA

Published March 1941. Introduced by Alberto Vila.

VERSE

I don't describe you when I say
You have immortal beauty,
Or when I say that you are wise
Or you're a slave to duty.
But you mean more to me
Than anyone before, by far.
You are

REFRAIN

Simpatica.
One look in your eyes and I knew you.
Touching your hand bound me to you.
You understand, for you are simpatica.
Simpatica.
You don't have to talk to inspire me,
Don't have to say you desire me.
Day after day you are so simpatica.
You speak and it's the sweetest music
I have ever heard.
You taught me how to live again

The day you taught me
That single word
Simpatica.
I know that our love must be deathless.
One little kiss leaves me breathless.
You must know this if you are simpatica,
And you are so
Simpatica!

WE'RE ON THE TRACK

Unused. Alternate title: "On the Track."

VERSE

When horses hear a shot
They're off!
And when the band gets hot
We're off!
It takes a thoroughbred
To win the race.
Horses are nose and nose—
We're face to face.
Now the weather's clear,
Track is fast
And we're ready to start at last.
We're off!

REFRAIN

We're on the track.
Each colt with his filly
Dances until he
Leads the pack
On the track.
We're in our stride.
With music to pace us
Who can outrace us
As we ride
In our stride?
If you never hold your reins in check
We'll be sure to finish neck and neck.
Bet all your jack.
With rhythm to cling to
There's not a thing to
Hold us back.
Dance! Dance! Dance!
We're on the track!

ENCANTO

Unused.

VERSE

Dreaming we would never have to part,
Softly I heard a plaintive tune.

Something at the bottom of my heart
Tells me he's going to leave me soon.
Too soon.

REFRAIN 1

Ay-ay-ay. I'm in love, encanto.
Don't go. Why deny you're in love, encanto?
Don't go from the sea to the high sierras.
They know I adore you so.
On the sea there's a storm, encanto.
Stay here close to me where it's warm, encanto.
My dear, why
Should I say goodbye
When I need you? Ay-ay-ay.
I'm in love, encanto.
Don't go.

REFRAIN 2

Ay-ay-ay. It's goodbye, encanto.
I go with a sigh. It's goodbye, encanto.
I go from the sea to the high sierras.
They know I will miss you so.
On the sea there's a storm, encanto.
Stay true but my love will be warm, encanto.
For you I have to say goodbye
When I need you. Ay-ay-ay.
I'm in love, encanto.
Farewell.

BY JUPITER
1942

Tryout: Shubert Theatre, Boston, May 11–30, 1942. New York run: Shubert Theatre, June 3, 1942–June 12, 1943. 427 performances. Earlier title: *All's Fair.* Music by Richard Rodgers. Lyrics by Lorenz Hart. Produced by Dwight Deere Wiman and Richard Rodgers in association with Richard Kollmar. Book by Richard Rodgers and Lorenz Hart, based on the play *The Warrior's Husband* by Julian F. Thompson. Directed by Joshua Logan. Choreography by Robert Alton. Settings and lighting by Jo Mielziner. Costumes by Irene Sharaff. Orchestra under the direction of Johnny Green. Orchestrations by Don Walker. Cast, starring Ray Bolger, included Constance Moore, Benay Venuta, Ronald Graham, Bertha Belmore, and Vera-Ellen (chorus).

FOR JUPITER
AND GREECE

Introduced by Bob Douglas, Mark Dawson, and male ensemble. Added to the show during the Boston tryout.

ALL: We're here to fight the Amazons.
[*Music*]
So far away from Greece we are,
And just as far from peace we are.
We're bellicose and grim
And muscular of limb.
The Amazons will fight us Greeks.
[*Music*]
They're only women, but we hear
They wield a mighty wicked spear;
At home or in the field
They're disinclined to yield.
You might like to ask us why we left
our home
And neighbors.
It's all because of Hercules and his
dozen labors.
Hercules enslaved himself
Because he misbehaved himself.
ACHILLES: And Jupiter issued the following
command:
From Jupiter,
To Hercules,
Via Mercury.
Hercules, sir.
You will proceed to embark from the port
of Piraeus on May 9th, inst. You will
proceed to the land of the Amazons. You
will proceed to contact Hippolyta, the
Amazon Queen. Around her waist she
wears the sacred girdle of Diana. You will

proceed to get it. Get it? Then you will
proceed to come home. Proceed.
ALL: Agamemnon, Achilles and Ajax.
We would rather have stayed home to
play jacks.
Though we're well equipped with
swords and knives
We've been fighting women all our
lives
And losing
Come, boys, we're going to smother
Each Amazon mother and niece.
Out of the trenches and after the
wenches
For Jupiter and Greece!

JUPITER FORBID

Published May 1942. Introduced by Benay Venuta, Rose Inghram, Martha Burnett, Kay Kimber, and Monica Moore. Danced by Robert and Lewis Hightower, Flower Hujer, and ensemble. The song segued to an elaborate vocal arrangement of the number.

VERSE

You ought to be proud,
Tickled to death
To get a breath
Of this good atmosphere.
You're one of a crowd,
All on parade,
All unafraid,
And no one that must fear.
Just look around
And you'll kiss your native ground.

REFRAIN

Maybe there's a place where people never laugh,
Maybe there's a place where kids don't kid,
Maybe there's a place for just the upper half.
Not here,
Jupiter forbid!
Maybe there's a place where people never sing,
Where you have to hide each thing you did,
Where they have a sign, "Keep off the grass," in
spring.
Not here,
Jupiter forbid!
Here we dance if we see fit;
When he and she fit
It's fun.

Bright and light as a dancer,
For we must answer to none.
Maybe there's a place where you're afraid to kiss;
You could only do it if you hid.
That will never happen in a place like this.
Not here,
Jupiter forbid.

LIFE WITH FATHER

Introduced by Ray Bolger. Reprised by Bertha Belmore and Ray Bolger.

VERSE

"Won't you step into my parlor?"
Said the spider to the fly.
Like him I'm meek,
That's my technique.
I learned ev'rything from Father,
Who apparently was shy.
They thought he was a sheep—
And then the wolf would leap!

REFRAIN 1

I used to love my life with Father.
He was awkward and shy but he had a
romantic glance.
'Twas always open house with Father.
You would never believe that a boy
could have eighteen aunts.
With no fuss and with no bother
He made Mother come to tea,
And I'm a living proof that Father
Had a glorious gift and he handed it
on to me.

REFRAIN 2

I used to love my life with Father.
He was pure in his mind but his
actions were very free.
When I walked down the street with
Father,
He was only a mouse, but a louse in
the house was he.
Not a stingy man, but rather
He was lib'ral as could be.
When girls got sick of life with
Father,
He was gen'rous enough and he
handed 'em down to me.

REPRISE

POMPOSIA: I used to love my life with Father.
He was terribly sweet, though he
    wasn't exactly bright.
A tired man all day was Father,
But he'd walk in my room like a
    flower in bloom at night.
When romance began to bother
In his eye a gleam I'd see.
SAPIENS: I'm glad you loved your life with
    Father,
'Cause the gleam in his eye was the
    reason for little me.

NOBODY'S HEART

Published May 1942. Introduced by Constance Moore.
Reprised by Ray Bolger.

REFRAIN

Nobody's heart belongs to me,
Heigh-ho, who cares?
Nobody writes his songs to me,
No one belongs to me—
That's the least of my cares.
I may be sad at times,
And disinclined to play,
But it's not bad at times,
To go your own sweet way.
Nobody's arms belong to me,
No arms feel strong to me.
I admire the moon
As a moon,
Just a moon.
Nobody's heart belongs to me today.

INTERLUDE

Ride, Amazon, ride.
Hunt your stags and bears.
Take life in its stride.
Heigh-ho! Who cares?
Go hunting with pride,
Track bears to their lairs.
Ride Amazon, ride.
Heigh-ho, who cares?

REPEAT LAST SIX LINES OF REFRAIN

COMIC REPRISE

Nobody's heart belongs to me.
Heigh-ho, that's bad.
Love's never sung her songs to me—
No one belongs to me.
I have never been had.
I've had no trial in the game of man and maid.
I'm like a violin that no one's ever played.
Words about love are Greek to me.
Nice girls won't speak to me.
I despise the moon
As a moon,
It's a prune.
Nobody's heart belongs to me today.

THE GATEWAY OF THE TEMPLE OF MINERVA

Introduced by Ronald Graham and ensemble.

VERSE

When the Acanthus leaves are
    green again
And for their homes the homing
    pigeons start,*
Turning to home like all
    home-loving men,
April in Athens will be in my
    heart.

REFRAIN

In the gateway of the Temple of
    Minerva
There's a lovely Grecian girl who
    waits for me.
She was praying in the Temple of
    Minerva
As I sailed across the blue Aegean
    sea.
Oh, the temple fires patiently are
    burning
And I know just what her
    welcome's going to be.
In the gateway of the Temple of
    Minerva
She'll give the gate to me!

---

*Earlier version of lines 2–3:
    And all the brooks in rippling rhythm start,
    Turning to home, the happiest of men,

INTERLUDE

HERALD: She sits on a throne
In a joint of her own
And boogies her trouble and cares
    away.
SOLO GIRLS
& ACHILLES: Ay-way.
SOLO GIRLS: Minnie Min-er-her-er-va.
HERALD: Minnie's the hottest shot
They got on Olympus today.
SOLO GIRLS
& ACHILLES: Hot to-day.
ONE
SOLO GIRL: And they're plen-hen-ty hep on
Olympus so-ho they say-hay.
ACHILLES: In her cozy little temple
SOLO GIRLS
& HERALD: Minnie
ACHILLES: Digs the rhythms of the latest jive.
In her cozy little temple
SOLO GIRLS
& HERALD: Minnie
ACHILLES: Keeps the joint a-jumpin' and
    alive.
SOLO GIRLS: While the temple gates are
    swingin'
ACHILLES
& HERALD: Minnie
SOLO GIRLS: Gets the temple gong a-dingin'.
ACHILLES
& HERALD: Minnie
ACHILLES: She's a dame with vim and
    verve-a.
SOLO GIRLS
& HERALD: Minnie
ONE
SOLO GIRL: That's why bus'ness is so-ho
    terrific today with Minerva.
ALL
SINGERS: Minnie has a funny way of makin'
    with a boogie beat,
Oh, Minnie.
Does it with her head and with her
    eyes and does it with her feet.
Oh, Minnie.
Ev'ry god from Ajax up to Zeus
Finds his way to Minnie's swing
    caboose.
Minerva—Minerva.
[Orchestra interlude]
In her temple of learning
They're burning the mi-hid-night
    oi-hoil.
Minerva—Minerva.
[Orchestra interlude]
And the fires keep swingin'
And bringin' the boog to a boi-hoil.

DANCING
GIRLS & BOYS: You are talkin'
About what goddess?
SOLO GIRLS
& BOYS: We are talking
About the hot goddess.
SOLO GIRLS: Min-er-her-er-va.
ACHILLES: The lady with the temple of jive.
EVERYONE
ON STAGE: Mister Apopolus
On the Acropolus
In fact the whole metropolis
Loves making with the boogie with
Minerva.

REPEAT REFRAIN

HERE'S A HAND

Published May 1942. Introduced by Ronald Graham and
Constance Moore.

VERSE

I've marched away,
I've gone to war,
Slew ten one day,
The next day more,
And that's how I learned about love.
A soldier learns to understand
He must be faithful to his land;
He must be strong, all else above;
Yes, that's how I learned about love.

REFRAIN 1

Here's a hand that's learned to fight
All for you.
But the hand with all its might
Needs you too.
Here's a hand I gave to the land I love,
Pledged to fight till I fell;
Take this hand in the hand I love, too,
And I'll love you as well.
Here's a hand that will grow warm
When you say, "I love you, soldier,
I'm at your command."
With the love it holds for you,
Here's my hand.

NO, MOTHER, NO

Finale, Act I. Introduced by Ray Bolger, other principals,
and ensemble. There are two versions of this number. The
early version is from the manuscripts Richard Rodgers
donated to the Library of Congress.

Early version

HIPPOLYTA: The pris'ners, the pris'ners.
Where are they?
BURIA: They've escaped.
HIPPOLYTA: Without being raped?
Go find them at once,
You long-legged dunce!
ANTIOPE: Wait! Wait!
Such things don't alarm me.
Who's afraid of an army?
Especially when
It's an army of men.
ALL: Just an army of men.
ANTIOPE: Why waste time over two of them?
I'd like to tackle a few of them.
Let's get ready and then
Take over that army of men.
HIPPOLYTA: Report! Report! Report!
Report! Report to your company.
Hurry.
Stub a toe and bump a knee
But report to your company!
Money makes the mare go.
ALL: She must pay her workers—ergo
Money makes the mare go.
Maybe there's a place where people
will not give,
Where they wouldn't do what you
just did.
Maybe there's a place where mean
old misers live,
Not here, Jupiter forbid!
HIPPOLYTA: Of the names I've called you
I'll make short shrift
And thank you, dear, for your
generous gift.
POMPOSIA: A gift! A gift!
A wedding gift!
HEROICA: A wedding gift.
POMPOSIA: A wedding gift.
ANTIOPE: So you'll marry that insect?
HIPPOLYTA: Don't be such a cat!
ANTIOPE: He may give you children.
D'j'ever think of that?
HIPPOLYTA: I'll get the equipment.
No baby bunting,
It would ruin my hunting.

SAPIENS: No, Mother, no.
You embarrass me.
No, Mother, no.
I simply cannot go.
No, I will not go.
No trousseau.
Not a decent sandal.
It would be a scandal.
POMPOSIA: There! There!
SAPIENS: No, Mother, no!
Look at my hair.
Isn't it a mess?
Look at this rag,
This tunic is a bag.
I look like a hag.
Folks will gag.
I want something stylish
This whole thing is vile-ish.
POMPOSIA: There! There!
SAPIENS: No, Mother, no!
HEROICA: Sapiens, do you take this woman
To be your lady and mistress?
POMPOSIA: Wife!
HEROICA: Wife!
SAPIENS: For life!
No, I don't believe it.
I cannot conceive it.
No wedding night.
No night of bliss.
I never dreamed of a wedding like
this.
No loving arms, not even a kiss.
I dreamed I'd be sleeping in marble
halls,
And not even a trip to Nigerian Falls!

Later version

[*An army of Greek men has landed; news reaches the
Amazons*]

HIPPOLYTA: The pris'ners, where are they?
BURIA: They've escaped.
HIPPOLYTA: Without being raped?
Go find them at once, you dunce!
ANTIOPE: Wait! Wait! That doesn't alarm me.
Who's scared of an army?
Especially when
It's an army of men.
ALL: An army of men—hah!
HIPPOLYTA: Report! Report! Report! Report!
Report to your company. Hurry!
Stub a toe and bump a knee
But report to your company!
ANTIOPE: Thank the gods and little fishes
Who fulfill my dearest wishes,
We've someone to fight at last.

ALL: Hooray!

POMPOSIA: Antiope—not so fast!
The little runner here
Has told me there are five thousand
of the Greeks.

HIPPOLYTA: Suppose that's true!
We have five thousand too!

POMPOSIA: Without wanting to cause undue
alarm,
You've only three thousand under
arm.

HIPPOLYTA: But you have enough equipment for
the other two thousand.

POMPOSIA: I don't want to be funny
But what will you do for money?
I must pay my workers—ergo
Money makes the mare go.

ALL: She must pay her workers—ergo
Money makes the mare go.

HIPPOLYTA: You see the need,
You see the urgency.
This is a national emergency

POMPOSIA: Come, Hippolyta, take heart,
Every Amazon must do her part.
Give your helmets, give your shirts,
We must all give till it hurts!
As a gift to the country I adore
I will equip two thousand more.

ALL: Hooray!

HIPPOLYTA: I'm sorry now that we ever tiffed.
I thank you, dear, for your gen'rous
gift.

POMPOSIA: A gift! A wedding gift!

ALL: A wedding gift!

POMPOSIA: A wedding gift!
To you and Sapiens.

HIPPOLYTA: So that's your price?
Very nice!

POMPOSIA: The gift of your hand is due to all
your faithful skirts.
Give! Give! Give! Until it hurts!

HIPPOLYTA: I can feel it already.

ANTIOPE: Steady, sister, steady!
We can beat them with three
thousand!
We can beat them with two!

ALL: Hooray!

POMPOSIA: I wouldn't be outnumbered if I were
you.
Or you'll remember what my tip
meant.

HIPPOLYTA: All right! It's agreed—*if* I get that
equipment.

POMPOSIA: Then you'll marry my Sappy?

HIPPOLYTA: Him or his pappy.

POMPOSIA: Oh, you've made me so happy.
[Exits]

HIPPOLYTA: Get Pomposia's order for the
equipment without delay.

BURIA: O.K.

ANTIOPE: So you'll marry that insect?

HIPPOLYTA: Don't be such a cat!

ANTIOPE: He may give you babies.
D'j'ever think of that?

HIPPOLYTA: Before he can kiss me
I'll rush right off to war.
No baby hunting
Is going to spoil my hunting.

BURIA: Your Majesty!
[Enter Pomposia, leading Sapiens]

ALL: Ah! Ah!

SAPIENS: No, Mother, no.
I'm not ready yet.
No, Mother, no.
I'm so badly dressed.
Take this monkey's vest
Off my pretty chest.
They have bound my tummy
Like a mummy, Mummy.

POMPOSIA: There! There!

SAPIENS: No, Mother, no!

POMPOSIA: Sapiens!

SAPIENS: No, Mother!

POMPOSIA: Sapiens! Your mother is wise.
[Two boys come in with a cap, headpiece, and veil]
Surprise! Surprise!

ALL: Ah!

SAPIENS: [Examines the cap]
Imported—dear me.
I can smell the sea,
[Two dressmakers are fixing him up. One of them sticks
him with a pin]
Ouch! This is uncanny.
[Gets another pin in the backside]
Ouch! Right in the —
Mother, I won't be married.
Not if I'm carried.

HIPPOLYTA: Tell the Sixth Battalion to fall in.

SAPIENS: This headpiece is a sin.
[To Hippolyta]
Do you want me now?

HIPPOLYTA: Let's take the vow.

SAPIENS: I never dreamed I'd be a war groom.

HIPPOLYTA: Who'll marry us?

POMPOSIA: Heroica will perform the ceremony.

SAPIENS: Now?

POMPOSIA: Sapiens, be quiet, please.

SAPIENS: Mother, you haven't even told me
about the birds and the bees.

HEROICA: Kneel!
Sapiens, do you take this woman to
be your lady and mistress?

POMPOSIA: Wife!

HEROICA: Wife!

SAPIENS &
HIPPOLYTA: For life!

HEROICA: You're wife and man. I did the stunt!

HIPPOLYTA: All right, Antiope, we're off for the
front!

ANTIOPE: Come! Follow me—we're off to the
fray!

ALL: Hooray!

SAPIENS: Stay!
No, I don't believe it.
I cannot conceive it.
No wedding night.
No night of bliss.
I never dreamed of a wedding like
this.
No loving arms, not even a kiss.
I dreamed I'd be sleeping in marble
halls,
And not even a trip to Nigerian Falls.
[Hippolyta moves toward him]
No, no—you must not go!

HIPPOLYTA: Listen, fool, my country calls.
Go by yourself to Nigerian Falls.

THE BOY I LEFT BEHIND ME

Introduced by Jayne Manners and ensemble. This number
opened Act I during the Boston tryout.

VERSE

You may talk of gin and beer
When you're quartered safe out here
A-serving of Her Majesty the Queen,
But every soldier's daughter
Will do her work on water
When fighting on a foreign front she's seen.
She won't miss the pies and cakes
That her dear old father bakes,
Or the cottage with the little spot of green,
But just ask May or Lily
Or any fighting filly
What sacrifice her leaving home will mean.

ALL: It's the boy!
It's the boy!

SHE: It's the boy I'll leave behind me.

REFRAIN 1

Oh, how I miss the little boy I left behind
me.
I miss my gentle, sentimental little mate.

I'll never need the socks he knitted to remind me
That he is waiting for me at the garden gate.
He is both mentally and physically attractive,
And we have fun if we just talk or we are active,
And when I'm fighting foreign battles, you will find me
Longing for the boy I left behind.

REFRAIN 2

Oh, how I miss the little boy I left behind me,
Because the girl behind the spear has little sport.
If I were smarter in the Navy you would find me,
Because a sailor has a boy in every port.
A lonely tent can make a soldier get so nervous,
Because at night she needs a bit more active service.
And when I'm slicing enemy gullets, you will find me
Longing for the boy I left behind.

EV'RYTHING I'VE GOT

Published May 1942. Introduced by Ray Bolger and Benay Venuta.

VERSE 1

SHE: Don't stamp your foot at me,
It's impolite.
To stamp your foot at me
Is not quite right.
At man's ingratitude*
A woman winks,
But such an attitude just stinks.

REFRAIN 1

I have eyes for you to give you dirty looks.
I have words that do not come from children's books.
There's a trick with a knife I'm learning to do,

In the published version, lines 5–7:
All I discover is,
You're not so fine.
I fear my lover is a swine.

And ev'rything I've got belongs to you.
I've a powerful anesthesia in my fist,
And the perfect wrist to give your neck a twist.
There are hammerlock holds,
I've mastered a few,
And ev'rything I've got belongs to you.
Share for share, share alike,
You get struck each time I strike.
You for me—me for me—
I'll give you plenty of nothing.
I'm not yours for better but for worse,
And I've learned to give the well-known witches' curse.
I've a terrible tongue, a temper for two,
And ev'rything I've got belongs to you.

VERSE 2

HE: Don't raise your voice at me,
That's very rude.
To raise your voice at me
Is rather crude.
It's wrong essentially when woman yells,
And confidentially, it smells.

REFRAIN 2

I'll converse with you on politics at length,
I'll protect you with my superhuman strength.
If you're ever attacked I'll scream and say, "Boo!"
And ev'rything I've got belongs to you.
I will never stray from home, I'll just stay put,
'Cause I've got a brand-new thing called athlete's foot.
I'm a victim of colds, anemia, too,
And ev'rything I've got belongs to you.
Off to bed we will creep,
Then we'll sleep and sleep and sleep
Till the birds start to peep.
I'll give you plenty of nothing.
I'll be yours forever and a day
If the first good breeze does not blow me away.
You're enough for one man, that's why I'll be true,
And ev'rything I've got belongs to you.

ENCORE

SHE: You may have some things that I can't use at all.
When I look at you, your manly gifts are small.

I've a wonderful way of saying adieu,
And ev'rything I've got belongs to you.
HE: You won't know how good I am until you try
And you'll let my well of loneliness run dry.
I've a marvelous way of telling you no,
And ev'rything I've got belongs to you.
And ev'rything you want belongs to me!
And ev'rything you need belongs to me!

REPRISE

VERSE

SHE: Life has no shape or form
And no design.
It isn't life without
That fool of mine.
I used to gad about
With any chap
And now I'm sad about my sap.

REFRAIN

He's a living thing that isn't quite alive,
He has brains enough for any child of five.
Oh, he isn't too rich in vigor and vim,
But ev'rything I've got belongs to him.
He's a naughty brat that can't be left alone.
He has eyes for ev'ry skirt except my own.
Even under a tree, he grabs for the limb,
But ev'rything I've got belongs to him.
Something beats in his chest,
But it's just a pump at best.
I'm for him, he's for him.
He gives me plenty of nothing.
When I see that funny face, I know
Something scared his mother twenty years ago.
But I'll never let go, he'll never be free!
Till ev'rything he's got belongs to me!

CODA

And ev'rything I've got belongs to him!
And ev'rything we've got belongs to us!

BOTTOMS UP

Introduced by Mark Dawson, Benay Venuta, Constance Moore, Berni Gould, Bob Douglas, Vera-Ellen, Flower Hujer, and ensemble.

HERALD: Hippolyta, I greet you from the
enemy.

ANTIOPE: That's Hippolyta.

HERALD: Great Hercules has come with noble
Theseus,
And Jupiter would smile with pride
could *he* see us.
Great Hercules in fame is
unsurmountable.
And we've so many men that they're
uncountable.

HOMER: Great . . .

HERALD: Great Hercules came sailing, to the
tussle bound.
When he was born, he was already
muscle-bound.
He's traveled down to Africa in quest
of you.
He doesn't give a hoot about the rest
of you.

HOMER: He's . . .

HERALD: He's made mistakes, but they were
unintentional.
He killed his kids, and that was
unconventional.
And so, twelve mighty labors he must
consummate
And hang your pretty little girdle on
some mate.
And . . .

ANTIOPE: Oh, nuts!

HIPPOLYTA: Antiope, you swear like a
longshorewoman.

HERALD: I wish you wouldn't interrupt me.
I've got enough trouble remembering
these damn tripe rhymes.

ANTIOPE: Why don't you talk straight?

HOMER: Why, I stayed up all night writing
this poem.

ANTIOPE: Why?

HOMER: Well, I don't sleep and . . .
Please: Will you let the herald do his
stuff?
Hercules wants the Queen . . .

HERALD: Hercules wants the Queen
To fight him single-handed
So he can win the girdle
As Jupiter commanded!

HIPPOLYTA: Where will he meet me?

HERALD: Between the two camps.

HIPPOLYTA: Good!

HERALD: Hercules is brave,
Gets over ev'ry hurdle.
His only stipulation
Is that you wear your girdle.

HIPPOLYTA: Drinks, Andromache.

ANTIOPE: Boy, you need one!

HOMER: Well, I've never been known to
refuse one yet.

HIPPOLYTA: To the fights, and may the gods help
Hercules!

HERALD: Bottoms up!
Fill the cup.
Bottoms up!
Refill the cup.
Get the feeling
That the sky's the ceiling
And you're high! High! High!
Elbows bend,
I'm your friend.
Elbows bend,
And voices blend.
Start believing
That the room is weaving
And you're high! High! High! High!
Have another and another and
another!
Then take another and another and
another!
Kiss me first,
Kill the thirst,
But the first
Won't kill the thirst.
Life means plenty,
It begins at twenty
When you're high! High! High!

CARELESS RHAPSODY

Published May 1942. Introduced by Constance Moore and
Ronald Graham.

VERSE

Music is the food of love
To get us in the mood of love.
It adds a tender tone.
A melody can light the spark
So let us both ignite the spark
With music of our own,
Sweet music of our own.

REFRAIN

Let's play a careless rhapsody
And let's set the music free.
I'll touch your heartstrings to make the tune
clearer
And you'll be nearer me.
Maybe a careless rhapsody
Will soon teach us both to care.

Strike all the chords that our fingers can find us,
Chords that will bind us there.
When you are the theme
Oh, it's wonderful
And I'll make that theme
Reach its greatest height,
So let's play a careless rhapsody
Deep into the night.

THE GREEKS HAVE GOT THE GIRDLE

Introduced by Ray Bolger, Benay Venuta, Bertha Belmore, and ensemble. Alternate title: "Finaletto."

HIPPOLYTA: The Greeks have got the girdle.
We have to get over that hurdle.
I still am the Queen.

SAPIENS: That remains to be seen.

HIPPOLYTA: The Greeks have got the girdle.

POMPOSIA: The girdle is gone.
The girdle is gone.

CHORUS: Oh! Oh! Oh!
The girdle is gone.
Gone! Gone! Gone!
The girdle is gone.
Gone! Gone! Gone!
We must get the girdle.
We must get over the hurdle.

SAPIENS: I will get the girdle.
I'll get over the hurdle.
I'm going to the rescue.

HIPPOLYTA: Who the hell are you?

SAPIENS: Who the hell am I?
I am the King.

HIPPOLYTA: You undernourished thing.

SAPIENS: The Queen's husband is the King.
Women having lost their power,
This is man's hour.

HIPPOLYTA: Prove you're the King,
You silliest of freaks.

SAPIENS: I'll save your sister myself.
I'll save her from the Greeks.
The girdle won't be gone.

CHORUS: Gone! Gone! Gone!

SAPIENS: I'll prove that I'm the King.

CHORUS: King! King! King!

SAPIENS: I'll prove that I'm the King.

CHORUS: He'll prove that he's the King!

WAIT TILL YOU SEE HER

Published May 1942. Introduced by Ronald Graham and ensemble. Apparently dropped from the show in April 1943. After April 25, 1943, it is no longer listed in the program.

VERSE

My friends who knew me
Never would know me,
They'd look right through me,
Above and below me,
And ask, "Who's that man?
Who is that man?
That's not my lighthearted friend!"
Meeting one girl
Was the start of the end.
Love is a simple emotion
A friend should comprehend.

REFRAIN

Wait till you see her,
See how she looks,
Wait till you hear her laugh.
Painters of paintings,
Writers of books,
Never could tell the half.
Wait till you feel
The warmth of her glance,
Pensive and sweet and wise.
All of it lovely,
All of it thrilling,
I'll never be willing to free her.
When you see her
You won't believe your eyes.

NOW THAT I'VE GOT MY STRENGTH

Introduced by Ray Bolger, Irene Corlett, Vera-Ellen, and ensemble. Added during the Boston tryout, it replaced "Life Was Monotonous."

VERSE

I'm coming out of my cloister,
I'm emerging from my sheath.
The lovely world is my oyster

And I'll crack the shell with my teeth.
Quite a guy—I!

REFRAIN

Now that I've got my strength,
Now that I'm big and strong,
I have learned from women what course to take.
A worm will turn if he gets a break
This worm has turned to a great big snake,
Now that I've got my strength.
Holding hands was my fashion,
Just a kiss was a feast.
Now I'm roaring with passion,
For today I am a beast!
Now that I'm big and strong,
I'll go to any length.
I've found my happiness, lost my doubt,
I really know what it is all about.
I only hope that I don't wear out,
Now that I've got my strength!

FOOL MEETS FOOL

Dropped before the New York opening. Introduced by Benay Venuta in Act II during the Boston tryout.

VERSE

Said I to my horse, said I,
We mares belong in battalions.
We never should bother with males at all,
So don't give a neigh to the stallions.
A neigh means yes to the stallions.
Let's bid all the males goodbye,
Said I to my horse, said I.

REFRAIN

Fool meets fool, fool meets fool.
It's all the same with birds or beast
And people are worse, to say the least.
Fool meets fool.
Sap meets sap, sap meets sap.
They do the same thing every night
And finally hate each other's sight.
Sap meets sap.
They call it love and make themselves absurd for
     it.
I met a Greek, he had a better word for it.
Fool meets fool, I'm that fool
Who'd do the ridiculous thing again.

LIFE WAS MONOTONOUS

Dropped before the New York opening. Introduced by Ray Bolger, Irene Corlett, Nadine Gae, and ensemble in Act II during the Boston tryout. Replaced by "Now That I've Got My Strength."

VERSE

One day was like the other;
I never saw a thing.
I played ball with my brother;
I heard my sister sing.
I went with boys, I went with girls,
I thought it was the same thing,
And now I think I understand
The whole darn blame thing.

REFRAIN

Life was monotonous, life was wet,
Life could have gotten us if we hadn't met
And discovered we were meant for us.
Life was monotonous, we felt old,
Blood wasn't hot in us, it ran awfully cold
Till we met and learned to make a fuss over each
     other.
We've discovered this and that in us,
Mother nature had a plan.
Now my spine is not gelatinous,
For today I am a man!
Life was monotonous, life was blue,
There was a lot in us that we never knew
Till we found we were adjacent.
That's why we are so darned complacent.
Life's not monotonous; I've got you!

NOTHING TO DO BUT RELAX

Dropped before the New York opening. Introduced by Ray Bolger, Benay Venuta, Constance Moore, Ronald Graham, and ensemble in Act II during the Boston tryout.

VERSE

The day is made for working,
For scrubbing floors and clerking.
Is this the time for shirking?
Yes, yes, yes.
We'll go where trees are fruity
And study nature's beauty.

Will we neglect our duty?
Yes, yes, yes.

REFRAIN

Nothing to do but relax
'Neath the eucalyptus tree,

Flat on our beautiful backs
Healthy and dumb.
Warm days are nice enough,
Summer has come.
And we'll bring ice enough
For our rum.

Nothing to do but make love,
Two demented butterflies,
Time with a flutter flies
While the bees make wax
And we have nothing to do but relax.

Lorenz Hart and Richard Rodgers

MISCELLANEOUS | 1940–1943
MISS UNDERGROUND | 1943

MISCELLANEOUS, 1940-1943

In the early 1940s Rodgers and Hart wrote a small number of songs not specifically earmarked for their own stage and screen scores. Most of these were written to boost morale during World War II.

NOW THAT I KNOW YOU

Introduced by Earl Oxford and Marie Nash in the Ted Fetter-Richard Lewine summer revue, *Two Weeks with Pay*, which was presented at the Ridgway Theatre in White Plains, New York, June 19–July 1, 1940. It has the same music as the original title song for *I'd Rather Be Right* (1937), which had been dropped before the New York opening of that production.

VERSE

When you know that someone loves you so
You know you'll never be alone.
I'm not smart, my brains are in my heart.
Behold in me
The one who'll be your own.

REFRAIN

Now that I know you,
Now that I know you won't forget,
You can leave me,
But you will leave me in your debt,
For I see now
How grand life can be now.
My world is in the making
And daylight is breaking,
All's well, for I know you at last.
I know your eyes, their expression,
Your thoughts in procession,
They're in my possession—
I know you, so you
Must be my future,
Just as you must have been my past,
For I really know you at last.

ALTERNATE VERSE

If by chance you stumble on romance
You're foolish to pass it by.
I'm not smart, my brains are in my heart.

But I don't see
The point in being shy.

KEEP 'EM ROLLING

Written for a film short, *Keep 'Em Rolling*, made by Universal Pictures in 1942. Introduced by Jan Peerce.

VERSE

It's fun to drive a brand-new car,
It's lots of fun to dine and dance
And think the wolf who's at the door
Just hasn't got a single chance.
But I don't need a brand-new car,
The old one's good enough to drive.
I'll work and save and save and work
To keep my Uncle Sam alive!

REFRAIN

The flame of freedom is burning,
We've lots of timber and coal.
The wheels within wheels are turning.
Keep 'em rolling!
We've got the goods to deliver
And that's our ace in the hole.
The logs are all in the river.
Keep 'em rolling!
In town and country,
Lowland and mountain ridge,
Let's build bridges
Instead of playing bridge!
Don't trust to one little ocean,
The land itself must be strong,
So keep the motors in motion,
Keep 'em rolling along!

BOMBARDIER SONG

Published May 1942. Written for the Army Air Force.

VERSE 1

Said the bombardier to the pilot,
"Give us a little ride."
The pilot said to the navigator,
"Won't you slide inside?"
The navigator looked around and said to the
    engineer,

"Your hands are dirty,
Your pants are dirty,
You're dirty behind the ear!"
Said the bombardier to the gunner,
"How are we fixed for lead?"
The pilot said to the radioman,
"How's the weather ahead?"

REFRAIN

The weather's fine for flying,
The fog has gone to bed;
There's such good visibility
You can see victory ahead!
Let's fill the air with bombers,
Let's fill the clouds with men,
And we will see
A world that's free
When we fly home again.

VERSE 2

Said the bombardier to the pilot,
"Give us the pretty crate,
And five degrees to the right will make it
Just as sure as fate."
The ship belonged to the bombardier, who
    opened his little bay.
He saw the target,
The lovely target,
And suddenly, "Bombs away!"
Said the bombardier to the pilot,
"Call it a day," and then
The pilot said to the radioman,
"Say, we've done it again!"

REPEAT REFRAIN

SHORTY THE GUNNER

Date of composition unknown. Found in the Rodgers and Hammerstein office.

VERSE

When the enemy comes through the skies,
Who is on his toes?
Who's on the job to keep the flies
Off the horse's nose?
The pilot steers the plane,
The bombardier is hot stuff,
But who's behind the gun,
And who's the one who's got the stuff?

REFRAIN

Who's in the hottest seat, cool as a breeze?
Who's short upon his feet, tall on his knees?
Who shoots a row of neat holes in the cheese?
Shorty, the plane depends on Shorty.
Shorty, Shorty, riding in the rumble,
Flying backwards only makes him grin.
Can't see where he's going in the rumble,
Bet your life he knows where he has been.
Who makes the buzzard screech, just for the
      sport?
Who has the longest reach? Shorty, the short.
Who steps into the breach, who is the one?
It's Shorty, the guy with the gun!

THE GIRL I LOVE TO LEAVE BEHIND

Introduced by Ray Bolger in the film *Stage Door Canteen*,
released May 1943.

VERSE

I have to leave my sweetheart
And yet I'm feeling fine
Although she's broken-hearted for me.
I met her on a Friday
In November twenty-nine;
That's how depression started for me.
All these years I thought I'd never get away
Till my uncle with the whiskers saved the day.

REFRAIN 1

She has hair that she wears like Veronica Lake,
So that fifty percent of her is blind.
She is known to her daddy as Mother's mistake.
She's the girl I love to leave behind.
She is silly for soldiers and mad for marines
And she can't get the Coast Guard off her mind.
She keeps doing the can-can in all the canteens.
She's the girl I love to leave behind.
After dancing her round the floor
It's a pleasure to go to war.
Oh, she giggles and gurgles and rattles around
Like the model that Henry Ford designed.
While I fight on the sea, in the air, on the
      ground,
She's the girl I love to leave behind.

REFRAIN 2

When you take her to dinner she eats every
      course,
She's a triumph of matter over mind.
For an entree she orders the hip of a horse.
She's the girl I love to leave behind.
She is good to her mother and sweet to her pop
And to all of her relatives she's kind,
But when I try to kiss her she yells for a cop,
She's the girl I love to leave behind.
If I live through this big romance
Then the Japs haven't got a chance.
Her deportment at parties would cause you to
      weep,
Lou Costello is slightly more refined.
While I fight in a tank, on a plane, in a jeep,
She's the girl I love to leave behind.

MISS UNDERGROUND, 1943

In 1943, while Rodgers was at work with Oscar Hammer-stein II on the show that became *Oklahoma!*, Paul Gallico approached Hart with an idea of writing a musical about the French underground. Gallico wrote the book, which he called *Miss Underground.* Emmerich Kalman (1882–1953), the revered Hungarian-born operetta composer, wrote the music, and Hart's close friend George Balanchine was to do the choreography. The show was never produced, as it proved impossible to raise money for it during wartime. In addition to the lyrics printed here, other lyrics believed to have been written or intended for the show are: "Alexander's Blitztime Band," "Otto's Patter Song," "Vendor's Song," "Otto's German/English Song," "Lucio's Victorian Family," "Otto and the Elephants," "The Bad Little Apple and the Wise Old Tree," "Get Your Man," "New York Number," "Jean's Magic Song," and "France Is Free." They are missing.

MESSIEURS, MESDAMES

Messieurs, mesdames . . .
Mesdames, messieurs . . .
Voilà nous avons
Une histoire de Paris . . .
But don't be afraid of me.

There's not a soul that must fear
That this show is in French.
That was only for atmosphere.
In this show when I'm supposed to sing in French,
I sing in English.
When a Nazi tries to occupy a weeping wench,
He growls in English.
And though we have battalions
Of equestrian Italians,
They'll sing presto and andante,
Like Signor Jimmy Durante,
"Am I mortified?"
What am I here for, you ask?
It's about time to let you know
That I'm the program of the show . . .
It's a cross section of humanity,
A story not without insanity,
Some country folks and others with urbanity.
Oh, vanity, thy name is just humanity!
For women are women, and cats are cats,*
Men are mice who think they're rats . . .

First on the program we get
Honest Jean—petite Jeanette.
Her name is Marge, and his is Jack.
He wolfs a little with the pack.
Marge plays the innocent Jeanette.
On the stage she's hard to get.
These are the kids who used to work us
To great excitement in the circus.
This is Lucio, who provided the mirth
For Ringling's greatest show on earth.
He rides a horse on his ear—
That takes endurance
But should he fall
The show has insurance.
This is handsome Mogador,
And this is Chita, the queen of the show.
Take a good look, brother—the answer is No!
So go.
For women are women and cats are cats,
Men are mice who think they're rats . . .

Rosita Moreno,
All the folks in our play know,
She's married and means it.
Rosie was the thrill
That enraptured Brazil.
Argentinians rage,
But the Latins despair,
They can't get anywhere.
She's a waste of talent off the stage.
And this is Jack Page,
Who is gay on the stage,

*This couplet, twice repeated in this lyric, appeared earlier
in "Love Is Queen, Love Is King" from the 1933 film version
of I Married an Angel (1933), page 191.*

But he leads his wife
A melancholic life.
He's tired and sad,
Thinking up how to be funny.
And that's why Mr. Page is in the money.
And here—well,
Well, well, well,
Isn't she stylish? Isn't she regal?
I'm Susan Sherlock Holmes.
You're Vivienne Segal
Let's hear a song from your latest show.
Come let us hear
That hit of last year.
This is our cast,
And foremost, but last,
I am Evans. Let your minds be at peace,
For I am Wilbur, not Maurice.
I am the one that Segal chases,
But I escape in the strangest places.
For women are women and cats are cats—
Men are mice who think they're rats.

IT HAPPENED IN
THE DARK

VERSE

Kissed and ran,
Made my conquest, or
Missed and ran.
I went right through my list and ran.
Sentimental, oh no!
Then you came.
To the coldest of men you came,
Threw a boomerang when you came,
And you melted the snow.

REFRAIN

One night it happened in the dark
And I could only see with the eyes of my heart.
My arms could never miss their mark
And all the whirling world couldn't tear us apart.
And through the canopy of night
You looked, and there was light
And my old love was new.
One night it happened in the dark.
But yet it wasn't dark,
Not for me, not for you.

MOTHER, LOOK,
I'M AN ACROBAT

VERSE

LUCIO: You must do this-a [trick]
You must do that-a [trick]
SUSAN: Oh no, not-a without a mat-a.
LUCIO: It's easy, you try-a [trick]
SUSAN: Easy, my eye-a [on her fanny]
LUCIO: Just-a practice you must-a.
SUSAN: I will till I bust-a.

REFRAIN

Mother, look, I'm an acrobat.
Baby's jumped in the ring.
Once I sat as a back-row bat,
Now I nip up and spring.
Hear your daughter yell, "Allez up!"
With the strong man I'll play.
Watch them lift this tamale up
And we'll rally up all the crowd there.
I have never groused about
Showing my form in tights
Or watching a clown or roustabout
In fights—
Join the circus and see the world,
Monkey and tiger pup.
Now my circus will be the world.
I'm an acrobat—"Allez up!"

THE ONE WHO
YELLS THE LOUDEST
IS THE CAPTAIN

The one who yells the loudest is the captain,
On battlefield, in business, or in bed.
The man who works the hardest is the private,
And virtue is its own reward instead.
A major may become a major general,
If his larynx and his pharynx are in shape.
But the one who yells the loudest is the captain,
Right from Peter Pan down to the Hairy Ape.

They think that I'm a Nazi,
What Winchell calls a Ratzi,
But don't throw any mud, son,
I come from the banks of the Hudson.
This joint could not be drearer,
And I'll never Heil the . . .
Ah, the hell with him.

. . .

I used to be a waiter,
Before I sailed that freighter,
In Fourteenth Street by Lüchow,
Where, boy, they sure serve you chow.
And then by an unhappy chance,
I took a vacation in France.
But I was born in Germany,
An unlucky son of a gun,
But that was twenty years ago—
So when the rats came to Paree,
The dirty skunks adopted me.

But still I'm not a Nazi,
What Winchell calls a Ratzi.
They should sprinkle this place with prophylaxis
And sprinkle right on the Axis.

No garden spot is flowery
If it's too far from the Bowery.
I wish that I could swim out
And look at that lousy dim-out.
That face could not be queerer
Of the guy they call der . . .
Don't worry. I won't mention his name.
He's the big shot and the proudest,
Because his voice is the loudest.

The one who yells the loudest is the captain,
Selling Lucky Strikes . . .
[Imitates tobacco auctioneer's jargon, at the end of
which he yells, "Sold!"]
Or selling fish.
The man who speaks the softest is the corporal,
And in his way is quite a dainty dish.
The man who suffers most is the civilian.
He looks right at his missus and he groans.
The one who yells the loudest is the captain,
Right from Mrs. Roosevelt down to Mrs. Jones.

DO I LOVE YOU?

VERSE 1

I'm no little boy full of sentiment
But I still take girls to tea.
In my early years ten or twenty meant
Just the quota of an average week for me.
Drained the cup a bit in my ballad days,
Yet I like a pretty face.
I've slowed up a bit
Since my salad days.
I'll be running like a fox and you can chase.

REFRAIN 1

Do I love you? Yes, I do not!
Do I love you? Guess I do not!
You are just a joke in my eyes.
You can't put that smoke in my eyes.
Though that spark has not got to us
We'll get married, but not to us.
Two hearts make one, yours and mine make two.
I'm not in love with you.

VERSE 2

When a negative meets a positive
They get mated on the spot.
I'm a positive, you're a positive.
With no negative around, we can't get hot!
Every bully boy gets a woolly girl
If he knows his way about.
You're a bully boy, I'm a bully girl.
We could step into the ring
And dish it out.

REFRAIN 2

Do I love you? Yes, I do not!
Do I love you? Guess I do not!
Love moves mountains into the sea.
I'm Gibraltar—try to move me!
When I'm hungry, I dine alone.
Eat your heart out—leave mine alone.
Tell your mother! Tell your daddy, too!
I'm not in love with you.

YOU CRAZY LITTLE THINGS

Alternate title: "Fall in Love." The melody was used later in Kalman's score for *Marinka* (1945).

VERSE

When I was young I was a fool myself.
I thought I ran the school myself.
I thought that I could rule myself.

You're just as bad as I—
When I was young I was no jewel myself.
Like everyone, I was a tool myself.
And now I know I was just cruel to myself.
You're just as bad—as foolish as I.

REFRAIN

You're in love,
You crazy little things.
Start to love,
You lazy little things.
Just put your arms
Where you should put your arms.
Why should you two care
Ever—anywhere?*
You're in love,
You crazy little things.
You're in love,
You pigeons without wings.
What can I say?
You are fools today
As I was many years ago.

Alternate version: Love is ev'rywhere

A CONNECTICUT YANKEE | 1943

A revision of the 1927 version. Tryout: Forrest Theatre, Philadelphia, October 28–November 14, 1943. New York run: Martin Beck Theatre, November 17, 1943–March 11, 1944. 135 performances. Music by Richard Rodgers. Lyrics by Lorenz Hart. Produced by Richard Rodgers. Book by Herbert Fields. Directed by John C. Wilson. Choreography by William Holbrook and Al White, Jr. Settings and costumes by Nat Karson. Orchestra under the direction of George Hirst. Orchestrations by Don Walker. Choral director, Clay Warnick. Cast, starring Vivienne Segal and Dick Foran, included Julie Warren, Chester Stratton, Vera-Ellen, Jere McMahon, and Robert Chisolm.

This was Lorenz Hart's last score.

HERE'S MARTIN THE GROOM

Apparently intended as the opening chorus of the 1943 revival of *A Connecticut Yankee*. John Cherry, Dick Foran, Robert Chisolm, and ensemble were to have introduced it, but the number is not listed in programs for the New York run of the show.

He's a jolly good fellow,
He's a jolly good fellow,
He's a jolly good fellow,
And he lives down in our alley—

JUDGE: Here's Martin the groom,
Ready for the tomb.
MARTIN: The groom beseeches,
No after-dinner speeches.
JUDGE: The groom beseeches,
No after-dinner speeches,
But I drink this glass of domestic Claret
To the groom, Lieutenant Martin
Barrett.
Tonight we kindle the last faint ember
And the rest of the speech I can't
remember.
I'm your friend who thinks you're
charming and pleasant.
This, my boy, is your wedding present—
MARTIN: Judge, please stop—don't say another
word.
That's the lousiest rhyme I've ever
heard.
JUDGE: To the boy who's about to marry my
niece,
We wish a life of love and peace—
My lovely niece Fay—my joy and pride.
ARTHUR: She's just about to become his bride.

JUDGE: Quiet!
Because I am a good psychologist
I give this armor to Martin—the
archaeologist.
That's a damn good rhyme.
So, Martin, take this armor with a
blessing and a benison.
MARTIN: Because I loved my Tennyson.
JUDGE: That's correct . . .
This is the armor of Sir Launcelot,
A noble knight who used to chance a
lot.
Because he wooed Guinevere,
King Arthur's Queen,
He lost his armor in a bedroom scene.
MARTIN: Because of every rule of etiquette he cut
He's a bad example for us sailors in
Connecticut . . .

THIS IS MY NIGHT TO HOWL

Introduced by Vivienne Segal and ensemble. Registered for copyright as an unpublished song by Warner Brothers, Inc., November 1971.

VERSE

When the church bells sound my plight
I'll look like a ghost in white,
But tonight I'm still a live one—
It's the kid's last fight.

REFRAIN

There's a marital knot and at noon I'll tie it—
All of my friends say I ought to try it.
If I must go, then I won't go quiet.
This is my night to howl!
I knew all of the boys who were well worth
knowing,
Sowed all my oats and I'm good at sowing,
This is the time when the hen starts crowing.
This is my night to howl!
"The prisoner ate a hearty meal."
I know what that means all right.
I'm tramping along that last long mile
With a hell of an appetite.
While I still am alive I am going to mingle
Till I throw in the towel.
I may be dead when the church bells jingle.
This is my night,
This is my night to howl!

YE LUNCHTIME FOLLIES

Introduced by Chester Stratton and ensemble.

GALAHAD: Prithee, One, Two, Three, Four, Five,
Six, Seven,
Eight, Nine, Ten, Gadzooks, and
Eleven.
Prithee, Alpha, Beta, Gamma, Delta,
Bend thy back, and pull in thy belta.
And by gums, by gees, by gollys,
Work ye out in ye Lunchtime Follies.
ALL: Instead of lunch—we get ye Lunchtime
Follies.
GALAHAD: This is station B-O-S-S
Teaching you to—
ALL: Yes! Yes! Yes!
GALAHAD: I give you lunchtime relaxation
So you won't need a summer vacation.
ALL: Prithee, One, Two, Three, Four, Five,
Six, Seven,
Eight, Nine, Ten, Gadzooks, and
Eleven.
GALAHAD: Today the boogie-woogie has become a
bugaboo.
We swing from swing to saccharine,
From saccharine to goo—
To the sentimental singer with a
sentimental song.
Our monarch is a crooner and our king
can do no wrong.

CAN'T YOU DO A FRIEND A FAVOR?

Published November 1943. Introduced by Vivienne Segal and Dick Foran.

VERSE

You can count your friends
On the fingers of your hand.
If you're lucky, you have two.
I have just two friends,
That is all that I demand.
Only two, just me and you.
And a good friend heeds a friend
When a good friend needs a friend.

REFRAIN

Can't you do a friend a favor?
Can't you fall in love with me?

Life alone can lose its flavor,
You could make it sweet, you see!
I'm the dish you ought to savor,
Something warm and something new;
I could do my friend a favor,
I could fall in love with you.

YOU ALWAYS LOVE
THE SAME GIRL

Published June 1944. Introduced by Dick Foran and
Robert Chisolm.

ARTHUR: 'Tis a jolly song in truth.
MARTIN: I learned it in my youth
    In quite another mundus
    From this genus Vagabundus.
ARTHUR: Mean-est thou hoboes?
MARTIN: Let's rest our boboes.
    I've walked so long I'm really out of
      breath.
ARTHUR: Thy galloping jeep did leap itself to
      death.
    'Twas thy fault we hit the willow tree.
    Thine eyes were never on the wheel.
MARTIN: There was something on my brain
    When the jeep jumped off the lane.
ARTHUR: 'Tis the maid, and I know how thou
      dost feel.

VERSE

MARTIN: I loved another girl once,
    In another world, in another land.
    I love another girl now,
    In this other world, in this other land.
    I don't think I'm a man to blame.
ARTHUR: Not if the girls were much the same.
MARTIN: Not much the same—but just the same.
    Explicitly—
    Implicitly—
    Illicitly the same.

REFRAIN

    You always see the same girl
    In every girl you love,
    Though one is dark, the other fair.
    It's not the eyes—it's not the hair.
    There's something very similar there
    In every girl you love.
ARTHUR: The moment that you meet her

You know you've met before.
If you love more than one or two
She's still the same, What can you do?
More power to you,
For you are not untrue.
BOTH: You always love the same sweet girl
    Or you would not be you.

TO KEEP MY LOVE ALIVE

Published March 1944. Introduced by Vivienne Segal.
Believed to have been the last song lyric written by Lorenz
Hart.

VERSE

I've been married and married,
And often I've sighed,
I'm never a bridesmaid,
I'm always the bride.
I never divorced them—
I hadn't the heart.
Yet remember these sweet words
"Till death do us part."

REFRAIN 1

I married many men,
A ton of them,
And yet I was untrue to none of them
Because I bumped off ev'ry one of them
To keep my love alive.
Sir Paul was frail;
He looked a wreck to me.
At night he was a horse's neck to me.
So I performed an appendectomy
To keep my love alive.
Sir Thomas had insomnia;
He couldn't sleep at night.
I bought a little arsenic.
He's sleeping now all right.
Sir Philip played the harp;
I cussed the thing.
I crowned him with his harp
To bust the thing.
And now he plays where harps are
Just the thing,
To keep my love alive,
To keep my love alive.

REFRAIN 2

I thought Sir George had possibilities,
But his flirtations made me ill at ease,

And when I'm ill at ease,
I kill at ease
To keep my love alive.
Sir Charles came from a sanatorium
And yelled for drinks
In my emporium.
I mixed one drink—
He's in memoriam
To keep my love alive.
Sir Francis was a singing bird,
A nightingale. That's why
I tossed him off my balcony,
To see if he could fly.
Sir Athelstane indulged in fratricide;
He killed his dad and that was patricide.
One night I stabbed him at my mattress side
To keep my love alive,
To keep my love alive.

ENCORE REFRAINS

I caught Sir James with his protectress,
The rector's wife, I mean the rectoress.
His heart stood still—angina pectoris
To keep my love alive.
Sir Frank brought ladies to my palaces.
I poured a mickey in their chalices.
While paralyzed they got paralysis
To keep my love alive.
Sir Alfred worshipped falconry;
He used to hunt at will.
I sent him on a hunting trip.
They're hunting for him still.
Sir Peter had an incongruity,
Collecting girls with promiscuity.
Now I'm collecting his annuity
To keep my love alive,
To keep my love alive.

Sir Ethelbert would use profanity;
His language drove me near insanity.
So once again I served humanity
To keep my love alive.
Sir Curtis made me cook each dish he ate,
And ev'rything his heart could wish he ate,
Until I fiddled with the fish he ate
To keep my love alive.
Sir Marmaduke was awf'lly tall;
He didn't fit in bed.
I solved that problem easily—
I just removed his head.
Sir Mark adored me with formality;
He called a kiss an immorality.
And so I gave him immortality
To keep my love alive,
To keep my love alive.

INDEX

This is an alphabetical index of song titles and first lines (*including refrains*) of Hart's lyrics. It includes individual song copyright information. All rights are reserved on all Hart song copyrights. All lyrics are used by permission. All music is by Richard Rodgers, except where otherwise indicated.

The following copyright information should be added to individual notices according to the corresponding numbers:

[1] Marlin Enterprises and Lorenz Hart Publishing Co., owners of publication and allied rights throughout the world. Made in U.S.A. All rights reserved, including public performance for profit. Any copying, arranging, or adapting of this composition without the consent of the owners is an infringement of copyright.

[2] Marlin Enterprises and Lorenz Hart Publishing Co., owners of publication and allied rights in the U.S. Made in U.S.A. All rights reserved, including public performance for profit. Any copying, arranging, or adapting of this composition without the consent of the owners is an infringement of copyright.

[3] Rights Assigned to CBS Catalogue Partnership. All Rights Controlled & Administered by CBS Robbins Catalog Inc.

[4] (c/o The Welk Music Group, Santa Monica, CA 90401). International Copyright Secured.

[5] International Copyright Secured.

A B C D E F G—, 271
A baby can only have one mother, 114
A bottle of Belasco sauce, 52
A drooping little daisy hid her head, 21
A Jane once was called Cinderella, 119
A kiss is just a kiss, 167
A knife does all the talking for the Tartar!, 128
A maiden with romance was once wed and won, 34
A mop! A broom! A pail!, 97
A nightclub hostess is one of those dames, 91
A nightclub hostess, without any aid, 91
A pretty girl and a bright young man, 259
A sailor man may sport, 118
A strolling player's just a nomad, 159
A tailor! A tailor!, 176
ACROSS THE GARDEN WALL (missing), 37
Act One, 199
ACT II, SCENE 3, *See* THIS RESCUE IS A TERRIBLE CALAMITY
After one whole quart of brandy, 272
Ain't it awful to be moral?, 18
Ain't it lovely in the store?, 88

ALE, ALE, ALE (missing), 56
ALEXANDER'S BLITZTIME BAND (missing), 291 (Music by Emmerich Kalman)
All alone, all at sea, 141
ALL AT ONCE, 230 Copyright © 1937 by Chappell & Co., Inc. Copyright Renewed.[5]
All court conversation, 110
All crowds are such a menace, 58
ALL DARK PEOPLE, 228 Copyright © 1937 by Chappell & Co., Inc. Copyright Renewed.[5]
All dressed up, 260
ALL DRESSED UP SPIC AND SPANISH, *See* SPIC AND SPANISH
All glorious epitome of light, 4
All my future plans, 64
All New York's a stage, 199
ALL POINTS WEST, 225 Copyright © 1937 by Chappell & Co., Inc. Copyright Renewed.[5]
All right. Then I'll tell you something, 234
ALL SET! LET'S GO!, *See* HERE SHE COMES
All the little men are little women, 67
All words are futile, 73
ALL YOU NEED TO BE A STAR, 21 © 1986 Warner Bros. Inc.
All you Shriners and Elks and Pythian Knights, 72
ALLEZ-UP, 75 Copyright © 1986 by Estate of Richard Rodgers and Estate of Lorenz Hart.[1]
Although I've lived so close to you, 152
AMARILLO, 278 Copyright © 1941 by Chappell & Co., Inc. Copyright Renewed.[5]
America has a sweetheart, 167
AMERICAN BEAUTY ROSE, 72 Copyright © 1986 by Estate of Richard Rodgers and Estate of Lorenz Hart.[1]
AND THEREBY HANGS A TAIL, 53 Copyright © 1986 by Estate of Richard Rodgers and Estate of Lorenz Hart.[1]
And who do you love?, 180
ANGEL WITHOUT WINGS, 247 © 1939 (Renewed 1966) by Robbins Music Corp.[3]
ANIMATED OBJECTS, 193 © 1933 (Renewed 1960) by Robbins Music Corp.[3]
Anna came to Havana, 90
ANOTHER MELODY IN F, 14, 29 Copyright © 1920 by Richard C. Rodgers. Reprinted by permission of The Trustees of Columbia University in the City of New York and Estate of Lorenz Hart.
Answer, please, to the name, 162
ANY OLD PLACE WITH YOU, 12 © 1919 Dorothy F. Rodgers, Mary Guettel, Linda R. Breckir, and Estate of Lorenz Hart.[2] © 1919 (Renewed) Warner Bros. Inc.
ANYTIME, ANYWHERE, ANYHOW (missing), 37
APHRODITE (missing), 12
APRIL FOOL, 47 © 1925 Dorothy F. Rodgers, Mary Guettel, Linda R. Breckir, and Estate of

Lorenz Hart.[2] © 1925 Edward B. Marks Music Company. Copyright Renewed.
Are not mine eyes fair to view?, 111
Are not my eyes fair to see?, 167
ARE YOU MY LOVE?, 224 Copyright © 1936 by Chappell & Co., Inc. Copyright Renewed.[5]
Are you sure you love this guy?, 265
AS THOUGH YOU WERE THERE, 142 Copyright © 1940 by Chappell & Co., Inc. Copyright Renewed.[5]
As you draw me near you, 158
At Lido life is very fast, 79
AT THE ROUND TABLE, 108 © 1927 (Renewed) and 1986 Warner Bros. Inc.
AT THE ROXY MUSIC HALL, 248 © 1938 (Renewed 1965) by Robbins Music Corp.[3]
AT THE SASKATCHEWAN, 99 Copyright © 1986 by Estate of Richard Rodgers and Estate of Lorenz Hart.[1]
ATLANTIC BLUES, 83 © 1926 Dorothy F. Rodgers, Mary Guettel, Linda R. Breckir, and Estate of Lorenz Hart.[2] © 1926 (Renewed) Warner Bros. Inc.
AWAIT YOUR LOVE, 125 Copyright © 1986 by Estate of Richard Rodgers and Estate of Lorenz Hart.[1]
Await your love with utter circumspection, 125
Away with Sunday shows!, 154
Ay-ay-ay. I'm in love, encanto, 279

BABBITTS IN LOVE, 34 Copyright © 1925 and 1986 by Estate of Richard Rodgers and Estate of Lorenz Hart.[1]
Babe, we are well met, 107
BABES IN ARMS, 228 Copyright © 1937 by Chappell & Co., Inc. Copyright Renewed.[5]
BABY BOND, A, *See* BABY BOND FOR BABY, A
BABY BOND FOR BABY, A, 237 Copyright © 1937 by Estate of Richard Rodgers and Estate of Lorenz Hart.[1]
Baby, how sweet to be, 235
BABY STARS, 201 © 1933 (Renewed 1960) by Robbins Music Corp.[3]
BABY STARS NUMBER, *See* DEVELOPMENT OF BABY STARS NUMBER
BABY WANTS TO DANCE, 31 Copyright © 1986 by Estate of Richard Rodgers and Estate of Lorenz Hart.[1]
BABY'S AWAKE NOW, 133 © 1929 Dorothy F. Rodgers, Mary Guettel, Linda R. Breckir, and Estate of Lorenz Hart.[2] © 1929 (Renewed) Warner Bros Inc.
BABY'S BEST FRIEND, A, 114 © 1928 Dorothy F. Rodgers, Mary Guettel, Linda R. Breckir, and Estate of Lorenz Hart.[2] © 1928 (Renewed) Warner Bros. Inc.

A NOTE ON THE TYPE

This book was set in Bodoni Book, named after
Giambattista Bodoni (1740–1813), son of a
printer of Piedmont. After gaining experience and
fame as superintendent of the Press of the
Propaganda in Rome, Bodoni became, in 1766,
the head of the ducal printing house at Parma,
which he soon made the foremost of its kind in
Europe. In type designing he was an innovator,
making his new faces rounder, wider, and lighter,
with greater openness and delicacy. His types
were rather too rigidly perfect in detail, the thick
lines contrasting sharply with the thin wiry lines.
It was doubtless this feature that caused
William Morris to condemn the Bodoni types as
"swelteringly hideous." Bodoni Book, as
originally reproduced by the Linotype Company,
is a modern version based not on any one of
Bodoni's fonts, but on a composite conception of
the Bodoni manner, designed to avoid the details
stigmatized as "bad" by typographical experts
and to secure the pleasing and effective results
of which the Bodoni types are capable.

Composed by The Haddon Craftsmen, Inc.,
Scranton, Pennsylvania

Printed and bound by Kingsport Press,
Kingsport, Tennessee

Designed by Dorothy Schmiderer,
following an original design by Holly McNeely